...How They Rose and Fell

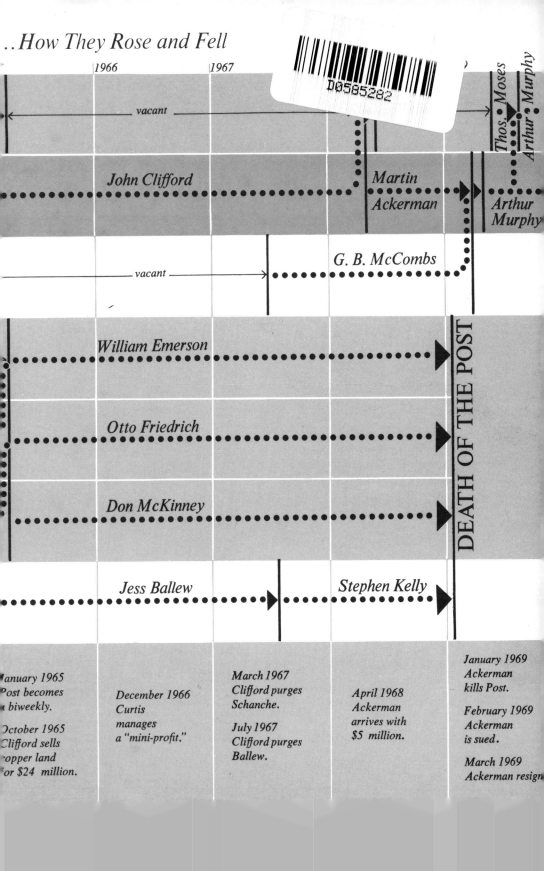

1966   1967

Thos. Moses • Arthur Murphy

← vacant →

John Clifford   Martin Ackerman   Arthur Murphy

← vacant →   G. B. McCombs

William Emerson

Otto Friedrich

Don McKinney

DEATH OF THE POST

Jess Ballew   Stephen Kelly

January 1965
Post becomes
a biweekly.

October 1965
Clifford sells
paper land
for $24 million.

December 1966
Curtis
manages
a "mini-profit."

March 1967
Clifford purges
Schanche.

July 1967
Clifford purges
Ballew.

April 1968
Ackerman
arrives with
$5 million.

January 1969
Ackerman
kills Post.

February 1969
Ackerman
is sued.

March 1969
Ackerman resigns

DECLINE AND FALL

DECLINE

AND

FALL

by Otto Friedrich

MICHAEL JOSEPH · LONDON

Grateful acknowledgment is made for permission to reprint the following:
Lines from *Murder in the Cathedral* by T. S. Eliot on page 175, reprinted by permission of Faber and Faber Ltd.
Lines from *The Cantos* by Ezra Pound on page 317, reprinted by permission of Faber and Faber Ltd.
Quotations on page 33 *et seq.* are taken from *The Curtis-Culligan Story*, by Matthew J. Culligan, copyright © 1970 by Matthew J. Culligan. Used by permission of Crown Publishers, Inc.
Saturday Evening Post covers and illustrations reprinted by permission of the Curtis Publishing Company.
Portions of this work have previously appeared in *Harper's* Magazine in somewhat different form.

First published in Great Britain by
MICHAEL JOSEPH LTD
52 Bedford Square, London, W.C.1.
1972

7181 0914 7

Reproduced and Printed in Great Britain by
Redwood Press Limited, Trowbridge & London
and bound by the Dorstel Press at Harlow

To Priscilla

Contents

Illustrations

The composing room in 1910
The subscription department in 1910
Walter Fuller (UPI)
Robert MacNeal
The Sharon Hill printing plant
High-speed presses
Ben Hibbs in 1942 (UPI)
"Freedom of Religion" (1943)
The Whittaker Chambers cover (1952)
A typical Norman Rockwell cover (1957)
Hibbs and Robert Fuoss in 1961
The cover of the disastrous "new" *Post* (1961)

The following are grouped in a special section at page 244:

THE YEARS OF CONTENTION

Clay Blair and Robert Sherrod (Copyright by Philippe Halsman)
Don Schanche (John Zimmerman)
Davis Thomas
Hank Walker
Matthew Culligan (*Media Decisions*)
Culligan in his helicopter
Serge Semenenko
Wally Butts (Wide World)
The article that libeled Butts (1963)
The Curtis board of directors (John Zimmerman)
Blair with Marvin Kantor after their suspension (Wide World)
John McLean Clifford (Wide World)
Gloria Swett with Clifford
Maurice Poppei
William Emerson after becoming editor
Emerson with Norman Rockwell
Emerson with Sharon Tate (Andrée Abecassis)

Emerson with Stephen Kelly
Asger Jerrild (Andrée Abecassis)
Martin Ackerman and his town house (*New York Times*)
Ackerman with G. B. McCombs
Mrs. Martin Ackerman, Bob Yung, Lavere Lund and Stephen Kelly
Ackerman laying out pictures (Burt Glinn—Magnum)
Ackerman at luncheon (Burt Glinn—Magnum)
Ackerman's plan

The following are grouped in a special section at page 340:

THE LAST DAY OF THE *Saturday Evening Post*

Emerson waiting for the death knell (Steve Shapiro—*Life*)
An editor receiving job offers (Steve Shapiro—*Life*)
Ackerman killing the *Post* (Sam Young)
Emerson as the *Post* is killed (Sam Young)
Rita Waterman weeping (Steve Shapiro—*Life*)
The oldest editor packing (Steve Shapiro—*Life*)
Don Allan giving roses (Steve Shapiro—*Life*)
Editors opening wine (Jill Krementz)
Emerson being kissed (Sam Young)
Emerson's farewell (Sam Young)
Ackerman during litigation (UPI)

Book I

THE REVOLUTION

We conferred endlessly and futilely, and arrived at the place from which we started. Then we did what we knew we had to do in the first place, and we failed as we knew we would.

> —Quotation from Sir Winston Churchill, mounted over the desk of Robert Fuoss, editor of the *Saturday Evening Post* from January to March, 1962

The supreme art of war is to subdue the enemy without fighting.

> —Sun Tzu, *The Art of War*

1

"Nobody knows how bad it really is"

On the first day I went to work for the *Saturday Evening Post*, early in September of 1962, everything I saw seemed symbolic of the magazine's awesome age and solemnity. The Curtis Publishing Company building in Philadelphia was itself symbolic. An eleven-story structure of white marble that had been shipped from Maine by Cyrus H. K. Curtis, it overlooked the somnolent gardens of Independence Square and the brick tower that contained the Liberty Bell. The lobby of the Curtis building was also symbolic. Stained-glass windows darkened the interior, and, at the rear, fountains splashed softly before a gigantic mosaic mural entitled "The Groves of Academe," created by Louis C. Tiffany from designs by Maxfield Parrish. The elevators were symbolic, lined with dark wooden paneling, and gently maneuvered upward and downward by Negroes in gray livery and white gloves. Even the towels in the lavatories were symbolic. There were no paper towels because there had never been paper towels. After washing one's hands, one took a clean towel from a large pile of folded linen; one dried one's hands and dropped the towel into a wicker hamper. At the end of every day, Negroes came to carry away the towels, launder them, and return them to service.

Six years later, on January 10, 1969, I watched the *Saturday Evening Post* being put to death. The end came, as it so often does nowadays, under the blinding lights of television. That afternoon, while New York City was staging a ceremonial welcome for the three Astronauts who had just completed the first trip around the moon, I stood at the back of a rather bleak auditorium in the Overseas Press

Club on West Fortieth Street and watched Martin S. Ackerman, a small, taut figure newly tanned from a vacation in the Bahamas, standing on a suitcase and squinting into the floodlights. The execution, the latest president of Curtis said briskly into a thicket of microphones, was "sad for me, for our employees, officers and directors; indeed, it is sad for the American public. However, no other decision was possible. . . ." Back at the *Post*'s last editorial offices on Lexington Avenue, the news seemed hard to accept. "I just said my prayers this morning and hoped that all this wouldn't be true," an eighteen-year-old secretary called Linda Leto told an interviewer from the *New York Times*. And the weeping old cleaning woman named Louise blurted out to us: "Oh, where was Saint Anthony?"

There had been, for six years, a kind of inevitability to the decline and fall. The gossips of Madison Avenue and Wall Street had repeatedly predicted the magazine's death, and the press had reported the details of every misfortune that could be discovered. But nothing is ever completely inevitable. The *Post* could have been saved from death at any number of points, including the day of its execution. The story of its last years, in fact, is partly the story of how a number of talented and dedicated people fought to save a magazine they cherished.

If the end was not inevitable, however, the odds against us were very long. In the autumn of 1962, when I came to Philadelphia as the *Post*'s foreign-affairs editor, Curtis and the *Post* were already in desperate trouble. On March 29, President Robert A. MacNeal, a rather remote and lonely man who seemed unable to understand the forces that were engulfing him, announced that Curtis had lost money for the first time since its incorporation in 1891. The loss—$4,193,000— was only a symptom of the problems and mistakes of two decades, and by this time the vulnerable corporation had begun to attract the interest of various Wall Street speculators. Early that summer, MacNeal was abruptly dismissed, in the middle of a European trip, and the board of directors turned to Madison Avenue for a new president who could bring in more advertising revenue. They chose Matthew Joseph Culligan, formerly of NBC Radio and the McCann-Erickson advertising agency, a rambunctious figure whose black eyepatch had become a sort of trademark.

Culligan's regime began with a storm of publicity about his travels by helicopter, his demonic talents as a salesman, and an extravagant *Post* editorial called "The Curtis Commitment": "The Curtis Publishing Company is committed to the goal of becoming the voice and conscience of the competitive free-enterprise system, which is the

foundation of a progressive economy and a democratic way of life."
Culligan's frenetic activities entertained everyone for a time, but the
company continued to lose millions of dollars, and Culligan consequently became the target of a conspiracy organized by two of his
chief executives. Clay Blair, the darkly temperamental editor who had
launched the *Post* on a new course of "sophisticated muckraking,"
and Marvin Kantor, the Wall Street investor who had become chairman of the Curtis magazine division, invited a dozen of the company's leading editors and publishing executives to Manero's steak
house in Greenwich, Connecticut, to plot Culligan's overthrow. I was
the only one of the conspirators who told Blair and Kantor that their
revolt was doomed, but the prophets of failure rarely win an audience, and later I could only listen stoically to Blair saying, as we
began the insurrection, "What do you call this, Otto? *Der Tag?*"

It all leaked out, inevitably, onto the front page of the *New York
Times*:

CURTIS EDITORS ACCUSE CHIEF OF MISMANAGEMENT

And just as inevitably—since confrontations were not fashionable
in those days—the leak brought on the counterrevolution. Blair's
insurrection was suppressed, and he and Kantor were both dismissed.
But Culligan, too, had to abdicate his throne. Almost by accident,
then, this still-wealthy and still-powerful company fell into the hands
of John McLean Clifford, a sour little man with a white crew cut and
black-rimmed spectacles, who had served as Culligan's cost-cutting
executive vice president. Clifford started out by firing two editors, and
so we immediately had a new confrontation.

Bill Emerson, then the reigning editor, resigned outright, and about
thirty of his lieutenants gathered in the *Post* conference room to
excoriate their new president to his face. "You have violated one of
the oldest traditions of the *Post*, the independence and integrity of the
editorial staff," one of the editors declared to Clifford. "You have done
a monstrous thing." Clifford sat silent and stared with cold blue eyes
at his own hands, clasped prayer-like before him. When the accusations subsided, he excused himself and departed, and we began a
new regime, a regime of pinching and parsimony, of caution and
fear, until one fine spring day when it turned out that Mac Clifford
simply couldn't pay the bills due to the various banks.

And so, in April of 1968, we acquired our next and last president,
Martin S. Ackerman, aged thirty-six and bringing $5 million with
him. He came in a whirlwind, bustling in at eight o'clock every
morning, lunching on sandwiches, and hurrying out at night with his

briefcase stuffed with articles to read. The *Post* was already near death by then, but Ackerman suddenly provided a huge infusion of energy, ideas, enthusiasm. One day, taking a break between two meetings with the bankers, he barged into my office, flung himself into a chair, tore the cellophane wrapping off a cigar, and began talking about the editorial page, which I regularly wrote myself. It turned out that Ackerman wanted to write editorials too, with his name on them. I just frowned at him. "Listen, I've put my five million dollars on the line, and my reputation too," Ackerman said. "So, I'm telling you, I'm going to *participate* in the editorial direction of these magazines, okay? Because if I can't participate, then I'm not interested in putting up my five million dollars, okay?"

And then he got up to return to work. He prepared himself by unzipping his trousers and tucking in his shirt. "It's worse than you guys can imagine," he went on, still tucking. "This company—worse than *anybody* could imagine. The book division alone lost maybe a *million* dollars last year. Things we never even knew about. And nobody really knows any of the figures, nobody knows how bad it really is." With that, he smiled his quick smile, stuck his cigar into his mouth, and darted out again, back into conference with the bankers.

The decline and fall of the Curtis Publishing Company has been called, perhaps a little hyperbolically, "the greatest corporate disaster in American history," and so it should be worth our while to consider some of the details of the disaster. "Since the end of the second world war," Andrew Hacker of Cornell observed in *The Corporation Take-over,* "the corporate form has emerged as the characteristic institution of American society. Its rise has rendered irrelevant time-honored theories of politics and economics, and its explosive growth has created new breeds of men whose behavior can no longer be accounted for by conventional rules of conduct." This is undoubtedly true, but it is also true that all organizations resemble one another, that they all grow and decay in similar ways, and that the perpetual struggle between king and barons may flare with equal violence in the corporation, the political party, the university, or the army. Still, if the corporation is our "characteristic institution," and if we may adopt Nabokov's reversal of Tolstoy's maxim by declaring that all unhappy families are "more or less alike," then the story of the Curtis Publishing Company may tell us a great deal about how our system of competition for the sake of profit really works—or fails to work.

2

"Our greatest bulwark in a time of crisis"

Gibbon began with a benevolent portrait of the Age of the Antonines, as a standard by which to judge subsequent disasters, and so, on a miniature scale, it may be fitting to begin this story with the saga of George Horace Lorimer. The Dickensian name evokes the age, as does the portrait. It shows a heavy man, with a strong nose, deep-set eyes, and a wide mouth, sober and dignified. He looks like one's father. Very few people at Curtis could still remember Lorimer as anything more than a portrait, but the details are recounted in the standard biography, *George Horace Lorimer and the Saturday Evening Post*, by John Tebbel. It is a sturdy story.

Lorimer was born in Louisville and grew up in Chicago, the son of a Baptist minister. While a sophomore at Yale, he encountered one of his father's parishioners, P. D. Armour. The meat-packer asked the student what he was doing, and then said, "Give up that nonsense and come to work for me. I'll make you a millionaire." Lorimer consulted his parents, left Yale, and appeared at Armour's meat plant. Armour could barely remember having met the student, but he gave him a job at ten dollars a week. . . .

Lorimer became interested in journalism, abandoned Armour, worked his way through Colby, went to work for the Boston *Standard*, then the *Post*, then the *Herald*. There was an announcement that Cyrus H. K. Curtis, owner of the successful *Ladies' Home Journal*, had just bought, for $1,000, a dying old periodical called the *Saturday Evening Post*. The announcement said Curtis was looking for an editor. Lorimer sent a telegram asking for a job. Curtis was on his way to Europe, stopped in Boston, and hired the young Lorimer—he was thirty—as literary editor at $1,000 a year. The editor then was William George Jordan, and there were conflicts. A year later, in 1899, Jordan was gone, and Lorimer took charge. . . .

The *Post* claimed to have been founded by Ben Franklin in 1728. In actual fact, Franklin published the *Pennsylvania Gazette*, which he sold, shortly before the American Revolution, to David Sellers, who then went into partnership with a man called Hall, whose grandson had a partner called Atkinson, and Atkinson had a partner called Alexander, and these two gentlemen changed the *Pennsylvania Gazette and Weekly Advertiser* into the *Daily Chronicle and Saturday Evening Post*, which finally became, in 1821, the *Saturday Evening Post*. Edgar Allan Poe published "The Black Cat" in the *Post*, and the other contributors included James Fenimore Cooper and Harriet Beecher Stowe. The early success faded after the Civil War, however. By the time Curtis and Lorimer took over, the *Post* was a sixteen-page sheet, edited by a Philadelphia newspaperman in his spare time, filled with material clipped from other newspapers. Its circulation was barely two thousand, and its advertising revenue totaled about $300 per issue.

Lorimer changed everything. He reduced the price from ten cents to five, lower than the price of any competitive periodical. He changed the *Post* from a weekly newspaper into a magazine. In September of 1899, it appeared with a cover in color for the first time, and that same issue contained stories by Stephen Crane and Bret Harte. Later that year, there were works by Kipling, Hamlin Garland, Edwin Markham, and Joel Chandler Harris. Everything was illustrated. There was also an article called "The Making of a Merchant," which first expressed the *Post*'s dedication to what Lorimer called, in all sincerity, "the romance of business." And the advertising began to come in. Singer Sewing Machine, the National Cloak Company, and the Mosely Folding Bathtub Company. The *Post* increased from sixteen pages to twenty-four, and then to thirty-two. "It promises twice as much as any other magazine," Lorimer wrote, "and it will try to give twice as much as it promises."

This was not easy. Curtis spent $250,000 to advertise his new magazine, and when circulation didn't climb fast enough, he said, "All right, I'll send another $250,000 after it to bring it back." Circulation increased, but advertising failed to make up the deficits, and the company treasurer told Curtis that the magazine was $800,000 in the red. "Well," Curtis said, "that gives us a margin of $200,000 more to make it a million. I like round numbers." The next day, he started a $200,000 advertising campaign. The circulation figures are astonishing—from 33,000 in 1898 to 97,000 the following year, to 182,000 the year after that. The *Post* reached half a million in 1903, a million in 1909, two million in 1913. Advertising followed, as the nature of American business gradually changed. The giant public corporation had appeared and was prospering, and it needed a national market rather than local ones. The first automobile advertisement in the *Post* was a twenty-one-line entry by W. E. Roach in 1900; by 1915, auto ads helped to produce a record issue of 100 pages; in 1929, the *Post* produced an issue of 272 pages. Advertising revenue increased from $8,000 in 1898 to $160,000 in 1899 to more than $1 million in 1905, $3 million in 1909, $5 million in 1910. By the end of the Twenties, it was over $50 million, and the *Post* collected almost thirty cents of every advertising dollar spent in magazines.

Lorimer remained a marvelously independent and idiosyncratic editor. He liked to hear from great men, and so every President from Grover Cleveland to Hoover (except McKinley) wrote for the *Post*. He sponsored some of the legendary characters of popular fiction—Tugboat Annie, Ephraim Tutt, Alexander Botts, Mr. Moto—but he also published the best writers of the period, Faulkner and Fitzgerald, Edith Wharton and Ring Lardner. For this, he was rarely appreciated, and Scott Fitzgerald once told him at lunch, "American magazines have always published the work of mediocrities and nobodies. They've taken no notice of real genius. It's a safe bet that nobody in this room ever heard of the most important writer of the early 1900's, Frank Norris." Lorimer couldn't resist the answer: "Then maybe I didn't go so far wrong after all when I bought *The Pit* and *The Octopus* from Frank Norris and serialized them both in the *Post*."

To his staff, Lorimer was always "The Boss," and just as he bought what he liked and published what he liked, so he fought off every interference. Early in his regime, Cyrus Curtis complained about a short story: "My wife doesn't think it's a very good piece to be in the *Post*." Lorimer promptly replied: "I'm not editing the *Saturday Evening Post* for your wife." As for the readers who criticized a 1931 serial, in which the first installment ended with a secretary dining at her boss's home and the second installment began with the couple having breakfast, Lorimer prepared a form letter: "The Post cannot be responsible for what the characters in its serials do between installments." And once an advertising man wandered into the art department and admired a cover painting of a golfer. "Gee, that's fine," he said, "that'll help us sell some pages of advertising." "I'm sorry you said that," Lorimer answered. "Now we can't use that cover."

It is hard to believe that Lorimer really did all that he is said to have done. According to the legend, he read a half-million words a week, edited copy, wrote ads, picked covers, wrote editorials, and yet he managed to take over all of the corporate management as well. In 1932, after the death of Cyrus Curtis, Lorimer became president of the Curtis Publishing Company; in 1934, he became chairman of the board. It was perhaps this incredible involvement in his job, and not just his native conservatism, that made Lorimer become so remote from his readers and his people. An admirer of Hoover, he wrote to a friend, "I'll fight this New Deal if it's the last thing I do." He called it "a discredited European ideology"; he railed against "undesirable and unassimilable aliens"; and the *Post* declared: "We might just as well say that the world failed as the American business leadership failed." The election of 1936 was a humiliating blow, which, according to one chronicler, left Lorimer "crushed and bewildered, a stranger in a land he loved."

He was also getting old, nearing seventy. He had a persistent cough, and he couldn't give up smoking. "For thirty-five years I've been in a squirrel cage," he said to a friend. "I want to get out and climb some trees." In the last issue of 1936, he announced his retirement; the following October 27, he died of throat cancer.

In the spring of 1963, there was an upheaval, and various editors were moved around. Bill Emerson became executive editor of the *Post,* and I replaced him as articles editor. I moved into his office and took possession of his desk. All the other editors had sleek modern desks, but the one in Emerson's office was an old-fashioned piece of cherrywood—a large table, really, with a set of shallow drawers on each side. A few weeks later, I had a visit from John Bird, who had preceded Emerson as articles editor and then decided to shift to writing.

"Well, I see you've got Lorimer's desk," Bird said.

"This? I thought it was just Emerson's desk."

"Well, it was mine too, but it was originally Lorimer's. It's a copy of a desk that George Washington once had. Lorimer used it for years, and then Ben Hibbs inherited it, but Sherrod didn't want it, for some reason, so I took it."

I was very proud to have Lorimer's desk, and when Emerson tried to get it back, I wouldn't give it up. "Does it really mean that much to you?" Emerson asked. "Yes," I said. And it did, and so I kept it.

"You want to know the truth about Lorimer?" said Clay Blair. We were sitting at the bar of La Grenouille, a fancy new restaurant just off Fifth Avenue. "You want to know what I think? I think Lorimer was the guy who sold out to big business. When McClure was doing all those exposés—Lincoln Steffens and Ida Tarbell and those people —really telling the truth about the outrageous things that were happening, graft and swindles and price-fixing and everything, Lorimer was saying that everything was just great. And big business rewarded him for it. That's how Lorimer became such a big success. He sold out."

It is a common mark of strong-willed men that they cannot pick worthy successors, and Lorimer was no exception. Walter Deane Fuller, as president of Curtis, and Wesley Winans Stout, as editor of the *Post*, were both narrow conservatives, and within a few years they were in serious trouble. In the wartime spring of 1942, while the *Post* was losing money during the first quarter, Stout blundered into print with an article entitled *The Case Against the Jew*. The reaction was thunderous—cancellations of advertising and subscriptions, threats of a boycott. Within a month, there was a new editor, and an apology on the editorial page.

Any such change is a profound shock to the nervous system of the organization, and the new editor, Ben Hibbs, did what new editors always do. He issued a statement announcing that there would be change but not too much change, progress but stability. After a lapse of more than a quarter of a century, we can still read Hibbs's statement as a paradigm of all statements by all new commanders taking over old commands. "I firmly believe," Hibbs said,

in the American system—freedom of living, freedom of enterprise. . . . The problems that confront the American people are staggering. It is our responsibility to weigh, analyze, and explain these problems. . . . New types of material will be introduced. We will make fundamental changes in typography, layout, styles of illustration. . . . We shall handle many of our subjects in much shorter length and we shall cover more subjects. But let me emphasize that [this] does not mean that the Post will become shallow. . . . Furthermore, new short features will enliven the pages. . . . We shall publish more material of interest to younger readers.

While the blueprint always remains the same, the execution obviously varies according to the nature of the new commander. Ben Hibbs, then forty, had grown up in Pretty Prairie, Kansas, a town of four hundred inhabitants, where his father was a lumber merchant. "There are thousands of Pretty Prairies throughout this land," Hibbs had written a year earlier in *Country Gentleman*, a Curtis farm magazine of which he was then editor, "and herein lies my faith in America. I don't mean to say that there are not plenty of fine and patriotic people in our great cities and within the ranks of organized labor. I merely say that, in the country and the country towns there is still a stability of life and thought which is our greatest bulwark in a time of crisis."

Tall, stoop-shouldered, Ben Hibbs even looked like an editor from Pretty Prairie, Kansas—the graying hair was parted a bit too high on the head, the mouth was thin and reticent, the eyes behind the horn-rimmed glasses were kindly but not gullible. An intelligent, capable, decent man—"easygoing and quiet but with iron in his soul," said the young Norman Rockwell—and many of the *Post* editors were enthusiastic about the change. "I wanted to stand up and yell with joy on his behalf," said one.

And so the *Post* entered what might be called its Silver Age. Hibbs and his lanky young managing editor, Bob Fuoss, reduced the emphasis on fiction and set out to cover World War II as "the greatest news story of our time." The *Post* then had only one war correspondent, who was home on leave in New York. Hibbs recruited MacKinlay Kantor, Samuel Lubell, Edgar Snow, Richard Tregaskis, Demaree Bess. C. S. Forester wrote about the sinking of the *Scharnhorst,* Ambassador Joseph E. Davies wrote from Moscow about the Russian front, and Norman Rockwell painted his version of Roosevelt's slogan, the Four Freedoms. In this silver age, the money came and went at an unprecedented rate. Hibbs spent $175,000, a record for extravagance at that time, for *My Three Years with Eisenhower,* by the general's naval aide, Captain Harry C. Butcher. He spent another $125,000 for the memoirs of Casey Stengel, and $100,000 for a biography of General Douglas MacArthur. The last of these, which had been commissioned without any safeguard as to its quality, was never published, and Hibbs referred to it, in a private office memorandum, as "my worst mistake in twenty years." At the same time, Hibbs willingly led the *Post* into a circulation war against *Life* and *Look,* and the *Post* bought its way up from 3.3 million to more than 6.5 million during his twenty-year regime. Advertising revenue rose just as spectacularly, from $23 million to $104 million a year.

Such figures tend to preclude criticism, but there was something hollow about Ben Hibbs's rural, familial, conservative *Post.* A promotional brochure in the late 1950's, for example, boasted of new features like "the I Call On series, evolved from Senior Editor Pete Martin's chatty, intimate technique of interviewing. . . . The first of these articles, I Call On Bing Crosby, appeared May 11, 1957. Others followed on Grace Kelly, Clark Gable, Phil Silvers, Helen Hayes,

Ingrid Bergman, Dick Clark, Marilyn Monroe and many more." Bob Sherrod, the managing editor who eventually succeeded Hibbs and Fuoss, used to look back in awe at the fact that a *Post* cover story on Arthur Godfrey had sold no less than two million copies on the newsstands, and it may be true that Arthur Godfrey in his day reached the same kind of Midwestern audience that Hibbs was trying to reach, but by 1960, in the era of Jack Kennedy, Fidel Castro, the civil rights struggle, and rock 'n' roll, the viewpoint of Ben Hibbs began to appear somehow irrelevant. The state of Kansas ranks thirty-first in population, and there is no longer any reason—if there ever was any reason—to think that this bleak prairie state represents the American spirit.

Perhaps Hibbs sensed this; more likely not. In 1960, he told Bob MacNeal that he wanted to retire, at the age of sixty, at the end of 1961. "I always said a magazine should change editors every twenty years," he declared. But as Hibbs prepared to turn over the magazine to his executive editor, Bob Fuoss, the need for more drastic change became more apparent. The *Post* was widely considered to be old and stodgy, edited by the old and stodgy to be read by the old and stodgy, and Ben Hibbs couldn't accept it. "The ad people were always hollering in my last year about the Norman Rockwell covers, that they were old-fashioned," he protested. "Heck, those were the *Post*'s most popular feature." And the books he kept buying kept becoming best sellers. "Dammit, we were hitting the American market," said Hibbs. "We had to be with that kind of record." And did someone say that *Post* fiction was unreal? "After all, the world is not entirely composed of hydrogen bombs, juvenile delinquency, race riots, mental institutions, heart disease and cancer," said Hibbs. "I can remember the time when people thought it was *fun to read*."

"You want to know the real story on Ben Hibbs?" said Clay Blair. "Listen, when he took over, in the middle of World War II, you couldn't lose because of the paper restrictions. The advertisers were begging for space. Then after the war, you couldn't lose because the big advertisers had to get their message across to the public. So for eight years, any idiot could make money in the magazine business. But then television came along, and the advertisers could buy a bigger audience for a lower cost per thousand, and Ben Hibbs was in trouble, and all the other people like Hibbs were in trouble. Because now the question was: Who are your readers, and what have you got to say to them, and are they really listening? And Ben Hibbs didn't have the answers."

It is easy to deride Ben Hibbs's old-fashioned *Post*. It is also easy to make the mistake of blaming the *Post* for the declining fortunes of the Curtis Publishing Company. In fact, however, the decline can more accurately be blamed on errors of judgment by Curtis management back in the 1930's and 1940's.

The essential misjudgment, of course, is always a misjudgment of people. Cyrus Curtis's famous dictum on the handling of editors had been: "Find the right man and then leave him alone." This maxim becomes dangerous, however, when the authorities select the wrong man. And while it may be dangerous to have the wrong man as editor, it can be ruinous to have the wrong man as president. When George Horace Lorimer grew weary of the paperwork that encumbered him in the corporate presidency, he turned the position over to Walter Deane Fuller, an accountant, a former bank clerk, a former salesman of dress patterns, a veteran of twenty-four years in the business departments of Curtis. And when Fuller also became chairman of the board in 1937, total authority fell into the hands of a man who publicly opposed Social Security, unemployment compensation, the "coddling" of labor unions, and the Democratic Party. Fuller was supported throughout this period, however, by the heirs of Cyrus H. K. Curtis, who still owned more than 30 percent of the company, and who spoke through the equally conservative voice of Cary W. Bok, grandson of the founder and treasurer of his company.

There is nothing intrinsically wicked about conservatism, to be sure, but it is possible to suspect that the traditional association of businessmen and right-wing causes may reflect little credit on either side, and that executives without much political perception may also lack foresight in the operation of their own corporations. Walter Fuller, in any case, determined to change Curtis from a great publishing company into a great printing company. The difference is not immediately easy to understand—Curtis's own management never did understand it—for it violates our instinctive sense of economic values. But the essential difference is this: Publishing is based on ideas—the *Saturday Evening Post* was really little more than a series of ideas—and ideas are valuable—they can be bought and sold. Printing, by contrast, is a manufacturing industry, and it is based not on ideas but on physical objects—printing presses, factory buildings, paper mills, tons of wood pulp, vats of ink, fleets of delivery trucks. To a mind that does not believe in the value of ideas, wealth and security can lie only in the accumulation of physical objects. And no such mind can ever understand publishing.

In fairness, it should be noted that Fuller's presidency began during the difficult days of the Depression, when Curtis and many other companies tottered near bankruptcy, and the value of ideas may well have seemed less obvious than it does today. And then, during World War II, the shortage of supplies convinced many an executive of the value of hoarding and stockpiling. Whatever his reasons, Fuller held to his empire-building philosophy with an exceptional singleness of purpose. He could have bought the entire Columbia Broadcasting System for $3 million, but he declined the offer; a few years later, he declined a similar opportunity to buy the American Broadcasting Corporation. Television, radio, the growth in book publishing, the so-called "paperback revolution," the rise of suburban newspapers, the increasing need for school texts—Walter Deane Fuller had not been blessed with a gift for prophesying such developments. Instead, just after World War II, he bought a 108-acre site on the outskirts of Philadelphia, shipped in twenty new printing presses, and constructed the gigantic Sharon Hill printing plant. It was, in its day, the largest and best-equipped printing plant in the world. And as late as 1950, when Fuller finally passed on the presidency to his protégé, Robert A. MacNeal, Curtis reaffirmed its dedication to machinery by investing $20 million to become full owner of a paper company in which it already held a controlling interest.

By 1960, then, the people actually employed in creating Curtis magazines represented only a tiny fraction of the armies engaged in manufacturing them. The editorial staff of the *Post* numbered about 125 people; the employees in the printing division numbered 2,600; the employees of the whole corporation numbered about 11,000. And in surveying the corporate assets, Curtis executives liked to boast that the company owned not just a few magazines but a $40 million printing plant, three large paper mills, 262,000 acres of timberland, and a circulation company that distributed 50-odd magazines through 100,000 outlets.

But all these boasts missed the essential point. The buildings and machines that served as monuments to the thirty-year rule of Fuller and MacNeal were all built and paid for by Ben Hibbs's *Post*. Even during Hibbs's later years, from 1956 through 1960, the *Post* brought in huge revenues ranging from $87 million to $104 million a year, while other Curtis enterprises consistently lost money, and even the corporate overhead rose from $7 million to $13 million. What happened during the early 1960's, therefore, was that a magazine that had supported regiments of accountants and printers and promotion men finally began to falter under the burden. It could no longer earn $100 million a year.

"I used to see MacNeal working alone and late," said Clay Blair, "sometimes eating by himself in the employees' cafeteria, after midnight. He was a cold, distant figure, with a white, pasty face and rimless glasses. One evening, he invited me to his gigantic office on the ninth floor, overlooking Independence Square. He was working away at his mahogany desk, which was loaded with enormous piles of confidential reports, charts, mail. There was a dim light from a little lamp. He didn't get up when I came in, but he asked me to sit down, and then he launched into a monologue in defense of himself for not less than two hours. He talked about Sharon Hill, and the paper company, and his cost-reduction program, and the Wall Street buyers of Curtis stock, whom he described as 'foreign-born.' MacNeal was drawing up a three-part 'Statement of Policy' to answer everybody. He was also preparing replies to a sixty-seven-point questionnaire from some stockholders. He was suspicious of everything, and he asked me a lot of questions about what I was doing, but I got very little chance to answer. He started pouring out more statistics, like the temperature of the press dryers. He made me think of Philip II of Spain, ruling his vast empire from the Escorial, scratching away fourteen hours a day on a lot of documents. While Philip scribbled, Spain went bankrupt."

Late in 1960, while Ben Hibbs was still the editor, the Curtis authorities decided that the *Post* needed a total renovation. No outsider can ever know who was responsible, who decided on which changes and why, for many of those involved later blamed one another for everything that went wrong. "Victory has a thousand fathers," said Jack Kennedy after the Bay of Pigs, "but defeat is an orphan." In any event, it was agreed that there should be a "new" *Post*. Bob Fuoss, the *Post*'s executive editor and Hibbs's heir apparent, took charge of a special staff that spent the spring and summer of 1961 in planning the changes. And nobody seemed to realize that the venture was doomed from the start.

It was doomed because of a sequence of misjudgments that were typical of Curtis, and perhaps of other organizations as well. For twenty years, the Curtis executives and managers had misguided the corporation, taking their profits from magazines and investing them mostly in machinery, and now that the profits were declining, they wanted to change not the machinery but the magazines. But Curtis's rulers had never understood that a magazine is an idea, and so they now set out to solve the problem not by developing new ideas but by changing the magazine's appearance. They were worried about advertising, and it was generally assumed that advertising executives do not read anything smaller than headline type. So Art Director Kenneth Stuart took charge of hiring fashionable designers like Herb Lubalin and Saul Bass to create a "new look," and Clay Blair began assigning expensive photographers to illustrate the articles.

In June, Fuoss gathered in the *Post* salesmen from all over the country to a convention at the Pocono Manor in the hills of Pennsylvania. Fuoss, Stuart, and Blair displayed their dramatic layouts for the "new" *Post*, and the salesmen rose to their feet and cheered. With a promotion budget of $1 million, Curtis began advertising the forthcoming magazine as a creation "like no other magazine you ever read before," one in which "suddenly reading becomes an adventure." And for this first version of the "new" *Post*, Madison Avenue bought $6 million worth of advertising, creating an issue of 148 pages, the largest in years.

But the "new" *Post* that appeared on September 16, 1961, was a peculiar mixture of new and old. The cover, by Norman Rockwell, showed an artist looking at various old *Post* covers and trying to puzzle out a new one. Inside, a new feature called "Speaking Out" ("a forum for all the nuts to sound off," Fuoss condescendingly remarked) was designed with an exclamation point instead of the letter "i" in the word "speaking," and the first offering was a polemic by Herman Kahn, entitled, "We're Too Scared to Think." The lead article, on the other hand, was that Hibbsian triumph, the memoirs of Casey Stengel, and one page was devoted entirely to a color photograph of the old man sniffing a rose. A new feature called "People on the Way Up" showed that nervous preoccupation with youth that is a familiar symptom of a magazine in trouble. But while some of the layouts were flashy, most of the issue contained the same kind of trivia that had typified the "old" *Post*. After the Stengel memoir came a short story called "Once upon a Treasure Hunt," another story called "Hit and Run" by John MacDonald, and another by Gerald Kersh. The articles included "Japan's Young Moderns," a widow's account of "Now I Walk Alone," and a long report on an American doctor doing good works in the jungles of Haiti. The look of the "new" *Post* infuriated its readers, and they wrote in to protest at a rate of ten thousand letters a week. "Idiotic . . . Please change it back. . . . Cancel my subscription. . . . I have been betrayed—and many others with me." As for Madison Avenue, for which the "new" *Post* had been created, it responded as it usually does to such efforts— with a shrug. "The mistake was," in the words of one cynical old *Post* editor, "that you forced them to read the magazine." From another point of view, the *Post* had erred by forgetting Edward Bok's old rule: "Come down to the level which the public sets and it will leave you the moment you do it." Basically, the *Post* had announced change and then attempted to counterfeit change, and the increased advertising didn't last a month. Over the whole year, in fact, advertising plummeted from $104 million to $86 million. The *Post* consequently went into the red by $3 million, and Curtis by $4 million.

During these important days of transition, Ben Hibbs kept fading away. Though Fuoss was more or less in charge, Hibbs's name remained at the top of the masthead throughout that autumn, and it was not until the last issue of 1961 that he departed from the editorial page with an appeal for everyone to "stand up on our hind legs and be Americans." In the editorial of the next issue, the first of 1962, Bob Fuoss tried bravely, and a bit awkwardly, to announce "Where the Post Stands." It would no longer be a Republican organ, Fuoss said, remarking that he himself had voted for Eisenhower in 1956 and for Kennedy in 1960. To this, he added the usual recommendations—support for free enterprise as "a matter of personal pride," an appeal for a more "imaginative" foreign policy, and domestic struggle against "ugly scars on the proud shield of democracy." In commercial terms, unfortunately, none of this really mattered as much as people thought. MacNeal's Curtis Publishing Company was as arthritic as the magazine that Hibbs bequeathed to Fuoss. Within a year, all three of these genuinely worthy gentlemen would be gone.

"The new *Post* was an utter, total, complete disaster," said Clay Blair. "The staff was shocked and bewildered. There wasn't an old *Post* any more, only a new *Post* that no one liked. We were hanging in mid-air, with staggering losses, and nobody had another plan. . . .

"The *Post*'s advertising director was still hopeful, and he asked me if I would call on some key advertisers and explain what we were trying to do with the *Post*. I made about forty speeches during October and November of 1961, and that brought me into close contact for the first time with the sales side of the *Post*. And I saw the same thing I had seen in circulation, in manufacturing, throughout all of Curtis—fat, age, incompetence, fear, fatigue, and plain laziness. It finally dawned on me that saving the *Post* was not simply a matter of changing a format, or assigning better writers to more timely articles. Saving the *Post* meant overthrowing the management of the entire Curtis Publishing Company."

3

"I am not afraid of anything"

I do not believe in fortunetelling. In January of 1962, however, my wife paid a visit to one of New York's more celebrated astrologers, a bewigged septuagenarian who practiced his craft on West Forty-fourth Street, within a block of the Harvard Club. "Your husband will have a very difficult spring," said Mr. McC——. "He must be patient. A change for the better will come, but he must do nothing to seek it. Other people will come to him, people who know his past work. The change will come in September."

The absurdity of prophecies is that one cannot understand them when one first hears them, and afterward, when they have come true, it is impossible to believe that they were true from the beginning. I took Mr. McC——'s prediction as quite reasonable, something he had somehow deciphered from my wife's conversation, since I was then the assistant foreign editor of *Newsweek,* and I expected to replace the foreign editor when he returned to London that spring. "A difficult spring." Yes, I was working very hard, and making plans for how I would run things when the promised promotion became official. Despite the promise, unfortunately, another foreign editor was appointed—"You don't have enough panache," one of the authorities explained to me—and I was left with a raise, some flattering words, and a sense of humiliation. I bitterly began looking for other jobs, so bitterly, in fact, that my wife telephoned Mr. McC—— to ask what had gone wrong with his prediction. "There was nothing wrong with it," Mr. McC—— retorted. "I said it would be a difficult spring. I said he should not do anything about it. Tell him to be patient. The other people will come to him."

In June, I got a telephone call from Don Schanche, a former Time-Life foreign correspondent then working in the Washington bureau of the *Saturday Evening Post*. "I might as well be frank," he said at the outset. "Would you be interested in talking about coming over to the *Post?*" Schanche, a blond, stocky man of about thirty-five, had been assigned to "run up the Jolly Roger," as one observer put it, and to recruit a new staff for the *Post* by raiding every magazine in New York. One major acquisition had already been arranged, Schanche informed me as we sat down to lunch in front of the huge Dali mural in the Berkshire Hotel. Bill Emerson, the *Newsweek* senior editor in charge of "the back of the book" (all the sections except national affairs, foreign affairs, and business), had just agreed to move to the *Post* as chief articles editor. The *Post*'s foreign-affairs editor was retiring, and Emerson had recommended me as a replacement. So Schanche and I sparred for a while, conversing learnedly about the recent political paroxysms in Laos. (An interest in Laotian politics is an acquired taste, but connoisseurs find the subject highly savory.) As for the job, I said I would be very much interested if the *Post* would provide a contract that paid enough, and I named a figure almost 50 percent higher than what I was getting from *Newsweek*. Schanche said he would have to arrange a meeting with Bob Sherrod, who had just succeeded Fuoss as editor of the *Post,* and a week or so later, I had lunch with Sherrod, this time at the St. Regis Hotel. I liked Sherrod, a nervous but rather courtly Southerner with a red face and a large nose—a paternal figure, then in his middle fifties. And once again, since he was also a former foreign correspondent—actually, a very distinguished war correspondent for Time-Life—we talked about the dreamlike politics of Laos. We also talked about the *Post,* and Sherrod finally said he would like to hire me as foreign editor, adding, "This job pays twenty thousand."

That was more than I was getting, but not what I had asked for, and I recognized the same trap I had fallen into several times before. When I was twenty-three, I wanted so much to escape from the copy desk of the *Stars and Stripes* that I eagerly agreed to work for the United Press in London for $75 a week, and later learned that the UP had been ready to pay me $85. When I eventually returned to New York, it took me three months to find a job, and I had three children, so I was happy to find work at the *Daily News* at the Newspaper Guild minimum wage of $134.50 per week. Three years later, having received only one "merit raise" of five dollars a week from the *News*, I thought I was lucky to get a job at *Newsweek* for almost twenty dollars a week more, $9,000 a year. Now I was five years older, and

five years meaner about getting a good salary, so I calmly said that
$20,000 a year just wouldn't do.

Sherrod said he would have to think about it some more. The next
week, I got another call, and yet another invitation to lunch, this time
at the Downtown Club in Philadelphia. Sherrod wanted me to meet
his managing editor, Dave Thomas, a slender and soft-spoken young
man with a droopy mustache. I brought my wife along to Philadelphia, and she went wandering through the art museum during my
negotiations, and when I finally found her among the Renoirs, I said,
"You are looking at the new foreign editor of the *Saturday Evening
Post*, starting the first of September." "You see?" she said, after the
congratulations. "It came out exactly the way Mr. McC—— said it
would."

I had agreed to join the *Post* on September 1, on the understanding
that the editorial offices would be moved from Philadelphia to New
York by then. But in a mix-up typical of everything that followed, the
move had to be postponed for a week. All the editors who had been
hired in New York had to come to Philadelphia, live in hotels, and
learn the office routine of an office that was in its last few days of
existence. We got very little work done during that week, but we did
get a unique farewell view of the *Post* as it had once been.

In several ambiguous meetings with my retiring predecessor, Marty
Sommers, I had tried to get him to explain how things worked, since I
had never before seen a magazine that had no reporters, no correspondents, no apparent contact with the outside world. I didn't even
know what questions to ask this amiable, rubicund little man, who
still parted his white hair in the middle, and he, after thirty years at
the *Post*, was equally puzzled at how to answer. "What do you—" I
ventured at one point, "what's the first thing you do when you come to
work?" "Well," he said helplessly, pointing to his In box, "I open the
morning mail." Perhaps he was remembering times past. "In the last
year of his life . . ." said the biographer of George Horace Lorimer,
"the Boss seemed more reflective. . . . He stopped often after work
to have a beer with a new Post editor, Martin Sommers, at the Belle-
vue-Stratford's rathskeller, and over the foam he lovingly recalled the
old days on the Post for this man who had never heard the familiar
tales."

"I work out of this little green box," Marty Sommers had finally
said to me. "Everything is in here." He flipped open a green metal
box, about four by six inches, filled with filing cards. I must have
looked puzzled because Sommers repeated his claim. "It may not look
like much, but everything's here. You'll see." Now that he was gone, I

flipped through the cards, and I saw that they did, in fact, contain "everything." They contained the names of every foreign correspondent that the *Post* had used for twenty years, and the cards listed not just the correspondent's name and address but personal details, his birthday, his wife's name, and the names of his children, and other useful information, like "Schanche, Don. Pronounced SKANK-ee." The cards also listed sources of information to be checked by telephone, ranging from Los Angeles press agents to New York police officials to the omniscient Colonel Grogan, who could never be publicly identified as what he was, press spokesman for the CIA. There were cards listing the simple comforts too—where to order a sandwich late at night, where to get a suit pressed, New York theater tickets, airplane reservations. The effort to contain the whole world in a little green box struck me as bizarre, but I kept it on my desk through all the years I worked at the *Post*.

The office where this round little man had worked was large and square, with a lofty ceiling. The walls held three or four paintings of World War II battle scenes, B-24's swooping low over Ploesti, the *Missouri* firing her sixteen-inch guns, all presumably painted for the *Post*, twenty-five years ago. The tall windows opened onto Independence Square, where insects buzzed and chirped in the September sunshine. Next to the window, a fan six feet high turned lazily from side to side. It was a beautiful office in which to watch the years go by.

Decade after decade, everything here had remained comfortably the same. The *Post* had no air-mail stationery, for instance, because it had never had air-mail stationery. Expense-account forms had a printed space for train fare but none for air fare. One didn't dial outside calls on the telephone—one asked for the operator—and for a private call, one received a bill for ten cents. Very few new people were ever hired, and so the average age of the editors was fifty-seven. Until quite recently, they had received their pay in cash in an envelope every week. That was the way things had always been done. To deliver materials from one part of Philadelphia to another, the company maintained a fleet of dark green electric trucks, acquired in 1913, which rolled along at about ten miles an hour and could not reach the printing plant in Sharon Hill because their batteries could not hold out that long. And in the men's rooms, according to one survivor's recollections, "They employed one gray-haired gentleman as a toilet-tissue splicer. It was his duty to take the nearly exhausted rolls of uncomfortably scratchy paper from the marble lavatories, splice them together, and place the neatly rolled results back in the john."

Since time immemorial, work had begun every day at 9:10 with the ringing of a fire bell. Bob Sherrod, like Hibbs before him, held a morning meeting with his chief lieutenants to give verdicts on the manuscripts that had been read the night before. Lesser editors spent their time dictating answers to the previous day's mail, for there was a "reading line" that dealt with all incoming material, passing anything good up to the editor, and it was a firm rule that every manuscript and letter had to be handled within seventy-two hours. (If a manuscript was accepted for publication, on the other hand, it required at least a month to reach the newsstands.)

At twelve noon, the editors began drifting next door to the Downtown Club. There, for years, a large round table had been reserved for them to sit, according to masthead rank, reading the afternoon Philadelphia *Bulletin* while they ate. Afterward, many of them retired to the clubroom for a nap. (Fuoss, by contrast, was still remembered as a fierce cribbage player during these luncheon hours.) At two o'clock, everybody trooped back to his desk. Soon after four, the editors began departing for the suburbs, the conscientious ones carrying attaché cases filled with new loads of manuscripts. By five, the offices were empty; by 5:30, the switchboard shut down, and massive fire doors slid into place, sealing off the editorial offices from the printing areas at the back of the building.

(Once a week," said Clay Blair, recalling the old traditions,* "there was a staff conference in a stuffy, windowless room at the rear of the building. The editors filed in and sat by rank at the long conference table. Hibbs opened the meeting with a tap of a little chrome school bell. Then he cleared his throat and announced the previous week's newsstand sales, and any staff births and deaths. Then we listened to the fiction editors give their long and incoherent accounts of their trips to faraway New York: 'John Marquand is sick again, but he may have a new novel finished . . . mumble-mumble . . . May or June . . . mumble-mumble . . . maybe another Hornblower . . . although it is . . . mumble . . . nonfiction . . . mumble . . . fight between *Hood* and *Bismarck* . . . and I talked to Harold Matson . . . Ruark . . . another novel on Kenya . . . mumble-mumble . . .'")

In every previous job, I had come to work for a boss, who had told me what he wanted me to do, but now I sat in Marty Sommers's huge,

---

* I am indebted here, and at a number of other points, to Clay Blair's unpublished memoirs, which he made available to me in manuscript.

silent office, listening to the whirring fan and the insects in Independence Square, and wondering how the system operated. At one point, on that first day, I started down the corridor to see if I could find somebody who knew more than I did. I wandered into the office of a pipe-smoking, gray-haired gentleman who looked like, and indeed was, a member of the old guard, and I asked him what he could tell me about how things worked. "Damned if I know," he said, none too cordially. "They've changed everything." Back in my own office, I received a visitation from a nervous old gentleman who introduced himself as Day Edgar, assistant to the editor. "*You're* a senior editor?" he asked. I acknowledged that I was. "Well, you're certainly the youngest senior editor *I* ever saw," he said, and away he went, and I never saw him again.

And then a young lady came and handed me a messy manuscript and said, "Mr. Sherrod would like you to read this editorial." It was a short statement supporting the UN effort to reintegrate Katanga Province into the Congo. "What do I do when I've read it?" I asked. "I don't know," the girl said. "Mr. Sherrod just asked that you read it." I followed her back through several corridors to Sherrod's office, which was three or four times as gigantic as mine, a throne room. Sherrod sat at the far end, between the purring fans, his desk awash with papers. As I approached, interrupting him, he looked up with the wild expression of a man at the limits of his endurance.

"This editorial . . ." I said.

"Oh, yes," he said, his flushed face relaxing slightly.

"It seems perfectly all right to me," I said, "although it's not very well written."

"Oh," he said. A pause.

"Would you like me to do some editing on it?" I asked.

"Why, yes, if you would."

I went back to my office and edited the editorial rather drastically and then returned it to Sherrod, who never mentioned it again. And so, several weeks later, I saw my first words in print in the *Saturday Evening Post*. It all seemed somehow too easy, as though nobody were actually in charge.

But Bob Sherrod's tasks during that week were beyond any rational comprehension. At the very least, he had to oversee the publication of a weekly magazine, plus the gathering together of a new staff, most of whom knew neither the magazine nor each other, plus the transfer of that whole staff and all its equipment from Philadelphia to New York. And yet there was still more going on. At the end of the last week in Philadelphia, Sherrod called his two dozen remaining editors together for the regular weekly staff meeting. Most of the chairs had already been shipped to New York, so we just stood, or sat on the floor. Sherrod began with some of his usual announcements—the free coffee wagon was being abolished, and coffee in New York would cost ten cents; the *Post* was not registered for Blue Cross in New York, but new forms would be distributed shortly—and then he turned the meeting over to Clay Blair. There had been "some misunderstanding about Culligan's memo," Sherrod said, and Blair would explain it.

At this point in time, September of 1962, I not only had never met Clay Blair, I had never even heard of him. Nor had I ever seen the mysterious memo that he was going to explain. I had come to work for Bob Sherrod and Bill Emerson, and if the *Post* was losing some money, well, somebody would eventually solve that problem. "Thank God," I had said to my wife, after my first lunch with Bob Sherrod, and after five years of serpentine intrigues at *Newsweek,* "I can finally work at a job that won't involve any office politics." I knew nothing, in short, about what was really happening at Curtis. I did not know that Sherrod was already engaged in a fight for his life—or rather, since he did not fight very hard, and had no chance of winning, I did not know that Sherrod had already been marked for slaughter. Nor did I know that Clay Blair, once his protégé, would be his slaughterer. I knew nothing of Blair's background, or of his ambitions; I did not know that he had recently been the *Post*'s managing editor, or that he had been named vice president of Curtis, or that he had spent the last two months in analyzing the corporation. And so I attached no particular importance to this important confrontation. I regarded Blair simply as a large, dark stranger, who began to talk, rather entertainingly, in fits and starts, about the anachronisms and absurdities that his "study group" had discovered within the Curtis Publishing Company.

"Let me give you just one example," Blair said. "Just one example. The mail. When you want to mail a letter, you put it in your Out box, and you probably think it goes to the post office. Well, it doesn't. The first thing that happens is, all this mail gets put into a *suitcase*—an unmarked suitcase—and a little man carries it down in the elevator, and then he loads it onto a handcart, and another little man wheels it over to Chestnut Street, through all that traffic, over to the Gimbel Building, and over there he takes the suitcase and puts it on another elevator—I'm not kidding—and it rides up to the tenth floor, and—" There was some laughter now, and Blair began playing to it, encouraging it. "And they take the suitcase out of the cart, and open it up, and dump all the letters out on a table, and then they put *stamps* on them—because this is the company mailing room, for everything—" more laughter by now—"and then they bag it for shipment, and put it back on the elevator, and then load it onto one of our electric trucks, and so it finally goes to the post office." Amid the laughter, Blair again offered that as just one example of how absurdly, desperately, Curtis needed modernization—and somehow, by God, it would be modernized.

"Now about this memo," Blair went on. "I want everything to be perfectly clear. Bob Sherrod is the editor of the *Post,* and he's a great editor, and I don't have any intention whatsoever of interfering with him. What I'm going to do is . . . questions like . . . should we buy this radio station or that one, or should we be doing more in the field of books, that kind of thing. Now, I reserve the right to change the editor of the *Post,* if I think that's necessary, but I want to say once again that I think Bob Sherrod is a great editor. In fact, I think he's maybe the greatest editor in America. So I don't expect there will be any problems at all." Blair then turned the meeting back to Sherrod, and Sherrod glumly said, "Class dismissed," and we all dispersed, understanding nothing.

We did not understand—or, more accurately, I did not understand —that the newly installed President Culligan had just appointed Blair to the position of "Editorial Director" of all Curtis magazines, and that the mysterious memo had provided Blair's own picture of the future:

The Editorial Director will be on hand and available to give guidance and suggestions. His responsibility includes the editorial content of the magazines, the operational staffing of the magazines, the public acceptance of the magazines. This responsibility will not be exercised on a day-to-day basis; the editors are still in charge of their publications. . . . Blair will attend the scheduling meetings of the publications, and will have responsibility for determining the final closing schedules and formulae.

We also did not know that Sherrod had interpreted the memo correctly and reacted properly. "I picked up the phone and called Joe Culligan in San Francisco, and I said, 'I quit,'" Sherrod said later. "He begged me not to. He said we couldn't stand the trouble. He told me to get together with Blair and talk about it." They had done so, and Blair apparently promised not to interfere with the *Post.* Thus Sherrod took Blair's public statement as a threat. "It was a double cross," Sherrod said later. "Blair went back on what he had said one hour earlier. In fact, he made everything worse."

I did not see Blair again for another two months. Then, in November of 1962, we were all summoned to the conference room of the new Curtis headquarters at 666 Fifth Avenue in New York. Culligan was the first to speak, and he told us with enthusiasm of a recent visit to the White House. "You know, Joe," President Kennedy had said to Culligan, "it's great to see an Irishman getting ahead in the business world.." Even after having heard himself tell the story many times, Culligan still seemed greatly moved by the President's condescension. And then, after offering a few good wishes, he turned the meeting over to Clay Blair and hurried away.

Blair's announcements were stunning. He started by declaring that he was taking over the *Post*, and that Bob Sherrod, the "great editor," now sitting red-faced and glassy-eyed at a nearby place on the dais, was "returning to his first love, reporting and writing on world affairs." To start with, Sherrod was being shipped off to India as the head of a "task force" that included Norman Rockwell and a photographer called Ollie Atkins, plus their wives, to produce a story on Nehru. And there would be other changes. Don Schanche was moving from Washington to New York to become executive editor. Dave Thomas would remain as managing editor, and Bill Emerson as assistant managing editor for articles. A Danish designer would become art director. A *Life* photographer was joining the *Post* as assistant managing editor for photography. The former picture editor had resigned.

"This magazine has only achieved about 50 percent of what it must achieve to survive," Blair said. "And now we're all going to have to get in there and try harder. . . ."

So Sherrod had failed. After ten years at the *Post*, as foreign correspondent, managing editor, editor, he sat there and heard himself sent into exile. It is easy to conclude that Sherrod was inadequate to the editorship of the *Post*, or perhaps simply too old to fight for the job, but this was not a man who deserved scorn. Sherrod had taken part in the most terrible battles in the Pacific during World War II—Tarawa, Iwo Jima, Okinawa—and the men who survived those battles will never forget the mere act of survival. Nobody who knew Sherrod during those years, and during the postwar years in Tokyo, has anything but respect for him as a correspondent and as a man. But hideous scenes of survival sometimes unfit the survivor for further combat. So Ulysses S. Grant, whom the people loved, was one of our clumsiest Presidents, and as I try to evaluate the end of Sherrod's reign, I remember primarily a series of small scenes of failure.

The scheduling meeting, to take only one example, is the essence of editorial power. This meeting decides what will go into a magazine, in what position, and at what length. The meetings should be small and short, directed by somebody who knows what he wants. Scheduling meetings under Sherrod were state occasions, held at a long table, and interminable. I remember attending one of them and seeing Sherrod helpless. "Come on now," he said to the ten or twelve silent lieutenants, "doesn't anyone have anything to propose as a lead? We have to have a lead after all. Doesn't anyone have anything?"

Within Sherrod's own staff, he could find little support, for Thomas and Schanche were already committed to Blair. "I've asked him to let me help him," said Emerson, the only editor of any importance who was both independent and sympathetic to Sherrod, "but he won't admit there's any problem. They're going to kill him, and he knows it, but he won't admit there's anything wrong."

There is a relationship between what people look like and what they are. Clay Blair was very large. He was tall, over six feet, and heavy, perhaps 220 pounds, but the huge bulk seemed to lack shape. He had neither the simple roundness of the fat man nor the proportioned size of the athlete but rather a quality of formless massiveness. And darkness. The dark hair lay flat on the heavy head, the eyes were dark, and the cheeks darkly shadowed. He glowered. There was an elemental energy here, not fully under control, but also a quality of vulnerability, of secret fragility. He spoke nervously, in a curiously blurred voice, the sentences tumbling forth without any hint of syntax, and the tongue lashing out in an odd flickering movement, like that of some lizard perched defensively on a rock.

Blair was a Southerner, born in Lexington, Virginia, in 1925, and he volunteered for the navy in World War II. His public life began then, and, as recounted in *Post* promotional material, it appeared to be a series of misfortunes remedied by blind bravery. In one episode, for instance, Blair reported that a Japanese submarine had fired two torpedoes at his sub, and that the helmsman had become paralyzed. "I grabbed the wheel and gave it a turn," Blair said, "and we went between the two torpedoes. It was one of those moments when any action, right or wrong, seems better than doing nothing." In another promotion booklet, Blair listed his "dedication to firsts" as the basis for his "spectacular publishing career." "He was the first reporter to make a simulated combat mission in a B-47 bomber, first to ride on the [atomic] submarine Nautilus, first to fly in a B-52 jet bomber, first to go through the sonic barrier in a plane, and first to be submerged in a submarine when it fired a missile." In the course of these autobiographical advertisements, Blair commented on what he had learned. "The real measure of a man is not how he performs in times of peace and prosperity but in times of adversity. I admire men who work and fight to the end under fire. . . . I am not afraid of anything, and I feel that fear is an indefensible emotion. Fear is something that a man feels when faced with an unknown, but he should probe the cause of his fear and learn what to do about it. . . . Fear should be a call to action."

Blair's real life had been somewhat less glamorous. His father was an electrical engineer, who moved his family through a series of Southern towns during the Depression—Memphis, then Valdosta, Georgia, then Bay St. Louis, Mississippi. And if Blair did not talk much about his childhood, he may have had good reasons. "As a small boy, a Catholic in hard-rock Baptist south Georgia, I was a sissy, a loner, a reader, something of a mama's boy," he recalled much later. "My ambition then was to be a poet. I was regularly beaten up by the town bullies, disrobed, humiliated. Later, as a teenager, I suppose I overreacted to that, and for a long time I did crazy things to test my fear. I was the first to smoke, drink, get laid, to own a car (and thus to drag race). . . . Hence, too, I think, submarines."

(The submarine experience turns out, on closer examination, to have been not quite what the *Post* promotion brochures claimed. "The war anecdotes, like most war anecdotes, were exaggerated," Blair said later. "When I heard the lookout cry, 'Torpedoes on the starboard bow,' I was scared out of my wits, as anyone would be, and everyone was. . . . But remember that the promotion booklet was prepared by Caskie Stinnett at a time when panic was widespread at Curtis, and the decision was to present Sherrod and Blair as two pillars of strength who were not afraid of anything. So it's wrong to say I have no fear. I could never have said, 'Fear is an indefensible emotion.' Caskie's words, maybe, not mine." I finally asked Caskie Stinnett, tall and stately and silver-haired, and by now the editor of *Holiday,* whether he had actually fabricated this quintessential expression of Blair's philosophy, and he smiled and shrugged, and said, "Well, perhaps I did make that up.")

After attending Tulane and the Columbia School of Journalism, Blair turned up at that Times Square of journalism, *Time* magazine, and got himself a job. "I was a glorified copy boy," he once said to me, but *Time* apparently thought well enough of him to send him to Washington within a year, and there he became a Pentagon correspondent. Blair made his way, and wrote his first book, *The Atomic Submarine and Admiral Rickover*. He also collaborated with James

Shepley, who later became president of Time Inc., on a book dealing with the controversy between Admiral Lewis L. Strauss, the Wall Street banker who was then the head of the Atomic Energy Commission, and J. Robert Oppenheimer, the distinguished physicist who was banned from the government's atomic program as a "security risk." The Shepley-Blair book was ardently on the side of Admiral Strauss.

After seven years in the Time-Life Washington bureau, Blair apparently decided it was time for a change. One day in 1957, he approached Bob Sherrod, who had been a Time-Life correspondent at the Pentagon, and asked for a job. "I was delighted," Sherrod said later. "Blair had been my assistant when he was about twenty-five years old, and I knew him as energetic, enthusiastic and resourceful—the very type I thought we needed on the *Post*. I classed him as my friend." Hibbs promptly agreed to hire Blair as an associate editor at $18,000 a year, and the newcomer spent the next three years in the *Post*'s Washington office, writing articles about political and military affairs.

On periodic trips to Philadelphia, however, Blair was struck by the general stagnation and inertia that marked the closing years of the Hibbs regime. When he grumbled about it, Bob Fuoss responded by inviting him to spend a month in Philadelphia during the summer of 1960 and to write a report on what he saw. Blair's report, the first of many he was to compose on this subject, sharply criticized all editorial operations—the aging staff, the lack of ideas, the general apathy. The result was that Hibbs brought Blair to Philadelphia as an editor, and that Fuoss disclosed his plans for a "new" *Post*.

There is probably a limit to the time any man can function as an heir apparent without suffering some loss to his capacity for independence. So Bob Fuoss, a modest but highly capable man who had served at Hibbs's right hand ever since Hibbs took over the *Post* in 1942, appeared to be stunned by the failure of the "new" *Post*. He was "disheartened even before he became editor," according to Sherrod, "and some time in February, his second month in office, he said he was going to resign. I could hardly believe him." When Fuoss did resign the next month, Sherrod succeeded him as editor and promptly appointed Blair as his managing editor at $30,000 a year. "I'm desperate," Sherrod said, according to Blair's recollection. "I need all the help I can get. You're the best man on the staff."

By this time, however, something surprising had happened to inspire Clay Blair with ambitions far beyond a managing editorship. Toward the end of 1961, Admiral Lewis Strauss, the Wall Street banker whom Blair had treated so benevolently in his book, *The Hydrogen Bomb,* telephoned about some now-forgotten editorial problem and then remarked, "I see you boys are having some financial troubles. If I can be of any help, please call on me. You know, I used to sell the *Post* when I was a boy." Blair was greatly impressed by the offer. "I sat at my desk, staring into Washington Square, thinking of the millions and millions of dollars Strauss could lay his hands on, if moved to do so. With a few phone calls, he could raise enough to buy the company, install new management, give the *Post* another chance." Blair sent a note to MacNeal, urging him to call Strauss, and when there was no answer, Blair flew to Washington to see Strauss himself. Strauss asked a lot of questions about stock ownership and financial problems, and Blair, who did not know the answers, promised to find out. He spent two weeks studying Curtis financial affairs and then wrote a fifteen-thousand-word report on the company's history, present situation, problems and prospects. The report urged that Strauss approach the Bok family with an offer to buy the family's 30 percent holding in the company. "I asked him, 'Do you really think you have a chance of being the new president of this company?'" said Don Schanche, who edited Blair's report to Strauss, "and he said, 'Well, yes, maybe I do.'" Bob Sherrod had a similar exchange: "Blair came to me and said, 'I know a lot about this company now. May I have your permission to try for president myself?' So I said, 'Go ahead, Clay, and good luck to you.'"

Not long afterward, Blair received a telephone call inviting him to New York for a meeting with Douglas Black, chairman of Doubleday & Company. It soon became clear that Strauss had interested Black in the idea of merging his book-publishing firm with Curtis. In a dinner at the Union League Club, Black and a new Curtis director named Milton Gould asked what Blair would do if he became president of Curtis. He gave the inevitable answer: "Dispose of the paper and printing plants, cut out the deadwood, and put the company's resources behind the *Post.*" Despite his own analysis of Curtis, however, Blair scarcely realized how bad the corporation's troubles were. Doubleday concluded its investigation by backing away from any attempt at a merger. Admiral Strauss's interest began to fade. Another prospective buyer began yet another study and was advised by his accountants that Curtis "didn't even have any figures worth looking at." The bankers who held Curtis notes for $22 million were pressing MacNeal for some sign of progress, but MacNeal had no plan. Instead, during the early summer of 1962, MacNeal simply flew off to Europe. "That trip, I think, was the final blow," said Cary Bok, grandson of Cyrus Curtis and chief trustee of his estate, "and it was obvious that MacNeal had to go." Bok himself held the title of acting president, in MacNeal's absence, but he had recently undergone surgery and then broken a leg. "Hell, I'm flat on my back," Bok said on the telephone to Philadelphia. "I resign as acting president. Work something out."

Ancient Walter Fuller, who had succeeded Lorimer as president back in 1934, had survived all these years and was ready to reassume his responsibilities. A tiny figure of eighty by now, bald, bony, and somewhat deaf, Fuller still was a power on the board. And so, in one sudden burst of activity, the board deposed MacNeal, appointed a four-man committee to find a new president, and, almost incidentally, made Blair a vice president with unspecified responsibility in editorial matters. The committee, headed by Fuller but dominated by the assertive Milton Gould, once again asked Blair what he would do as president, and Blair drafted a written response that he entitled "Tomorrow Morning's Plan."* It began with "Appointment of new executive team," and it listed the best available candidates, starting with

  a. Clay Blair, President—(ready)
  b. William Buckley,† Exec. Vice-Pres.—(ready)
  c. Jesse Ballew, Vice President, Publisher of SEP—(ready)

and so on for twelve top positions.

Blair's recommendations were Draconian. For one, he recommended the liquidation of the *Ladies' Home Journal*, which was losing large sums of money during the last days of the twenty-year regime of Bruce and Beatrice Gould, and *American Home*, which was also losing several million dollars a year. He recommended selling the Curtis building in Philadelphia, getting rid of the paper mills, tightening the Curtis Circulation Company, moving everything except printing and distribution to New York. For the *Post* he recommended a deliberate reduction in circulation from 6.5 million to 5 million—for much the same reasons that a similar move was finally made six years later, too late:

  a. Lops off expensive unstable top 1½ million circulation.
  b. Gives SEP high quality, definable audience, noncompetitive with

---

* For this document, the quotations from Cary Bok, and other background material, I am indebted to *The Curtis Caper*, by Joseph C. Goulden, published in 1965.

† A former vice president at such publishing firms as Holt and World, not the William Buckley who edits the *National Review*.

Life, Look, TV. Fulfills promotion policy of high quality reading magazine for influential people, in class alone, like *New Yorker.*

c. Reduces greatly cost per thousand in ad rates, enables some advertisers to return to magazine, offers new opportunity for advertisers. Enables reduction of and dependence on costly, futile split-run advertising.

In summation, Blair said, "The foregoing recommendations are designed to reshape Curtis in order to direct, emphasize and support the SEP, which is the only property held by Curtis capable of making large amounts of money. . . . The suggested moves are drastic. But such moves are required to save the company."

The proposals might have saved the company, but they may also have doomed Blair's chances for the presidency. "Walter Fuller invited me privately to his office, a gloomy, oak-paneled room with a fireplace, on the fourth floor of the Curtis building," Blair recalled. "It was Fuller who had 'integrated' Curtis, bought the paper companies, built the Sharon Hill printing plant—his monuments. Now he seemed disturbed that I wanted to divest them. . . . The committee's legal counsel, Milton Gould, meanwhile had found Joe Culligan, by way of Barney Gallagher of the *Gallagher Report.* Neither I nor anyone else at Curtis took seriously the Gallagher proposal that Culligan be considered for the presidency. But Culligan met Gould in Gallagher's office, and afterward Gould declared, 'Boy! This guy's got moxie!' "

So it was Joe Culligan, then only forty-four, the one-eyed magician from Madison Avenue, the necromancer of advertising revenue, who was going to be swept into the vacant presidency of the Curtis Publishing Company. But while Milton Gould was arguing his views before the frightened presidential committee, he was also staging a bizarre bit of theater. He summoned both Culligan and Blair, who barely knew one another, to a private office in downtown Philadelphia and left them alone together. Culligan, who later called this meeting "the oddest I had in almost twenty years in business," quickly deduced that Gould had "decided just to throw us together and see 'who'd come out on top.' " Blair walked into the office, recognized Culligan, and introduced himself.

"I started asking him some questions about Curtis, which he at first answered," Culligan recalled. "As the probing got deeper, he suddenly fixed me with a suspicious stare and demanded: 'What is your interest in Curtis?' I said, 'I may join Curtis.'

" 'In what capacity?'

" 'As president,' I answered.

"Blair's reaction was violent. He gasped and went ashen, staring at me with an expression I could not quite read. Had Gould warned me of Blair's ambition to be president, I would have been prepared.

"Believing that Blair was in a mild state of shock, I took the offensive immediately. He was quite easy to handle. . . ." Blair, on the other hand, later called Culligan's account of this confrontation "ridiculous." "You can imagine that I was surprised by his pronouncement," Blair said. "But I didn't gasp. I was relieved, frankly. Compared to MacNeal, Culligan looked like a real winner. I was much impressed."

"This magazine has only achieved about 50 percent of what it must achieve to survive," Blair was saying to the assembled editors. To explain what he meant, he had taken the latest issue, the Thanksgiving issue, torn it to pieces, and tacked the pieces on the walls of the conference room. Now he poked at them with a schoolroom pointer. The magazine's cover, to start with, was an old-fashioned cartoon. Timed for Thanksgiving, it showed a truck driver staring in dismay at a flat tire on his truckload of gibbering turkeys. It was a pleasant little joke, but it had sold poorly on the newsstands, and Blair now denounced it as typical of the *Post*'s failure to change. "The gag cover is an anachronism," he said. "We've got to go beyond that. We've got to have covers that have something timely to say." Next came the weekly department of dissenting opinion called "Speaking Out." Blair said it was full of "nonentities," speaking out on trivial subjects. "I want important people speaking out," he said, "like Admiral Rickover, and Edward Teller, names that people really want to hear from."

Then we came to the lead, which I had edited and which I was proud of. It was a two-part report on the obscure war that was just getting under way in Vietnam, and it included the first major story on North Vietnam in any American magazine. The author, Bernard Fall, had interviewed Ho Chi Minh and Premier Pham Van Dong, he had toured factories and military bases, and he concluded, oddly enough, that the United States should stop Ho by bombing the North. Blair was not satisfied. This was just a story about "gooks," he said. "The American people don't want to read about gooks. If we have to do a story about gooks, we ought to tell it in terms of what the Americans are doing out there, not what the gooks are doing."

The moving finger passed on. We had just published a profile of Geraldine Page, and Blair didn't like it because Geraldine Page was too old. Henceforth, stories about show business would involve pretty girls. Then we came to the question of chili. Every issue in those days was supposed to contain one article of "women's interest," and the one in this issue was a little feature about chili con carne, illustrated with a color photograph of what looked like, at best, dog food. Blair suggested a more vulgar analogy and vowed that the *Post* would never again publish an article on such a subject. Blair's criticisms were not without justification, of course, particularly as he reached the back pages of this unfortunate issue. There was a two-page picture story devoted to an ice cave in Wyoming; there was a memoir by a colonel about the difficulties in arranging a Thanksgiving turkey dinner during the Korean War, and, finally, there was an article by Ben Hibbs, who was easing into his retirement by writing, about a ranch for delinquent boys in Texas.

"The *Post* is a good magazine, but it's still too aimless and bland," Blair announced. "I think we have to make the magazine compelling—I mean, I *know* we have to make the magazine compelling. The purpose of the *Post* should be not only to inform but to crusade, and every issue has to land with impact. Not with sensational yellow journalism but with real hard-hitting articles that are timely and mean something to somebody. I'd like to see the magazine generate electricity, verve." In theory, I agreed with the demands for more timeliness, more youth and energy, but the tone of Blair's whole speech reduced me and most of the staff to a state of mutinous resentment. For within three months the *Post* had already absorbed its newcomers, just as Imperial China had once absorbed barbarian invaders. I, who had been brought to the *Post* as an agent of change, had already become an enemy of change, a defender of the status quo. I judged Blair to be an aggressive reactionary, a propagandist for the military, and something of a Yahoo.

When the meeting broke up, I retreated angrily into my office, with Gerry Astor, another newcomer, who edited "Speaking Out." I slammed the door and launched into a tirade against our new editor.

"Gooks!" I shouted. "How the hell can anybody work for an editor who thinks the war in Vietnam is nothing but a bunch of gooks?"

"And what about 'Speaking Out'?" Astor joined in. "How can anybody call it a forum for dissenting opinion when all Blair wants to hear from is the right-wing establishment? Teller! Rickover! Who cares what they say?"

Bill Emerson, sensing the trouble, opened my door and stuck his head in to see what was going on. "Gooks!" I shouted at him. "The gooks are going to take over the world, whether Clay Blair likes it or not."

"Don't get so excited," Emerson said. "We'll work everything out."

4

"You are putting out one hell
of a fine magazine"

In every man's life, there comes an adventure or experience that changes the shape of everything that follows. Often, we do not recognize the experience at the time, as we do not recognize the angels who move among us, or, perhaps more accurately, we do not understand our act of recognition.

Clay Blair, who partly understood, summoned his newly acquired editors, on the second day of his reign, so that he could tell them a story about a meeting in Rock Creek Park. "I was all alone in the Time-Life office in Washington," he told us, "when this man called, and so I picked it up, and this guy told me that he had an important story that he wanted to tell somebody. You've probably all had calls like that, and you've probably all said, 'Yeah-yeah-yeah,' and turned the guy off, and I guess I have too, but I was just a kid then, and I didn't know enough to say 'No.' So this guy said he couldn't talk on the telephone, had to meet me somewhere—another sure sign of a nut, right?—but, as I say, I didn't know any better—so he said there was this boulder in Rock Creek Park. He described it, what it looked like, and he said he'd meet me there at eight o'clock on Sunday night. I was just dumb enough to go, and I met this man, there by the boulder, right where he said he'd be, and he said he had a story about the United States Navy, about a terrible injustice that the navy was committing. He said there was a brilliant captain called Hyman Rickover, a man nobody had ever heard of, and the navy was suppressing him because of his ideas and ambitions, and something ought to be done about it."

Blair looked around at us. Nobody said anything.

"And by God, it was all true!" Blair went on. "I started to look into that story—remember, now, that nobody had ever heard of Rickover in those days—and nobody paid any attention to—well, they'd ask me where I got this story, and if I said I'd just met some guy in Rock Creek Park—well, but it was all true! So I started a *crusade* for this unheard-of guy called Rickover. I dug out the facts, and I made them public—and we took on the whole Navy Department—started a Congressional investigation—and we won! And if it hadn't been for that, Rickover's nuclear submarine, the Polaris missile, our strongest deterrent against the Russians right now—well, that's how it happened."

Blair looked around at us, breathing a little heavily. He seemed to expect something from us—a murmur of surprise and applause—but we were not sure what he wanted, and we were still too new to one another to respond easily, and so we all just sat there, looking back at him. "Well, that's the story," Blair said. "I just thought you'd like to hear it."

Blair may have realized that his meeting on his first day had been somewhat less than a success, or perhaps his lieutenants convinced him that he had angered many of the editors he would need to put out a magazine. In any case, he called for this second meeting. Now, instead of telling us what he didn't like about the *Post*, he tried to explain more specifically what he wanted. He told us that he had been thinking about our readers' interests, and he had catalogued all matters of interest into ten categories that he wanted us to keep in mind: (1) war, (2) natural disasters, (3) royalty, (4) sex, (5) crime, (6) religion, (7) medicine, (8) adventure, (9) movie and television stars, and (10) big names. Don Schanche, who was a little embarrassed by this whole exhibition, interrupted to suggest that the ideal *Post* story henceforth would be the story of "an American nun of royal blood raped in Vietnam." To which I added, "During a high wind." There was laughter, but Blair did not laugh. He looked at us, Schanche and me, with some puzzlement, and then he called the meeting to attention and went on with his lecture.

He wanted, he said, "crusading journalism." But when asked for more details on the nature of the crusade—"Where is our Jerusalem?" somebody interrupted—Blair had difficulty in explaining what he meant. He wanted articles that were "meaningful." He wanted them to "serve a purpose." Still, someone asked again for specific plans, and as Blair began spewing forth ideas, one of the editors attempted to take notes:

Air safety crusade: Point up crash causes—Rickover blast—poor standards of inspection—box with Rickover's picture—editorial.

Blast at letting French have atomic sub. "Bunch of lousy, wine-drinking security risks."

Slap at *New Yorker*. "Increasingly dull sheet."

Politics are obsolete. "Must recast whole damn Republican Party." War on machine—anatomy of an election—We have to have a whole new way of doing things—Dictatorship?—Need a new platform. "I'll draft it later."

Replica of Columbus ship landing soon. Build up suspense about being lost at sea.

The Shame of the American Woman. Her problems. (Schanche: "Yeah, she's giving it away when she could be selling it.")

Blast at Civil Defense. Nation in peril . . .

Blair had scarcely taken command of the *Post* before he steered it into a major crisis. At the executive end of the corridor, there was a great deal of scurrying around, the rescheduling of an issue that had already started going to press, the announcement of a switch in covers, and a lot of telephoning to Washington. To most of us, however, the scrambling remained a mystery. Blair had turned Sherrod's corner office into a sort of combat headquarters, and he confided only in the very few editors he knew and trusted, leaving the rest of us in Limbo. We asked one another what was going on at the far corner of the office, and all that anyone could learn was that there was a new story involving Cuba.

We had recently passed through the Cuban missile crisis, an event considerably beyond the *Post*'s capacity for news coverage, but Schanche had expressed the Blairian view by saying at the start: "I think this is one of those times when we ought to be doing something even if we don't know what we're doing." What the *Post* had actually done was to assign its Washington editor, Stewart Alsop, to write the traditional sort of article on how the Kennedy administration had functioned during the crisis. But Alsop, in turn, had joined forces with Charles Bartlett, a newspaper columnist who was known to be on very friendly terms with President Kennedy. Now the results were in, and Blair was tearing up the December 8 issue, and refusing to let anyone see what Alsop had written.

When the story finally appeared, there was a great uproar over Alsop's treatment of Adlai Stevenson, because Stevenson had urged that the United States negotiate with Castro, and some official had declared that "Adlai wanted a Munich." Stevenson himself complained of "irresponsible journalism" because the secrecy of the

National Security Council "has been seriously breached." Much of the press supported this view and accused the *Post* of partisan politics. What everybody seemed to ignore (aside from the curious fact that Alsop's article had added two new phrases to the language: "eyeball to eyeball" and "doves and hawks") was that the article was essentially true. "No one knew that the insider Alsop had quoted was John F. Kennedy himself," Schanche said later. "The President read the Alsop-Bartlett piece twice before it went to the magazine, and he wanted the quotation published." Despite the criticisms, Blair was delighted with all the publicity, and understandably so. The *Post* with turkeys on the cover was gone, and now it would be a battle to stay with and in the news every week.

And so we all went back to work. If Blair did not want a foreign editor to produce articles about "gooks," then I could do other things. The *Post* had assigned a reporter named Peter Maas to investigate the activities of Igor Cassini, who wrote a society column for the Hearst press under the by-line of Cholly Knickerbocker, and Maas had found good evidence that Cassini was an unregistered lobbyist for the Trujillo regime in the Dominican Republic, and also that he used his gossip column to promote the clients of his own public-relations company. I was sitting at Blair's conference table when Blair said, "Cassini is spreading the word all over town that he got this story killed, so we're going to run it, see? But this lead is just a mess." Emerson quickly said, "Otto can fix all that," and Maas, red-eyed with exhaustion, said, "Sure, I don't care what you do." So I took the clumsily written manuscript home that night and sent my wife to bed and sat up at the typewriter until four o'clock and then brought in a new version of the story the next morning. Blair had called another meeting on how to handle the Cassini case, and Schanche handed him the new manuscript and said, "Here, it's all done for you." On the basis of Maas's story, Cassini was removed from his job and taken to court, where he pleaded *nolo contendere* and was placed on probation.

Just about then, we read that a replica of Christopher Columbus's ship, the *Nina*, was missing at sea during an attempt to duplicate Columbus's voyage. Then we learned that Blair had been subsidizing the adventure, that he had a friend on board, keeping a log, that the missing ship had been sighted, that Blair was chartering a plane to land a reporter and photographer aboard the *Nina*, that the reporter wasn't much of a writer, and that Blair was wondering whether I could produce a new story of about ten thousand words within the next two days. I did produce the story, and Blair, in search of more such tales, promptly signed up his friend and protégé, Bob Marx, as the *Post*'s adventure editor. (In a strange way, Marx's real purpose was to act out Blair's fantasy life. A lean, wiry young man with a piratical mustache and a skin burned dark by the sun, Marx was a fearless explorer, but he was also wildly impractical, and Blair subsequently wasted tens of thousands of dollars in sending his alter ego to hunt for treasure, dive among sharks, and sail the oceans in a leaky Viking ship.)

Blair really needed only a few weeks, all in all, to change the entire magazine—not just what it published, photographic covers, investigations and exposés, fiction by celebrities, and raucous editorials, but the way it operated. Instead of letting editors putter along in their departmental specialties, he insisted on getting everyone involved in the continuous uproar. And at the end of these first few weeks, in January of 1963, he sent us all a memorandum: ". . . You are putting out one hell of a fine magazine. The articles are timely, full of significance and exclusivity. The . . . visual aspects have improved tremendously. . . . [Fiction] could be one of the great breakthroughs in magazine publishing. The final yardstick: We have about six lawsuits pending, meaning we are hitting them where it hurts, with solid, meaningful journalism." It was typical of Blair to scatter boasts and praises in all directions—and also to revel, like a man collecting albatrosses, in the accumulation of troubles. Some disaffected editor promptly sent the memo to *Newsweek*, and there it was published without comment—a damning piece of evidence in every lawsuit that was to come.

Foreign news did not disappear, of course, despite Blair's original criticisms, and I continued at the pleasant task of pursuing every foreign correspondent I had ever admired—James Morris of the Manchester *Guardian*, Max Frankel of the *New York Times*, Sanche de Gramont of the *Herald Tribune*, Stanley Karnow of *Time*, to name a few—for since I had no staff to worry about, I could ask anyone in the world to write on foreign affairs for the *Post*. Nor was I limited to journalists. For an assessment of the Sino-Soviet conflict, for example, I called on George Kennan, and when Pope John fell ill, I persuaded Evelyn Waugh to write the obituary. By far the best article I got during that spring of 1963, however, was a story called "I'm Hit! I'm Hit!" by Jerry Rose, a talented young correspondent who had quit *Time* to take on his first assignment for the *Post*. The U.S. Special Forces were still fairly new then, and Rose was the first correspondent to write a really detailed account of their life in the Vietnam highlands (Rose himself died not long afterward in a plane crash near Saigon). This was the cover story of the March 23 issue, and I complacently thought of it, as all editors complacently do, as "my" issue. I did not pay any attention to the fact that I had not received an advance copy—Blair had several times "embargoed" advance copies because of one secret project or another—and it was only while riding to work on the Long Island Rail Road that I read in the *New York Times* that some Southern football coach was protesting about an article in "my" issue.

THE STORY OF A COLLEGE FIX

Not since the Chicago White Sox threw the 1919 World Series has there been a sports story as shocking as this one. . . .

With that title and that boast, we blundered into the disastrous Butts-Bryant affair. At the time, it seemed to epitomize all of Blair's hopes for "crusading journalism," but ultimately it undermined all his plans and cost us millions of dollars. It is ironic, therefore, that this was not Blair's idea at all, and if any mere editor had proposed such an article, it might never have been published. The *Post*'s own lawyers, however, had been engaged for some time in defending the magazine against a libel action by Paul (Bear) Bryant, head coach at the University of Alabama, who complained of an article that had accused him of encouraging unnecessary roughness. The *Post*'s lawyers, consequently, were a natural audience for the story of an Atlanta insurance salesman named George Burnett.

Burnett's story, as he later testified, was that he had been making a telephone call, the previous September, when the lines became mysteriously crossed, and he found himself listening in on a telephone conversation between Coach Bryant of Alabama and Coach Wally Butts of the University of Georgia. Butts told Bryant the secrets of Georgia's offensive and defensive plays, according to Burnett, who testified that he listened for a quarter of an hour and took notes on what he heard. Nine days later, Alabama defeated Georgia by a score of 35–0, considerably more than the difference predicted on the gamblers' boards.

Burnett took his story to a variety of people. He took it to Johnny Griffiths, who had replaced Butts as coach when Butts became Georgia's athletic director. After an investigation, Butts resigned. But Burnett was questioned harshly, particularly about a conviction for bad checks. He also took his story to the Atlanta newspapers, which declined to publish it. And he took it to the Alabama law firm of Beddow, Embry & Beddow, which was representing Curtis against Bear Bryant. Beddow passed the story to Curtis's Philadelphia law firm, Pepper, Hamilton & Scheetz, and one of that firm's partners, Phil Strubing, brought it to the attention of the *Post*.

It is difficult now to assign the blame for the Butts-Bryant story, but the ultimate responsibility must rest with Blair, not only because he was the editor of the *Post* but because the whole incident illustrated what we had come to view as the Blair style. There are channels of command, however, and, as we learned at Nuremberg, nobody is ever wholly innocent. The first telephone call from Strubing went to Dave Thomas, Blair's managing editor, and Thomas called in Roger Kahn, the sports editor. Thomas hoped that Kahn would write the story himself, since Kahn was a man of considerable ability, but there was a company rule against paying editors extra money for writing articles, so Kahn turned the project over to Frank Graham, Jr., a shy, introverted young sports writer with relatively little background in police reporting. Kahn liked Graham, however, and was encouraging his modest literary talents.

"The first time I heard of the Butts story was late in February," Kahn recalled. "I was starting down the hall, in my coat, going to lunch, when Dave Thomas shouted, 'Hey, Roger,' and then, 'Wait up.' He told me a few details of the story, and I thought it sounded odd, but Thomas was in a state of high excitement. He said, 'This is a story that's so big, everybody's going to be talking about it, and you're going to write it.' I said, 'I don't write unless I get paid to write.'

"I am not much of a fan of Southern college football, and I didn't like the story anyway," Kahn said. "When I was at *Newsweek,* I once wrote a cover story on gambling, and I came across three pretty solid rumors of fixes, one in boxing, one in baseball, and I forget the third. And I convinced myself that there was no sense in trying to print these reports because they were legally unprovable. So here was more of the same.

"But Schanche *was* a Southern football fan, and he argued that, at the very least, we ought to find someone reliable to check on this story. So I mentioned Frank Graham, who had already done two nice pieces for the *Post*. He was conservative, and safe from charges of ax-grinding. We all agreed on Graham, and I sent him to Georgia, and when he came back, he said, 'I got Burnett's affidavit.' Next day, we joined with Thomas and agreed that Graham should write a rough draft. At about this time, my thoughts changed from 'This is a joke' to 'This is a hell of a story.' I learned that *Sports Illustrated* was after it.

So was *Newsweek.* I began to be swept along. All my training goes toward 'Get the story.' Graham wrote a draft. I pointed out holes, rough spots. He came back Saturday, and I worked on the manuscript some more. Thomas's secretary was called in to type it, and then I wrote the precede about the White Sox."

Whenever Kahn raised any question about the legal risks, he said, Thomas replied that Curtis lawyers had the matter in hand. There still seemed to be some doubt late that Saturday, but Blair and Thomas and the lawyers were going to talk some more. "It was Thomas who kept urging secrecy," Kahn said, "which, in view of the story, seemed reasonable."

This secrecy, so characteristic of the Blair regime, was the final error, for it prevented other editors from advising caution, or even common sense. Bill Emerson, then the articles editor, never saw the Butts-Bryant story; neither did Don McKinney, his assistant; neither did Spike Haines, the *Post*'s regular libel lawyer. Liberals and conservatives alike have learned, over the centuries, the value of checks and balances, but Blair was neither a liberal nor a conservative but rather a nonideological radical, who had learned a certain lesson from the man by the boulder in Rock Creek Park. The lesson of Rock Creek Park was that the world is divided into the good and the bad, that the bad operate by conspiracy and the good by publicity, the bad by darkness and the good by light. And if there are times when "any action, right or wrong, seems better than doing nothing," why should anyone hesitate when the story of a conspiracy is brought by one's own lawyers? Blair later said that he had warned his disciple, Dave Thomas, "Be absolutely sure—we don't *need* it." But when it finally came to printing the story, there was very little hesitation.

"The Story of a Football Fix" was indeed shocking, and it sounded very believable—Graham was not without talent, after all—and the targets fought back for their lives: Butts and Bryant each sued the *Post* for $10 million. There were criticisms in the press too, particularly in the South, but Blair responded with defiance. "We believe that anyone who rigs a football game should be exposed," said the *Post* editorial page (written, in this instance, by Kahn). "We will continue to cling to this radical belief despite what our detractors in and out of publishing may say about us." The *Post*'s lawyers encouraged Blair in his defiance by declaring repeatedly that the lawsuit should present no insuperable difficulties.

The lawyers' confidence was not wholly unwarranted. Georgia's Attorney General Eugene Cook had investigated the case and formally concluded that the evidence "indicates that vital and important information was given about the Georgia team, and that it could have affected the outcome of the game and the margin of points scored." Once the Butts trial began in Atlanta that summer, however, Blair began to discover some of the unfortunate truisms of the legal profession, that plausible accusations are hard to prove beyond a reasonable doubt, that friendly testimony can be canceled by the testimony of the other side, and that cross-examination can be quite embarrassing. In court, it turned out that Graham had never seen Burnett's notes on the celebrated telephone call, and that some of the characters in his story had never said the things he had quoted them as saying. Graham did not help matters by claiming that "reconstructed quotes" are a standard practice in journalism—which is true for some of the trivia of sports but not true for matters that lead to lawsuits.

Blair himself had to undergo a strenuous examination about a *Newsweek* story in which he had been quoted as saying that the *Post* would dedicate itself to "sophisticated muckraking." Blair now said that his words had been distorted. He was also confronted with that embarrassing memo about pending lawsuits.

Q: Just taking the quotation I have just read you: "The final yardstick is the fact that we are hitting them where it hurts . . ." Now, who is them, "hitting them"?

A: Them is the general phrase to refer to the whole United States of America.

Q: Hitting everybody in America where it hurts? Is that the meaning you intended to convey?

A: Not quite so literally as this . . . I can't answer without telling you what my philosophy is.

Blair eventually escaped from the trap only by testifying that he had intended his statement as "facetious."

"To me, personally, there was a nightmarish inevitability about the trial," Blair said later. "As I sat in the court, hearing my own words distorted, twisted, the hard work that we had done ridiculed, my own integrity and the integrity of the *Post* blackened by Butts's lawyer, I wanted to leap up and scream in his face." When the verdict was announced, Strubing said, "Oh, my God!" The verdict of $3 million in punitive damages, plus $60,000 in actual damages, was the highest libel judgment ever inflicted on a magazine, and though it was later reduced to $460,000 on appeal, the court's decision cast a pall over the *Post*. One immediate result was that Curtis, having lost in Georgia, where the terrain was relatively favorable, lost its nerve at the prospect of fighting the same battle in Alabama. It agreed to settle with Bear Bryant by a tax-free check for $300,000.

"I returned to New York in low spirits, almost in shock," Blair said after the trial. "I went to Culligan's suite at the Regency and offered my resignation. But Joe was chipper, all sunshine. 'It could have been worse—ten million,' he laughed. He refused my resignation." Culligan, however, subsequently cited this as the turning point in their relationship. "Blair was in terrible shape when he came back from Atlanta, badly upset about the damage to the *Post*. That trial did something to him. He was never quite the same again."

The intangible damage was hard to assess, but it was substantial. The *Post* had lost a dangerously large part of its reputation for accuracy and responsibility, the reputation on which all its other stories had to rest. The news magazines and newspaper columnists wrote scathingly about the whole affair. Several major advertising executives were equally critical. And from that point on, even the most implausible suit against the *Post* became news, and the news stories surrounded the magazine with an aura of scandalmongering and sensationalism.

Partly to restore its reputation, partly because it was convinced that the Butts-Bryant story was true, the *Post* fought back in a series of legal appeals. And it had a new weapon. Shortly after the *Post* settled with Bryant, the *New York Times* won a major case, *Sullivan* v. *New York Times Co.*, which established the "Sullivan rule," that a public official could not recover damages for libel, even if the defamatory statement was false, unless he could prove that the defendant had known it was false or had shown "reckless disregard" for whether it was true or false. That ruling buoyed up Curtis lawyers through the long months of appealing the Butts case all the way to the Supreme Court. On July 16, 1965, the United States Third Circuit Court of Appeals rejected the *Post*'s arguments; on June 12, 1967, by a vote of five to four, the United States Supreme Court did the same. Despite the Sullivan ruling, said Justice Harlan's majority opinion, the *Post* was guilty because "elementary precautions" had been "ignored," because the evidence on how the *Post* had prepared the story "cast serious doubt on the adequacy of the investigation."

But that was far in the future. Now we return to the spring of 1963, and Clay Blair, content that his team of editors has the *Post* on the right course, wants to take over the *Ladies' Home Journal*. It is worth remembering that the *Journal* was once the biggest and richest magazine in the country. Back in the 1870's, when Cyrus Curtis was producing a four-page weekly called *Tribune and Farmer*, Curtis himself provided a column, "Woman and Home," which he cribbed from other magazines. "Who gets up this column?" asked Mrs. Curtis, according to legend. "I do," said Mr. Curtis. "If you really knew how funny this material sounds to a woman, you would laugh," said Mrs. Curtis. "If you think you can do it any better, why don't you try it?" asked Mr. Curtis. The result was Mrs. Curtis's column, then a page, then an eight-page supplement, then a magazine. When Mrs. Curtis retired in 1889, the *Journal* already had a circulation of 440,000, larger than any other women's magazine. Her replacement was a Dutch-born bachelor of twenty-six, whose only close contact with a lady was with his elderly mother, until, seven years after taking over Curtis's *Journal,* he married Curtis's only daughter. "Bok's attitude towards women was that of avoidance," he wrote about himself in *The Americanization of Edward Bok.* "He did not dislike women, but it could not be said that he liked them. Nor had he the slightest desire, even as an editor, to know them better, or to seek to understand them." Edward Bok was a kind of genius, however, and perhaps because of his very isolation from women, he talked to them as they had not been talked to before. He told them about venereal diseases and civic planning and the slaughter of herons for feathered hats. He started a lovelorn column ("Learn to say no," he advised), and he provided a doctor who answered readers' questions about the care of children.

In a way, the golden age of Bok's *Journal* paralleled that of Lorimer's *Post* (the two men fought repeatedly, with Lorimer usually victorious), and the silver age of the *Journal* under Bruce and Beatrice Gould matched that of Ben Hibbs's *Post.* In 1961, the year that Hibbs decided to retire, the *Journal* had to announce that it had lost money for the first time since the 1930's (some insiders argued that it had been losing money for years, but that internal bookkeeping disguised the losses). The following year, the Goulds turned over their magazine to their managing editor, a blond, thirty-two-year-old cherub named Curtiss Anderson. Anderson did reasonably well during his first year, bringing to the magazine a fitful sort of rejuvenation, notably with a series called "The World We Want." He also benefited from the fierce salesmanship of the *Journal*'s new publisher, "Hungry John" Veronis, who increased the advertising lineage during the first half of 1963 by more than 20 percent over the previous year.

Anderson cut costs severely, reducing his staff from 170 to 80, and consolidating the *Journal*'s scattered offices into its main headquarters on Sixth Avenue, but this was not enough for Blair. He wanted the *Journal* reconsolidated from Sixth Avenue over to the

Post's headquarters on Fifth Avenue—a move that would help to create an integrated Curtis editorial staff. Why, Blair reasoned, should the *Post* and *Journal* have separate libraries, separate copy-checkers, separate equipment for making layouts? Why, for that matter, should the *Journal* and *American Home* have separate testing kitchens, and separate systems for photographing interior decorations?

To any cost-efficiency expert, the duplication of facilities among Curtis magazines was extravagantly wasteful, and yet the various editors had good reason to mistrust Blair's drive toward integration. It was scarcely a secret that Blair had misgivings about the very existence of the other Curtis magazines. For a time, he had urged the liquidation of both the *Journal* and *American Home;* then he had become interested in the idea of changing both the *Post* and the *Journal* into biweeklies, appearing on alternate weeks. Whatever happened to the magazines, however, he left no doubt that he intended to take charge of them. "There has been too little close supervision and coordination of the Curtis publications," Blair's study group had reported to Culligan the previous year, "no one to needle and cajole, to criticize or offer suggestions and assistance." The group recommended that Curtis abolish the traditional independence of its editors and make them subordinate to an Editorial Director, someone who would be capable of what it called "flaming leadership," namely, Clay Blair. "The Editorial Director would have broad responsibility for the editorial material of the magazines," the report continued, "the operation of the staffs of the magazines, editorial innovations, etc., somewhat like an editor-in-chief."

Most editors do not appreciate the idea of suddenly acquiring an editor-in-chief, and Curtiss Anderson was understandably hostile to Blair's proposals for integration. He argued that a merger would "destroy the identity and individuality of the magazines," and he added that if the plan were carried out, he would consider himself "the wrong editor at the wrong time." Blair was conciliatory at first, and Anderson decided to treat himself to a brief vacation in the Virgin Islands. While he was away, somebody in the office of Publisher John Veronis complained about an article on birth control, and Blair took it upon himself to decree that the article was "too frank and explicit." He turned to the *Post* and instructed Dave Thomas and the science editor to "fix it." When Anderson flew back to New York, there was a strained confrontation.

"Are you going to be the editor of the *Journal?*" Anderson demanded.

"No, but neither are you," Blair said.

And so the invasion began. "On the following day, I also fired the three key men in the *Journal* art department," Blair said. "The managing editor, Geraldine Rhoads, resigned to go to *McCall's*. I fired the entire *Journal* fiction department. I let go the whole Reader Service Unit. By coincidence, the food editor was in the process of resigning to take another job. Dr. Spock resigned in a huff, saving me the trouble of letting him go."

For mysterious reasons, Blair replaced Anderson with Hubbard Cobb, a mild, round, blond little man who until then had been peacefully employed as the editor of *American Home*. The first problem Cobb had to face was an office in a state of feminine hysteria. A number of editors were determined to leave with Anderson, and others were doomed by the staff integration—for Blair had ordered everyone to move to *Post* headquarters forthwith—and now they milled about, weeping and crying out: "I've been fired!" It was all rather too much for Cobb. "He doesn't dare talk to his staff because they all keep bursting into tears," said Bill Emerson, who, like most of us, regarded the crisis as a comic diversion from our own problems, "so he keeps running back to *American Home* and hiding in his old office, because everybody loves him there." At the end of the week, Blair decided to celebrate his triumph by staging a cocktail party to welcome the *Journal* editors to their new home at 666 Fifth Avenue. We expected, some of us, a flock of pretty young things, but our new colleagues turned out to be a band of grim, gray-haired ladies, many of them in fierce little hats. From their side of the room where the party was given, they eyed us with suspicion and hostility.

By now, Blair had fired or lost every principal editor on the *Journal,* and it had become clear that Hub Cobb had no stomach for his new assignment, so Blair blithely shipped Cobb back to *American Home* and put the *Journal* mess in the hands of Dave Thomas. By raiding the *Post* inventory of articles, by calling on *Post* editors and writers— there was Roger Kahn, for example, the sports editor, rewriting an article about Doris Day to appear under somebody else's by-line—and by capitalizing on the fact that the *Journal* published only bimonthly during the summer, Thomas somehow managed to get a magazine to press.

And thus he became the new editor of the *Ladies' Home Journal*. It may seem surprising that Blair entrusted a position of such importance to a man of very limited editorial experience, but he had a high opinion of Thomas's various qualities. "Dave was very hip on women's stuff—food, fashions, etc. (his wife is a designer)," Blair said later. "Besides, there was the political situation. The power struggle had begun. The *Journal* would be a power base, an important one. I wanted a man there who was completely loyal. Dave was."

The chief critic of this plan was Dave Thomas himself, who still cherished the idea that he might become the editor of the *Post*. He thought he was going only temporarily to the *Journal*, but he had no sooner gone than the door closed behind him. Schanche replaced him as managing editor of the *Post*, the Number Two position under Blair. Emerson replaced Schanche in the Number Three slot as executive editor, and I replaced Emerson as assistant managing editor for articles.

While Blair was expanding his power over the editorial façade of the Curtis magazines, however, his own independence was being strongly challenged from inside the corporation. Blair had not only failed to win the presidency of Curtis, he had failed even to win autonomy for himself, and that failure left him vulnerable. His vulnerability, in turn, left him feeling both puzzled and cheated. For after Milton Gould had staged the mysterious confrontation between Blair and Culligan on the day of Culligan's takeover, the little lawyer had come bustling into the office to make peace between the two men, and he had offered them both a proposition. Blair recalled it as "a comical scene":

" 'Culligan,' Gould said, 'you're Mr. Outside.' Then, turning to me: 'Blair,' he said, 'you're Mr. Inside.' He paced the floor and puffed on a huge cigar. 'Culligan, you bring in the advertising and straighten out the image of this company. Blair, you keep the books, fix the products, and deal with manufacturing and the rest of it.' It was an eloquent proposition, and when he finished, Culligan and I took the deal, with Culligan pledging then that 'No one will ever come between us.' We shook hands all around."

It would be hard to imagine a man more unsuited by temperament to the assignment of "keeping the books . . . and the rest of it" than the mercurial Clay Blair. But he apparently interpreted Gould's suggestion as an agreement that made him the Number Two executive at Curtis. Joe Culligan never confirmed this assignment, however, and his own plans for the management of the corporation were undoubtedly somewhat different. "At home one evening, after I had been at Curtis about six weeks," Culligan said, "the telephone rang, and the long-distance operator said that J. M. Clifford was calling from Santa Barbara, California. I knew that he was living there, having been 'put out to pasture' by RCA. . . . Clifford was at odds with

[President] Robert Kintner . . . and so was thrust out. . . . His opening line—'I just called to congratulate you on your new job'— did not fool me at all. I was immediately sure that he was looking for a job. . . . I was elated, because Clifford was the perfect man for the cost-reduction and control job to be done. . . . Over the years, Clifford had become hardened and cynical. . . . He would take and follow orders to the letter and could fire hundreds, even thousands, of people with no outward show of emotion."

Culligan promptly hired John McLean Clifford, at a salary of $100,000 a year, as his executive vice president and true "Mr. Inside." And Clifford immediately began to act accordingly. After a preliminary inspection of Curtis, he announced that the situation was worse than Culligan knew, and that every department should cut its costs immediately by 20 percent. In the editorial department, the Clifford view and the Clifford style became apparent as early as November of 1962, when a memo from Clifford announced: "Effective immediately, there are to be no additions to or replacements of personnel without my prior consent. Likewise, no salary or wage increases are to be granted without similar approval."

The conflict between Clifford and Blair came quickly and inevitably. They fought over every one of the technical and financial problems that lie at the heart of corporate power. "During 1963, Clifford got a throttle hold on the company," Blair said later. "He took over circulation, manufacturing, and paper mills, then accounting, personnel, and legal. He brought in three obnoxious lieutenants: Maurice Poppei, comptroller; Gloria Swett, legal; Sidney Natkin, personnel. By summer, Clifford's control of money and people was so complete that nobody, including me, could hire or fire or give a raise or sign a check without his specific approval."

To overcome unjust warlords, according to the teachings of Chairman Mao, we must organize at every level, and so Clay Blair created a new organization that he called the Curtis Editorial Board. In principle, it consisted of the chief editors of all the Curtis magazines, but the magazines were not equal in importance, and the editors of Blair's *Post* naturally dominated the group. "Ultimately," Blair said afterward, "I intended that this board should become the most powerful decision-making body within Curtis, beneath the board of directors. For me it might serve as a political tool to offset the tremendous corporate political drives of Culligan and Clifford."

To every manager of every institution, there inexorably comes a moment when the job gets too big to handle. Consciously or unconsciously, he must then confront the alternatives—manage every detail and become a prisoner of routine, or delegate authority and lose control. For a time, Blair fought off the inevitable choice. Even while he was arguing with Clifford over corporate budgets, he once sent Schanche a list of fifty articles that he had previously requested, demanding a response on what had happened to every one of his ideas. That in itself was proof that Blair had been too busy to maintain control, and Schanche's response was still further evidence of the change that was taking place. He had to ask Emerson, and Emerson had to ask me, and I gave the traditional answer of the entrenched bureaucracy—the good ideas were already being worked on, and the bad ideas were "under consideration."

Here, too, the Butts case had its effect. Blair, Schanche, and Emerson all shared a vain belief that "investigative journalism" could somehow overcome a failure in legal planning, and therefore they all spent a good deal of time in wandering through the South and investigating the affairs of Butts and Bryant. They wasted not only thousands of executive man-hours in this venture but thousands of additional hours that they demanded from *Post* writers, reporters, stringers—even the mustachioed explorer, Bob Marx, was assigned to investigate an Atlanta bar, and ended, according to Emerson, "being chased down the street by the irate patrons." And then it came to be vacation time, and the ranks thinned, and so Blair's tight control of the magazine relaxed, weakened, faded.

Gradually, over the months, a new kind of magazine evolved. A lot of the ideas and a lot of the energy had come from Blair, but one-man rule cannot long survive the one man's absences. And "crusading journalism" is not really a viable form of the craft, particularly if the crusaders have never succeeded in finding their Jerusalem. And so there came to be a more collective editing, one in which Blair's views, filtered through Schanche, were modified and shaped by Emerson and me, and by the rest of the senior editors who had come to the *Post* with us the year before, particularly Don McKinney from *True* and Bill Ewald from *Show Business Illustrated*. "Collective journalism," as used by the editors of *Time*, has become a dirty word, meaning that everybody second-guesses everybody else, and mucks with everybody else's copy, so that the final result reads like the work of a machine. But at the *Post*, while a collectivity of editorial judgment superseded Blair's autocratic whims, the final responsibility for an article remained in the hands of the man who wrote it.

And so, while we began turning aside the tipsters who telephoned us about secret scandals, we began publishing articles like Martin

Mayer's "Last Chance for Our Schools," Budd Schulberg's "Return to
the Waterfront," and Ben Bagdikian's pioneering report on poverty in
America. One fairly typical issue that summer contained the "Auto-
biography" of Yevgeny Yevtushenko; Peter Maas's disclosure of Joe
Valachi's confessions about the Mafia; a "Speaking Out" by Jackie
Robinson attacking the GOP failure to help Negroes, and a profile of
the Countess Paolozzi by Gay Talese. There were occasional complaints about the *Post* trying to be a news magazine, which we always
piously denied. But, in fact, the *Post* did begin developing into a
wholly new kind of news magazine. Blair had compressed our publishing "lead time" to eleven days, and while we did not attempt to
report the previous week's events, we did try to carry out Ben Hibbs's
original statement in 1942 that "America's life will be affected by
what happens in Brazil—in Turkey—in Hong Kong—in Russia . . .
[and] the *Post* will report and interpret those happenings." And in
that course, we also tried to carry out George Horace Lorimer's
promise in 1899, "to present the best and largest weekly magazine in
the world."

The test came during the hideous final weekend of November. It
has been said that everyone over a certain age will always remember
where he was on the afternoon of April 12, 1945, and now the same
statement is true for the hours just after noon on Friday, November
22, 1963. Bill Emerson and I were having lunch at a French restaurant on East Forty-ninth Street, Le Marmiton, with Joseph Wechsberg
and two agents, Paul Reynolds and Malcolm Reiss. Emerson was
expansively proclaiming the virtues and goals of the *Post* when a
waiter came wandering past, calling for "Mr. Frederick." He said
there was a phone call for me, then added numbly, "President Kennedy has been shot." Most people in the restaurant were still noisily
eating and drinking and talking, but there was already a cluster of
waiters hunched over the portable radio next to the telephone at the
bar. The robot-like voice at the other end of the phone told me that
Blair wanted everybody back at the office right away, and then
Emerson was grabbing me by the arm and saying, "Come on!"

All that Friday afternoon, we sat around Blair's conference table,
trying to figure out what the magazine could do, had to do, would do.
Blair himself seemed in a kind of daze. He would sit staring into
space for fifteen minutes at a time, ignoring the talk around him,
then emerging with a shake of his heavy head to say nothing more
than "It's fantastic—unbelievable." In the midst of the turmoil,
Schanche, Emerson, and I, and the rest, began to fill in the outlines
of a new magazine. We had stopped the presses, of course, and we

were still able to discard about half of an issue that we had long since closed. The cover had been devoted to, of all things, Hong Kong clothing fashions, and now we had to decide on what single image could illustrate what had happened. A photograph of the Dallas motorcade? A picture of the funeral? A portrait of the new President Johnson? Suddenly Schanche pointed to the wall of Blair's office. There hung two paintings that Norman Rockwell had done for the *Post* during the 1960 campaign, portraits of Nixon and Kennedy. The Kennedy painting, rimmed in black, immediately became our new cover.

Who could write a "Speaking Out" against the outbreak of violence in this country? Emerson telephoned an old friend, Ralph McGill of the Atlanta *Constitution,* who stayed up all night at his typewriter until he had to run through the streets at dawn to meet his cable deadline of 5 A.M. Saturday morning. Now, would President Eisenhower write an article on the transition of power facing the country? John Bird, who traditionally wrote Eisenhower's articles for the *Post,* hurried to Gettysburg and camped there until the article was finished. Now, who among Kennedy's advisers could most fittingly write a eulogy? We asked Dean Acheson, who said it was too much for him. Then we asked Arthur Schlesinger, and the result was carried to New York aboard a Saturday night shuttle by Stewart Alsop's secretary, who also brought along Alsop's own profile of the new President. (Alsop had protested, when I told him on that Friday that he had twenty-four hours in which to write the story, that he was in bed with a severe case of flu. "Stew," I said, "it is absolutely forbidden to have the flu at a time like this." "I know," he said.)

Ben Bagdikian had already flown to Dallas to write a profile of Lee Oswald, and Peter Maas and Anne Chamberlin were with the Kennedy family. And everybody was telephoning. Every writer in America, represented by every agent in New York, had something he wanted to write about Kennedy, or Dallas, or violence, or the state of the nation. Even Leroi Jones sent us an article, denouncing Kennedy as an enemy of the underprivileged, and his representative was not surprised when I rejected it. Some articles were assigned, written, bought, edited, and set in type—a portrait of Dallas, for instance—and then thrown out because better stories came in. Some came quite unexpectedly, like Jimmy Breslin's vivid account of the scene in the Parkland Hospital emergency ward. And as soon as a batch of new stories had been processed, an editor flew them to the Philadelphia printing presses in Joe Culligan's personal helicopter. The television sets were going all that weekend, and I never saw any of it, because there was no time even to sleep. On Saturday night—or was it Sunday?—Schanche and Emerson and I checked into a hotel at 6 A.M. and were back at work at 9:30. And even at the last possible hour, when we were closing the Bagdikian story on Oswald, I got an idea for a better lead, and Schanche said, "Leave it alone, it's okay the way it is," and I shut myself in an office, while the television was showing the funeral, and wrote the new lead. Our job was to try to tell what had happened, and by Monday afternoon, seventy-two hours after the shooting, we had ripped up twenty-one pages of an issue that had theoretically gone to press, and had sent to press nine completely new articles covering every aspect of the tragedy.

Inside the corporation, however, nothing matters so much as the control of the corporation's own affairs. Assassinations, wars, elections, earthquakes—such events have little relevance to the things that really count: the checking of expense accounts, the authorization to buy material, the right to hire and fire. After Clay Blair had evicted most of the staff of the *Journal,* he had to acquire some new people, and the employment of new people involved personnel requisitions, and the man who now approved such requisitions was Mac Clifford, and he chose not to approve them. He simply kept them, all twenty-four of them.

At this point, Blair decided to try out his new weapon, the Curtis Editorial Board. On October 9, he called the group together, and they drew up a manifesto to be presented to Culligan:

The editors . . . are finding it increasingly difficult to function effectively because of the steady encroachments into editorial operations of the Curtis business department. . . . Business office delays, interference, and harassment are undermining the Curtis editorial operation, lessening its ability to compete with other publications, occupying too much of the time of the editors, and lowering the quality of our magazines. The Curtis Editorial Board asks for immediate and permanent relief from this interference.

Culligan tried for a time to mediate the dispute, but Clifford was adamant in calling the editors "a bunch of goddamn lunatics," and so Culligan removed him from direct financial control of editorial matters. And to mollify the editors, Culligan and Blair somehow decided on a grand vacation.

"I'd like to take the key men in *Post* editorial on a junket," said Blair, "someplace where we can have a long meeting under pleasant circumstances. One problem we have is that everybody is exhausted from overwork."

"A great idea," said Culligan. "And see that you take the wives."

Clay Blair passionately loved the Caribbean, loved swimming and skin-diving and the easy life of the beach, and so he decided to reward the *Post* editors, who were now "his" editors, by inviting all of them and their wives to a week's free vacation at Huntington Hartford's Bahamian resort of Paradise Island.

Ostensibly, since the junket cost $14,000, we were all there to "rethink" the future of the *Post*, and there were indeed brief daily meetings of editors in shorts and sweat shirts, with the waiters bringing in round after round of whiskey. But the primary purpose, I think, was to enable Blair to express his sense of triumph by an ingathering of all his children. After a year as editor, he felt that his magazine was a great magazine, and he wanted all those who had contributed to it to share in his triumph. He led bands of editors and wives on skin-diving expeditions—bursting a blood vessel in one of the less athletic—and late at night he would commandeer the piano in the Paradise Island hotel dining room and play old-fashioned boogie-woogie until three in the morning.

Blair was right in thinking that the *Post* was once again a great magazine, but he was wrong in thinking that it was his, and he was even more wrong in thinking that he could use his domination of it as a weapon that would enable him to win control of the Curtis Publishing Company. For just as the tough and skillful editors beneath him were determined to publish their own kind of magazines, the executives above him were determined to retain control of their rich offices, their perquisites and powers.

5

"The answer to all our problems"

In the fall of 1963, the United States welcomed a visitor, one of the phenomena of the day, Madame Nhu. During the past few years, we had become enmeshed in Vietnam largely on the pleading of Ngo Dinh Diem, a fierce, stubborn autocrat whom we had installed as President of South Vietnam after the departure of the French. Diem, who believed in the feudal traditions of family rule, relied heavily on his equally fierce brother, Ngo Dinh Nhu, who served as Minister of Interior. And since Diem was a bachelor, his sister-in-law, Madame Nhu, became his official hostess, Minister of Women's Affairs, arbiter of national morality, and chief emissary to the American press. Madame Nhu was very beautiful, judging by her photographs, and very outspoken. When a number of Buddhist monks began to immolate themselves in protest against Diem's dictatorship, Madame Nhu cheerfully dismissed the hideous sacrificial pyres as "barbecues." With a mixture of fascination and revulsion, the American press made her a celebrity, and when she came to America, she came as royalty.

Clay Blair, too, was fascinated, and he instructed Bill Emerson to invite Madame Nhu to dinner, "to meet a few people." Emerson rented the "library suite" of the St. Regis Hotel, so named because the walls of the reception room were lined with bound sets of collected works, but Emerson himself had to make a speech somewhere on the night of the dinner, so I was the only other editor to be invited. Madame Nhu, a tiny figure in pink silk, swept in under the escort of a Vietnamese Embassy official, and trailed by her eighteen-year-old daughter, also in pink silk. There were fresh drinks, some desultory conversation, while Madame Nhu tried to determine who was important, and then Blair, with some heavy laying of hands on shoulders, maneuvered Madame Nhu to a seat at the head of the table, with himself on one side of her and Joe Culligan on the other. There were about twenty of us, seated around the slender vases of red roses, and for an hour or so we quietly ate our dinners, as though this were the way we dined every evening. Then, while the waiters began clearing away the raspberry sherbet, Clay Blair arose to introduce Madame Nhu, and to tell us a little about the background of her embattled nation of Korea.

"For many years, many years," he began, his voice a little slurred, "until—what? 1954?—Korea was a French colony. . . ." Madame Nhu looked on impassively, without surprise. Perhaps she had already endured similar introductions during her tour of America. "Now some of the Korean rebels were Communists," Blair went on, "and some of the Koreans fought on the French side, and some were just nationalists, neither pro-Communist nor pro-French, but simply pro-Korean, and one of these was Madame Nhu's brother-in-law, whose name is pronounced—uh—wait a minute, we've got it right on this card—it's pronounced 'No—Din—Zee-yem'—how about that? Now in 1954, when the French got licked, we decided that Diem was our man, and so we backed him as the President of all the southern half of—of—say, have I been saying Korea?" Nervous laughter. "Isn't that the goddamnedest thing?" More laughter. "Vietnam is what we're talking about, of course—my apologies, Madame Nhu—the southern half of Vietnam . . ."

Madame Nhu was there to answer questions, and her answers soon fused into a monologue, built out of all the familiar terms, "the defeat of Soviet Communism . . . aggression from the North . . . need for strong leadership . . ." Madame Nhu's doll-like beauty, so striking in photographs, proved to be, on closer examination, exactly that of a doll, rouged, powdered, and without expression. Only her voice expressed the shrill, self-echoing determination of the shrew. It is asking a lot, perhaps, to ask a Vietnamese lady of fashion to achieve, in English, in her five hundredth speech, before a dozen ignorant American businessmen, the rhetorical power of Sir Winston Churchill. But I was there too, and I knew what was happening in Vietnam, and Madame Nhu, knowing that people like me were dangerous enemies, addressed much of her monologue to me. It served only to convince me, the more she spoke, that our regime in Vietnam was doomed.

At any dinner party, of course, any political celebrity can strike the skeptical guest as surprisingly small and plain. I have seen a reasonable number of presidents and cabinet ministers and senators, and my reaction, more often than not, has been that of Lamiel's discovery: *"N'est-ce que ça?"* Once I even met the heavyweight champion of the world strolling down Fifth Avenue, and he seemed astonishingly small, a head shorter than I and ten pounds lighter. *"N'est-ce que ça?"* So now that Madame Nhu is gone, last seen writing her memoirs in a retreat outside Rome, I remember not just her and her entourage but the peculiar variety of corporate warriors arrayed around that rose-bedecked table. I have already noted, on either side of Madame Nhu, Clay Blair and Joe Culligan. And now I met, for the first time, Milton Gould, dark, heavy, blustery, grayhaired, a partner in the law firm of Gallop, Climenko & Gould, and a man who had already declared himself by saying, "We're not liquidators; we breathe new life into companies. But if the wolves are chasing the sled, you may have to throw one baby off to save the others." With him now was a matronly lady, Mrs. Gould, one of only two American women present.

And then let me introduce the ravaged-looking figure of C. L. (Bud) MacNelly, an advertising agency executive whom Culligan had installed as publisher of the *Post.* Fiftyish, his face mottled, heavily lined, the gray-blond hair combed straight back, MacNelly considered himself an artist, literally, a painter of portraits. Blair often referred to him as "the Mississippi gambler." And then let me introduce "Hungry John" Veronis, tall, thin, marked by a bad complexion, only recently an ad salesman for the *Ladies' Home Journal,* then made publisher of the *Journal,* then publisher of both the *Journal* and *American Home,* then head of the Curtis magazine division, advancing so rapidly that he couldn't get raises to keep up with his promotions, so that he ended up making less money than some of the people who worked for him.

Trying to avoid the wolves and foxes, I had singled out the one pleasant person I could find, and I maneuvered myself into a seat next to her at Madame Nhu's dinner table. On my other side was a rotund Mr. Dodge, whom I took to be somebody of commercial importance, and so we spoke intermittently of Curtis and the future of publishing, but I devoted most of my attention to the handsome lady on my left, a small and friendly housewife, unassuming and unimposing. We spent much of the dinner hour talking about her three children in Queens and my five on Long Island. She occasionally referred to her husband, and when I asked what he did, she said he "works in Wall Street," and as dinner was breaking up, she finally introduced me to him. Marvin Kantor was a small, sharp-looking man, with an oddly Oriental face and a rasping voice, and we shook hands and said hello and forgot about each other.

Kantor was then thirty-five, president of the Wall Street brokerage house of J. R. Williston & Beane, in which Joe Culligan's father-in-law happened to be a partner. Kantor might have had good reason to think that after years of ferocious competition he had finally become a success, but he was actually resting on the brink of disaster. One November morning of that year, 1963, Wall Street began to learn that a fat, bespectacled man named Tino De Angelis had been dealing in vast quantities of vegetable oil that didn't exist. Within a month after the discovery of the so-called "salad-oil scandal," De Angelis's creditors found themselves holding worthless receipts for $150 million worth of nonexistent vegetable oil, and among those creditors was the firm of J. R. Williston & Beane, which reported it had lost $2.4 million and was soon absorbed by Walston & Company. By that time, however, Marvin Kantor had nimbly left Williston and moved to Curtis as chairman of the magazine division, a position that was publicly described as "second in rank only to Matthew J. Culligan."

I am an inadequate witness to the career of Matthew J. Culligan because we were always strangers. The first time I ever saw him, he was on a dais, introducing Clay Blair as the new editor of the *Post*, and the second time I saw him we were walking along an office corridor, he with his black eyepatch on the side away from me, so I didn't realize who he was. I saw only a tall, husky, graying man walking next to me, and heard him say, "You fellas are certainly putting out a great magazine." I just grunted, not knowing what he wanted, or why he seemed to be trying to curry favor, and he went on, "That last issue—just great," and I shrugged, and we parted, and only then did I see the black eyepatch that enabled people to say at once, "That's Joe Culligan." About three years later, after a variety of conferences and confrontations, I received my last official communication from Joe Culligan. I had been one of the fifteen executives who signed a public indictment of him, and now he wrote me a letter, signed in green ink, to say that the damage I had done him "cannot be undone," but that there was still time for me to repent and retract before he took action against me for my "outrageously libelous statements." I did not answer his letter, but I saved it, since it seemed a kind of documentary testament to the fact that I never knew him, and he never knew me.

The official story provides the official background. Culligan was one of five children of immigrants from Ireland. His father, a Treasury Department tax agent, died when Joe was ten. Joe, born in 1918 in Eastchester, New York, grew up in Washington Heights, played football and boxed at All Hallows Institute (a Catholic school), and got a job as a greeter at the New York World's Fair of 1939. His recent book, *The Curtis-Culligan Story*, passes quickly through these years, but it does provide one strange observation: Culligan tells of a day when he was nine years old, and he and his best friend climbed out onto the ice of a frozen reservoir, and the ice cracked, and the friend drowned, and Culligan adds: "My emergence from this tragedy, and similar deliverances from later ones, has given me a spooky feeling that I am either the luckiest of the lucky Irish, or being spared for something down the road, maybe to be hanged."

Culligan entered the army as a private, passed through Officer Candidate School, became a first lieutenant, reached Europe on the eve of the Battle of the Bulge, and there a German hand grenade exploded just over his left eye. Surgeons took out the eye at a field hospital in Liège, Belgium, and the young lieutenant appeared to be unusually stoical about his wound. "Unable to see at all for two days," he said, "I resolved never to complain if I came out with one good eye. I did, and I haven't." Somehow, Joe Culligan, now twenty-six and horribly wounded, managed to pull himself together and create for himself a whole personality based on energy and optimism and the will to believe. He sold ads for *Good Housekeeping*, then got a job with more responsibility at *Modern Bride*, turning its losses into profits. NBC hired him to help the *Today* show. It was losing money, but Culligan raised it, in less than a year, to profitable billings of $10 million. He became an NBC vice president and took charge of NBC Radio, which, under the crushing influence of television, was losing $3 million a year. He began selling the fact that millions of Americans listened to car radios, he emphasized fast news breaks, and he had a cost-cutting assistant named Mac Clifford. Within three years, the network was in the black, and Culligan moved on to the advertising galaxy called Interpublic, Inc.

At about this time, unknown to Culligan, a rather odd group of men became interested in buying shares of Curtis stock. One of them was a small, volatile Italian named Peter Treves, who ran the stock brokerage house of Treves & Company in the triangular Times Tower at the foot of Times Square. Another was Marvin Kantor, who was then a partner in Treves's firm but later moved downtown to become president of J. R. Williston & Beane. Still another was Milton Gould, who served as attorney to both Treves and Kantor but also represented the investments of his brother-in-law, Richard Rosenthal, president of the Cities Utilities Corporation. And finally, there was the investment house of Loeb, Rhoades, where Treves had served an apprenticeship, and for which he was still a "correspondent firm." This loosely allied syndicate followed the theory that there was money to be made not only in the growth stocks that were fashionable on Wall Street but in the stocks of moribund companies that needed new capital and new management. According to this theory, new investors could force changes that would increase the value of their investments. In 1960, they tried out this theory by buying into Twentieth Century Fox, which was then in considerable trouble. John Loeb and Milton Gould won seats on the board of Fox, and Gould had a grand time investigating the movie business and holding press conferences about his plans for the company. Unfortunately, Darryl Zanuck, a founder and major stockholder of Fox, returned from Europe and took possession of the company, and that was the end of that.

The Curtis Publishing Company looked almost as promising, however, and somewhat more docile. Its major stockholders, the Bok family, appeared to be dormant. In January of 1961, therefore, Marvin Kantor took a train to Philadelphia, where he had never been before, and then went to Independence Square to inspect the marble headquarters that Cyrus H. K. Curtis had built for himself a half-century earlier. Kantor was vastly impressed by the sight of the building, standing massive and eternal in the thin, winter sunshine. He brought out a Polaroid camera and took pictures of the Curtis building and Independence Hall. Then he hailed another taxi and rode out to the Curtis printing plant in Sharon Hill, another gigantic edifice built to last until Judgment Day, and there he struck up a conversation with a guard at the gate. The guard politely answered Kantor's questions about the age of the factory, the number of people employed, the types of machinery. After half an hour of questioning, Kantor thanked the guard, took a taxi back to the station and a train back to New York. He spent a good deal of time thinking about what he had seen: "In a word, wealth . . . solid and impressive wealth, accumulated through the years and standing like a fortress."

So Kantor and Treves began buying shares in Curtis during the winter and spring of 1961. The price of Curtis shares climbed to a high point of 16, and Wall Street heard many rumors that the company was being bought—by the former Senator, William Benton, now head of the Encyclopaedia Britannica, or by Samuel Newhouse, the newspaper magnate, or by Loeb, Rhoades, acting on behalf of someone or other. By the following January, 1962, the syndicate had invested about $3 million and bought about 400,000 shares of Curtis, somewhat more than 10 percent of the total. (There were published rumors that the syndicate held as many as 700,000 shares.) At this point, Gould journeyed to Philadelphia to demand two seats on the Curtis board, but Bob MacNeal was noncommittal, and Gould returned to New York in frustration, denouncing MacNeal as a dull accountant. After some consultation, the syndicate turned Gould around and sent him back to Philadelphia to repeat his demands, more threateningly, and this time MacNeal surrendered. "We have only 32 percent," Cary Bok said later. "We were unsure what the other people had. In a situation like that, a threat is sometimes as good as an actuality."

And so Milton S. Gould, who was to play a key role in the life and death of the *Post,* took his place on the Curtis board of directors, bringing with him the representative of Loeb, Rhoades, a tall, imposing Canadian named Robert Maclean Stewart, who had made a good deal of money in banking and oil ventures. The Curtis board did not dismiss anyone to make room for these newcomers. It simply increased its membership from eleven to thirteen, but that increase caused a fundamental change in the nature of the board itself. The so-called "Philadelphia directors," those aged gentlemen who had placidly watched the company decline through the years, still held a majority. But there was no longer a majority for the "inside directors" —Cyrus Curtis's daughter and grandson and the four chief executives of their corporation. These six, dedicated to the corporate status quo, had been able to control a board of eleven members, but the expansion to thirteen turned the board room into an arena for combat, and in such an arena there was nobody ready to stand up to the noisy new director, Milton Gould. It was Gould who demanded that MacNeal must go, and Gould who demanded a place as counsel to the committee of directors that would search for a new president. The leaders of this committee were Walter Fuller, then aged eighty, and his ally, M. Albert Linton, then aged seventy-five, retired president of the Provident Life Insurance Company of Philadelphia, so it is quite likely that Gould, a vigorous man in his fifties, seemed a figure of boyish enthusiasm.

Since none of these searchers had any great knowledge of the publishing industry, however, the search led into a number of curious byways, including the files of the Madison Avenue tip-sheet editor and job broker, Bernard P. Gallagher. "On June 18, 1962," Gallagher later declared, "Peter Treves phoned me, stating that Bob MacNeal could be replaced as president of Curtis, if he had a candidate acceptable to the board. He asked my recommendation. After a search of my files, I recommended Joe Culligan. Next day, June 19, I introduced Culligan to [Gould] and Peter Treves in my office. I later counseled Joe on his contract. . . . I accept the responsibility of having selected Joe Culligan. If I made a mistake, I am willing to admit it."

It seems astonishing, in retrospect, that the committee charged with finding a president for a $125 million corporation devoted so little time to the task and apparently interviewed no candidates except Culligan and Blair. But that is perhaps no more astonishing than the action of the full board in dismissing MacNeal without having any replacement as president. The essential fact was that this rich, staid old corporation had no real management at all, and that the exposure of its hollowness could only benefit an aggressive bargainer like Gould, for Gould was willing to act while all the distinguished old men simply sat and wondered what was happening.

"I am the primary witness to testify that Milton Gould did contribute mightily to the saving of Curtis in the spring and summer of 1962," Culligan said later.

Without him, the executive committee would have vacillated about the selection of a president, and if Curtis had remained without a president for just one more month, I firmly believe it would have been in bankruptcy by the fall of 1962. . . . I was asked to stand by in Philadelphia, but not in sight of the press or of Curtis employees. I was told to go to the Public Ledger Building, across the street from Curtis, to the office of Walter Fuller. . . . I waited there for several anxious hours. . . . The telephone rang. . . . I walked dazedly to the elevators . . . through that marble lobby, across the street, up the sweeping stairs fronting the Curtis Building, between the towering columns. . . . I stepped into the cavernous, dimly lit, paneled boardroom. The twelve directors stood. Each extended his hand as I moved around the table. As I shook each hand, its owner said, "Welcome, Mr. President." . . . Linton . . . continued as chairman of the meeting . . . [and this] gave me time to settle down and look around. First I glanced at Bob MacNeal, who seemed to have shrunk since our previous meeting. He huddled in the massive boardroom chair, saying not a word and looking dreadfully ill. . . . Several times I asked myself, "What the hell are you doing here?" I knew I was in over my head.

"For eighteen months," said Cary Bok, when asked why the Curtis directors had turned over their company to a comparative stranger like Culligan, "it looked like a good decision." The new president set

out on an orgy of salesmanship, with press agents keeping track of
every move. It was said that he traveled 3,500 miles a week to sell
ads. It was said that he flew to Detroit and made presentations to
General Motors, Chrysler, and Lincoln-Mercury all in one day. It was
said that he signed $30 million in new ads within his first month.
"From late fall of 1962 through the spring of 1963," said Culligan, "I ran Curtis almost entirely by telephone, memo and crash
personal meetings at airports, in cars roaring along turnpikes, in the
Curtis plane (a sturdy old twin Beech), and even a helicopter, which
I leased, to cut down the time wasted getting from New York to
Philadelphia." To the editors, in that first statement from the dais at
666 Fifth Avenue, he expressed his philosophy by saying, "I had two
choices. I could have stayed in Philadelphia and listened to everybody's problems, or I could go out and start selling, and let the problems take care of themselves."

It is an inspirational philosophy, but problems have a way of not
taking care of themselves. For every new account that Joe Culligan
sold, some other account faded away. Despite all the feverish selling,
advertising revenue in the *Post* continued shrinking, from $104
million in 1960 to $86 million in 1961 to $66 million in 1962 to $60
million in 1963. Curtis's losses, which had been a shocking $4 million
in 1961, the last full year of the old regime, soared to $18.9 million in
1962, a year for which Culligan was half responsible.

New presidents like to shrug off such disasters as the work of their
predecessors (the three worst years in recent Curtis history were
Culligan's first-year loss of $18.9 million, which could be blamed on
MacNeal, Clifford's first-year loss of $14 million in 1964, which could
be blamed on Culligan, and Martin Ackerman's loss of $18.3 million
in 1968, which could be blamed on Clifford), but Culligan's second
year, 1963, required some substantial gains. By this time, he had
brought in the fierce little Mac Clifford and his chief adjutant,
Maurice Poppei, and both of them had started to cut costs. Cost-
cutters are a special breed, who seem to achieve both sensual and
moral satisfaction from firing people and imposing new regulations,
all designed to make a corporation smaller, neater, and more easily
manageable. Clifford and Poppei were of this breed, and so, while Joe
Culligan looked outward and upward, singing and selling, the cost-
cutters chopped the payroll by about 2,200 out of 10,000 people.

That helped to cut the losses from the $19 million of the previous
year to not much more than $10 million for 1963—but then there
was another complicated maneuver that Culligan later described as
"a great stroke of luck." The Philadelphia manager of the accounting

firm of Price, Waterhouse—eager to get the new management's business—studied the Curtis accounts and realized that the corporation was still charging itself for the full price of every subscription it sold. Other publishers, he pointed out, deferred the income for all subscriptions of more than one year, and thus postponed the liability for fullfilling those subscriptions.

That sounds complicated. The basic thing to remember is that whenever a publisher sells a subscription, he is not making a profit but incurring a loss. Specifically, when Curtis sold a two-year subscription to the *Post* for, say, $7.95, it first had to pay a large share to local subscription agents, so that it netted only a dollar or two. And at the same time it incurred an obligation to deliver not just $7.95 worth of magazines but 100 issues, which cost $20 to produce and deliver. Should all of that loss be charged to this year, or should it be spaced out over the two-year life of the subscription? Once Curtis adopted a new system of accounting, the losses for 1963 magically shrank to $3,393,000—not much better than 1961, perhaps, but a lot better than 1962, and so the optimists could say that things were improving at a great rate. There was even a small profit in the last quarter of the year, and the miracle was repeated in the first quarter of 1964, a profit totaling $96,000, just enough to cheer up the stockholders at the annual meeting that spring.

"So Joe called me up one night," said Marvin Kantor. We were driving along the Jersey Turnpike at night, in Kantor's brown Cadillac, returning home from a Curtis board meeting in Philadelphia. Kantor was a terrible driver, swerving from lane to lane without signaling, one arm drooping over the wheel, the other arm on the window sill, and he must talk, and I must listen. "And he said, 'Do you know Serge Semenenko?' And I said, 'Sure, I know Serge.' And Joe said, 'Well, you know, I just met this little guy at a party, and I think he may be the answer to all our problems.' "

Despite all appearances, the worst problem at Curtis in the early 1960's was not a matter of editorial quality or advertising sales. It was the problem of the banks. Within a month after Joe Culligan had taken over the company, the banks asked him how he proposed to repay them the $22 million that was due to them on August 16, 1962. The money was due to the four banks because MacNeal had borrowed it without collateral and without amortization—it was a "demand" loan that the banks had made, just as though the Curtis Publishing Company were a worthy citizen who happened to be temporarily short of cash. Culligan had no possible way of paying, of course. But with his customary enthusiasm, he talked the banks into giving him a year's extension. He even talked them into increasing the loan by $4 million. But the main bank in the group, the First National City Bank of New York, made it clear that it was unhappy, and that this extension would be the last.

And so Culligan had to begin struggling with the chronic and almost insoluble problem of the Curtis preferred stockholders. It is a situation too complex for anyone but a specialist, but it is also a situation that must be understood, because it bedeviled the corporation to the end. There are three important facts to remember. The first is that the owners of Curtis preferred stock, an issue created by Cyrus H. K. Curtis in 1925 in a moment of paternalistic generosity, had first claim on all assets of the company. (During that year, specifically, when Curtis made a huge profit of $17 million, the company issued 900,000 preferred shares and guaranteed the holders an annual dividend of $6.3 million—this was reduced by Cary Bok to $2.1 million in 1940—and it also guaranteed that the dividend payments would never be missed. If the company couldn't pay during a bad year, it would consider the unpaid dividend as a debt to be paid in some future year.)

The second fact to remember is that because the preferred shareholders had first claim on all major corporate assets, the company could not take out a mortgage on anything without the approval of these same preferred stockholders. This was why Bob MacNeal had been unable to negotiate a normal bank loan, and why he had borrowed millions of dollars in "demand" loans that could be called in whenever a lending banker felt nervous.

The third fact to remember is that people who own preferred stock are not generally people who care very much about what the stock represents, or what the company produces; instead, they are inclined to feel, like the legendary loan sharks of the slum ghettos, that an investment of twenty or thirty dollars should continue to pay dividends to the investor forever and ever. When Joe Culligan tried to convince the preferred stockholders that he had to pledge some of the company assets for a long-term loan in order to liquidate the demand loans, the preferred stockholders responded by demanding payment of the dividends that were in arrears. At the 1962 annual stockholders' meeting, they voted down Culligan's plan to refinance the $22 million debt at the expense of their holdings. And so it was that Joe Culligan found his salvation in Serge Semenenko. "Were it not for Semenenko," Cary Bok said later, "Curtis would have been dead."

Semenenko, I'm sorry to say, is the only major character in this chronicle whom I never met, but perhaps that is as it should be, for Semenenko's whole public-relations persona is that of the mystery financier, a phantom who can be recognized only by the exquisite calling card he leaves behind. He was born, in 1903, in one of the least exotic of cities, the Black Sea port of Odessa. When the Russian Revolution broke out, the family fled to Constantinople, and then the young Turk moved on to the Harvard Business School. At twenty-one, he became a $25-a-week credit clerk for the First National Bank of Boston. For the next forty-odd years, then, he led one of Boston's more conservative banks into one risky venture after another— Warner Brothers, Hilton Hotels, Hearst newspapers, and all those other enterprises, which, precisely because of their glamour, tend to frighten Boston banks, but which, despite their glamour, are not really risky at all. In those forty-odd years, Semenenko acquired a certain celebrity as a banker who had never lost a loan, and, like all mystery men who shun publicity, he had his own publicity man, Bob Taplinger of Taplinger Associates.

Curly-haired and vaguely dissolute-looking, with thick pouches under those sad Odessa–Constantinople–Harvard Business School eyes, Semenenko had been relaxing in recent years. He cruised the Mediterranean in his yacht, the *Shemara;* he staged parties in Acapulco; he maintained an extravagant suite at the Pierre Hotel in New York; and he donated large sums to a Russian Orthodox Church on East Ninety-third Street. The only information that came freely from his publicity man, Taplinger, concerned his charities and good works.

According to one very flattering account in the *New York Times,* however,

Mr. Semenenko got some unlooked for and unfavorable publicity last year [1963] when Representative Wright Patman, Democrat of Texas, who is chairman of a Congressional subcommittee investigating tax-exempt foundations, disclosed that he had ready access to huge amounts of credit from a group of charitable foundations for dealing in the stock market and invested in shares of companies that he served as banker. . . .

These foundations were all controlled by David G. Baird, a New York stockbroker and close business associate of Mr. Semenenko's. Mr. Semenenko was by far the most active user of credit facilities made available by the Baird Foundations. In 1956, he tapped them for more than $6 million to finance the purchase of 160,000 shares of Warner Brothers stock, a deal that Mr. Patman claims made him at one point Warner's second-largest stockholder. He also borrowed to buy shares in Universal Pictures company, the American News Company and Olin Industries, which was later merged into Olin Mathieson Chemical. In all, Mr. Semenenko's borrowings from the foundations totaled well over $20 million between 1951 and 1961, with most of his investments in companies he serves as banker. . . . Mr. Semenenko . . . denies that there was anything illegal or unethical in his dealing with the foundations. He says that he did not . . . employ the foundations to gain any business advantage.

Semenenko and Culligan apparently enjoyed one another, as the telephone call to Kantor had predicted, but it took several months for them to organize a business relationship. Semenenko brought in two young assistants, and these two spent much of the summer of 1963 investigating Curtis. They concluded with an optimistic report that said: "A credit of $40,000,000 can safely be made to the Curtis Publishing Company. The job of reconstruction of an all but defunct company is well along and is in the hands of an extremely capable management." This report, to the delight of Joe Culligan, completely contradicted the increasingly disagreeable views of the First National City Bank, which wanted to call in its loan of $7 million. The bank had even gone so far as to write Culligan a stern letter saying, among other things, "In order to bring this matter to an ultimate point of resolution, we request that you furnish us within the next thirty (30) days, or before September 16, with a plan satisfactory to us for the payment of both the above mentioned notes before the end of this calendar year."

Culligan took the bank's letter to Semenenko in his office suite at the Pierre Hotel.

"Serge, it's now or never," said Culligan.

"Joe, my dear," said Semenenko, "you can tell our friends at the City Bank that Serge Semenenko has entered the Curtis picture."

With considerable speed, Semenenko arranged a six-bank, twenty-year loan of $35 million to Culligan and Curtis. Semenenko's own bank, First National of Boston, put up $10.5 million, and the five other banks, two in Philadelphia, one on Long Island, one in Houston, and one in Los Angeles, were persuaded to provide the rest. Among Semenenko's major conditions, however, was that the preferred stockholders surrender their first claim on Curtis assets. Culligan and Kantor devoted much of that autumn to courting the preferred stockholders, and at a special meeting in December the stockholders gave in, accepting a token payment on their arrears ($3 per share) and voting away their claim on the assets.

In theory, therefore, Culligan had achieved a fiscal miracle. He had floated a $35 million long-term loan, liquidated $22 million in short-term demand loans, placated the preferred stockholders, and acquired the use of about $5 million in new working capital. As he himself viewed it, he had saved the Curtis Publishing Company. In public, Semenenko agreed. He broke his own rules and gave a press luncheon at the Hotel Pierre. Huge posters illustrated the theoretical reduction in losses since Culligan's arrival, and Semenenko praised the "young and dynamic" Curtis president for a "phenomenal" improvement in the company's affairs. "I can see the pattern of a very important publishing company in the making, and I'm delighted to be part of it," Semenenko said.

In private, Semenenko knew that he had made a very satisfactory loan. He had acquired first claim on all the Curtis assets. He had a management pledge that all major decisions would be "reasonably satisfactory" to him. He also collected $87,500 as a "service fee" for making the deal in the first place. And he charged a rate of interest 1 percent above the prime rate. Until then, Curtis had only paid one-quarter to one-half percent above the prime rate. A difference of one-half percent on $35 million amounts to almost $200,000 per year, which, over twenty years, would add up to a difference of almost $4 million. "Mr. Semenenko's financing arrangements produced tidy profits," the *Wall Street Journal* observed on the occasion of his retirement a few years later.

The six banks charged Curtis a full percentage point more than the prime interest rate . . . and First National of Boston got an additional ¼ of 1% interest for acting as agent for the banks. The banks probably also profited in ways that weren't announced. One source says Curtis was required to keep hefty compensating balances that earned no interest on deposit at the banks. This meant that Curtis actually had use of only part of the loan but was paying interest on the full $35 million. The source says Curtis also switched some $38 million of company pension funds from another bank to Old Colony Trust Co., a First National of Boston affiliate. Institutions receive substantial fees for managing company trust funds.

And as a final touch, our paychecks, from that time on, were drawn every week on the First National Bank of Boston.

One day toward the end of 1963, Marvin Kantor walked into the office of Clay Blair.

"What do you do around here?" Kantor asked.

"I stand with my back in the corner," Blair said, "with a sword in one hand and a stiletto in the other."

Kantor was impressed. He saw something in Blair that he liked, or something that he could use. He was still new to Curtis, still new to the magazine business, and Joe Culligan had been doing his best to make sure that Kantor entered the company under Culligan auspices. "He bragged about 'winning Kantor over to our side and making a friend of him,'" Cary Bok said later. "Culligan went after him, cultivated him, finally put him in as head of the magazine division. Bad decision." In retrospect, it seems obvious that Blair needed Kantor to provide him with the figures that would document his suspicions of Culligan and support his own drive for power, but why did Kantor agree to join forces with Blair? The obvious answer is that he wanted more power for himself, but I have a different theory, perhaps too romantic. It is based not on facts but on my inferences from facts, for the facts themselves are full of contradictions.

On the day of Kantor's dismissal from Curtis, within a year of his arrival, the *Times* attempted to write his biography and concluded that he was a "mystery man." It noted that he was not listed in *Who's Who in America* and complained that "few of his former associates would say anything." The *Times* reported that Kantor was born in New York City on August 13, 1928, that he attended Syracuse University "for a while" and then Brooklyn College "for 2½ years," and that "his business career began in March, 1946, when he was named manager of the Loveland Apartments Realty Corporation of Brooklyn, a post he held through 1965." The *Times* did not say that Kantor never finished college, though that seems likely when someone begins a business career at the age of seventeen. Then came an interruption that the *Times* did not mention. The Korean War broke out, and Kantor was called to duty as a second lieutenant in the reserves. "It was sort of strange," Blair said later. "He was with this platoon that was searching through some kind of a barn, and a Chinese jumped Marv with a bayonet and stabbed him in the side, practically killed him. He hates to talk about it nowadays. He gets sore when you even mention it."

"He next appears," the *Times* story said, "as secretary-treasurer of the Beaver Lumber Corporation, also of Brooklyn, and then for twelve months in 1954 in a similar post with Color-Age Stores of Jackson Heights." The *Times* did not speculate on what the business world of Brooklyn and Queens must have looked like to a young man returning from Korea, nor did it suggest what he did to escape it. Actually, his escape route was quite unusual. He bought a ticket in a church bazaar and won a new Cadillac. He drove the Cadillac around the block and then sold it back to the church for $3,500 in cash. With this money, he opened a stock-trading account at Merrill, Lynch, and within a year he ran his winnings up to $10,000. As Kantor himself laconically described this sequence of events, "A free-spirited individual often finds his life influenced by the unexpected. The raffle episode was my admission ticket to Wall Street."

"From January to April, 1955," the *Times* continued, "Mr. Kantor was a trainee with Hirsch & Co., a member firm of the New York Stock Exchange. Two months later, he joined Harris Upham & Co. as a registered representative." Kantor had started with Hirsch at $200 a month, but he was ambitious and restless, and he changed jobs frequently. In 1957, he shifted to Gude, Winmill & Company; in 1959 to Treves; in 1961 to Williston & Beane; in 1963 to Curtis.

In the penultimate paragraph, the *Times* biographer described Kantor as "a small man, rather pleasant looking and very polished in his manners and bearing," but that description is somewhat more flattering than propriety requires. Kantor was small and bright and quick and energetic, but he was not exactly pleasant looking. His complexion was sallow, his eyes bulged slightly, and his thin mouth twitched nervously. And if speech is an indicator of "manners and bearing," then "polished" is not quite the word to describe him. Kantor literally used the Winchellian pronunciation "colyumist," and when he wanted to criticize his enemies for splitting hairs, he accused them of "splitting infinitives." ("Splitting *hairs,* Marv," Schanche said with some exasperation, the second or third time it happened. Kantor looked at him with hurt surprise, restrained his competitive instincts, and passed on to the next point.)

It would be easy to say that Kantor had taken a lot of blows and was used to fighting for his life, but I think there was more to him than just combativeness and quick wit. One evening, we were driving out to Queens, and he was going to leave me at the railroad station in Jamaica before returning home to Kew Gardens. The destination itself was symbolic. Kew Gardens was a genteel housing development of the 1920's, an island of miniature lawns and brick respectability in the ocean of Queens, and I suspect that the district's roster of $80,000-a-year publishing executives then numbered exactly one. But I also suspect that in the mythology of Brooklyn realty corporations, Kew Gardens must have represented something very special, something like the green beacon that Jay Gatsby saw at the end of the pier, and certainly something not to be abandoned. But we didn't talk about that—driving over the Fifty-ninth Street Bridge in Kantor's brown Cadillac, high above the shivering lights of the East River— but about farming.

Both of us had grown up on farms, both run by fathers who saw in the farm some mystical escape from the world of commerce and violence. My own father, orphaned at seventeen in Germany, had dreamed of supporting the rest of his family by raising rabbits, but he had been forced to go and earn a living in the coal mines of Holland. For the next half-century, he tried to reconstruct another Eden in Vermont and New Hampshire, raising sheep and cattle, chickens and ducks, soybeans and alfalfa, quince and roses. Kantor's father had settled on a farm outside Syracuse—we were now driving along Queens Boulevard, mile after mile of grocery stores, wallpaper stores, liquor stores, linoleum stores, delicatessens, and red lights—and decided to raise onions. "He wanted to pass it on to the three of us someday, me and my brothers," Kantor said, "but I just couldn't see myself raising onions on a farm outside of Syracuse, so I left. I didn't run away or anything, I just left, and then my brothers left too, and then my old man got so sore that he sold the farm and retired to Florida—and now I want to go back."

So Marvin Kantor of Kew Gardens was spending his weekends looking at cattle farms in Dutchess County. His wife, Sibyl, didn't want to leave Kew Gardens, and neither did his three children, "but she lets them come along with me on Saturdays, and we look around, and they're getting to like it." Marvin Kantor of Kew Gardens said he now subscribed to magazines published for producers of beef cattle, and he liked to spend weekends studying them, and I told him that I had grown up with the spectacle of my father poring over the *Jersey Breeder's Journal*, and suddenly he asked whether I wouldn't like to stop off and have dinner in Kew Gardens. It was nearly nine o'clock, and I was sure that such a move would dismay his wife just as much as my own, and so I begged off. We drove on through the neon confusion of Queens, and, at a red light just a block from the Jamaica station, I thanked him for his kindness, declined his invitation once more, and scrambled out of the Cadillac, leaving him to go his own way home.

From then on, I always liked Marvin Kantor, and I always thought that I was the only one who understood him. When he acted aggressively, it was because that was the way he had learned to do business when he was a young real-estate manager in Brooklyn. When he joined forces with Culligan, he saw this, I think, as just another deal, larger than any he had encountered before, perhaps, but not really different. He saw the figures being manipulated, and lies being told, just as things were done in Brooklyn. That was the way the game was played. And then he encountered, in Blair, something rather novel—a visionary preaching patriotism and moral regeneration and the art of the impossible. They were the most unlikely partners—Blair large and effusive, Kantor tiny and wary; Blair seeking glory, Kantor inclined toward cynicism—and yet each saw in the other something he himself lacked and needed. Blair could dream; Kantor could figure. Blair could talk; Kantor could count. Kantor could analyze and solve Curtis's financial problems; Blair could provide the perspective that made the solutions worth fighting for. These two found not only complementary strengths and virtues in one another, but they also acquired a mutual affection and admiration that overcame all the dissimilarities in their backgrounds.

Only in retrospect is it possible to see the extent to which both Blair and Kantor misunderstood one another. Blair relied, for commercial support, on a man who, despite his skill and intelligence, was alien to the conventionbound world of most banks and board rooms. And Kantor relied, for editorial vision, on a man who really was no longer editing magazines, who had become obsessed with the pursuit of power. Both of them, for that matter, were obsessed with that same pursuit. Together, they shared a belief in a world based on conspiracy, and together they planned the conspiracy that led to their own ruin.

6

"Goodbye, apogee. Hello, perigee"

At the beginning of 1964, the year that was to wreck both Culligan and Blair, the salvation of Curtis appeared to be almost in sight. The corporate losses had been cut by almost 80 percent, a long-term bank loan of $35 million had been approved, and the new management could face the future with high hopes. In fact, however, the battles between Blair and Clifford had torn the company apart, and Culligan seemed unable either to restore peace or to revive a sense of purpose.

"Total civil war raged," according to Blair's recollections. "Clifford had denounced me to Semenenko and his lieutenants. Editorial, in turn, was firing mortar shells at Clifford. . . . John Veronis and *Post* Publisher Bud MacNelly were locked in hand-to-hand combat. . . . All over the company, there were hundreds of other skirmishes in progress. The Business Review Meeting in January, a meeting of all Curtis brass, erupted into venomous name-calling, which Joe Culligan was powerless to stop. As I told him afterward, he had 'lost control' of the company, of management. I was fed up. I wanted to resign." Despite the difference in viewpoints, Joe Culligan's recollection of this period is strikingly similar. "For almost two years . . . I ran Curtis," he said. "Then Curtis started to run me. . . . Exactly when and precisely how the change occurred, I do not know. What I do know is that it happened [in the spring of] 1964. I reached my peak at Curtis in December 1963, but I lacked the experience and wisdom to capitalize on it. . . . I should have forced the Curtis-Bok family to sell its stock to a syndicate organized by me . . . but I didn't."

Various observers have offered their own explanations for the apparent disintegration of Curtis management. Cary Bok, for one, has compared Culligan to Jack Kennedy, for whom he apparently had a very limited regard. "Culligan had the same Irish enthusiasm, the same wit, the same easy flow of talk and banter," Bok said. "But he lacked stability. We needed a manager, a president who could settle down to the hard decade of rebuilding which our company needed. Culligan wasn't like that. After eighteen months, he had done all he knew how to do. . . . The long-range Curtis job was unglamorous, and Culligan wasn't interested in it."

In the case of Clay Blair, the political analogy is somewhat different. "Something happened to Blair in the first six months of 1964," said Don Schanche. "He was thinking about more than the magazine." Blair would not have denied this, of course. He was thinking about all the magazines, about the whole company. But even if Blair's most ambitious dreams had been fulfilled, if he had become, at the age of thirty-nine, the president of the Curtis Publishing Company, that probably would have been only a beginning, a plateau from which he could look to greater things.

Nobody can tell how specific Blair's plans were, but we may find some clues in the May 16 issue of the *Post*, which appeared the week before the Oregon primary. Barry Goldwater was already sweeping toward the Republican presidential nomination, but the press didn't know that then; we thought the Republican "liberals" would unite to block him, and the only question was which of them would be the beneficiary of this unity. The Oregon primary—a free-form competition in a liberal state—seemed the perfect setting for a resounding victory by Henry Cabot Lodge. The former senator, who was serving as the United States Ambassador in Saigon, placed first, just about then, in a Harris Poll on Republican candidates. Blair insisted that we put Lodge on the cover of that May 16 issue, and the editorial page, on which Blair still kept tight control, said, "We believe that Lodge's strong showing with Republican voters indicates that the people want a modern, progressive, responsible party, and that Lodge is the *kind* of Republican they prefer. We wish him well."

The cover and the editorial were not based entirely on objective observations. Blair had once written a profile of Lodge for the *Post*, one that placed great emphasis on Lodge's patriotism and sense of public service, and both author and subject thought it a splendid piece of work. Blair had also been corresponding with Lodge in Saigon, hoping that Lodge might announce his candidacy exclusively in the *Post*; Lodge remained politely noncommittal. It does not take much imagination to suggest a scenario that might have occurred to Blair: Lodge wins the Oregon primary, and then the nomination and then the election. Blair uses the *Post* to "crusade" for Lodge throughout the campaign, but the question remains the same as in 1932, when Jim Farley asked of Roosevelt's supporters, "Who was for us before Chicago?" Now Lodge would remember, "Who was for us before Oregon?" Clay Blair was. And what might the rewards be? White House assistant? Secretary of the Navy? One of the major embassies? Time is a harsh judge of scenarios, unfortunately. It brought victory in Oregon to Nelson Rockefeller, and for Lodge a retirement from electoral politics.

So let us return to the politics of the Curtis Publishing Company in the spring of 1964. The fight between Blair and Clifford, mediated by Culligan, wearied everyone to such an extent that a vacuum developed at the center of power, and into this vacuum stepped Marvin D. Kantor. By joining forces with Blair, Kantor immediately acquired a program—the long-ignored reports of Blair's study group, more than three hundred pages of detailed recommendations on how to streamline every part of the company. By joining forces with Blair, Kantor also acquired a personnel policy. He dispatched two of Blair's key rivals, Magazine Division President John Veronis and *Post* Publisher Bud MacNelly. He almost got rid of Mac Clifford too, but Culligan moved in to protect his old ally. He told Kantor that Clifford was suffering from internal cancer—"Mac has the big C," Blair quoted him as saying—and so he could not cause anyone trouble for long. Then Culligan gave Clifford a $20,000 raise and moved him off into the nebulous area of mergers and acquisitions. "Clifford took the change badly," Culligan said. "[He] sulked for a time. . . . He brooded and waited." These shifts created vacancies, of course, and Marvin Kantor was quite ready to fill them—one of his mottoes was "Power is what power says it is." Within three months of his arrival at Curtis, Kantor had taken charge of editorial, advertising sales, manufacturing, and just about everything else that interested him. What came next, then, but the presidency?

At this point, Culligan was doing his best to portray Curtis as a company that had been saved, a company that had already moved from paralyzing losses into a state of profit by the end of 1963. Once Kantor got access to the ledgers, however, he began expressing suspicions of Culligan's optimistic predictions. In March, Curtis neared the limits of its bank credit, and Kantor brought in some new cash by selling Curtis's one, halfhearted venture in book publishing, a one-third interest in Bantam Books, for $1.9 million. Culligan got the board to agree to new investments in Curtis's printing and paper

plants, but Kantor, after looking into the plants, began arguing that
they should be sold, just as Blair's group had said two years earlier.
And when Kantor checked Culligan's advertising forecasts for the
Post, he decided that they were going not up but down (in actual fact,
Post ad revenues for the first six months of 1964 eventually proved to
be 17 percent lower than similar revenues for 1963). All in all,
Kantor told Blair, Joe Culligan was leading Curtis not to salvation but
to ruin. The company would again lose heavily during 1964, Kantor
said—perhaps another $10 million. Blair was appalled.

From the *Gallagher Report, March 4, 1964:*

CURTIS AT THE CROSSROADS. Now run by banker Serge
Semenenko. Chairman-president Joe Culligan in back seat. Joe's "team"
cut to pieces. Marvin Kantor, magazine division chairman and company
director, now official spokesman . . . J. M. Clifford, executive v-p finance
and operations, ready to be retired . . .
Strong management needed. One year ago The Gallagher Report
. . . said: "The problem is not financial. It is management." Joe Culligan,
recommended and introduced to Curtis principals by GR, did good "selling"
job in first year. Has outlived usefulness. Inclined to let ego cloud objec-
tivity. Weak on administration, policy making.

Among the Curtis editors, who were busy in the creation of
magazines, none of these corporate maneuverings had much reality.
Few of us had ever met Kantor or Gould or Clifford, and we knew
very little about their arguments. On the editorial floor, the most
notable event of early 1964 was the death of Ted Patrick, the editor
and virtually the creator of *Holiday*. Blair was not a great admirer of
Holiday (nor was I, for that matter), and to the horror of Patrick's
several underlings, each of whom wanted to be the new editor, Blair
turned the magazine over to Don Schanche. It seemed strange to me
that anyone reared in journalism would want to leave the *Post* for so
moribund and essentially pointless a magazine as *Holiday*, but
Schanche had reached an age when the exhausting routine of managing a weekly magazine no longer brought him enough satisfaction. At
Holiday, he thought, he could not only run his own magazine but
relax and enjoy life a bit.

By natural progression, Bill Emerson advanced from executive
editor to managing editor, and so he became, in effect, the top man at
the *Post*. My own ambition was not to replace him as executive editor,
a job traditionally encumbered by paperwork, but rather to abolish
that job, and in one fiercely argued scene with Emerson, I succeeded

in doing so. I thus retained control of the whole process of assigning, buying, and editing articles, and from now on there would be nobody in charge of me but Blair and Emerson.

We have observed Blair in some detail, and now it is time to discover Emerson. He will eventually become, in many ways, the nearest thing to a hero that this chronicle can provide, but since there are no real heroes in a story of decline and fall, it might be better to introduce him simply as a unifying character, both a leader and a one-man chorus, who will periodically attempt to explain the meaning of events from now until the day of our death.

William A. Emerson, Jr. (the A. stands for Austin, which was his name as a child, but during the critical years at the *Post* he liked to say that the initial stood for Appomattox) was a large, noisy, paradoxical, funny, and altogether overwhelming personality. Physically, he was even more bearish and misshapen than Blair. He was well over six feet tall, perhaps six three, about two hundred pounds, with a shuffling walk and a protruding belly. He had small but expressive blue eyes, bright square teeth, and a mass of brown hair emerging from a rather low forehead, all of which gave his face an oddly Neanderthal quality. His health broke down several times during the Curtis years—he had a chronic irregularity of the heart, and at one point he had to be trussed up in a sort of corset that held his spine in position—but he never abandoned the idea that life was a physical experience, to be physically enjoyed. "I'm sick of men who are scared of their own secretaries," he burst out during one of the dark days of the Ackerman regime, the last year of the *Post*. "I like people who like to eat and drink and fornicate. If a man's innards are going to give out on him, they ought to give out because of too much booze, not just venality."

Emerson's unique language illustrates the uniqueness of the man, but it almost defies the arts of quotation. Dick Schaap, writing a profile in *Atlanta* magazine, did manage, though, to capture a few good examples:

Bill Emerson never simply compliments anyone. Instead, he says, "Sir, you have the heart of a Capetown lion!" He never calls anyone stupid. He says, "I am surrounded by cretins and miscreants." . . . When problems arise, which is fairly often at the *Post*, Emerson bellows things like, "Goodbye, apogee. Hello, perigee." . . . Once, when the editorial staff of the *Post* was undergoing a shakeup and the management had cautioned everyone against speaking to reporters, Emerson could not bring himself to say, "No comment." Instead, he parried the press with, "The wisdom of the ages is crying out for silence at this very moment."

Since all these elaborate phrases emerged in a thick and deep-voiced Southern accent, it was possible to mistake Emerson's language for the traditional Southern rhetoric. It was not that functional, however; it was even counterfunctional. Some of Emerson's images occurred simply because the vividness of the perception appealed to him. A man might have "the soul of a scallop" or "the warmth of an arctic eel"; he might fall into "a den of pit vipers," or he might deserve to be "pressed between giant stones," or he might be forced to "swim through a swamp full of owl shit." Other phrases had little or no meaning at all, except through Emerson's constant repetition of them—"bulldog opacity," for example, or "gimlet-ass," or the dictum that a "pissant" (one of his favorite insults) was the equivalent of five (or was it ten?) "sappin'paws," each of which, in turn, was the equivalent of five or ten "ninnyhammers." ("Great God," he said, after explaining this to a *Newsweek* writer named Frank Trippett, "even a cretinous pifflesniffer ought to know that.")

Emerson loved polysyllabic surprises, so words like "eleemosynary" and "serendipitous" and "pusillanimity" appeared in his conversation not as occasional displays of virtuosity but as a regular practice. Yet the language was never under control—indeed, what made the language interesting, to him as to his listeners, was its state of being out of control. Mispronunciation was commonplace, so "pusillanimity" emerged with the first syllable pronounced like the word "pus," and "unconscionable" came out as "unconsciousable." This was not ignorance so much as experimentation, for Emerson quite deliberately pronounced "enormous" so that the last syllable sounded like the small rodent, and he liked to manipulate a word to make it more impressive, as in "fornification." And when the mood struck him, and his mind was reaching for a word that did not exist, he invented one, like "horribilous" or "preposterosity." His command of the written language, I should add, was equally precarious—his handwriting was an illiterate scrawl, his syntax often unintelligible, and he was the only man I have ever met who spelled the name of Hitler's party "Natzi."

Language can be a social disguise, and there are people who knew Emerson in the 1940's and testify that he then spoke orthodox English in an orthodox accent. There is a pattern here—a feint in one direction, then an exaggerated move in a different direction, creating a sense of uncertainty and surprise. He was born not in the Southern metropolis of Atlanta, for which he became an almost professional booster, nor in Bottom Dollar, Tennessee, an imaginary birthplace that he created for comic effect on the speech-making tour, but in

Charlotte, North Carolina. His father was in business, and his background was entirely conventional, until World War II began a process of transubstantiation. Emerson was shipped off to China and served with the Chinese Army as a member of a three-man American combat-intelligence team. It must have been the strangest three-man combat-intelligence team in all of China, since the other two members were the future Senator Frank Church of Idaho and a Philadelphia Main Liner named Ramsay Nathaniel Pennypacker.

Emerson had started college at Davidson, a small institution in North Carolina, but after the war he finished his undergraduate years at Harvard. We were classmates there, in the class of 1948, but, as is typical of Harvard, I was an editor of the *Crimson,* the daily newspaper, and he was an editor of the *Advocate,* the literary magazine, and so we never met. The next stages in his life he described in the same *Post* promotional brochure that spoke of Blair's "spectacular publishing career." Emerson's entry—we wrote our own accounts of ourselves—was characteristically different:

He came to New York almost by accident in 1948 with two pairs of socks in his pocket. To his consternation, he was hired by *Collier's* as an editorial assistant, and the very day his class was graduated from Harvard College, Emerson was already toiling in the magazine field. Progressing to associate editor, he worked at *Collier's* for three years as one of the three key articles editors and in 1951 became a staff writer and opened a regional bureau in Atlanta. In 1952, exercising what a friend called "his instinct for sinkings," Emerson left *Collier's* for the perilous business of producing and directing news features on a free-lance basis for network television. Then he joined *Newsweek* and for nine years covered the Southeastern United States and the Caribbean. His specialties were riots, revolutions, and everyday politics; and since this was a lively decade he reported the Negro revolution. It was in 1961 that Emerson was made a senior editor of *Newsweek*. For the following year he ran all critical, cultural and scientific sections of the magazine.

During these fifteen years, Emerson acquired not only his revived Southern accent but layer upon pearl-like layer of protective personality. He was always acutely conscious of social distinctions, and I could not help suspecting that somewhere at the center of that rambunctious, laughing, blustering whirl there was the remnant of a small boy uncertain of his own place in the world—but never mind; if this had ever been a problem, it was one that Emerson had solved to his own satisfaction. "I never lie," as he said, "I just bullshit 'em." By being more hillbilly than a hillbilly, and then dropping in some quotation from Yeats, Emerson learned to make everything he said sound as though he might mean more than he seemed to mean.

In his heart, for instance, he had the inevitable feelings about Negroes, but, as a member of the enlightened South, he felt he had to be in favor of civil rights, and he convinced himself that he really was in favor of civil rights. Yet, as a Southerner in the alien North, he refused to remain on the defensive, and so he adopted the pose of a Mississippi sheriff, guffawing and profane over the fate of "Niggers" —or, as such people prefer to pronounce such things, "Nee-ger-oes," or, from time to time, "blue-gummed Senegambians."

This ethnic consciousness extended to include every possible minority. Jews were obvious targets, of course. Emerson often described them as "Hebrew" or "Levantine" or "Oriental," and he seemed to believe quite sincerely that they were sinister and unscrupulous beyond the understanding of ordinary people. Yet he was just as suspicious of Armenians, and not only suspicious but *aware* of their Armenian-ness, as aware as only another Armenian could be. The most familiar groups and the most exotic were equally suspect. One editor, for example, was Irish, and Emerson attributed his various faults to his Irishness, but another was of Pakistani origins, and Emerson was just as wary of that. I am sure that in his mind I was always a dogmatic Prussian, and he even used terms like that to describe Don Schanche, until I convinced him that Schanche was really Norwegian, whereupon Schanche became, in Emerson's mind, a cold-blooded, rockheaded Scandinavian.

The disguise would have failed if, like most people, Emerson had kept his prejudices secret. So he made them as public as possible. And after every outrage, he would turn on his victim and say, "I hope I haven't outraged you." The hillbilly disguise would only work, you see, if everybody could be informed that it was a disguise. You were supposed to see through that, down to the next layer of disguise. Emerson being orthodox was not particularly impressive, and he knew it, whereas Emerson the false hillbilly was funny and charming—but he couldn't bear to be laughed at. And so, in the midst of his hillbilly talk, he would insert an aphorism from La Fontaine, or a recollection of his travels with Lyndon Johnson, or, if things got more esoteric, a comment on the fine points of Chinese cooking as he had tasted it in Yünnan Province.

And ultimately he judged you. He had four ways of categorizing people. Like any man, he divided them up into people he liked and people he didn't like. Like any editor, he divided them into the talented and the untalented. Like any political figure, he divided them

into the useful and the useless. And then there was another category
that he considered at least as important as all the others. He called it
"character," but that wasn't really what he meant. It was more a
matter of class distinction. This man who swore and shouted and
ogled secretaries would never let anyone else hold open a door, or
divide a restaurant check, nor would he violate any of the other rules
that he considered part of the division between those who were
gentlefolk and those who weren't. All categories are unfair, and all
judgments are unfair, but Emerson was at least consistent. His trust
and respect came very slowly indeed, and until you had earned them,
you were always on trial, always under suspicion. But once he had
decided in your favor, he was profoundly loyal. He would listen to
your problems and do his very best to solve them. He would praise
your successes and help to cover up for your failures. These were, in
my opinion, very rare and very admirable qualities.

On the morning of April 16, 1964, I wandered into Blair's office,
and I found everyone there—Blair, Kantor, Emerson—in a state of
euphoric hysteria.

"Most fantastic thing!" Blair said. "They've found copper on our
land."

"What land?"

"Up in Canada—here, look at the paper—35 *million* tons—the
stock has gone crazy."

"They've stopped trading in it," Kantor said. "It jumped four points
in an hour, and then they stopped trading."

"Most fantastic thing," Blair repeated dreamily. "After all we've
been through with these magazines, busting our asses to save the
Post—now we're going to get rich on *copper!*"

In this first moment of euphoria, Blair insisted, as editor of the
Post, on sending a writer to Timmins, Ontario, to produce a story on
the great copper strike. I tried to argue that nobody knew much about
it at this point, and that most of our readers were not interested in
the state of copper in Ontario, but I finally had to agree to send a staff
writer to take a look. I telephoned one of our best feature writers,
Lewis Lapham, and told him he would have to go to Ontario.

"But it's cold up there," he protested.

"It's not cold; it's already April."

"But that's Ontario. They've got six feet of snow."

"Look, I just sent you to Florida on three easy stories in the sun, so
you owe me this one."

Lapham was a writer who found interesting people wherever he went, and he soon found a major copper speculator who had an organ installed aboard his private plane and played Rodgers and Hammerstein tunes while the aircraft flew across the snow-covered forests of Ontario. Within a few days of the assignment, however, Blair had become suspicious of the whole discovery. What he wanted from his writer now was not publicity but an investigation.

Timmins, in Kidd Township, was about five hundred miles north of Toronto. Here, in 1946 and 1947, some 110,000 acres of timberland had been acquired by T. S. Woollings Company, Ltd., a subsidiary of the New York & Pennsylvania Company, a paper-making firm, which was, in turn, a subsidiary of Curtis. Woollings had made a few attempts to see whether the land contained any valuable minerals, but it was not until November of 1963 that a geological team headed by Kenneth H. Darke, of the Texas Gulf Sulphur Company, discovered a gigantic lode of copper, zinc, and silver. Darke and Texas Gulf kept the discovery as secret as possible and began buying land and mineral rights all around the lode. On February 4, 1964, Texas Gulf signed an exploration contract with Curtis. In April, finally, Texas Gulf confirmed rumors of the discovery and estimated the value of the lode at $2 billion—but as Curtis shares began sailing upward on the New York Stock Exchange, there was surprisingly little evidence of what Curtis actually owned in Timmins. Blair insisted on commandeering the Curtis company plane and flying to Timmins himself. Lapham, still under the impression that he was supposed to be writing a story on the copper strike, introduced Blair to Ken Darke, but Darke refused to escort Blair to the scene of the strike. Back in Philadelphia, Blair discovered that the contract with Texas Gulf had been signed by Mac Clifford, for whom he had little regard, and he thought it strange that this document had never been submitted to the board of directors for approval.

As for the contract itself, it impressed a newcomer like Blair as unconscionably favorable to Texas Gulf. For the relatively small sum of $50,000, Texas Gulf acquired a three-year right to explore 46,000 acres of Curtis land surrounding its own properties in Kidd Township. Each year, Texas Gulf had to relinquish these rights on the least-desirable one-third of the land. At the end of the three years, it could buy any two thousand acres it chose for a modest ten dollars an acre. Texas Gulf had the right to dig out any copper it could find, paying to Curtis a mere 10 percent of the net profit—meaning 10 percent of whatever profit might remain after all expenses, taxes, and depreciation. Experts in mining described this as a "standard contract," which seems reasonable when dealing with trackless acres of Canadian woodland, but it is worth remembering that Texas Gulf signed this contract two months after its own geological surveyors had discovered a major lode of copper on adjoining land. And as Clifford finally said a year later, "If we knew we had those riches there, we wouldn't have shared it with anyone. We had no knowledge of the ore being there."

Every spring, there came a time when I would get sick to death of commuting and answering office telephones, and so I would take two weeks off and plant flowers and play the piano and sleep late. This time, after two or three days, I got a call from Norman Ritter, Blair's new administrative assistant, who said he wanted to read me a manifesto by the Curtis Editorial Board.

"Oh, God," I said.

"No, this is really important," Ritter said.

The manifesto announced that the Curtis editors were grievously concerned about the company's continuing losses (Culligan's six-month interlude of profit was about to end with a $3.7 million loss in this second quarter of 1964), that they thought Curtis needed stronger management, and that they were unanimously in support of establishing a triumvirate of Culligan, Blair, and Kantor.

"So you see, that's why I'm calling you," Ritter said, "so it'll be unanimous."

"But what does it really amount to?" I asked, having forgotten, apparently, all the lessons of Roman history. What a triumvirate means is that one or two ambitious men are not yet strong enough to seize power.

"It means we're all backing Clay and Marv," Ritter said.

"Is everybody else signing it?"

"I'm just now calling them all to get their agreement. Clay has to have it when he goes to the board meeting."

"Well, if everybody else signs, then I'll sign too."

This manifesto was only one maneuver in the Blair-Kantor spring offensive. The two insurgents apparently began by taking their case directly to Culligan himself. "I urged Joe to relinquish his job as president and give it to Kantor," Blair said later. "Instead, Joe proposed that both Kantor and I be named executive vice presidents, and that we form a committee—the executive committee—consisting of the three of us—to run, and fix, the company. The executive committee met once. We agreed on a fifteen-point program of action, steps that would cut overhead, reduce losses, and tighten up the company. The two major decisions were to dispose of the paper company and

Curtis headquarters in Philadelphia, a marble palace built for an eternity of success.

The Philadelphia Years

THE
Pennſylvania *GAZETTE*.

Containing the freſheſt Advices Foreign and Domeſtick.

From Thurſday, September 25. to Thurſday, October 2. 1729.

THE Pennſylvania Gazette *being now to be carry'd on by other Hands, the Reader may expect ſome Account of the Method we deſign to proceed in.*

Upon a View of Chambers's great Dictionaries, from whence were taken the Materials of the Univerſal Inſtructor in all Arts and Sciences, which uſually made the Firſt Part of this Paper, we find that beſides their containing many Things abſtruſe or inſignificant to us, it will probably be fifty Years before the Whole can be gone thro' in this Manner of Publication. There are likewiſe in thoſe Books continual References from Things under one Letter of the Alphabet to thoſe under another, which relate to the ſame Subject, and are neceſſary to explain and compleat it; theſe taken in their Turn may perhaps be Ten Years diſtant; and ſince it is likely that they who deſire to acquaint themſelves with any particular Art or Science, would gladly have the Whole before them in a much leſs Time, we believe our Readers will not think ſuch a Method of communicating Knowledge to be a proper One.

However, tho' we do not intend to continue the Publication of thoſe Dictionaries in a regular Alphabetical Method, as has hitherto been done; yet as ſeveral Things exhibited from them in the Courſe of theſe Papers, have been entertaining to ſuch of the Curious, who never had and cannot have the Advantage of good Libraries; and as there are many Things ſtill behind, which being in this Manner made generally known, may perhaps become of conſiderable Uſe, by giving ſuch Hints to the excellent natural Genius's of our Country, as may contribute either to the Improvement of our preſent Manufactures, or towards the Invention of new Ones; we propoſe from Time to Time to communicate ſuch particular Parts as appear to be of the moſt general Conſequence.

As to the Religious Courtſhip, Part of which has been retal'd to the Publick in theſe Papers, the Reader may be inform'd, that the whole Book will probably in a little Time be printed and bound up by it ſelf; and thoſe who approve of it, will doubtleſs be better pleas'd to have it entire, than in this broken interrupted Manner.

There are many who have long deſired to ſee a good News-Paper in Pennſylvania; and we hope thoſe Gentlemen who are able, will contribute towards the making This ſuch. We aſk Aſſiſtance, becauſe we are fully ſenſible, that to publiſh a good News-Paper is not ſo eaſy an Undertaking as many People imagine it to be. The Author of a Gazette (in the Opinion of the Learned) ought to be qualified with an extenſive Acquaintance with Languages, a great Eaſineſs and Command of Writing and Relating Things cleanly and intelligibly, and in few Words; he ſhould be able to ſpeak of War both by Land and Sea; be well acquainted with Geography, with the Hiſtory of the Time, with the ſeveral Intereſts of Princes and States, the Secrets of Courts, and the Manners and Cuſtoms of all Nations. Men thus accompliſh'd are very rare in this remote Part of the World; and it would be well if the Writer of theſe Papers could make up among his Friends what is wanting in himſelf.

Upon the Whole, we may aſſure the Publick, that as far as the Encouragement we meet with will enable us, no Care and Pains ſhall be omitted, that may make the Pennſylvania Gazette as agreeable and uſeful an Entertainment as the Nature of the Thing will allow.

The Following is the laſt Meſſage ſent by his Excellency Governour Burnet, to the Houſe of Repreſentatives in Boſton.

Gentlemen of the Houſe of Repreſentatives,

IT is not with ſo vain a Hope as to convince you, that I take the Trouble to anſwer your Meſſages, but, if poſſible, to open the Eyes of the deluded People whom you repreſent, and whom you are at ſo much Pains to keep in Ignorance of the true State of their Affairs. I need not go further for an undeniable Proof of this Endeavour to blind them, than your ordering the Letter of Meſſieurs Wilks and Belcher of the 7th of June laſt to your Speaker to be publiſhed. This Letter is ſaid (in Page 1. of your Votes) to incloſe a Copy of the Report of the Lords of the Committee of His Majeſty's Privy Council, with his Majeſty's Approbation and Order thereon in Council; Yet theſe Gentlemen had at the ſame time the unparallel'd Preſumption to write to the Speaker in this Manner; You'll obſerve by the Concluſion, what is propoſed to be the Conſequence of your not complying with His Majeſty's Inſtruction (the whole Matter to be ſaid

A celebrated *Gazette* feature was this cartoon urging the pre-Revolutionary states to unite.

JOIN, or DIE.

Original Tales.

THE BLACK CAT.

WRITTEN FOR THE UNITED STATES SATURDAY POST, BY EDGAR A. POE.

For the most wild, yet most homely narrative which I am about to pen, I neither expect nor solicit belief. Mad indeed would I be to expect it, in a case where my very senses reject their own evidence. Yet, mad am I not—and very surely do I not dream. But to-morrow I die, and to-day I would unburthen my soul. My immediate purpose is to place before the world, plainly, succinctly, and without comment, a series of mere household events. In their consequences, these events have terrified—have tortured—have destroyed me. Yet I will not attempt to ex-

Poe was one of the *Post's* early authors. Others included James Fenimore Cooper and Harriet Beecher Stowe.

Cyrus Curtis bought the *Post* for $1,000 in 1898 and made it the center of his empire.

In George Horace Lorimer's 35-year editorship, the *Post* became America's favorite magazine.

Lorimer introduced color paintings to the *Post*'s cover in 1899.

One of Lorimer's ardent themes was "the romance of business."

Like all new editors, Lorimer tried to appeal to youth.

1900: "Why wars are becoming rarer and religions better."

1907: There were cover girls, but glamour was restrained.

1913: The *Post* published Jack London's attack on liquor.

F. Scott Fitzgerald, William Faulkner, Edith Wharton, and Ring Lardner were *Post* writers.

Even before World War II, the *Post* suspected Russia.

Curtis made a good thing of its Independence Square address:
readers felt it practically unpatriotic not to subscribe. The grandiose
Curtis lobby (above) boasted a Maxfield Parrish mural executed
by Louis Tiffany.

The company's fleet of electric trucks (top), which cruised Philadelphia at ten miles per hour and were kept in use for half a century, symbolized the Curtis pace. The truck above advertised a typical *Post* article of the 1950's: "I Spent 30 Years Trapping Smugglers."

The composing room at Curtis, modern in 1910, looked very much the same when the *Post* folded in 1969.

Eventually, however, Curtis did buy a computer to replace these ladies of the subscription department.

Under Walter Fuller (above), the company splurged on machinery but failed to buy into television. Fuller's protégé, Robert MacNeal (right), presided over Curtis's first losses.

The Sharon Hill printing plant was Fuller's delight, but it became an albatross. When the *Post* began to languish, there wasn't much other work for its expensive high-speed presses.

In 1942 Ben Hibbs, a young man from Pretty Prairie, Kansas, took over the faltering *Post*.

Hibbs's *Post* reached an early
peak with Norman Rockwell's
"Four Freedoms" paintings.

The Saturday Evening
POST

February 9, 1952 · 15¢

IN THIS ISSUE

One of the Great Books of Our Time:

WHITTAKER CHAMBERS'
OWN STORY OF THE
HISS CASE

*

A story that, for the first time, will show you the true dimensions of the communist threat to America

Always conservative, the *Post* took vigorous part in the Cold War.

The Saturday Evening
POST
May 25, 1957 · 15¢

I Call on Groucho
By PETE MARTIN

How Will America Behave
IF H-BOMBS FALL?

Norman Rockwell

In 1961 Hibbs (left) bequeathed the editorship of the *Post*—once again faltering—to Robert Fuoss.

For forty years Rockwell's covers illustrated mid-America's folksy image of itself.

September, 1961: Rockwell did the cover for the first issue of the "new" *Post*. The revamping was a disaster.

the Curtis building in Philadelphia. The money realized would be
used to pay off the bank loans."

This was essentially the old Blair study-group plan to liquidate the
manufacturing facilities and mobilize behind the *Post,* but Culligan
had little enthusiasm for anything so negative. "The one, simplest,
quickest solution to virtually all Curtis problems was a merger with
a well-rounded, glamorous company," Culligan said. "Of all possibilities, I was most attracted to the Columbia Broadcasting System."
Culligan therefore entered into discussions with CBS President Frank
Stanton on the possibility of some kind of merger, or, failing that,
the joint creation of a new magazine to be called *CBS News Post.* CBS
Chairman William Paley listened carefully and then declined the
proposal on the grounds that "The magazine business is too hard."
Culligan, undaunted, went on to a new plan, an attempt to interest
the Ford Motor Company in acquiring Curtis. And when that failed,
"I tried to revive the Doubleday Company merger proposal, another
ideal match for Curtis. . . . There were others—Warner Brothers,
Seven Arts; Gulf & Western, and so on—but Curtis looked so in-
credibly messy from the outside that all efforts . . . were futile. In
desperation, I even had involved conversations with the head of
Dominion Tar and Chemical of Canada." To Blair and Kantor, on
the other hand, all these adventures appeared extravagantly irrelevant. "Culligan immersed himself in wild schemes," Blair complained.
"He talked to *Variety* about a merger, talked to Herb Mayes about
merging the *Journal* and *McCall's,* talked to a brewery in Los Angeles
about selling *Holiday.* He drew up plans to 'go public' with the circulation company. . . . The list of his capers is almost endless."

The two insurgents decided, then, to go to the board of directors
with their demand that Kantor become the new president. They
arranged a secret meeting with Cary Bok to make sure that the ruling
family would not oppose the insurrection. Bok nodded and smiled
politely, and they believed, mistakenly, that he favored their views.
They had another conference with Semenenko's two young adjutants,
and these two also listened and smiled and nodded—and then reported back to Semenenko.

In the midst of all this, Mac Clifford was attempting a similar
Putsch. He, too, saw that the company was still in great trouble; he,
too, had a reorganization plan, with himself as president; and he, too,
paid visits to Semenenko and Bok. This prospect of a Clifford revival
was so grim that Blair made a new appeal to Culligan. "I warned Joe
that Clifford was about to decapitate him. Joe refused to believe it. I

begged Joe to step down, or aside, and give Kantor full control before it was too late."

Culligan's answer was predictable, and so was Blair's response. With the new manifesto from the Curtis Editorial Board in his pocket, Blair set off for the May board meeting in Philadelphia, preparing for open combat in the board room. But Mac Clifford also arrived in Philadelphia, carrying by hand a letter from Semenenko declaring that "No change in the management of Curtis is acceptable to the banks."

"We received the news of Semenenko's decision the night before the board meeting, while dining at the Barclay Hotel," said Blair. "I was sick. After dinner, Kantor and I strolled through Rittenhouse Square, and I said that I had had it, once and for all, that I would resign at the meeting tomorrow. Kantor had reached the same decision. We shook hands on it. Going back to the hotel, we encountered Milton Gould, who had just arrived from New York. We told him our plans. He seemed shocked. 'No, no!' he said. 'It would destroy the company.' For two hours we argued: Either Joe Culligan went or we went. 'You can't oust Joe,' Gould said. 'You don't have the tickets.' Gould wore us down."

When the board met the next day, it did not want to hear about internal problems. It wanted to hear the latest news of the great copper strike in Timmins. And Blair, who quickly saw that he indeed did not have "the tickets," never even took the editorial manifesto out of his pocket.

"It's been really hairy," Emerson said. "Very secret but very hairy." I had just returned to work, having heard nothing about Curtis politics since I had agreed to sign the April manifesto, and we were eating lunch at a French restaurant on Forty-ninth Street called the St. Germain. "Blair kept saying he was going to walk out—resign— quit—tear down the magazines. Just because he couldn't be president of the corporation. And Hank Walker, that big hero, saying, 'We gotta fight!' Waving his arms around and shouting, 'Fight!' Calling everybody else chicken if they weren't ready to fight.

"That's when Schanche and I turned against Blair, and we really gave it to him. We said, 'Do you want to be known for the rest of your life as the wrecker?' And he was shouting and carrying on and saying, 'I resign!' And Walker was saying, 'Fight! Fight!' And we said, 'If you try to wreck these magazines, there isn't a place in the world that would ever hire you again for anything, or any of us either.' And then we said that if he was really looking to replace Culligan, he ought to find some compromise candidate who could get the support of the board. And we even suggested Bill Buckley, said the editors could support him, but that just made him furious at Buckley. So we said, 'If you're making all this noise just so that Kantor can be president for you, then count us out of it.' And he said, 'You're all chicken! Coxey's Army!' And so we all resigned, and Walker resigned, everybody resigned."

Emerson sipped his coffee and shook his head at the recollection.

"But Culligan was just as bad," he went on. "I was out in Akron with him to make a speech to the tire people when the whole thing blew—he found out about the editors' manifesto and the list of names attached—and the worst of it was that Joe and I were sharing the same damn suite at the hotel. So he naturally asked why we were trying to chop his head off. And I said, 'Joe'—and I kept circling around toward his blind side, the way you do when you're in a knife fight with a one-eyed man—I said, 'Joe'—still circling, because Joe, in spite of all that spinning and weaving, is a pretty raw, basic kind of cat—I said, 'Joe, I had my reasons for doing what I did, so let's not try to settle the whole thing now. Let's just try to keep the advertisers happy for once.' And then he had to go out and give the introduction to my speech. And he did it."

The effect of the Timmins copper strike, obviously, was to crush Blair's spring offensive. If we were now the owners of a mountain of copper, what did it matter whether we sold our decrepit paper plant? What did any of these internal quarrels matter if the copper strike had made us all rich?

For a time, Blair fought back with the fanaticism of the prophet in the wilderness. He started by arguing that the copper strike might have been faked, and when that proved absurd, he argued that there might not be any copper on Curtis land, or, at the very least, that Curtis would never profit from it. He was dismayed and outraged that Curtis stock was climbing (from 6 to 19 within a fortnight) on the basis of what he considered false rumors. He declared that the Texas Gulf deal was "a giveaway," and that "this whole thing sounds like a stock deal." Careful stock buyers apparently were also skeptical. "The commission houses have been doing tremendous business . . . on orders from the public," the *Herald Tribune* reported in May. "Institutional houses have had relatively little of the action."

If "the public" was buying, Blair reasoned, somebody had to be selling (more than half a million shares were traded during that April), and Blair thought he knew who. He came to me with his dark suspicions of his antagonists at Curtis (curiously enough, one of those who later turned out to have sold their Curtis stock at the peak price was Marvin Kantor), but I frankly confessed ignorance of the whole world of stock-market manipulation. I passed him on to Sandford Brown, our business editor, who was a talented and honest man. Blair ordered Brown to start investigating the whole deal, investigate Texas Gulf, investigate Canadian copper mining, investigate the entire stock market. Brown could find little evidence of wrongdoing, but each negative report only convinced Blair that Brown was naïve. When Blair persisted in his accusations, Brown urged him to call in the Securities and Exchange Commission, and Blair did. He also began leaking his suspicions to the press, so that one *Herald Tribune* headline in May, for example, asked:

IS CURTIS DISSATISFIED?
SECOND THOUGHTS REPORTED
ON TEXAS GULF TIE-UP

To Joe Culligan, I think, the details of the Texas Gulf contract were probably of relatively minor importance at this particular time. As long as the terms of the contract remained secret, most people thought that Curtis now owned a fortune in copper, so why shouldn't a smart salesman make the most of it? What is a credit rating, after all, what is "the confidence of the business community," except the general impression, true or false, that one will be able to pay one's bills? The official company line—to avoid ruffling the investigators of the SEC—was that Curtis was still a simple publishing company, which was just beginning to look into the implications of its copper interests. Yet Curtis officials kept releasing statements—the public-relations firm of Taplinger Associates now represented Curtis management as well as Semenenko—implying that the copper would make us rich. At one point, Curtis even sent out thousands of reproductions of a clipping from an obscure Canadian newspaper, giving a highly optimistic report on Curtis's prospects as a copper company.

As late as that summer of 1964, when I was the highest *Post* editor to be found on the premises, Culligan asked me to attend a lunch he was giving for the business press in a private dining room of the Twenty-One Club. His official purpose was to announce that the *Post* would abandon its reduced schedule of forty-five issues a year and return to full-time weekly publication in the following year; his real purpose was to create some good news to disguise the fact that Curtis would soon have to announce a large loss for the second quarter of that year. To further that real purpose, he just happened to have brought along a heavy, dark-gray metal cylinder, about two inches thick and six inches long, which he insisted on passing from hand to hand. Curtis was not in the copper business, of course, but he thought the reporters might be interested in seeing a sample of "the first ore" actually drilled "from our land."

The SEC, which had its suspicions, duly questioned Culligan and other Curtis officials, but while there was a great uproar about Texas Gulf executives' benefiting from their inside knowledge of the copper strike, no evidence of fraud or deceit was ever charged to anyone connected with Curtis. Culligan, characteristically, met all this with great aplomb. "If you see me walking down Madison Avenue with a piece of ore in my hand and an enigmatic smile on my face," he said in one speech, "you'll understand why."

7

"We may be bankrupt within thirty days"

Like the peace in Europe during the 1930's, our peace during the summer of 1964 was a period of helpless anticipation. In the outside world, this was the summer in which the Republican Party nominated Barry Goldwater for President, and the nominee declared that "extremism in defense of liberty is no vice." Clay Blair went out to San Francisco to watch the spectacle, and he came back somewhat shaken by the fanaticism of the crowds, but then he went off to Bermuda to finish his summer in the sun. Culligan was off somewhere too, and Kantor went to England, and Emerson made his annual pilgrimage back to Georgia, and so I edited the *Post* in relative peace and quiet.

The inevitable autumn crisis began exactly on schedule. Blair returned from Bermuda just in time to attend the September 3 meeting of the board of directors, a ritual that occurred on the first Thursday of every month. Late that same afternoon, he summoned his principal editors to his office so that he could report on the board meeting. "It was a shambles," he said several times. "A complete and utter shambles."

Blair and Kantor had apparently reopened the controversies of the previous April as though nothing had changed. They argued, as before, that the company was going bankrupt, that it was Culligan's fault, that his promises of improvement were false, that their own plans for salvation had been cast down or ignored. "Finally, old Cary Bok took the floor," Blair told us, "and he turned to Culligan and asked in this quavering voice, 'Mr. Culligan, we have just one basic question: Can you save this company?' And you know what? Joe suddenly got very solemn and said, 'Yes, if we can just get all these people to work together, then I believe I can save this company.' Fantastic! And you know what Bok said? He said, 'Thank you. That's all we wanted to know.' And then he just sat there. I tell you it was fantastic. Because in case you all don't know it, that's all a lot of bullshit. As Marv Kantor can tell you, this company is going under, and I mean that. There just literally isn't any cash, no money to pay the bills. I don't know how long we can last, maybe a few weeks, but we may be bankrupt within thirty days. Now I leave it to you all, what we should do, because I've got to go to another meeting with Marv and Joe, but you just sit there and decide what we should do, because whatever you all decide is okay with me."

Don Schanche acted as though Blair were not really leaving. "I think you'd better get right straight up to Boston and tell the bank what's going on," he said.

But Blair really was leaving. "Well, if that's what you all agree on," he said, "that's—listen, whatever you say. But you think it over now. Because this is it, the showdown, and the only strength we have is if we all stick together, the editors who really put out these magazines. We've got control of these magazines now, and we can beat 'em."

With that, he cheerfully walked out, leaving us all looking at one another. We were sitting in Blair's own office, part of an imperially vast complex of office, conference room, anteroom and bathroom, but there was an oddly makeshift and temporary quality about the place. We had just moved, a few days earlier, from 666 Fifth Avenue into this new building at 641 Lexington, and the corridors were full of exposed wiring, painters' equipment, and misplaced furniture. Blair's own office was lined with paneled bookshelves, totally empty of books. Now, in late afternoon, nobody seemed to know where the light switches were, and we sat in gathering darkness.

The first to speak was Hank Walker, the assistant managing editor for photography, a thick, heavy man who had evidently not evolved much since his days as a Marine combat photographer in World War II. As Blair's most blindly loyal follower, he had brought written notes outlining what he (or Blair?) wanted from the editors. "We gotta put our jobs on the line," he said. More specifically, he had two proposals for us to endorse. The first was that all the editors fly to Boston, to invade Semenenko's home territory, to march into the offices of Lloyd Brace, chairman of the First National Bank, and to tell him the impossible problems confronting Curtis and the solutions proposed by Blair and Kantor. The second was that all the editors give Blair their written resignations, to use for whatever bargaining purposes he pleased. "We gotta put our jobs on the line for Clay," he said once again.

The other editors, who had not been in the Marine Corps, were less pugnacious. We all agreed that we should support Blair in whatever he wanted to do to save the corporation, but a few of the more cautious conspirators, namely Caskie Stinnett and I, wondered aloud whether a Boston bank president would be favorably influenced by a delegation of editors barging into his office, and whether anyone at all would be impressed by a sheaf of undated and unreasoned resignations from various Curtis editors.

"If that's all the support you guys can give Clay," Walker said, "he won't even go to Boston, or to Philadelphia, or anywhere else. I know he won't."

"Well, that's up to him," I said. "He wanted to know what we thought."

"I don't know about the rest of you guys," Walker warned, "but he's got my resignation whenever he wants it."

Don Schanche, who was in a relatively militant and evangelical mood at this stage of the crisis, refused to let Walker assume the role of the supreme loyalist. "Look, Blair hired me, and Blair promoted me, and Blair put me in my present position," he solemnly announced to us, "and any time he asks me to resign he can have my resignation. And I think that's true of everybody in this room, Hank. Let's see." Being an exceptionally methodical person, Schanche asked for verification from the man on his right and then began calling out the names of everyone else in the circle.

As each man said "Yes," and Schanche's pointing finger came closer and closer to me, I faced for the first time the hateful kind of moral quandary that I was to face many times in the next few months, and, for that matter, the next few years. I did not realize then the considerable difference between quitting and resigning. Quitting is what wage-earners do, a unilateral act, and then you walk out and go to work at another job—which, if you have any sense, you have already found before you quit your first job. Resigning is what executives do, and it isn't real, like quitting, but rather the beginning of a new and more intensive state of bargaining with your employer. I had quit a number of jobs, but I had never resigned, and I had no intention of quitting now. Five children and all that. On the other hand, I couldn't face the prospect of being the only one in the room to announce that he would be a scab, or that his weekly paycheck meant more to him than anything else.

And so, as Schanche's finger came closer and closer, I found that my powers of sophistry were even more acute than I had previously suspected. It would be a lie for me to say that I would willingly resign, and I didn't want to tell a lie, but, on the other hand, what did it mean to say that one would resign if one's superior officer asked for that resignation? It meant—did it not?—that one simply acknowledged the editor's obvious right to fire the assistant managing editor. It took me only a few seconds, while Schanche continued his one-question interrogation of the other editors gathered in that circle, to decide that I would have to lie after all. I would have to pledge a resignation that I had no intention of carrying out, if I could help it, but I had found a rationalization to explain my lie. Having decided all that within a minute or two, I hoped for an absurd moment that Schanche might accept a tacit consensus and end his inquisition, and when he finally pronounced my name, I pretended to be engrossed in eavesdropping on a murmured conversation between Emerson and Dave Thomas. But Schanche only repeated my name, somewhat louder and more peremptorily—*"Otto?"*—and I adopted the coward's course of saying what everyone else had said.

It was agreed, finally, that we were all for Blair, that we supported him in any course he chose to adopt, that we would all resign any time he asked us to, but that we didn't really know what to do next.

It may seem perverse to interrupt this story for a survey of our surroundings, but just as the giant marble building in Philadelphia was a symbol of the Curtis-Lorimer regime, we now were inescapably the prisoners of the new offices in which we lived and worked. Most of us spend more of our waking hours in our offices than in our homes, after all, and so our offices, like our homes, either reflect our sense of what an environment should be, or, by violating that sense, cause us a deep and mysterious unhappiness.

In theory, every office should be of a decent rectangular size, not less than, say, ten feet by twelve, and it should have the one most important thing of all—a window. Unfortunately for theory, however, the average new office building in midtown New York is a skyscraper that occupies much of a block. Each floor, therefore, contains a vast central area where no natural daylight is ever seen, and where nobody would work unless forced to do so. How this floor space is used governs the quantity of unhappiness set loose in the corporate headquarters, or, more accurately, the kind of unhappiness.

The Tishman Building, 666 Fifth Avenue, where we lived during our first two years in New York, was a new skyscraper that fulfilled all the standard requirements—a subway station in the basement, a cigarette stand and even a bank in the lobby, a restaurant on the top floor, and, finally, an artistic waterfall next to the main entrance. But it was a strangely impersonal building. The windows couldn't be opened, and the dribbling waterfall came to be known as *"le pissoir."* Upstairs, on the third floor, the gigantic editorial area was divided into three sections. To the left, the *Post* editorial floor plan consigned senior editors to a row of small but windowed offices, lesser editors to the communal cubicles of a central work space. To the right, *Holiday* and the *Journal* occupied a similar area, organized in much the same way. In the dark center, there was nothing but a huge and empty corridor, richly carpeted, and illuminated by spotlights that shone on a long series of magazine illustrations and mounted photographs hanging on the endless walls. At the far end of this vaguely ominous pathway, one emerged into the executive area, still without daylight, where a row of executive secretaries guarded the doors to the offices of Joe Culligan and his chief vice presidents.

At the time, I railed against these offices of ours. As a senior editor, I had a sort of den, with a window looking out over the Episcopal Church of St. Thomas, but, because of the bustling in the corridors, it was impossible to concentrate unless I shut my door, and then, because the window couldn't be opened, I soon began to suffocate. What was even worse, in my opinion, was the organization's dedication to office protocol. When any senior editor quit or was fired, every other editor was supposed to root up all his paraphernalia and move to the next office up the line, one step closer to Blair's center of power. Conversely, when someone was installed above the rank of senior editor, all the senior editors were supposed to decamp once again and move one step back down the line. In addition to this constant moving to and fro, protocol dictated that the top editors have offices of double size, and so our two years at 666 Fifth were spent in periodic clouds of plaster because of the ceaseless destruction and reconstruction of interior walls. The builders could never keep up with Blair's executive changes, of course, and so, at one point, Managing Editor Thomas and Executive Editor Schanche had to share a single office, and, at another, Executive Editor Emerson had to occupy a windowless cubicle—all because we were waiting for the builders to rebuild our offices for the fifth or sixth time.

During the summer of 1964, Marvin Kantor arranged for us to move to cheaper quarters at 641 Lexington Avenue. Here, in a somewhat smaller building, and in a less fashionable but actually much more pleasant neighborhood, we acquired the second-through-fifth floors, plus the penthouse suite, in what was to become the Saturday Evening Post Building. And here Blair hoped to solve all the problems that had plagued us at 666 Fifth. Culligan, Kantor, and all the other Curtis executives were relegated to the thirty-second floor, while Blair designated himself the king of the editorial fourth floor. He ordered for himself a suite of three offices—his own nest, with blue plush chairs and those empty bookshelves, a conference room with a magnificent conference table and a dozen tan chairs, a separate room for his secretary, a long white-tiled bathroom just for himself, and finally a set of mahogany doors that were alleged to have cost $500 apiece. What the specially installed private bathroom cost, God only knows.

The curious thing was that our new offices, while physically better than our old ones, created certain psychological difficulties that Blair had never anticipated. At 666 Fifth, the central areas, away from the windows, were filled with junior editors and secretaries, all creating the noise and bustle that annoyed me at the time. At 641 Lexington, this central area was devoted to a library and a photo lab. Thus the core of the office was devoted not to people but to silent machines and supplies. The people were strung out on a long corridor extending from corner to corner of the outside walls, and so virtually every editor, even the most junior one, had his own window. But precisely because of this, we lost something that was to prove important. The turmoil was greatly reduced now, but so was the sense that we were all working together on the events of the day. The noise, specifically, had been a nuisance, but the new absence of noise was to exercise a peculiarly deadening effect on the entire office. Because there was no center of activity, the editors in their long row of offices came to feel isolated and irrelevant, to feel that nothing they did mattered very much. My own office now overlooked the Lutheran Church of St. Peter, and when I got depressed, as I often did, I could shut my door and open my window and look down over Fifty-fourth Street and forget that there ever was such a thing as the Curtis Publishing Company.

It takes years of reflection and retrospection to understand how one's environment has affected one's state of mind, how such details as the opening of windows or the location of a photo lab can affect one's supposedly objective views on whether a corporation will succeed or fail. And yet once those years have passed, one can only look back and wonder why nobody foresaw what was to come.

When Kantor had confirmed the deal for the new building on

Lexington Avenue, Blair wanted to write an editorial about it, and so he suggested the idea to Emerson, and Emerson suggested it to me. The most notable view on new buildings, it seemed to me, was that of C. Northcote Parkinson. One of the minor but nonetheless significant sections of Parkinson's canon of laws decrees that an organization's decision to create a new headquarters for itself is usually a sign that the organization is near death. The Cathedral of St. Peter, Parkinson pointed out, was completed on the eve of the Reformation, and the League of Nations Building on the shores of Lake Geneva was completed at about the time that the League of Nations became obsolete. To me, it seemed only reasonable to cite these examples in an editorial about the *Post* moving into its new headquarters, to cite them ironically and with some sense of the limitations on one's own importance.

Such limitations played no part in Blair's plans, however, and he threw away my editorial with some annoyance. In its place, the editorial page displayed a huge picture of the new *Post* building, "shown in the artist's conception," and Norman Ritter's editorial said:

By the time we occupy our new quarters, The Saturday Evening Post Building will already be an established landmark on the ever-changing skyline of New York. The illuminated sign on top of the building, adapted from the logotype on our cover, will be a familiar beacon to millions who will see it from miles around. Its light shining through the night will be a token of the energy with which we dedicate ourselves to the job ahead.

Now that we had occupied our new headquarters, however, there was no beacon at all on top of the building. We heard vague excuses about problems with labor unions. The artist's conception remained an artist's conception. And our occupation of the new building provided splendid new evidence of the accuracy of Parkinson's Law.

The day after Blair precipitated the crisis, September 4, I came to work prepared to work, but no sooner had I arrived than I was summoned to another conference in Blair's barren office. The men around the table were the same—"the Blair men"—Schanche from *Holiday*, Thomas and Stinnett from the *Journal*, Emerson, Walker, Ritter, and me from the *Post*. This time, however, Kantor was going to tell us all about the financial situation. There would be huge losses in the second half of the year, Kantor said, adding up to a total of about $10 million for the whole of 1964. The basic problems, as Kantor saw them, remained unsolved—the inefficient paper company was not being sold, the unneeded headquarters building in Philadelphia was not being sold, the company was being bled white by Culligan's constant acquisition of new consultants and advisers and legal firms, in addition to Culligan's coterie of overpaid and underworked vice presidents, almost thirty of them. Kantor's remedy, which he repeatedly referred to as "our eleven-point plan," would reverse all this, sell the paper plants, close the Philadelphia headquarters, dismiss the unneeded executives, cut the losses.

Kantor had gone through these points so many times at so many meetings that his speech wandered, and when he finally asked for questions, I was the first to break in. Since Blair had told us yesterday that the company was literally running out of money, I wondered what the cash flow was. How much money was left and how long would it last?

"There's not an immediate problem," Kantor said. "It's a little tight right now, but there'll be enough to get us through this year, and if the ad forecasts are accurate, there shouldn't be any cash problem for the first quarter of '65."

Kantor then went on with his report on the company's problems, and I looked at Blair, who remained silent, without any change of expression. I looked at Schanche, at Emerson, and nobody seemed to realize what Kantor had just said. Nobody seemed to realize that Kantor had quite calmly contradicted and destroyed Blair's essential argument of the previous day. If there was no cash crisis—if the company was not running out of money—why were we being mobilized to overthrow Joe Culligan?

While I was trying to work out the implications of what Kantor had said, and while Kantor himself droned on about the advertising forecasts for the first half of 1965, the door suddenly opened and in walked, smiling his ruddy smile, Matthew J. Culligan. There was an absurd outburst of greetings, handshakings, hellos. Culligan claimed he had just dropped by to see if Blair was free for lunch. Now he was invited to stay, so he moved over to the corner and sat down at Blair's own desk, while Kantor, sitting next to Blair on the sofa, resumed his monologue. He had been interrupted during a fairly cheerful discourse on the bright prospects for advertising in the *Post,* and so he continued his recitation while Culligan sat and smiled fixedly at us from his seat in the corner.

I once attended a performance of *Die Meistersinger* at the Paris Opéra when all the lights blew out in the midst of a chorus. The pragmatists on the stage stopped immediately, the idealists faded away in a cacophony of wrong notes, and the technicians in the orchestra pit struggled on until they realized that they were performing all alone. The last to stop were a group of first violinists, finally overcome by a sense of isolation, and by the thunderous rustling of an audience trapped in total darkness. Kantor's monologue died out in much the same way, the narrative becoming increasingly fragmentary, the pauses longer, the audience restless. Finally, during one of those pauses, Don Schanche proved to be the only man with enough poise and, as Emerson used to say, "certitude" to stop the charade. He turned to the rigidly smiling Culligan and said, "Joe, in a way we're glad you came. I assume you know what we've been talking about, and I think we'd all like to hear your ideas on what's been happening and what the prospects are."

"Well, I'd be glad to answer," Culligan said, "because we've all come a long way together, out of the darkest depths, and I frankly can't understand why anyone would choose this moment to turn against the company. . . ." I could not, as he spoke, take my eyes off that black eyepatch. It forced itself on you, like the open wound of a beggar. Was this the simple secret of Culligan's salesmanship, an unspoken appeal to revulsion and pity? No, he was not like that. The last time we had collectively seen him was at the last meeting of the Curtis Editorial Board, after the collapse of the spring offensive, after he knew that we had unsuccessfully but unanimously voted for his demotion. "I will not be coerced," he had declared then. "And I will not be threatened. I am doing my job, and I expect you to do yours. I'm willing to be judged by how I do my work, but I'll also judge you by how you do yours." Then he had pleaded an engagement and left the meeting, and now, four months later, it was obvious that we had judged him and found him wanting. Why were we going to lose $10 million this year?

Culligan's explanation was surprising. Like all salesmen, like all politicians and stunt pilots, he was a great believer in the self-fulfilling prophecy. A company that was rumored to be in trouble would get into worse trouble because of the rumors, whereas any sign of a trend toward improvement would bring real improvement. And now he talked openly about events that had occurred during the darkest days of 1962, when Curtis was widely believed to be at the brink of bankruptcy. Culligan and the board had apparently agreed that an announcement of more than $20 million in losses might be very damaging. And so, by counting things one way rather than another, they had arrived at a figure of $18.9 million. The following year had been better but not enough better, and then, thanks to the sudden deferral of long-term subscription liability, the loss had been fixed at $3.4 million. But just as repeated face-liftings become less and less effective, leaving the face subject to sudden collapses, now the company had apparently run out of stratagems, and thus the 1964 loss, though actually smaller than that of 1963, would look somewhat larger. "So you see, it's really just a bookkeeping problem," Culligan said with a smile, as though that solved it, as though nothing so lowly as bookkeeping could represent any real problem, "because we're really much better off than we were a year ago."

Puritans believe (and perhaps bookkeepers do too) that past deceptions eventually return to bring retribution on the deceiver, but Culligan, unlike me, was not a Puritan. He believed in salvation through faith more than in salvation through mere good works. Faith had brought advertising contracts, and Serge Semenenko's loans, and ingots of copper from Timmins. "And all I ask of you men," he was saying, "is to have faith in me, trust me to lead this company into the black, as I've pledged that I would."

The door opened again, halting Culligan almost in mid-pledge, and this time a band of blue-overalled workmen marched in. Pretending to ignore us, and pretending to believe that we could ignore them, they began feeling around behind the bare bookshelves on the walls, apparently in search of some electric wires. While most of us sat in embarrassed silence, Culligan cleared his throat, and looked nervously around, and Dave Thomas finally walked over to the workmen and muttered to them to leave. They straightened up and looked at us as though they couldn't understand our objection to their work, and then they filed silently out the door. Culligan looked inquiringly around, ready for the next scene.

Hank Walker was the first to bestir himself. He shifted his heavy body and then asked: "We'd like to know what happened to the three-man committee of you and Clay and Marv. We thought that was going to be a step forward, but—"

"I beg your pardon, beg your pardon," Culligan interrupted. Then he became very formal. "I am not prepared to violate confidences, and I cannot tell my side of that story without the permission of the other two members who are sitting there." There was a pause. "Do I have that permission?" Culligan asked. Blair grunted. Kantor stared into space. "Marv?" Culligan insisted. "Whatever you want, Joe," Kantor snapped.

"All right, I take it that I'm free to speak," Culligan went on. "And now my next question is whether anybody in this room, and I mean *anybody*, is suffering from the mistaken impression that the president of this corporation, or any other corporation, could surrender his executive responsibilities to any sort of committee. Because if any of you have that impression, you couldn't be more wrong. There's only one president of this corporation, responsible to the board of directors and the stockholders, and that president is me, and that's all there is to it."

Once all these preliminaries were concluded, Culligan turned to the specific matter of the triumvirate. Blair and Kantor, he charged, had attempted to make a move affecting a production department in Philadelphia, and they had deliberately not consulted him on the move. He would not, said Culligan, participate in an executive committee with people who deceived him, and so he had dissolved the committee. On hearing this explanation, Schanche asked the silent Blair and Kantor for their answer to it. Blair, staring into space, cleared his throat and said he would let Kantor answer, and Kantor, also staring into space, said he would not "dignify such charges by engaging in debate."

It seemed to me that this was an odd response. If an honest man is falsely accused, does he refuse to answer because of his dignity or does he answer with an indignant denial? While I was puzzling over this question, somebody mentioned a rumor that Culligan planned to fire Blair, and Caskie Stinnett now spoke up in considerable agitation to say that he was sorry that he had ever mentioned the subject. And then it turned out that Stinnett had encountered someone who had quoted Culligan as saying that Blair would be out of a job within a few months, and that Stinnett had told Blair both the rumor and the source of the rumor. And if this had caused any trouble for anyone, Stinnett repeated, he was very sorry. Culligan then seized the opportunity to be magnanimous.

"Listen to me now," he said. "I put Clay Blair in the job he has because I believed in him, and I've kept him there and supported him, and I have always told him, as I tell you now, that I respect and admire the independence of the editorial staff. And as far as I'm concerned, whatever differences of opinion there may have been, there will be no change of editors and no change in the freedom that the editors now have."

I was impressed, I must admit—not only by Culligan's words but by the sullen silence of Blair and Kantor—but apparently I was alone. Hank Walker, apparently still thinking about the mass resignations he had demanded the day before, was determined to announce his dogged loyalty. "I just want it understood," he declared, "that if Clay goes, I go too." Culligan responded coolly. "Well, frankly, I couldn't care less," he said.

Then the door opened again, and the men in blue overalls reappeared and said that they were going out to lunch, and that if they couldn't get started on this job, they were going to charge a lot of overtime, or refuse to do the job at all, or both. "Go on, go on," Dave Thomas shooed them out again, promising them that they could begin work as soon as this meeting ended. By now, Culligan was ready to end it himself. As he moved out, once again claiming an engagement, circling around behind the chairs of his enemies, he was talking all the way, and not just talking but pleading. There would be no dismissals and no recriminations, and if we worked together, we could all save this great company, and if we ever heard any rumors about him, we should come to him for an explanation. "Just give me the benefit of the doubt, that's all I ask," he said. "Just put as much confidence in me as I put in you, and give me the benefit of the doubt." And then, standing at the door, still smiling, his one blue eye sweeping nervously over us, and that black patch so hideously strapped across his head, he turned and was gone.

There was a long moment of silence, finally broken by a burst of laughter from Blair. "Wasn't that fantastic?" he asked. "Have you ever seen anything like that in your whole life?"

"He certainly has the brass of a second-story burglar," Schanche agreed.

"No, but I mean all that same old con about how he's leading us to better days ahead. He just isn't real. Not real. Okay, from now on, what we want is to move one step at a time. No more frontal assaults. We don't need them. I think we've taken a big step in here this morning, because now we know we're in charge, we're running this thing, and nobody can stop us."

The rest of them went off to Dawson's Pub for a late lunch, but I did not follow. This was a Friday, and I was going on a short vacation the next day, and so I lagged behind to catch Emerson. Since it was already after three o'clock, we went to the Brasserie, which is open all day and all night.

"Okay," I said, "I'm going on vacation, so I don't know how this will turn out, but let's forget everything we've heard from Blair and start asking some questions about this so-called crisis."

"Okay, tiger, you go ahead and talk and I'll just eat," Emerson said.

"The first question is why Blair told us yesterday that we were running out of money, and Kantor told us today that there was no cash problem. If Kantor is right, there's no real crisis at all. So the next question is why Schanche and Walker were so insistent yesterday that everybody resign so that Blair could go and threaten the banks, or threaten Culligan. And since Blair's best friends were so eager for a showdown yesterday, the next question is why Blair told us just now that we shouldn't have any showdowns, just one step at a time. And for good measure, why couldn't Blair and Kantor find any answer when Culligan accused them of lying about the dissolution of the executive committee? If someone accused you of lying, would you say that you refused to dignify such charges with an answer?"

"No," Emerson said, "I'd kick the s— out of him."

"Okay, would you like to hear a new theory? Did you notice how upset Caskie Stinnett got about the fact that he'd passed on some rumor that Culligan was going to fire Blair?"

"How could I miss it?"

"So suppose that Caskie heard the rumor, and passed it on to Blair. Wouldn't Blair figure that he had to strike first? And how would he strike first? Exactly the way he just did. How does that sound to you as a theory?"

"A very interesting theory," Emerson said.

On the evening before we made that move from 666 Fifth to 641 Lexington, there was an orgiastic party in the central production room of the old building. It was orgiastic not because an orgy occurred but because it could have, because the production room was hot and noisy, and full of rock 'n' roll, and people were sweating and rather drunk, and because the abandonment of the old offices gave everyone an unconscious sense of abandon.

I was wandering around, gin and tonic in hand, through the empty corridors—the company movers had already come and gone—and on the top shelf of the main coat closet I spotted three colored boxes, each about the size of a telephone book. I took down one of them, a speckled black and white one, and opened it. Inside was the manuscript of a novel entitled *Impersonation*, and the first sentence was unforgettable. "Garland Lee owed much of her glamorous success to the fact that she looked like the wholesome girl next door."

The authorship was unmistakable. Clarence Budington Kelland, then in his eighty-third and last year of life, had been selling stories and serials to Lorimer and Hibbs for forty years—does anyone still remember his most celebrated creation, a Yankee promoter called Scattergood Baines?—but there had come a time when even Hibbs couldn't bear to publish any more, and couldn't bear to reject the old man either. So Hibbs had bought Kelland's last three novels, for

$50,000 each, and then left them behind for his successors to deal with. And Clay Blair had said, "Kill them."

I wandered back into the party, where Blair was standing in a corner, sweat pouring down his fat cheeks, with Kantor standing nearby in a black shirt, both of them very much out of things, and I held out the speckled box and said, "Guess what this is?" Blair looked and saw what it was and said, "Be goddamned." I said, "There's two more of them out on the top shelf of the coat closet—$150,000 worth of fiction lying on a closet shelf." Blair said, "Tell somebody to take care of it. Somebody ought to take care of it." But I didn't. I just put the box back on the shelf and finished my drink and went home.

About a year later, when Blair and Kantor were gone, one of Mac Clifford's nervous bureaucrats asked me whether I would join him in opening "the vault." Vault? What vault? "The editorial safe," the bureaucrat said. "Nobody could find the keys after Blair left, and it's taken us all this time to get a duplicate set made, and I want somebody of authority with me when I open it up, because there's no telling what might be inside." I shrugged. "Can't be terribly important," I said. "I never knew we even had an editorial safe."

Together we walked back through the photo lab into some storeroom that I had never seen before, and there stood a gigantic old black safe, not less than fifty years old. The bureaucrat fumbled with his keys while I stood by, feeling like a grave-robber, and then the inner door creaked open. "Go on, see what it is," the bureaucrat said.

"Good Lord, here's that MacArthur book," I said. A Ben Hibbs project, costing $100,000, never published. "And this just looks like old correspondence, Sherrod's contracts with various people. And here—Jesus Christ!" There lay the boxes filled with Clarence Budington Kelland's last three novels.

"What should we do with all this stuff?" the bureaucrat asked.

"I don't know—I'll take it," I said. There was a glass-fronted bookcase in my office, with some extra space on the bottom shelf, a suitable resting place for a quarter of a million dollars' worth of Ben Hibbs projects. And for the remaining years of the *Post*'s life, they lay there in peace.

After two weeks' vacation, I returned to work in late September and heard from Emerson that the crisis was still continuing. "Wolf, wolf," I said. It seemed hard to believe that so many executives of a major corporation could spend so much time conspiring against one another, never really settling anything but endlessly writhing and squirming like the sons of Laocoön. As Bill Buckley said at one point, "I know that Blair has convinced all of you that Culligan is nuts, but do you realize that Culligan is convinced that Blair is totally screwy?"

There was to be another board meeting the following Thursday, at the Curtis headquarters in Philadelphia, and I got a telephone call from Culligan's secretary, announcing that he was inviting me to "a social gathering" that same afternoon in Philadelphia. I checked with Emerson, who had received a similar invitation and was equally baffled. We both accepted.

That Saturday, Emerson telephoned me at home to say that the crisis was now truly critical, and that Blair had convoked a meeting the following evening at a restaurant called Manero's near his home in Greenwich, Connecticut. I usually spent my weekends working on *Post* manuscripts, and I told Emerson that I was sick of wasting time at Blair's meetings. "If he just wants to gather the clan for another blood oath of loyalty to himself," I said, "I will absolutely refuse to sign."

"I may refuse to sign too," Emerson said, "but I really think you'd better come to the meeting."

8

"I'll sign anything"

At about five o'clock on Sunday afternoon, I drove from my home on Long Island to Bill Emerson's house, a turreted Victorian place in Larchmont, just north of New York. Expectant and a bit nervous, I planted myself at Lucy Emerson's grand piano and played several preludes and fugues from the *Well-Tempered Clavier*, which I play tolerably well, and then, in honor of the occasion, Chopin's Revolutionary Etude, which I play very badly. Don Schanche, who also lived in Larchmont, rescued the Emersons by arriving in his white sports car and driving us to Greenwich. It was a dull drive along the parkway, and we did not talk about what lay ahead. I don't think that either Schanche or Emerson knew much more than I did about what Blair planned to do, and I'm sure that neither of them expected that as a consequence we were all going to appear on the front page of the *New York Times*.

Manero's steak house, when we finally arrived, was conventional enough. We parked in the usual parking lot, walked toward the usual building, low and square. The only thing a little out of the ordinary was an adjoining butcher shop with rows of beef carcasses hanging white and orderly on fierce steel hooks, a convincing display of the freshness of Manero's steaks. Inside, Norman Ritter was standing by the stairway, waving people upstairs, and at the head of the stairs, Blair was shaking hands.

He had ordered a private dining room, and now he ushered us into it, to eleven seats around one very long table, and then the waiters began taking the orders for drinks. Scotch or gin or vodka for most of

us, Jack Daniel's for Emerson. The steaks were thick and good, the
wine was plentiful, and there was little talk of Curtis problems until
everything was eaten. No dessert, thanks, just coffee, and then Blair
called for silence. A little quiet, please. He had called this meeting, he
said, because we had reached a state of grave crisis. The company
was in real danger of going under, and now we would all have to
decide what to do next. Before coming to any decisions, however, he
wanted to have Marvin Kantor review the whole situation, okay?
There was a shuffling of chairs and a clearing of throats, and then
Kantor began his familiar recitation of all the problems and grievances of the past year—the continuing losses, the vain prophecies of
better times ahead, the failure to sell the paper mills and other facilities, the general disorganization of the Culligan regime. Most of
us—the *Post* editors—had heard all this several times before, and we
sat nodding over our brandy while Kantor droned on. What we did
not realize was that the Blair-Kantor strategy had reached a new
phase, and that the primary purpose of this meeting was to recruit
three newcomers. The three, whom we barely knew, were Jess
Ballew, the newly appointed publisher (i.e., advertising manager) of
the *Post;* Jack Connors, his chief deputy; and Mike Hadley, publisher
of the *Ladies' Home Journal.*

On all successful and well-run magazines and newspapers, there is
a deep division between the editors and the business managers. In
theory, this preserves the independence and integrity of the editors.
In practice, as Blair had realized, it also preserves the independence
of the business managers. What Blair had realized, in other words,
was that his control of all the Curtis editors was not a strong enough
weapon to coerce the board of directors and thus to capture the company. In the view of these old men—bankers, railroaders, insurance
executives—the editors were spendid artisans, to be supported and
encouraged in the practice of their craft, but the management of any
corporation should and would remain in the hands of people who
"understand business." By this, they meant not the creation of any
useful or valuable product but the supervision of payrolls, preferred
stock issues, insurance costs, depreciation of inventory—in short,
numbers. This, more than the mere lack of proxy votes, may have
been what Milton Gould really meant when he told Blair and Kantor
during the spring crisis that they couldn't overthrow Culligan because
"you don't have the tickets."

The three advertising executives, therefore, were intended to become "the tickets." If the editors alone walked out, an aggressive
business management might keep the magazines functioning long
enough to find some new editors, but if both editors and business

executives agreed to a strike, then Blair and Kantor might finally have the power to enforce their will. And to the three newcomers, Kantor's speech was a series of astonishing revelations. They had known nothing of the previous editorial insurrections; they had known nothing, or next to nothing, of the Blair-Kantor charges against Culligan, of the demands for a rule by triumvirate, of the campaign for the liquidation of manufacturing facilities. "We sat there with our jaws hanging open," Jess Ballew said later.

And during Kantor's recitation, an important new element appeared. He said he had discovered evidence implying that special favors were being granted to certain advertisers. The word "kickbacks" appeared for the first time. And Jess Ballew expressed the view that there was "something funny" about some of Joe Culligan's biggest advertising deals. One, in particular, involved a large Chicago manufacturer, who had bought $2 million worth of advertising in Curtis magazines and had received a large discount in exchange for mysterious "services." Ballew said that some kind of secret contract had been signed at the *Post*'s office in Chicago, and that he himself had been forbidden by Culligan to see this contract. Jack Connors, Ballew's deputy, brought up a similar case, involving another large advertiser. With these disclosures, Blair and Kantor acquired both their key recruits and what looked like a key issue—an issue involving not just disagreements about the management of the corporation but actions that appeared to us to be improper and immoral. And even though nobody really knew what the facts were—Ballew and Connors promised to get more details—the meeting quite suddenly became revolutionary.

Revolutions cannot be plotted by working-class hours, however, and this one failed to take sufficient account of the restaurant waiters' desire to go home. Kantor was still in mid-speech at about midnight when we began to get preliminary signals of the restaurant's closing. Blair responded with an impatient wave of the hand. Threatening growls from Walker. The waiters went away, but only for fifteen minutes, and then they were back again, leaving the doors open so that we could see the lights being turned off outside. It seemed an ignominious conclusion to a revolutionary meeting, but Walker proposed a solution.

"Hey, listen," he said, "my house is only a few minutes' drive from here, and there's plenty of room, so why don't we go over there and get this thing settled?"

We had little choice. The waiters were determined to leave, and to shut down the restaurant when they left, and so we trailed down the stairs again, and out into the clear, cool September night. The midnight air was a bit dizzying, and we paused again to stare at the beef carcasses hung in the spotlit window. They were bigger than we were, those carcasses, the flesh deep red, the fat white, the legs sawed off at the lower joint, and all now hanging neatly and bloodlessly from silvery hooks in the light of a showcase window. Wasn't that what happened to Admiral Canaris after the failure of the July 20 plot? But let us not think morbid thoughts. We were off again, through the deserted streets of Greenwich, taking the curves a bit too fast for the tires, to the large white house where Hank Walker lived. The door was unlocked. The lights were on. Walker went to look for his wife, Alma, and found that she had fallen asleep in front of the television set on the second floor. He came down alone, determined to play the host. A tray full of whiskey bottles. A white plastic bucket full of ice cubes. Help yourselves, you guys.

And now Kantor, like a tape recorder stopped and then restarted, resumed his chronicle of woe. Another one of the novelties in this two-hour speech was the announcement that Culligan had proposed to get rid of his critics by settling their employment contracts. Blair was to be paid $300,000 if he would resign from the corporation, and Kantor was to get $150,000. Blair corroborated this. They both said that the settlement was to be announced at next Thursday's board meeting— this was presumably the purpose of Culligan's "social gathering." Now, after a certain amount of jocularity about Blair being worth twice as much as Kantor, both said they had rejected the proposal.

"Okay, okay," Jack Connors broke in. "I think we all agree that this situation can't go on, that we've got to do something about Culligan. How about if we all just put it on the line?"

"Damn right!" Walker grunted.

"What is that going to involve, putting it on the line?" somebody asked.

"It's a very simple issue," Ritter said. "Are we willing to go on working for Culligan and his people? I mean, it's a moral issue, isn't it?"

"Yes, it damn well is," said Jess Ballew.

I was surprised, from the beginning, at how sure of themselves they all seemed. I had never paid much attention to the business side of Curtis, assuming that somebody else was taking care of such things, and I could not understand why everyone was so suddenly demanding a revolution. So I sat on Hank Walker's white sofa, at one o'clock in the morning, watching all these people make impassioned statements, and I said nothing at all. But Marvin Kantor, who was sitting next to me on the sofa, seemed bothered by my silence.

"I notice you haven't said anything for quite a while," Kantor said. "How do you feel about all this?"

"You really want to know?" I asked. I had not planned to say anything, only to watch and listen and see what happened. But if Kantor wanted to know what I thought, I was perfectly willing to tell him.

"Yeah, sure," Kantor said.

"I think you've all gone crazy," I said.

"Crazy? What do you mean?" Kantor asked, genuinely surprised.

"I mean, I'm only interested in editing the *Post* and making it a good magazine, and I really don't care much about paper companies or printing costs or P-and-L statements or any of that stuff—"

"But you don't seem to realize that we're going over the cliff," somebody said.

"Okay, maybe I don't realize it, but if the *Post* is going to die, I'm planning to edit the last issue, and I'm going to make sure that it's a good one. But as for the rest of this stuff we keep talking about, it just strikes me as sort of irrelevant to the job of editing a magazine."

There was a babble of protestations, and Blair cried out from across the room, "Why, you talk as though the *Post* were some kind of personal possession of yours."

"Well, that's the way I feel about it," I said.

"As far as I'm concerned," Ritter said, "I think we ought to plan for a general strike on the *Post* and shut it down if we have to."

"You're not going to shut it down as long as I'm there," I said.

"Everything you say would be perfectly reasonable in a normal corporation," Mike Hadley said, acquiring the floor. "But you've got to realize that this isn't a normal situation—this corporation is going broke because of the people who are running it."

"So what?" I shouted back over the uproar of people trying to get into the argument. "So maybe Culligan's no good—I don't know—but if you get rid of him, there'll probably be some new Culligan running things."

"Otto thinks all businessmen are crooks," Bill Emerson offered on my behalf. "And you may not agree with him, but he has a right to his opinion."

"The point is that I don't think it's up to us to decide who runs Curtis," I went on. "I don't care whether Culligan runs it, or Blair, or Kantor, or Gould, or somebody we've never even heard of. As for me, all I want to do is put out a good magazine."

"Well, that's completely unrealistic," Dave Thomas said in his soft but merciless voice. "And if I may say so, it's exactly the line the Germans took under Hitler."

"Oh, the hell it is," I retorted. "But one thing that happened to the July 20 plotters was that a lot of the generals wouldn't join in because they'd signed a loyalty oath to Hitler, and I'm not signing any more loyalty oaths to anybody."

"Nobody's asking you to sign a loyalty oath," Kantor said quietly.

"Why are we arguing about this anyway?" Thomas asked the group at large. "It seems to me that the majority is agreed on backing Clay against Culligan, so all we have to do is draw up the terms, and anybody who doesn't like it can just leave."

I suddenly felt the way a loyal Mafioso must feel when he has disputed the consensus of his "family." People who were once friends begin to look at you in a different way, not exactly hostile but cool and mistrustful. And so my isolated resistance served only to bring the meeting to an end. It was almost three o'clock in the morning, and Walker had run out of ice, and Blair was simply sitting and staring into space. We all decided to go home, and to meet again at noon on the following day.

Monday was normally a heavy workday. The lead story had to go to press, and the late-closing story at the back of the magazine had to be ready to go the following day. Despite all the work, I found it hard to concentrate. I assumed that I was in disgrace, but I was also curious about the flow of executives drifting along the corridor to gather in Blair's office. At noon, I simply joined the flow and walked in.

About twenty people were milling around Blair's conference room in an atmosphere of noise and frenzy. Blair and Kantor were sitting at the conference table in earnest conversation with several people I knew only slightly or not at all. These turned out to be the people who had been missing from Manero's—Caskie Stinnett, executive editor of the *Journal;* Garth Hite, advertising director of *Holiday;* and Hub Cobb and John Collins, the editor and the publisher of *American Home.* I found Bill Emerson and asked him what was going on.

"Well, we've reached the real showdown," Emerson said.

"Again?" I said.

"No, this is really going to be it," Emerson said. "Blair and Kantor have brought in whoever they thought they needed from the other magazines, and they're briefing them on the situation now, over there. And I can tell you that the charges against Culligan sound worse and worse, and I'm ready to go along with Blair. Now you're going to have to make your own decision, and whatever you decide is perfectly all right with me."

So Kantor and Blair finally had all their pieces in place, all the top editors and all the top advertising executives on all the magazines, all mobilized and ready to march, and I seemed to be the only one who not only considered the whole venture irrelevant to the task of editing magazines but also suspected that the whole venture was doomed. Still, assembled armies with flags flying always manage to look impressive—as when Xenophon set out on the march to Persia, and it was only when the Greeks reached the battlefield on the Euphrates that the invading army proved wholly inadequate. And no matter what I might suspect or fear, I also had to reckon with the possibility that Blair might win this great battle of his, and that anyone who deserted him today would be flogged tomorrow. No matter what course I took, in other words, I foresaw the prospect of very unpleasant consequences. And that brought me to the conclusion that misery would love company. I had come to work for Emerson, and so I concluded that I might as well stick with him.

"I'll decide by leaving it up to you," I said. "If you go along, I'll go along."

Emerson, to whom every action was a political action, promptly reached out and clutched Blair, a mountainous figure wandering around through the turmoil. "Clay," he said, "I just wanted you to know that Otto has decided that he's with us, as you probably knew he would be."

"Course I knew that," Blair said coolly, and we shook hands on it. "The only thing that disturbed me was the contempt he has for me."

"Contempt?" Emerson echoed.

"Utter contempt," Blair repeated, and now I understood why he had stared into space for the last hour of the meeting at Walker's house. "Equating me with Culligan and Gould and those people. Calling me a crook."

"Listen," Blair suddenly turned on me, his finger jabbing at my chest. "I used to have your job, I used to do exactly what you do, a working editor, and I've had to listen for hours to those guys telling me that editors don't know anything about business, and now you tell me that I'm just another business con man."

"Come on, Clay," I said. "I didn't mean it that way."

Emerson waved me away and then took Blair aside and mollified him. I could see Emerson talking to him, and laughing, and Blair shaking his heavy head like a disgruntled bull.

With the "briefings" completed, Blair took his place at the head of the long mahogany table and told everyone to quiet down.

"Okay, this is it," he said. "Armageddon—what do you call this, Otto?—*Der Tag*—the day—this is *it*."

Blair asked whether we were all prepared to act together to achieve the overthrow of Joe Culligan. If so, please raise your right hand. Everyone raised his right hand—and, with a number of people turning to stare at me—*pax vobiscum*, Count von Stauffenberg—so did I. With that vote of confidence, Blair designated Caskie Stinnett, the publicist who had once produced Culligan's "Curtis Commitment," as the "chief manifesto writer" and assigned him to the next office to draw up the manifesto. (Emerson shrewdly asked to accompany Stinnett and take part in the drafting.) So for another fifteen or twenty minutes, we continued to mill around, and then Stinnett returned to read his manifesto. It announced that we, the assembled editors, publishers, and advertising managers of the Curtis magazines, did accuse the president of the Curtis Publishing Company, Matthew Joseph Culligan, of inefficiency and incompetence, that his continuation in office would mean the bankruptcy of the company, and that if he were not removed from power at the next board meeting, we would all resign "at the close of business on that day."

"Damn good," said Hank Walker as a rumble of general approval welcomed Stinnett's reading of the manifesto. Stinnett, however, had no sooner finished than he raised a question. "Are we all sure that we want to sign an ultimatum that cannot be accepted? Are we all sure that we want to commit ourselves to a move that is doomed to failure?"

The phrasing of the questions put a certain chill on the enthusiasm of the insurgents. Somebody asked Stinnett to explain what he meant by saying the move was doomed.

"Well, we all ought to know perfectly well that the board can't get rid of Joe on Thursday," Stinnett said. "It'll take time for them to look into all this and make their decision. So if we all promise to walk out of here on Thursday—and I'm perfectly ready to join you if that's what you all want—we ought to agree now that we're ready to kill all the magazines on Friday morning."

It was an artful point, artfully made. Kantor, for his part, argued that the manifesto didn't really commit us to walking out on Friday, and that it was important mainly as a statement of intent, to compel the board to take action. Kantor's lawyer urged that we give the board more time, and I joined in this argument, as did several others. Dave Thomas then proposed a later date for the ultimatum, like November

1, and the meeting soon began to dissolve in a chaos of proposals about various dates.

In the midst of all this, there was some question about whom we should honor with our manifesto. The natural candidate was M. Albert Linton, the seventy-seven-year-old chairman of the Curtis board's executive committee. But although someone had placed a call to Linton, he could not be found, and when he finally received the message that Kantor was trying to reach him, he refused to accept the call.

And so we ended in the confusion characteristic of this rebellion, as though we were all followers of Jack Cade. We were all prepared to sign a manifesto, but we couldn't agree on the wording of it; we were all prepared to resign on a given date, but we couldn't agree on the date; we were all prepared to threaten the reigning authorities, but we weren't sure whether they would listen to us, or even who they were. Just as characteristically, Blair resolved the problems by inviting everyone out to a leisurely lunch that lasted until four o'clock in the afternoon. And later that day he spread the word that the crisis was off again, that this was not *Der Tag* after all, that we must proceed carefully and gradually.

The next afternoon, Tuesday, I was summoned once again to Blair's office, to a seat in one of the four deep-blue plush chairs in the center of the room, and this time the ultimatum was already written. Sometime in the preceding twenty-four hours, Schanche's Puritan compulsion to get things settled had driven him to telephone Phil Strubing, at Curtis's Philadelphia law firm of Pepper, Hamilton & Scheetz, to warn him that there might be an editorial walkout if Linton refused to hear the charges against Culligan. Strubing suggested that if the editors had charges to make, they should be put in writing and delivered to Linton. So Schanche had done the deed, and now that I was almost the first of the rebels to arrive in Blair's half-darkened office, Hank Walker shoved the letter at me across Blair's marble coffee table.

"Ya gonna sign?" Walker asked, not threateningly, but not very cordially either.

"Okay," I said. At this point, like Rubashov in *Darkness at Noon*, I could only think: *I'll sign anything. Even if it gets us all fired, and all the magazines shut down, let's get it over with. . . .*

"Dear Mr. Linton," the letter said,

. . . We are, quite frankly, in a state of revolt on the simple moral premise that we cannot, in good conscience, continue to contribute our skills and our reputations to what we view as an immoral deception of our fellow employees, our readers, our loyal advertisers, the directors and the stockholders of Curtis. We fear that the Board of Directors has been deluded by Mr. Culligan and is unaware of the many instances of questionable and perhaps even illegal conduct of the company management. There have been shocking instances of advertising kickbacks, which we understand may be illegal under the Robinson-Patman Act. There have been consistent misrepresentations to us and to the public of the truth about the company's extremely bleak financial position. There has been consistent frivolous waste of the company's funds. . . .

The letter did not demand Culligan's dismissal, but it did demand that he "be quietly stripped of his executive power but left nominally in charge for the sake of appearances only." While the board investigated Culligan's activity, the letter continued, the company should be governed by an executive committee consisting of Linton, Blair, Kantor, and Poppei (the comptroller). No time limit was set for these changes, but if the board failed to act, the letter said, then none of the signers "can continue to participate in what he knows to be deceitful and wrong." It concluded that we were all "determined to terminate our employment," if necessary, because we all preferred "to see these great institutions die with honor than expire, as they are now doing, under a corrupt leadership."

I skimmed through this document, full of dubious and certainly undocumented charges, and even more full of Schanche's moralizing rhetoric—*and he doesn't even write very well,* I thought—and then I signed my name at the head of the list, before all others. I was still quite sure that the manifesto would do no good, but I was acting out of solidarity rather than out of belief. Even as I was signing, the rest of the revolutionaries began drifting in—Ritter, Ballew, Connors, Thomas, Hadley, Schanche himself. There were fifteen in all. They silently read the letter and then signed, and that was all there was to it.

Once Linton had been informed by telephone that this document existed, he became very anxious to receive it before the next day's meeting of the executive committee, and so Ritter was delegated to get on a train and carry the letter to Philadelphia. Actually, Linton didn't live in Philadelphia but in Moorestown, New Jersey, but when Ritter arrived at his door that night, he found that the old man's real concern, like that of every other Philadelphian, was for the Phillies. With scarcely a month remaining in the baseball season, the Phillies had been six games ahead and apparently on their way to their first pennant in fourteen years—but then they began losing, game after game. Night after night, everyone in Philadelphia sat in front of the television set and watched the disaster come one step closer. Ritter arrived at Linton's house during the sixth inning and spent a fretful half-hour discussing the crisis at Curtis, and then the old man dispatched him with a promise that everything would be settled at the executive committee meeting the following day, or the board meeting the day after that. As soon as Ritter left, Linton returned to his television set and watched the last inning of the game. The Phillies lost again.

9

"We're going to win"

While the Curtis directors gathered in the marble fortress on Independence Square, Blair mobilized his revolutionaries in a different kind of fortress. The Marriott Motel stood beside a superhighway on the outskirts of Philadelphia, but it was quite isolated from the life of the city, belonging instead to that spidery metropolis inhabited by all the motorists on all the expressways. Here one could pause, after a day of driving, and dine at the Steak 'n' Saddle or the Tahitian Room. Outside, all day and all night, the traffic sounded like the rush of restless surf.

We still did not know the directors' reaction to our manifesto, which Norman Ritter had so ceremoniously delivered at the home of M. Albert Linton, but the great confrontation had already been scheduled. On this morning of September 30, 1964, Kantor was to argue the case before the board's executive committee, of which he was a member. On the following day, Kantor and Blair would both argue the case before the full board. For his own moral support, or possibly for a cavalry charge, Blair wanted all his rebels to come to Philadelphia with him. We were not supposed to go to downtown Philadelphia, however, because, as he put it, "everybody'll see us." Nor were we supposed to tell anyone in New York where we were going, or why. Our "cover story"—Blair loved to devise cover stories —was that we had all gone somewhere to confer in privacy on the Curtis editorial budgets. And so Ritter had booked us all into this isolated motel, this trap.

The lobby was full of potted palms, and loitering delegates to some business convention, and after I had checked in, the bellboy took my suitcase not to an elevator but to a kind of miniature jeep, which circled the vast barracks until it reached the proper entry to my room. We had all been instructed to report promptly to Blair's suite, but our only purpose there was to wait. From Blair's sixth-floor balcony, we could look out over compounds of apartments, walkways, swimming pools, and beyond that there was the relentless whooshing of cars racing past on the speedway, through a landscape without trees or houses, where no one could live or even take a walk, where there was nowhere to go and nothing to do.

And so we waited. Hank Walker organized a gin rummy game at a table in one corner. The morning newspapers were passed from hand to hand, and we all learned, in due time, the complete contents of the Philadelphia *Inquirer,* including news of local social events and school budget problems. At about two o'clock, when there was no word from the executive committee meeting, Schanche telephoned room service to order lunch, a dozen variations on ham and eggs. And a lot of Coca-Cola. We were all staying totally sober, since we theoretically might be summoned at any moment to appear before the elders of the executive committee. The lunch left a litter of dirty plates and empty Coke bottles, and still we just sat and waited, nodding over the newspapers, listening to the cars droning past in the hazy distance.

And there were the jokes, the compulsive, monotonous jokes that keep pouring out when a group of bright, nervous people are confined in one room with nothing to do. Emerson, predictably, was the only one who could really make us laugh. He gave us an elaborate and graphic description of a Texan technique of love known as "smother-f——," in which, once the action has begun, the cowboy lifts the lady's skirt over her head and does his best to smother her. The lady's writhing struggle to escape, according to Emerson, adds a novel element to the familiar experience. As a specific example, Emerson described the adventures of a rancher's wife in Pecos County, who suddenly found that the sensation of smothering was somewhat stronger than she had expected. She thrashed her way out of the bedroom, down the stairs, and all the way across the newly redecorated living room before achieving the climax next to the kitchen range. "She said it was an interesting experience," Emerson concluded, "but not one that she wanted to repeat."

What was never mentioned during those long hours of waiting, oddly enough, was the specific evidence that Blair's new allies in the advertising department had finally produced against Culligan. That morning, Ballew and Connors led Emerson and me into a private room and told us for the first time the details of their charges of large discounts to favored advertisers. In the two major cases, they had obtained copies of the contracts and learned that the sums involved totaled more than $600,000. The discounts, they said, were not only uneconomical, meaning that Curtis would be publishing the advertisements at a loss, but unethical, since both law and custom forbade favoritism to any one advertiser. They were particularly disturbed by the fact that they themselves had signed contracts promising major advertisers that no other advertiser would get a better rate. If the details of these two secret deals were ever disclosed, they said, it would cause a major scandal and do ruinous damage to Curtis.

In addition to all this, the discounts seemed to have angered Ballew and Connors in a more personal way. To put it simply, they were salesmen too, and they thought they were probably just as good as the famous Joe Culligan, and when they learned of the large discounts he had given, they resented his celebrity as a supersalesman. "Give Joe the same rate card that any other salesman has to use," Connors said bitterly that morning, "and then see what happens—hah!"

I did not think it my function to serve as the devil's advocate, and I knew relatively few of the facts about the *Post*'s advertising sales operations, but as I listened to Ballew and Connors pouring out their accusations, I could not help imagining a case for the defense. The basic problem, I would argue, was much bigger than rate cards and official discounts. The basic problem was that the *Post* was going bankrupt, and the biggest single reason that it was going bankrupt was that the advertising industry had lost faith in it. In such a situation, everybody on Madison Avenue imitates everybody else, and it is much safer to sit still and do nothing than to risk one's reputation and one's money on a magazine that everybody else thinks will fail. The only way to change such a situation, I would say, is to begin achieving a few successes, and then to use those as the route to further successes. And if I were Joe Culligan, I would rather give away a Cadillac ad for nothing, free, and then use that to help me sell a million dollars' worth of business to Ford—I'd rather do that than sit around and quibble about percentages and rates and discounts. This was not Culligan's defense, you understand, for Culligan had not yet been accused of anything specific, and he might deny that he needed to offer any defense, and he might deny, above all, that he needed me as his defender.

(As it turned out, five years passed before Culligan finally made public both the charges and his own defense. And his defense consisted in acknowledging the details of the two supposedly secret contracts and insisting that there was nothing wrong with either one of them. In his book, *The Curtis-Culligan Story,* Culligan said:

(Kantor got the support of Jesse Ballew. . . . Ballew seized on two joint-venture programs, one with Admiral, one with Longines, as evidence of more than mismanagement—he and Kantor distorted them into "advertising kickbacks." The Admiral situation developed this way: The Chicago advertising manager, Jim Hagen, sent an urgent message to me to call on Ross Siragusa, President of the Admiral Corporation. Hagen had a good plan calculated to appeal to Siragusa. It involved the purchase by Curtis of the names of Admiral customers who had warranties on expensive merchandise, if Admiral would purchase over $2 million in advertising space in Curtis magazines. . . . I had the plan sent to Maurice Poppei, treasurer, and Allison Page, legal counsel, for advance approval. Both gave an OK, and I made the presentation. Siragusa bought the idea on the first call. . . . Television set buyers at that time were a very desirable socio-economic group in the United States, and their names and addresses were extremely valuable to people in the direct mail business. Such lists of names were salable at rates of up to seventy-five dollars per thousand. . . . A similar kind of deal was also made with the Longines-Wittnauer Watch Company. . . . There was no Robinson-Patman violation involved because Curtis was at all times prepared to offer the same arrangements to any advertiser who had something of equivalent value to offer to Curtis. . . . The Longines and Admiral contracts were admittedly out of the ordinary but extraordinary measures were needed to meet extraordinary conditions.

(In addition to the lists of names, both corporations agreed to provide various other services—Admiral, for instance, promised to "conduct a national survey of magazines," and Longines promised to hire a consultant "to develop different mailing subscription offers." One basic question, of course, is whether these names and services were worth the prices Culligan agreed to pay—$238,000 for Admiral and $400,000 for Longines. Five years after the fact, Joe Culligan still said the names and services were very valuable; several of his critics said they weren't; and the Curtis Circulation Company, for whom these services were contracted, declined to say anything at all.)

When a struggle for power nears the point of decision, it is important to pause and reconsider two fundamental questions: What is the object over which we are struggling? And who really has power over that object?

Magazines (and newspapers, too, for that matter) are quite different, as objects of value, from other products of the economy. The *Saturday Evening Post* consisted of one essential asset: the words that made up its name. It was basically a set of ideas, as I have said, and the name simply provided a label by which anyone could recognize the new set of ideas contained in each weekly issue. Other than its basic ideas, then, what does a magazine really own? Its second greatest asset—some would idealistically argue that this is the greatest—is its staff of editors, writers, photographers, but all of these are rented talents, like actors signed up for a Broadway musical. They, too, are a set of ideas. After these two main assets, the value of the remnant diminishes rapidly. First there is the list of names of subscribers, which can be bought or sold or rented as a market for other products, but these names have no more intrinsic value than a telephone directory, or, better, a copy of *Who's Who*. Their real value depends entirely on the use that someone else can make of them (i.e., on the value of someone else's idea). Next, there is the "inventory," but in contrast to a steel plant, which may have an inventory of steel ingots that can be sold at any time, a magazine has an inventory consisting of nothing more substantial than a few manuscripts and pictures—more ideas—all gradually going out of date.· This inventory may have cost a million dollars or more, but, depending on the talent of the editorial staff, it may be worth more than that, or a lot less, or nothing. And finally, after the intangible name and good will, the volatile staff, the impersonal lists of subscribers, and the evanescent inventory, there is nothing left but a few rented offices containing some used desks, chairs, and typewriters, some copy paper and pencils.

These concepts used to baffle the accountants who were assigned to watch over us. Once or twice a year, they would voyage northward from Philadelphia, always traveling two at a time, in the manner of nuns, policemen, and prostitutes. They had long lists marked "Inventory," and when the inventory showed that we had bought an article, they wanted to see a copy of the manuscript to make sure that it was really there. But when we advanced $500 to a writer to go somewhere and report on a story, that advance, too, had to be listed in the inventory—since all our expenditures had to conform to one or another of the official categories of accounting—and then the accountants couldn't understand what we had received in exchange for the $500. Maurice Poppei, the comptroller, used to ask why all outstanding advances couldn't be "settled" or "wiped out." I would try to answer him in the language of business, arguing that such payments represented investments in the raw materials necessary for the production of magazines, and the only way they could be "settled" would be for us to close the books and go out of business. Maurice Poppei could only look at me and shake his bald old head and conclude that I did not understand financial affairs.

But who really controls a magazine? Where does the real power lie? The editors, naturally enough, often declare that they are solely in charge of their pages. And it is true that they do decide, most of the time, what they will print and when and in what form, with little interference from the business managers. There are two reasons for this. One is that editors are technicians, with certain skills that cannot be easily replaced, and the business management needs technicians to get the job done. But the second reason for the editors' cherished independence is that it usually doesn't matter very much, in a commercial sense, what editors publish, and therefore there is no reason for the business management to interfere.

This apparently cynical observation should not be taken too literally. Obviously, some stories do matter, and, just as obviously, a certain minimum level of professional competence must be maintained. But in the general run of magazine articles (or newspaper stories), most profiles of athletes and movie stars are relatively interchangeable, and so are, for that matter, most reports on men fighting in Vietnam, foreign ministers conferring in Paris, or Negroes demonstrating in ghettos. They may all be worthy stories, but in commercial terms, in terms of publishing magazines for a profit, they don't vary a great deal from one version to the next. Cyrus H. K. Curtis, who might in a later incarnation have become a great television tycoon, expressed this view quite succinctly many years ago to a group of advertisers: "Do you know why we publish the *Ladies' Home Journal*? The editor thinks it is for the benefit of the American woman. That is an illusion, but a proper one for him to have. But I will tell you the publisher's reason. . . . To give you people who manufacture things that American women want to buy a chance to tell them about your products." Curtis was not alone in his view. Henry Luce, who had a high regard for editorial independence, nonetheless told a group of advertising agency people: "Yours is the only court in the land to which I hold myself accountable. My only law is the concordat between advertiser and editor to give the people what they want . . . be it anything from a bottle of beer to the hope of immortality."

A magazine, then, has publishers, people who are supposed to see to it that the bills are paid, and that the publishers' income exceeds expenditure—that the magazine makes a profit. These people are generally known, in the language of business, as "management." They are not wholly separated from the basic functions of production, distribution, and sales, but they are valuable not because of their skill in those fields but often in spite of it. A true salesman, for example, will never be content with simply managing a company but will continue, even if he is president, to go on making sales. Similarly, a producer, a man who has devoted his life to making things, will probably insist on supervising production. As Joe Culligan was an obvious example of the first type, so was Lorimer, who continued to edit copy when he was president of Curtis, an example of the second.

Let us return to specifics. The object of the struggle was not the *Post* itself, which Blair's rebels already controlled, or even the five Curtis magazines, which the rebels equally controlled, but the Curtis Publishing Company, the legal owner of all the magazines. It is important that the distinction between the organizations be kept clear, because two different concepts of the publishing business could imply two different conclusions. On the editorial side, we technicians believed that the magazines had long been carrying the whole company, and that the company's other divisions, which should have existed to serve us, were doing just the opposite. When we wanted a better grade of paper, for example, we found that we could use only what our own paper mills gave us. More important, the centralization of the printing process in Philadelphia still required a journalistically ruinous delay of two weeks between the time we went to press and the time we reached the newsstands all around the country—still required, in other words, that we impose limits on the kind of stories we printed. And yet even while they dictated the technical rules of what we could publish, the lords of the mechanical divisions insisted that they were the sources of Curtis profits, and that we, who supported them, were to blame for the company's losses. So unless we could acquire control of the whole company and change the system that governed it, we believed, the Philadelphia oligarchs would blindly sacrifice the Curtis magazines to the preservation of their own fiefs.

But in Philadelphia there was quite another view of the company's problems. In this managerial view, the Curtis magazines might once have been profitable, but they now were draining money from an otherwise successful corporation, and the Blair revolt was an effort not to rescue the corporation but to destroy it. To the editors, the murder of *Collier's* during the Christmas week of 1955 provided an ugly precedent for the death of the *Post*. But the Philadelphia managers saw the precedent differently. Had the Crowell-Collier Corporation collapsed along with its magazines? On the contrary, the suspension of the magazines had saved the corporation, which had merged into Crowell-Collier-Macmillan and was now highly prosperous. To put it another way, a magazine can be bought or sold, but it must always remain a magazine, even when there is no market for it, whereas a corporation can adapt itself to changing conditions and become anything that its managers think will make a profit. "The corporation itself, as an abstract form, is a creation of art wonderful to behold," Martin Mayer wrote in his book on Wall Street.

A corporation comes into existence when it is needed, and dies when its usefulness is done. It can own property and money and other corporations; it can buy and sell rather eminent men. It can . . . expand, contract, manufacture all goods, perform all services. It needs no sleep, takes no vacations. It can borrow and steal, and even beg. . . . Exactly what a corporation is, nobody knows; that is one of its beauties.

The Curtis Publishing Company, in this autumn of 1964, included these things: a large printing plant at Sharon Hill, Pennsylvania, valued at something between $10 and $40 million, depending on who was doing the valuation; the Curtis Circulation Company, a wholly owned subsidiary, which distributed 50-odd magazines through 100,000 outlets and claimed it was making a profit of several million dollars a year; the gigantic brick and marble headquarters building on Independence Square, worth somewhere between $5 and $15 million; two paper mills in upstate Pennsylvania, of uncertain value; a collection of forest lands totaling 262,000 acres, including natural gas wells and a vast amount of copper; and finally, of course, the five magazines.

As an indicator of relative importance, the *Post* editorial staff now numbered less than 100 people on the Curtis payroll of about 8,000. The *Post* editorial budget of $5.3 million, which included everything from secretarial salaries to the payment for a short story to the settlement of a libel suit, was about one twenty-fifth of the Curtis budget of $130 million. Obviously, if only a few hundred of Curtis's employees were engaged in creating magazines, the thousands of other employees were engaged, at salaries totaling more than $50 million a year, in all these other areas of the company's activity. At one time, presumably, these other labors had been started in support of the magazines, but that time was long past. Printers are technicians too, and so are papermakers, and by now these subsidiary baronies had become quite autonomous, as feudal baronies usually do. Their function was no longer to support the magazines but simply to exist, for their own sake, and the magazines now had to pay whatever they were charged for goods and services by the feudal barons.

Structurally, the army of Curtis employees worked for a hierarchy of supervisors and administrators, which had grown in proportion to the number of employees—more personnel workers keeping records on more payroll clerks—quite irrespective of the amount of work done. At or near the control room of this machine, about thirty vice presidents (of whom Blair was the only one with any editorial function whatever) reported to the president, Matthew J. Culligan. If Culligan had considered himself an administrator, he could have kept himself fully occupied solely in administering this machine, but, as he himself told us in that first meeting, "I had two choices—I could have stayed in Philadelphia and listened to everybody's problems, or I could get out and start selling."

It has never been determined exactly what a corporation president should do with his time and talent, and, since the job is really more than any one man can handle, the average president does what he thinks he can do best, and leaves the other aspects of the job to his subordinates. Thus a salesman-president, like Culligan, remains a salesman and hires a Mac Clifford to take care of administration; an administrative president, as Clifford was to be, stays in his office and does paperwork, leaving the salesmen to do the selling. But under any system, the laws of feudalism apply. If there is a strong, wise, and ruthless king, who works hard to dominate all areas of his kingdom, then he will truly be king. This rarely happens, however. And if the king is weak or foolish or softhearted, or if he spends too much time at falconry or prayer or gluttony, the feudal barons reassert themselves as quasi-independent rulers, capable of defying the king whenever they choose.

One of the essential inefficiencies of the feudal system was the uncertainty about ultimate authority, and the history of those medieval years is the history of interminable quarrels, of dynastic rivalries, of ferocious civil wars. But although the American corporation generally conducts its routine operations along feudal lines (I do not deny the existence of efficiently autocratic corporations, in which all decisions are made at the top and carried out through the ranks, but such corporations must remain relatively small, or else they require chief executives with a will and talent far beyond the executive average), it cannot accept the confusions of unresolved warfare between king and barons. The War of the Roses would be too expensive nowadays.

On top of the old-fashioned political structure, therefore, the corporation superimposes a tribal court that is both newer and older than anything in our political history: the board of directors. The directors are truly tribal, since they are elected by the stockholders as a kind of council of elders, a form of government that can be traced back to the caveman. From a more positive point of view, the directorial system brings the processes of democracy to the conduct of business. Every stockholder, by investing his ten or twenty dollars, becomes a voter and full participant in the fortunes of his company. Corporation executives like to perpetuate this theory by referring to themselves as "your management," and there have been efforts to popularize terms like "people's capitalism." The flaw in the theory is that the system does not provide for a loyal opposition. There are a few professional gadflies who appear at the annual stockholders' meetings, to be sure, but there is no means of providing an informed critical review of the company's operations. And even if there were— this is the ultimate problem—the nature of the average stockholder is such that his critical questions would not deal with the quality of the company's work or the value of that work to American society. On the contrary, his questions would almost certainly involve nothing but demands for higher profits.

And yet the board retains the ultimate responsibility. The board represents the stockholders, and thus it speaks with the voice of ownership. The board alone has the right to depose the president and to replace him with a new president. So when a civil war breaks out within the management, a rebellion that the president fails to crush, the conflict comes before the board, the final arbiter, the supreme court of all our problems.

Who, then, controlled the Curtis board of directors? Unlike many boards, which are acquiescent allies of the reigning management, the Curtis directors were divided into a number of factions, which not only were hostile to one another but scarcely even comprehended one another. The chairman was Joe Culligan, who counted on the support of his own appointees—Clifford and Poppei—but their loyalties were less than certain. Clifford, having been demoted from the Number Two position by Kantor, apparently believed that he himself would be a more efficient president than Culligan. Poppei's loyalties seemed to belong partly to Culligan, partly to Clifford, partly to the discipline of the accountant's profession. On the insurgent side, Blair spoke only for himself and the editors. Kantor had made himself an ally of Blair's but still had ties to the stock interests that had brought him to the board in the first place. The most ambiguous of all these new directors was Milton Gould, once the attorney for Kantor, once the discoverer of Culligan. Gould was also a partner in the law firm of Gallop, Climenko & Gould, and since the *Post* alone paid more than $600,000 a year for legal expenses, Gould had a natural interest in this aspect of Curtis.

Since none of the main antagonists could create a majority, their conflicts served as a kind of ballet staged for the amusement of the old board members, who represented a plurality of the stock, and who retained a veto over any attempts to save the corporation. Of these old board members, the basic group was known as "the family," which owned 32 percent of all common stock and officially consisted of two people: Mary Louise Curtis Bok Zimbalist, then aged eighty-eight, the daughter of Cyrus H. K. Curtis, who occasionally was wheeled into critical board meetings by her Negro servants; and her son, Cary W. Bok, aged fifty-nine, who was in rather poor health but periodically came to Philadelphia, dressed in the old khakis that he liked to wear at his country place in Maine. (There was another son, Curtis Bok, who might have helped to save the company, but that was not to be. Lorimer had denounced him a generation earlier as "that damned Bolshevik," and things were arranged so that Curtis Bok would never have a voice in the operation of the Curtis magazines. He went on to become a distinguished judge, and his son was recently made dean of the Harvard Law School.) As for Mrs. Zimbalist, let us remember her by a story told by a retired executive. Once a year, according to this chronicler, Mrs. Zimbalist would engage in exactly the same colloquy with Walter Deane Fuller, who was then president of the corporation. "She would very respectfully ask Mr. Fuller that her salary as a director be doubled. Very gravely he would reply that economic conditions were such that this could not be done. She would thank him and sit down. Of course, her salary was only one dollar. But she and Mr. Fuller seemed to enjoy the byplay."

The rest of the old directors tended to support "the family," to the extent that they could determine what the family wanted, but Mrs. Zimbalist and her son rarely attended board meetings during these declining years—refusing either to sell the stocks they had held all their lives or to exercise the authority that those stocks gave them. The old directors were thus left to decide matters for themselves, and for this, they were of an age and distinction that would have done credit to the United States Senate. The most senior of them, of course, was Walter Deane Fuller, the tiny, bald gentleman of eighty-two, who had joined the accounting department of Curtis in 1908 and worked his way up to be president and board chairman for more than twenty-five years. Next came M. Albert Linton, seventy-seven, retired president of the Provident Life Insurance Company of Philadelphia and now chairman of the board's executive committee, assigned to deal with our accusations. Then there was Walter S. Franklin, aged eighty, retired president of the Pennsylvania Railroad; and Ellsworth Bunker, aged seventy, former president of the United Sugar Company, former U.S. Ambassador to India, former president of the American Red Cross; Moreau D. Brown, aged sixty-one, partner in the private banking firm of Brown Brothers, Harriman; Harry C. Mills, aged sixty-three, retired vice president of J. C. Penney; and Curtis Barkes, aged fifty-eight, executive vice president of United Air Lines.

Once the managerial civil war had broken out, it soon became apparent that this board, this ultimate court of appeals, knew relatively little about the Curtis Publishing Company and was quite bewildered by the problems that were being placed before it. More than half the directors were over sixty—"Why," someone asked Clemenceau, "are the presidents of France always octogenarians?" And Clemenceau replied: "Because we have run out of nonagenarians" —and most of them, except for the actual combatants, were weary of combat. Thus, when Blair and Culligan wanted to accuse each other of guilt for Curtis's condition, they had to carry their case before this ancient tribunal, which, in consenting to hear the arguments, denied that the ultimate guilt was its own.

At about four o'clock we got a telephone call saying that the executive committee meeting was finally over, and that Kantor was on his way back to the Marriott Motel. Shortly before five, Kantor suddenly burst in, full of the exhilaration of battle. He took a seat on top of a television set and started to describe what had happened. "It was a donnybrook," he said gleefully. "Culligan was just furious. He accused us of lying and scheming and—get this—irreparably damaging his business reputation." Kantor gave a short laugh. "But I paid him back. I said we were charging corruption and mismanagement. I tell you, it was a real donnybrook. Linton and Brown kept asking whether we could prove our charges, and I said, "Listen, we wouldn't be here if we couldn't prove our charges.' "

It sounded very good, very confident and solid, and some of our more militant rebels, Walker and Ballew and Ritter, nodded soulfully at every declaration, like witnesses at a revival meeting. But there was something wrong with Kantor's testimony, some false note. "And that's when I said to him," Kantor was saying, " 'Doc, why don't you just go back to your bank and stay there?' " I had never met the elderly Moreau D. Brown, partner in Brown Brothers, Harriman, but I suspected that this was not the best approach to convince him of anything. I began wondering, then, whether Kantor was being carried away by his role as a battler against these ancient gentlemen of the establishment.

In any case, we had achieved nothing at the executive committee meeting. The committee had simply listened to the accusations and counteraccusations, and then it had deferred action until the full board meeting on the following day. Our problem, therefore, was how to prepare for that full meeting. In search of a wider variety of advocates, we began dispersing in a number of directions. Somebody brought in Phil Strubing, the lawyer, red-faced and gray-haired, an amiable and moderate man who represented "the family" and a number of other board members. He told us that the board was deeply concerned by our charges and would do its best to evaluate them and act on them, but he urged us not to act rashly, and not to issue ultimatums. The bankers, too, were on hand. Semenenko himself was yachting off the coast of Spain, and apparently in telephone communication with Culligan, but he did not interrupt his vacation to fly back for the critical board meeting. Semenenko's two assistants were in Philadelphia, however, and Ballew headed a delegation to call on them, tell them the details of our case, and persuade them that Semenenko should give up his commitment to the Culligan regime.

In the midst of all this lobbying, we had dinner in the motel's Steak 'n' Saddle restaurant—steak and whiskey and baked potatoes in tinfoil—where else could we go, after all?—and then we drifted back to Blair's suite, heard Ballew's optimistic report on his meeting with the bankers, and talked on and on about what would happen. At about eleven o'clock, I began to have the feeling that we were all back at Hank Walker's house in Greenwich. Various people were talking, but nobody seemed to notice that Blair and Kantor were just sitting in silent isolation, spectators. Blair, in fact, had said nothing for several hours and seemed to be simply staring into space, so I got the floor, told everybody to be quiet, and asked Blair what he planned to do at the board meeting the next morning. Blair's only answer was to glower at me, and then to look at Kantor. Kantor said he would answer for both of them, and he launched into yet another speech on the Blair-Kantor plan to save the company. The only novelty was his announcement that he planned to offer his own resignation to the board, but nobody took that seriously. Then, as the hubbub began again, someone spoke up and said, "I still think Otto's question deserves an answer," and so I turned again to Blair. "Come on, Clay,"

I said. "You've just been sitting there for three hours. You're the one who has to speak for us tomorrow, so what are you going to say?"

Blair finally felt sufficiently stung to shake himself to attention. "You know, I really don't know what I'm going to say," he answered, not snappishly, but simply with that vagueness that periodically overcame him. "You know, I think it would be a mistake to try to plan this thing too much. I mean, I know all the facts, all the figures, all the arguments, so I think I'll just play it by ear. Okay?" I did not answer him, since I did not realize that I was supposed to answer, but I was wrong. "Okay, Otto?" Blair repeated. "Okay if I just play it by ear?" I silently nodded, and Blair accepted that as his answer.

By now, everyone was rather dazed with a long day of strategy, planning, arguments, and, finally, drink. Like an opera chorus, voices from smoke-hazy corners agreed that it was best to play it by ear, not to have plans. And just as the opera chorus keeps repeating banalities as it troops off the stage, people began filtering out. Some of them had a purpose—Ritter was going to draw up a document listing Ballew's charges against Culligan, and Ballew and Connors were going to provide all the details—but most of them just wandered off. I myself intended only to finish my drink, but since my glass was half full, and since people were leaving very rapidly, I soon found myself all alone on the sofa, with Kantor stripped to the waist in preparation for bed, Blair still staring into space, and Dave Thomas and Caskie Stinnett passionately lecturing Blair on the need for leadership, strategy, confidence.

"Ah, what're you talking about?" Blair suddenly erupted. "Listen, I don't need any lectures from you guys. There's Otto over there, practically accuses me of being a crook."

"That isn't true," I snapped back at him.

"Come on, Clay," Thomas pleaded in his oddly soft and serpentine voice. "You're the one we all look to as our leader. You can't act as though—"

"Listen," Blair turned on him, "I don't owe you guys anything. Nothing at all."

"The hell you don't," I said. "You led us into all this, and we followed you into it. You think a general has a right to turn on his troops in the middle of a battle and say, 'It's been nice knowing you'? The hell he does!"

"He's right, Clay," Thomas added, almost pleading. "You've got to realize that we're all behind you in this. We're all behind you in that meeting tomorrow. You've got to realize that."

Kantor had stood watching this scene with some bewilderment, and now he broke in to say, in that curiously rasping, nasal voice, "Well, we're certainly going to do all we can. No question about that. But I'm also going to go through with my determination—and nobody can dissuade me from this—to resign from this board."

"Oh, come on, Marv," Thomas said.

"You just don't know what he's been through," Blair burst in. "You have no right to tell him what to do."

"Nobody's trying to tell him what to do, but—"

"Can't we stop all this talk of resigning?" I said.

"That goes for you too," Blair said.

"Look, the idea is to win, right?" I said. "And we can't win if people keep resigning."

"Well, look, it's two o'clock, and I think we'd all better get some sleep," Kantor said.

"Okay, don't worry," Blair added, suddenly conciliatory. "We know what we're doing, but we have to play it the way we see it."

By the time we woke up the next morning, October 1, the battle was already joined, and we could only sit and wait. The tension of the previous day had worn off. We were fairly sure we would never be summoned to the board meeting; indeed, there was some doubt whether the board even knew we were in Philadelphia. Breakfast was leisurely. There were some phone calls to New York to find out what was happening back at the office. It was only after lunch that we again gathered in Blair's suite, again rustling through the much-read newspapers, again drinking Coca-Cola and listening to the intermittent chatter of jokes and wisecracks.

Suddenly the door flew open, and Blair marched in, followed by Kantor and Ritter, all bursting with triumph. "We're going to win," Blair announced, and everyone pressed around, shaking his hand and shouting congratulations. "Thank you, thank you," Blair was saying, "we've really got him on the run now." The hand was held out to me, and I could only think, *Well, maybe I was wrong,* and so I was shaking it too, *and no hard feelings.* "He's dead and he knows it," Kantor shouted. It seemed like a great triumph.

As the tumult died down, Kantor began describing what had happened. He told how Culligan had taken the offensive, accusing his accusers of a power-mad plot to seize the corporation, charging them with irresponsibility, denying that he had ever done anything wrong. Kantor told how he had fought back, citing all his examples—"I had the facts after all"—of Culligan's own irresponsibility, his failure to carry out promises, his extravagances and deceptions.

"Wait a minute, wait a minute," Blair broke in. "Tell 'em about the Goldwater editorial."

"No, you tell 'em," Kantor said.

The "Goldwater editorial" had been Blair's last major act of editorial license. Traditionally, and quite properly, the editor of the *Post* had exercised complete control over the editorial page, but Blair rarely had time to write editorials himself, and so he worked out an arrangement to buy them from a *Life* writer named William Miller, who had once been chief editorial writer for the New York *Herald Tribune*. Miller was a strange addition to our empire—a very large man, well over six feet and well over two hundred pounds, but curiously pixyish, with a high voice, a tripping laugh, and a vague, otherworldly manner. Since *Life* disapproved of its writers' working for other magazines, everybody pretended that Miller would write editorials in great secrecy. Despite his anonymity, however, Miller was an emotionally dedicated liberal and an effusive writer. His editorial manuscripts, which never appeared before the deadline, would generally turn out to be shaggy perorations that included denunciations of segregation, appeals for Christian charity, snatches of half-remembered poetry, and some facts and figures from whatever he was then writing for Time Inc.

Although I heard from Emerson that Miller had produced a wild diatribe against Goldwater—"It's the hairiest thing you ever saw," Emerson said. "It's got hairs that long all over it"—it was not until the printed preliminary copies appeared that I saw what Blair had allowed Miller to do. Obviously, the *Post* should have come out for Lyndon Johnson against Goldwater, but it should have done so in a thoughtful, well-reasoned, and coolly written editorial. Miller's harangue was as extreme as anything Goldwater himself had ever said. "Goldwater is a grotesque burlesque of the conservative he pretends to be," said that editorial in the September 19 issue. "He is a wild man, a stray, an unprincipled and ruthless political jujitsu artist. . . . For the good of the Republican Party, which his candidacy disgraces, we hope that Goldwater is crushingly defeated."

The results of this editorial were extraordinary. Conventional liberals, who applaud any action that serves their purposes, naturally cheered. More fair-minded readers, however, resented the shrill polemic tone. And at the other extreme, conservative readers began canceling their business. The subscriptions were relatively unimportant, a loss of something like ten thousand, but the loss of advertising was later estimated to be at least $3 million, and perhaps considerably more. The important point in terms of Blair's regime, however, was that he had not written the editorial, had not seriously edited it, and had rushed it into print without any serious discussion among the other editors.

"Let me tell you," Blair laughed now. "Once Culligan brought up the Goldwater editorial, I got up and I formally introduced a resolution of censure against that editorial. Yeah! No kidding! Listen, I worked this out at four o'clock this morning. I got up and presented this resolution for the board to censure that editorial. And the next thing you know, old Walter Fuller was saying, 'If you think this board is going to intrude in the editing of the Curtis magazines, you're quite mistaken.' And then they're all in there *defending* the editorial. See? See how it worked? I conned the board into defending the editorial."

Amid the general laughter, Blair sat chuckling to himself and repeating the phrase, "conned the board." Marvin Kantor, meanwhile, went on with his recitation. He told how he had carried out his plan to resign, how he had told the board of his long labors for the sake of this moribund corporation, his efforts at reform and reorganization, his suffering of calumny, and now he resigned.

"I tell you they were stunned," Blair cried. "They were absolutely stunned. And Gould got up and shouted: 'Nobody resigns! Nobody resigns! We're all in this together, and we're going to work it all out.' "

"And that's when I gave 'em my spiel," Blair went on.

"Clay was great," Kantor said. "He was really great."

"I told them all the things we'd been through, day after day," Blair said. "The anxiety, the struggling, the effort. Every night, I go to bed, and I can't sleep because of this damn corporation. Month after month. I told them what it was really like to try to save this goddamn company. I even cried. I tell you, I had to stop, and I really cried."

"Clay was great," Kantor repeated.

"And then I said this just couldn't go on this way, and they really— they're finally going to do something."

"It was the moral issue that finally got to them," Kantor said. "That was the thing. I'm not kidding. We finally convinced them that they've been failing in their duty, just sitting there, and that finally got to them. Even Poppei, Culligan's own financial man. He said to me, 'You fellows may really have something here.' "

"So what did Culligan do?" somebody asked.

"What could he do?" Kantor said. "He just sat. He knows when he's licked."

"And I want to tell you what Linton said," Blair added. "He said, 'I want you to tell those boys that we won't let them down.' Meaning you guys. We really got to him, and he wanted us to tell you, 'We won't let them down.' "

So the board had decided to investigate. Linton, Brown, and Gould were to form a special committee to study the specific charges against Culligan, and to report back to another meeting—the session had merely recessed—in two weeks. We all shook hands on our triumph, for we all accepted the euphoric statements by Blair and Kantor that we were winning. Nobody bothered to ask why Culligan would simply abandon his presidential powers, or why the board would turn the corporation over to two executives so troublesome and so inexperienced as Blair and Kantor. Nobody, in other words, really analyzed what was at stake, or what had happened, or where we all stood now. It was much more pleasant to revel in the prospects of victory.

Late afternoon. That same day. Kantor wheeled his brown Cadillac out of the motel parking lot and asked whether anybody wanted a ride back to New York. Everybody did, of course, but only two of us—Dave Thomas and I—had the temerity to speak up.

"Well, it must be a great relief," I said as a beginning, as Kantor steered his Cadillac out onto the expressway. Kantor smiled his wintry smile and started a monologue that lasted all the way back to New York.

He began with the board meeting, and the spectacle of old Mrs. Zimbalist being wheeled in. "She was dressed all in white, and her face was about the whitest face I ever saw, and she just sat there, smiling and nodding every once in a while. And then at lunchtime, they wheeled her out again, right in the middle of the meeting."

As we spun through a series of traffic circles on our way out of Philadelphia, Kantor talked of the other old dignitaries who had attended the meeting. "Even Bunker," he said, "who has hardly attended a single board meeting since I've been with this company. He sat there too. And Cary Bok in his khakis. I tell you, it was a fantastic scene."

The conversation inevitably turned to Culligan, whom Kantor managed to portray as a protégé of his. "He knows the job is too big for him—he's told me as much. But as long as there's enough good times, Joe's happy." Then he spoke bitterly of Semenenko, and his vast suite at the Hotel Pierre, filled with icons and paintings and tapestries. And Semenenko still had a Russian accent, which Kantor considered an annoying affectation. "After all," Kantor said, "he's been in this country for forty years, so there's no reason why he has to keep talking like an immigrant, unless he wants to talk that way."

And Kantor was still indignant about Mac Clifford, whom he had displaced, and whom he now denounced with a string of insulting names. And he was outraged that Clifford had promoted a former secretary, Gloria Swett, to the position of corporate secretary at a salary of more then $25,000 a year. Then there were two vice presidents whom Culligan had hired at $50,000 a year—Kantor said one was known primarily for his skill at playing golf and the other primarily for his position as a "socialite." And then there was another of Culligan's adjutants who had taken a boatload of advertisers out for a boat ride. He had become so drunk, according to Kantor, that he had ordered the entire crew of the boat to jump overboard. Kantor had fired him, he said, but Culligan had countermanded the order, telling his friend to "lie low for a while," and telling Kantor, "I've given him sick leave."

It had grown dark as we sped northward along the Jersey Turnpike, and in the darkness, listening to Kantor's droning voice, I realized that he was obsessed with other people's sense of morality. He was outraged by people who maintained suites in New York hotels, outraged by people who drank too much, outraged by anyone who indulged himself—or even enjoyed himself. (At one point during these maneuvers, Joe Culligan had encountered Kantor in a corridor. "Well, how's the president of the moral indignation society?" Culligan had asked. "Indignant," said Kantor.)

In the spotlit darkness, Kantor finally drew up before the last toll booth and paid his fees to the New Jersey Turnpike Authority, and then he drove on, still talking. We were now entering the evil-smelling tunnels under the Hudson, and it was possible to conclude from Kantor's monologue that he was quite overwrought about everyone else in the corporation. This, for example, was his response to one of the Semenenko-Culligan merger efforts: "Joe, you want *Curtis* to be associated with *gamblers*, with *crooks*?" Or, again, his response to a plan by G. B. McCombs, head of the Curtis Circulation Company, to distribute a girlie book called *Jayne Mansfield for President*. " 'G. B.,' I said, 'you want the *Curtis* Publishing Company to distribute garbage—*shit*—like this?' "

Well, yes, G. B. McCombs would indeed distribute just about anything that would make money for the Curtis Circulation Company, just as Joe Culligan would probably approve of any merger within reason so long as it proved profitable. But Marvin Kantor had become infected with strange ideas during the past year or two, and the strangest of all was the idea that corporate profits should be subordinated, in some instances, to the preservation of a corporate image.

For this was not just any publishing company that Kantor was fighting to control but the *Curtis* (the word was almost always underlined when he spoke it) Publishing Company. It was the headquarters of *Curtis* that Marvin Kantor had come to Philadelphia to photograph, on that thin, cold January day, with his Polaroid camera. Somehow, he would save this hapless company from itself, from both moribund Philadelphians and immoral New Yorkers. And by saving the Curtis Publishing Company, with all its traditions and all its innocence, Marvin Kantor would reach, finally, the light at the end of the pier. "His dream must have seemed so close that he could hardly fail to grasp it. He did not know that it was already behind him, somewhere back in that vast obscurity beyond the city, where the dark fields of the republic rolled on under the night."

10

"Curtis editors accuse chief"

Conspiracies and power struggles undoubtedly occur within many organizations, but the antagonists almost unfailingly maintain the rule of secrecy. Any embarrassing inquiries from the outside world receive the polite response that there must be some mistake, that any reports of trouble are wholly unfounded. One reason for this rule of secrecy, of course, is that stories of internecine warfare inevitably damage the entire organization; the other reason is that anyone who speaks out knows he will be punished for the damage caused by his own indiscretion.

The Curtis directors had all promised at their October 1 meeting that they would say nothing about the Blair-Kantor manifesto, and consequently we have no way of knowing how Bernard P. Gallagher broke the story in the October 7 issue of the *Gallagher Report:*

EXPLOSION AT CURTIS PUBLISHING. Due shortly. Tense October 1 meeting could have serious consequences. "Palace rebellion" reportedly headed by editor-in-chief Clay Blair. Ultimatum issued to oust chairman-president Joe Culligan. Magazine division chairman Marvin Kantor said to be disenchanted with Clay. Both Clay and Marvin would like to get Culligan's job. . . . Curtis directors would be wise to oust Blair and Kantor. . . .

The item in the *Gallagher Report* was dangerous but not, in itself, disastrous. Gallagher's newsletter was a weekly chronicle of office politics on Madison Avenue, including many reports of threats, confrontations, and impending disasters, but most of this gossip never got far beyond the audience of the newsletter itself. On the following day, however, the mighty *New York Times* bestirred itself. At the late-afternoon story conference held daily in the office of Managing Editor Clifton Daniel, someone declared that there was something interesting happening at Curtis, and that the *Times* should look into it. The financial editor, Tom Mullaney, brought these tidings back to his own department and asked his assignment editor, Bob Bedingfield, to "get a man on it." The department was short-handed, and so Bedingfield began making telephone calls himself. "I started with the proxy fighters," Bedingfield said later, "and then I began calling all the directors."

"This whole thing is going to blow very soon," Don Schanche warned Emerson that afternoon. "The *Times* has a man calling everybody."

In retrospect, it might be interesting to know why the *Times* began this investigation in the first place. The *Gallagher Report* provided a tip, of course, but the *Times* did not generally devote much effort to checking on tips in the *Gallagher Report*. Five years after the event, Tom Mullaney said that he could not remember who had brought up the matter at Clifton Daniel's story conference. And Clifton Daniel also said, very politely, that "nobody here seems to remember just how the Curtis rebellion first came to our notice." In any case, Bedingfield's telephone calls confirmed the report that there was trouble at Curtis, but they provided him with very few details. "I knew Semenenko, and I talked to him, along with all the others, but what he told me was very clean, and all I had for the first edition was a box, a couple of paragraphs."

"During that afternoon," Norman Ritter said later, "Blair received a call from Bedingfield, but he didn't have a chance to return it because he was leaving for Detroit to make a speech at the Economic Club. Clay asked me to call Bedingfield because he thought it was poor policy to ignore a *Times* reporter, and so I returned the call at about eight o'clock. Bedingfield was not in the office, but Douglas Cray took the call. I had known Cray since the days when we both worked for Time-Life in Washington. Cray told me that Bedingfield was about to go to press with a story saying there was a management dispute at Curtis and that the board was soon going to ask Blair and Kantor to resign. There was no mention in the story of any of our complaints against Culligan's management or any indication of why Blair and Kantor were questioning it. The story was going to press at 8:30. I told Cray that there was more to this story, and that I would try to call him back in a few minutes. I tried to call Blair. I left a message for him at the gate at LaGuardia, but his flight had already left. In the next few minutes, I composed a short news story reporting the recent events in the dispute. At about 8:30, I called Cray and began to dictate the story to him. . . . You know the rest. 'Our' story supplanted the original Bedingfield version and made page one instead of the financial section."

There were also efforts to reach Marvin Kantor that night, but he was engaged in a theater party for *Post* advertisers. "It was that play about Ben Franklin in Paris, starring Whatshisname—Bob Preston— and we figured that Ben Franklin's magazine should celebrate it," said Jess Ballew. "So we invited about thirty media directors to see the show, and then we took them to dinner at the Hotel Pierre, and during the middle of the dinner, I remember, Jack Connors passed me a matchbook cover, and I still have it, and Jack had written on it: 'Joe has blown the whole story.' "

In fact, however, Joe Culligan was remarkably silent. "I was trying to call Joe all that night, and he wouldn't return my calls," Bedingfield said, "and that in itself was significant, of course. Finally, very late, I talked to his wife and said that I was going to have to go with this story as it was, and that it could be very damaging, but he still didn't call back." Culligan's own recollection is that he was in bed. "Bedingfield called my home shortly before 2 o'clock the morning of October 9 and told my wife that he would be forced to run the story in the morning edition. He wanted to hear my side of it. I signaled my wife to say nothing."

The headline on the front page of the *Times* the next morning said:

CURTIS EDITORS ACCUSE CHIEF OF MISMANAGEMENT

Under the by-line of Robert E. Bedingfield, the story began by stating the essential facts: "A group of 15 editors and production personnel of the Curtis Publishing Company have leveled charges of mismanagement against Matthew J. Culligan, chairman and president of the company."

The story told me nothing that I did not already know, and so I failed at first to understand that all our lives would be different from then on. The difference was simply that the story in the *Times* made us public figures. I had spent twenty years reporting and writing news, and yet, because nobody had ever reported or written about me, personally, I had never really understood the difference between private life and public life. It is a difference that is hard to define but impossible to exaggerate. Into every action in public life, into every decision, even every perception, a new element intrudes: How will it look in the newspapers? The answer, unfortunately, is that it will probably look bad. This is not because the story will be told incompletely or inaccurately—though this will probably happen, partly because the people who really know the facts usually have no reason to believe in full disclosure, partly because the average newspaper reporter is, like other mortals, fallible—but because it is generally a sign of trouble that one is in the news at all. And when one is in trouble, as we now were, all one's actions look vaguely suspicious—particularly when seen, as the press sees things, through a glass, darkly.

Businessmen, who spend billions of dollars on public relations, are usually horrified when any real news about their operations reaches the newspapers. M. Albert Linton, who was identified in the first *Times* story as Arthur B. Linton, reacted in the traditional way by issuing an absurd press release. The *Times,* too, reacted in the traditional way by treating the press release, which was wholly imaginary, as a statement of fact. So the second-day headline on October 10 said:

CURTIS AIDES VOW
TO PRESS GROWTH

Linton also acted in the traditional manner by ordering everybody in the company to say nothing to the press. He may have hoped in some vague way that a reaffirmation of the customary silence of the business world would cause everybody to drop the subject. But the press—Bedingfield for the *Times,* Barry Gottehrer for the *Tribune,* A. Kent MacDougall for the *Wall Street Journal,* and a bevy of young researchers for the news magazines—was in full pursuit. For the next five years, in fact, even the most insignificant events at Curtis were treated as though this venerable publishing company were a topic of major national concern.

Some people have inferred malicious intent in this exhaustive coverage, which undoubtedly injured the company's efforts at recovery, but I think the explanation is simpler. "The *Saturday Evening Post* was different from any other magazine," Bedingfield said later. "When I was a kid, I sold more copies of the *Post* than any other boy in Oak Park, Illinois." For Linton to dream of shutting off such an emotionally inspired flow of gossip and nostalgia only demonstrated once again how little Linton knew of the business in which he was a director. The main effect of Linton's order was to silence the most conscientious people involved in the controversy and to turn the whole process of public information into a series of leaks and counterleaks. Each day's newspaper account of our activities on the previous day thus became an account not of what had actuallly happened but of what various executives wanted other people to think had happened. And inevitably there developed an ebb and flow between private and public information. What really happened might never get into the newspapers at all, while, conversely, a leak to the press might affect what happened in private.

The second-day story, the one headlined with the "vow to press growth," was a mosaic of these managerial leaks. Officially, everyone was very proper. Culligan "could not be reached for comment directly," and Blair, out in Detroit for a speech, would say nothing more controversial than that he would "continue to do everything I can to help this company." Further down in the story, it became apparent that somebody was talking. On the one hand, Culligan was portrayed as a humanitarian who had resisted efforts to sell the printing plant because he was "unwilling . . . to be forced to embark on a wholesale staff layoff of production workers." On the other hand, the story portrayed Blair as a reluctant rebel who had to be "asked by several staff executives to arrange the Sept. 27 meeting" at Manero's.

This sparring lasted only one more day, and then, on the grounds that the ban on press publicity had been violated, Linton struck. (I say Linton, since he had temporarily assumed the role of commanding officer, but at this point the man making the major decisions was undoubtedly Serge Semenenko.) And the next day's *Times* put the story back on the front page:

CURTIS SUSPENDS
2 CULLIGAN CRITICS

———

*Blair and Kantor Relieved
of Duties in Policy Rift*

My weekend began at seven o'clock in the morning when I was waked out of bed by a telephone call from Bob Sherrod. He himself had been waked at six and told to telephone all major editors and read them a communiqué. The communiqué, signed by Culligan, announced that Blair and Kantor had been suspended, and that Curtis hoped all editors would report for work as usual on Monday morning.

"Well, what can I say?" I said groggily. "I'll think about it."

"I understand," Sherrod said. "All they asked was that I call the key editors and relay this message."

At a somewhat more normal hour, about ten o'clock, Emerson telephoned to say that there would be a meeting at the apartment of Dick King, one of Ballew's associate advertising managers. "God— another meeting?" I protested. "Well, that's sort of the way we all feel," Emerson said, "but we might as well carry on. Blair said he didn't want any more meetings, but Schanche and I told him that he wasn't the editor any more, and we'd come to enough of his meetings, so he'd better come to one of ours." Then Dave Thomas called to change the time of the meeting, and then Emerson called to change it back again. Then I got a call from Harold Martin, a kindly, courtly Georgian who had worked as a writer for the *Post* for about twenty years. He said he had been summoned from Atlanta to the Regency Hotel in New York, which happened to be Culligan's headquarters, to "be on hand" in case of any editorial walkout. He said he wanted to see me as soon as possible. I said I would telephone him as soon as the meeting with Blair was over.

At one o'clock in the afternoon, I parked my car near the corner of Second Avenue and Eighty-fifth Street and proceeded to Dick King's apartment. It was a large and conventionally furnished place, which had, however, a convenience we had lacked in all our previous meetings—a pretty and good-natured hostess, who managed to keep twenty noisy strangers supplied with food, drink, and clean ashtrays. When I arrived, Blair was already loudly engaged in telling his version of the event that flickered on and off all afternoon: Who leaked the story to the *Times*? The question was fundamental because the charge of leaking the story had become the cause for the suspension of Blair and Kantor. According to Blair, who by now had hired and brought along his personal attorney, the first tip to Bedingfield had come from someone associated with Semenenko. Ritter had only "corrected" the leak by disclosing his own version of the crisis. At this point, Ritter was already trying desperately to reach Bedingfield to get him to confirm in writing that the first leak had not come from him. Bedingfield said he would have to consult with his superior, Harrison Salisbury. Salisbury said we could use Bedingfield's verbal statements in any way we chose, but any written statement would have to be cleared by the *Times* authorities.

And now, the manifesto-writing urge took over once more. Don Schanche retired to a bedroom and drafted another one of his proclamations, a telegram informing the board of directors that Blair and Kantor must be reinstated forthwith or everyone would walk out.

When he read it aloud, there were rumbles of approval from the militants, like Walker and Ritter, and complaints and criticisms from the conservatives, like Caskie Stinnett and me. Schanche then staged another one of his finger-pointing, around-the-room demands that everybody state his position, but the old coercive power was no longer there. The consensus was that there should be a statement of protest to the board, but that it should be more temperate. Schanche returned to the bedroom to write a new draft. And while he wrote, the flow of argument and chatter and stating of positions became a bedlam. At one point, Jess Ballew was asked, as publisher of the *Post,* to give an expert opinion on how long the magazine could survive without the reinstatement of Blair and Kantor.

"It couldn't survive a fortnight," Ballew said.

"Oh, how the hell can you know that?" I protested.

"That's his job—he knows all right," Hank Walker declared.

In the midst of this argument, the phone rang. It was Harold Martin, calling to ask Emerson what had become of their meeting, and of his meeting with me, and warning Emerson that a triumvirate of senior writers—namely Bob Sherrod, Stewart Alsop, and Martin himself—had been summoned to New York by Culligan to take over in case of any walkout by Blair's rebels. Emerson refused to discuss the crisis on the telephone, but he told Martin to get himself to King's apartment as soon as possible, "and bring the rest of the goddamn triumvirate with you."

Blair, meanwhile, had been skulking in another bedroom for some time, and now he emerged with the announcement that he wanted to make a statement. He said, very slowly and very softly, that he and Kantor had discussed the whole situation, that the news of their suspension had really come as "a kind of relief," that he and Kantor had had a festive dinner together the night before, and "we felt as though a great load had been lifted off our backs." The twenty-four-hour-a-day effort to save Curtis, he said, now looked like "a kind of madness"—all those months, all those sleepless nights—"*Why* should we be killing ourselves for this hopeless corporation?"

Now, however, after twenty-four hours, he and Marv had thought it over, and he and Marv were angry, and he and Marv were going to fight. "But it's our fight and ours alone." He, Blair, had no financial considerations at stake. He had only $2,000 in his savings account, but he was going to fight the Curtis Publishing Company until he got his rights. As for the rest of us—whom he had recruited and trained as revolutionaries—he now told us all to disband. "I think you all should stop this talk about a telegram to the board," he said. "I think you should all just think about your wives and children, and your future careers, and then make your own decisions. But I don't ask you to support Marv and me. And I think we should break up this meeting and all go home."

Amid the murmurs of dissent and dismay, Bill Emerson, sitting cross-legged on the floor, shouted: "Clay, I have a one-word answer to that little statement—*bullshit!*"

And the machinery continued to revolve. Schanche emerged from the bedroom with another draft of the manifesto. It said about the same thing as before, but slightly less belligerently. It said that we the undersigned believed Linton had "acted on the basis of misinformation" in suspending Blair and Kantor, that we understood the move had been made because of the disclosures to the *New York Times,* that we could produce testimony from the *Times* reporter to show that Blair and Kantor were innocent of the original disclosures, that the suspension of Blair and Kantor would be disastrous for the future of the *Post* and Curtis, that we demanded their reinstatement "immediately," and that we made this demand "a condition of our continued employment."

In the prevailing atmosphere of hysteria, almost everyone roared his approval. Emerson turned to me and asked, "Should we sign it?"

"Oh, why the hell not?" I said with a shrug.

"See, even Otto is for it," Emerson shouted.

There were some defectors, however—Caskie Stinnett, for one, and Garth Hite, the advertising director of *Holiday.* In addition, two of the original "rebels" did not come to the meeting—Publisher John Collins and Editor Hub Cobb of *American Home.* On the other hand, there were two new recruits, our host, Dick King, and his colleague, Joe Welty, the Numbers Three and Four men in the advertising hierarchy of the *Post.* And so there were eleven of us who signed the new manifesto, and Ritter telephoned it to Western Union as a telegram to M. Albert Linton.

At about six o'clock, the doorbell rang, and in came what Emerson had called "the goddamn triumvirate"—Sherrod, Alsop, and Martin. Those of us who knew them welcomed them with a mixture of affection and apprehension. Bob Sherrod had not been a very successful editor of the *Post,* but we still held a certain regard for him. Alsop, ruddy, wary-eyed, wearing the brown trench coat of the traditional foreign correspondent, had a rather grand sense of his own importance, but he was basically an able and likable man. Martin, square-faced, silver-haired, and very paternal, had not an enemy in the world. Once their coats were off, they were ushered to the three seats on Dick King's three-part sofa. Blair sat at a nearby desk, ready to take notes, while the rest of us gathered into a surrounding and accusing semicircle. It is hard to believe that any three men ever sat so ill-at-ease, so defensive, and so thoroughly unhappy.

Sherrod adopted the role of spokesman and told us that the three had been designated to make sure that the *Post* continued publishing. The three had no point of view and took no stand. "We are absolutely neutral," Sherrod said. "And since the board can't take any action until its meeting on the nineteenth, we have been charged with keeping things going until then."

"It might be well," Schanche interrupted in his dry, naval-officer voice, "for you to know the latest developments." Not without pride of authorship, he handed Alsop a copy of his new manifesto. Alsop read it, nodding sagely, until he reached the last sentence. " 'As a condition of our continued employment,' " he quoted. "That's pretty strong." He looked around as though someone might admit that we didn't mean it. "Damn right," Hank Walker said. Alsop passed the message to Sherrod, who read it mutely and passed it to Martin. "Well, our only purpose," Sherrod said again, "is to make sure that the *Post* goes on. That's all we're concerned about."

"Listen, let me ask you one very basic question," Bill Emerson said. "Do you have any idea of the charges that have been made against Joe Culligan? Have they told you any of that?"

"Well, no, not in any detail," Sherrod said.

"Then you don't really know what this is all about, do you?" Emerson persisted.

"We're just writers and editors, just like you," Martin said helplessly.

The oddity was that neither side knew, now that we had come to open warfare, what the other side planned to do, or even what it was capable of doing. To the beleaguered rebels, it seemed quite likely that Semenenko and Culligan, having suspended Blair, had now appointed these three distinguished but inappropriate gentlemen to take over the editing of the *Saturday Evening Post*. To the beleaguered management, on the other hand, it probably seemed quite likely that Blair's suspension would lead to an editorial strike, a total walkout of everybody who knew where anything was, and thus a breakdown of the *Post*'s weekly production schedule.

In this void, Emerson summoned up his old friendship with Harold Martin and appealed to the triumvirate to disband and go home. Martin said he would be happy to oblige, but he first needed to know whether Emerson was prepared to continue at his job. "I was," Emerson retorted, "until the three of you appeared on the scene, trying to take over the magazine." All three promptly protested their innocence of any such plan.

"Hell, we're not editors," Alsop said, "but we don't want to see everything wrecked."

"You're just cat's-paws in a power struggle that you don't know anything about," Emerson cried. "You've been swindled and misled and taken in by that bunch, to do their dirty work for them. And you're f—— up the last chance we have to save this magazine."

At that point, the argument became general, and the three trium-virs seized their chance to escape from the sofa, and so we all stood around arguing, some half-drunk, some coldly sober, some sitting idly by, some going in and out of the apartment on various errands. In front of me, as I sat in a great easy chair, I saw Jack Connors shout at Harold Martin, "This is a cowardly thing you're doing—cowardly— you're all behaving like cowards." I saw Martin, who had been under enemy fire in at least three wars, flush and tighten but restrain himself as he swirled the ice around in his whiskey glass and stared silently back at his accuser. Martin turned to me, then, and said he was surprised to see "such a logical person" at "a revival meeting like this."

"Well, sometimes I travel in unusual circles," I said.

"Let me ask you one question, as a personal favor," Martin said. "Are you going to be at work on Monday?"

"Well, let me ask you—if we come in, are we going to be working for the three of you?"

"God, no," Martin protested. "I think you and Emerson are great editors, and I'd like nothing better than to go back to Atlanta on Monday afternoon."

"Okay, I'll think about it," I said.

Then he faded away, as people do at cocktail parties, and Stew Alsop faded in, and he, too, wanted to know what I was doing at a confrontation like this. Alsop and I had a rather peculiar relationship, since I edited almost all of his copy, and therefore I felt obligated to pose as a figure of authority. In other words, the editor-writer rela-tionship had cast Alsop, a leading figure of the Washington establish-ment, in the role of a frisky literary colt, while I, several years his junior, had to adopt the role of an aged Chiron.

"Go home, Stew," I said to him now, following Emerson's argument that the distinguished triumvirs should be treated like mischievous children.

"Jesus Christ!" Alsop protested. "All I'm trying to do is to help keep the *Post* alive."

"Back to Washington, Stew," I repeated. "You don't realize what you're involved in here, and you're better off that way."

In the midst of this uproar, Blair had vanished, and now he was back, furious. A circle quickly gathered around him, as people gather around anyone who is sputtering and gesticulating. Blair had gone back to the office, for some reason, and a band of Pinkerton agents had stopped him. They had prevented him from taking anything from his office, and now he turned on Sherrod.

"You did this!" he cried. "You're responsible for this."

"I didn't want to have any trouble," Sherrod protested.

"Let me tell you one thing," Blair shouted, his eyes flashing, his huge body quivering. "I'm going in there Monday to clean out my desk, and get my things, and *nobody better try to stop me.*"

Sherrod already had his coat on, and now, with a series of embarrassed farewells and muttered good wishes, the three men trooped off. And as soon as the door closed behind them, everybody else was ready to go. Good-bye, Mrs. King. Thanks for everything. You've been great.

I shook hands with Blair, and it never occurred to me that, except for a couple of brief encounters, I would never see him again. At the beginning, only two short years ago, I had mistrusted and resented his portentous announcements of what he planned to do with the *Post,* but in due time I had come to like him. And even when I disagreed with him, which happened often, I admired his dedication and his enthusiasm. He was what the Germans call a *Mensch.* And so I had joined his suicidal assault on the Curtis management, an assault that I had never believed in, but now that it was all over, I could not realize that the end had really come. I somehow assumed that there would be more telephone calls, more meetings, but it was not so. As far as Blair was concerned, the battle had ended.

("For me personally, I suppose, the fight itself, the chance again to test my fear, was controlling," Blair said long afterward. "And even if we had won, it would have taken a miracle to save the company. But what general can look back on his conduct of a battle and not think of it as a shambles of mistakes, poor decisions, inept timing, a thrust when a withdrawal was needed, and so on? No battle goes according to plan. The losing battle is especially susceptible to fault-finding. In the flush of victory, all the horrendous mistakes are forgotten. Or reshaped by historians.")

My weekend concluded, finally, with another telephone call from

Bob Sherrod. It was nearly midnight on Sunday night, and I was watching the snowflakes flurry through a late movie on television, when the phone rang. Sherrod did not tell me many details of what had happened. He did not tell me whether he had hoped the triumvirate might lead to his regaining the editorship of the *Post*. He did not tell me that Alsop and Martin, battered by that evening's arguments, had persuaded him to give up any such ideas. All he said was: "I've recommended that the triumvirate be dissolved. I told them that they might as well let Emerson edit the magazine." And all I said was: "I think that sounds fine." Then we said good night, and I went back to watching the snowflakes on television.

From the *Gallagher Report*, October 14, 1964:

REVOLT AT CURTIS PUBLISHING . . . *Management overhaul urgent.* Board should appoint new president & chief executive officer. Possibilities: former president of Curtis magazine division John Veronis, publisher of McCall's Ed Miller . . . Saturday Evening Post needs new editor. . . . *Must go.* Kantor and Blair. Attorney-director Milton Gould. SEP assistant managing editors Otto Friedrich, Norman Ritter, Hank Walker. Editors Don Schanche (Holiday), and Davis Thomas (LHJ). Publishers Jesse Ballew (SEP), Mike Hadley (LHJ) . . . *Quick action needed.* Last chance to save company.

Blair's departure brought an important change in our perception of events. We no longer had any inside knowledge of what was happening at the upper levels of the corporation itself. In the view of the surviving management, generically known as "Philadelphia," the editors were rather like prisoners of war, not to be mistreated but to be isolated and ignored. The management had no time to think about editorial matters anyway. It was desperately trying to deal with its own commercial problems, and we could learn of them only in the *New York Times*.

On October 13, the *Times* told us that Linton and Poppei had spent the day conferring with publishers and advertising executives of all the Curtis magazines on "the seriousness of the charges levelled . . . against Matthew J. Culligan." On October 14, these discussions had gradually turned into hints that Culligan would follow Blair and Kantor into exile. He would go less abruptly, his path eased by clouds of publicity releases, but he would go. Without ever declaring that Culligan might be guilty of wrongdoing—for that would implicate not only his corporate associates but the corporation itself (and the

corporation, like the king in chess, must ever be spared from violence)—the directors and managers had seized on the charge of
"mismanagement" and turned it to their own purposes. There was no
proof of any serious mismanagement, of course, but perhaps it could
be said that administration just wasn't Joe Culligan's greatest talent.
Toward the end of that day's story in the *Times,* an anonymous
source disclosed the corporation's line of argument by claiming that
"the search for [a] new chief had been under way even before the
recent mutiny by the Curtis staff. Once Mr. Culligan could be freed of
administrative duties, he said, he would be free to give his full attention to advertising solicitation, in which he is recognized as one of the
top men in the industry." The story added that Culligan was "cooper-
ating fully" in what amounted to his removal and ultimate ban-
ishment.

Culligan's own account of these events was somewhat less placid.
"As I made the long, two-hour trip to Philadelphia, that afternoon,
October 18," he wrote,

. . . [I realized] what my instincts had been telling me: I was finished at
Curtis; it was just a matter of time. I had been asked the day before by
Cary Bok to attend an informal meeting of "some directors," as he put it,
in his apartment, the night before the board meeting, around 8 o'clock.
After I had checked into the Warwick Hotel, I called him and said cheerily,
"Hello, Cary, what time do you want me at your place?" His chilling
answer: "Joe, a group of us have been meeting for some time. The meeting
is about over. Really no need for you to come." [I said:] "That sounds
ominous, Cary." He said, "Joe, we think it would be better all around if you
resigned as president tomorrow." "Thanks, Cary," I said. "I'll think about it."

It took almost a year for Culligan to find out what had really
happened at that meeting of directors in Bok's apartment. Then, in
an arbitration hearing, which had been called to consider Culligan's
demand for payment of personal legal fees, it turned out that Mac
Clifford and Maurice Poppei had followed the Blair-Kantor attack
with an attack of their own. At the meeting in Bok's apartment,
according to Culligan's account of the testimony,

Clifford and Poppei had . . . continued to criticize me to some of the
directors, and at the critical point had delivered an ultimatum. It was not
as brazenly stated as the Blair-Kantor ultimatum, but it was more effective.
Under oath, Page [Allison Page, the attorney representing Curtis] stated
that Clifford and Poppei had said, "We cannot continue to do our jobs if
Culligan remains as President and Chief Executive Officer." Coogan [Cul-
ligan's attorney, William Coogan] made Allison Page repeat the comment

several times. As he said it the third time, a remembrance of poor Bob
MacNeal flashed through my mind. Some of the same Philadelphia directors
who had bowed to the ultimatum of Milton Gould in that instance had in
my case let themselves be influenced by Clifford and Poppei, the very ones
who had been the original cause of the editors' anger. . . . The thing that
disgusted me most, however, was my exclusion from the meeting at which
my fate was decided.

There was another striking parallel between MacNeal's fate and
that of Culligan—it was the second time in two years that the Curtis
directors had precipitously dismissed a president without any plan
for finding a replacement. Having repeated this error, they now had
to reenact the search for a president, this time with Serge Semenenko
trying to control the decision, and with the press loudly announcing
each development. On the battered editorial floor, we read the papers
with morbid interest.

On October 14, the *Times* said that Curtis had narrowed its search
for a president to two men, whom it identified as "Mr. X" and "Mr. Y."
The source for this story acknowledged that there had been rumors
about the presidency being offered to Frank Stanton, president of
CBS, but he denied the truth of the rumor. He declined comment on
another rumor that Mr. X was a Californian named Raymond DePue
McGranahan, former president of the Wilshire Oil Company, former
vice president of the Los Angeles Times-Mirror Company (a job he
had left that August). To deny one rumor and decline comment on a
second is tantamount to confirmation, and the next day's headline
duly announced:

CURTIS SEEKING FORMER OFFICIAL OF TIMES MIRROR

The following day's *Times* went a step further:

CURTIS DIRECTORS
SET TO OUST CHIEF

Who, then, was Raymond DePue McGranahan? Photographs in the
newspapers showed an amiable and portly figure, with the hopeful
smile of an aging salesman, and with three children named Christopher, Candace, and Cynthia. The *Times* described him as fifty years
old, an enthusiastic golfer, and an "active communicant" in the All
Saints (Episcopal) Church in Beverly Hills. In his two-year stay at
the *Times-Mirror*, according to the *Times*, he had "general responsibility for the conduct of the company's subsidiaries," apparently

including the printing division, "whose principal business is printing telephone directories."

To an amateur in the methodology of corporate politics, there seemed to be no visible reason why the Curtis board of directors should have selected Raymond DePue McGranahan as their new leader, but there were rumors that offered explanations. One of the simplest rumors was that the Bank of America, headquartered in California, had touted McGranahan as "a good man," and that the word of a big bank carried a great deal of weight among Curtis's nervous creditors. Specifically, McGranahan was said to have considerable support from Serge Semenenko. Another theory, considerably more ingenious, was that Curtis's expensive, high-speed presses, which could operate efficiently only by printing very large numbers of one thing, would stand idle if the Post were killed, and that one major use for such presses would be the printing of telephone directories, about which McGranahan presumably knew something. Still another rumor, widely spread, was that McGranahan was "a Goldwaterite." This, according to some observers, might appeal to Curtis corporate authorities seeking a way to attract the support of big business. As for McGranahan himself, he told the *Times:* "I haven't been a part of any of this stuff. I don't even know what's going on."

We did not, of course, spend all our time puzzling over the *Times* and wondering about the qualifications of Raymond DePue McGranahan. Almost all of our time, on the contrary, was devoted to editing and publishing an exceptionally good weekly magazine, and in this October of 1964, the problems of the Curtis board of directors really amounted to very little in the world. In one week of that month, while the Johnson-Goldwater campaign was sweeping to its conclusion, Nikita Khrushchev was fired from the premiership of Russia, and the Chinese detonated their first atomic bomb.

By the happy circumstance that optimists call foresight and pessimists call luck, we had already scheduled a lead article by Defense Secretary Robert McNamara, rejecting the Republican charges of U.S. weakness and reasserting America's military supremacy over the Russians; now, at this time of crisis in the Kremlin, the story acquired a wholly new relevance. We also had on hand a long and very good article by Harold Martin, who had spent the summer in Russia in an attempt to discover the details of Khrushchev's youth; that, too, had a new interest now. At the same time, Stew Alsop, who had dreaded trying to write his slow-closing political column around election time, had already booked passage to Moscow, and our

Moscow correspondent, Ed Stevens, was amassing the background material on how Khrushchev fell. And from our Paris correspondent, Edward Behr, came a cable saying that he had met and talked with Mao Tse-tung just before the Chinese bomb exploded. Tearing up issues and getting all these stories into print was our real function that fall, and the one we really enjoyed. But we could never escape the fear that any given issue of the *Post* might be the last.

The October 19 board meeting, which was supposed to settle everything, ended with the following statement:

The board . . . today announced the election of Mr. Raymond DePue McGranahan to the board of directors and the executive committee. Mr. Culligan volunteered his resignation as president of the company, which was accepted by the board. He continues as chairman of the board. The election of a president is expected to be announced in the near future.

The rest of the story in the next day's *Times* filled in or implied some of the details. McGranahan, apparently increasingly aware of the problems confronting any future president of Curtis, not only had not taken the job but had not even gone to Philadelphia to attend the board meeting. Blair and Kantor, who could not be involuntarily removed from the board except by a vote of the stockholders, had come and gone in their hired Lincoln. The rest of the board had then conducted business at a lunch at the Downtown Club. The net result was that Curtis had deposed one president, had failed in its efforts to acquire another president, and now had no president at all.

It may be argued, I suppose, that a corporation can survive for a time without any president, that the bureaucratic machinery simply continues to operate on its own authority, and that it would be better to have no president than the wrong president. But the best argument against that, in turn, was the spectacle of the Curtis board wallowing in a trough of indecision as it vainly searched for a new chief executive. The aged directors were helpless, once again, and because of their helplessness, the corporation itself turned into a rudderless hulk. As a consequence, the most important result of the October 19 board meeting occurred almost by accident. As soon as Culligan's resignation as president had been accepted, Mac Clifford, who was supposed to be concerning himself with remote areas of merger and acquisition, but who still held the title of executive vice president, suddenly and automatically became the corporation's "chief executive officer."

For a few days, nobody quite realized what had happened. Then, at about eleven o'clock on the morning of Friday, October 23, Tom Marvel, the head of the *Post*'s production department, knocked on the door to my office and said in a choked voice: "Otto, I want to introduce you to the new production chief, Jack Pauley." I shook hands vaguely with a smiling, dark-haired stranger, assuming this was some new official in the Philadelphia printing plant, and the two of them continued on down the corridor. Then another editor came into my office and said, "Have you heard? They've fired Tom Marvel." Marvel's assistant, a girl called Flo Conway, had just come into my office, and I looked up and saw that she was in tears.

"What the hell's going on around here?" I demanded.

"They just fired Tom," she said.

"And they're firing Ritter," somebody else said. By now, a whole flock of people were swarming into my office.

"Who the hell is they?" I asked.

"Clifford and Poppei," somebody said.

"And Poppei told Tom to have his desk empty and be out of the office in half an hour."

"And Ritter too."

11

"There's nothing we can do"

There had been strange intimations of trouble on the previous day. Emerson and Ritter and I were all walking toward Grand Central Station after work, and Emerson said to Ritter, "Did you save your secretary?"—adding to me, "They fired Ritter's secretary today."

"You're kidding," I said.

"No, but I'm going to get it stopped," Emerson laughed. "But maybe they're trying to tell us something."

"Yeah, maybe that's it," Ritter said. He laughed, too, but not so confidently as Emerson.

Now that the storm had begun, I went out into the corridor and found Tom Marvel, a short, square young man with a heavy jaw. I brought him back to my office, where a dozen editors were already milling around.

"Now what is all this?" I asked.

"They've fired me," Marvel said, almost in tears. "Poppei said to get out in half an hour."

"Have you told Emerson?"

"No, he's in with Clifford."

"Well, you can't just walk out without even talking to Emerson. We all work for Emerson now."

My theory at the time was that we could resist the managerial counterrevolution by simply rejecting it. ("They can't fire me because I won't go," I explained the theory to Emerson, "and if they cut off my pay, I can go on working without pay, and what can they do then?" Emerson found this hilarious. "They'll call back the Pinkertons just for you," he said.) It is hard to guess how my strategy might have worked, but it could not possibly work when Marvel's only desire was to grope his way to the door. I made him promise to telephone back in an hour, and not to leave the area until I could talk to Emerson. But he had no sooner left than Ritter came in, already wearing an overcoat, carrying an attaché case, and grinning with the nervous bravado of a college student who has just been expelled.

"Well, good-bye, Otto, it's been good working with you," Ritter said.

"Why do you just leave?" I asked, gradually realizing the impossibility of getting people to resist when they didn't want to resist. Ritter shrugged.

"Have you talked to Emerson?" I asked.

"Sure, but what can he do?"

A few minutes after Ritter's departure, Emerson himself finally steamed into my office, like an ocean liner caught in a sudden outbreak of naval warfare. "By God but this is the *goddamnedest* business," he roared. "Those goddamn little butchers, just walking in here and starting to fire people—boy, did I give them *hell!*"

"You've got to do more than that," I said. "We've got to get Ritter and Marvel back to work before the end of the day."

"That's not going to be so easy, old friend." Emerson looked around at some of the editors accumulated in my office—Don McKinney and Bill Ewald, the two chief articles editors; Tom Congdon, a national affairs editor; David Lyle, foreign editor; and three or four more. "What do the rest of you all think?"

We had begun, then, what might be known as the post-Blair phase of operations. Blair had always proclaimed himself the sole defender of editorial integrity, telling us that every other division of the corporation wanted to encroach on our independence, and, in fact, to sacrifice the editorial pages to the task of pleasing advertisers. (He had never told us, of course, that we, in our insurrection, were violating the independence of other departments, that Marvel had been assigned to harass the printing division, and that Ritter had even been dispatched to Philadelphia at one point with instructions to fire Poppei. "Poppei just chased Ritter out of his office," Emerson said.) If the great rebellion failed, Blair had warned us, and if we failed to walk out together, we would all be picked off, one by one. Now that the rebellion had indeed failed, and now that we had failed to walk out, now that Blair's theory of integrated editorial operations had gone with the departure of the editorial director himself, each remaining editor was isolated and vulnerable—and none more so than Emerson, for he was not even the editor but only the managing editor, branded as a "rebel" but without the authority that traditionally belonged to the editor of the *Post*.

Most of the other *Post* editors shared Emerson's dilemma, feeling that Ritter and Marvel should be immediately restored to their jobs, but uncertain how to proceed. We had no reason to think that Clifford and Poppei would be susceptible to persuasion, and in a test of strength what strength did we have? Only the ability to walk out in such numbers that the *Post* would be badly damaged, or even shut down. But then we had to face the question that Blair had usually ignored: What would we accomplish by ruining a magazine we all loved? Or by turning it over to our enemies?

Emerson was ready to resign, and Jess Ballew, who had joined the crowd in my office, was ready to subscribe his own name to Emerson's resignation, but we still struggled to find some alternative. I persuaded Emerson to telephone Linton, to tell him that we had all followed his wishes that we continue at our jobs, and that we were now being attacked by corporate officials interfering with our work. Linton, who apparently thought he had successfully completed his brief regency, proved evasive. Although he was not aware of the two firings, he said, Clifford was now in charge of things, and any complaints should be addressed to Clifford, not to him. At that, there seemed to be no alternative to another session between Clifford and Emerson, who took it to be the consensus of the editors that the abrupt dismissal of Ritter and Marvel was totally unacceptable. In fact, he apparently felt that all of us wanted him to resign over the issue. He went off to find Clifford, the other editors began drifting back to their own offices, and I shut my door and tried to get some work done.

Suddenly the door flew open, and Mike Mooney burst in, his normally red face flushed with indignation.

"Are you all going to get on your high horses about this Ritter-Marvel business?" he demanded.

"Damn right we are," I said.

"But you can't walk out now!" he cried.

"Why the hell not?" I retorted. "If they start barging in here and firing people?"

Mooney gave a deep sigh.

"Listen," he said, "do you realize what I'm doing? I'm trying to sell this whole damn company, and I've got a couple of buyers lined up, but if you people all walk out, you'll queer the whole deal."

"Who ever authorized you to sell the company?" I asked.

"Nobody ever authorized me to do anything," Mooney said, "but this company has got to be sold, and I've got buyers."

Mike Mooney had been a strange and splendid phenomenon ever since he had wandered into my office the previous February. He was looking for a job, and both Schanche and Emerson wanted to hire him as an articles editor, and so they sent him to me to see what I would make of him. An immensely Irish Irishman, with protruding ears and curly blond hair, Mooney had won an Olympic gold medal for sailboat racing at eighteen, operated his own public-relations agency at thirty, helped to found the *National Review*, and hoped to run for Congress from the North Shore of Long Island. But then, having broken with the *National Review* for reasons that were never quite clear, and having inherited enough money so that he didn't need any job that didn't interest him, he said, "I don't know why they insist that I talk to you, but they do, so here I am." I said, somewhat stiffly, "They want you to talk to me because I'm in charge of the articles in this magazine, and the articles editors work for me."

Mooney had never been trained as an articles editor, and yet he was so bright and quick and self-confident, so full of ideas and enthusiasm, that I joined in the Schanche-Emerson theory that there must be something we could do with him. Unfortunately, I soon realized that I had only a limited need for editors who were still learning the craft, and so Mooney passed into a kind of Limbo, in which he spent his days drawing up charts and memoranda on what the *Post* should and should not do.

After a time, I persuaded Emerson that Mooney would be useful to Blair as a liaison man in the fields of advertising, circulation, and promotion. Blair and Mooney took to each other immediately, but Mooney couldn't or wouldn't fit into Blair's coterie. One crisis soon occurred when Blair went vacationing in Bermuda, leaving Ritter in charge of administrative affairs. Mooney tried vainly to call Blair about some problem, and Blair's return call was intercepted by Ritter, who said he would handle the matter. Mooney's reaction was unequivocal. He walked out of the office and took the next plane to Bermuda, at his own expense, rented a motor scooter, rode up to Blair's house, rang the doorbell and said, "There's a problem I want to discuss with you, and for some reason, I haven't been able to reach you by phone."

A larger crisis occurred when Mooney began pursuing the theory that the Curtis indebtedness should be refinanced, to get rid of Semenenko. Mooney had argued, and Blair had apparently agreed, that Semenenko would probably continue to back Culligan against any Blair *Putsch*. Mooney had therefore offered to find new bankers to take over the Curtis debt. But when Kantor discovered that Mooney was about to begin discussions with the Morgan Guaranty Trust Company, there was a stormy meeting with Blair. Kantor forbade Mooney to go to the bank. Mooney retorted that the bankers were personal friends of his, and he was going to see them. The following week, Mooney was back in the Limbo of an articles editor with no articles to edit. "Blair doesn't need any more liaison," he said bitterly to me. "He's got too much liaison going on as it is. And I tell you: Whenever people say they have a problem in communications, it always means that they do have a problem, but the problem never has much to do with communications."

Mooney had theories about everything, and one of his theories was that Curtis could not be saved so long as the Curtis-Bok-Zimbalist family owned one-third of the shares and represented a fatal force for inertia on the board of directors. His solution was quite simply to find someone to buy them out, and my question as to who had authorized him to do so simply showed how little I had so far learned about the operations of American business. Authorizations and official channels apply only in stable corporations, steaming along in peaceful prosperity. In times of crisis, all the lines of feudal authority become blurred, and anyone who can work out a solution to the crisis automatically becomes the new ruler. I had seen this actually happen at *Newsweek* in 1960, when the death of the owner and the resignation of the editor suddenly brought the magazine to the state that physicists call "the critical mass." In about a week of feverish negotiations, Osborn Elliott, then the managing editor, and Benjamin Bradlee, then a Washington correspondent, maneuvered the sale of the magazine to Philip Graham and the Washington *Post*. The result was the inevitable elevation of Elliott to editor and Bradlee to Washington Bureau Manager, and those who had previously been their superiors were compelled to step aside. At Curtis, at about that same time, Clay Blair had hoped in vain for similar rewards during his discussions with Admiral Strauss and the other kingmakers. But although those maneuvers were past, similar possibilities kept arising in the distance.

"So you want to become publisher of the *Post*?" I asked Mooney at one point.

"Publisher?" Mooney echoed. "That's Jess Ballew's job. I don't want anything like that."

"You mean you want to be the president of the whole company?"

"Why, obviously," Mooney said.

In several weeks of soundings, Mooney now reported, he had found at least three interested buyers. The best prospect was Eric Ridder, of the prosperous Ridder newspaper chain. The other two were millionaires interested in diversification—Allan Kirby of the Alleghany Corporation, and William Moore of Moore-McCormack Lines. In retrospect, I have no way of telling how much of this discussion was real and how much was just social chatter at the Seawanhaka Yacht Club in Oyster Bay, where Mooney liked to spend his evenings, but at the time of all the other maneuvering, this seemed as real as anything else. "But they won't buy a corporation that isn't functioning," Mooney was saying. "They know the fifteen 'rebels' are putting out the magazines, and they want the fifteen as part of the package."

"Well, there are only twelve left, at last count, and there aren't going to be any at all if Clifford and Poppei keep screwing up the works."

The door flew open again, and Emerson stormed in, and my office was once again filled with a babbling chorus of editors, writers, secretaries.

"Now you've done it, old tiger," Emerson said to me, aside. "I have resigned. I'm through—out."

All I could think of to say was: "As of when?"

"I don't know—I don't care."

"Mr. Clifford—" Emerson went on to announce, shushing the general tumult—"Mr. Clifford wants to meet with all the senior editors in Blair's conference room in fifteen minutes."

Within ten minutes, we were all assembled around the dark mahogany table, where, less than a month ago, Blair had sounded his battle cry for Armageddon. There were about the same number of people, but Blair's people had been jubilant, mobilized from all the magazines to begin the great offensive. Now there were only the editors of the *Post*, cornered, besieged, and intent simply on defending the citadel. Into this crowded conference room marched two figures whom we had heard much about but had never actually seen—Mac Clifford, short, stocky, weatherbeaten, with crew-cut white hair and startlingly bright blue eyes behind dark-rimmed glasses, strode to a seat at the head of the conference table; Maurice Poppei, tall, bulky, with very white skin and rimless glasses, stood by the doorway, as though ready for escape. In the confrontation of these two triumphant bureaucrats with about thirty righteously indignant but totally unorganized editors, there was more hatred than should ever be confined within the walls of one room.

Emerson, in a state of shock, announced that he had resigned, and then introduced Clifford.

Clifford began by brusquely recapitulating the events of the day. He held his hands out on the table, palms down, fingers spread. As chief executive officer of the Curtis Publishing Company, he said, he was in charge of seeing that the company was run "in a businesslike way." He had fired Ritter and Marvel because they were "disruptive influences."

"Now Bill feels very strongly that we should not have done this without consulting him, and he has offered his resignation—"

"I *have* resigned, Mr. Clifford," Emerson said, staring down at the table.

"But I have not accepted his resignation, and I'm not going to accept it," Clifford went on. "Of course, if he insists on walking out, I can't stop him, but I hope he won't. And I hope none of the rest of you will either. We've had a lot of trouble, but I hope it's over now. I realize that we made a mistake in not consulting Bill, and I've apologized for it, and I can promise you that it won't happen again. All we want to do is to get these magazines back into the black and start making some money. There are no hard feelings on the side of management so long as you people just go on doing your jobs. As far as I'm concerned, the past is past, and if you put out good magazines, we won't interfere with you. And as long as Bill Emerson is willing to stay, he's in charge here. He will report to Mr. Poppei, and Mr. Poppei is your boss. That's all I have to say."

"If Emerson's in charge," I promptly asked, "can he hire back Ritter and Marvel?"

"No," Poppei answered sharply from the doorway. "That's an irrevocable management decision. They weren't editorial employees anyway. They were on the corporate payroll."

"But they were two of us," I cried. "And why is any decision irrevocable?"

"We have our reasons," Poppei said. His face never showed any expression. I couldn't help suspecting, though, that he now savored the recollection of Ritter's unsuccessful attempt to fire him.

"What reasons?" I demanded. "Whatever they did, they did because Blair told them to do it. That's not a reason for firing them."

"We don't choose to have them working for this company," Poppei said. "And that decision is irrevocable."

As I shrugged in hopelessness, Don McKinney broke in to address Clifford. "You know, most of us had nothing to do with Blair's operations. All we've been trying to do is put out a magazine, and

Ritter and Marvel were doing that too, and if you wreck this group, you'll wreck everything that the *Post* has been moving toward for these last two years."

"If Emerson leaves—" Bill Ewald began. "I hope you realize that if Emerson leaves, many of the other editors will leave too."

"He doesn't speak for everybody," someone else broke in. It was John Hunt, who now edited the column of dissent called "Speaking Out." Hunt had been my choice for that job, since it was his nature to dissent from any majority on any subject, but I scowled at his dissenting now. So did McKinney. "Come on, John," he said sharply. "Knock it off."

"No, let me talk," Hunt persisted. "I just want it understood that Ewald was not speaking for all of us when he said we'd walk out."

There were a few other dissenting opinions too. Jeannette Sarkisian, the woman's editor, sat brightly birdlike near the middle of the table, taking notes on a large pad of lined yellow paper, and acting as though this were just another staff meeting. "I think a lot of us are talking too emotionally," she said. "As for myself, I want to know what the facts are." She, too, was answered by glares.

From the side of the room, Tom Congdon, stammering in indignation, brought the focus back to Clifford. He had worked at the *Post* for eight years, Congdon said, longer than many of these people, longer than Clifford or Poppei. "And I want to protest against what you have done. You have violated one of the oldest traditions of the *Post*, the independence and integrity of the editorial staff. You have done a—a—a *monstrous* thing!"

Clifford sat in apparent indifference to all these speeches, his head turning from speaker to speaker, his mouth working nervously. Poppei had made it very plain that nothing was going to change, and so, after about half an hour of rhetoric, when the speeches began to become repetitious, the two new rulers began to make their departure. They had made their point, they had listened to our protests, and there we were, helpless. Once they had gone, we turned to Emerson, but he would only repeat, "I'm sorry, but I have resigned." They turned, then, to me, and asked what I was going to do. After all, if Blair remained suspended, and Emerson had really resigned, I became, *faute de mieux*, the ranking editor of the *Post*. And I had no answer to offer.

"I don't know," I said. "I'm going to think it over."

"What do you mean, 'think it over'?" John Hunt demanded.

"I mean exactly what I said," I answered angrily. "What's the matter, is there some law against thinking things over?"

"What an awful-looking pair Clifford and that other man are," said someone in a far corner, Rust Hills, the fiction editor.

"Sure they're awful, but we've got to live with them," said one of the older editors, Bob Johnson.

"Why do we have to live with them?" I asked. Johnson shrugged.

"So now what?" somebody else asked.

"Look, they've apologized, and they've promised it would never happen again, so nothing very drastic is likely to happen right away," I said. "And we can't decide anything right now. Let's break it up and see how things develop."

My first objective was to get the meeting disbanded. Unlike Blair, I was convinced that no meeting that included twenty or thirty people, with twenty or thirty different gradations of complaints, tactics, and objectives, could ever accomplish anything. Ritter and Marvel could not be retrieved—that was obvious. So if we wanted to retain control of the magazine, the main thing was to get Emerson's resignation canceled, so that we could mobilize around him and turn him into a figure who would fill the void that Blair had left.

It was about seven o'clock that evening when I cleaned up the day's work and went into Emerson's office and found Mike Mooney and Bob Johnson both at work on the same project.

"But I *have* resigned," Emerson was saying once again. It was fairly clear that he didn't want to leave, but he also didn't want to back down.

"And your resignation has been rejected," I said. "Clifford said he wouldn't accept it, and he gave you an apology. As far as I can see, that's the end of it."

"Just what I've been saying," Johnson said.

"But I've got to go down to Philadelphia and present my resignation to the board on Monday," Emerson said.

"The hell you do," I said. "Once it's presented and rejected, it's a dead letter."

"Listen to him," Mooney said to Emerson.

"Look," I said, "it all boils down to one basic fact. After all the battles, this magazine is in your hands now, and it's up to you to take charge of it. If you insist on resigning, you hand it over to them, and they'll wreck it. All this resigning is a lot of nonsense, and as long as you're here, it's all yours, so why give it up?"

"Listen to him," Mooney said again.

Emerson didn't submit his resignation to the board the following week, and, in fact, never resigned again. But he never forgot or forgave what I had done—or what he claimed I had done. In every subsequent crisis, in all the years ahead, he would accuse me of having demanded on this occasion that he resign, and then that he withdraw his resignation. In some way that he would never quite specify, I, Warwick, had humiliated him. Perhaps it was nothing more than the fact that I had seen that he wanted to be king.

Mike Mooney had a theory. "Every organization needs a mythology, and mythology is made out of conflicts and confrontations that the organization has lived through together. Look at Mao and his Long March, or Castro and the boys landing on the beach. Blair understood that when he took all the *Post* editors down to Paradise Island. You all came back with a different relationship to one another, and to him. Same thing with the meeting at Manero's. The real rebels were the ones who were there that night. Now that's all gone. But you'll see—if Emerson survives, and if the *Post* survives, one of the reasons you'll all survive is that you'll all remember that meeting in that room with Clifford. That's why Henry V made the St. Crispin's Day speech, and that's why Jack Kennedy loved it."

If I thought that Bob Sherrod had given up on the *Post* when he gave up on the triumvirate, I was mistaken. He now reappeared in the crisis, announcing that he had been asked to serve as an intermediary between the corporate management and the disaffected editors. At the milder levels, this meant that he took me out to lunch at Sardi's East and reminded me that he was the one who had originally hired the present editorial staff. At a harsher level, it meant that he would frequently telephone me, or Emerson, or some senior editor, and complain about some detail that he had spotted on the page proofs.

The honor of reading page proofs is an ambiguous one, since, by the time a story is finally set in pages, it is too late for anything to be changed without considerable trouble, and anybody with the authority to make such changes should have a good deal of responsibility for what reached the page proofs in the first place. In the *Post* editorial department, the only people who read page proofs were the senior editor and copy editor in charge of a specific story, and the person responsible for the final okay (Emerson or me). It was obvious, therefore, that Sherrod was getting page proofs directly from the printing plant in Philadelphia, but nobody had ever told us what responsibility he might have for ordering changes. He would telephone us with his complaints, and then we would answer that we were right, or that we would look into the matter, or that nothing could be done.

We were baffled, however, by the question of why Sherrod was doing whatever he was doing. The most sinister interpretation—and Emerson always favored sinister interpretations—was that he was building a case against us in preparation for his own return to the editorship. My more commonplace interpretation was that Clifford still mistrusted us and relied on Sherrod to see that we made no disastrous mistakes. An even more commonplace interpretation, and most probably the correct one, was that Clifford couldn't see what Sherrod did to earn his $50,000 salary as an "editor-at-large," and that he thought it would be proper for Sherrod to become a sort of supervisory editor, vaguely responsible for seeing that everything was all right.

One morning, as we were discussing the Sherrod problem—Emerson, McKinney, Congdon, and I—Congdon suddenly went to his own office and returned with Xerox copies of a letter that he had sent the day before, by special delivery, to the ancient Walter Deane Fuller. Without a word, Congdon handed copies to us, and we read this extraordinary document:

Oct. 28, 1964

DEAR MR. FULLER:

I write this letter to you—without the knowledge of my superiors—because I share with my fellow senior editors an intense concern. We are afraid that, simply through poor communications, the Board of Directors may be about to make a tragic mistake. . . .

I came to the *Post* in 1956 and was reared in my profession by Ben Hibbs, Bob Fuoss and Bob Sherrod. Two years ago, in a short space of time, many of the editors I had worked with were fired and many others were employed. When I came up from Philadelphia to join this drastically revamped staff, I was full of bitterness and doubts. . . . I couldn't have been more wrong. The new men who came in just below Sherrod and Blair and Schanche were remarkably decent and—even more important—remarkably able. I speak of Bill Emerson, Otto Friedrich, Don McKinney and Bill Ewald. Several of them proved to be truly brilliant. All of them worked long and hard and well together, neglecting their private and personal lives, giving all their energies to the *Post*.

You know what happened: Blair pushed past Bob Sherrod and took control. What you may not know is that almost immediately Blair became so involved in corporate affairs that, practically speaking, he did not edit this magazine. This is a crucial point: *For considerably more than a year the Saturday Evening Post has been edited not by Clay Blair but by William Emerson and Otto Friedrich.* They did not engineer this. They received the

job by default. Blair knew they were doing the job extremely well and
wisely refrained from interfering with them.

The letter recorded Clifford's dismissal of Ritter and Marvel, and
the meeting that followed:

One after another the editors stood up and tried to explain that editors
do not work primarily for money. . . . We work out of loyalty to the
quality of our publication, and to our working relationships with one another. We said we hoped to God that Mr. Clifford understands that Emerson and Friedrich could not be undercut or humiliated without all of the
senior editors feeling personally attacked. . . . Blair's suspension (despite
the pro forma telegram the dissidents sent out some two weeks ago) did
not mean a great deal to the editors because for some time Blair had not
in fact been their editor. Emerson and Friedrich *are* our editors, and they
are damned good ones. Losing Blair actually solved some problems for us;
losing Emerson and Friedrich would break our hearts and spell disaster.

The letter went on to observe that Clifford might have felt threatened and might strike back. One possibility was the return of
Sherrod, but the letter called this "folly" and said that "most of the
editors . . . would not want to work for him again." The other alternative was the imposition of a new editor from the outside.

No one . . . could predict what might happen if this step were taken
(much may depend on who the man is); I would not be optimistic. But the
pathetic fact is that both steps—the imposition of Sherrod or of an outsider—are so unnecessary. Emerson and Friedrich are doing an excellent
job, and their only passion is to keep on doing it. They are not "Blair men"
—not by a long shot. . . . They have no ambitions in the company beyond
the operation of *Post* editorial. The Board, instead of agreeing to an agonizing reorganization of the *Post*'s staff, should kneel and thank heaven that
this vital department of the Curtis Publishing Company is in good shape
and eager to proceed.

"Well, I'm very touched," I finally said, "but Jesus Christ!"
Congdon would listen to nothing until he had told the sequel.
Fuller had telephoned him that very morning to say that he had taken
the letter immediately to Linton, and that Linton had said, "You tell
that young Mr. Congdon that we appreciate this very much."
It took me a little time to realize all the implications of the letter,
and then to bring myself to denounce Congdon. I told him that the
letter might do us some good (and, of course, it would do us a lot of
good), but that I was glad I had not known about it because I would
have forbidden him to send it, and I forbade him ever to do anything

like this again. Congdon looked dismayed and said he couldn't understand why I was so hostile.

"Do you realize what that letter does to Blair's position?" I asked.
"It takes away the only weapon he has left—it makes him out to be a
fraud—it destroys him."

"Well, all right," Congdon said defiantly. "But he was prepared to
destroy this magazine. The trouble with you, Otto, is that you're too
stoical. You just watch things instead of doing something about them.
You're ready to see this magazine die, but I'm not. I want it to live."

The Congdon letter may have eased Linton's mind, but his course
of action had already been determined. The Linton-Brown-Gould
committee had been studying the charges against Culligan, and it had
come to its conclusion. These charges, oddly enough, had mysteriously grown from the original complaints expressed at Manero's into
a whole dossier containing every grievance that Blair and Kantor had
ever held against Culligan. In Blair's subsequent account, "The group
decided to throw in everything else, including the kitchen sink—the
whole long anguishing history of Culligan's 'frivolous waste' and
'mismanagement' and 'questionable behavior.' (The charges were
filed under those headings.) The latter charges were hastily thrown
in and somewhat lacking in detail. Joe, meanwhile, holed up in his
office, preparing written replies." This final indictment was an extravagant collection of accusations—ranging from vague allegations
of Mafia associations to complaints about the expense of Culligan's
suite at the Regency—all strenuously denied by Culligan. It was
never even seen, much less endorsed, by the fifteen editorial rebels.
And so, at the October 29 board meeting, Linton's investigating committee simply rejected all these superfluous accusations. But the
conclusion of Linton's report was scarcely favorable to Joe Culligan.

Culligan had shown a clear inability to lead or maintain an
effective management of Curtis Publishing, Linton declared. Throughout the company, he continued, there had been conflicts and intrigues, and a general breakdown of confidence. Linton quite directly
blamed Culligan for this situation and recommended to the board
that Culligan be removed from any position of authority in the company. The board accepted this verdict, and then decided that the
Linton report should be buried away forever. Blair, however, was
making elaborate notes, and, as he later recalled, "I requested that
Linton reread the statement so that I could check, precisely, my
notes." Moreau Brown, who had joined Linton in drafting the report,
subsequently confirmed that Blair's version was substantially ac-

curate, though he complained bitterly about the details being made public. The chief goal of the directors was to get rid of all the combatants with a minimum of unpleasantness. For the public record, Linton and Brown composed a much milder letter to Culligan:

The examination revealed no irregularity on your part (as could be inferred from the wording of the [Blair-Kantor] letter) nor any profiting by you personally from Curtis business transactions. It did reveal a very few joint venture cases which, although they had been cleared with counsel, involved what the Committee felt were errors of business judgment. However, the Committee does not feel that the errors were such as to warrant your dismissal from the office of President as demanded in the [editors'] letter nor to justify the vituperative language used in the letter. Your voluntary resignation as President was to expedite the appointment of a successor to that office in line with your prior recommendation that someone be found to furnish the company with additional administrative personnel.

The main item on the agenda that day was a motion to dismiss Blair and Kantor, and, after what one director called a "heated discussion," this motion carried by a show of hands, eight to three. At that point, according to one chronicler, Blair rose to his feet, pointed an accusing finger and uttered one last, confused outcry: "I thought the day would never come when I would have to suffer the indignity of being in the room with this board of directors." Blair walked out, followed by Kantor, and they held a press conference in that marble-floored, stained-glass-windowed lobby of the Curtis building. They insisted that they had done no wrong, had obeyed all rules, and had been "fully sustained and vindicated" by the resignation of Culligan. Blair's closing statement was, once again, at the very frontiers of coherence: "I devoted eight years of my life to the Curtis Publishing Company. The last four years, I have given it everything I had, including my family, which is about the most any man can give a company. I want to say I think the action of this board is a disgrace not only to me personally but also to Marvin Kantor—who devoted three years of his life to the company—and the entire competitive system."

One of the wonders of the corporate system is that the board of directors can fire an executive who may be getting $100,000 a year, but it cannot get that same executive off the board; that is the prerogative of the stockholders. So the board met again that Thursday, November 5, with Blair and Kantor in vociferous attendance, and then it quickly adjourned to the Downtown Club to conduct its business without them, in peace. That same day, Blair and Kantor sued

Curtis for "unlawful discharge." They listed their salaries as $75,000 for Blair and $80,000 for Kantor, and they claimed their employment contracts had a combined value of $500,000. Through their attorney, they served summonses on Curtis and on Semenenko's bank, First National of Boston. A messy situation. Blair made it even more messy by announcing that he would write a book about the whole affair. It was known that he had been keeping a diary of the crisis, and in fact he did begin but never finished a book entitled *The Crack in the Liberty Bell*.

It took almost two months for the company to settle that problem. On December 28, Blair and Kantor agreed to accept $75,000 each in exchange for their contracts, their suit, and their silence—specifically, "not to take voluntarily any action directly or indirectly injurious to the company for a period of two years." At the end of two years, the management thought, in an outburst of enthusiasm, the *Post*'s problems would be solved or the *Post* would be dead.

There was another irony. Several years after the crisis, according to Culligan, an intermediary said that Marvin Kantor wanted an interview, and so the two enemies finally met again at the Terrace Club of LaGuardia Airport.

"Kantor came in," according to the Culligan account,

approached me uncertainly and put out his hand as though he wasn't sure whether it would be shaken or shaken off. He said, "It's been a long time." After some inconsequential talk, he finally said, "Joe, my only reason for wanting to see you was to tell you I made a terrible mistake and that I'm sorry." "It takes a man to admit that, Marvin," I answered. "Thanks. But I'll never understand how you could have been suckered into such a bonehead ploy. . . . [Blair's] attack would have been laughable if you had not got the publishers involved."

"I know, I know," Kantor said. "There was a kind of madness in the air—I don't know what happened to me."

In this time of crisis, the Curtis board decided that it was holding too many meetings. Normally, the board paid each of its members $250 per month for a few hours of conferring on the first Thursday of that month. This cost the company $40,000 a year. Now, when the board had to meet twice or even three times a month, the members felt they should maintain their own pay scale of about $75 per hour, and so they voted to pay themselves $250 for each meeting.

On a more serious level, the company was compelled by law to confess on November 6 that its net operating loss for the first nine months of 1964 was just over $8 million—exactly as Blair and Kantor had predicted several months earlier. There was no sign that the final quarter would be any better, and there were quite a few signs that it would be much worse. And while Raymond DePue McGranahan continued to worry over the vacant presidency, the board turned to executive employment agencies in its desperate search for a savior. I was told later that the presidency had been offered to at least six men, at salaries up to $175,000 a year, and not a single one had been willing to accept the impossible job.

Late on Wednesday afternoon, November 11, I got a telephone call from an old friend named Peter Wyden, articles editor at *McCall's*. A Berliner by birth, he was very self-assertive, but also round, funny, charming, and very able. Wyden had worked with me at *Newsweek*, moved to the *Post* and tried to hire me there, then moved to *McCall's*, and turned down my effort to hire him back to the *Post*. We had periodic lunches to exchange gossip, and now he was telephoning to say, "I've got good news." A new team of two good men would soon take over at Curtis, he said. One of them would be Ed Miller, publisher of *McCall's*, whom he described as intelligent, pleasant, dedicated, and the potential salvation of Curtis; the other would be Newton Minow, former law partner of Adlai Stevenson, former head of the Federal Communications Commission, the man who had first described television as a "vast wasteland."

"You're really in favor of this?" I asked.

"Absolutely," Wyden said. "Just remember, you didn't hear it at *McCall's*."

The next day's *Times* was to confirm the rumor. The front-page story, by Bedingfield again, began by saying:

The Curtis Publishing Company has decided to place its management in the hands of a new team of prominent executives. Newton N. Minow, chairman of the Federal Communications Commission under President Kennedy, has been offered one top position at the rebellion-torn company, and is reportedly ready to accept the job. Another top position will be given to A. Edward Miller, who resigned yesterday as publisher of McCall's magazine. A third high post has been offered to an unidentified executive, but his acceptance has not yet been received. Directors of Curtis are expected to act at a meeting in Philadelphia today on the hiring of both Mr. Minow and Mr. Miller and to designate titles for them. The two men will share the executive direction of the company. Indications last night were that Mr. Miller would be the senior executive—probably with the title of president—in charge of the company's publications. Mr. Minow would be the chief executive officer in charge of the company's non-publishing activities.

At midnight, my telephone rang. Bob Sherrod was calling from Philadelphia. He said that great changes were about to take place, and that he wanted me to be aware of them. The most definite change was that the *Post* would have to give up weekly publication and go biweekly as soon as possible. And the fast eleven-day closing that Blair had won for us would have to be abandoned—too expensive. We would have to go back to the previous minimum of nineteen days' printing time.

"Look, I'd appreciate a chance to argue against all this," I said.

"I know you won't like it, but I'm afraid it's all settled," Sherrod said.

"But there's a good case to be made against it," I said, "and all I want is a chance to present that case."

"I'm afraid it's all settled," Sherrod said again. "There's nothing we can do." (*"Nous sommes foutus,"* said General Goltz. *"Oui. Comme toujours. Oui. C'est dommage. . . . Rien à faire. Rien. Faut pas penser. Faut accepter."*)

"Say, what about these rumors of a new regime?" I asked.

"I haven't seen the papers, but I had somebody read me the story in tomorrow's *Times*," Sherrod said.

"Well, I've heard reports that Ed Miller and Newton Minow are taking over the company," I said. "Have they approved our giving up weekly publication?"

"Well, the *Times* story talks about Miller and Minow," Sherrod said, "but I asked Mac Clifford about it, and he says the *Times* story is poppycock. That's the word he used—poppycock."

We all came to work quite cheerfully the next morning, because we had all read the *Times* story announcing that the managerial crisis had finally been solved. For months beyond counting, before, during, and after the Blair rebellion, the editors at Curtis had a desperate feeling that nothing they did could ever save the corporation from its managers and directors. Blair had exploited this feeling to mobilize his insurrection, but it outlasted him because it remained basically true. And now, after months of crisis and confusion, there seemed to be some possibility that Curtis might actually be saved. In whatever was said about them, Miller and Minow were generally reputed to be men of intelligence, energy, experience, and good will.

Since an announcement was expected by noon, there was little

work done that morning. Mike Mooney, whose prospective buyers had
all blanched and balked after a closer inspection of Curtis's managerial problems, now declared that the corporation might at last be
salable again. Bill Ewald stopped by with some bit of gossip and the
latest Polish joke. I then had a long visit from a relatively new actor
in this melodrama, Asger Jerrild, the Danish art director whom Blair
had hired almost two years earlier. Throughout those two years,
Jerrild had been crushed by Hank Walker, but now that we were
banishing Walker, Jerrild sprouted up again and began to assert himself. He wanted to sing me his praises of Semenenko, and of Bob
Sherrod, who, he said, might yet regain the editorship, with Semenenko's blessing. And so we waited for news from Philadelphia.

The critical board meeting on this morning was delayed, however,
because of the death of Walter Deane Fuller, aged eighty-two, protégé
of Curtis and Lorimer, past president and board chairman of the
Curtis Publishing Company, guardian of the shrines during all those
long years of depression and war, builder of the printing plant and
buyer of the paper mills. If, after all these years, one had to single out
one person and brand him as the man most responsible for the situation in which Curtis now found itself, would not Walter Deane Fuller
be high on the list of candidates? But could anyone deny the traditional explanation—that Fuller had acted for the best of reasons and
the best of motives?

The board did finally meet, but there was no immediate announcement, and so I waited around for Emerson, who had been summoned
to Philadelphia on the seven o'clock train that morning. He finally
stormed in at two in the afternoon, calling on anyone available to join
him for lunch, and then marching on into his office. I followed him
there and heard him on the telephone to his wife.

"No, it's all bad. . . . No, I didn't get to see them. . . . No, that
was all a lie. They never had them at all. . . . Miller was last seen
running screaming into the night, with Semenenko chasing him
through the streets, shouting, 'Wait! Wait!' . . . And that—Whatshisname—Minow, the *fingerling*, he slipped through their clutches
too. . . . No . . . *Clifford*, I tell you . . . No, I'm telling you it's all
bad. . . ."

Mooney was still full of good cheer when we picked him up for
lunch, and so was McKinney, and Congdon. And Emerson wouldn't
say anything until we had settled ourselves down, in a Third Avenue
bar called the Green Derby. There he ordered a double Martini and
began to tell us what had happened in Philadelphia.

"It's very simple. Nobody ever got any real commitment from either

Miller or Minow. So after some hard bargaining, both of them turned down whatever jobs were offered them. And that drove the banks into hysterics. And that was when Clifford made his bid."

"Clifford!" I cried.

"He's it, tiger. He's the new president."

"You've got to be kidding."

"Read it in tomorrow's *Times*. And in the meantime, order me another double Martini."

It would, of course, be announced in the usual way. John McLean Clifford, whom Blair had repeatedly denounced for his harsh methods, whom Culligan had demoted for being unable to keep the peace, whom the board had ignored during the long, vain search for a president, was dutifully described in the next day's *Times* as "a tough, decisive, all-business businessman with a penchant for personal and corporate trimness." He was a Westerner, born of Mormon stock in Salt Lake City in 1904, and after graduating from the University of Utah, he got a law degree from Southwestern University. He worked fourteen years for the Securities and Exchange Commission, then became State Land Commissioner in California, then switched to the legal staff of RCA in 1943. Over the course of twenty years, he worked his way up to the executive vice presidency at NBC, where, according to the formal statements, he was "responsible for most of the network's staff functions . . . the financial operations . . . international operations . . . the legal and accounting departments, the engineering department, and all the network's film operations." Since there was little to say about his talents or graces, the *Times* kept repeating its one leitmotif of trimness: "Mr. Clifford, who is 5 feet 7 inches tall and keeps himself lean by strict diet control, is a cost-conscious executive who belongs to the clean-desk set. . . . He is a hard-driving, plain-talking man who can and does fly his own plane."

Clifford had already begun to exert his "penchant for trimness" over the exhausted board of directors. "Clifford and Poppei have that board programed like a computer," Emerson said. "They feed in the figures and the board members all nod their heads." This meant that the board had approved, without any real debate or consultation, the cost-cutters' idea of changing overnight from all the tradition inherent in the very name of the *Saturday Evening Post* to the cheaper expedient of biweekly publication ("The Every-Other-Saturday-Evening-Post," someone soon named it). And there was more. Emerson had never even seen the board of directors but only Maurice Poppei, and Poppei had said that biweekly publication would naturally mean a reduced budget. Bob Sherrod, the intermediary, riding home with Emerson on the train from Philadelphia, said that Poppei "didn't have the heart" to admit the planned figure—a cut of 40 percent in the editorial staff, in the buying of manuscripts, in all editorial expenses.

"I mean, am I wrong in thinking this is anything but a disaster?" Emerson asked us. Nobody disagreed. Biweekly publication could be defended as a merchandising idea—*Look,* after all, had grown large and prosperous as a biweekly—but as a journalistic idea, biweekly publication seemed hopelessly remote from the flow of the news— and as a cost-cutting operation under the aegis of Mac Clifford, it seemed to promise nothing but failure.

"What went wrong with Miller and Minow?" Mooney asked.

"Who the hell knows?" Emerson said.

"Miller resigned from *McCall's* yesterday to join Curtis, so he must have seen something since then—"

"And ran," Emerson said. "Ran screaming in horror."

("I came in ready to sign a contract that morning," Ed Miller said later. "The amount of money was almost embarrassing—$150,000 a year. But I had other conditions. One was that the banks guarantee a period of grace of twenty-four months, without anybody blowing the whistle, because no miracle would work in less than twenty-four months. Then the other element was John Kluge, the head of Metromedia. We talked to him about taking over the financial responsibilities, and Kluge loved the idea, but his bankers didn't see it in the same light. So that morning, I learned that neither of these conditions would be met, and I said, 'To hell with it,' and walked out.")

By the time we got back to the office, the news of Mac Clifford's election was already out, and everybody was milling around in the corridors. The first word had appeared on the Dow Jones ticker, along with a statement from Semenenko that Curtis "doesn't need any more cash," meaning that Curtis wouldn't get any more cash, and providing a plausible explanation for the sudden flight of Miller and Minow. Then somebody called from the *Wall Street Journal.* Then it was on the UPI ticker. Then Emerson called a meeting of the entire staff.

Before an audience of editors, writers, secretaries, and anyone else in the building—many angry and resentful at the news, others unaware of what was happening—Emerson began by bellowing out the results of that morning's board meeting. Mac Clifford, "whom we all know and love," was now the new president of Curtis, and the fast-closing weekly *Post,* to which we had all committed ourselves in the past year or two, was finished. As the chief survivor of the Blair revolt, he seemed to be in charge of things, he said, and so he would like to tell us a story.

There had once been a farmer in the back country of Georgia, and he got himself a wife and she bore him two children, and he raised his hogs and grew his corn and prospered mightily. And then there suddenly came a mysterious blight that killed all the hogs and shriveled all the corn. And the farmer raised up his face to heaven and asked, "Why me, oh, Lord? Why me?" From the sky, there came only an answering rumble.

And so the farmer and his wife and his children set to work and planted new crops and grew new herds, and once again they all prospered mightily. And once again there came a mysterious blight that killed all the hogs and shriveled all the corn. And the daughter ran off with a traveling salesman, and the son was stomped to death by a mule. And the farmer raised his face to heaven and cried out, "Why me, oh, Lord? Why me?" And from the sky, there came only an answering rumble.

By this time, the fifty or sixty people packed into the production room were completely an audience, straining to hear, laughing at every arabesque in the story, forgetting the reason they had been summoned. Then the phone rang, once, twice, and somebody picked it up and said it was for Emerson, and Emerson waved it away with a sweeping gesture of his arm. And he told how the farmer had started all over again, with only his wife to help him rebuild, and he planted new crops, working from dawn until midnight, plowing, harrowing, and finally harvesting. And then there came a great thunderstorm, and the lightning set the barn on fire and destroyed the harvested crop and killed the farmer's wife. And the man lifted up his face to heaven and cried at the top of his voice, "Why me, oh, Lord? Why me?" And the heavens rumbled, and a great voice spoke out and said, "I don't know why, but there's something about you that just *pisses me off!*"

In the midst of the laughter, Emerson waded through the crowd to take the phone call. It was from Dick Ficks, the little public-relations man who was just now calling to transmit the Philadelphia news to New York.

"Richard!" Emerson bawled into the telephone. "You're a great American! With the heart of a Capetown lion! An ornament to the organization!" In his outcries, Emerson carried his audience with him, so that the telephone became no more than a stage prop. "Yes—yes, we know about old Mac. The news was greeted here with cries of joy all up and down the corridors. More news? Yes? Ed Miller has agreed to become a consultant? Well, that's a bold and dramatic move. Who? Minow has also agreed to become a consultant? That's truly inspiring news. It makes us all feel warm and come all over peculiar just to think of the number of high-powered consultants we now have on the premises. Yes, sir—sure thing. Never in the history of the Curtis Publishing Company has there been a moment of glory quite like this. Right. Good talking to you . . .

"That was Dick Ficks," Emerson told us. "He says Mac Clifford is the new president."

In his theatrical way, Emerson had managed to convince his staff that nothing disastrous had happened, and to encourage them to continue going about their business as usual. But though they all returned to their offices relatively cheerful, the fact was that business could not go on as usual because something really disastrous really had happened. The battle between Blair and Culligan had ended in mutual defeat, and in the abrupt abolition of half of the *Post*'s weekly issues. Unable to find a new president, the bankers and the directors had simply turned over the wreckage to the senior survivor of the old regime, and nobody expected that he would be much n.ore than a caretaker. The imagination and intelligence and sheer work that would be required to save the corporation would have to come from some yet undiscovered leader. And despite the legends about the inevitability by which a Caesar or a Napoleon finds his historic mission, the events of the past few months had demonstrated that a leaderless organization may very well remain perpetually unable to find its true leader.

As soon as the staff had dispersed, I cornered Emerson in his office and asked him what he really planned to do about the change.

"I'll tell you very simply," he said, still in an emotional state. "I'm going to go on running this magazine just as long as it *amuses* me. There's no other reason to go on, and there's not going to be any other reason. But right now, the whole f—— thing *amuses* me. It entertains me. I *enjoy* watching all these pissants f—— around with things. But the minute it stops entertaining me, then I say: 'F—— the whole bunch of them!' "

Book II

THE COUNTERREVOLUTION

There have been oppression and luxury,
There have been poverty and license,
There has been minor injustice.
Yet we have gone on living,
Living and partly living.

—T. S. ELIOT, *Murder in the Cathedral*

12

"It seems I'm the new editor"

"I just saw the goddamnedest thing," Bill Emerson said, "the god-damnedest knife fight I've ever seen. Listen, let me tell you—I was walking up Third Avenue, right around the corner, to have lunch at that French place—what's the name? the Mole?—and I heard this screech of brakes, and I turned around, and I could see that a car and a taxi had just had a near-miss. And both the doors swing right open, and the two drivers get out. The taxi driver is a big, tough Negro, and the other driver is a big, tough Puerto Rican, and the Puerto Rican starts coming at the Negro in a way that you just *know* there's going to be bloodshed."

By now, Emerson was marching up and down the floor of my office, acting out both roles.

"So the Puerto Rican is coming at the Negro, like nothing's going to stop him, and they don't say a word, but the Negro just stands there waiting for him, and when the Puerto Rican gets into range, the Negro just hauls off and *whomps* him in the jaw. And the Puerto Rican staggers back about three or four paces—like this, like this—and then he reaches down, like this, and slowly pulls out this switch-blade, and goes—*flick*—and out comes this knife. And then with his other hand, he pulls out his whole belt, and it's got this big, heavy buckle on it, and he gets the belt swinging like a bullwhip, and then he starts coming for the Negro again, and the Negro just stands there waiting for him. And they're coming closer, slowly, like this, and then the Negro takes another swing at the Puerto Rican, and that knife goes out like *that*, and the Negro's arm is slashed from here to here.

And then the Negro tries to kick the Puerto Rican in the groin, and that knife goes out again, and the Negro's leg is sliced open from here to here—I tell you, that Puerto Rican really knew how to use a knife."

"What were you doing in the midst of all this?" I asked.

"I kept hollering, 'Stop, stop, the cops are coming.' Then I went running into this antique store and told them to call the cops. When I came out again, this Negro had somehow got his taxi meter out of his cab, and he was waving it around his head like this, like a club—and then he threw it at the Puerto Rican—but he missed him. And the Puerto Rican let fly with that belt and hit the Negro right across the cheek, and the blood started pouring out from under his eye. And they're circling around the cab, out into the street, and you know the goddamnedest thing? That Negro just would not give up. He's got nothing but his bare hands against this guy with the knife and the belt, and he's bleeding from the leg and the arm and the face, and all he has to do is run, but he absolutely would not give up.

"So while they're circling around this cab, I went back into the antique store—and they hadn't even *called* the cops—and I start looking around for something to use as a club on this crazy Puerto Rican before the Negro gets himself killed, and I come out of that store with some kind of an antique walking cane in my hand, and then I see a policeman is finally there. And he's got a gun in the Puerto Rican's back, and the Puerto Rican just sort of goes limp, you know, the way it can happen when high tension suddenly stops, and the policeman takes them both away. Now wasn't that the goddamnedest thing to see, on Third Avenue, in broad daylight, when you're just going out to lunch?"

The battle took place on the day after Mac Clifford's ascent to the presidency of the Curtis Publishing Company. It was, granted a little hyperbole, a foretaste of the life we were to lead for the next few years.

I had come to the *Post* in 1962 with some hope of helping to save it, but after my first encounter with Mac Clifford, when he started out as chief executive officer by firing two members of our staff, I became convinced that the *Post*'s chance of survival was almost nonexistent. Since I was near the center of the crisis, I thought it would be worthwhile to begin keeping a day-by-day record of the *Post*'s last few months. And so I began to set down every sign of lesions or bleeding, every symptom of the inevitable death. Who could have guessed that these last few months would drag on for more than four years, that the journal would grow to the size of a Russian novel, and that the *Post* and I would both outlast Mac Clifford?

In these lean years of survival, there was little of the drama of the Blair rebellion, or of the Ackerman upheaval that was to follow. Whereas Blair had fought for control of the company, and whereas Ackerman tore the whole company to pieces in an effort to make it function, Clifford simply sat stiffly at the controls and hoped for the best. There were some people high in the company who considered Clifford only an interim president, a sort of regent who would carry on administrative affairs until a new monarch appeared, but Clifford soon made it clear that he intended his regency to last indefinitely. This is not without relevance to the general functioning of the American corporation. Clifford's system for running a company, not too different from the way Bob MacNeal had run Curtis in the 1950's, is quite standard. There are hundreds of corporations ruled by some elderly but still energetic executive who doesn't really contribute much but sees to it that the annual report shows a respectable profit for the stockholders. In a prosperous corporation, the system works well enough, just as it does in a peacetime army, or in a city political machine between elections. When a corporation reaches a crisis, however, many of the flaws in the system become clear, because the system that seemed to work well enough really doesn't work at all.

If the Clifford regime lacked melodrama, it nonetheless contained certain elements of interest. There was, first of all, the peculiar personality of little Mac Clifford himself, grumbling and snorting over the smallest details of the baffling corporation he had somehow acquired. Clifford prided himself on a rugged Western approach to things, and he enjoyed recalling the day some labor union negotiators had threatened to throw him out a twelfth-floor window. He also liked to fly the company plane, ignoring all the perils that might trouble an aging and out-of-practice pilot. A less stubborn man, finding himself in need of help on a difficult job, might have surrounded himself with experts and advisers, but Clifford scarcely even tried to recruit any new men into the management of the corporation. Instead, he preferred the company of familiar faces.

The most unusual of these was Gloria Swett, a name that was supposed to be pronounced "Sweet." She had started as a secretary at RCA, where she had developed a close relationship with Clifford. He had brought her with him to Curtis and made her the secretary of the corporation, a job that paid her $28,000 a year. She was a rather tall woman of about forty, with a pale complexion and a receding chin. She was also efficient, ambitious, and determined to have her own way. And once Clifford became president, she took charge of personnel, public relations, legal affairs, and, it seemed, anything else she felt strongly about. She was a power, to be treated with considerable caution.

Clifford's other power, slightly more conventional but no less worthy of cautious treatment, was the enigmatic Maurice Poppei, whom we had met during our confrontation with Clifford over the firing of Ritter and Marvel. Poppei, who pronounced his name like that of the flower, was the very image of an accountant, which was his training, occupation, and spiritual vocation. A graduate of the Temple University School of Commerce, Poppei had worked for more than twenty years in the statistical departments of RCA, eventually achieving the post of Manager of Business Analysis. "I can tell a man's character," he once said, "by his budgets and expense accounts." Clifford had brought him to Curtis early in 1963 to help in the takeover of all financial operations in the company. Now, as comptroller, he had complete charge of the money.

The only other major member of Clifford's entourage was a man who had survived every change at Curtis for a generation. G. B. McCombs, a thin, gray-haired Texan with a pointed face and shining teeth, had come to Curtis in 1930, when he was just twenty-one, and over the years he had worked his way up to the presidency of that fief called the Curtis Circulation Company. Dave Thomas used to be fascinated by his name and called him Gonly Bonly, insisting that G.B. had no real first names. When G.B. went into the navy as a young man, according to Thomas, the navy stenciled all his equipment with his surname and with his initials—"G(only) B(only)." Much the same sort of thing had happened in the Curtis bureaucracy, and one of the secretaries had started the nickname of Gonly Bonly. Emerson, a bit more charitable to a fellow Southerner, liked to call him The Gray Fox of Waxahachie County.

(There was a splendid Emerson story attached to the name of that county. A wandering theatrical troupe once came to Waxahachie, Emerson recalled, and the leading lady promptly ran off with a plumbing-supply salesman. The director of the company searched all over town for someone to act in the play that night, and finally he found a girl who looked about right. He told her that it was really a very small part—all she had to do was to run onstage at the end of Act III, and then the hero would shoot her with his cap pistol, and she would fall down, and the hero would cry: "Oh! What have I done?" Whereupon the curtain would fall. Evening came, and everything went smoothly. Act III was drawing to a triumphant close, the girl ran out, the hero shot her with his cap pistol, the girl fell to the floor, and the hero cried, "Oh! What have I done?" And in the third row of the stunned audience, a grizzled old farmer struggled to his feet and cried out, "What have you done? I'll tell you what you've done, you sonofabitch! You've just killed the only whore in Waxahachie County!")

From any objective point of view, Mac Clifford's managerial team was a comic quartet—all of them known by ludicrous nicknames: Mac the Knife, Sweet Gloria, Popeye, and old Gonly Bonly from Waxahachie County. Yet the Curtis board of directors, the supreme authority, had designated John McLean Clifford as the newest heir to Cyrus H. K. Curtis and George Horace Lorimer, to preside over our fate and over the fate of the Curtis Publishing Company. And Clifford, in turn, had designated those three companions, the secretary, the accountant, and the circulation man, as his chief lieutenants—Poppei in charge of the money, G.B. in charge of the magazines, and Gloria in charge of miscellaneous details. They paid themselves, with the board's approval, almost a third of a million dollars in salaries, with Clifford alone taking $126,000.

Under this management, it seemed to me, the death of the *Post* was inevitable. As it turned out, the patient outlived the doctor. This miraculous survival, however, was no indication that the doctor ever knew of any cure.

It is not easy to cut a budget by 40 percent, as Clifford had ordered, nor is it pleasant, nor is there a standard way to do it. For the budget is a political manifesto, subject to all the vicissitudes of politics. The first problem was to figure out what was actually in the budget, since the last one had been drawn up by Blair, approved by Kantor, and administered by Ritter, all of them now gone. To me, the editorial budget itself was a novelty, a document I had never even seen before. Rental of equipment? Outside employee services? Maintenance? What were all these things? Who authorized these payments, and what did we get for them? It is exasperating to discover, for the first time, the real cost of doing business—to discover, for example, that the cost of a secretary is not just her salary but her Blue Cross and unemployment insurance, or that the accumulation of telephone calls from one relatively small department can cost tens of thousands of dollars a year.

Once all these areas have been explored and grumbled at, however, there are only two ways to make substantial reductions in a budget. The first is to slice away at the amount you spend on raw materials. In our case, this item was called "materials used," meaning the amount we paid for material actually published in the magazine. This was not difficult to cut, at least on paper, not only because we would need a lot less material for twenty-six biweekly issues than for forty-five weekly ones, but because we would not know for months how much we had actually paid for material over the course of a year, and by then the battle of the budget would be long past. But although any imaginative budget is full of white lies, it is unwise to promise a program of total fantasy, since the accountants can easily break down the budget into average monthly expenditures, and the white lies, if too large, will soon become apparent. And since it is dangerous to make really substantial reductions in raw materials—even Congress spends a certain amount of time investigating bridges that crumble and guns that don't fire—the only other way to cut the budget, and the only way to make immediate savings, is to cut the payroll.

So we started drawing up lists of who could be fired—or moved, in some gentler way, off the payroll. At the head of his list of expendable people, Emerson boldly placed the name of his supposed superior, the "coordinator," Bob Sherrod. "I can't justify paying him $50,000 a year out of *editorial*," Emerson snorted. "If they think he's that valuable to the corporation, they ought to put him on the corporate payroll." It was a daring gambit, which brought a cold smile to the lips of Maurice Poppei, but Poppei accepted the reasoning and agreed to transfer Sherrod to the corporate payroll.

From then on, Emerson used every stratagem he could think of to avoid dismissals. He transferred one senior writer off the payroll by offering him a free-lance contract, and the writer took a leave of absence and went to the *Reader's Digest*. He took an editor whom Schanche had originally hired for the *Post* and persuaded Schanche to transfer him to *Holiday*. He heard of an opening at the *Times*, and he promptly got on the telephone to praise the virtues of one of the editors on the dismissal list. The fact was that Emerson hated to fire people, and even when he had to do it, he did his best to blur the humiliation with a cloud of rhetoric. "When I get through with them," he said, "they thank me for giving them their freedom, the new opportunity they'd always wanted." By one device or another, Emerson managed, over the course of a few weeks, to cut the *Post* editorial staff by 40 percent without actually firing a single person.

The new administration didn't object to such legerdemain, but its own actions followed a somewhat different style. Clifford and Poppei fired people right and left, and with very little tenderness. And while Emerson could maneuver and dissemble for the people on his editorial payroll, he could not protect the ones who worked directly for this management. So, for example, the new regime struck down poor old Gladys Mueller, old not in years but in service to former masters. Every corporation has or needs to have a Gladys Mueller, a kind of court chamberlain, who knows where everything is, who will undertake any assignment, and who lives only to oblige the crown. On the wall of her office, where other people might hang travel posters or pictures that entertained them, Gladys Mueller had her icon, an autographed photograph of Ben Hibbs. She had served Fuoss and Sherrod as she had served Hibbs, worrying, fretful, shaking her head at the strange changes that kept taking place, and so she had served Blair, too, disapproving, not because he had overthrown the old gods but simply because he was untidy. Blair, understanding her value, put her to work on a wide range of bookkeeping-housekeeping problems, and at some point during those labors, she may well have come into conflict with the new powers. And so now, after more than twenty years at Curtis, Gladys was fired, effective immediately, without even her pension. Emerson and Schanche led a small delegation of protesters to the office of Maurice Poppei, but they reported that Poppei had said Gloria wanted her out, and that Poppei declined to oppose her. Gladys came to Emerson's office to say good-bye, and Emerson characteristically put his arm around her and told her that everybody at the *Post* still loved her, at which she burst into tears and ran out of the office.

From the *Gallagher Report:*

Saturday Evening Post assistant managing editor Otto Friedrich has good chance to become SEP editor. Caskie Stinnett, executive editor of Ladies' Home Journal, expected to replace editor Davis Thomas. . . . SEP needs ad director. Publisher Jesse Ballew good salesman. Weak as manager . . . Curtis needs someone to call the shots—particularly in sales. . . .

It is traditional, at this time of year, for New York corporations to give Christmas parties. Traditionally, nothing much happens, beyond what normally happens when people drink too much. Some men make passes at the secretaries, and some of them insult their bosses, and many of them have hangovers the next day. In the pre-Christmas week of 1964, however, Maurice Poppei announced that Curtis could not afford any Christmas parties. That sounded fine, because it meant that we could have our own party, and so each editor contributed ten dollars to turn the photo studio into a vast discothèque. We invited the staffs of the other magazines. We even invited Clifford and Poppei to come to the party they had refused to finance. They were too timorous to come, but several hundred people did, and Mike

Mooney, who had organized much of the revelry, appeared in a Santa Claus suit, reading aloud a long list of prophecies. All evening long, the rock 'n' roll roared from the tapes, and the psychedelic lights flashed, and we celebrated Christmas with grand defiance.

And in the last weekly issue of the *Post*, December 12, 1964, a very dark time, I wrote this on the editorial page:

. . . Before we change to biweekly publication, we are going to indulge ourselves in an evaluation of the year past. With all due allowances for editorial vanity, we feel that this constantly changing but uniquely traditional magazine is completing a year of extraordinary excellence. In fact, we'd be prepared to match our 1964 record against that of any magazine any year anywhere. . . .

We'd like to cite Roger Kahn's dramatic report on Harlem, *White Man, Walk Easy;* Edward R. F. Sheehan's penetrating survey of the Catholic Church in America, *Not Peace, but the Sword;* John Hersey's moving account of a proud Mississippi Negro's determination to win his constitutional rights, *A Life for a Vote.* . . . During 1964 . . . the *Post* published articles by four different presidents: Truman, Eisenhower, Kennedy, and Johnson. . . . The *Post*'s fiction, too, has been unique. Saul Bellow's *Herzog,* currently the No. 1 best seller . . . was first excerpted in the *Post* last August. Arthur Miller's controversial play, *After the Fall,* appeared in its entirety in the *Post* last winter. And the stories have come from such distinguished writers as James Gould Cozzens, John Updike, Graham Greene, and Louis Auchincloss, with no less than 12 contributions by John O'Hara.

I ended on an elegiac note, and Emerson found that too depressing, so he added this postscript:

. . . At this turning point in our history, we rededicate ourselves to our readers. We will have more time to plan, to polish, to perfect, and we will make good use of it. We will produce a more important, more lustrous magazine than ever before. And we hope to leaven it with wit, humor and grace.

The *Post* was not, of course, the only Curtis magazine under fire. They were all in convulsions of one sort or another, and some of their convulsions now were worse than ours.

The first crisis came at *Holiday.* Unlike the *Post*, *Holiday* had no long institutional tradition. It was largely the creation of one man, Ted Patrick, who had become the editor in the magazine's first year, 1946, and remained there until his death in 1964. In those last few years, Patrick was repeatedly engaged in beating off the encroachments of Clay Blair, but within twenty-four hours of Patrick's death, Blair imposed Don Schanche on the stricken staff. There seems to have been no clear difference of policy between this staff and its new editor, but rather a difference in approach. The staff thought the magazine was fine just as it was; Schanche wanted it to be younger and livelier. The staff wanted things to continue in the old way; Schanche wanted things done his way. Throughout the Blair rebellion, *Holiday*'s senior staffers dithered over their disagreements and fretted at Schanche's frequent absences. Then, by a miracle of bad timing, they chose the first week of Clifford's presidency to send him a written denunciation of Schanche, a denunciation that curiously echoed Schanche's own draft of the manifesto against Culligan:

"We, the signatories to this letter, are the senior members of the editorial staff of *Holiday* magazine," the letter solemnly began. Then, after a brief statement of their efforts to work with Schanche, the dissidents continued: "We have now reached a point where our standards of excellence and Mr. Schanche's view of the magazine's function diverge so widely that, in our belief, further cooperation is not possible. We feel that Mr. Schanche is not qualified to be the editor of *Holiday*. He lacks the experience, the scope, the taste, and, above all, the imagination to guide the progress of this magazine."

The four signers—Albert H. Farnsworth, executive editor; Harry Sions, editorial director; Frank Zachary, art director; and Louis Mercier, picture editor, all of whom had been with *Holiday* from the beginning—issued no ultimatum, made no threats, set no deadline. They asked only for a chance to "discuss this urgent problem." Once the quarrel had reached the stage of written accusations, however, there was little hope for any discussions. Clifford conferred with the four dissidents and asked them to be patient for a time and to avoid any publicity. Poppei apparently encouraged them by saying that he had been "aware of the situation," and that it would be "taken care of." Schanche, meanwhile, drew up a flashy blueprint for a "new" *Holiday*—"the bible of our new, actively rewarding world of leisure"—which made a considerable impression on the new management. Schanche thus was able to tell the dissidents that he had won a "vote of confidence" from the management, and that "you'll have to make up your minds whether to give me loyal and complete support." The dissidents went back to Poppei to complain, and Zachary emotionally declared that he would not tolerate "immorality, venality and pusillanimity," upon which the four editors all walked out. Schanche announced to the staff that the four had resigned; word leaked to the press; the four said they hadn't resigned. Clifford angrily told them: "You are guilty of the same thing as Blair and Kantor." He told them to make their peace with Schanche on any terms that Schanche would accept, and so all four departed. "Someone has to run the show and I have been assigned to that task," Schanche announced. "I intend to do the job."

One afternoon early in the new year, Mike Mooney said that the fifth floor (meaning the *Journal* and *Holiday*) was alive with rumors that "an outsider" would be appointed editor of the *Post,* and that the announcement would be made "tonight or tomorrow." The story seemed so specific that we thought we ought to check it. We tried for several hours, and every telephone call indicated that the rumors were untrue.

The next day everything seemed relatively placid, but I asked my secretary, an amiable and attractive girl named Jane Russell, whether she had heard any rumors.

"What kind of rumors?" she asked.

"There's a board meeting going on, so there have to be rumors, and secretaries are supposed to know all rumors so their bosses will be ready to duck."

She laughed and went out and returned half an hour later to say: "The rumor is that Dave Thomas has been fired, and the editor of *McCall's* is going to be the next editor of the *Journal.*"

"Really? That sounds crazy."

"Yes—and, Mr. Friedrich, there's another rumor—that all the editors who signed the letter against Mr. Culligan will be out within a year."

"Well, that's ridiculous," I said. "You can forget that."

The rumor about Thomas was soon confirmed, however, and the next day's *Times* announced that John Mack Carter, thirty-six, had been designated to replace Davis Thomas, also thirty-six, who had resigned. (Carter also brought with him the irrepressible Peter Wyden, returning to Curtis as the executive editor of the *Journal.*)

Poor Dave Thomas. In 1961, after Thomas had worked six years as a *Life* checker and reporter, Schanche had recommended him to Blair, and Blair had hired him as a picture editor. And largely because of the incredible vacuum in the editorial headquarters in Philadelphia, Thomas had taken less than a year to become photography editor and then managing editor, second only to Sherrod, whom he hoped to replace. And then, in that fall of 1962, when he was almost singlehandedly putting out the magazine, on the brink of disaster, he had suddenly been overwhelmed by a wave of newcomers—Emerson, me, McKinney, Ewald—and then, that winter, another wave, Schanche, Walker, Jerrild. Blair had moved Thomas to the *Journal,* and now he had apparently been summoned to Philadelphia early in the morning and told to resign. And so he had resigned. "Thomas's last act at Curtis," Emerson said, "was to write an impassioned letter to the management, explaining why he should be made the editor of the *Post*."

And poor Joe Culligan. Almost unnoticed in that day's news about the *Journal* was an announcement that a few more buttons had been snipped from the former president's uniform. He was still chairman of the board, but at this day's meeting, presumably run by Clifford, the board removed Culligan from its two main committees, the executive committee and the finance committee. The move left Culligan with very little to do, except to collect his salary of $110,000 a year, and look forward to the additional deferred payments of $40,000 a year that would begin in 1967.

At this point in our lives, New York City officials decided, for some reason, that we didn't have enough fire protection, and so they attached new fire extinguishers every thirty feet or so along the main corridor of the editorial office. This prompted a number of lugubrious jokes, but Bill Ewald surmounted them by attaching a white card above one of the shiny metal devices. It said:

FIRE EXTINGUISHER

By Andy Warhol

1965

After John Mack Carter took over the *Journal*, I chided Mike Mooney about the falsity of his rumor. It was not false, he said. They were still looking for an editor for the *Post*.

Ed Miller, the *McCall's* publisher who had declined the Curtis presidency, had by now become a major figure as a "consultant." He had asked every Curtis editor to write an outline of what he wanted and planned for his magazine. Schanche had done so, with great success—all his dissenting subordinates had been removed. Dave Thomas had failed to write his outline, and now John Mack Carter, from Miller's former company, had come to replace him. Emerson, too, had failed to produce an outline. *Ergo* . . .

While the rumors continued endlessly, I drew up a list of all the people whom I had heard mentioned, in one way or another, truly or falsely, as future editors of the *Post*: (1) Ed Thompson of *Life*, (2) Jack Fischer of *Harper's*, (3) Norman Cousins of the *Saturday Review*, (4) Reuven Frank of NBC, (5) Wade Nichols of *Good Housekeeping*, (6) John Mack Carter of the *Ladies' Home Journal*, (7) Don Schanche of *Holiday*, (8) John Denson of the New York

Journal-American, (9) Oz Elliott of *Newsweek*, (10) Murray Rossant of the *New York Times*, (11) Clay Felker of *New York* magazine, (12) Bob Manning of *Atlantic Monthly*, (13) Lawrence Gittelson of *Coronet*, (14) Jim Bellows of the New York *Herald Tribune*, (15) Eric Sevareid, (16) Ted Sorensen, (17) Pierre Salinger, and (18) Bob Sherrod. And there may have been others. In fact, I knew of at least one other, a middle-aged man who had never had a major job at a major magazine. He turned up one day under the auspices of a "management consultant" firm and let it be known that he had been offered the editorship of either the *Post* or *Holiday*. He was quickly shown to the door.

After the *Journal* upheaval, I decided, in a small, doomed, bitter way, that we had been on the defensive too long, that we had drifted too long, that we had hoped for too long that if we cut the budget, produced the magazine, and behaved ourselves, we would be rewarded. The history of autocracies provides no evidence for such expectations; on the contrary, people who carry out orders and do their duty are quite likely to be rewarded with a shot in the back of the neck. At the very least, I thought, I could start some movement flowing in the direction we all wanted. In contrast to Blair's belief in the mass ultimatum, I thought I could work best by persuading a variety of people, one at a time, that Emerson had done a good job for three months as the acting editor, that the entire staff was united behind him, and that continued indecision about the editorship was bad for morale and bad for business.

I started by going to see Jess Ballew, for, although he was officially a "rebel," he was also the publisher and theoretically in charge of the commercial future of the *Post*. He agreed strongly with my approach, promised to take the case to Poppei that same day, and to see Clifford within the week. I next tried Bill Buckley, a vice president and head of the book division and syndicate, and a neutral party on cordial terms with everybody. Buckley answered by criticizing Emerson's volatility and eccentricity, and then he added an interesting question: "Don't you think that you yourself would be a better editor of the *Post* than Emerson?" I paused for a moment, since I had my own views on the subject, but then I said that there was no possibility of a management choice between Emerson and me but only between Emerson and some outsider, with, in the latter case, the certain prospect of another upheaval. "What I want," I said, "is for Emerson to be the editor."

I then went to see Don Schanche, even in the midst of his troubles, and he was fairly optimistic. "I think they'll get around to making Emerson the editor as soon as they can get themselves organized," he said. And then to Peter Wyden, who claimed to have friendly ties with both the new consultants, Ed Miller and Newton Minow. He had once offered to help "if problems become really critical," and I told him now that the critical time was already upon us. "They keep looking for some outside Mr. Big," I said, "but we don't need any Mr. Big, and we don't want him, and we won't put up with him." Wyden seemed startled at my vehemence. "They know you feel that way," he said. "They already know that."

My purpose in all these maneuvers—and I extended my reach to quite a number of people—was not to rely on any one of them to carry the message to management, but rather to create a situation in which any inquiry from any quarter, from management or its various advisers and consultants, would always produce the same answer: The *Post* staff wants Emerson. Still, the problem remained: Why was the editorship of the *Post* being hawked around New York? Partly at my urging, partly because of his own exasperation, Emerson carried the question directly to Clifford. He reported afterward that Clifford had done his best to be reassuring. There had been a search for a new editor, Clifford acknowledged, but it had been discontinued, and Emerson would be consulted before any important move was made.

By then, Emerson had already embarked on his own course for the editorship. Because I could run the magazine in his absence, and because Jess Ballew desperately needed help in convincing advertisers that the *Post* was still alive, and because those doubting advertisers wanted to hear about the editorial prospects of the magazine, and because Emerson himself loved to talk, he undertook an enormous campaign of selling ads. Week after week, he would telephone me from some place like Cleveland and tell me that everything had gone well and ask whether there were any problems and then announce that he was flying on to Detroit. When he was back in New York, writing cover billings or approving the editorial page, he would suddenly say, "My God, I've got to finish my speech for tomorrow in St. Louis." Then he would call from St. Louis and say he had to fly on to Dallas.

He told them about his childhood in Bottom Dollar, Tennessee, and about his great-uncle who was called They'll-Never-Take-Richmond Emerson. He told them about the curse on the Plotnick Diamond— "The curse," she said, "is my husband, Mr. Plotnick"—and about the shooting of the last whore in Waxahachie County. But he also told them about Marshall McLuhan and the decline of linear perception— "Someday," he liked to say, "you'll all be able to get the *Saturday Evening Post* in the form of a pill, somewhat larger, I hope, than the pills labeled *Life* and *Look*"—and about Buckminster Fuller's theory of the city as an information-retrieval system. And also about how he had labored with Martin Mayer over an article on the schools and how he had told Stew Alsop to rewrite a profile of Secretary McNamara. "You can't imagine how they sit there, absolutely fascinated," said Mike Mooney, who went along on one of Emerson's sales trips to Detroit. "They really love the *Post,* and they're a little tired of ad salesmen, and finally they get to see somebody who can tell them how things are done. Every time Emerson goes out on the road, he sells millions of dollars' worth of ads. *Millions.*"

"The funny thing is," Emerson said, "that Ed Miller is supposed to be a consultant to Clifford, but Clifford is leery of him, so everything Miller may say against me makes my odds better with Clifford. In fact, you know, I have a funny feeling that Clifford almost *likes* me."

"That's because you're about the only person I know who seems to like him," I said.

Thursday, March 4, 1965. As I arrived at work, I met Emerson mysteriously leaving. It was that first Thursday of the month, when the board of directors—which I had taken to calling "The Mistake of the Month Club"—traditionally met. "I've got to go to Philadelphia," Emerson said. "I just got the word last night. Don't spread it around. I'll call you as soon as I can."

So the long day began. Thursday was also the day when Mooney staged his weekly lunch at the Stanhope Hotel on upper Fifth Avenue. His theory was that if the *Post* regularly invited two celebrities from two totally unrelated fields, plus a couple of advertising men, plus a couple of *Post* editors, the editors would get valuable story ideas, they would surreptitiously create the image of a successful and fashionable magazine, and, precisely because no sales pitch was ever made, they would get advertising. I had originally agreed to the plan as long as it was understood that I wouldn't have to attend any lunches, but on this occasion it all sounded fairly low-keyed—the only celebrity was the actor-playwright Ossie Davis, accompanied by an agent—and since I was nervous and worried, I thought I would join in. The lunch was marvelous, lamb chops and string beans that I can remember to this day, but the conversation was dully predictable: the Negro Problem. In the midst of this, Mooney picked up a telephone call from the office. The news was that Joe Culligan had finally resigned from all connection with Curtis, and that Curtis had lost almost $14 million during 1964.

When we got back to the office, there was an announcement on the bulletin board, which elaborated the ironies of the situation. The financial loss was disastrous. President Culligan, who had once predicted profits for 1964, had been replaced by President Clifford, who had predicted a "small loss" for the final quarter. The loss for that final quarter alone, the three months following the Blair-Kantor assault, was now disclosed to be $7,624,000, more than half of the full year's loss of $13,947,000. The cumulative figures on Culligan's two years as president showed that Curtis had borrowed about $35 million from Serge Semenenko and lost almost two-thirds of that amount—more than $20 million, all gone.

On this occasion, Culligan issued a statement:

I am gratified to have been able to make a contribution to Curtis during some of its most difficult hours and am reassured by the personal realization that all my efforts were directed toward the good of this historic institution. It is in the best interests of all that Curtis now be given the time without harassment to continue to improve its magazines and market them more effectively to advertisers and the public.

For the duration of his contract, Culligan would continue to receive his $150,000 annually for working on "special projects." One of these was suitably nebulous: He would "seek to develop broadcasting opportunities for the company." The other project deserved some kind of award for imaginative corporate planning: He would write a history of Curtis up to the end of 1963. In the next day's *Herald Tribune*, Culligan went beyond his formal statement and spoke to Joseph Kaselow in words that showed him both irrepressible and incorrigible. "I guess I should say that I long for the obscurity I undoubtedly deserve," he said. "What has been overlooked is the tremendous job I did from July, 1962, through December, 1963. I saved the business. Somebody later asked me, was I prepared for what happened [the revolt]? The answer is, was the captain of the *Titanic* prepared for hitting the iceberg?"

But Emerson had not been summoned to Philadelphia to witness the casting out of Joe Culligan. He was apparently expected to spend most of the afternoon waiting. "I waded up and down through that pool in the lobby," he said later, "until I got something stuck between my toes, so I had to come out." He had wandered off, then, across the street to look at the Liberty Bell—"Biggest damn crack I ever saw in a Liberty Bell." All that afternoon, I waited for Emerson to call, and every time I left my office, I told my secretary where to find me. At six o'clock, I was at the far end of the editorial floor, trying to get a layout redesigned, when my secretary finally came bouncing down the corridor and gasped, "It's the phone call you've been waiting for." As I hurried back to my office, Bill Ewald grabbed me by the arm and gleefully said, "Emerson's the editor—nobody else knows." In my office, I found that Mooney had taken over the phone, guffawing, with another secretary standing in the doorway. I chased everyone out and shut the door.

"Tell me everything," I said.

"Well, you talk about the Mistake of the Month Club," Emerson said, "it certainly has been a day, and a curiously structured sort of day, they've got me structured right into the 1964 statement of losses."

"Listen," I said, "you haven't told me anything yet. What the hell is going on?"

"Well, it seems I'm the new editor."

"Really?"

"Absolutely."

"Is that official? Is it being announced?" I still didn't trust anybody.

"Yes, they're drawing up a release right now as Clifford's announcement."

"Well, damn, congratulations!"

Outside in the corridor, as I went back to settle the layout problem, the only question I kept encountering was: "Is it true?" Yes, it was true. Only as I passed Ewald did I burst out with what I felt: "We've won!"

The next day, the celebrations started at about ten in the morning and continued all afternoon. There were speeches, telephone calls, photographs, and a vast lunch, organized by Mooney, for all the twenty-one editors who had been at that apocalyptic meeting five months ago when Emerson had resigned in front of Clifford. There was champagne and shouting, and Emerson told stories all day long, until his wife Lucy came to fetch him off to a cocktail party at eight that night. She had already prepared their house in Larchmont with balloons floating from the trees, and a giant sign that said, "Now doesn't he think he's really *it*?" As they left the Post building, Emerson carried a vast horseshoe of carnations that all the editors had presented to him that morning. It bore a bright red ribbon that said "CONGRATULATIONS" and a small white card that said:

From all the crew members
of the Titanic

13

"The time for change is now"

As soon as Emerson became editor, I naturally replaced him as managing editor. This was duly announced in the *Times,* and I got my own share of congratulations. One came from the first editor I had ever worked for, on the Brattleboro *Reformer,* in Vermont, twenty-one summers before. The nicest one came from the late Filmore Calhoun at *Newsweek,* who, remembering that my failure to become foreign editor had been due to my alleged lack of panache, now sent me a telegram saying, "All of us here covered with our own panache." The strangest one came sealed within a series of envelopes, all marked confidential. "Congratulations on your promotion to M.E.," said Clay Blair. "I hope it lasts beyond July. Or whenever the turning point is. Beginning with the October 30 CPC board meeting, when I was fired (following suspension) I urged, at board meetings (right into December), your appointment as *editor.* This probably hurt you now that I think back on it. If the magazine is to be salvaged, you will have to do it."

For a few days, it was pleasant to think that everything would now be all right. In actual fact, however, we were still in terrible trouble. There had been a nominal first-quarter profit of $36,000, but this failed to satisfy the stockholders at the annual meeting on April 20. They listened restively while Mac Clifford read a formal statement on the prospects for the future. "Your new management . . . has moved aggressively to reshape the editorial excellence of Curtis publications, sell vigorously the magazines and other products and services marketed by Curtis, intensify cost reduction and improve finances. . . ." Then, when Maurice Poppei tried to present a series of charts illustrating the high readership of Curtis magazines, the stockholders began to protest. "This is all double-talk," one of them shouted. "It doesn't mean anything." Clifford responded by threatening the stockholder with expulsion.

It is traditional, in the mythology of American business, to regard the common stockholder as the ordinary citizen of the commercial community. Once a year, at a kind of town meeting, the stockholder is invited to the corporation's headquarters and asked for his opinions and his votes. Thus, in theory, the corporation remains a democratic institution. It is pleasant to imagine corporation presidents trembling at the need to answer their accusers' questions—and managements do indeed tend to avoid trouble during the weeks immediately preceding the meeting—but the realities of stockholder meetings have little to do with the theory. They are, in the words of A. A. Berle, "a kind of ancient, meaningless ritual." Of the thousands of Curtis stockholders, only about two hundred appeared in Philadelphia, and most of those who spoke up were professional critics who make it their business to harass corporate executives. It is important to remember, moreover, that the stockholders not only have little knowledge of how a corporation runs (in this area, they are supposedly represented by the board of directors, and we have already seen how that system works), but they also have little concern for how well (as distinct from how profitably) the corporation does its work. "Forgive me for saying it," said one stockholder who was criticizing the extravagance of executive salaries at that 1965 meeting, "but we want profits." If this is democracy, it is a democracy in which the voters judge their rulers entirely on one issue, the rate of government handouts.

And if the stockholders' criticisms were supposed to change Mac Clifford's system of management, they achieved no such effect. Clifford not only had no plan to make a profit in 1965; he admitted as much. When a stockholder named Philip Kalodner asked whether the *Post* would lose money in the coming year, Clifford simply said, "Yes." Kalodner, a Philadelphia lawyer who would someday find himself president of Curtis, then asked whether Clifford had any estimate on how much the entire company might lose. "I do have, but I'm not publicizing that figure," Clifford answered. Clifford did have proxy votes from the big stockholders, however, and every measure that required a vote was decided in management's favor by a majority of a million votes or more. The only consolation for the critics came from the rhetoric of Bill Emerson, who told the unhappy stockholders, "For years we've heard nothing but the snap of jackals and seen nothing but buzzards overhead. Now it's time to get a crop in."

With so little hope of profits, it seemed inevitable that the *Post*, or all the Curtis magazines, or the entire company, would be sold or liquidated. And by a peculiarity of the tax laws, our losses had become one of our greatest assets. For if we merged with a profitable company, our new owners could deduct all our losses of the past five years—more than $40 million at this point—from their own income. This phantasmagorical possibility was called our "tax loss carry-forward," and since it enabled us to bring to any merger negotiation a potential tax benefit worth millions of dollars in cash, we heard flickering rumors of such mergers for month after month. One day, for instance, an editor came to me and said he had heard that Curtis had just been sold to McCall's. "And this is past tense, man," he said. "It's already over, and tomorrow we'll be looking for jobs." Another time, we were supposedly being bought by the Encyclopaedia Britannica, or by Philip Morris, or by two brothers in Ohio. In May, Patrick J. Frawley, chairman of Eversharp, Inc. and a well-known supporter of ultraconservative causes, said publicly that he was "interested" in buying the *Post*, which filled us all with dread. We knew that Clifford himself was extremely conservative, and so, we thought, he might consider it quite patriotic to turn the *Post* into a right-wing propaganda organ. But nothing ever came of Frawley's interest.

The worst effect of these constant rumors was a constant erosion of staff morale, which took the specific form of people seeking and getting other jobs. Editors are a fairly volatile lot, and it is standard to shift from one place to another every few years. What keeps good editors in one place for a time is not just money but the feeling that a newspaper or magazine is worth publishing, and that it is moving forward. When it becomes stagnant, the editors begin to look around for better things. The core of the *Post* staff held together throughout these last years, but in the trying days of 1965 there was a crumbling at the edges. One editor, whom we had hired from *True*, was offered several thousand dollars more to come back again as executive editor, an offer we could not match. Our chief Asian correspondent now got a better offer from the Washington *Post*. The photography editor went to Los Angeles to edit *West*, and one of his best assistants went to *Life*. People like this were not easy to replace, and now, in our depleted state, we had very little time even to look for the replacements.

The atmosphere of failure was not just a matter of rumor. The first-quarter profit of $36,000 proved as temporary and as meaningless as one might have predicted. In the second quarter, and thus for the first half of the year, Curtis lost more than $2.5 million.

The newspapers were getting a little tired of us by now, however, and when newspapermen get tired, power shifts to the public-relations man. How could a public-relations man make the loss of almost a million dollars a month look good? He could send out an announcement that the loss was 34 percent less than last year's second-quarter deficit of $3.9 million. Would anybody take such an announcement at face value? The *Times* headline the next day said: "CURTIS REDUCES ITS LOSS BY 34% ."

At times of loss and confusion, a corporation often turns to consultants, and that was how we got so deeply involved with A. Edward Miller.

In theory, it seems to me, no well-managed corporation should ever employ a consultant for anything but highly technical problems, since the arrival of a consultant contradicts the very idea that the corporation is well managed. In all its major areas of activity, the corporation should have its own executives at work. Ideally, it should even have a few ministers without portfolio, executives of such versatility that they can be assigned to whatever new problems arise.

If this were true, there would be very few consultants. Since there are a great many of them, it follows that, if the theory is true, there are a great many badly managed corporations. For the essential premise of the consultant is that he can analyze a problem better than the corporation's own managers, and that he can offer a solution that never occurred to any of them. The secondary premise is that the consultant is so much better at problem-solving than the regular executive that it is not worth the consultant's time to stay with any one corporation, since there are so many others that need and will pay for his part-time services.

It was perhaps not Ed Miller's destiny to be a consultant. His background did not indicate a predilection for part-time work. On the contrary, it implied a man completely dedicated to the commercial application of statistical research. A. Edward Miller was twenty-five years old when he began doing market research for Time Inc., and after sixteen years at *Life,* where he rose to the position of assistant to the publisher, and five years at *McCall's,* where he was the publisher, he was still essentially a votary in the religion of statistics. He taught a course in market-research psychology at City College, and he took part in such organizations as the Market Research Council, the American Marketing Association, and the American Statistical Association.

You imagine, I suspect, a human computer, someone thin-lipped, gaunt, and bloodless, but Ed Miller was the very opposite of that. He was large, soft, and corpulent, with a mottled complexion and a rather high voice. He was nervous, vulnerable, defensive, and rather shy. If you had to guess what course he taught in college, you would not guess statistics; you would guess something more nebulous, like sociology. He wanted to be liked, as we all do, and so, to illustrate his empathy with literary people, he once told us that his wife, "who teaches English," had thus and such an opinion on thus and such a short story in the *Post*. The look I gave him must have been a cold one, as I recalled George Horace Lorimer's splendid answer to a similar comment from Cyrus H. K. Curtis: "I'm not editing the *Saturday Evening Post* for your wife." To be liked, professionally if not personally, the sensible method was to ask people what they thought of you, and what they wanted of you. If you asked enough people, and analyzed their responses accurately, and then gave them what they wanted, you would be not only popular but rich as well. Wasn't that the secret of television? And of the great industries? And of successful presidential campaigns?

It is important to remember, because of what followed, that Ed Miller was not just a time-study expert who had come to survey our operations. According to the *New York Times*, he had been offered the presidency of Curtis, and although that prospect had evaporated, we still looked to him, in our innocence, as a possible savior. While Mac Clifford was talking about budget cuts, Miller was talking about "investing money in editorial quality." We innocents did not realize that budget-cutting is an attribute of people who have to meet payrolls, and that the ones who talk about investing in quality are generally the consultants. By now Curtis had acquired consultants on everything from public relations to accounting to legal problems, so it was quite in order for Miller to become the consultant on editorial questions. His fee for this was reputed to be $1,000 a day, the equivalent of the salaries of ten or fifteen senior editors, or, to put it another way, the equivalent of about one-quarter of our entire editorial payroll. On the other hand, if any consultant could have solved the basic economic problems at Curtis, he would have been cheap at almost any price.

Miller's first step was reasonable enough, in terms of the way consultants work. He asked the editor of each Curtis magazine to write an outline of what his magazine was, what its audience was, what its purpose was, and where it was going. Schanche, as we have seen, took several days off from work and wrote a manifesto that suited its purpose brilliantly. Dave Thomas, on the other hand, had never done so. As for Emerson, he just dithered and worried, writing several drafts and throwing them away. Perhaps it was at this point that Emerson began iriritably referring to the rotund consultant as "Flubber." It is· not an easy task, however, to explain one's existence, and to foretell one's future, nor does it have much to do with editing magazines; it is largely an exercise in publicity and self-promotion. Each time Emerson showed me a new draft of the required blueprint, I said it was terrible. Then I myself wrote a draft, which Emerson showed to Mooney, and Mooney said that was terrible too. "The only effect this blueprint will have," Mooney said, "will be to convince them that they need a whole new editorial staff."

So we did nothing, and while we did nothing, we drifted into the Luce crisis. At least a year earlier, Blair had assigned John Kobler, an editor-at-large, to write a long article about Henry Luce and all his magazines. I suspect that Blair wanted an "exposé" of his former employer, but he never asked for one, and never really gave any specific instructions of any kind. Since I was in charge of articles, I undertook the job of shepherding Kobler through his assignment. We had innumerable lunches and conferences, and the 25,000-word manuscript that finally emerged was, while scarcely profound, an interesting and unprecedented account of the press lord's rise to power. We scheduled it for publication in November of 1964. But soon we got urgent requests, through Sherrod, to postpone it "for a couple of weeks," along with hints that high officials of Time Inc. were involved in the sale or merger of Curtis. Despite the outcries from Kobler—"We may go under," said he, a querulous and rather turkey-like figure, "but we can at least go with *honor*"—Emerson agreed to the postponement. But we promptly rescheduled it for the first issue of 1965. "That has a certain symbolic significance," Emerson said. On December 4, however, Emerson got a brief note from Miller saying that "for reasons I don't have time to explain, I wouldn't count on running the Luce story."

Blair had said it would be like this—the budget-cutting, the piece-meal dismissals, the interference in editorial decisions—and this seemed a point on which to resist. " 'For reasons I don't have time to explain,' " Emerson quoted. "Well, f—— him!" Emerson telephoned Miller to say that we were going to run the Luce article on schedule, and that if he had any objections, he had better find time to state them now. Miller offered a number of ambiguous criticisms. He said the article was "too long." He said it was "wrong in places." He said there was "a question of taste" in criticizing other magazines. He said he would discuss the problem over the weekend with a number of other people. Emerson then called Clifford, reported the conversation with Miller, and said that if there were any "discussions" over the weekend, he wanted to take part in them.

The next morning, a Saturday, I telephoned Emerson at home to find out what had happened. Lucy Emerson said that her husband had already gone in to New York to start fighting the battle. "Clifford called at eleven o'clock last night," she said, "and Bill was being his most persuasive when the chair collapsed underneath him, and he fell right on the floor, and there he was, in the middle of all the debris, but with the telephone still clutched in his hand, and still talking." So they sat around a table all that Saturday—Clifford, Emerson, and Miller—arguing over every comma in this book-length manuscript. They argued over the accuracy of this and the source of that, and yet they never mentioned the real problems. They never mentioned, in other words, our dubious corporate involvement with Time Inc., which appeared to be concerned at the prospects of Curtis's going bankrupt. They never discussed the question of James A. Linen, president of Time Inc., agreeing to give Mac Clifford some of the Time Inc. printing and circulation business, and also some of the names on the Time Inc. subscription lists—all of these offerings being worth several hundred thousand dollars, and enabling Linen to say later that he had "saved" Curtis. Did they discuss, for that matter, the reports that Linen was one of those who had urged Miller, one of his ex-employees, to take the presidency of Curtis?

It was scarcely an ideal time for us to be publishing an article about Henry Luce, but at seven o'clock that night, Emerson called me, said he had resigned approximately every hour on the hour, and concluded: "Well, we're going to have to recheck a few things, and clear a few things with the lawyers, but we're going to run it." So we did, and among the various people who liked it was Henry Luce. And a month or so later, when we were in some new trouble, Mooney remarked: "That Luce piece is saving Emerson. He had to fight for his life to get it into print, but now it's saving him. Whenever anybody asks what the *Post* is doing, or where it's going, all he has to do is to point to the Luce piece and say: 'There! That!'"

Despite these conflicts, Emerson still hoped to conciliate Miller, to win him to our side as Blair had once won Kantor, and so he invited Miller to come to our regular Friday staff meetings, bringing his new statistics with him. For Miller's second step as a consultant, after asking the editors to tell him their plans for the future, had been the inauguration of a series of readership studies. After declining the presidency of Curtis, Miller had become president of the polling firm of Alfred Politz Research, Inc., so it was only natural that he should recommend, as a consultant to Curtis, a Politz poll of the readers. Since Clifford had misgivings about Miller and all his expensive theories, it was just as natural that he should demand that this polling be kept to an absolute minimum.

The compromise that resulted, known as "the Miller poll," was a statistical marvel. Every fortnight, a week after the *Post* had been delivered to the subscribers, the Politz interviewers appeared at the home of two hundred *Post* subscribers and began asking them about the last issue. These two hundred subscribers lived in four small cities in various parts of the country—Hartford, Connecticut, for example, was the representative of the Northeast—and the polltakers then subdivided them by sex, age, education, and income. They were asked (as they had been when Hibbs conducted similar polls—Blair had ordered them discontinued) about every single item in the magazine—whether they had read all of it, part of it, or none, and whether they considered it excellent, good, fair, or poor. In so small a sampling, obviously, a variation of two or three housewives in Hartford would provide huge variations in the so-called "readership," but Miller now presented these statistics to us with infinite condescension. We, in producing the magazine, had merely guessed, while he, in reporting the results, offered scientific conclusions. We listened in amazement, occasionally trying to refute one result or another, but always failing. Miller's standard answer was that if there were inaccuracies in this sampling, he could rectify them with a larger sampling, but that was too expensive at present. In the meantime, he said, this small sampling was "relatively" accurate.

And, of course, it was true. If we did not accept what Ed Miller's wife thought about a short story, how many of us accepted the views of our own wives as an expression of "the woman's viewpoint"? How many of the country's editors, for that matter, listen mainly to their friends and neighbors and relatives and then consider the results a sampling of "public opinion"? How many, if they heard the same opinion echoed by twenty or thirty acquaintances, would consider this an example of "what the people are talking about"? How many editors, in short, ever hear the opinions of two hundred people on whether some story they published was any good—or on any other question?

So even while we protested the inaccuracy of Miller's polls, we had the opportunity to learn something about our work, about what effect we had on those mythical readers whom we liked to consider our reason for publishing a magazine. At the very least, we could see patterns, over the course of several months, in what these subscribers read and what they considered "excellent." We learned, first, that the readers were surprisingly conscientious, and quite willing to devote some time to their reading. Aside from cartoons, which didn't really count, these readers favored the long and serious articles, the articles that promised to tell them something important that they hadn't known before. Specifically, they read the lead articles, and they read those long projects that Blair had christened "big acts." The profile of Luce, for example, was almost twenty thousand words long in its final form, and on a somewhat special subject, but the subscribers read it and liked it. They read and liked those "problem" pieces— Mafia influence in the Bahamas, scandals in housing for old people, a new program for teaching slum children to read.

On the other hand, they did not read most of the lighter material that we had put into the magazine primarily on the theory that people wanted some entertainment. They did not read fiction, for example— good stories and bad stories, sophisticated and unsophisticated, all got ratings between 10 and 20 percent. Similarly, because some people had said the magazine was too gloomy and problem-ridden, we had inaugurated a humor column, to which we devoted a great deal of time and effort and money, but the readers didn't read it. And because some people said our articles were too long, we made a great effort to publish what we called "compacts"—articles of only two thousand words, complete on one two-page spread—but the polls showed that the readers didn't read them and didn't like them.

It would be possible, of course, to argue simply that we did these things badly, that our fiction was bad fiction and our humor columns weren't funny. Or one could argue that our readers were square and old-fashioned. Or that such limited polls provided no accurate measurement of anything at all. But I myself found the polls, though erratic, rather satisfying. It seemed to me that our readers gauged us quite accurately, that they liked what we liked, that they shrugged off all the trivia we offered them, that they wanted the best we could give them, and when they got it, they appreciated it. In principle, then, the Miller polls generally confirmed our main theories on how to edit a magazine.

What we failed to realize, however, is that people do not spend thousands of dollars just to confirm that everything is all right, and that the purpose of statistical research is not just to support the status quo. On the contrary, the purpose is to provide a quasi-scientific basis on which to make changes. If statistical surveys showed that 80 percent of the *Post*'s readers never finished a single short story, then—then Ed Miller, having made those statistical surveys, asked us the inevitable question: Why did the *Post* continue to publish fiction? It was a difficult question, and most of the answers we offered were hopelessly unscientific. We argued in terms of tradition, since the *Post* had published fiction for generations; we argued in terms of image, since fiction helped to make us different from *Life* and *Look;* we argued in terms of intangible values, since fiction provides a perception of the world that we don't get from articles. But finally, we had to fall back on the most impractical argument, and the only correct one—we published fiction because we wanted to publish fiction, because we felt we ought to publish fiction, and because we liked to publish fiction, and that was all there was to it.

The statistician recoils in the face of unscientific vehemence, but consultants cannot abandon the field simply because they are misunderstood. If we must publish fiction, then why couldn't we publish more popular fiction? "Wouldn't it be a good idea?" Ed Miller asked, "if we could get some of the scripts of *Bonanza* from NBC and get somebody to convert them into short stories?" We looked at him, Emerson and I, like thunderstruck cattle on one of those *Bonanza* shows. "No," one of us finally said, "it really wouldn't be a good idea." "But those are stories of proven popularity," Miller said.

Miller, it turned out, had lots of ideas. One day, he came and said that he had been at a cocktail party with Herman Wouk, and he thought we should make a large bid for Wouk's next novel. Had he read it? No. Was the manuscript available for reading? No. Then perhaps it would be better to wait. Another day, Miller noted that President Johnson had suggested an exchange of TV speeches by the White House and the Kremlin. Miller sent Emerson a memo arguing that this was unfair to magazines and proposing that the *Post* offer its pages to both capitals for written statements of policy by the two leaders.

It is difficult to keep saying "No" without acquiring a reputation for being negative, or for lacking imagination, and Emerson periodically worked himself up into paroxysms of rhetorical intrigue in his efforts to turn aside this constant flow of proposals. But when he asked me for advice and help, I could only resort to my old argument: Just say "No."

My own poll, of myself: In the first few months of 1965, after Kobler's piece on Luce, we published Ed Linn's excellent article on the Black Muslims, Roger Kahn's excellent article on the Mark Fein murder case, Harold Martin's excellent article on the Protestant ministry, Lewis Lapham's excellent article on a Broadway flop, Bill Heinz's excellent article on the Selma March, and Dick Armstrong's excellent article on the New Left, the first such article in any major magazine. And also a series of good short stories by Frank O'Connor, Shirley Jackson, William Saroyan, V. S. Naipaul, Stanley Elkin, Evan Connell, Thomas Berger, and Warren Miller. There never was such a magazine—but the Curtis Publishing Company still had no plan to avoid bankruptcy.

Early in June, when Emerson was off in Chicago to sell more ads, I got a telephone call from Mac Clifford. This was the first time we had spoken, I think, since the stormy meeting that followed Clifford's firing of Norman Ritter the previous fall. It would be easy to pretend that one takes such a call with nonchalance because it is easy to tell lies. In fact, one discovers, on trying to say hello into the telephone, that one has a scratchy feeling in the throat.

Clifford, to my surprise, tried to be as amiable as he could be. He inquired about my health, and about the general state of things.

"The reason I'm calling, actually," he said, "is this meeting you fellows had last Friday—"

"What meeting?" I said.

"Well, wasn't there some kind of meeting?" Clifford asked. "You and the other editors? Ed Miller must have been there too."

"Oh, that," I said, having thought he meant some new conspiracy. "That's just the regular staff meeting. We have that every week, and Miller wanted to come, so Emerson said okay."

"Well, what really happened at this meeting? Wasn't there a lot of criticism of the *Post*?"

"I guess so, but there always is," I said. "That's what the meetings are for, so we can all critique the magazine, see what we're doing right or wrong, deal with anybody's questions or complaints."

"I see," he said, but I suspected that he didn't see.

"It wasn't rebellious, if that's what you mean," I said.

"No, it isn't that," Clifford said. "Tell me this, frankly: Do you think the *Post* would be better off under a different editor?"

"No," I said promptly, "I don't."

"Well, tell me this: Are Miller's polls any use to you?"

"Oh, some, but it's such a small sampling that you can't really trust the figures very much, and the questions are so limited that they don't really tell you a lot."

"I see," Clifford said again. "Look, I'll tell you why I called. I've got a long memo here from Miller, saying that you all had this meeting when Emerson was away, and that you all criticized the *Post* and said it was no good, so I'm just trying to get the sense of the meeting, what the atmosphere really was."

"Miller must have got it all wrong," I said. "Sure we criticized the *Post*, but the day we stop doing that we'll be dead. We don't have any real trouble here, except that the budget's awfully tight, and we said that to Miller too, but we're basically okay, and the *Post*'s okay."

"Well, good, that's all I wanted to know," Clifford said. "I appreciate your help, and I'll show you a copy of Miller's memo the next time I'm in New York."

As soon as Emerson got back the following day, I told him about Clifford's call, and he was outraged. He tried to call Clifford immediately, but Clifford was busy at the monthly board meeting. When Emerson finally reached him, Clifford was cordial but secretive. "Otto gave me all the information I needed," he said, and he would give no details of what was in Miller's memo. It was later that day, and from G. B. McCombs, that we heard that Miller's memo was "a strong personal attack on Emerson," and that the board was much concerned.

The following week, a certain number of issues became clearer when Clifford, Emerson, and Sherrod all had lunch together. Sherrod, to whom Clifford had given the vague title of vice president and "editorial coordinator," had been in consultation with Miller, and now he abandoned his former claim to neutrality. He denounced all of us, according to Emerson, declaring specifically that I was "narrow" and "despotic," and that Emerson was to blame for letting me "tyrannize" him and "ruin the magazine." It also turned out that Sherrod was to speak before the board the very next day on the subject of the Miller report. Emerson demanded the right to speak at the same board meeting, and when this was refused, he insisted that it be made clear that Sherrod did not speak for him or the editors. "You're the enemy now," he told Sherrod. "You're the antagonist."

The most specific result of the lunch was that Emerson finally obtained from Clifford a copy of the famous Miller report. It was a relentless indictment of Emerson, and, more generally, all the editors and publishers:

In my opinion The Saturday Evening Post . . . is not in its present form a magazine that is editorially capable of attaining the success we are struggling to achieve. We have done a number of editorial readership studies. We have made comparisons with the Post in the 1957–61 period when the Post was already on its extended downtrend. The Post—to oversimplify—is providing the reader with one, possibly two worthwhile articles in each issue and very little else. . . .

The reasons for these inadequacies are simply lack of skill and experience and judgment on the part of the editors. I have no doubt that they are working hard and conscientiously, but there are basic elements of taste, judgment and planning which simply do not exist and in my opinion will not develop. . . . I have discussed these matters quite directly with the editors and there appears to be a slow recognition of the brutal facts. . . . A meeting I held with the editors on May 28th was the most revealing of all. In Bill Emerson's absence there was a fairly widespread agreement that this seventh issue of the year which we had just analyzed and discussed was another mediocrity. Again for the seventh time there was a plea for a need for creativity, imagination, spark, freshness, all of which was completely lacking. . . .

Please treat these remarks confidentially because if they are reported back to the editors it will destroy my ability to be effective with them. At the moment I am the only real link to the editors. I think I have provided them a measure of inspiration. I think they are trying to do a better job so that they can get better "Milleratings." I do not believe the present editors and the present budgets will permit any significant change or improvement. I believe the funeral procession has been slowed down but it continues its inexorable path to the grave. . . .

WHAT DO WE DO ABOUT ALL THIS?

I would urge that we hire a new editor for the Post. As you know, we have developed a few candidates—all superior to the present editors in my opinion. Eric Sevareid would in my judgment have made a great editor for the Post. There are others who could do a job that is superior to what is now being done. It seems to me that this need is urgent and basic and should not be postponed any longer. Bill Emerson while a delightful guy is simply not doing the editorial job. There is need for new management on the publishing side. . . . I respect the need for a period of stability but I believe the time for change is now.

Our first reaction—Emerson's, Ballew's, McKinney's, mine—was indignation, an angry desire to answer back to Miller. He had misunderstood everything—the magazine, its editors, our meetings, his own statistics. But the more immediate problem was that Sherrod was going to address the board on this matter the next day. Ballew was determined to try to prevent him, but Sherrod proved elusive. His wife said he was at his office; his office said he was out. Emerson had guests coming for dinner, but as he began worrying about whether to ask Lucy to delay the meal, Ballew's promotion people suddenly announced that a documentary movie about Emerson would have to be made this very evening or they would lose, for some unexplained reason, $10,000 in production costs. There was no script prepared either. So at 6 P.M., just as the air conditioning went off on this July evening, the spotlights went on, and, with Ballew still trying to reach Sherrod, and Lucy wondering what to do about her dinner, Emerson had to start improvising a movie about the historic qualities of Ben Franklin's magazine.

In actual fact, Sherrod spoke rather mildly before the board, and in retrospect it seems quite possible that Miller's report was a dead issue the minute he submitted it. For what we failed to realize at the time was the depth of Clifford's hostility toward his celebrated consultant. We failed to remember that Miller had once been chosen as president of Curtis, and that Clifford had received the job only by default. If Miller had then decided to become a consultant, it was presumably not at the request of Mac Clifford.

We failed to realize, finally, that Clifford considered it his personal decision to make Emerson the editor and that any challenge to this decision was a challenge to him. "We're in this together," Clifford later told Emerson. "I put you in that job." It would be nice to think that this decision had been made entirely on merit, but there were other elements too. Perhaps Clifford really did like Emerson, or perhaps Emerson was simply the kind of editor he wanted. Royal courts have gone out of style, but cronyism is still a recognized form of government, as we saw during the administrations of both Eisenhower and Johnson, and Emerson knew quite well how to play the role of joke-telling crony. Indeed, he used every trick he had, including some that were a little unpleasant. After one of his critical meetings with Clifford, for example, he reported a rather nasty joke he had told. "And Clifford laughed and laughed," Emerson said. "I know all his little prejudices, and I don't mind playing on them."

For some reason that I never understood, our good issues came in seasonal cycles, year after year—early fall, late winter, early summer. And so, in this difficult season, we finally began to encounter a little luck.

We had decided to do a cover story on Sean Connery as James Bond for the July 17 issue. On the deadline day, Emerson was away, and Asger Jerrild was sick, and the cover illustration was so awful that I could only tell the art editor, Frank Kilker, to throw it away and do the best he could with whatever photographs he could find. In a crisis, Kilker could scramble, and by the end of the day he had produced a portrait of Connery, which he superimposed on a series of little pictures that looked like film strips, showing girls, boats, guns, and all the rest of the mystic paraphernalia that caused the popularity of the Bond movies. After we sent the cover to press, we were dismayed to see *Look* come out a week ahead of us with a cover of Connery lying on a beach, but that made it all the more impressive that our Bond cover outsold theirs by 100,000 copies.

Our next cover was a photograph of the tiresome Fischer quintuplets (a story we had bought with a long-term contract during the Blair days), but even though the quints were all coming down with colds, the photographer had organized them and some baby ducks into a charming portrait. That, combined with Tad Szulc's critical report on the Dominican invasion, gave us our second sellout in a row.

And then, with all the cards falling in our favor, we stumbled into that summer's Kennedy sweepstakes. The most valuable of the Kennedy memoirs, it had been generally agreed, would be those of Theodore Sorensen, and *Look* had won that bidding with an offer of $150,000. We ourselves had decided, back in the Blair days, that the story we wanted was that of Arthur Schlesinger, and so we had telephoned him with an offer of $50,000. His answer was a dry laugh, since he had already received a bid of more than $100,000 from *Life*. We then withdrew from the whole sweepstakes—until, at the very last minute, we received a copy of a tearful little memoir by Kennedy's devoted secretary, Mrs. Evelyn Lincoln. It had already been turned down by all the other big magazines, but that was because the other big magazines had failed to perceive its maudlin virtues. What none of them had realized was that Mrs. Lincoln had observed Kennedy a lot longer and a lot more closely than most of his entourage, and although she might have nothing more to say than that she picked up Kennedy's socks after his nap on the White House sofa, that was all the average reader needed. Very few people really cared about the political revelations in these memoirs—who can now remember the details in any of them?—for what everyone wanted was simply a retelling of the legend, a sense of reunion with the fallen prince, and thus a momentary feeling that he was not really dead. So for $15,000 we bought Mrs. Lincoln's little book, and, with a handsome cover portrait of Kennedy by Karsh, we outsold both *Life* and *Look*.

It may seem crass to speak so commercially of these things, but the competition was, after all, a commercial competition, and we were fighting for our lives. And now, with three sellout issues in a row, some strange things began to happen. John Mack Carter, who had rejected the Evelyn Lincoln story at both *McCall's* and the *Journal*, dropped in to compliment us on our success. Bob Sherrod came by to tell us what good issues we were publishing these days. And there even came a letter from Ed Miller, of all people, praising Emerson for the improvement in newsstand sales. The statistical method of making judgments had finally become epidemic.

I do not know how many thousands of dollars were ultimately paid to Miller and Newton Minow and all the other consultants, or what real effects their advice ever had. A lot of the former, I suspect, and relatively little of the latter. For the consultant system requires not only a management that is uncertain of what it is doing but a management willing to be told what to do. That was not Mac Clifford's style. He was willing to listen to supposedly expert opinion, but not to accept it as a higher authority. He was, by God, the president, the king, the boss, and if he made mistakes, they would be his own mistakes. And if anyone thought Bill Emerson was one of those mistakes, then so be it.

14

"You have to send a train through there somewhere"

One of Mac Clifford's first moves on becoming president of the Curtis Publishing Company was to seize the large corner office on the editorial floor, which Clay Blair had built, at great expense, for himself. It was neither a very attractive office nor a very efficient one—the walls lined with half-empty bookshelves looked gloomy rather than scholarly, and the heavy blue plush conference chairs were designed for receiving visitors rather than getting work done—but Blair had insisted on all the executive perquisites: a private bathroom, a separate chamber for his secretary, a built-in color TV set, a refrigerator, and the mahogany doors that allegedly cost $500 apiece. Here, while the workmen were still laboring to install the imperial ornaments, Blair had convened us in the previous autumn to join in overthrowing Culligan, and here we had all signed the great manifesto. When Blair's downfall left this executive suite empty, Mac Clifford may have felt about it some of the loathing that a man might feel after capturing a vampire cavern. Somewhere in these dark and forbidding rooms, the cursed spirit of editorial rebellion could be staked through the heart and put forever to rest.

Having claimed Blair's office as his own, Clifford went to unusual trouble to make some use of it. His main headquarters was still in Philadelphia, and the only space available for his executive conferences was on our thirty-second floor, in the eyrie originally designed for Culligan and his vice presidents. Still, Clifford tried his best to occupy our fourth floor, bustling in at the unearthly hour of 8:30, a tiny figure determined to assert his authority but confounded by the emptiness of the long corridor of editorial offices. From then on, as the morning hours passed and the other offices gradually filled, Clifford remained trapped inside his citadel, like some Chinese warlord surrounded by the hostile peasantry. When he finally left, marching out through the corridor, a stiff smile fixed on his face, no one spoke to him, or even looked at him.

After a time, Clifford came less and less frequently to Blair's haunted office, and in the fall, at my urging, Emerson finally got him to give it up. And just as no haunted house can withstand the invasion of a half-dozen children, so Blair's gloomy office gave itself up to Emerson. He filled the refrigerator with beer and wine and cheese, and the empty bookshelves with whatever he could find. He hung on the wall a gigantic Norman Rockwell painting, once a *Post* cover, of an election headquarters bedecked with streamers saying "Win with Casey," and, in one corner, the defeated and exhausted figure of Casey himself, sitting on the floor. Emerson brought in his own pictures too, photographs of himself receiving awards from various Southern institutions, and he brought his toys, a Bahamian taxi horn that he squawked at people when their backs were turned, a gigantically long-necked musical instrument that was called a Polkalele, and a tiger that growled and crawled around on his desk whenever he pushed a button. As for the rest of us, we all moved up one step, somewhat more quietly. I took over Emerson's old office, Don McKinney took mine, and so, a year after Blair's insurrection, the editors finally regained possession of the editorial floor.

I have said too little about these editors, perhaps, for my purpose is to describe the decline of an organization rather than the editing of a magazine, and the two stories are quite different. At the top levels of Curtis, there was constant controversy and turmoil—four presidents in seven years—but on the staff of the *Post*, the key editors who had arrived with Emerson in the fall of 1962 were still there when the last issue went to press early in 1969.

The most notable of these was Don McKinney, a stocky man of about forty, with very short gray hair and a rather compact face (Emerson used to make fun of him as "Beebee-eyes"). He had wasted a number of his early years at jobs like writing comic books (and even serving as an assistant to a marriage broker) before he finally settled down as an articles editor at *True*. He worked there for eight years, learning every aspect of nonfiction magazine editing, not only who all the writers were but how to deal with them and get the best work from them. *True* underpaid him grievously, and so when

Schanche began his pirate raid to recruit all the discontented editors in New York, McKinney signed on. As chief articles editor of the *Post*. he was sensible and competent and quick, but his greatest value was his extraordinary good nature. He was genuinely friendly, cheerful, optimistic, utterly without malice, and these characteristics gave him an exceptional advantage in dealing with our ragged regiment of writers. When anybody needed someone to listen to his ideas or his problems, McKinney was unfailingly ready with counsel, sympathy, and even solutions. This was more than just a matter of spreading good will, for writers need a phenomenal amount of shepherding in order to produce the ingredients of a magazine. McKinney was our chief shepherd.

The other editor who played an important part in every issue of the *Post* was Bill Ewald, assistant articles editor, a man as strange and convoluted as McKinney was simple and outgoing. Ewald was also about forty, partly bald and shaped like an egg. He had been trained and developed during eight years at the United Press, where he became the agency's first television critic and columnist, and so, like McKinney, he was quick and professional. But Ewald, fiercely conscious of his plebeian childhood in Brooklyn, now let his aesthetic tastes luxuriate. He filled his apartment with paintings, not the conventional modern but the avant-garde. The most extreme jazz group, the latest style in neckties, the current fad in stock-market investments—whatever was new or unusual, Ewald pursued with the dedication of the obsessed.

Then came the senior editors, among whom there were several of considerable talent and dedication. Tom Congdon and Mike Mooney have already appeared in these pages. Jim Atwater, a lanky, high-strung New Englander whom we had hired from *Time* as a contract writer, became an editor of phenomenal energy and eclecticism; he took charge of sports, adventure, military affairs, and space as a matter of course, and moved easily into politics, religion, education, or civil rights whenever some extra work needed to be done. Dick Lemon, another contract writer, formerly at *Newsweek*, mild and soft-spoken, came into the office and edited articles for a year, when we were short-handed, and proved exceptionally skillful at it. And more: Bob Johnson, a meticulous craftsman and one of the few surviving veterans of the Hibbs regime; David Lyle, the fiercely mustachioed and fiercely independent foreign editor; Bob Poteete, another dedicated craftsman who had come to us from the ruins of the *Herald Tribune;* Jack Nessel, a bright and inquisitive young Californian who had been, and later went back to being, managing editor of *New York*.

What do such men really contribute to a magazine? It is widely believed that magazine editors simply arrive at their offices in the morning, open the mail, pick out the manuscripts they like best, and send them to the printers. Theoretically, it is possible to produce a magazine this way, for New York is full of professional writers and literary agents who will inundate any editor who seems receptive to their ideas, outlines, and manuscripts. But any magazine edited in this way will be a lifeless, lusterless anthology of miscellaneous contributions; on a well-edited magazine, by contrast, the initiative comes largely from the editors themselves.

Ideas, in short, are the first ingredient of a good editor. With a mixture of intelligence, skill, and experience, he can discern what will interest people before they know it themselves. But a story idea by itself is of limited value, and an editor hears every day someone proposing a new report on lobbying in Washington or a profile of a Negro militant. An idea begins to take shape only when a writer has been found, to give it the shape that his imagination dictates, which means, in turn, that an editor must know the special interests and talents of all the best writers in the country. Here, too, though, it is easy to conjure up abstractly interesting assignments—send Norman Mailer to Vietnam; get Truman Capote to interview Greta Garbo—but it is also easy to get the answer that Truman Capote doesn't want to interview Greta Garbo, and Norman Mailer is busy just now. The second ingredient of a good editor, then, is a personal relationship with writers, an understanding of both them and their work, and an ability to guide and encourage them.

There are not nearly enough good writers to fill up all the major magazines, unfortunately, and an editor must accept mediocre work every week in the year just to keep his readers supplied with their regular rations. Helping good writers is interesting and relatively gratifying, but mediocre writers need just as much care and atten- tion—in fact, more. Their egos are just as vulnerable, their insecu- rities just as painful, their need for alimony payments just as demanding, and the only difference lies in their relative lack of talent. They believe themselves entitled to the same freedom as good writers, but the editor must curb their ambitions and revise their stories. The third essential skill, then, is the ability to take a pencil and make a manuscript better. This means that a good editor should also be a good writer—better than many of the men whose work he edits—and yet he must resist the temptation to turn someone else's story into a story of his own. The rule was best formulated by Wolcott Gibbs of *The New Yorker:* "Try to preserve a writer's style, if he is a writer and has a style."

Perhaps I am being too abstract in describing these basic functions of an editor, for no editor, not even a bad one, works according to abstract principles. On the contrary, he tends to think of the needs and interests of his readers in terms of his own needs and interests. Clay Blair, for example, had talked with great passion about improving America, and he seemed to feel a genuine sense of moral purpose in "exposing" such familiar villains as the Mafia and the Teamsters Union. At the same time, his fondness for skin-diving filled him with an equally passionate enthusiasm for assigning teams of underwater photographers to take pictures of murky figures groping for largely mythical treasures buried under the Caribbean. And his strong feelings about what the *Post* should publish applied just as strongly to what the *Post* should not publish. He abhorred the whole subject of homosexuality, for example, and this taboo extended to anyone who was even rumored to be tempted by unnatural practices. Blair's widely varied prejudices were never officially codified, however, and so it was only after I had bought and edited a memoir by Birgit Nilsson that I found Blair was implacably opposed to anything connected with the opera.

Bill Emerson's interests and prejudices were equally unpredictable. For example, he was deeply concerned with religion—he even tithed to the Presbyterian church—but he favored only a certain rather oldfashioned kind of religion. He was profoundly suspicious of radical clergymen who worked in the slums, and the whole God-Is-Dead movement irritated him so much that we never got an article on the subject into print. On the general subject of the Negro rights movement, he struggled through the years in a state of almost total disagreement with his entire staff, for he really believed that Martin Luther King was an irresponsible demagogue, and that the best of Southern sheriffs knew far more than ignorant Yankee police about handling crowds of Negro demonstrators. Our younger editors therefore expected arguments whenever they wanted to assign articles on some new wave of Negro militants, but their expectations represented a misunderstanding of Emerson's point of view. He actually seemed in a way to relish the wildest demands for black power, for that fitted his own image of Negroes at their worst. The only people on whom he adamantly did not want any articles were Indians. Every time the matter came up, he gave the same answer: "They have fleas."

Don McKinney, by contrast, extended his sympathetic interest not only to homosexuals and opera stars, not only to Negro militants and Indians, but to all varieties of people in what he considered interesting situations. Half a dozen times a day, he would send me memoranda proposing stories on guilt-ridden mountain climbers, unhappy circus clowns, art forgers and second-basemen, or some surburban family that had made a home in its living room for a ferocious reptile. Nothing in the world bored him, it seemed, except precisely the subjects that struck me as essential, and so it was left to me to argue for articles on topics like DNA and quasars, the brain drain, the dollar deficit, and the influence of computers on decision-making.

These differences among the editors were a matter not only of subjects but also of approach. Although this may seem relatively unimportant, the story that appears in a magazine generally reflects the editor's choice of a writer and his instructions to that writer. And every editor, of course, believes that his own technique is the best. Clay Blair, for the most part, liked simply to report his inspirations to subordinate editors and then leave the details to them. When a gang of British bandits robbed a mail train of $8 million, for example, he demanded that we assign Agatha Christie to write the story. The fact that this octogenarian lady was not interested in such assignments impressed him as relatively unimportant—any famous English thriller-writer would do as well—and so we spent weeks investigating the availability of people like Graham Greene and Eric Ambler before settling on one of our regular contributors to get the job done.

Emerson, on the other hand, mistrusted the journalistic abilities of celebrated novelists. With his news magazine background, he believed that any competent magazine writer could handle any assignment if only he had enough research reports from other correspondents. Any time he assigned a story, therefore, he began telephoning a whole network of past and present *Post* writers, *Newsweek* stringers, Southern newspapermen, and anyone else he knew who might help deluge his protégé with information. I myself resisted this technique, preferring to pick a writer I trusted and rely on him to do all the reporting he might need. I usually began, however, with a fairly clear idea of the story I wanted, and I would provide the writer with a long memorandum outlining what I expected him to write. To McKinney, my system seemed as constricting as Emerson's system seemed chaotic. His own theory was that a good writer assigned to a good idea should be left free to find—or lose—his own way.

At best, the variety of our interests provided a variety of articles, a variety of styles and tones, but there were inevitably some fierce arguments. The only real quarrel I ever had with Emerson, for example, came after he had received a tip from some fellow Georgian that Martin Luther King's Southern Christian Leadership Conference had been infiltrated by Communists. He urged the story on me, and I urged him to forget it. Soon afterward, I found him in McKinney's office, making a new attempt to arouse support for the story. I told him again that we should leave it alone.

"Are we supposed to be King's *protectors?*" Emerson demanded. "I'm damned if I can see that we have a mandate to keep those people's secrets for them."

"We're not protecting them," I said, "but we don't have a mandate to smear them either."

"We're not going to *smear* them," Emerson retorted. "I just think it's journalistically dishonest to refuse to look into a legitimate story. I'm not making this up, after all. I'm told that the FBI already knows about it. So all we're going to do is raise the question."

By this time, McKinney's head was swiveling to and fro with each argument, as though he were a spectator at a tennis match.

"Even just raising the question is smearing them," I said. "It's like saying, 'Is the State Department infiltrated by Communists?' Once you print the question, it doesn't even matter very much if the answer is no."

"I don't mind," Emerson said doggedly. "I don't mind asking questions. I wouldn't mind asking questions about the Krupps either, for that matter, but I didn't see you hurrying to assign that when I asked about it."

"What have the Krupps got to do with anything, for Christ's sake?" I demanded. "Everybody who knows anything about Europe knows that's a dead dog of a story."

"Well, I just said I don't mind asking questions," Emerson repeated. "So I'm going to ask questions about King."

I was so angry that I immediately assigned an article on the new Ruhr industrialists who were rising to take the place of old dynasties like the Krupps. But though Emerson assigned half a dozen writers to file research reports on Communist infiltration of the civil rights movement, I told everyone whom he tried to involve in the project that I was strongly opposed to the story and would do my best to see that it never ran. And partly because of Emerson's technique of making assignments, the flow of research reports ended up in various folders in various desks. In due time, we published an article by Welles Hangen on "The New Ruhr," but the article on Communists in the civil rights movement was never even written.

The editorial process—it should be clear by now—followed no

easily definable set of rules. My five-year-old son, as a matter of fact, once came to my office to see what I did and later reported to his mother that I really did not work at all. "All he does," he said, "is type and talk to people and look out the window." But the essential element of my work, the story ideas, came from everywhere, from writers, agents, other editors, and sometimes simply from the contemplation of the stolid gray walls of the Lutheran church outside my window. Some ideas were obviously good ones, and a senior editor was promptly put in charge of turning the idea into an article. Others were just as obviously bad—old, dull, trivial, or formless—and they were promptly rejected. Still others underwent a period of purgatory, in which their fate was argued, their purpose redefined. Sometimes, news events might change a bad idea into a good one, or vice versa. And in some cases, the life or death of an idea depended largely on whether it had a strong advocate among the senior editors. Such an advocate could appeal a proposal over my head to Emerson, and sometimes Emerson overruled me. Sometimes, in fact, he approved an assignment not because he liked it but because he believed that any editor who felt strongly enough about an idea should have the freedom to carry it out.

At any given time, we had about one hundred assignments outstanding, enough to fill ten or fifteen issues, but between the idea and the reality, between the conception and the creation, stands the writer. John Hersey was a splendid example of a writer who knew exactly what he wanted to write, a story of the Negro vote-registration campaign in Mississippi, and who produced a story that could be published almost exactly as he wrote it. Evelyn Waugh, at the other extreme, accepted an assignment to write an obituary of Pope John and then proved surprisingly unable to say anything worth publishing at all. I wrote a letter to his agent, requesting certain revisions and expressing disappointment at the lackluster prose; the manuscript came back with the revisions completed and a piteous explanation: "Mr. Waugh says he has done the best he can." Most writers, however, were neither so confident as Hersey nor so helpless as Waugh. One writer accepted my judgment that his natural opening had been buried on page 37 and should be brought up to page one; another balked at a similar judgment and vowed he would never write for the *Post* again; still another telephoned me at home three times on a Sunday afternoon to read me so many different beginnings that I finally told him I would accept whichever one he decided on by himself.

All the senior editors spoke for their favorite projects, but it was up to me finally to decide, subject to Emerson's approval, what we bought and what we published. Every two weeks, I would hold a scheduling conference with McKinney and the heads of other departments (art, fiction, and production) and decide what to put in the next issue, in what position and at what length. From that point on, it was largely up to the senior editors to exert their technical skills— editing the copy for clarity and concision, consulting with the art director on the selection of pictures, making sure that everything had been checked for accuracy and legality, and finally writing titles, subtitles, and captions. Then everything went back through me again before being sent to the printers.

The system worked quite efficiently, but never without arguments at every stage of the process, arguments about which articles to run, arguments about the space to be allotted to pictures, arguments with writers who didn't want their copy cut, and with lawyers who lived in terror of new lawsuits. The most fundamental arguments of all, though, were the continuing and basically irreconcilable arguments about what the *Post* stood for. We had happily abandoned Blair's concept of muckraking in favor of a less partisan kind of journalism —the *Post* was, in fact, the only mass magazine that specialized in sending writers out to report on all aspects of what was happening in the world—but no two editors could ever agree completely on what *was* happening.

These were times of very rapid change, not only in terms of news events but in terms of what could be said about those events. I could remember Blair deciding, with some misgivings, that if writers like John O'Hara insisted on using words like "God" and "damn," then the old *Post* rules against profanity would have to be set aside. Then, as the barriers fell, word by word, we began permitting "sonofabitch," and "bastard," and finally "f——." This may seem ridiculously squeamish nowadays, but the new permissiveness is still not as widespread as many people think. Even in our last year of publication, we regularly got letters from readers who wanted to cancel their subscriptions because the *Post* had become "filthy."

On a more serious level, the evolution of the civil rights movement kept bringing into the news a whole series of more and more militant blacks, and at each stage we argued about how to deal with them. Emerson gave way on Martin Luther King, of course, but he was disturbed when I bought a favorable article on CORE, and he was aghast when I insisted on putting Malcolm X on the cover to announce our publication of his *Autobiography.* But this came to seem a halcyon period when we arrived at the point of assigning articles on people like Rap Brown and Ron Karenga and Eldridge Cleaver. Emerson found them repugnant, and so did I, and so did most of our readers, but the younger editors, notably Ewald, Congdon, and Atwater, kept fighting for a greater involvement in the newest events, and often they won their way.

It was the celebrated youth movement, though, that precipitated the most vehement and irreconcilable arguments. Emerson, who had two adolescent daughters, regarded the whole phenomenon with a mixture of horror and fascination. His commercial instincts, however, convinced him that this was a subject that would sell millions of magazines. We had published our first Beatles cover during the Blair regime, and Blair had insisted that we find a sociologist who would "explain" the Beatles' popularity. But after that issue sold out, and a second Beatles cover did the same, Emerson knew that nobody cared very much about explanations. A cover story on Sonny and Cher sold very well too, and so did one on Bob Dylan, and Drugs on the Campus, and Teen-Age Drinking, and the Peril of Pep Pills. Our younger editors were still not satisfied with this paternalistic approach, however, and in time the youth fad became almost a religion among magazine editors, and so we went along with the herd in publishing stories on body paint and old-costume fashions and various weird rock groups.

Whether this was really good journalism was a matter of endless debate. I myself strongly opposed the whole trend, arguing that most Americans do not dance to rock music or smoke marijuana, after all, that all the teen-agers together represent a relatively small part of the population, and that the median age in this country is not getting younger, as many people think, but older. In short, as the times changed, my own role gradually changed from that of the young militant to that of an aging conservative. I could remember demanding that Blair approve a profile of a celebrated writer who was generally known to be a homosexual, but now, when the younger editors wanted to do a story about a long-haired Lebanese with a falsetto and a mandolin, I vetoed the whole subject of Tiny Tim.

Although editors may disagree among themselves, any organization inevitably acquires its own power structure, based not so much on theory as on the personalities of the top executives. Men who have to work together come to know each other's strengths and weaknesses, and they tend to fill in each other's gaps.

Traditionally, the great editors of the past have acquired reputations for being authoritarian. Men like George Horace Lorimer, Carr

Van Anda of the *Times*, Harold Ross of *The New Yorker*, seemed to know what they wanted and to inspire their subordinates with a mixture of awe and terror. I suspect that these legends are greatly exaggerated, however, and that the supposedly authoritarian methods of the famous editors consisted of a brusque manner rather than real tyranny. They were all intelligent men, after all, and every intelligent executive knows the importance of permitting and even encouraging dissenting opinions on his own staff. But it is often difficult to explain why one wants things done one way rather than another, and it is particularly irritating to have to argue the case with people who prefer the wrong course to the right one. Sometimes, for that matter, there is no reason for a choice at all, except that a choice must be made. "Suppose you were a railroad man," Monroe Stahr tried to explain in Scott Fitzgerald's *The Last Tycoon*. "You have to send a train through there somewhere. . . . You've got to decide—on what basis? You can't test the best way—except by doing it. So you just do it. . . . You choose some one way for no reason at all—because that mountain's pink or the blueprint is a better blue. You see?"

Bill Emerson, however, did not like to make decisions this way. He would have assigned an engineer to choose the best railroad route, and then, while reserving the right to countermand the engineer's choice, he would probably have supported him. He was, in short, an extremely permissive leader. This was partly a matter of convenience. "Any editor," he once remarked, "who would carry home every night a satchel full of manuscripts that the magazine might not even print, the way Ben Hibbs used to do, has got to be wasting time." But it was also a matter of conviction. Like President Eisenhower, the most notable practitioner of the theory, he genuinely believed in delegating authority to any subordinate who showed he could handle that authority in the best interests of the organization. He himself preferred to remain a judge of the finished results, and a court of appeal for any dissensions among subordinate editors.

I myself, in defiance of all the management textbooks, do not really believe in delegating authority. Much as I admired Lorimer for his reign at the *Post*, I admired him even more for continuing to edit his magazine while he served as president of the corporation. There are limits to the amount of work that anyone can do, granted, but it is only at these limits, I think, that one should begin delegating—starting with the least important responsibilities. There are important distinctions here. The Eisenhower system consists in delegating everything but the supreme authority, and its weakness is that it often leaves the chief executive with no alternative but to approve or disapprove of his lieutenants' *faits accomplis.* The opposite system, in which our own President Clifford fretted over raises for secretaries, condemns the chief executive to such a mass of trivial detail that he has no time for planning and over-all supervision. And the danger of both systems is that they lull the executive into mistakenly thinking he has done his job—one kind feels he is making the big decisions, despite the inadequate options, while the other makes so many small decisions that he feels justified in ignoring the major problems. The difficulty lies, obviously, in deciding what is really important, but just as obviously, I think, a good executive wants to keep as much control of events as he can, and to delegate only what is relatively insignificant.

If this theory is true, then Emerson was probably derelict in delegating so much of his authority, but it scarcely becomes me to criticize him on this point, for I was the chief beneficiary of his dereliction. I had started two years earlier, on becoming articles editor, by securing my right to assign and buy the articles I wanted. Then, when Schanche went to *Holiday,* I moved into the area of logistics—inventory, budgets, expense accounts. (Mac Clifford, incidentally, was making a series of similar moves under Culligan. We both knew—he by experience, I by instinct—that the basic step toward power is to get control of the flow of money.) When Blair left, I began writing the editorials, and the cover billings, and I ran the scheduling meetings that decided what each issue would contain. Now, in the fall of 1965, I took over the supervision of all fiction and began a certain amount of harassment of the art director.

I cite all this neither as a boast nor as a confession but in an attempt to explain the unorthodox Emerson-Friedrich relationship that by now governed the editorial policies of the *Post.* Magazine editors like to pretend that they assign all the stories, pick all the pictures, and edit all the copy, but it is largely pretense. "An editor's main job nowadays is not editing his magazine," as Don Schanche once said from sad experience, "but making speeches that will help sell advertising." Emerson did maintain a supervisory control of the *Post* editors, and he read through every page before it went to press, but his position inevitably required him to make flying trips to Detroit or Los Angeles, to deal with all the harassments of Mac Clifford and his entourage, and generally to lead a public life. "It's like carrying the Liberty Bell around on your back," he used to say. Actually editing a magazine, by contrast, means leading a relatively private existence—reading, thinking, fixing copy. By some happy circumstance, Emerson preferred the public life and I preferred the private life, and so, because we trusted each other, we were able to divide up the work according to our preferences.

The result was that I kept acquiring new responsibilities without delegating old ones, and each change brought me a new degree of power. When I was younger, I had never really thought much about power. I worked hard at my various jobs and did what I was told. I never thought of power as something that one acquired, or even hoped for—it was something that other people had, older people, the bosses, the establishment. Only as I grew older myself, and saw various bosses fighting with each other, did I realize that I didn't always have to do what other people said, that, on the contrary, I could often make them do what I said. The knowledge of power, in other words, is simply the knowledge that we can get whatever we really want. I suspect that this is also a fatal sign of middle age—a realization that we can no longer look to our fathers, because we ourselves have become the generation of fathers.

Perhaps I am too fond of theorizing. My power was really infinitesimal, after all, compared with that of any major political figure. I was not even the editor of a magazine, but only a chief of staff under a lenient commander, who was, in turn, responsible to a caretaker president and an antiquated board of directors. And the magazine to which we devoted ourselves had fallen far from its position of a generation ago. When it roared, no one trembled, and when it bled, no one came to help. As for any claims to power that I might have, then, they were rather like those of a prince from some moribund Balkan monarchy. Underestimation can be an error too, however. Quite aside from its great name and traditions, the *Post* still carried its message to almost seven million homes every fortnight and still grossed nearly $40 million a year. This sum is relatively meaningless until one gets a share of it, but our editorial share was $3 million, and that is a substantial sum if one has the power to distribute it according to one's own likes and dislikes.

In the simplest terms, that was my power—the power to provide anyone with several thousand dollars in cash and an audience of millions. It is not so much as an army, perhaps, but it will serve to illustrate general theories, for it brought me many of the conditions that greater power brings to greater men. It brought me, for example, more friends than I had ever had before, or ever wanted. Regardless of what I did or said, politicians and publicity men and even an occasional movie star forced themselves to smile on me as though I were the most parfit gentil knight they had ever encountered. I also acquired more enemies than I had ever had, or wanted. For every idea I approved, for every manuscript I bought, I inevitably had to reject ten or twenty more, and every man whom I rejected began creating dark images of me as the cursed nay-sayer. I was surprised, at first, that people took everything so personally, but I soon learned not to depend on new friendships and not to get angry about new enmities. Machiavelli said that *il principe* should try to be both loved and feared, but if he could not be both, then it was better to be feared. Before I was ever in a position to test these propositions, they impressed me as unreal, abstract, but when it came time to experience them, I found them true to the point of banality—and, more important, not really relevant. For there is another rule: *Il principe* must try to do what he thinks best without excessive regard as to whether it makes him loved or feared. And that is the way it generally happens.

But power, like wealth, also provides many small rewards that accumulate into a different way of life, and a different way of looking at life. A man of power looks different—walks differently, speaks differently—simply because he gets accustomed to having people do what he says. At the beginning, it is a novelty even to have a secretary, and one gains from her the first experience of seeing a woman do whatever one tells her to do, but in due time everything becomes a bad habit, and then we have the spectacle of the rich man requiring his flunkies to spend their own money to buy him a newspaper or a shoeshine. "Who's got some change?" the millionaire casually asks, not even watching to see who steps forward. Is this really a pleasure, or, more generally, do men who have power really like it? Yes. Yes, I liked it. Yes, all men like it. And the more power they can get or keep, the better they like it.

One of the reasons that Clifford took over Blair's office was that he had the very practical idea of getting rid of the whole executive suite on the thirty-second floor. Joe Culligan clung to his roost there for a while, but by the end of 1964 Culligan's whole executive team had been abolished, and the beautiful glass-walled offices stood empty. A receptionist still sat in the dark foyer, nodding over a paperback novel, and a couple of secretaries typed desultorily in the dark center space (one of the problems with glass-walled executive suites is that the executives' assistants get no sunlight at all). The only survivor who still held one of the big, bright offices was our "editorial coordinator," Bob Sherrod.

For several months, Clifford tried to sublease this penthouse establishment, but perhaps he asked too much money, or perhaps there simply are not very many customers for penthouse office suites. In any case, Clifford did not find a tenant, and so, in a fit of thrift, he abruptly decided to get his money's worth by filling up these haunted offices with all the executives who could be categorized as "miscellaneous." Bill Buckley, for instance, head of the Curtis syndicate and book division, suddenly found himself swept up to the thirty-second floor. Ron Diana, our company lawyer, who had been lobbying for more room, now became the master of a miniature suite. Dick Ficks, the head of public relations, wasn't sure he wanted to move away from the editorial floor, and he asked for some time to think it over. "They said," he reported later, " 'You have exactly one minute to make up your mind.' "

The sudden influx of executives brought an equivalent influx of secretaries, who were flung together at relatively close quarters in the central arena of the executive horseshoe. One of these secretaries was a rather hot-tempered girl who had once worked for me but had later been transferred to Bob Sherrod. And now, as a consequence of some unknown and unknowable secretarial conflict, she was banished from the secretarial area and told to move her desk inside Sherrod's office. It may be hard for an outsider to believe that these things are important, but office life makes them seem so. Such an order was an unbearable affront not only to the secretary but to Sherrod, the "editorial coordinator." Shortly after that, Sherrod went all the way to Philadelphia to see Clifford about "a personal matter." The consequence was that the "editorial coordinator" departed from the glass-walled thirty-second floor and moved to a small office on the second floor, with his secretary trailing behind to a desk outside in the corridor.

On every newspaper I have ever known, the editorial page always seemed to be born by a kind of daily self-ovulation. In a separate area of the building, an autonomous editorial department would commune with itself and then announce what the newspaper thought about any subject on earth. At the *Post*, when I first arrived, Bob Sherrod maintained a somewhat similar system. An editor based in Washington flew north with his manuscript every Wednesday and loitered in our corridors until Sherrod had time to join him in a discussion of the week's editorial page. Then came the experiment of Blair trying to write the editorial page himself, and repeatedly forgetting about it until the deadline was upon him. And then the bizarre system of Bill Miller moonlighting editorials at *Life* and sending them across town by messenger for $250 apiece. With Blair's departure, this system became an embarrassment, and so I took on the job of writing the editorial page myself.

At first, it seemed a great honor to speak through the trumpet of George Horace Lorimer. The editorial page, theoretically, was the voice—the very soul—of the *Post*. And when it spoke, it spoke to millions, telling them not just some writer's opinions but the *Post's* authoritative views on the state of the world. Within a few months, however, the job seemed somewhat less of an honor, for I now realized how those newspaper editorial departments of my youth had arrived at their Olympian conclusions: the *Post's* editorial view on all questions was, subject to Emerson's approval, whatever I chose to say it was. *N'est-ce que ça?* It is always a little disillusioning—it is the basic disillusionment of power—to discover that one's own views are accepted as those of the final authority, that there is no one else who can provide a cure for one's own ignorance.

If I was going to speak in the name of the *Post*, then, I decided I would start to speak about the war in Vietnam. I began cautiously, with some sarcastic remarks about South Vietnam's new dictator, "a bizarre 34-year-old pilot named Nguyen Cao Ky [who] wears purple scarves and flies a purple airplane." In the next issue, I tried a more philosophical tone:

> Now that the war in Vietnam reaches ever more dangerous levels of violence, it appears easy for the ignorant and the forgetful—on both sides —to talk about "toughness" and "teaching a lesson." . . . Someone once said that the worst crime was to treat human beings as though they were objects, and that is what the slogans of belligerence imply—that we cannot settle our differences except by blind outbursts of destruction, that we have some kind of commitment more important than our commitment to human life.

And again, two issues later, as our bombing of civilians increased:

> It is easy—and inadequate—to answer that war is hell. It is easy—and inadequate—to say that the Communists have committed atrocities. It used to be axiomatic that there could be no victory in Vietnam without the support of the Vietnamese people. . . . Our commitment to the people of South Vietnam is a commitment to protect them, not to destroy them in the name of "the free world."

In retrospect, such declarations may seem as mild as cottage cheese, but very few people were saying anything like this back in 1965. This was the year in which Lyndon Johnson began his bombing of North Vietnam and announced that American forces would have to be increased from a mere 75,000 to a mere 125,000. The country, as usual, supported its President in waging war. The polls were over-whelmingly in his favor, and the press was quiescent. Other mass magazines like *Life* and *Look* docilely supported the government. Only the previous summer, for that matter, Senator Fulbright had guided the Senate to a virtually unanimous approval of the so-called Gulf of Tonkin Resolution, approving any measures the President might decide to undertake in Vietnam. On a smaller and more personal scale, then, I felt I had to move gradually in persuading millions of traditionally patriotic readers that their government was leading them into quicksand. I had to move gradually in persuading Emerson, too, for he was also very patriotic, naturally combative, and he believed instinctively in the doctrine of "my country right or wrong." In other words, he dreaded every editorial I wrote on Viet-nam, and he hated having to defend them against irate readers and advertisers, but he also knew that I was determined to go ahead, and he acknowledged that I might be right.

By the end of that year, 1965, when the confident predictions by President Johnson, Dean Rusk, and Robert McNamara appeared regularly on the front pages, I had become convinced that the Communists were going to win in Vietnam, and that our intervention could not and would not prevent their victory. I did not try to carry the *Post* that far, but I did keep moving it in that direction. During this period, Soviet Premier Kosygin granted an interview to James Reston of the *New York Times* and berated him for American interventions in Vietnam and the Dominican Republic. Reston, like a good *Times* man, upheld the official views of the U.S. government and got much the worse of the exchange. "Force should never be used for political ends," said Reston. "This war in Vietnam," said Kosygin, "this reflects your doctrine of peace? I cannot agree that you have the right to kill defenseless people." To me, Reston's air of injured innocence seemed a perfect example of the way we mirrored the Communists: "We say we are fighting for the liberty and indepen-dence of the people of Vietnam. The Communists say they are fighting for the liberty and independence of the people of Vietnam. We say we will stop the bloodshed if they will stop their aggression. They say they will stop the bloodshed if we will stop our aggression."

Late in the afternoon, after I finished writing this editorial, I found Emerson closeted with Jess Ballew and worrying about what effects my comments would have on the advertisers. It was a change, I acknowledged, from the old days of the *Post*. What would George Horace Lorimer say about a *Post* editorial that equated American efforts to combat Communism with Communism itself? In his anxiety, Emerson used all the favorite euphemisms by which he signaled his desire to avoid trouble. The *Post* was now "at a critical juncture." In a few months, we would be "in a stronger position." And that ultimate argument: "We have lots of freedom, if we just don't abuse it." In response to these fears and anxieties, I got very mulish. We always seemed to be at some "critical juncture," I said, and the "stronger position" had been receding into the future ever since I had been at the *Post*. And Jess Ballew—bless him—reacted just as a publisher should. The editorial, which he didn't really agree with, was soundly argued, he said, and it seemed to represent what the editors thought, and that was what editorials were for, and if there were any complaints from advertisers, he would deal with them.

Each editorial represented a new bench mark, a point that had theoretically been conceded by Emerson and demonstrated to the readers and could therefore be used as a base for future forays. By that autumn, in fact, the *Post* editorial page had become quite fierce.

In this "just" struggle against Communism, we are killing civilians as surely as any Communist ever did [I wrote]. Our bombs drop on friend and enemy alike; our napalm burns them alive, friend and enemy. We are just carrying out someone's orders, of course, like all soldiers, and we are certainly not Nazis. We provide doctors to treat the children we have bombed. We hold "elections" so that we can reassure ourselves of popular support. And we promise that we will provide money someday to rebuild the land we are destroying. But what if the ends do not justify the means? Not as a philosophical principle but as a matter of fact? What if the surgical experiment is a success but the patient dies under the knife? What if no future form of "freedom" or "self-government" can ever make up for the pain being inflicted now? . . . Someday we will wonder why we failed to realize that greater and ever greater amounts of force do not always solve a problem. Someday we will remember that there are no "final solutions." Someday we will wonder why we keep on being sheep.

Lyndon Johnson went to Vietnam just about then, and told the American troops to "come home with that coonskin." And so it seemed reasonable to denounce him somewhat more directly:

. . . The theory of "aggression" is . . . virtually worthless. Vietnam is one country, torn by the agony of civil war, and the major outside intervention is our own. We can justify this, of course, as all great powers justify their use of force—by claiming that might makes right. . . . We can claim that we have a right to veto who will govern South Vietnam—or anywhere else. We can claim that we have a right to kill anyone who stands in our way. . . . But patriotism is not a justification for everything, nor was the world designed to suit our convenience, and in due time we all learn to judge our leaders by the wisdom and justice of their causes, and not by the amount of blood they shed in their quest for shining victories.

I barely got that demagogic last sentence past Emerson, but it reached its target in the White House. Emerson got an unhappy telephone call from Douglass Cater, an assistant to the President, who invited him to Washington for a series of high-level conferences "before you run us out of here." Emerson evaded that confrontation, but I made us some interesting enemies in Congress too. When I wrote an editorial arguing that strategic bombing was "one of the clumsiest, messiest, bloodiest and least efficient ways of waging war," and that our raids north of the 17th parallel were "the least effective and least defensible aspect of our war in Vietnam," Senator Stuart Symington denounced this issue of the *Post* before the Senate Armed Services Committee and even interrogated an Air Force officer about the various points I had made. The Air Force officer denied everything I had written.

It is reasonable to ask whether such controversies mean a great deal. Editorial writers suffer from two occupational diseases—the illusion that everybody is listening and the fear that nobody is listening. I got a personal satisfaction from the fact that the *Post*'s editorials against the war made it the first major magazine to take this stand—and for several years, it was the only one to do so—but it is difficult to determine what effect this had on anyone. Over the next few years, more and more people began to oppose the war, but who converted them? And during those same years, President Johnson steadily increased the violence of the war, so what value did any of our sermons have? What value, for that matter, do any sermons ever have? Is the pen really mightier than the sword, or was that familiar comparison conceived by someone who had never used a sword at all?

Jess Ballew was right in thinking that my Vietnam editorials would not cost us any advertising, but Emerson was equally right in worrying about the problem. The celebrated 1964 editorial attack on Goldwater had cost us an estimated $10 million, after all, and it was evident that the advertisers did to some extent base their advertising decisions not just on the *Post*'s rates but on what the *Post* published.

Traditionally, of course, the advertisers' views should have no influence on a magazine's editorial pages. Idealistic editors like to proclaim their independence of commercial pressures, and even the most aggressive businessmen feel some obligation to honor the theory of a free press. This is good business, too, since readers who believe in a magazine tend also to believe the advertisements it publishes. On the other hand, businessmen are only human, and it is human to believe that one's own opinions of the world are shared by all men of good will and common sense, and that there must be something wrong with anyone whose opinions are radically different. And since the loss of even one advertising page in the *Post* meant a loss of about $40,000, not even the most quixotic editor could easily ignore the businessmen's reaction to the magazine.

In areas as complex as Vietnam, the advertisers seemed willing to believe that the *Post* had expert knowledge to support its views, but there were other areas in which businessmen believed they knew just as much as anyone else. Morals, for instance. While the advertising agency people on Madison Avenue might feel that a magazine should be bold and dashing, the men who actually ran the great corporations out in the midlands felt quite differently. "They're not just square," Emerson would say after one of his speech-making forays, "they're octagonal." Many of them had liked the old *Post* of Ben Hibbs, and they regarded our periodic reports on motorcycle gangs and mari- juana-smoking as a misguided attempt at sensationalism. At one point, Jess Ballew even urged us not to put Elizabeth Taylor on the cover of an issue that contained many advertisements for new automobiles. A Taylor cover guaranteed high newsstand sales in those days, and so most large magazines ran one every time they needed increased circulation, but the magnates of Detroit apparently disapproved of Miss Taylor's numerous marriages. "They think she's immoral," Ballew said, "and they don't like to have their ads in the same issue with her."

The one topic about which every advertiser felt really passionately, of course, was his own product, and everything related to it. When we published a picture of someone using a Sunbeam mixer, for example, we could expect a cry of protest from General Electric. When we reported on the controversy over the California redwoods, we aroused the suspicions of the wood-products advertisers. And even by occa- sionally using the word "booze," we apparently inflicted grave damage on the whiskey distillers' yearning for respectability.

Clay Blair had started his career as a muckraker by publishing an article that probed into the causes of an airliner crash and put part of the blame on equipment manufactured by Boeing. Blair defiantly cited the subsequent cancellation of Boeing advertising as evidence of the *Post*'s courageous independence, but by the time I began running the articles department, I found that the enthusiasm for this particular kind of independence had waned. In an article on the automobile industry, for example, Blair insisted that the statistics on death rates be cut to a minimum and moved far down in the story; an article about a critic of the big banks survived only by being entitled "The Oddball Crusade of Congressman Patman"; an article reporting the dangers of excessive use of vitamin pills never ran at all; and when I sent Emerson a memo asking tartly just how much revenue we received from drug-industry advertising, I got a quick answer: $3 million a year.

In the spring of 1964, there had been constant rumors of corruption and graft surrounding the construction of the New York World's Fair, but we decided that it would be the better part of valor to ignore the whole fair. There were major advertisers taking part in this enterprise, however, and they kept asking what plans we had made to extol the great event, and so Blair ordered us to produce a special issue devoted to the glories of New York and its new fair. We dutifully produced the conventional sort of tribute—beginning with eleven pages of color pictures by one of Hank Walker's minions and following up with "New York fiction" by people like Louis Auchincloss, John Updike, and Warren Miller—but the regular feature called "Speaking Out" was traditionally devoted to dissent, and we had permitted one of our more irascible writers, John Skow, to produce a commentary entitled "Who Needs the World's Fair?" We subtitled it in the most ingratiating manner: "A spoilsport among the happy crowds takes a maverick view of the world's greatest fair." But the sad fact was that Skow had found fault with the Ford exhibition, and he particularly disliked the noisy Pepsi-Cola theme song, "It's a Small, Small World."

Blair was dismayed. He wanted all such criticisms taken out. I, in turn, declared that they absolutely could not be taken out. We had already made Skow rewrite the article so that his criticisms changed from outright denunciations into ironic expressions of personal distaste. And as Skow himself put it, "If the muckraking *Post* can sternly accuse the President of the United States of 'deception' about a new fighter plane [that had been Blair's word and one of his pet projects], why can't it mildly accuse Pepsi-Cola of bad taste?" The simplest answer was that Lyndon Johnson was not a major advertiser, but editorial arguments of this kind are never fought out on such terms. Blair's line of attack was that he had been to the fair himself, and he had liked it, and he had particularly liked the Pepsi-Cola exhibit. Emerson, caught in the middle, had to argue simultaneously for the writers' right to express their views and the editors' obligation to be responsible. As a compromise, he devised a way of toning down five of Skow's more caustic comments. I agreed to that, bitterly and reluctantly—but Blair didn't.

"Okay, you're responsible for the articles in the magazine," Blair said desperately, "but I just want to tell you that you might as well kiss the Pepsi-Cola account good-bye. Hell, it took a lot of diplomacy to get them over that last case, when they paid for the whole center spread and then we ran a full-page picture of a guy drinking a Coke. And now this . . . It's just a couple of hundred thousand dollars' worth of business, that's all, but that's up to you. . . ."

Emerson warned Blair that I might resign, for I was by now in a state of high indignation, and that there had to come a point at which we defended our writers against commercial pressures. Blair grudgingly gave way, and the article ran. I do not know what Pepsi-Cola ever said about it, but I got an outraged letter from Skow, denouncing me for having "emasculated" his story.

Yet Blair not only had believed in editorial independence; he had also been in a relatively strong position to fight advertising pressures. Emerson, as the inheritor of a badly battered magazine, could only rely on his own prudence to avoid further advertising losses. And so, when we published an article on air pollution in an issue filled with auto advertising—yes, the *Post* was the first major magazine to start campaigning against pollution back in the mid-sixties—we accommodated Mac Clifford's anxieties by inserting a few lines about Detroit's efforts to devise cleaner engines. When we published an article on Senator Thomas Dodd's questionable relations with various corporations, we deleted the names of several of the corporations that had helped to make his life more comfortable. And then there were other subjects that we decided to ignore altogether—the high cost of life insurance, for example, and the news that cigarettes cause cancer. "Those are fascinating stories," said Emerson, who had the unpleasant responsibility for making decisions on such matters, "and when we decide that we want to go out of business, we'll publish all of them in our last issue."

It would not surprise me to hear that *Life* and *Look* and many other large magazines occasionally encountered similar problems, and came to similar solutions, but I am speaking only from my own experience. And in all fairness, I should acknowledge that I know of no single instance in which any advertiser actually threatened us for publishing or not publishing any specific article. The system never works that way. It relies instead on the fact that editors will censor themselves for the sake of that higher goal known as survival. From an editor on another magazine, however, I heard a very forthright statement of the business point of view. This editor happened to encounter the head of a large corporation, which regularly bought advertising to express the industrialist's conservative views on taxes, labor unions, and other economic issues.

"You know, I think you people are hypocrites," the industrialist said to the editor. "You pretend to be neutral and nonpartisan, but you're really in favor of the Democrats in this election, so why don't you be honest and come right out and say it?"

"Okay, suppose we did come out for the Democrats," the editor said. "How would you react to that?"

"I'd admire your integrity," the industrialist said, "and I'd cancel my ads."

One autumn day, Sandy Brown, a senior editor at the *Post*, fell off a ladder while putting up storm windows and cracked his skull. While he recovered from brain surgery, the Curtis bureaucracy set to work to get him off the payroll. There was a Curtis rule book that contained a company policy to cover every contingency, and the personnel and accounting departments contained a number of functionaries who spent their time discovering and applying rules. One of these rules was that any employee who had missed more than a month of work was cut off the payroll—secretly—and could not be reinstated except at the request of his departmental chief.

What happened, therefore, was that a November payday went by, and Brown didn't get his paycheck. It took several days for Mrs. Brown to inquire about it, and several more for Emerson to discover the old rule, and several more for the reinstatement request to go to Philadelphia—and get lost there. All this time, according to the system, the Curtis Publishing Company was theoretically saving money by not paying an employee while he lay in the hospital.

Every ten days or so, Emerson would voyage to Philadelphia with a ten-day accumulation of problems like this, and then he would sit in Mac Clifford's office and argue and wheedle and tell jokes until everything was straightened out. In the case of Sandy Brown's paycheck, nobody seemed able to find either the reinstatement request or the official who had last seen it. It was Gloria Swett's responsibility, as head of personnel, but she had not received the required document, and neither had her administrative assistant, and neither had the head of the personnel department. After about half an hour of detective work, which consisted of summoning various officials to

Clifford's office for interrogation, the missing paper was finally discovered in the hands of some tertiary bureaucrat, who confessed that he had been hiding it in his desk.

"Why in hell were you keeping it in your desk?" Emerson demanded.

"Because I was afraid Miss Swett might disapprove of it," the paralyzed functionary answered.

I have not yet finished my observations on this mysterious relationship called power. There are, I think, two basic kinds of power, which might be designated as statutory power and functional power. Statutory power comes by decree. General So-and-so receives authorization to take command of an army, and the army waits to carry out his orders. Everyone must obey because he is the commanding officer. Functional power descends from an older kind of army, in which a general won the right to command because he was a stronger warrior than any of his soldiers.

In the first full-time job I ever had, at the age of twenty-one, I experienced my first taste of statutory power. I was put in charge of men who knew more than I did, and I shall never forget the contemptuous tone in which one of them responded to a request by saying, "Well, okay, if you want, but that's an awfully half-assed way of doing things." The trouble was that he was right, and I had to admit that he was right. Ever since then, I have preferred to take charge of things only when I was sure I could do all the work better than anybody who worked for me. It is this skill, not age or experience, that provides the most basic kind of confidence, and confidence is indispensable in telling other people what to do.

This introduction may serve to explain one of the oddities of the *Saturday Evening Post*—that it consistently looked dull or vapid or ugly or tasteless, or all four, and that I did little or nothing to solve the problem. As a matter of fact, the problem had existed since time immemorial. During the long regime of Ben Hibbs, according to one critic, the magazine "looked like a seed catalogue," and when the authorities decided to launch a "new *Post*," they concentrated heavily on visual improvements. Clay Blair took charge of photography; Kenneth Stuart, who was then the art director, called in various designers to create stylish layouts. The result was generally considered a disaster, even by the art experts who subsequently tried to heap the blame on each other. When Blair eventually became editor, he hired Hank Walker from *Life* to take the responsiblity for photography, and he brought in the Danish designer, Asger Jerrild, to handle illustrations and typography. Walker generally overrode Jer-rild, and so the *Post* often looked like a mediocre imitation of *Life,* but after Walker left and Jerrild took charge as art director, the magazine began to look vaguely unreal, full of boxes and long lines and other marks of the graphic designer.

I had no particular training or experience in photography or design, and so I tried to stay out of this whole field, hoping that all the people who claimed to be experts could somehow produce layouts that would meet with general approval. But I found it astonishing, over the years, that all the experts' efforts were so consistently unsuccessful. One reason, of course, is that many people like to claim an expert understanding of photography and design that is based on nothing more substantial than the traditional statement of I-may-not-know-much-about-art-but-I-know-what-I-like. On the other hand, the real experts, the men with training and experience, often seem to have very little judgment, or even taste.

For the next three years, in any case, the visual appearance of the *Post* was the responsibility of the enigmatic Asger Jerrild. After having been hired by Blair and then pushed aside by Walker, Jerrild had cultivated friendships with various minor potentates in Phila-delphia, and in due time some of these minor potentates became major potentates. In the shambles of 1964, then, Emerson learned that Jerrild had been secretly producing dummies of the way he thought the *Post* should look—full of lines and boxes—and that he had the full support of the new management. It thus became our job to decipher this indecipherable figure and fit him into his place on the staff, and this was a job more difficult than it might seem.

Emerson called Jerrild "The Green Noodle," but the nickname did not really describe him. He was tall, perhaps six foot two, but pudgy, not really fat in terms of his over-all size but round and flabby in the individual features—jowls, dumpling cheeks, thick-fingered hands. He moved quickly, darting through doors, but with an oddly rolling motion like that of a shorebound sailor. When he sat down, he ap-peared nervous, fidgeting with his cigar, or dabbing at his hair, which was gray and curly, receding high over the temples, combed straight back.

His language was fluent but inexpert, strongly accented and quite unstoppable. And in the course of his career, he had learned the mysterious dialect that all art directors speak. Phonetic spelling is always a dubious technique for capturing the intonations of speech, but I cannot convey our difficulty in communicating with Jerrild unless I offer a brief glossary, recording some of an art director's favorite terms:

Veezhul excitement—what art directors strive for
Jost nossing—what art directors think of text editors' views
I'm so hoppy weezit—the photographer did a good job
Eezat really sotch a good story?—the photographer failed
Vary strrong—dark, murky colors
Vary clessy—effete, pastel colors
Beezy—too much text
Clottered—same as "beezy"
Sateerical—the quality of European illustrations
Fonny—same as "sateerical"
Too sopheesticated for oss—dirty pictures

But the difficulty in communication illustrated a more general problem. ("Whenever people say they have a problem in communications," Mike Mooney had remarked, "it always means that they do have a problem, but the problem never has much to do with communications.") The problem, at least for editors, is that art directors think in a rather special way. They focus on patterns, spatial relationships, elements of color. They try to show rather than to explain. They often avoid reading—or, when they do read an article to be illustrated, they often concentrate entirely on its visual aspects—for they instinctively consider a sequence of words primarily as something to be looked at—a pattern of gray superimposed on white. "Get an art director and put him at a drawing board [and] put a tape over his mouth," one of the men who helped to design *Life* once warned Henry Luce, "because whatever he has to state should drain off through his fingers onto paper. Never let an art director talk."

In any event, there are obstacles to the production of a handsome magazine that have nothing to do with the art director. One is that the system of magazine illustration has lagged behind and below every other aspect of magazine publishing. In a time when magazine editors bid competitively for the best writers available, the best artists do not do magazine work, and so a collection of people who call themselves "commercial artists" still turn their routine talents to the routine paintings that appear, on commission, in every mass magazine. And what can any art director do with people who make their living by being mediocre?

Photographers present exactly the opposite problem, for the good ones do work for magazines but refuse to limit themselves to illustrating text. On one occasion, for instance, we sent John Launois, a good photographer, to accompany Bill Heinz, a good writer, while Heinz created a memoir for the twentieth anniversary of the Battle of the Bulge. Every time Launois asked Heinz for suggestions on what to photograph, Heinz was baffled, for the Battle of the Bulge was long past, and most of the story was inside Heinz's head. Finally, when they came to a town where Heinz had once had an emotional encounter with a colonel, Heinz pointed out the scene.

"Over there," he said. "You could take a picture of that building where I met the colonel."

"That building!" Launois exploded. "Do you think I came all the way from New York to France to take pictures of buildings?"

In his heart, every good photographer thinks that he can tell any good story entirely in pictures, and that the only function of writers (known collectively as "text people") is to write an occasional caption. Another photographer, Larry Schiller, expressed this view succinctly when he said, "The trouble with text people is that they're not really creative, the way photographers are." ("If Friedrich ever hears you say that," Emerson answered, "he'll kill you.") To produce a good picture magazine, therefore, one must give most of the space to the photographers, with only a few paragraphs of text to provide a pretense of substance to each two-page spread of pictures. It was generally agreed, however, that the *Post* was a text magazine, and that the average story involved a manuscript of five thousand words or more, and that there just wasn't room for the photographers to tell their own version of the same story with five thousand pictures. They tried, Lord knows, they fought, they sulked, they argued their philosophy of life, but in a conflict between text and pictures, the text editors generally won. This was a matter not just of space but of the basic philosophy that governed what we published. On a picture magazine, like *Life* or *Look*, when good pictures come in, they are published, and some junior editor writes a little block of text to go with them. On a text magazine, by contrast, good pictures are rejected unless there is a story to justify them—but a good story gets published whether there are any pictures or not. The art director of a text magazine, therefore, is a man doomed to frustration.

Eventually, as a matter of fact, the years of frustration drove Asger Jerrild to a minor rebellion all his own. Brooding over the comparative ugliness of the *Post*, dominated by gray pages of solid text, he once again began producing a secret series of new layouts designed to show the authorities in Philadelphia what he thought the magazine should look like—"like a Danish picture magazine," as Emerson put it. The presentation was undoubtedly handsome, for Jerrild was not without talent, but he did not show it to Emerson or me. The oligarchs in Philadelphia were baffled by this sudden appearance of *Post* layouts, however, so they passed them around among themselves and wondered what to do next. Gloria Swett had rather liked Jerrild's plans, and his courtly attentions, but Clifford said, "It's Bill's magazine, and he can do what he wants."

As for me, I avoided the art department as much as I could, partly because I was uncertain of my own judgments and partly because I thought the whole matter of illustration was sufficiently unimportant to be delegated to other people. And in this, of course, I was wrong. Illustrations are critically important to a magazine, not because of their inherent value, or because readers like them, but because many of the people who play a decisive part in the publishing business simply do not read the text in text magazines. On both Wall Street and Madison Avenue, they flip through the pages to get an impression of quality or mediocrity, success or failure, and they act accordingly. A magazine that looks good is consequently thought to be good, even though a really handsome magazine is almost necessarily one that has sacrificed ideas and substance to the need for expanses of white space and glowing color.

There is one final irony. If an editor and an art director actually do produce a magazine that looks truly impressive, so that Madison Avenue will be impressed, Madison Avenue will express its pleasure by inserting ads that will ruin the lucky magazine's appearance. There are a few exceptions, like *Fortune, Vogue,* and *The New Yorker,* which look glossy and opulent primarily because their wealthy audiences attract lavish advertisements, but in a mass magazine, it is safe to predict that a handsome opening page will emerge opposite a sales spiel for deodorants, and that an article about the future of the presidency will be illustrated with a photograph of a woman grimacing from a headache. The visual excellence of a magazine, in short, is important primarily to attract attention in the market place, and the rulers of the market respond to that excellence with the embrace of Kali.

"The thing I can't figure out," said Mike Mooney, who had become a sort of office philosopher, "is, what is our circulation policy?"

"What do you mean, what's our circulation policy?" I retorted.

"I mean, what are we trying to accomplish?" Mooney persisted. "Are we sending the magazine to the right people? And are they paying us the right price?"

"Well, that's what the circulation company is supposed to be in charge of, isn't it?" I said, still clinging to the theory that somebody in the business departments must be handling the business side of the magazine. "Why do we have to worry about that?"

"Because the circulation company guys are only worrying about making a profit for the circulation company. Who's worrying about us? As far as I can make out, nobody."

Mooney was right. The *Post*, virtually alone among magazines, had no circulation director. There was only the circulation company, which charged us handsomely for its services, and which also circulated more than fifty other magazines, including *Look*, our main competitor. In fact, the *Post* did not have a single employee, then or on the day of its death, who was paid solely to see to it that the magazine reached its proper customers and made a profit in the process. Not a single one. It was as though Curtis's rulers had somehow forgotten, decades ago, what the basic rules of business are.

For some reason that I cannot quite explain, it became an avocation of mine, from then on, to attack the circulation problem—the problem being, basically, that we kept selling cut-rate subscriptions at $1.95 a year (eight cents a copy) to provide a mass audience for advertisers who no longer wanted to reach that kind of audience. I sent long memoranda to Emerson, I cajoled Ballew; I pleaded for an increase in the price of subscriptions, and for the hiring of a circulation manager. And because I think this question is absolutely essential to the business of publishing, it will reappear from time to time in the following pages. I realize, of course, that circulation problems are not of widespread public interest, and so the reader may skip a few pages whenever he encounters tiresome terms like "subscription fulfillment" or "A and B circulation." (By similar skips, we may perceive all of history as a series of cavalry charges, and the development of corporate capitalism as a series of amusing anecdotes about Charles Goodyear melting his galoshes and Alexander Graham Bell calling for help from the next room.) In any case, the problems of circulation were never solved during the reign of John McLean Clifford. It was only when a new president took over the debris of the Clifford regime that we started serious work on the circulation question, and found that we had run out of time.

What obsessed Mac Clifford throughout that year of 1965 was that Curtis owed the banks $37.3 million, and that its publishing operations would lose more money in every quarter. In May, Clifford had managed to sell the paper mill in Lock Haven, Pennsylvania, for

$10.3 million, and to use $8 million of that for a reduction in the debt. The company's operating losses in the second quarter had devoured another $2.5 million, however, and the third quarter had taken yet another $1.1 million. Curtis stock was traded very actively on Wall Street all year, and there were constant rumors of mergers and takeovers, rumors that someone would come and rescue us, or destroy us, but still Mac Clifford clung to the joystick, determined to figure out something.

To a man like Clifford, with a background in Western mining rights, Curtis had one asset incomparably more valuable than its magazines and printing presses. It had 110,000 acres of timberland in Ontario, and 13,000 of those acres lay athwart the Kidd Creek Mine that the Texas Gulf Sulphur Company had discovered outside Timmins late in 1963. Texas Gulf executives had chosen to keep their discovery secret—a decision that later caused a bitter quarrel with the SEC and some stiff penalties for the defendants—and they had negotiated a contract that permitted them to dig copper from Curtis land for a mere 10 percent of the net profits. By now, after almost two years of exploration, it had been confirmed that the Texas Gulf mine consisted of about sixty million tons of copper, zinc, silver, and lead, worth an estimated $2 billion. It was also evident that Curtis's contract, which Clifford himself had signed, gave Curtis only a minimal share of the wealth under its own land. With the government applying pressure to Texas Gulf, and several of Curtis's own stockholders suing to demand a better contract, Clifford began new negotiations with Texas Gulf.

The negotiations were ˜strenuous and unpleasant—at one point, according to subsequent testimony by Milton Gould, Curtis threatened to sue Texas Gulf for fraud—but in October of 1965, Clifford was finally able to announce an agreement "in principle," which was made official at the end of the year. Curtis sold to Texas Gulf all its 110,000 acres in Ontario plus its 141,000 acres of hardwood timber in northwestern Pennsylvania. Curtis gave up its right to a 10 percent share in mineral profits from the 13,000 acres directly over the mine, but it retained a share of possible profits in land farther away from Kidd Creek. And in exchange for all this, it got from Texas Gulf the sum of $24 million in cash.

For a nearly bankrupt corporation, it was an overwhelming sum. Twenty-four million dollars in cash. That was about six times as much as the current operating deficit, about 80 percent of all the money owed to the banks. It was, in short, salvation—again. Four years later, when the company finally foundered, many people tried to analyze the causes of failure. Very few asked the real question: How did such a company ever survive so long? World War II and the postwar boom had provided a temporary prosperity, of course, and Curtis had sunk its profits in printing plants and paper mills. In the early 1960's, when the company appeared in danger of collapse, Joe Culligan had found Serge Semenenko and negotiated a loan of $35 million. Both men felt, not without justification, that their deal had saved the corporation. But that was just a loan to be repaid. Now, Mac Clifford had acquired $24 million that would be Curtis's own money—to pay off Semenenko—and Clifford had good reason to think that it was he, not Culligan, he, Mac Clifford, whom the board had chosen only when it couldn't find anyone else, who now had truly saved the Curtis Publishing Company.

15

"Hell, we're making money right now"

In the following year of 1966, the Curtis Publishing Company, like a half-submerged hulk lunging mysteriously to the surface, managed once again to make a profit. It was not a very large profit—$347,000 —but it was just about the only profit that Curtis achieved during the entire decade of the 1960's. Because of Mac Clifford's peculiar sense of public relations, this news item, which Joe Culligan would somehow have brought to every household in the country, remained a matter of almost total secrecy—announced in Philadelphia on the day before George Washington's birthday and relegated to one paragraph on page 54 of the *Times*. Still, the profit was perfectly real. Was it possible, then, that Mac Clifford had some kind of managerial talent that we had not hitherto suspected?

On the *Post* editorial floor, the year began with an epic failure, the last Ben Franklin issue. In the old days, at least through the 1950's, Ben Hibbs had celebrated the founder's birthday every January 17 by publishing a cover that combined a portrait of Franklin and one of his pithy sayings. Since Hibbs's departure, the *Post* had dedicated most of its covers to the search for novelty, and Clay Blair had even removed Franklin's portrait and signature from the magazine's regular colophon page. Now, in an effort to recapture some of the tradition that Blair had so lightly discarded, we commissioned the satirical illustrator Blake Hampton to design a cover showing Franklin and his printing press, for which we selected a Franklinian text that embodied many of our personal hopes: "Be at war with your vices, at peace with your neighbours, and let every New-Year find you a better man." It was not a bad issue, by any means, but it was one of the thinnest in history, a pitiful sixty pages, of which only nine were advertising pages. And that Ben Franklin cover, appearing during the Christmas season, went to a miserable death, selling only 58 percent of the copies offered on the newsstands.

Even before the returns were final, Emerson began to discount the Ben Franklin issue as the last failure of the old year, and to demand that the next issue be a resounding success. "Birth control!" he cried. "Where the hell is Steve Spencer's piece on birth control? I want a cover on birth control!" And so the cover of the next issue cried out: "The BIRTH CONTROL REVOLUTION/ The effect on MORALS/ The progress in SCIENCE/ The role of the CHURCH/ The changes in LAW/ The new freedom." And so on. Historic traditions didn't sell magazines, perhaps, but the traditional feature stories still did. The newsstand sale of the birth-control issue jumped by 135,000 copies, 35 percent higher than poor Ben Franklin.

After the failure of Ben Franklin, in other words, we launched the new year with considerable effervescence.

And we finally saw the last of Joe Culligan. On January 18, it was announced that our former president had gone to work at a new job—as a consultant to the William J. Burns International Detective Agency. To celebrate the move, he gave an interview in which he announced that the detective agency had a great future in the field of "communications." It was also announced that Culligan had flown south the previous month as "a member of an inspection team of the United States Information Agency mission to Costa Rica."

"Costa Rica!" one cynical editor exclaimed. "Other people get sent on missions to Paris or London or Berlin or Vietnam—but Costa Rica!"

The next sign of progress in the new year was that G. B. McCombs, the czar of Curtis circulation, agreed to increase the newsstand price of the *Post* from twenty-five cents to thirty-five cents. This may seem like a small thing, but it was of considerable symbolic significance. And the move was made, of course, for the wrong reasons.

Newsstand sales are widely thought to be the measure of a magazine's success. They fluctuate from issue to issue and therefore provide an indicator of comparative sales for successive issues of a magazine, and, more important, for competitive issues of different magazines. Advertising agencies take these figures very seriously, which makes magazine managements take them very seriously indeed. At the same time, newsstand circulation is relatively profitable, because newsstand prices are higher than subscription prices. The basic question, therefore, is this: Should a publisher concentrate on making a profit at the newsstands by charging a high price and selling relatively few copies, or should he gamble on the theory that low newsstand prices would increase sales and therefore impress rich advertisers? A few years later, most publishers finally came to the right decision and increased their prices, but at the beginning of 1966, each publisher was waiting fearfully for the others to make the first move.

Just before Christmas of 1965, Emerson happened to mention that G. B. McCombs had summoned him to confer on an increase in newsstand sales.

"Why would they want to do that?" I asked.

"They think it's evidence of growth," Emerson said. "They want to sell at least 100,000 more copies, maybe even 200,000."

"How on earth do they plan to do that?" I asked. "Unless they want to put naked ladies on the cover, the only way to sell that many extra copies is to spend a lot more money on promotion, and I bet they don't plan to spend a nickel."

"They'll have to," Emerson said. "They're not *that* stupid."

In the afternoon, at the meeting with G.B., Emerson, and Ballew, I found that I had not underestimated our management. G.B. told us that Maurice Poppei was trying to draw up a 1966 budget that would show a profit, and he had fallen short. He had simply decreed, therefore, that the *Post* would earn an extra $500,000 in annual revenue by selling an extra 100,000 copies on the newsstands every fortnight.

"How much is Poppei going to invest in extra promotion money?" I asked.

"Well, frankly," G.B. said with a laugh, "frankly nothing."

"Then how are we supposed to sell 100,000 extra copies?"

"Well, we'll all just have to try harder," G.B. said.

What does one do when ordered to charge an impregnable fortress? The best alternative is to propose some wholly different course of action. If we were committed to a theoretical increase of $500,000 in newsstand sales, why couldn't we achieve it by simply setting a higher price? "That way, we at least have a chance of making it," I said, "whereas trying to sell an extra 100,000 copies . . ."

Emerson and Ballew added their views in favor of a price increase, but G.B. was noncommittal. He said only that he would feed some new figures into the computers and then see what Poppei said. Ten days later, we met again, and G.B. began cheerily by asking, "Well, are you boys ready to put out a thirty-five-cent *Post*?"

"We sure are," Ballew said.

"Okay," said G.B. "The price is going up on the next issue."

"That sounds almost too easy," Emerson said.

"Yeah, I guess it does," G.B. agreed.

Poppei and G.B., it now turned out, had had no intention whatever of increasing the price. They had asked some statistician what the effect would be, and the statistician had promptly answered that sales would decrease by 10 percent, and that this decline would jeopardize the minimum rate base of 6.5 million that we promised our advertisers. Then, however, it came to light that somebody in charge of the computers had made a terrible mistake and had somehow *lost* the names of 100,000 subscribers. Or, to put it another way, we had 100,000 more subscribers than we thought we had, and we were sending out 100,000 more copies of every issue than we thought we were sending out—100,000 copies for which we weren't charging the advertisers anything at all. Because of this ludicrous mistake, Poppei now wanted to sell fewer copies on the newsstands, and therefore G.B. was making the smiling announcement that we were being granted our price increase. Still, we could only accept our blessings and keep asking for more.

"While we have you here, G.B.," I pressed on, "can't we do something about subscription prices? Why do we have to keep giving the magazine away at $1.95 a year?"

"Well, we have to stay competitive with *Look*," G.B. said.

"But isn't there some way we could get together with them and say, 'Listen, we're both losing money this way'?"

"That's a violation of the antitrust laws," G.B. said with a grin.

"But there's got to be some way around that."

"I'll think about it," G.B. said.

Within a month after we had increased our newsstand price because of the mistake in the computers, *Look* announced the same change in rates. The failure to increase the price of subscriptions, however, was a problem that would haunt us to the end. In fact, it was a major cause of that end.

Our most critical need early in 1966 was neither editorial excellence nor newsstand sales, however, but more advertising revenue. We had lost another $3.5 million during the confusion of 1965, when we scarcely expected to survive at all, and now it was up to Jess Ballew to start bringing in more money. Ballew was a phenomenal work horse, and his love of work was matched only by his enthusiastic optimism about the results of that work.

"The business is coming in," he would say every time I saw him. "Every issue is going to be up from last year, and we'll be hitting a hundred pages soon."

I did not believe him. In fact, his buoyancy irritated me. It reminded me of a toy that was popular at the time, a ball of some material that produced extravagant bounces. "What Jess Ballew really is," I complained to Emerson, "is a superball." This delighted Emerson, who told the next meeting of the editorial staff all Ballew's predictions and then added: "Otto thinks that Jess is exaggerating, and he called him a superball."

As it turned out, Ballew's prophecies were not so wild after all. His ads pushed the *Post* over one hundred pages by March—bringing a profit on each issue—and the average for the first six months of 1966 was a solid ninety-seven pages.

Despite the loss of $3.5 million during 1965, Mac Clifford emphasized that there had been a $400,000 profit during the last quarter of the year. The annual report showed that although assets had been reduced from $112.6 million to $88.9 million, liabilities had been reduced much more, from $103 million to $68.4 million—thus increasing the stockholders' equity from $9.5 million to $20.5 million. In addition to all this, Clifford now announced the first-quarter profit for 1966—$251,000—about seven times as much as the nominal profit during the first quarter of the previous year. "With a continuation of the economy on its present basis, we would expect a successful year for the company," Clifford said. "Hemlines are going up, and so are Curtis's fortunes."

Despite all these signs of progress, however, we were already learning that prosperity and poverty were strikingly similar under the reign of Mac Clifford. Or, to put it another way, prosperity would bring us very few of the benefits that we had hoped for during our poverty. As early as March, when it became clear that we might end our losses for the first time, Clifford announced that we must all "tighten our belts" so that the company could make a respectable profit. As a first step in that direction, he abolished the *Post*'s traditional advertising-editorial formula, whereby an increase in the sale of advertising pages also permitted the publication of more editorial pages. Henceforth, editorial pages would not go beyond fifty-one, no matter how many ads were sold.

Prosperity also enabled Clifford to begin thinking about new purges

The Years of Contention

Clay Blair (left) began as a protégé of *Post* editor Robert Sherrod
but soon took the editor's chair for himself.

Blair's aide Don Schanche (left) recruited a new staff to replace the old *Post* editors. Davis Thomas (left, below) and Hank Walker also were devoted Blair lieutenants.

The Blair forces opposed Matthew Culligan, the supersalesman
who became president and vowed to save Curtis.

A showman, Culligan used a helicopter to dash around the country soliciting ads. At right, Serge Semenenko, the mysterious financier who rescued Curtis with a $35,000,000 loan.

Wally Butts sued the *Post* over a 1963 article accusing him of rigging a football game. He denied it and won $460,000.

THE STORY OF A COLLEGE FOOTBALL FIX

GEORGIA VERSUS ALABAMA

The sharply divided board of directors posed for a harmonious group portrait (clockwise from Blair, nearest camera): John Clifford, Marvin Kantor, Walter Franklin, Harry Mills, M. Albert Linton, Mary Curtis Bok Zimbalist, Matthew Culligan, Gloria Swett, Cary Bok, Walter Fuller, Moreau Brown, Curtis Barkes, and Milton Gould.

The revolt of Blair and Marvin Kantor against Culligan ended in the departure of all three. Above, Blair and Kantor talking with reporters just after their suspension.

After a fruitless search for fresh talent, the Curtis presidency
fell to Culligan's deputy, John McLean Clifford.

Clifford's secretary, Gloria Swett, soon came to exercise substantial powers in the company. Controller Maurice Poppei (right) administered drastic cuts in the Curtis budget.

The *Post* staff members rejoiced when ebullient William Emerson
became editor.

The editor's job required diplomacy: Trying to revive shattered *Post* traditions, Emerson (left) sought to rehire Norman Rockwell, in vain.

The editor also had to entertain visiting celebrities, such as Sharon Tate. Emerson ran an article on her called "Sexy Little Me."

More diplomacy: The desperate need for ads put Emerson in an uneasy relationship with publisher Stephen Kelly (right, above). And criticism of the *Post*'s appearance prompted disputes between Emerson and art director Asger Jerrild (right).

Entrepreneur Martin Ackerman put up $5,000,000 to take over
Curtis and ran it from his Park Avenue townhouse.

In the euphoric early moments of his regime, Ackerman was surrounded by hopeful executives like G. B. McCombs (left).

From left: Ackerman's wife, his aides Bob Yung and Levere Lund, and publisher Kelly.

"The magazine must reflect me," said Ackerman (center); he tried his hand at laying out pictures.

Ackerman enjoyed presiding at business luncheons, and when he spoke the table chatter ceased.

The Plan: Ackerman's scribbled sketch for a drastic overhaul of the tottering corporation.

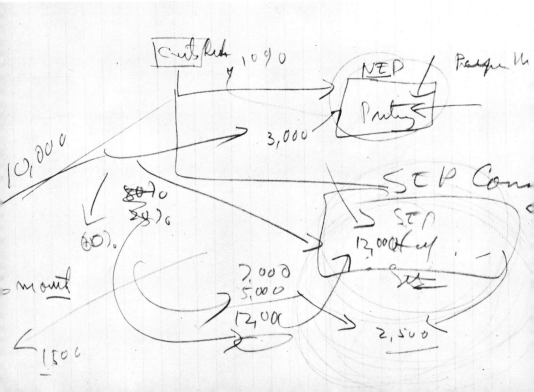

of the staff, purges that he had been reluctant to undertake during the uncertainties of the previous year. On the *Post*, his main target was none other than the publisher, Jess Ballew. Although Ballew was selling a lot of ads, he had neglected one of the basic rules of corporate warfare by failing to keep his own base of operations protected. He had several ambitious lieutenants, and they had intimated to Clifford that Ballew really wasn't doing his job as well as it might be done. They suggested, among other things, that Emerson might become editor-and-publisher. Emerson rejected the suggestion, however, and he implied that he might resign if Ballew were fired. Clifford by now liked and trusted Emerson, and so he drew back from the attack, grumbling and muttering.

Clifford's other main target was *Holiday*, for in this year of recovery, when the *Post* increased its advertising by 16 percent during the first six months, the *Journal* gained 20 percent and *American Home* 42 percent, but *Holiday* sank by 9 percent. It was not, indeed, an exceptionally interesting magazine. I don't think it ever had been, or ever could be, for there are narrow limits to what can be done with any magazine devoted primarily to travel. Don Schanche, in his two years as editor, had made all the conventional moves to attract an audience of young vacationers, but Schanche had never really been the ideal man for the job. *Holiday* needed, if it was to be successful at all, an editor who was stylish and elegant and even somewhat frivolous, a flamboyant figure who would appear at all the right parties in all the right resorts. Schanche, for all his abilities, was earnest and somber, a journalist rather than a *bel esprit*. The man most directly responsible for *Holiday*'s commercial success or failure, though, was a cultivated but equally somber gentleman named Garth Hite, the advertising director. And as Mac Clifford contemplated the magazine's decline, he presumably recalled that both Schanche and Hite had been among Blair's rebels. In fact, their days were numbered.

The first actual victim of Clifford's slow purge, however, was the ghostly figure of Bob Sherrod. Only about three years earlier, Sherrod had been the editor of the *Post*, a man of eminence, with the respect and affection of much of his staff, but these last three years had not treated him well. Various management oligarchs had tried to use him for their various purposes, treating him as a man who would make unpleasant telephone calls and generally carry out orders. Sherrod had drifted into the ambiguous position of "editorial coordinator," an executive without executive authority. Editors who had once worked for him eventually had no choice but to rebuff his suggestions—and this had its effect. He seemed to become more and more diffident and unhappy.

Just before Christmas, Sherrod had made one last effort to reassert himself as an "editor-at-large." A friend in some Western embassy in Moscow had invited him there for a party, and he asked whether we could use an article on current developments in Russia. To Emerson's horror, I said we could, for we had published nothing about the changes in the Soviet Union since the fall of Khrushchev in the previous year, and so Sherrod set off once again as a foreign correspondent. The results, however, were thin. Sherrod brought back little more than the conventional street scenes and embassy gossip, and we published his story mainly because of his name and former position.

By May, Clifford had decided that Sherrod was not working out as a corporate vice president, and so he asked Emerson whether we could use him as a writer. For old time's sake, Emerson was willing to experiment, but only if Sherrod could accept a substantial salary cut that would bring him down to the level of our regular writers. Emerson's decision must have delighted Clifford, but he told Sherrod nothing more detailed than "Go and make your peace with Bill." It fell to Emerson, therefore, to explain the new salary and the new conditions to the man who had once hired him. Sherrod reacted by asking time to think it over, and then he proposed a plan to escape from the whole problem. He wanted to go back to Asia for three months, he said, to write a major story, twenty thousand words, called "The Chinese."

"I've lived there for several years, and I know the Chinese," Sherrod said. "What I'd like to do now is to make a tour of the whole periphery of Southeast Asia."

"Isn't that necessarily going to turn into a piece on the overseas Chinese?" I asked. Sherrod and Emerson had inevitably brought the problem to my office, and I happened to know that Sherrod had been unable to get a visa to China.

"Oh, no," Sherrod said. "I have good contacts in the government, and they can fill me in on what's happening on the mainland."

"Lord, I don't think the government itself has any idea of what's happening on the mainland," I said.

Sherrod only smiled a thin smile at this, and Emerson stood in silence, waiting to see what would happen next.

"In any case," I said, "I think it would be a mistake to attempt a major story on the Chinese without going to China."

This seemed to me perfectly reasonable, even self-evident, but Sherrod suddenly flushed a dark red.

"Well, there certainly wouldn't be any point in undertaking such a story," he said, "if the editors have serious reservations about it."

"I'm sorry," I said, "but as far as I'm concerned, I do have serious reservations."

"All right, then," Sherrod said, turning to Emerson. "I'll be thinking about what you said."

We shook hands stiffly, and that was our parting. A month later, I heard from Emerson that Sherrod had complained to Clifford that working for us would be "insulting." Clifford quoted Sherrod as saying, "They want to tell me what stories to write." Emerson said he had told Clifford: "Damn right! And we'll tell him how to write them too." Another month elapsed, and then the *Times* of July 8 declared:

The Curtis Board is understood to have accepted the resignation of Robert L. Sherrod as vice president and editorial coordinator. Mr. Sherrod has been the principal editorial officer of the magazine publishing company since the fall of 1964, when it was engulfed in an editors' rebellion. . . . J. M. Clifford, new president, in a telephone interview from the company's Philadelphia headquarters, denied that Mr. Sherrod's resignation had been accepted. . . . "There is nothing final yet. . . . No action has been taken by the board. It hasn't happened."

That same day, I was talking with the company lawyer, Ron Diana, an amiable young man who managed to hear a lot of gossip, and I asked him whether Sherrod had or had not resigned.

"I can't tell you that," Diana said. "I can't tell you that he resigned, and I can't tell you that his resignation was accepted."

"What else can't you tell me? Can you tell me why Clifford denied it?"

"No, I can't tell you that it was just another example of Clifford's fear of publicity. I also can't tell you that Sherrod's going to set up a private office in the East Sixties, and that he has two good job offers, from Time Inc. and the *Reader's Digest.*"

"Now can you tell me why he hung on through these last three years? Why didn't he leave when he lost his battle with Blair?"

"Well, how can you ever know?" Diana said.

It took four days before Clifford's formal announcement of Sherrod's resignation appeared on the bulletin boards in the familiar posters with the red borders. Could it be that Clifford had denied a true story simply because his official forms hadn't yet been printed and distributed? It seemed absurd, and yet that was the way Lyndon Johnson was currently carrying out personnel changes in Washington, and it was the traditional method of making such changes in Moscow. Why should Mac Clifford be any less petty?

And so Sherrod was gone. He subsequently went to Vietnam for *Life* and then moved to Washington to write a book about the American flights to the moon. How long it had been since our first lunch at the St. Regis, when he had first offered me a job on the *Post*. And how much better it would have been for both of us if I had never seen all the things that had happened to him.

On May 2, 1966, a heart attack killed M. Albert Linton, aged seventy-nine, long-time president of the Provident Mutual Life Insurance Company of Philadelphia. As chairman of the executive committee of the Curtis board of directors, he had sat in the seat of judgment during the Blair-Culligan fight, and consequently he was perhaps the one man most directly and specifically responsible for the way the battles of 1964 ended, and for the way the company was now organized. And yet the obituary, which must sum up a man's life in a few paragraphs, always tells us surprising things. Linton's photograph showed the bland, starched expression we would expect of an insurance-company president, but the obituary itself said that Linton was also "an ardent mountain climber." He had climbed the Jungfrau four times (most recently at the age of sixty), and also the Matterhorn and a variety of other mountains in the Alps and the Rockies. Furthermore, according to the *Times*, he was an amateur ornithologist of some note, who published "erudite treatises on birds." In fact, one species of Ecuadorian flycatcher was officially named Lintoni "in recognition of his work in its identification."

In the spring of every year, the corporation's salesmen begin to yearn for their annual sales conference. It is a strange tradition, this insistence on regular gatherings at golf clubs, but there are good reasons for it. One reason, obviously, is that the salesmen get a free vacation, away from the office in St. Louis or Chicago but also away from the wives and children who dominate the conventional family vacation. This does not mean, as wives suspect, that the sales convention is an orgy of vice and debauchery. The salesman is a simple soul (and the corporation likes to convene at country clubs that are remote from carnal temptation). He genuinely likes to spend his days playing golf and his evenings playing poker, and his nearest approach to vice is that he drinks too much whiskey and gets raucous.

But there are also business reasons for this conviviality. One is that it gives the salesmen a good opportunity to compare notes. Scattered over the country, they all face similar problems in isolation, and the only way they can learn from one another's experiences is to gather and talk about what has happened to them. And when they gather, the home office has its best chance to explain to all of them what it is that they are selling—which is more complicated than one might think. (This is why editors are summoned to try to define the function and goal of their magazine.)

The most important reason for these meetings, though, is that salesmen are not like normal people. They do not get their satisfaction from making things, or even from fixing things, but from the quasi-erotic act of selling things. I say quasi-erotic because selling is based on a relationship of aggression and submission, flirtation and acceptance. For the successful practice of this art, it doesn't really matter what is being sold, but it does matter that the salesman feel a profound and visceral sense of confidence in whatever he is selling. One analyst, Antony Jay (*Management and Machiavelli*), has even compared the salesman's task to that of the missionary: "Other members of the corporation see only each other—it is easy to be a good Catholic in the Vatican. But the salesman travels alone to a spiritual Limpopo with only the strength of his faith to sustain him. He meets men who laugh at his god and deride his priests with tales of missed delivery dates and unmet specifications."

Because of the salesman's passion for golf, and because the corporation considers this a harmless way for a salesman to work off excess energy, sales conferences are generally held in remote resort hotels. The first one I ever attended, while still at *Newsweek,* took place at an isolated country club near the coast of New Jersey. My first *Post* sales conference brought me to the rain-swept hills of central Pennsylvania, and another one occurred on a virtually inaccessible mountain in West Virginia. I can only assume, therefore, that the hotel rates in Puerto Rico are cheaper than those at any East Coast resort—it is the kind of thing Mac Clifford would have insisted on—for in mid-May of 1966, I found myself and my wife disembarking among the palm trees in the bright, hot sunshine of San Juan airport. Then, in a Volkswagen bus, we rode through the clamorous city and its outskirts until we reached a beach enclave about ten miles to the West, the Dorado Hilton.

We soon realized that we were prisoners here, with nowhere to go and nothing to do, but the salesmen seemed to enjoy being prisoners. They sat around the swimming pool, in their trunks and sports shirts, and fed on hamburgers on paper plates and beer in paper cups. The waiters were rather sullen, as they seem to be all over the Caribbean, helpless natives in this American occupation zone, but the management did its best to make things cheerful. In the evening, there was a rum party on the glass-walled upper terrace overlooking the ocean, and then a spare-ribs barbecue by the swimming pool, to the accompaniment of a Calypso band.

The next morning, there were more than one hundred salesmen packed into the golf clubhouse, air-conditioned to the point of subterranean chill. In the back row, somewhere, sat Gloria Swett, taking notes. Emerson gave a little introductory spiel about the roles of the editors who were going to address this group, and then I had to step forward and start talking. Knees shaking, hands trembling, throat parched, I began to tell the salesmen how things had changed since our last meeting in Hershey, Pennsylvania, how Blair had fallen and the weekly *Post* was gone, and how the slower closing had forced us away from trying to cover the week's news, but not away from the essential process of journalism. "SPEAK SLOWLY AND CLEARLY," I had written at the top of every page of notes, and so I lumbered on. I told them that we still claimed the constitutional function of journalism, to inform the public about what was happening, so that people could make the decisions they needed to make in order to govern themselves. I told them how I used to scramble through a day's news at the United Press and then have nothing to tell my wife at the end of the day, and I offered one definition of news: something that's worth telling your wife when you come home from work. And I quoted Ezra Pound to the effect that history is news that stays news, and I told them that this was what we were trying to report.

The stony faces stared back at me, without the faintest signs of approval or interest or anything else. There are no faces so inhuman, it occurred to me, as the faces of an audience, passive, without emotion. It occurred to me, too, that I would never again go through this awful experience of making a speech, never for any reason or any price. But before I could leave this podium, I had to get through this last speech. I turned another page of notes and saw once again the warning: "SPEAK SLOWLY AND CLEARLY."

I began to tell them about Vietnam. I told them how we used to cover the war in news magazine style, with our own correspondent, Stan Karnow, reporting on each major development. That was no longer possible, I told them. No single correspondent could provide continuing coverage of a war of such complexity. We needed more information from Washington, like Stewart Alsop's recent interview with Secretary McNamara, and Senator Fulbright's article calling for peace talks. As for scenes of combat, we would have to go beyond ordinary journalism to find stories like that of Captain Roger Donlon, who had recently described in the *Post* the ferocious battle in which he had become the first American in Vietnam to win the Congressional Medal of Honor. Our newest correspondent in Vietnam, I added offhandedly, had just spent a day in a fighter-bomber raiding North Vietnam. But we were not covering the war if we reported only our side of it, and so I cited Sanche de Gramont's unprecedented report from Vietcong territory. De Gramont was an exceptional representative for a stuffy old Philadelphia magazine like the *Post*, I told them—a French aristocrat, an intellectual, a veteran of the Algerian War, an experienced reporter for the Associated Press and the *Herald Tribune*, winner of a Pulitzer Prize for work done under deadline pressure. When I had asked him what his wife would think of his assignment to Vietcong territory, he said he wouldn't tell her what he was doing, and so I had said, "Go."

But then I told them that journalism, despite all the talk about "reporting in depth," was not just a matter of facts, that the facts were pointless unless we told people what they meant, and that as far as Vietnam was concerned, we were against the war, and we were going to say so and keep on saying so. Here, I said, holding up the latest issue of the *Post*, here was an article by Joseph Alsop, claiming that we were winning the war. I conceded Alsop's right to say what he thought, but I also insisted on our own right to put Alsop's article in perspective, and so I pointed to an editorial I had written in the same issue, which said, stealing an old line from John Steinbeck, that "our military victories may represent no more than the victory of flies conquering flypaper."

The faces of the salesmen remained stony. I could not tell whether they disapproved or whether I was just boring them. By now, in any case, I was near the end. "SPEAK SLOWLY AND CLEARLY." I told them how I had discovered, back in 1964, a history of the *Post*, and how I had suddenly realized that we were failing to preserve one of our most priceless assets, our great tradition. I told them how I had begun accumulating office treasures, how I was proud to have Lorimer's desk and Hibbs's chair and Blair's conference table and Marty Sommers's maps of the world. I told them, finally, how I had recently had lunch with an editor I was trying to hire, and how that editor had asked me what the *Post* was and where it was going, and how I had said that I didn't really know the answer to that familiar question, that we had no rigid formula for what we published, that the *Post* was simply a magazine to be written by good writers and read by intelligent readers, that its function was to explain what was happening in the world, and that its purpose was to be the best magazine in the country. I thought it had already achieved this purpose, I said, and its goal now was to become still better. The End.

I was shuffling my notes together and abdicating the platform, vowing to myself never to make another speech, when I realized that the salesmen had all risen to their feet, applauding wildly, frantically, as though they had just witnessed some divine revelation. At the time, it seemed an incomprehensible outburst, but that was because I did not realize how desperately these salesmen needed a sermon. It had been two years since they had even seen the editorial staff, and then it had been the staff headed by Blair. Since the Blair insurrection, which had left the salesmen in bewilderment, they had heard pep talks from Ballew and jokes from Emerson, but it was hard for them to keep the faith in a climate of doubt and cynicism, and now finally a new group of editors had started to give them a new *Summa* of the faith that they were expected to keep. And so they stood there for several minutes, beating their hands together, some even shouting, while I stumbled dazedly back to my seat, reveling in the fact that my opening turn was over. All I had to do from then on was to listen to the other editors, McKinney and Congdon telling stories about the proper treatment of writers, Mac Farrell explaining the purposes of contemporary fiction, and Asger Jerrild showing slides to illustrate our changing policies on graphic design.

That afternoon, we went to San Juan, leaving the salesmen to their ritual golf tournament, and we returned only in time for the evening's ceremonial dinner. First we gathered in the golf club to drink a very strong rum punch (this was Puerto Rico, after all, and rum is the *vin du pays*), and then, with dinner, we had wine and whiskey and more rum. The atmosphere was fairly mellow by the time we began the presentation of awards to those who had sold advertising for Curtis for twenty-five years, those who had sold for twenty, those who had sold for fifteen, and finally those who had won various events in the afternoon's golf. Then, in some curious fit, Clifford asked that everyone who had been at Curtis for less than ten years raise his hand. About half of us dutifully raised our hands, and Clifford bellowed that we were the ones who had been doing all the work, and he wanted to pay us $25 each. Nobody moved. "I'm serious," Clifford said, peering about him with the jerky neck motions of a rooster. "Turn in your names at the desk here." Once again, nobody moved, and so Clifford gave up. (Several months later, I was surprised to receive a check for $25, with a note from Clifford that simply said, "I meant what I said.")

When it came time for the official speeches, Jess Ballew climbed to the rostrum and made a brief introduction, in which he presented Mac Clifford as "a hard-nosed, two-fisted sonofabitch businessman," which everyone seemed to consider a high compliment. (I am prejudiced, I suppose, by the fact that I was brought up to think that business was not really a worthwhile way to spend one's life, and that successful businessmen were generally of questionable character. This is snobbery of a sort, I know, but is it possible to imagine someone being introduced to a public gathering as a "hard-nosed, two-fisted sonofabitch teacher"? Or lawyer, minister, violinist, doctor, or farmer? No, the businessman likes to take his imagery from the worst of the competitive, combative professions. That introduction would have served equally well to present a policeman or a prize-fighter.)

Clifford began by telling the salesmen that Curtis was improving. Things were looking up. If we could just have team work. And communication. There were some wonderful people working for Curtis, and everybody should be grateful to them. Like Maurice Poppei, who couldn't take the time to come down here to Puerto Rico but was doing a great job for all of us. And Gloria Swett, who was also doing a tremendous job. She was "important not only to my life but to the lives of all of you," Clifford said. And then, when he tried to go on, he began to falter. He paused and looked around him, confused. "Not as articulate as I might be," Clifford said thickly. There was no way for him to stop in mid-speech, however. We were all staring up at him, on the podium, all the bright-eyed salesmen waiting for the word from our president. Tell us, Mac Clifford, tell us how it's going to be, you stubby, white-haired, hard-nosed, two-fisted sonofabitch businessman, tell us about our golden future, tell us about the rabbits. "Not as articulate as I might be," Clifford said again. "Maybe had one too many."

All he had to do, then, was to introduce the final speaker. "Bill Emerson—a man you all know—has done a great job. Emerson will become one of the great figures in the history of magazines." There were murmurings from the floor. "He already is," several of the salesmen chorused. The interruption seemed to push Clifford into a new and less amiable direction. "Emerson and his team are putting out a great product," Clifford said, "but you people aren't doing enough to sell it." The salesmen looked numb. Was this the way the Central Committee used to hear Comrade Stalin announce the new production goals? "*American Home* is up 56 percent," Clifford said, "*Ladies' Home Journal* is up a lot, even *Jack and Jill* is doing better. So all of you are going to have to work harder to make the kind of progress we need." Clifford's speech struck me as insulting, but the salesmen did not seem to mind. The lash was part of their pep rally. Hit 'em again, harder, harder. And when Clifford ended by presenting Emerson, everyone applauded wildly in a kind of cathartic release.

Emerson, unfortunately, had an insoluble problem—this whole regiment of salesmen had heard virtually every joke in his repertoire. They already knew about his uncle in Bottom Dollar, Tennessee, who had taken him down to the crossroads "to learn how to hang around"; they had heard about his Aunt Sina's funeral, when the post office lost the special-delivery letter that contained her ashes; they had heard about the last whore in Waxahachie County and the curse of the Plotnick Diamond and the rooster that had said, "If you want to f—— a buzzard, you have to play the game." In short, he did not have a new speech ready, but he did know what the salesmen needed and wanted—a sense of unity—and so, since I had already delivered the sermon, he simply told them how he had watched Joe A. do a great selling job among the Boeing people in Seattle, and how he had gone with Joe B. to argue with the hostile establishment in Dallas, and how he had got drunk with Joe C. in Chicago, and how he and Joe D. had sold a half-million-dollar contract in Cleveland. It was not a speech so much as a series of recollections and pledges, but while Clifford obviously had very little personal relationship with his sales staff, Emerson just as obviously knew all of them and all of their problems, and when he was done, they all felt, for no reason, that they were seven feet tall.

The sales conference continued for another day, but they didn't need editors any more, and so we set off on a tour of the island. When we got back that night, we found that the prisoners of the Dorado Hilton had finished their meeting and were all searching for enjoyment. The only place to go, after dark, was the hotel's own nightclub, a dark and crowded place called La Fuente, and at the entrance we encountered the welcoming blast of nightclub jazz. Inside, there were perhaps two hundred salesmen and golfers and tourists, not all ours but indistinguishable from ours, and out of the darkness loomed Jess Ballew in a plaid jacket and scarlet trousers.

"Hey, I know you're not worrying too much about business right now," Ballew said, "but you've always been so interested in circulation that I thought you'd like to hear that they've agreed to increase the subscription prices at the end of the year."

"Well, that's great," I said. "How much of an increase?"

"I think it's a dollar a year, to $4.95. But I've got to go now."

I watched Ballew work his way through the crowd to a place at the bar, where Mac Clifford stood in a circle of supporters and subsidiaries. I could not help wondering about "their" decision to increase the price. I wondered whether G.B.'s computers had made some new mistake, or whether some other kind of miscalculation had driven our leaders to this measure. La Fuente was not a place for reflection, however. Bands of salesmen, who had heard the editorial speeches from the anonymous safety of the audience, popped up from their tables and offered introductions. This is Harry, from the San Francisco office. Good to meet you, Harry. And Charley, from Atlanta. Say, would you let us buy you a drink? And Sam is from the Chicago office, and he shot a 73 today. And hey, will you look at that?

Out on the darkened dance floor, lit only by a pair of spotlights that cut through the clouds of cigarette smoke, Sweet Gloria Swett was dancing all alone with a young salesman from one of the regional offices. The little band had faded to a series of lazy improvisations, interrupted from time to time by trumpet bursts from the bearded bandleader, and Gloria undulated in the rhythm of her own improvisation. Her partner, inhibited both by the social situation and by the current rules of dancing, stood at a distance, swaying, pretending to maintain a partnership. But Gloria was really all alone, her eyes dreamy, looking at nothing; her white dress, cut very short, swinging from side to side as she danced. Not a figure that you would expect to see dancing with an advertising salesman in Puerto Rico, but nonetheless chief of personnel and public relations, of raises, office space, and all the details that can make office life pleasant or unpleasant. And, for these few moments, in the half-darkness and the smoke, perhaps all the unpleasantnesses of life might float away. Then the music stopped, and the band trooped off the little stage, and Gloria Swett and her partner looked at one another with an embarrassed uncertainty about what to do next. We looked at Gloria, we the watchers, and our eyes followed her and the young partner toward the bar, where we saw Mac Clifford, the two-fisted sonofabitch businessman.

And to our surprise, we also saw Mac Clifford in animated conversation with Tom Congdon. From a distance, it looked a little perilous, Congdon breaking in on the president, Clifford staring back with the look of a turtle disturbed while at rest. But Clifford actually was in a euphoric mood, it turned out, and he wanted to talk about his capacity for decisive action. It was because of him, Clifford, that Bill Emerson had become the editor of the *Saturday Evening Post*, and that all the rest of us had survived in Emerson's shadow. Several members of the board had been against Emerson's appointment, Clifford said, but he, Clifford, had said to the board: "Either Emerson becomes the editor or you'd better find yourselves another president." It was the right decision too, by God, Clifford said, his head weaving a little from side to side, and we would all benefit from it. "All of you editors who were there during the dark days and helped save the *Post*," Clifford told Congdon, there at the bar of La Fuente, "all of you will be rewarded."

Flo Conway was a tiny, fierce girl of twenty-three, who played the violin and worried over the *Post*'s printing problems. When Mac Clifford had fired Flo's boss, Tom Marvel, chief of production, Flo had simply taken over Marvel's whole department and run it splendidly. Reconciling the problems of the editors and the problems of the printers was a job calculated to drive anyone mad, however, and Flo finally told us, in this spring of 1966, that she was quitting the *Post* to go out to the University of Oregon to get a master's degree in something called "communications."

"Why are you doing that, Flo?" I asked her. "What on earth are you going to do with a master's degree in communications?"

"I'm going to be an executive," said Flo. I did not offer the obvious answer, that Flo had no experience in selling things or keeping accounts or performing any of the other routine jobs that supposedly lead to an executive position. But I wondered what had inspired this girl to such an ambition.

"An executive?" I echoed. "Just because of a master's degree?"

"Well, just look at these people around here!" Flo cried. "Look at G. B. McCombs! The first time I saw G. B. McCombs, I thought he was a nice old man, but when I learned that he was an *executive*, in *charge* of things—why—why anything that G.B. can do, I can do, I'm absolutely positive of that!"

I wondered whether G.B. would be pleased to know that he had served as an inspiration to a young girl with executive ambitions. Perhaps not. In any case, Flo went West, and we replaced her with her own assistant, Miss Rita Ortiga, who was also twenty-three, but tall and slim and glamorous, with long black hair. Once, as a secretary, she had typed Tom Congdon's letter to Walter Deane Fuller, about who really edited the *Post*. Now, by coincidence, Congdon and Rita and Bruce Jay Friedman and I all entered the elevator at the same time, and Congdon introduced Rita to Friedman as "our new chief of production." Friedman paused and stared for a time, and then he finally said, "You could certainly win a lot of money on *What's My Line?*"

In good times and bad, the corporate machinery continues to run by itself, unaffected by any external reality. The Curtis legal department sent me a memorandum announcing the formation of the Curtis Trademark Committee and asking my attendance at its first meeting. Something happened to prevent my attending, and so I received another memo announcing that the Trademark Committee had met and reached its first decision. It had decided that, for the protection of our trademarks, the legal and official names of the Curtis magazines were, in fact, the *Saturday Evening Post, Ladies' Home Journal*, the *American Home, Holiday*, and *Jack and Jill*. Any changes, the memorandum informed us, would jeopardize our proprietary interest in these names.

From the *Gallagher Report*, June 14:

NEW CURTIS PUBLISHING UPHEAVAL. Due shortly. Involves two corporate offices, one editor. President "Mac the Knife" Clifford ripe for retirement . . . Former McCall's publisher "Steely Blue" Kelly listens to offer. Probably on Holiday. Times-Mirror, Metromedia, McCall Corp. candidates to acquire Curtis. Latest prospective buyer: Dow Jones . . .

On June 27, Emerson informed me that "they" had removed Garth Hite, and that the new publisher of *Holiday* was Steve Kelly, late of *McCall's*. He said that Schanche didn't yet know of the change, that "they" would inform him on the next day. I said that if the change had been made primarily to create an opening for Kelly, then we ought to get Hite transferred to the *Post*. Emerson agreed and called Ballew, but it was already too late. Hite was gone.

From the *Gallagher Report*, July 12:

"Steely Blue" Kelly expected to appoint travel editor Caskie Stinnett as new editor of Holiday . . .

Throughout these years, there was very little contact between the management in Philadelphia and the editors in New York. Ever since that first meeting at which the editors had denounced Mac Clifford for firing two editorial people, both sides seemed wary, mistrustful, and a little afraid of one another. For three years, therefore, Bill Emerson served us all as intermediary and envoy plenipotentiary, telling each side what the other wanted or did not want. One day in

July, however, when Emerson had taken his wife and children on their annual vacation to Georgia, I had to play his substitute at a managerial meeting, and so I got a brief but overwhelming view of the Clifford management as it now reigned in full power.

Gloria Swett telephoned me early in the week to "invite" me to Philadelphia to take part in a meeting of the board of directors of the Curtis Circulation Company "to see if we can't get this scheduling business settled." I had no idea what she meant, but I couldn't admit that. I asked whether I should plan to speak or just listen. She said I should be "ready to take part in the discussion, and bring along any figures you may need." In hope of some enlightenment, I called Jess Ballew and found that he was also going to the meeting, and that he knew as little as I did.

The only way to get from Long Island to Philadelphia in time for a morning conference is to arise at the sepulchral hour of five-thirty and catch a train that leaves from Penn Station at eight. This sequence duly brought me to Philadelphia almost an hour before the meeting, leaving me nothing to do except wander around. It seemed strange to be in Curtis's capital city once again—the first time since the Blair conspiracy had brought me to the Marriott Motel two years earlier, the first time downtown since I had come to work for Bob Sherrod four years earlier. Compared with New York, Philadelphia always seemed moribund, the narrow streets empty, the air hot and motionless. It was as though nothing ever happened here, and nobody cared.

Shortly before eleven, I entered again the marble palace on Independence Square, and one of the liveried Negroes maneuvered the dark, paneled elevator to the eighth floor. A gray-haired lady blocked the corridor to the board room and ushered me into a thickly carpeted anteroom. The only other person there, looking very lonely, was Don Gold, managing editor of *Holiday*, another substitute like me. But more people soon began filing in. Steve Kelly, the newly appointed publisher of *Holiday*, a heavy-set man of nearly fifty, silver-haired, with bright blue eyes and a very smooth, in-charge-of-things manner. And John Mack Carter, editor of the *Journal*, giving me a quizzical look and asking, "Have you heard anything?" Meaning, since this was the deadline for competitive bidding on William Manchester's book on the death of President Kennedy, that he had already learned of our preposterous bid of $155,000 (which turned out to be not so preposterous as Carter's own bid, and not nearly preposterous enough to win—that honor going to *Look* for about $650,000). No, I hadn't heard anything yet. Desultory chatter.

Gloria Swett finally appeared to summon us, and we trooped off after her, down a corridor and then to the throne room. This, then, was where all those battles had taken place—Blair against Culligan, Clifford against Kantor, and, for all I knew, Lorimer against Bok. We first entered another antechamber, about fifteen feet square, entirely paneled from floor to ceiling, and serving no apparent purpose except to house a giant portrait of the white-bearded Cyrus H. K. Curtis. Then left, through glass doors, into the board room itself. It was about twenty feet by eighty, dominated by one enormous table. The walls had ornate wooden panels, and the high ceiling was covered with curlicues and arabesques. The directors' chairs were heavy, with high, straight backs, covered with faded brocade. In front of each chair lay an array of equipment, yellow pad, needle-sharp pencils, glass ashtray. And around this baronial table, in this baronial council chamber, sat an extraordinary collection of courtiers.

At the far end, looking very small in that high-backed chair, so that one suspected that his feet did not quite reach the floor, sat Mac Clifford, very clearly occupying the seat of power. At his right hand sat Gloria Swett, no longer the voice of authority, nor the Puerto Rican swinger, but now just the corporate secretary, taking notes, a demure figure of service. And up and down both sides of the long wooden table sat all the other familiar figures—Maurice Poppei, round and white and nerveless, sometimes making me think of a human *bockwurst;* and G. B. McCombs, genial and wary, wary and genial, the great survivor; and Leon Marks, with his mottled and slightly misshapen face, who had served these many years as feudal lord of the printing plant. Then there were the attendant lords— Marks's chief of staff, Mort Schilbred, a beefy man who was going to get control of Marks's printing division but didn't yet quite have it; and Poppei's adviser, a crew-cut young accountant called Don Ziegler, on assignment from Price, Waterhouse. And finally, in addition to all these, there sat the old retainers and consultants and chamberlains, white-haired and creaky of limb, who looked up in surprise as we filed into the council chamber.

The Curtis Circulation Company had just finished its board meeting, and since all the main officers of Curtis served on the board of its subsidiary, Clifford simply wanted to keep them all together while he talked about our failures to meet production deadlines. The Circulation Company, Clifford said, must deliver all magazines to the wholesalers six days before the newsstand date so they could be bundled up in a new computerized operation. So there must be no more missed deadlines. As of now, according to Clifford's figures, late delivery of editorial and advertising copy had been costing $1 million to $2 million a year. This must stop. Now he wanted to hear suggestions as to how the problem could be solved. He turned the floor over to a rotund Southerner named Noble Acuff, who had recently been put in charge of all Curtis circulation problems, and Acuff repeated all the main points. Delays must stop. Next it was the turn of Don Ziegler, the man from Price, Waterhouse, and he said he had worked out a solution. He would recommend the creation of a "production coordinator" on each magazine and a "production control group" in Philadelphia. It was hard to see how this differed from the system we already had, but we all knew that the degree of difference mattered very little. One of the traditional ways to solve a problem, after all, is to create a managerial title. Then the problem becomes the new manager's problem.

Next came red-faced old Leon Marks, who was ready, as usual, with a long, thin chart that nobody at the table could even read, much less understand. Two of Marks's minions held up the chart from opposite sides of the table, and Marks pointed a stubby finger at it from time to time as he made his speech. He was curiously defensive. The manufacturing department had not done all it could, he admitted, he knew that, but it was taking firm and positive action to remedy its faults. (*God knows what that means,* I thought, *or what proven failures compelled Marks to this public confession.* Obviously something was seriously wrong, but nobody except Marks and Schilbred could understand the labyrinths of the printing plant schedules.) As this chart would show, however, Marks continued, there had also been serious failures on all the magazines. In terms of advertising copy, he said, the *Post* was 34 percent late. He then began to read a list of similarly mysterious figures (34 percent of what?) for the other magazines, all of which were worse than the *Post*. As for the editors, he went on, the *Post* was 21 percent late, *American Home* 34 percent, *Holiday* 36 percent, and the *Journal* 42 percent.

All these figures, all displayed on the incomprehensible chart that sagged across the table, were entirely meaningless. The "percentage" of late *Post* editorial material was actually zero—and even if it had really been late from time to time, there would have been no way to measure it in terms of such percentages. But it had become fashionable, particularly since the advent of Secretary McNamara to the Pentagon, to "quantify" everything, and even though the figures might be meaningless, their very existence was considered a scientific step forward in what was coming to be called "the decision-making process." So it was that Vietnamese villages where nobody knew what was happening became statistics and emerged from the computers with a rating of 60 percent government-controlled. And on the basis of such figures, our distinguished board member, Ellsworth Bunker, now Ambassador to Saigon, reported that we were making progress.

At any organizational meeting, it is bad form to offer the basic criticism—that we are talking nonsense—or to ask the basic question—what are we really talking about?—for we are all still feudal lords, even in the age of computers, and our first duty is still to protect our own fiefs. In a defensive operation of this kind, it is best not to counterattack until necessary, and so, since there were eight categories to be criticized, and eight people to speak in defense of them, and since *Post* editorial had received the best "rating" from Marks, I decided to say nothing at all while the other seven barons protected their own territories. John Mack Carter, with the worst rating, turned out to be quite eloquent in his *mea culpa*. He was trying to make the *Journal* a more contemporary magazine, he said, more in keeping with the times, more relevant to the news. Sometimes, this required last-minute changes, he said, but he hadn't realized that these changes were causing so much trouble and expense, and he would try, as much as would be consistent with his editorial mission, to reform. The other barons were more evasive. Mike Hadley, publisher of the *Journal*, said he could never get an accurate figure on how much it cost to put an ad in late. John Collins, publisher of *American Home*, blamed certain ad agencies for missing deadlines. Steve Kelly, speaking for *Holiday*, said that the lead time on ads had to be kept as short as possible so that *Holiday* could remain competitive with its rivals.

For an hour of this inconclusive talk, Mac Clifford sat beatifically at the head of the table, touching his fingertips together in the priestly mannerism that he affected, and showing no sign that any of the talk was having any effect on him. Nor was there any reason, really, why it should. To us, the barons, a meeting of the royal council inevitably seemed an affair of considerable importance, a time for great decisions. To Clifford, however, it was just another staff meeting, a matter of routine. The fact that most of us had traveled for three or four hours to attend it, and would require another three or four hours to get home, was not really of any consequence to the king. And so, just after noon, Mac Clifford smiled at everyone and said that he hadn't expected to solve anything at this meeting, but he wanted everyone to be aware of the problems, and now we could all go to lunch.

Lunch meant that bastion of the old Curtis Publishing Company, the Downtown Club. It was a short walk along the edge of Independence Square, with the insects chirping in the heat, and into the bank adjoining the Curtis building, up to the top floor, where one's feet sank in the thick carpeting and the washrooms seemed to be made entirely·of marble. Here it was that Bob Fuoss used to play cribbage every day while his fellow editors napped through the years. I had been to lunch in the main dining room the last time I was here, but now we proceeded to a smaller and more distinguished chamber, the Cyrus H. K. Curtis Room. Here again, as in the board room, an oil portrait of the founder stared down from the wall. After some preliminary maneuvering, G. B. McCombs and I took our seats beneath this portrait, at the right-hand side of Mac Clifford, who sat at the head of the table with his hand clenching a Martini, his second. Clifford raised the glass to his lips regularly and often, staring stiffly into space, with the desperate haste of a man about to run for a train.

"You know," G.B. said softly, glancing up at the portrait and then at Curtis's successor, "Mr. Curtis never allowed anyone to touch a drink in his presence."

"Times have certainly changed," I said.

"Have you heard this one?" Clifford said suddenly, looking vaguely around him to see who might be listening. "How do you tell a blind man in a nudist colony?"

There was an appropriate pause, and then Clifford said, "It isn't hard."

G.B., sitting between Clifford and me, demonstrated his appreciation with a burst of laughter. At that, Clifford himself indulged in a cackle. Poppei, on the other side of me, engrossed in some financial conversation with the Price, Waterhouse man, sensed that he had missed a cue, and so he dutifully joined in the laughter. The Price, Waterhouse man, less adaptable, turned in bewilderment, saying, "What? What?"

"Tell it to Don," G.B. said, still chuckling.

"Hell, Mary was the one who told it to me," Clifford said. "You tell it, Mary. Tell him, over there, about the blind man in the nudist colony."

Mary, bearing a tray of soup cups, was one of those elderly Irish ladies who wait on tables in places like the Downtown Club.

"No, no," said Mary, trying to get on with the serving of the soup.

"Go on, Mary," Clifford said. "Tell it to Don."

Mary's white hair was tightly curled, and she had a look of rigid respectability, but in some momentary lapse she had told this lewd riddle to old Mac Clifford, and now he insisted on making her repeat the lapse in public.

"Go on, Mary," he said again, more commanding.

"Go on, Mary," G.B. echoed. And so Mary gave in.

"How can you tell a blind man in a nudist colony?" she finally said, quickly, in a low, toneless voice, addressing nobody in particular. She made a very short pause and then gave the punch line. The Price, Waterhouse man, for whom all this had been staged, gave an appropriate guffaw, and the old men broke up all over again. Clifford, G.B., Poppei, they all acted as though they had never heard anything so funny. And then we settled down to our cups of tomato soup, with Saltines.

Poppei was a little worried about the Manchester book.

"Is there any chance that you or Carter might get it?" he asked.

"A chance, but no more than that," I said.

Poppei wanted to know how much it would cost per magazine page. I made a quick guess and said $2,500. That would be more than double the average cost, Poppei said. I knew that, I said, but the book was very interesting and would attract a lot of attention. How many pages would it require? Poppei asked. Maybe seventy-five, I said, guessing again.

"Well, maybe we could justify that if we could keep the returns low enough," Poppei said.

"Returns?" I said. "I don't think there will be any returns. You could increase the draw to a million, in fact, and it would still sell out."

"Well, you don't know that," Poppei said. "You can't be sure."

This may sound like technical shop talk, but it illustrates an entire philosophy of business. The "draw" was the number of copies we printed for newsstand distribution—a figure that varied with each issue but was now running at about 700,000. The higher the draw, the higher the sale, of course; but the higher the draw, the higher the risk, the higher the "returns," those copies that remained unsold and had to be destroyed. In a properly managed publishing company, a decision as basic as how many copies to print would be made by the magazine's editor and publisher and circulation director, but at the *Post*, which had no circulation director, these decisions were made by technicians in the circulation company, without great regard to what the *Post* was publishing in any given issue. And when there were any disagreements, the final decision went to Poppei. Emerson, out of editorial enthusiasm, and Ballew, out of the need to boast of newsstand sales, both asked repeatedly for higher draws, but Poppei preferred to print less and sell a higher percentage of what we printed. The desire to avoid gambles and losses made good sense on routine issues, but what surprised me now was that Poppei had no intention of printing more copies even if we bought a very expensive best seller with the express intention of getting higher sales. It was Poppei's view, in short, not as an economy measure but as a rule of business, that it was better to lose a sale than to print an extra copy that might not be sold.

"By the way," I said, just out of curiosity, realizing now that it really didn't matter very much whether we got the Manchester book, which we were unlikely to get anyway, "I hope you have some promotion money to spend on this project."

Poppei looked at me as though I had just made an indecent advance toward his daughter. His rimless spectacles gleamed.

"How much did you have in mind?" he asked warily.

"How much have you got?" I countered.

"Well, nothing, actually," Poppei said.

"Believe me, this is going to be the biggest book of the year," I said. "Do you want to publish it in secret?"

"Well, look at it this way," Poppei said. "If we could publish it at a profit of $7,000 with no promotion, and if we had to waste $8,000 on promotion in order to make $15,000, then there wouldn't be any point in promoting it, would there?"

Poppei smiled at me, condescendingly, a cold, mirthless smile. He seemed confident that a few statistics from the comptroller should silence a mere editor, and he seemed to have no idea that his figures themselves were self-condemning. Poppei was talking in terms of $15,000 when we had already bid ten times that much—and our bid was the smallest one submitted by any major magazine. But the most deadening aspect of Poppei's figures was the philosophy that underlay them, a sort of parody of Ben Franklin's Poor Richard—a penny saved, a penny earned; cut costs, think small, do less.

There are some people who are at their least likable when they are trying to be likable, and Poppei, munching on his pot roast, was trying, though not very hard, to be likable. He smiled and wiped his lips and predicted good things in the future. "I'm convinced we can get the *Post* into the black next year," he said. I nodded appreciatively, thinking to myself: *Not if you people are still in charge.* And on the other side of me, the conversation was equally cheerful. G.B. was talking to Clifford about some forthcoming project, and he used the phrase, "When we're making money again." Clifford stopped him short. "*When* we're making money—*hell!*" Clifford said, looking

owlishly about him to see if any of the courtiers were listening. The
courtiers always listened, of course, but only with a dozing ear, carrying on their own gossip while they remained attentive to any outburst
from the head of the table. "Hell, we're making money right now,"
Clifford went on, his speech a little slurred, the words coming out
slowly and carefully. "Not a whole lot, but we're making it."

Clifford had had four Martinis before the main course was served,
and by now the effect was noticeable. The conversation eventually
shifted back to the one basic subject, and it never again shifted to
anything else. Poppei told of a South American who liked to smoke a
cigar while enjoying a lady, and he demonstrated how the South
American had to pause every once in a while to knock the ashes off
his cigar. The court guffawed. Somebody else told of being interrupted
at a similar moment by a telephone call from the office, and of asking the boss to call back later. More guffaws. There was talk about the
expense of having children, and one of the older executives said he
had waited eight years until he thought he could afford it, "until
finally my wife said, 'To hell with that! Come on in here!'" More
guffaws. Clifford, snickering, described in some detail a cover that
had been planned for *American Home.* It had featured a mushroom,
and, according to Clifford, "It was the sorriest-looking p——— you ever
saw." Gloria Swett took one look at it, Clifford went on, snickering
more than ever, "and Gloria said, 'What are you going to call it? "Sex
in the kitchen?"'" Gloria Swett herself, sitting at the far corner,
smiled serenely across the listening table. "And Gloria said," Clifford
persisted, laughing so hard now that tears started to his fierce blue
eyes, "Gloria said, 'Look, they haven't even circumcised it!'" At this,
there came an explosion of laughter from the assembled courtiers,
and Clifford, wiping his eyes on his napkin, repeated Gloria's punch
line. "Look, they haven't even circumcised it."

This, then, was the president of the Curtis Publishing Company, in
its second century of existence, holding court beneath the blind gaze
of the founder's portrait.

From the *Gallagher Report,* July 6, 1966:

CBS INC. EXPECTED TO BUY CURTIS PUBLISHING . . . Deal will
be on a stock-swap basis. Require several weeks of negotiations . . ."

For several years, a number of people had considered CBS and
Curtis as natural candidates for a merger. CBS, which then owned
nothing in the field of publishing, was enormously profitable and
eager for expansion; Curtis, desperately short of cash and manage-

ment, controlled a vast quantity of stories, articles, ideas—the grist of television. Joe Culligan had discussed the possibility of a merger at least three years earlier, and he had even tried to promote the idea of a CBS news magazine inside the *Post*. It was not until the spring of 1966, however, that Mac Clifford and CBS President Frank Stanton got together and decided, in the words of one insider, "to really look into this." They commissioned the accounting firm of J. K. Lasser to make a thorough study of Curtis, and Lasser, operating under the disguise of an efficiency study for Clifford, assigned about twenty management analysts to spend several months studying every aspect of Curtis.

The conclusion of the study, delivered on July 27, 1966, was surprisingly optimistic:

Curtis is a bargain purchase today at the current market prices. It is, however, a bargain only for someone who wants it, who knows what to do with it, and who is willing to recognize its liabilities as well as its potentials. Further, it is a bargain purchase only if management can be strengthened and if patience and courage are exercised to reposition the company and to take full advantage of the opportunities it offers.

In working out these general prescriptions, the Lasser analysts had inevitably followed the same line of reasoning that had convinced every previous analyst of Curtis affairs—except, of course, for Curtis's own management. This line of reasoning invariably dictated the re-creation of Curtis as a publishing company, the sale of its manufacturing facilities ("Hell, I'd just as soon *give* them away," said one of the analysts), and the reinvestment of manufacturing money in new and diversified publishing ventures. Since Curtis needed what Lasser politely called "strengthened management," the Lasser analysts went so far as to interview some new managerial prospects. And since our gigantic "tax loss carry-forward" was still available to any merger partner, they worked out a tax strategy whereby any buyer could acquire control of Curtis for as little as $7.8 million, which, at CBS, would be hardly noticeable.

The idea of buying Curtis, however, was only one of many that came under the scrutiny of CBS Chairman William Paley and President Frank Stanton. They had just bought, to take one example, the New York Yankees. They had just bought a company that made guitars. They were investing heavily in a new, black-sheathed CBS building on the Avenue of the Americas. And when they considered buying into the publishing field, they undoubtedly wondered whether it might not be more sensible to acquire (as they finally did acquire) a relatively small but promising book publisher like Holt, Rinehart & Winston. . . .

On August 2, Emerson, back from Georgia, called Clifford to ask about the CBS rumors. He quoted Clifford as answering: "Remember when they were merging us with *McCall's?*"

"That isn't a very straight answer," I said.

"That's what I told him," Emerson said, "and he just laughed."

On August 11, a CBS spokesman denied that its accountants were surveying the Curtis books, admitted that the purchase had been considered during the past four years, but said that CBS had decided that Curtis "was not something to latch onto."

Somewhat later, Stewart Alsop encountered William Paley at a party and heard that CBS had come "within an ace" of buying Curtis.

"Then why the hell didn't they?" I asked.

"He said they didn't have enough extra executives to take charge of Curtis and operate it," Alsop said.

Few people still remembered that there had been a time, back in the 1930's, when the relationship had been exactly the opposite. Powerful Curtis had had a chance to buy the fledgling CBS for $3 million and had rejected it because "our business is magazines."

Under the kind of management we now enjoyed, the most important event of the corporate year was the approval of the budget. The budget is a symbol of the corporation's over-all prospects, the expectations of profit or loss in the coming year. The budget also symbolizes the status of every department within the corporation, and the standing of every departmental leader. An executive in the good graces of the president gets an increase in his budget; an executive in disfavor begins to hear about the difficult state of the economy.

Ultimately, all the departmental budgets have to add up to a corporate budget at the beginning of a new year, but the budget can become so involved, so political, so subject to negotiation and renegotiation, that it must be started months in advance, before anyone has any real idea of what the conditions in the coming year will be. In our profitable year of 1966, we began to work on the next year's budget in early August. And since Clifford seemed to be in a euphoric mood, it seemed none too early to start asking for a share of the anticipated profits. Specifically, we wanted $180,000 more for salaries—some for raises, most for an increase in the editorial staff— plus $100,000 more for editorial material. In this maneuver, our failure to acquire the Manchester book was a great help. The publicity about the money that other magazines had bid showed how far our austerity had left us behind our competitors.

In theory, budgets should be discussed with the vice president for finance, but Gloria Swett was by now the vice president in charge of getting things approved by Mac Clifford, and so Emerson invited her out to lunch. He invited her to a very expensive restaurant on East Fiftieth Street, the Lutece, a house with a garden and only a dozen tables. It was one of those places where there was no menu, where, after the opening round of drinks, the proprietor appeared, a handkerchief sprouting from the pocket of a blue blazer, and discussed the food to be served, and where, at the end, the bill arrived in a silver box. In these surroundings, and with an overwhelming effusion of Southern gallantry—the pulling out of chairs, the lighting of cigarettes, the inquiries about the right wine, and perhaps one or two just slightly off-color jokes—Emerson persuaded Gloria Swett to agree to all the increases in the budget, staff increases, raises, everything. And when Gloria Swett agreed, there was no further argument in Philadelphia. Even the board of directors, which still had to approve any raise to anyone earning more than $25,000, voted approval at its September meeting. At that same meeting, the board elected Gloria Swett herself a vice president of the corporation.

When the autumn sales figures started coming in, however, Clifford's season of euphoria was over. On November 3, the company had to announce that "because of the customary summer lull in the publishing business," Curtis had lost another $1,830,000 during the third quarter. That was a bigger loss than during the third quarter of the previous year. It amounted to $20,000 for every day of the quarter, a noble figure, worthy of our traditions. It also wiped out the profits of the first two quarters and gave us a loss of $1,462,000 for the first nine months of the year. In spite of all this, Clifford clung to the predictions that the fourth quarter would bring a redeeming profit of $1.5 million. "There is every indication that, for the first time since 1961, Curtis will not report a loss for the fiscal year," he declared.

But the autumn losses filled Clifford with a cold dread. He called together all his editors and publishers and warned them that he had "bad news" for them. This did not mean that the losses were worse than the announcement. No, on the contrary, he wanted to reaffirm that Curtis would make a profit in this year, and furthermore, he wanted to announce that Curtis would increase its profit next year toward a target of $5 million. The only way to do that, particularly in view of predictions of a softening economy in 1967, was for every department to cut its budget. There were murmurs of protest and complaint—the budgets had already been drawn up and approved—but Clifford growled everyone into silence. He wanted the revised budgets for 1967, cut by 10 percent, on his desk within two weeks, and that was that.

It could be argued, of course, that this new cutback simply showed a soldierly determination to achieve victory. Remember Marshal Foch: "My right flank has broken, my center is crumbling—very well, I attack!" But it could also be argued that a bureaucratic management in a time of crisis can only respond like a porcupine, curling up into a ball of prickles and hoping that the danger will somehow pass. What struck me most of all, however, was the realization that we would never be free from the demands for profit. When we were losing money, we had to cut our staffs and budgets and materials, all for the sake of survival, saving the magazines. But now it turned out that the same was true even when we were making money, that the demands of the management, on behalf of the stockholders, were limitless. Even if Curtis made a profit of $10 million in 1967, Clifford would demand for the insatiable stockholders at least $11 million in 1968.

At about this time, I received a form letter, at my home address, inviting me to subscribe to the *Post*. It offered me a sweepstakes prize of $25,000, free cars and free TV sets, if I would just subscribe to the *Post* for $1.95. I found it hard to believe. After a year of lobbying, I had been told in Puerto Rico that we were going to stop giving magazines away. "Well, they changed their minds," the circulation man said when I telephoned him. "They're still planning to go to a three-dollar minimum some time in '67, but they're afraid of any drop in circulation right now."

"Well, if we're going to lose money on every new subscription," I said, "let's just hope that nobody subscribes."

"You're perfectly right," the circulation company man said, "but they're the ones who are running this company."

"Yeah, great," I said. "Do you happen to know how much they're wasting on this new mailing?"

"It'll cost about a million dollars," the circulation man said.

That was the equivalent of the entire editorial budget for four months, and now we had to begin a series of meetings on how to cut it by 10 percent. In 1965, when we had changed to biweekly publication and had to cut everything by 40 percent, Clifford's hatchet men had demanded a $2.9 million budget, but we had convinced them that it was impossible, and so we got $3.1 million for that year, and again for this one. Now Clifford wanted to cut back to $2.7 million, a lot less than what couldn't be done in the bankruptcy year of 1965. Oddly enough, though, nobody thought Clifford really expected his orders to be carried out. One theory was that he simply wanted to produce a profit-showing budget so that Curtis would be ready for any merger negotiations. In any case, Emerson eventually submitted a revised budget of $3 million, including false promises of cuts in the materials we would buy for the second half of the year, and that was the last we heard of the budget.

This, then, was the managerial magic by which Mac Clifford ultimately produced a profit during the year 1966. The technique was simple. The conscientious employees worked hard at their jobs, because that was their nature, and then the supreme command ordered everyone to cut costs until the year's activities came out even on the balance sheets. This was not simply a matter of operating expenses. It was a philosophy of life. In November of the profitable year of 1966, we learned that Poppei had found yet another way of saving money. On all future issues, the printing plant's knives would be adjusted so that they would shear off an extra one-eighth of an inch along the top and bottom of each copy of the *Post* and an extra one-sixteenth along the sides. We first heard that this trimming would save the implausible sum of $250,000 a year in paper costs for the *Post;* then that it would save $250,000 a year for Curtis, including $100,000 on the *Post.* Then Emerson said that G.B. had told him that the saving would be $75,000. It was typical of all problems at Curtis that any inquiry about exact statistics would bring a spewing forth of supposedly authoritative but constantly varying figures. I myself was quite convinced that the decision to snip a fraction of an inch off the edges of the *Post* would not save any money at all, and that even if it would save a little money, nobody in the company had any idea what the right figure might be. It was a perfect example, however, of the cost accountants' system of doing business—to cut, shrink, tighten, until we reached the theoretical goal of not producing anything at all. Or, as Emerson put it, "It's like being nibbled to death by ducks."

16

"When a ball club is in trouble . . .
you replace the manager"

After having devoted a hard year to making a profit, Mac Clifford suddenly learned that it might all be taken away from him. The economic forecasts for 1967 were ominous. And as the accountants from Price, Waterhouse surveyed Clifford's budgets for the coming year, they judged him too optimistic. Ignoring his original target of a $5 million profit, they refused to certify even a budget that promised the company would break even, and Clifford had to have their certification before he could present his figures to the annual stockholders' meeting in the spring. What Price, Waterhouse demanded was that Clifford take his cherished 1966 profits and put them all in escrow to pay for new losses predicted in 1967.

Clifford could not bear to accept that. He summoned Jess Ballew and his two chief assistants to Philadelphia on a Sunday morning early in January, and then he began applying the thumbscrews to them. The company must announce a profit, Clifford said, and therefore Ballew must somehow turn predicted sales into real sales, so that the accountants would approve the budgets. Advertising predictions —to explain the technical terms briefly—fall into two basic categories: the "forecast" (which Ballew figured as half of all prospective sales on which the chances of success were at least 60 percent, plus a quarter of all prospects that had some chance of success) and "order position" (which was definite business, so-and-so-much space in such-and-such an issue at such-and-such a price). Now "forecasts" for 1967 were not bad, a little ahead of 1966, but the advertisers were delaying their specific orders because of the queasy state of the national economy, and therefore the figures on "order position" had slumped. The accountants from Price, Waterhouse apparently considered "order position" the only reliable figures on which to base a budget—hence their prediction of a loss for 1967—hence Mac Clifford's command to Ballew to start getting "forecasts" turned into concrete "orders." Specifically, Clifford said, Ballew had three weeks, until January 31, to sell $5 million worth of advertising. This was not going to be easy, since the total of orders at a comparable time the previous year was only $3 million, but Clifford authorized bonuses of $20,000 for the salesmen who brought in the business, and then it was up to Ballew.

I told Emerson that Ballew would inevitably fail, and I wondered what would happen then. Emerson said that Clifford would "turn against Jess." I said that I thought Clifford was already against Jess. Emerson shrugged. He said Clifford had told Ballew that he would have replaced him some time ago if he had thought that would solve anything, but now it was too late, because the annual ad schedules were being made up. Ballew had said he knew Clifford wanted a new publisher, but Ballew was one of those warriors who ignore all predictions of defeat. Under orders to sell twice as much as had been sold before, and with those orders issued by a commander who wanted to dismiss him, he marched forth and started selling.

Toward the end of January, I encountered Ballew standing with a suitcase on the corner of Lexington and Fifty-fourth Street, and we shared a cab to the air terminal, where Ballew was leaving for San Francisco. I had not seen Ballew for some time, and so I asked him how the great campaign was going, and he answered, to my surprise, "Not bad." He and his people had already sold 380 of the needed 600 columns, he expected to get 100 to 150 more during the final week of the campaign, and he thought that 500 columns would be all that Clifford really had to have.

"You getting any sleep?" I asked.

"Not much," Ballew said. Then he seized his suitcase, jumped out of the cab, and disappeared into the crowd.

Ballew was right again, it turned out. By the time of the deadline, he got enough advertising to convince the accountants that we would remain profitable for another year, and so they certified Clifford's figures. But as often happens, unfortunately, the accountants had been right the first time. Ballew's feat could only temporarily postpone the certainty that we were going to lose a lot more money during the coming year. Indeed, if the events of 1966 demonstrated how cost-cutting can turn a money-losing corporation into a profitable one, the events of 1967 demonstrated the limits of cost-cutting as a philosophy of business. This was the year, in other words, of our disintegration.

The time clocks provided the first clear evidence. Once the budget figures had been settled, Clifford summoned all Curtis editors and publishers to a conference on a problem that he found personally exasperating. He had repeatedly noted that quite a number of editorial secretaries were failing to keep proper business hours. People were just drifting in at 9:30 or 10. He had even had some efficiency studies made, and he had finally decided, damn it, on a solution. From now on—and he didn't want any goddamn arguments about this—there were going to be time clocks on every floor, and everybody would have to punch in and punch out. Punch in at 9. Punch out at 5:30. Every day. He didn't want to have to be disagreeable about this, Clifford said, or have it turn into a big issue, but we needed a little more law and order around this company, and now, by God, we would have it.

The time-clock crisis lasted through all of one absurd week. Emerson began by declaring that he had protested vehemently against Clifford's decree, but once the orders had been issued, Emerson seemed unable to treat them simply as orders. Instead, he called several meetings of the grumbling editors and secretaries to explain, argue, and persuade. This was not an issue on which to fight, Emerson said, not an issue worthy of rebellion. There were a number of editors who actually preferred the earlier hours, but Emerson's meetings and speeches somehow made the time clocks more important than they had been before, and when the workmen finally came to install them, a number of people felt inspired to acts of sabotage. The main clock required plywood backing, and someone stole the plywood as soon as it appeared. When the clock was finally installed —a gray metal box, about a foot square, with a slot at the top for the time cards to be inserted—somebody poured water into the slot. And when that dried out, somebody poured in coffee.

It took about three days for the pranks to stop, and then everybody punched the time clocks.

Mike Mooney said: "New York State law says that if you have time clocks, you have to pay overtime, and we don't even have any budget for overtime. Did anybody tell that to Clifford? Did anybody tell him that his bright ideas for saving a few pennies sometimes end up by costing more?"

From the *Gallagher Report*, February 28:

CURTIS PUBLISHING PERSONNEL TURMOIL. Due to prolonged acquisition negotiations. Low morale despite company turnaround to $347,-
000 1966 profit . . . Saturday Evening Post publisher Jess Ballew's future
questionable. Despite Post 22% revenue rise . . .

Bill Emerson was in a low mood. He had just returned from a
speech-making trip to Louisville and St. Louis, and he wanted to
indulge himself in a good lunch. We went to Giovanni's, a proudly
independent place that displays no sign out in front and accepts no
credit cards. The white-haired proprietor takes every order and sees
to it that the food is good.

Emerson spoke jokingly, and then more seriously, of my aloofness
toward Clifford. "I want them to think of you as the natural successor," Emerson said, "in case anything happens to me."

"What's supposed to happen to you?" I asked.

"Oh, you know," Emerson said.

These had been hard times for Emerson. About a year earlier, he
had waked up one morning and found that he couldn't bend his back,
couldn't tie his shoe, and that any sudden move brought a stab of
pain. The official diagnosis was that he had mysteriously suffered a
"herniated disc," and, as usual with major medical problems, there
was no known cause or cure. There were various treatments and
therapies—a corset containing fierce metal braces, a regimen of daily
exercises, and so on—but the collapse of the back seems also to have
some psychological element, seems to be caused partly by stress, and
seems particularly common among executives. Mac Clifford, it turned
out, had suffered a similar collapse, and his sympathy toward Emerson was almost paternal.

Such a blow necessarily fills a middle-aged man with thoughts of
his own mortality—or, more accurately, thoughts on the erosion of
life in the service of a mundane cause. In one's twenties, one never
thinks about problems of the back or heart or stomach, but when
these parts begin to give way in the late thirties, the deterioration
changes one's sense of all other values. In my youth, once, when I
had a really exquisite toothache, I suddenly realized that my tooth
had temporarily become the center of my universe, that its outcries
were more important than anything else, and that I would do absolutely anything to placate it. And as one gets older, and starts worrying about cancer, one becomes more and more conscious of the
fragility of the whole body, and with that consciousness comes a new

and degrading kind of fear. It is degrading because it strengthens the desire to survive on any terms, and the desire to survive on any terms is the most base of all our instincts.

Emerson had also experienced, during the past year, another and even more wounding experience of middle age. His father had been dying, painfully, grudgingly, one operation at a time, and each assault by the surgeons left him weaker in his next confrontation. The impending death of one's father is not easy to imagine or accept, and when it inevitably comes, it fills one with foreboding about all the prospects of one's own life. A number of times, when I went into Emerson's office to ask him about some current problem, I found him staring out the window and waiting for the next telephone call from Atlanta. When his father died that summer, I wrote Emerson a conventional note of condolence and got back a strange reply: "Thank you for your letter about my father's death. I think one reason I was so devoted to him was that he was so little like me. . . ."

At Giovanni's now, Emerson paused for a moment and then went on. "Well, to say it plainly—out in St. Louis, I felt this terrific chest pain, and I had a sudden feeling that if I'm going to die, I don't want to die selling advertising in St. Louis."

"Come on, now, don't be a baby," I said.

"No, I mean it," Emerson said. "This job is ruining my life. It's ruining my family. It's turning me into a bad husband and a bad father—and besides, I hate the climate around here."

The first casualty in our year of disintegration was inevitably Don Schanche. He was very vulnerable—*Holiday* had been losing money, and after Steve Kelly became publisher in place of Garth Hite, the magazine continued to lose money—and so Emerson wandered into my office one day in March and remarked, "Well, they finally got Schanche's ass—told him to get out of his office by noon." The announcement on the bulletin board was more formal: "Effective immediately, Caskie Stinnett becomes the editor, Holiday. The editor, Holiday, will report to the President."

And so went the best and toughest of Blair's real rebels, the pirate raider who had originally persuaded me to come to the *Post* five years earlier. The official announcements offered no explanation except "strong policy differences with the management," but Schanche's own account provides an interesting light on the state of competitive powers at the upper levels of the corporation.

"In mid-March, I was approached by Steve Kelly, with whom I had enjoyed the greatest friction and hostility ever since he had joined

Curtis," Schanche later recalled. "He said: 'A senior officer of the
company asked me to quietly pass along this word to you. You have
been running filler ads in support of the United Nations. Certain
members of the board of directors have complained. Find another
charity for your filler ads.' I gathered from the context of the conversation that the 'senior officer' was Gloria Swett, speaking for Mac
Clifford. I told Kelly to tell her and the complaining board members to
go f—— themselves, in those words, honest.

"On March 29, I was summoned to Philadelphia to see Mac
Clifford, and he opened by saying, 'Don, it looks like we're going to
have to have a change on *Holiday*.' He offered me another job in
Curtis, but I declined, and we arranged a settlement. Then he said, 'I
want you to know this wasn't my idea. I fought to keep you.' I was
intrigued enough by that to ask him to join me for dinner, which he
did two hours later at the Barclay Hotel, overlooking Rittenhouse
Square. We had quite a few drinks and wine and spent the most
comradely three hours I ever spent with Mac. Honest to God, it was
astonishingly friendly. During the evening, Mac explained that the
subject of UN filler ads ('Support the United Nations,' UNICEF, etc.)
had been brought up by Milton Gould at the previous month's board
meeting, and it was informally decided that I should be ordered to
stop running them. After my reply was relayed, Mac said, Gould took
the initiative and canvassed the board. A majority wanted my resignation. Mac didn't name the majority, but said that it included Cary
Bok, who had never approved of my editorship. Mac said he opposed
it but was having so many other problems with the board that he
couldn't refuse the majority demand. Maybe I'm crazy, but I believed
him and I still do. End of story."

The stockholders' meeting that spring was somewhat less euphoric
than the year before. Mac Clifford offered relatively good news—not
only the profit of 1966 but an increased profit for the first quarter of
1967, a total of $362,000 as compared to $265,000 during the
previous year. He also announced another ruinous increase in *Post*
circulation, from 6.5 million to 6.7 million, which most of his
listeners presumably considered further good news. But there were
signs of turbulence amidst all this good fortune. The *Gallagher
Report* and other tipsters kept predicting an imminent takeover, by
Philip Morris, CBS, or Encyclopaedia Britannica. These predictions
were reinforced when the octogenarian Mrs. Zimbalist resigned from
the board of directors in favor of an investment banker named Robert
Patterson. And the watchful Philip Kalodner arose, as he did now at

every annual stockholders' meeting, to offer his criticisms. This year, in fact, Kalodner claimed to represent more than 1 percent of the preferred stock, and so he demanded a seat on the board and filed suit to get a complete list of stockholders. This delayed the completion of the annual ritual for five days, but Clifford still held the proxies from the major stockholders, and that was enough to end all arguments.

The increase in circulation, however, would haunt us. The return on our last mailing, the one that again offered the *Post* at $1.95, had startled the Curtis management. At $1.95 a year, lots of people wanted to buy the *Post*. Indeed, they were flooding our Philadelphia offices with their checks and orders. There were about 200,000 more subscriptions than expected, and our thrifty management did not want to spend money hiring people to process the orders. By late spring, the backlog of paid but unfulfilled subscriptions had reached 100,000, and Mac Clifford himself had a personal backlog of 15,000 unanswered letters complaining about our failure to send subscribers their magazines. The readers, those long-neglected customers, were displaying the strength that had once built the *Post* and would eventually help to destroy it.

There were many reasons why the *Post* managed to live beyond its time, and one of the most fundamental reasons was the absence of labor unions. I realize that it is considered illiberal and improper to blame labor unions for the destruction, during the past two decades, of celebrated papers like the New York *Sun,* the Brooklyn *Eagle,* and the New York *Herald Tribune.* The unions always offer some interesting explanation to show that the collapse was somebody else's fault, but it remains true that the *Post* could never have wallowed into the mid-1960's if any unions had been snapping at its heels.

The reason we had no unions was that Curtis had always taken exceptionally good care of its employees, paying them better wages than any union shop could command, paying for their bad health and their old age. But under the Clifford system of cost-cutting, the generous treatment of employees was considered inefficient and wasteful. And in this year, on June 23, it was announced in the Sheraton Hotel in Philadelphia that Curtis was finally accepting a three-year contract with the International Brotherhood of Bookbinders and Bindery Women's Union of Philadelphia; the International Brotherhood of Firemen, Oilers, Power House Operators, Ice Plants Employees and Maintenance Mechanics; the Lithographers and Photoengravers International Union; the International Association of Ma-

chinists and Aero-Space Workers; the International Printing Press-
men and Assistants' Union of North America; and the International
Stereotypers and Electrotypers Associations of North America. The
Newspaper Guild, which is supposed to represent editorial employees,
never organized Curtis.

On the very same day that these contracts were announced, we
heard from the unions in a way we had never heard from them
before. The lead article in our newest issue dealt with the racial
conflicts in Cleveland, and the title said: "In Cleveland It Has
Become: Whitey versus the Niggers." The unions' views came in the
form of a telephone call from Mac Clifford to Emerson. If the word
"Niggers" wasn't changed, the message said, the newest issue of the
Post would end up at the bottom of the Schuylkill River.

It was useless to argue that the terms "Nigger" and "Whitey" were
supposed to represent each side's insult of the other side. Union
leaders were no more interested in the actual contents of an article
than were Madison Avenue media directors. But if we could not argue
a case on its merits, then we would have to argue it on a basis of
power politics. By what right were the printing-plant unions trying to
edit the magazines? In actual fact, the company and its new antagonists were so disorganized that it was impossible to negotiate or even
discuss these conflicts. For all we knew, a few idle complaints had
turned into implacable "union demands," passed on by inexperienced
foremen to equally inexperienced management. Was it not intrinsically absurd, after all, for the president of the corporation to be
telephoning the editor of a magazine to report that some workmen
wanted the title of an article changed?

"Tell them to go to hell," I said.

"Well, that's easy to say," Emerson retorted, "but if we don't change
the title, they're likely to change it on us in Philadelphia, and then we
can all resign if you want, although I never noticed anybody being
very keen on that when it came to a showdown."

"Why do you always talk about resigning?" I snapped back. "All
I'm trying to do is to stop people from interfering with us."

"Do you want to talk to Clifford yourself?"

"No, you talk to Clifford."

"I already have, and he's terrified."

"Oh, screw it," I said. "I never liked that title anyway. Let's go back
to my original title, which was 'Can Cleveland Escape Burning?' But
if this ever happens again . . ."

I then submitted to Emerson, for forwarding to Clifford, an angry
memorandum saying that we were making the change only under

protest, and that if this was a precedent for union interference in the editing of the magazine, we might as well cease publication immediately. It did not set a precedent, however, and the unions never again made an attempt to influence editorial actions. But they may well have remembered that Clifford's tough-talking management was not so tough as it sounded. Under pressure, it crumbled.

Because the accountants had been right, because even Jess Ballew could not overcome the downward trend in the magazine industry, *Post* advertising began to decline in the spring. As early as May, G. B. McCombs told Ballew to prepare a report for the worried board and to enliven it with some figures that promised hope. Ballew promptly reported that the bad second quarter was only 2 percent below the second quarter of the previous year, that order position for the second half was already ahead of the figures for last year, and that no other Curtis magazine could make this claim. This quieted the board for a time, but when all magazines announced their advertising figures for the first six months of 1967, the statistics refuted Ballew's optimism. In fact, they challenged the whole argument that the *Post's* newest decline was part of an over-all slump. Some magazines— *Time, Newsweek, Esquire*—had made substantial gains and were making substantial profits. It was the general mass magazines that were in trouble—*Life* down 2 percent, *Look* down 5 percent, the *Post* down 6 percent—and the *Post,* which had held the weakest position to begin with, was obviously in the worst trouble.

"It was Monday, July 11," Ballew later recalled, "and G.B. called at 11:45—I was just going out to lunch with a media director—and he said he wanted to see me right away. And G.B. came right out and said, 'When a ball club is in trouble, you don't get rid of the ball club, you replace the manager. And what we've decided to do is to replace the manager of the *Saturday Evening Post.'*

"I said, 'What does that mean? Going back onto the ad sales staff, the way I did before?' " (Ballew had been demoted in a similar crisis several years earlier, and he had gone out to sell ads with such a fervor that he had worked his way back up to the managerial level.)

"And G.B. said, 'No, we want you to resign. In fact, we've written a letter of resignation that we want you to sign.'

"Well, I didn't want to sign anything until I'd talked to Clifford, but he was unavailable. He was out at Beechcraft, out in the Middle West, testing the new airplane that he wanted to buy for the company. I tried to phone him, but I couldn't reach him. I wrote him a letter, but he never answered it. I never heard from him again."

I heard the news from McKinney when I came back from lunch, and so I immediately went to see Ballew, who was sitting at his desk in a state of shock.

"I've been hearing bad things," I said.

"They're all true," Ballew said.

"Is there anything I can do?" I asked.

"No, not a thing."

"Aren't you going to shout or scream or something?"

"I wouldn't give them that satisfaction," Ballew said fiercely. He appeared to accept his fate as part of the competitive system—businessmen live by the sword and die by the sword—but he still wanted vindication, and even in this moment of defeat, he could not suppress the salesman instinct. "The damnedest thing is—" he went on, reaching for a book of statistics—"look here—this happened just when things were beginning to pick up—you can see it right there—things finally getting better." Then he slammed the book shut and put it to one side. I said nothing. Optimism is not part of my nature, and I had never believed Ballew's predictions, even when they were correct. On the day the *Post* went bankrupt, I reflected, Ballew would still be predicting its triumph, and he would do the same at every future job, and he would believe his own figures as profoundly as I would disbelieve them.

"The thing is," he said, and there were tears in his eyes, "that these past two years have been the greatest years in my life just because of working with people like you and Bill and all the other editors. I know this sounds corny, but I really love the *Post*."

"Well, we all do," I said, "and you've helped it an awful lot."

"I've been proud to be here," Ballew said, "and now . . ." His voice trailed away, his Adam's apple bobbing up and down, his big, muscular hands twitching unhappily. He was right, poor man, there was nothing that could be done for him.

Back on the fourth floor, I tried to call Emerson, who had just gone on his regular Georgia vacation the previous week, but a sudden switching of telephone connections, as mysterious as the famous Butts-Bryant call, put me on the line with Gloria Swett. She said it would be "a smart thing" if I called the editorial staff together and told them the news, and if I told it to them "in positive terms."

"What positive terms should I tell them?" I inquired.

Gloria Swett did not react to irony. "Tell them that the management believes this is a good move for the future of the *Post*," she said.

I have always been in favor of doing the "smart thing," and so I called together the staff and told them that Jess Ballew was resigning, that Steve Kelly was becoming the new publisher of the *Post*, and Jack Connors was moving from advertising director of the *Post* to publisher of *Holiday*, that I anticipated no changes of any kind in the editorial plans and policies of the *Post*, and that Gloria Swett had suggested that I tell them that "the management believes this is a good move for the future of the *Post*." Then I sent them all back to work.

"Oh, God!" Emerson groaned when I finally got him on the telephone. "Those sonsofbitches, those goddamn sons-of-*bitches!*"

"Okay, okay," I said, "but the basic question is what can be done, if anything."

"I can resign, that's what can be done," Emerson shouted.

"What good would that do?" I asked.

"It would make me feel good and make them feel bad."

"But not very," I said. "Listen, Jess himself isn't making any trouble, so what's the point? These people are masters of the *fait accompli*."

It was, in fact, a well-timed stroke. Clifford must have decided quite a bit earlier to dispose of Ballew (the portents were certainly all there, open for inspection), and the last serious obstacle was "the reaction of the editors." This meant Emerson, since he was the only editor the management knew, and Clifford must have decided simply to bludgeon his way through. Emerson, having just gone to Georgia, could do nothing; Ballew, cut off and isolated, proved unable to fight back; Clifford, in seclusion, let the passage of time make his orders irreversible. All that was left was for Emerson to fly to New York and reach an understanding with Kelly, which he promptly did.

"I guess I ought to tell Kelly that I don't blame him for what happened," Emerson said as we joined forces to plan the meeting.

"That kind of approach is going to get you absolutely nowhere," I said. "Because it will never have occurred to Kelly that anybody could blame him for getting a promotion—you might as well say you don't blame him for existing."

"Well, what then? Am I supposed to pretend to be his best friend?"

"No, but you're supposed to show that you're in charge of all editorial affairs. You should make it clear that everything in the editorial department is progressing peacefully, and you wish him all the best on his side of the operation, and if you can be of any help, he should let you know. The main point is that you're the sovereign prince of a sovereign state, and your sovereignty isn't affected by a mere change in publishers."

The meeting apparently went well, for Emerson later brought Kelly around to shake hands with the various editors. Kelly was in one of his immaculate gray suits, but he looked a little worn and numb, quite a bit less ebullient than he had been when I first saw him in Philadelphia a year earlier. Then Gloria Swett appeared, and Emerson closed his doors again, and then Emerson was waving farewells in the corridor as he rushed off to catch a plane back to Georgia. I asked his secretary, Barbara O'Dwyer, whether he had said anything about what had happened at the afternoon's conferences. "All I know is that Gloria thinks too many secretaries are wearing miniskirts," Barbara said. "She seems to think something should be done about it."

In retrospect, the firing of Jess Ballew was another one of the increasingly frequent milestones on our route to disaster. The arrival of Steve Kelly solved none of our problems, of course, for our problems were too fundamental to be affected by changes in advertising executives. And our advertising revenue—perhaps because of the switch in publishers, perhaps in spite of it—continued to decline. At the same time, the downfall of Ballew marked a significant change in Emerson's authority over the *Post*. His authority had depended partly on his influence in the business departments, and now that influence would inevitably fade. Ballew had been a steadfast ally; Kelly would become a rival, to be met with caution rather than trust. Even more important, perhaps, Emerson had played a bold hand against Clifford and seen that hand defeated; his talk of resigning if Ballew was fired had proved worthless. If Emerson had carried out any such threat, it would have done no good and considerable harm, and that was why I argued against it—the threat of resignation is always an awkward and self-destructive weapon—but whenever a bluff is called in a game of power, the game itself changes for everyone who is playing. "Emerson groaned when he heard the news about Ballew," said one editor, "because he knew that it meant they had his number."

The newspapers of July 17 disclosed the unannounced retirement of Serge Semenenko from the First National Bank of Boston. He was sixty-four, and one year away from mandatory retirement, but I couldn't help wondering whether the newspapers told the full story. "He has chosen to leave early, he said," according to the *Times,* "so he could devote himself exclusively to major corporate problems." It did sound a little odd. "Mr. Semenenko disclosed that he had delayed his resignation," the *Times* continued, "until he felt sure that the Curtis Publishing Company, his most celebrated corporate case, had 'turned the corner.'" It was good to know that our corporate strength was now so great that it enabled Semenenko to retire with an easy conscience.

The *Wall Street Journal* was a bit more critical, however. It quoted Semenenko directly: "I try to save companies and build them up. Look at Curtis Publishing Co.—I saved it from the ash can." The *Journal* then inquired a bit further into what happened when Semenenko saved things. It cited the higher interest rates, the service charges, the transfer of pension funds into banks affiliated with Semenenko. "Mr. Semenenko profited personally, too," the *Journal* went on. "He bought tens of thousands of dollars' worth of Curtis common stock for his personal portfolio shortly before Texas Gulf announced its ore strike. When Curtis announced the lode extended under its timberland . . . Mr. Semenenko sold his shares at a profit —shortly before a Curtis management revolt against Mr. Culligan made headlines." From all of this, we could draw one basic conclusion: Just as thrifty relatives used to tell us that it is very expensive for a person to live on credit, so it is perhaps even more expensive for a corporation to live on bank credit, particularly if the creditor happens to be someone as shrewd as Serge Semenenko of the First National Bank of Boston.

Clifford's secretary was very polite. She asked whether I could possibly come to his office on the thirty-second floor, and we both shared in the pretense that I might be too busy to see him. After mature reflection, I admitted that I was available.

Clifford's office, the same one that Joe Culligan had briefly occupied, was a vast, loftlike area that seemed designed to prevent any serious work from being done. Next to the stunning picture-window view over Manhattan, Clifford occupied an oval table, totally bare except for one gigantic glass ashtray. There was no Out box, no In box, no place to put papers and no sign of papers anyway. Clifford waved me into a chair, a fragile, modernistic creation, and then ground out a cigarette butt as he resumed his telephone conversation with Emerson.

"Not all of us have the time to spend lying around on vacations in Georgia," Clifford said. There was a rumble from the other end of the phone, and then a cackle from Clifford. "But seriously," he went on, lighting another cigarette, puffing, then carefully placing the butt on the edge of the great glass ashtray, "we're going to have real trouble meeting our payroll in September, and the only solution I can see is that we're just going to have to tighten our belts." There was another rumble at the other end of the phone, and Clifford sat back in his chair, took up the cigarette and inhaled deeply, and it suddenly occurred to me that he was not really listening to Emerson, that this was just a formality that he felt was required.

"Specifically," Clifford said, "it means the *Post* will have to drop two editorial pages per issue for the rest of the year, or until the advertising revenue takes an upward turn." There was a rumble at the other end of the telephone. "That means cutting from 51 pages to 49, or 204 colums to 196." Rumble. "Oh, yeah?" Clifford said. "Well, I understand that Madison Avenue thinks pretty well of Kelly. I've heard a lot of good things about that switch." Rumble. "Well, one way you could cut down is to quit running stories about Negroes in every single issue." Rumble. "Listen, all joking aside, we lost $700,000 in the second quarter, and that's a hell of a lot of money, and the third quarter doesn't look one damn bit better, and if Detroit has a strike, we're going to be in trouble in the fourth quarter too. Now they tell me this move will save $700,000 a year." Rumble. "Here," Clifford said to me, "he says he wants to talk to you." Now I heard for myself all of Emerson's rumbling, protests of how hard he had fought, and how he was ready to die rather than give up the editorial columns. It struck me as a futile resistance; the reduction was inevitable. "You think we have to go along then?" Emerson asked with some relief. "We haven't got any choice," I said.

As soon as Emerson returned from Georgia, Clifford spent an hour and a half lecturing him on the editorial shortcomings of the *Post*. He didn't like the dissenting opinions in "Speaking Out." "That's all bullshit," he said. He also disliked "Points West," the column by Joan Didion and John Gregory Dunne. "That's bullshit too," he said. What he wanted, Clifford continued, was "a series of Horatio Alger–type profiles of successful businessmen."

"Like who?" Emerson asked.

"Like General Sarnoff."

Emerson refused Clifford on all counts, and Clifford growled his displeasure.

"The trouble with you," he said, "is that you're getting negative."

Despite all our difficulties, the Curtis stock kept climbing. Often the volume of trading was more than 100,000 shares a day, and by late July the price reached 19¼, the same peak it had reached shortly after the discovery of copper in Timmins. The *Wall Street Journal* attributed this frenzy to rumors of a takeover by some large and prosperous corporation.

The stock-market rise provided no help for Mac Clifford, however, and the trimming of a few editorial pages solved nothing. On August 8, Clifford announced the second-quarter loss of $732,000, which wiped out the first-quarter profit and left us $370,000 in the red for the first half of the year. In his desperation, Clifford evolved a plan to escape from the problems by floating a new securities issue. Curtis would raise $5 million, according to this plan, through a public offering of subordinated income debentures with warrants attached. The immediate purpose was acknowledged to be an increase in working capital, but Curtis also alleged that it wanted to be "in a position to seek acquisitions and entertain merger and consolidation proposals." The *Times* delicately remarked, however, that "the company has no specific plans along any of these lines now pending."

The real purpose of the maneuver was to somehow buy off the preferred stockholders, whose unpaid dividends kept piling up as a company debt, taking precedence over the company's other obligations and thus blocking the company from raising new capital. Specifically, arrears on the $4.00 preferred stock now totaled $15.75 per share, and arrears on the $1.60 preferred totaled $3.15 per share. The plan seemed to be to persuade the preferred stockholders to take the new debentures in exchange for the owed dividends, but the details remained curiously obscure. "The warrants attached to the planned debenture offering," according to the *Times*, "would entitle the holder to purchase shares of common stock of the company in an amount not yet determined. The price of the common stock to the purchaser exercising his warrant also has yet to be fixed."

Somebody inside Curtis, very probably a board member, provided an optimistic account of this maneuver to the *Gallagher Report*, which consequently predicted an improved future: "CURTIS PUBLISHING BAILS OUT. Recapitalizes arrears on preferred stock. New setup in effect by October 15. Leading board members expect to find buyer by end of year." Gallagher argued that there was a "new team at top," that Semenenko and the Boks had both faded away, and the key figures on the board now were Milton Gould, Moreau Brown, and Curtis Barkes. If these directors could sell Curtis to one of the newly powerful conglomerates like Ling-Temco-Vought or Gulf & Western, then Clifford would be outnumbered in the board room. "Mac likes job," Gallagher added maliciously. "Foresees retirement of self, Curtis Publishing secretary Gloria Swett under new management. Not anxious to leave apartment in Philadelphia, new company Beechcraft jet . . ."

Over the next two months, however, the stock offering failed totally, and Gallagher, who had once predicted that this deal would lead to Clifford's departure, now blamed Clifford for having bungled the deal itself:

Situation hopeless. GR recommends liquidation of Curtis Publishing. "Mac the Knife" Clifford makes offer to holders of prior preferred stock to exchange preferred shares for common stock plus 6.5% subordinated income debentures. Offering will fail. Mac wasted $100,000 in registration, legal fees. Preferred stockholders not foolish enough to give up preferred priority for common stock of failing company. . . .

In the editorial department, Peter Wyden had a simple explanation of both past and future. The company's commitments to its preferred stockholders had wrecked two separate merger attempts, he said. So if this attempt to buy off the preferred stockholders failed, there was only one other course. "We'll have to go back to selling off some more of the office chairs," he said. "That's the only way we've been living for five years now, selling the chairs and the bathroom fixtures."

Mike Mooney had an even simpler explanation of what had gone wrong. When the board of directors voted in August to approve the new stock deal, some directors, who themselves controlled substantial amounts of the preferred stock (notably the representatives of the Bok family), did not surrender their own preferred shares on the same terms that the board was proposing for outsiders. "That deal was doomed from that very minute," Mooney said. "It was doomed before it ever left that board room. And everything that happened after that was just a waste of money."

As we kept losing money, we kept shrinking. The 196-column *Post* that Clifford had decreed in the summer lasted less than two months. One day in late September, Emerson reported that Clifford had been on the phone three times that afternoon, that ads were falling out right and left, and that we might lose not the $1 million we had expected but $4 or $5 million.

"He's already talking about changing the *Post* to a monthly," Emerson said excitedly. "I told him, 'Forget it.' I said, 'We might as well fold as try that.' And I let him know that I might walk out if he insisted on it. And then he said, 'How about dropping two or three issues in bad times?' And I told him the same thing. I said, 'Forget it.' So then he said we'd have to reduce the size of every issue by four more pages, and I decided I had to agree to that."

"Four pages!" I exclaimed. "I wonder if he offers us the worse alternatives first so that we'll accept what he had in mind from the start."

"Well, would you rather drop whole issues?" Emerson asked bitterly.

"I'd rather do anything that's part of a plan to make a profit," I said. "We could make money as a monthly, or at any book size, but Clifford doesn't seem to know how to do it, and I don't think Kelly does either."

And so we kept shrinking. Shortly before Clifford took over, Culligan had announced a resumption of weekly publication, which would have meant a minimum of 10,600 editorial columns a year. We actually published, during 1964, about 9,400 columns. Clifford began his regime by making the *Post* biweekly, meaning only 5,300 columns, and his new plan would cut us to less than 4,600.

"He's desperate about going into the red again," Emerson said. "And Price, Waterhouse is going to make him put aside still more money for still more losses next year."

On November 3, the *Times* published the obituary of Robert E. MacNeal, sixty-four, "in poor health since he was retired by the [Curtis] company's board of directors in 1962."

MacNeal had been the son of a glassblower, the obituary said, and had begun working in a glass factory when he was thirteen. It said he had educated himself through night classes and business correspondence courses. It said he began working for Curtis in the scheduling department, and then in the industrial engineering department, where he designed a new folding machine which permitted the *Post*, for the first time, to publish issues of more than two hundred pages (oh, happy day). "I always kept looking around for some mean, unpleasant job that no one would do," he said, "and I pitched in and did it." Named assistant secretary of the corporation, then secretary, then a vice president, he became president in 1950, and so he presided over a good number of the business mistakes and misjudgments that were to ruin us.

As with Walter Fuller, the irony is that MacNeal meant well and worked hard. "I think he actually worked himself to death," said Ben Hibbs, and the *Times* obituary went on to say: "This was the price Mr. MacNeal paid for a success that was as much a romance of American life as any his magazines ever printed—and then for a failure he could not prevent."

De mortuis, of course, but a question keeps recurring: Why couldn't a president prevent the failure of his own corporation? Why

was it so inevitable that in more than a decade of rule, he could do
nothing?

Ruddy, silver-haired, impeccably dressed, Steve Kelly always
looked like the very model of a successful magazine publisher. His
credentials looked equally impressive. He was a veteran of twenty-
four years at Time Inc., first an advertising representative for *Life*,
then advertising director of *Sports Illustrated*. He had moved on from
there to become publisher of *McCall's* and vice president of the Mc-
Call Corporation, and when he came to Curtis he seemed, in Jess
Ballew's words, "a very valuable acquisition" and "quite a catch for us
to have made."

But Kelly's career in recent years had been somewhat turbulent.
After leaving Time Inc., he had spent only eighteen months at *Mc-
Call's* when, according to a *New York Times* account, "he returned
from a business trip and was unexpectedly dismissed by the McCall
Corporation. At that time, Arthur R. Murphy Jr., president of Mc-
Call's, said that he had 'asked for the resignation' because of 'policy
differences regarding McCall's magazine.' No further information
was forthcoming." At Curtis, then, Garth Hite was removed as
publisher of *Holiday* to make way for Kelly, and when that change
failed to make *Holiday* profitable, Don Schanche was dismissed from
the editorship. Then came the firing of Jess Ballew, and so Steve
Kelly, at forty-nine, had moved into his fourth major job in three
years.

In sharp contrast to Ballew, who was almost childish in his
enthusiasm, Kelly seemed inclined to periods of gloom. Emerson got
his first real glimpse of this when the salesmen gathered for another
one of their conferences at a country club in Connecticut. Emerson
gave his usual talk on the editorial prospects and then drove back to
New York with Kelly. They stopped for lunch and had several
Martinis, and Kelly appeared very discouraged. He said the ads
weren't coming in, and there was no sign of them coming in in the
near future, and he couldn't understand how the salesmen could
spend the afternoon on the golf course.

"They didn't ask me whether they could play golf," Kelly said,
according to Emerson. "They just went ahead, the way they always
have. With all the problems we face, they spend the afternoon
playing golf."

"I liked him much better in that state than when he's pushing,"
Emerson told me later. "And I got a much better purchase on him
than I ever had before."

I myself never did get a purchase on Kelly, nor did he on me, though we both kept sparring and maneuvering to see what the risks might be. The odd thing was that Kelly rarely brought us any glad tidings from the commercial battle fronts, the way Ballew used to do; on the contrary, he seemed to come to the editorial floor in the hope that we would have cheering news for him. When Emerson was around, he could usually fabricate some hopeful prospects, but when he was away, there was nobody who could cure Kelly's blues.

One day toward the end of that disintegrating year, Kelly invited me out for lunch, and we found ourselves talking about circulation. Kelly had just been to a meeting of the Curtis Circulation Company, in Florida or Texas or some Southern resort, and he claimed he had "opened up new channels of communication."

"What are the chances of our getting some control over our own circulation policies?" I asked. "How many copies we want to print, how much we want to charge for them—"

"Ah, well, now you're getting down to the roots," Kelly said.

"I know," I said. "That's why I'm asking."

"Well, for the time being," Kelly said, "we'll just have to do our best with what we have."

This meant that the magazine's basic problem would remain unsolved, because Kelly, like all his predecessors, regarded the *Post* not as a salable product in itself but simply as a vehicle for advertising. I tried to interest Kelly in the circulation question by arguing the case in his own language. If we charged more money for the *Post*, surely our readers would more nearly resemble the kind of audience that the advertisers wanted to reach. And if our readers paid more, surely it would convince advertisers that our readers were devoted to the magazine and paid attention to what it said.

"Well," said Kelly, drawling the word in a tone of faint contempt. ("Waal" was the way it sounded, but with a flat, grinding sound to the vowel, and I suddenly realized what Kelly's voice reminded me of. He spoke with exactly the intonations of Nelson Rockefeller. And I just as suddenly realized that Rockefeller's supposedly prospering presidential candidacy was doomed, because people instinctively don't like to be talked to in that domineering tone of voice.) "Well," Kelly was saying, "you can talk figures all day, but the thing that really counts is whether you've got a hot book." What were "hot books"? Well, *Newsweek*, for one. And *Esquire*. And what made them hot books? Kelly saw the situation in an unusual light: "Look, there are only about twenty thousand people in the advertising community, and the important guys in that community all know each other and talk things over with each other, and those are the guys we've got to impress."

"Community" is an interesting word, for its use in this sense always implies that there are myriad groupings of people who consider themselves part of some self-serving collectivity. "Diplomatic community," for instance, is a fairly common term, meaning that the ambassadors who meet in the corridors of the UN have probably met before in other corridors, equally protected from the outside world. "Academic community," similarly, means that a professor of linguistics in Oregon can fairly easily become a professor of linguistics in South Carolina, and all the rules will remain the same. And since all these communities exist primarily in the minds of their members, one can probably speak with equal accuracy of the tennis community, the psychoanalytical community, or the rose-growing community. The point to be remembered, though, is that a man who thinks of himself as a member of a "community" often gives to that group a loyalty as great as any he may owe to any employer. To me, the idea of an "advertising community" meant little more than the spectacle of a lot of nervous people competing against one another in a rather unsavory business, but to Kelly, this "community" was a society in which he had lived for thirty years, a society that had trained him and supported him—and would continue to support him, in one job or another. And maybe he was right. Maybe that is the way much advertising is sold, much business transacted—by impressing the leaders of whatever commercial community one inhabits.

How, then, does one impress the leaders of the community? One impresses them by being successful, which means never failing. The *Post* was undeniably failing, and therefore it needed a new image, and the logical scapegoat had to be Bill Emerson. The "advertising community" needed a reason to advertise in the *Post*, not a reason based on statistics, readership, and all that, but something that would turn an image of failure into an image of success, something that would make the media director who recommended an ad in the *Post* feel that it was a smart move, and that nobody would laugh at him for his decision.

"The advertising community still doesn't get the message from the *Post*," Kelly said wearily. "Those Emerson speeches about 'getting at the truth,' they just don't work. There's not enough sell to them."

I looked back at Kelly without saying anything. The fact that Emerson believed in what he was saying appeared to strike Kelly as irrelevant.

"Now Alsop," Kelly went on. "What do you think of Alsop?"

"I like him," I said. "We've had our arguments, but they've usually been friendly."

"I think he's pretty impressive," Kelly said. "He comes across as an important man. Someone who is listened to."

"You have to beat him on the head occasionally, though," I said, "just to keep things in balance."

"What about you?" Kelly said. "What do you see ahead for the field of magazines?"

"Trouble," I said. I wasn't getting the point of Kelly's questions.

"Well, put it this way, where is the *Post* going?"

"Wherever the world goes," I said.

"Ah, come *on*," Kelly said, flushing in irritation, his voice more Rockefeller than ever.

"I mean it," I said. "Where's the *Times* going? Where's *Newsweek* going? That's where we're going."

Kelly shook his head dolefully and said nothing. But I had suddenly developed a theory about what was happening. My theory was that Kelly was thinking of deposing Emerson, and that he was looking around for possible successors. I was one of the obvious candidates, but I did not want the editorship on any terms like these. I did not want to be Kelly's protégé, and I did not want to devise a spiel to impress "the advertising community." But since Kelly never offered anything, I could not reject the offer. Instead, I just played dumb. Nothing ventured, nothing lost.

From this point on, everything began deteriorating very rapidly.

Emerson and I were returning from lunch in mid-January of the new year when we encountered old G. B. McCombs, who took Emerson by the elbow and led him off to the thirty-second floor. An hour later, Emerson returned with the news.

"We're supposed to cut another $340,000 out of the budget."

"This is getting to be a regular event," I said. "I thought it had been all settled."

"It had been."

"Would this new cut settle it for good?"

"Not necessarily."

"So what did you tell him?"

"Told him it couldn't be done."

"But I suppose it can be."

"I'm just going to take it out of the budget for materials," Emerson said. "Then we'll just spend more than the budget says, and by the time they catch us going over the budget, they'll either have more money or it'll be too late to matter."

One day I came back from lunch and learned from Emerson's secretary, Barabara O'Dwyer, that Maurice Poppei had come by to visit us.

"What does he want now?" I asked.

"He just wanted to say good-bye to Bill, because he's retiring on the first of February."

Yes, I had heard that, a great secret, a few months earlier. Maurice Poppei was getting old and tired, but the money that he had raked in during these last few years would soothe the troubles of old age. And for what he had done at Curtis, Poppei was not without admirers. One independent expert described him as "brilliant" and added that throughout the Clifford years, "Poppei was the man who held the company together." I would always remember him, though, as the white-skinned figure who had taken part in so many firings. "But Bill wasn't here," Barbara added, "so he just said good-bye to me and went away again."

"So good-bye to Maurice Poppei," I said. "I wonder who's going to count the money from now on."

"Nobody seems to know."

One of our staff writers needed an expense account paid within a week, but the bookkeeper didn't think this was possible.

"I'm sorry, but Philadelphia hasn't paid any bills since the tenth of the month, and that's two weeks ago," said the bookkeeper, Elena Dardano.

"What happens to the payment forms we send down there?" I asked.

"They just pile up. For about six months now, they haven't been paying anything between the tenth of the month and about the twenty-fifth. Then, in the last week of the month, some advertising money comes in, and then they pay the first-of-the-month bills, with a little left over for whoever has been complaining loudest."

From the *Gallagher Report* there came a weekly drumbeat of dark prophecies:

January 16:
    CURTIS PUBLISHING IN DESPERATE STRAITS. Needs cash. Can't find buyer till settlement of preferred stock is arranged. . . . Valuable tax loss evaporates. . . . Saturday Evening Post should be folded immediately. . . .

January 23:

Curtis Publishing estimated loss for 1967: $4 million. Kills last hope for turnaround without merger. Top management looks for merger partner. Alternative: fold Saturday Evening Post in June. . . .

January 30:

CURTIS PROPERTIES RIPE FOR ACQUISITION. By highest bidder . . . President "Mac the Knife" Clifford in hopeless situation.

February 13:

Curtis Publishing president "Mac the Knife" Clifford investigates legality of loan from Curtis pension fund.

February 27:

CURTIS PUBLISHING FACES CROWELL COLLIER ROUTE. History repeats. . . . Curtis collapse would be major blow to entire magazine industry.

Having won his way with the time clocks, Mac Clifford was determined to solve another problem that irritated him—editorial vacations. According to the Curtis personnel policy rule book, which had undergone only minimal changes since the death of George Horace Lorimer, vacations were organized by seniority—two weeks off per year during the first five years of employment, three weeks during the next five years, and four weeks after that. These rules were supposed to apply equally to editors and office boys. In the outside world, unknown to Clifford, the principle of a month's vacation for senior workers had become fairly widespread, but Clifford seemed convinced that the idea of the editors' getting more than two weeks' vacation was an outrage to propriety. He forbade it in 1965, in 1966, in 1967, and each time we simply defied him.

Now, in February of 1968, barely two months before his own downfall, Clifford had G.B. summon a conference of the editors of all Curtis magazines. These were difficult times for the whole company, G.B. said, and there would no longer be any "extra" vacations for editors.

"Mac is going to hold the line on this," G.B. said firmly.

"Mac can go f—— himself," Emerson said.

For the salesmen, however, the golfing days were coming to an end. From Joe Welty, advertising director, a "confidential" memo went to all regional sales offices: "We have changed our plans concerning a 1968 National Sales Meeting. The announced meeting in April at Ponte Vedra will not be held. . . ."

17

"Nobody cares any more"

Every week or two, Mike Mooney and I would wander over to the Brasserie, a scene of noisy disorder in the basement of the Seagram Building, and have a large bowl of onion soup for lunch. I had always found Mooney good company, but this ritual had other functions too. Mooney had spent the past year not in editing articles but in working out his theory that *Post* material could fairly easily be converted to television as a weekly "magazine of the air." In collaboration with an independent TV producer, he had put together a pilot film for presentation. And in the course of maneuvering through the managerial ranks at Curtis, and in wandering through the demimondes of Madison Avenue and Wall Street, Mooney had acquired an astonishing amount of information about our financial difficulties.

Now, in early March of 1968, the conversation with the onion soup made it clear that we were nearing the last month of Mac Clifford's reign. "You have to remember the essentials," Mooney was saying. "No business is an abstraction. It has to take money in and pay money out, and the two have to add up. When they didn't add up, the company went and borrowed money from the banks, and now it's time to pay it back. Just like *Faust*."

The rumors of Clifford's trying to borrow more money were all true, Mooney said. Clifford had to raise $9 million by the end of March, just a month from now. "So all he can think of," said Mooney, "is to sell the old Curtis building in Philadelphia. Once they thought it was worth something like $15 million, so they turned down an offer of $12 million. All that marble, you know. Historic Philadelphia landmark. What would Mrs. Zimbalist say? So now he's got to negotiate over an offer of about $7 million, and he just hopes to hell he can bring it off in time. But he hasn't got much time left, old Mac Clifford. The bells are starting to toll, and the whole Curtis Publishing Company may turn into a pumpkin before our very eyes."

Mooney guffawed and snorted and spooned up some more of the onion soup. He was not a man who talked simply to convey information. Instead, each claylike fistful of information had to be sculpted into an image, a legend, and then all dramatized, vivified. Mooney would play various parts, muttering through his nose in imitation of Mac Clifford or rising to a squeaking soprano to represent Mrs. Zimbalist.

Clifford had never really wanted to sell Curtis, Mooney went on, because he enjoyed running a company, but things had become so desperate lately that he had once again approached CBS. "So little Mac Clifford, the tough negotiator, two-fisted—" all this spoken through the nose, with a bang on the table—"wanted to offer them a deal. He offered to sell them all the Curtis magazines for $15 million, provided they'd give him a printing and distribution contract. And the CBS people all sat there and stared at him." Here Mooney's blue eyes widened and his lips tightened into the expression of wary skepticism with which a TV executive would presumably confront a maniac. "They were just dumfounded."

"Okay, I'll bite," I said. "Why were they so amazed?"

"Because they'd all read the study that J. K. Lasser did for them, which is about the best study ever made of Curtis, and the Lasser study says that if you liquidate all those Philadelphia operations, the printing plant and all that, just close them all down or get rid of them somehow, then the magazines alone could make a profit of maybe $10 million a year. After all, the magazines, ruined and debauched as they are, still earn more than $80 million a year, whereas everything in Philadelphia ought to be sold for scrap. But the people who run it—G.B. and Leon Marks and all those old fogy-boppers have convinced everybody that the magazines are wasting all the money being earned by their great printing company. And now here comes Mac Clifford, honk-honk, the tough little businessman, honk-honk, and he wants to sell to CBS the only money-making parts of his own company so that he can keep the money-losing parts. I tell you, they were speechless."

"Well, okay," I said, "but he obviously wouldn't sell unless he could stick CBS with a printing and distribution contract that would guarantee him a profit. That's been the problem all along."

"And it's the problem right now, but that's the only thing that's holding up a sale. The fact that CBS isn't stupid."

"So we're back where we started from—nowhere."

"No, we aren't," Mooney said. "You've forgotten the essential fact, which is that Clifford can't pay the bills. And if he won't deal with CBS, he'll have to deal with somebody else. He might even have to deal with me."

"Ah," I said, watching Mooney savor the revelation. "You finally have a wealthy buyer waiting in the wings?"

"Right."

"You vouch for his character?"

"Absolutely."

"But you won't tell me who he is."

"Sorry."

It is useful to recall, from time to time, Cary Bok's statement of what he had found critically lacking in the regime of Joe Culligan: "We needed a manager, a president who could settle down to the hard decade of rebuilding which our company needed." The statement indicates that some of the powers at Curtis had an occasional insight into the nature of the company's problems, even though they had very little idea of how to solve those problems. Having decided that they needed a manager rather than an advertising salesman, they had evidently decided that Mac Clifford filled that need. What they forgot was that they needed a manager who would rebuild, not just a manager who would preside numbly over the breakdown of the machinery.

By March of 1968, Mac Clifford had had more than three years, a third of Cary Bok's decade, in which to rebuild. Unlike his predecessor, he had been blessed with three years of peace, both external and internal. The national economy had gone bumping upward through the Lyndon Johnson boom, rising from one peak to the next, and the Curtis Publishing Company had drifted along, relatively free of civil strife. Except for the flurry at *Holiday* early in 1965, there had been no insurrections, and the only editors or publishers who had left had done so at Clifford's own pleasure. But in the three years that could have been dedicated to rebuilding—which essentially means hiring talented new executives and encouraging them to get the organization moving—Mac Clifford had left the entire company in the hands of his cronies, Poppei, Sweet Gloria, and G.B. With these four at the controls, no executives of any significance were brought in from outside to renew the management of the corporation. And so, with the acquiescence of a docile and apathetic board of directors, the fundamental problems of the Curtis Publishing Company remained not just unsolved but almost untouched.

As for the *Post,* Clifford failed to deal with the difficulties of getting the magazine to its proper readers at a proper rate. Once or twice, he had edged up to the necessity of increasing the price of the magazine, and then edged away again. These misguided circulation policies doomed the *Post* to continue its total dependence on the favors of advertisers—and advertisers, by and large, weren't interested any more. This had relatively little to do with the *Post's* editorial contents or appearance—despite the views of would-be judges on Madison Avenue—but rather with its value as an advertising medium. In the course of a decade, a mass magazine that still charged $40,000 per page had simply become a bad buy. While smaller magazines could promise a richer audience, at a much cheaper advertising rate per page, television could promise a much larger audience, at a much cheaper advertising rate per head. To these realities, Mac Clifford's reaction was classic. He demanded that Jess Ballew try harder, fulfill impossible goals, and then, when Ballew failed to reach the goals, he was dismissed and replaced by Steve Kelly, who was given a new set of demands and goals. Clifford thought he had made a clever move, because Kelly seemed such a model of Madison Avenue, but the change made no substantial difference. Under Ballew, the *Post* had gone from 1,407 pages in the weekly issues of 1964 to 992 in the biweekly of 1965, then fought upward to 1,160 pages in 1966 (the year of Clifford's profit); under Kelly, the figures dropped to 1,052 in 1967 and 940 in 1968. As for the company as a whole, during those three peaceful years of nonbuilding, while Clifford fretted about time clocks and two-week vacations, the Curtis Publishing Company lost another $8 million.

The Mooney bid was a peculiarly angled shot because of Clifford's reluctance to sell, and his reluctance even to talk to prospective buyers. Of these, Mooney had two. One was a young man named C. Henry Buhl III, who was described by one observer as "an amiable jet-setter." While Mooney's father had been an executive at General Motors, Buhl's grandfather had been an early associate of the Fisher brothers (Fisher bodies), and so he became one of the largest stockholders in GM. Young Buhl, still in his thirties, had worked for a time on Wall Street and then gone to Europe, where he was now associated with the overseas stock investment empire of Bernie Cornfeld (Investors Overseas Service, the Fund of Funds, and all that). Mooney had spoken glowingly of Buhl as a man of limitless energy and imagination. On one occasion, when Buhl wanted to interest a stuffy Swiss banker in some South African gold mines, according to Mooney, he had led the Swiss banker aboard a plane to South Africa, driven him to the mines, and taken him, protesting, down the shaft for a firsthand study of what the mine actually produced—a story which, whether true or not, illustrated Mooney's views on how a business should be run and what kind of a businessman should be brought in to run Curtis.

During this critical period, unfortunately, Buhl had commitments that kept him in Europe, and so the negotiations were handled by Mooney and his other key figure, Robert Vesco, another young entrepreneur in his early thirties, head of a modest conglomerate called International Control. On Wednesday, March 6, the day before the last board meeting before the fatal bank loan would come due, Mooney and Vesco made their proposal to Cary Bok and William Bodine, a partner in Pepper, Hamilton & Scheetz, representing the Bok family's huge trust funds. According to this proposal, Vesco would arrange a merger of the two companies, through an exchange of stocks, and Buhl would invest $10 million in new capital, in exchange for working control of Curtis. Bok's answer was ambiguous. "Work it out with Mac Clifford," he said.

Mooney told the news only to Emerson, telling him as little as possible, and Emerson told me only what he could not keep to himself. "If they ask me whether I've told anybody, I'm going to lie and say I haven't," he said, "so you'd better be prepared to lie too." As usual, we listened to rumors. The February 27 *Gallagher Report* had already said that "Curtis could go Crowell-Collier route" and added: "Bad news coming at March 7 directors meeting." Now, on the day of the directors' meeting, Henry Raymont of the *Times* was calling various editors to ask confirmation of reports that the *Post* had just folded. The only official announcement from the board meeting, however, was that the company would be unable to pay its April 1 interest on its 6 percent debentures, and that it was postponing the annual stockholders' meeting from mid-April until May 29.

At about four o'clock, I saw that Mooney had finally returned to his office, which was just across the corridor from mine, and so I walked in and asked him what was going on. Mooney simply stared at me in a state of mute exhaustion.

"You look weary," I said.

"I am weary," he said, and paused. "But one thing I want to tell you, one thing I've been telling myself for the last three days: *Blair was right!"*

"Hell, that's no news," I said. "The only trouble with Blair's theories was Blair's tactics."

"This morning, I was sitting in one of these anterooms," Mooney went on, his eyes coming back to life as another story began to take shape in his head, "and I had to wait for half an hour to see one of these idiots, and so I pulled out a piece of scrap paper and wrote down in six paragraphs the six definitions of *evil*." Mooney guffawed. "That must have been what happened to Blair."

Clifford's reaction to the continuing losses on the *Post* was, as before, to cut off a few more fingers and toes. The news came through Steve Kelly, who wondered how we should react to a management proposal to drop two summer issues, in effect changing to monthly publication during July and August. My first response was that we should challenge Clifford to close down the *Post*, but this was rejected as a counsel of anger. A few days later, we heard that Clifford's technicians had already gone beyond proposals and had worked out all the figures for the elimination of three issues, not only two in the summer but one in December. Killing these issues, according to one report, would save $285,000; according to another report, since no managerial decision at Curtis ever involved less than two contradictory sets of financial statistics, the saving would amount to $850,000.

Obviously, some kind of cut was going to be forced on us, and so we tried to consider alternatives. One, if it was purely a matter of money, would be to lobby for the abolition of circulation advertisements, which dribbled away more than a quarter of a million dollars a year. But if Clifford were determined to shrink the *Post*, then, instead of dropping three issues a year, it would surely be more discreet to keep all twenty-six issues and to make still further cuts in each issue, another 12 percent or so. Emerson snatched at that as a splendid solution, a salvation of the biweekly schedule, one that he would urge on Clifford in Philadelphia the following week, one that Clifford could not reject.

Ten days after Mooney's offer, we were again having lunch at the Brasserie, where we encountered and joined forces with Mooney's brother John, an architect. Mooney, who had once been very secretive about his deal, now spoke openly and bitterly of the obstacles that prevented its consummation. He claimed that the Boks couldn't provide a warranty as to what would be included in a sale of the company. "Even the building, for Chrissakes!" Mooney cried. "They claim they can't be certain whether the Philadelphia headquarters building goes with the company or goes separately. There was supposed to be a deal on the building last week for $7 million, but did they close the deal or not? Cary Bok tells us to 'work it out with Mac,' but Mac is still stalling us while he tries to sell the magazines to CBS."

Mooney said he was going to "get together with the bankers and see if we can't just do something about Mr. Clifford." By bankers, he meant not only "the bank," the First National of Boston and its partners, but two Wall Street investment houses that had large holdings in Curtis—Loeb, Rhoades and White, Weld & Company.

"What does that mean, 'get together with'?" I asked. "What can they do?"

"You've forgotten the essential thing again, Otto. Mac Clifford can't pay the company's bills, and these bankers are people who believe in bills being paid."

"That's all fine talk, but the bankers are responsible for Clifford in the first place. They approved his becoming president back in '65."

"That's because nobody else ever came up with a plan. Banks don't think they're responsible for making changes."

"Why in hell not? If they have veto power over changes?"

"Because banks don't want to run corporations. They just want to protect their investments."

Emerson spent an entire day in Philadelphia, arguing with Clifford and the accountants from Price, Waterhouse, who still had not closed the books on 1967. If he did not want to drop three issues a year, they said, he would have to drop seven more editorial pages from each issue. Emerson then offered to eliminate the circulation advertisements instead. The circulation company complained bitterly, but the accountants greeted it as a simple saving. Then we would only have to drop three pages from each issue. Emerson telephoned me at home that night with the news of this great victory. Effec 've with the next issue, therefore, another 7 percent of the mutilated *Post* would be amputated.

Mooney's meetings with the bankers proceeded quite satisfactorily, or so he thought. After the first session, he quoted one of the bankers as saying, "We'll settle this thing at about 10 P.M. on March 31." And Clifford's own attitude seemed to be changing. A few days before, it had been impossible to reach him at all, and now he himself was calling Mooney to "see if we can't get this whole thing worked out."

They did meet during that last week in March, and, although Mooney had again become as secretive as Clifford himself, he was obviously trying to negotiate a peaceful transition. Clifford himself would stay on as a powerless chairman of the board. The details were all subject to bargaining, but Mooney seemed to have no doubts about the outcome.

"Are you still alive?" I asked him after that confrontation with Clifford.

"Very much so," he said, and laughed.

"Did he really give you an answer to your deal?"

"Well, in principle, he agrees to it."

"I'll be damned!"

It is easy to forget, in recording the death throes of a corporation, that we were still primarily occupied in publishing a magazine of considerable quality. The conventional way to support such a statement is to list some of the works we published during these last few months of Mac Clifford's regime, early in 1968—*The Price* by Arthur Miller, "We Can Get out of Vietnam" by James Gavin, "The Triumph" by John Kenneth Galbraith, "Iberia" by James Michener, "The Picking of the President, 1968" by Russell Baker, "True Grit" by Charles Portis, "Has This Country Gone Mad?" by Daniel Patrick Moynihan, "One Very Hot Day" by David Halberstam, "Above the Law: The Tragedy of Senator Dodd" by James Boyd. Inevitably, though, such lists place too much emphasis on best-selling books and "name" authors, when an editor's real pride and satisfaction generally come from works that do not lend themselves to such listing. A relatively unknown writer named Rebecca Morris, to take one example, sent us during this same period a warm and funny and beautifully written story, "Bellevue Circus," on the unlikely subject of life in the women's tuberculosis ward of a New York hospital. Another talented but relatively uncelebrated writer, Bil Gilbert, had been assigned to report on the effects of Vietnam on a small town, but he had gone beyond that to write a vivid portrait of the town itself, "The Great World and Millersburg." Still another writer, Lewis Lapham, had been sent to India to describe the lair of a phenomenally popular Hindu sage, and I happily entitled his story, "There Once Was a Guru from Rishikesh."

Of all my pet projects, the one in which I was most personally involved was an assignment that had been known for several years as "The Jew in America." It was originally another editor's idea, and several writers had been suggested and even tried, but I finally assigned it to Roger Kahn, and his agent sold the idea to a book publisher, and contracts were signed, and Kahn was turned loose to spend the next year investigating the situation of Jews in America. Kahn being Kahn, he took more than two years, wandering all over the country, interviewing hundreds of people, amassing mountains of notes, and then discovering that much of what he had to write was a book about himself and his own generation. It is dangerous, of course, to let any assignment cover such an expanse of time, and so I met periodically with Kahn to check on his progress, to listen to his tales of woe, to argue over what he had found and what conclusions he drew, and to reassure him that all this work would come to a splendid conclusion. And so, finally, it did.

On the business and managerial side of Curtis, however, the whole project was regarded with fear and hostility. In the distance, haunting the magazine like some ancestral curse, was the famous article of 1942, "The Case Against the Jew," by Milton Mayer. It was remembered, even by people who had not been there, as an unparalleled disaster—a storm of canceled ads, newsstand boycotts, rage and denunciation. Curtis officials tended forever after to think of Jews as a fierce and vengeful group, to be regarded with dread. This dread was not entirely free of guilt either. For many years, there had been no Jews in the top management of the corporation, or any of its magazines, and even now, in 1968, the number of Jews was so small that each of them was an exception that proved the rule. To the princes of the corporation, then, Jews were strange and incomprehensible people, best left alone.

Mac Clifford had officially asked several times that Kahn's project be canceled, but Emerson, though he had little enthusiasm for the assignment, argued that no decision could be made until the manuscript had been read. Steve Kelly, with similar misgivings, had been given a similar answer. And now, suddenly, we had bought the manuscript, entitled *The Passionate People*, and scheduled it for the May 18 issue. So on the same day that Mooney thought he had won agreement from Mac Clifford, a whole new crisis began with a visit from Steve Kelly.

"I just want to emphasize," he said, "the seriousness of our publishing an anti-Semitic article at this time."

"What anti-Semitic article?" I said.

"This Roger Kahn thing, 'The Jew in America'—God, the title alone gives me the shivers—Emerson says it will make a lot of Jewish readers unhappy."

"There must be some misunderstanding," I said. "He couldn't have meant that, because the vast majority of Jews are going to think it's just fine."

"Well, look, I've got a copy here, and so I won't say any more until I've read it, but I just want to be sure that you realize that a relatively small number of Jewish advertisers control millions of dollars' worth of advertising, and if we offend them . . ."

Kelly shook his head dolefully at the thought of the consequences that might follow. I tried to reassure him once again that there would be no serious trouble from Jews, only from our own management's anxiety about Jews, but he left with the look of a man doomed. The next morning, when I found him once again in Emerson's office, he had read the manuscript and seen the nature of his doom—to appear in the Colosseum. "Listen, I'm just telling you guys," he said, "Jews don't like to be singled out in any way." "That's ridiculous," I said. "Why do you think there's a magazine like *Commentary?*" Kelly kept shaking his head despairingly, and now it became clear what his role in the Colosseum would be, that of some brave but helpless animal, a bear from Hibernia or a Gallician ox, destined to charge blindly at bands of little men with swords until it was brought to earth.

In a desperate effort to avoid this fate, Kelly had decided on the drastic expedient of appealing an editorial question over the heads of the editors. Having annotated Kahn's manuscript, citing specific examples of passages that he thought would cause offense, he had turned it all over to G. B. McCombs, whom he blandly described as "our boss." I could recall no precedent for old G.B. ruling on the merits of a manuscript, and after stiffly ushering Kelly out of the office, Emerson and I quickly decided that we would not abide by any managerial ruling on our publishing Kahn's story. If there were specific objections, we would consider them—no more—and then make our own decisions. "How big a problem is this going to be?" Mike Mooney suddenly asked, worried, because his deal was based on the existence of an editorial staff. "Depends on them," I said. "If they want to make trouble, it will be big trouble."

The next day, Emerson had to go to Philadelphia to make a speech to the advertising officials of the Campbell Soup Company, and so it fell to me to go to G.B.'s office on the thirty-second floor and join battle over the Kahn manuscript. G.B. kept me waiting for almost half an hour in the "conference room," a rarely used chamber furnished with out-of-place mementos from Philadelphia, a dark wooden table, upholstered chairs, two cityscapes painted in the Rockwellian manner. Despite these homey touches, the room was dominated by picture windows that provided a view extending miles northward across Central Park. I rarely came to the thirty-second floor, and whenever I did, I found it haunted by the ghosts of Culligan and Kantor and all their scrambling vice presidents.

When G.B. finally came bustling in, smiling and dapper in a dark-blue suit, he brought the Kahn manuscript with him. "Now I know I'm not an editor," said G.B., gasping slightly through his shiny teeth, "and I have no intention of trying to override the editors, and I don't even know whether I *could* override the editors. . . ." I nodded in agreement—*that's true, G.B.*—but we both knew that there was a catch. "But when I feel that the company's business position may be threatened, then I feel it's my duty to speak up. You understand that, don't you? It's for the sake of the company."

"Sure, G.B. I understand."

So now we set to work.

In the very first paragraph, Kahn had written: ". . . but for Jews—for the loud Babbitts and the agonizing rabbis . . ." "Now that's talking down," G.B. complained, leaning back in his chair. "I'd hate to see us talking down to the Jews like that." The first problem, of course, was to find out what it really was that bothered G.B. In this instance, it was not just the word "Babbitts"—I convinced him that this was harmless because it had been conceived as a name for *gentile* businessmen—but the word "agonizing," which he misread as a description of people who make a fuss about nothing. I suggested that we change it to "agonized," and G.B. was content.

Kahn had written: "The secular variety of Jews is wider still. There is no American Jewish viewpoint on the war in Vietnam, or on Stokely Carmichael. There is, broadly, no American Jewish position on anything, except possibly anti-Semitism. Jews oppose it. . . ." G.B. objected. "That makes it sound as though we were saying that Jews are spineless," he said. I argued for a while and then suggested that we change it to read "no uniform American Jewish viewpoint." G.B. was content.

Kahn had quoted a Chicago businessman who said, "My kid was raised a Jew. We filled his head full of tradition from the time he was two. So what happens? All he wants to do is go to Mississippi and help the shvartzes, and he goes around bragging that he's an atheist. How do you figure that?" G.B. objected to every reference connecting Jews to Negroes, even to a mention that two Jewish civil rights workers had been murdered in Mississippi. "You know it, and I know it, and they know it," G.B. said, "but they don't want to be reminded of it." I didn't concede the point, but I didn't need the Chicago businessman either, so we cut him.

Kahn had told a story about Al Rosen, the baseball player, who had tried out for football and been told by his coach, "You're different from most Jews. Most Jewboys are afraid of contact." G.B. objected that this was an insult. I said it was supposed to be an insult; the point was to show the kind of life that Rosen had led. "Of course, it's true, they *are* afraid of contact," G.B. said. Again, once I could understand the objection, I could figure out a solution. In this case, we settled for "Many Jews don't like contact."

And so we labored on for an hour and a half, arguing not so much about what Kahn had written, or even about what Jews might think about what Kahn had written, but about what G. B. McCombs of Waxahachie County, Texas, representing a generation of Philadelphia dignitaries, thought about the world that was rising to threaten the Curtis Publishing Company. And he wanted me to know that he was not prejudiced.

"You know, Curtis used to not hire Jews," G.B. said, abruptly.

"I know."

"Or Catholics either," G.B. went on. "I was the one who hired the first Jew."

"And what happened?" I asked.

"Nothing." G.B. laughed.

Having hired the first Jew, G.B. nonetheless believed many of the myths, like the one that Jews feared physical contact, but then he wanted to tell me a story. Many years ago, his daughter had fallen down the cellar stairs, and she had to have three brain operations. She had recovered fully, but the bill was $9,000, and when G.B. went to pay it, he was told that it had already been paid by three anonymous donors. He had demanded to know who they were, and he had learned that they were three Jews, business associates, and he had paid them all back. But he was still moved by the story, and as he told it, his voice became vague and dreamy and he seemed near tears. "I'll never forget that," he said.

Bargaining is a strange business, and although I felt that I was right on every point, and that I should not have been making these bargains in the first place—is this the spirit at every peace conference?—I knew that it would be impolitic to claim my rights on each issue. I found myself, therefore, granting and refusing to grant for no other reason than the manipulation of my antagonist. In other words, I resisted on points that I could easily have conceded, just so that G.B. would not feel he was getting his way too easily, and I conceded other points unnecessarily just so that he would not feel he was getting nothing for his troubles. And finally, as a matter of principle,

I left a few points unresolved, not because they couldn't be resolved but because I didn't want the negotiations to be too simple. Having started with eighty-odd passages marked as dangerous by Kelly and G.B., we ended with six still unsettled, requiring further reflection.

The day after my conciliatory meeting with G.B., Kelly appeared in my office again, more anxious than ever. "There's just no way for us to win on this one," he cried. "Just no way at all." What troubled Kelly, I began to see, was not a matter that could be settled rationally but rather a hallucinatory vision of the vengeance of the Jews. Kelly had already described it to me once before, but with each passing day, the vision seemed to become more and more vivid. It was a scene that could have taken place in a number of corporations or advertising agencies, where various Jews might gather and condemn the *Post* to oblivion, but for some reason Kelly envisioned the scene in the office of Edgar Bronfman, Jr., president of Seagram's. "I can just see a guy like Eddie Bronfman putting down that issue of the *Post*," said Kelly, "and saying, 'Goddammit, no Curtis magazine is ever going to get another nickel that I have anything to say about.' "

It would not have been polite for me to suggest that Bronfman might have commercial reasons for his commercial decisions, and that he might think Curtis magazines failed to give him his money's worth; it would not have been polite of me to remind Kelly that Curtis had refused for years to accept any advertising from Bronfman or any other liquor producer, and that some liquor industry executives still cherished, as a supreme example of business blundering, the official statement in which Curtis haughtily announced that it was finally willing to accept liquor advertisements. Instead, I could only repeat, doggedly, that if Bronfman actually read Kahn's article in the *Post*, he would think it was splendid, because it really was splendid. But Kelly now wanted a more expert reading. He had a Jewish consultant, he said, who was paid to "help on the Jewish accounts," and he wanted another copy of the manuscript for this gentleman to read. I agreed, but only with a warning that it was a waste of time.

"If he doesn't like it, that's not going to stop us from publishing it," I said. "And if he does like it, that's still not going to convince you that every other Jew in the country will like it."

"Well, I've said before that I don't think we can win on this one," Kelly said, "but I want to be proved wrong. I really want to be proved wrong."

It was agreed, finally, that Emerson, Kelly, and G.B. would all meet in Philadelphia the following Monday, April 1, and settle the six unresolved questions in the Kahn manuscript. But this was the last weekend in March, in which the million-dollar bank loans came due, and on Saturday, G.B. anxiously telephoned Emerson and told him to prepare some other article for the May 18 issue in case "a postponement" of the Kahn became "necessary." Emerson called me to ask my views, and I said this would give the management too easy an alternative course. Our official answer should be that we didn't have any substitute article ready.

"I thought we had this practically settled," I added. "What's got into them now?"

"Well, now they're worried because Loeb, Rhoades is Jewish."

"God Almighty! Loeb, Rhoades is mad at them for financial incompetence, not for publishing articles about Jews."

"I know, but it's hard for them to realize that. The banks are pressing Clifford very hard, and this goddamn Kahn book has become for them a symbol of everything else."

"Well, it has for me, too," I said.

I expected a big crisis on Monday, but it was April Fool's Day. Emerson telephoned from Philadelphia that morning and said, "There won't be any trouble about the Kahn book. And Clifford got an extension on his loans."

The extension was announced without detail. The *Wall Street Journal* quoted one of the bankers: "The extension isn't for 'too long,' he said. 'They're not in very good shape.' Recalling the mineral find on Curtis timberland in Ontario four years ago, the bank executive added: 'They had one miracle before, and maybe they'll have another one.' "

That same weekend, Clifford released the annual report to stockholders, beginning with the glum statement: "The Curtis Publishing Company recorded a net loss in 1967 of $4,839,000." Clifford blamed this on an advertising decline "due primarily to softened national economic conditions and costly strikes in key industries," and he quickly added: "However, advertising orders are on the upswing and there is every expectation that this promising momentum will be maintained throughout the remainder of 1968." The *Wall Street Journal*, reporting that *Post* ad pages had actually declined 19 percent during the first quarter of 1968, commented: "Mr. Clifford's projections have sometimes been overoptimistic."

Aside from the speculation about advertising, the annual report provided some interesting statistics on the company's finances. As of the end of the year, current assets had declined by more than $6 million, liabilities had increased by more than $1 million, and actual càsh in hand had dropped from $10,102,000 at the start of 1967 to $425,000 at the start of 1968. Obviously, for a company that was operating on a budget of almost $130 million a year, a cash supply of $425,000 was virtually no cash at all.

The crisis that didn't come on Monday didn't come on Tuesday either. On that day, Emerson and G.B. and I met for half an hour and settled the six items in the Kahn manuscript and shook hands on the settlement. But on the next day, Wednesday, Emerson brought me into his office, and there sat G.B., looking nervous and unhappy.

"Well, the fact is," G.B. said, "we just can't afford to publish that Kahn piece. It will offend too many people."

"G.B., I thought we had this all settled," I said wearily. "You can't afford not to publish it."

"I don't see what you mean by that," G.B. said.

"Well, it'll probably mean a front-page story in the *New York Times*."

"Oh, I don't think so," G.B. said.

"Well, how are you going to explain the fact that we're reneging on a public commitment to publish the book?"

"Why, we can just say that the management decided that we couldn't get a satisfactory excerpt from it."

"That's a slander and a lie," I said.

"Well, I'm sorry," G.B. said, flushing at my accusation, "but we just can't afford to offend a lot of important readers at a time like this."

"It will *not* offend important readers," I said again.

"That's a decision that has to be made by the management, and so the management has decided."

"Then the management had better decide who's going to edit its magazine, starting right now."

"Well, I'd certainly hope that you two would go on editing it," G.B. said, genuinely surprised.

"Not me, thank you, because I won't be here," I said.

"Are you really serious this time?" Emerson asked.

"Absolutely," I said.

"Now, you see?" Emerson said bitterly to G.B.

"Look, we don't want to play editor—" G.B. said placatingly.

"Oh, yes, you do," I retorted.

"—but just this once—"

"That's like saying a virgin can oblige just once with no harm done," I said.

"Well, all I can say is that when we think the company's survival is at stake, we have to intervene," G.B. said.

"You talk about survival," I said, "but you're the ones who are wrecking the whole thing."

At that point, G.B. decided he wanted to postpone all further discussion until he could talk to Clifford, and so we decided to meet again after lunch. Just before that meeting, Emerson and I encountered Don McKinney and told him of our ultimatum. He paused for a moment and then said, "Well, I guess it's a good time of year for us all to go looking for work." So we took him along with us to the thirty-second floor for the new confrontation. G.B. had not been able to reach Clifford, however, and so there was really nothing new to say. Emerson spoke bitterly of his long service to the company and asked what it would cost if the *Post* were to lose its three top editors. "I don't know," said G.B., "but I think this book is even more dangerous than that." He had become adamant by now, and he offered only one other solution: "We could try emasculating it." Everybody looked at me, and I simply said, "No thanks."

Steve Kelly, who had precipitated the crisis, had subsequently disappeared into the far reaches of Oklahoma, where some kind of "Saturday Evening Post Day" was being celebrated in connection with an automobile industry award to an Oklahoman who had been named "Car Dealer of the Year." Now, early on Thursday morning, while Emerson was still stretching and twisting in his living room, carrying on the exercises prescribed for his damaged back, he got an anguished telephone call from Kelly. The resignation of the three top editors would be far more damaging than anything in the Kahn manuscript, Kelly said, and he had urged G.B. to drop the whole matter. But when G.B. himself finally telephoned at about noon (there was a board meeting in the process of electing two new members in Philadelphia), he only offered another version of what he had requested before—drastic re-editing and the elimination of anything that anyone might consider controversial. Once again, I gave the same answer: No. We would publish the article as it had been edited and agreed on. At this, Emerson suddenly blew up.

"God, I'm so *sick* of this whole business!" he cried, storming out of my office. He reappeared in a few minutes in an overcoat, looking dangerously red-faced with anger, but also slightly ludicrous because of the flat tweed cap that he affected. "It's Barbara's birthday," he shouted at me, gesticulating vaguely in the direction of his secretary, who hovered in the doorway, "and I'm taking her over to Barbetta's to buy her a good lunch."

"Okay, don't get so excited," I said.

"I tell you, I'm sick of all this pissantry," Emerson retorted, still shouting. "And I'm going to call G.B. from Barbetta's and tell him that I'm leaving this place."

"Suppose they give in?" I asked.

"Then I *may* stay."

It took another day for our collective intransigence to make its proper impression on Mac Clifford, and then he responded properly. He called Emerson and said, "Hell, you're the editor, and you're the one whose judgment I have to rely on. You do what you think is right."

Having won this great "victory," Emerson told me that he was returning to Georgia at the end of the week to watch the Masters Golf Tournament. "I can't stand the sight of these people any more," he said. "I feel I want to get into fist-fights with them. And it's your theory that physical confrontations should always be avoided."

"It's not my theory," I said. "It's Mao Tse-tung's theory."

"Okay, but the Kahn article is your project, and you got your way, so you take charge of getting it off to press, because I'm going away for a while."

It might be thought that we would have reveled in our great "victory," but, as Emerson's exasperated departure indicated, our joy in victory was less than our dislike of the whole episode. Our victory, after all, consisted simply of our continuing to edit the *Post* without more than routine interference. If we had ever admitted to an already discouraged staff that we had won this battle, we would also have to admit that we were now subject to strafing attacks from the management any time we wanted to publish anything that the management considered controversial. And so we kept our great "victory" a secret from the editorial staff, and even, above all, from the author of *The Passionate People*.

It was impossible to suppress, however, a general atmosphere of demoralization and disintegration during this spring of 1968. The editors all read the financial statements and heard the constant rumors of collapse. One of them, David Lyle, senior editor for foreign affairs, had acquired an increasingly radical view of both the *Post* ("irrelevant") and American society ("racist" and "pre-Fascist"), and he now resigned his job and took his family to live in France. Stewart Alsop, less unworldly in his views, received an offer from *Newsweek* that he considered "too good to turn down." And even among those who remained, there was a restless sense of things gone wrong, of erosion and decay. Our three best text editors, Bill Ewald, Tom

Congdon, and Jim Atwater, joined forces as a kind of *ad hoc* committee of malcontents and asked for a chance to express their grievances to Emerson and me. We listened, none too cordially, to their charges that we ourselves were too cautious, too negative, too unimaginative, too unwilling to take risks. When we asked for specific suggestions for improvement, they had none to offer. But that wasn't their point, they said. They felt that the magazine was going under, and they wanted to help. We tried to be sympathetic rather than truculent, but what was there that any of them, or any of us, could do?

"In April of 1945, with Allied tanks clanking past the shattered windows of the party's offices, the Führer's faithful were working out the paper-clip requirements for the third quarter of 1945." This was the observation of Gerhard L. Weinberg, who directed the study of captured Nazi archives at Alexandria, Virginia. The archives disclosed the views of the most prominent German officials, but they also showed that great numbers of Nazi functionaries remained heavily engaged in paperwork right to the end. "Had the stencil and carbon paper factories been placed at the top of the strategic bombing offensive's priority list," Weinberg continued, "the whole system might well have collapsed earlier."

On a more modest scale, it remains extraordinary that any organization, even in times of great crisis, continues to produce organizational spoor. In fact, it is possible that extreme crises cause some kind of internal spasm that increases the quantity of spoor left on the trail. During the last month of Mac Clifford's reign, on the brink of bankruptcy, a tracker would have found these three specimens:

On March 21, a memorandum from the company comptroller, W. E. Meyers, stated: "There will be no direct outside deliveries, including lunches, to or from any individual office. It will be necessary for deliveries to be picked up at the Second Floor Reception Desk or to be processed through the regular interoffice mail delivery."

On March 28, another memorandum stated: "Instead of using the complete address of our Paris office when sending cables to Paris, please use the following cable address: CURTISPUBCO Paris. This eliminates the address and cables will reach our Paris office efficiently and with much less expense."

On April 11, another memorandum stated: "The Advertising Detail Division in Philadelphia has been redesignated the Advertising Services Division."

At some point during these early days in April, Mike Mooney's grand dream of acquiring the Curtis Publishing Company began to fade gently away. The fact that Mac Clifford got an extension on the loan might have been a signal that there was something wrong with his plan, but Mooney did not read it that way. He said that the banks had no choice, because Clifford had no money, and that the moves toward the sale of the company were still progressing. Less than a week later, he claimed that Armand G. Erpf, senior partner in Loeb, Rhoades, was now "directing the board of directors, through Milton Gould and Moreau Brown." He considered this a step forward for him.

"I remember," I said, "when Clay Blair thought he had won Milton Gould over to his side, just before the debacle."

Mooney laughed. "You know what Erpf says? He says: 'Anybody can figure out how to drive the Curtis buggy, but nobody can figure out how to get into it.' "

From the *Gallagher Report*, April 9:

CURTIS PUBLISHING BOARD LOOKS FOR NEW PRESIDENT. Ouster of President Mac (The Knife) Clifford imminent. Directors, banks upset. . . . Logical successor: Former McCall's Corp. President Art Murphy. Revised board strengthens position of investors, money men. . . .

By the second week in April, when I again had lunch with Mooney at the Brasserie, it began to become apparent that Mooney's deal was dead, and that Mooney knew it but could hardly bear to admit it.

"Nobody seems to be able to find out who's in charge," he complained. "Cary Bok says, 'Work it out with Mac.' But Mac Clifford doesn't own anything. So you keep coming back to the damn board of directors, which now means that you come back to Milton Gould, and Gould doesn't want to deal."

"Why does Gould always seem to have so much power anyway?"

"Well, he represents a big block of preferred stock, him and his brother-in-law."

Partly because of this stock, Gould had just won a new strength that was not widely realized at the time. At the previous week's board meeting, on April 4, two vacancies had been filled. One was that of Newton Minow, former Federal Communications Commission Chairman, who had arrived as a bright hope for Curtis in the fall of 1964 and now was wearily relinquishing his $31,250-a-year position as an unheeded consultant. The other was that of Raymond DePue Mc-Granahan, who had also arrived in 1964, as a prospective company president, but had scarcely been mentioned in public since then.

Into their places moved Gould and Harry Mills, who until now had sat on the board as representatives of the preferred stockholders. That change, in turn, opened up the two board positions officially reserved for the preferred stockholders, and into those positions came Lawrence R. Kessel, sixty-five, and Thomas S. Hyland, fifty. Their election seemed a little puzzling, since both were identified primarily as directors of the Delaware & Hudson Railroad Corporation, and of various other companies quite unconnected to publishing. There was no indication of what might qualify them either to help direct a publishing company or to represent its preferred stockholders. In time, that indication became clear: On important matters, they generally agreed with Milton Gould.

There was another way in which Gould acquired power, the way that Clay Blair had dramatized when he commandeered the helm of his submarine under Japanese attack. At times of organizational crisis, as we had already observed at Curtis, the guidelines of purely hierarchical power fade or disappear because the people authorized to exercise that power are either unable or unwilling to act. When the crisis reaches a point at which the survival of the organization is threatened, almost anyone can move into the vacuum by loudly promising action and survival. Milton Gould was a lawyer—lawyers seem to have a reputation of being men who know how to do things— and he was a lawyer who appeared ready and able to act. In his harsh, rasping voice, which he did not mind raising at moments of conflict, Gould neatly outlined to the board the problems that confronted the company and the solutions that he wanted. The leaderless organization yearns for leadership, and the only leadership that the Curtis board now could see was that of Milton S. Gould.

At the same time, while the disintegrating organization suffers from a lack of central authority, that very lack of authority prevents it from making any rational judgment of any outsider seeking to take power. Thus, while Mike Mooney might wander through the maze of Curtis authorities, seeking someone with the capacity to sell him the company, those impotent powers responded with doubts and misgivings about Mooney and his associates. In other words, Gould, already on the board, could assert his own power by simply declaring it, and could assign that power to anyone of his choice, but Mooney, lacking Gould's approval, was just another pleasant and inexperienced young man, knocking on the doors of the haunted house and crying vainly for someone to sell it to him.

"So all you may get out of this is a nice no thanks," I said.

"All I may get out of this is that I may not even get a Christmas card," Mooney said.

From a journal: April 16:

. . . The demoralized staff seems to be even more demoralized than usual. Emerson is demoralized. The third and fourth floors, and probably the 32nd, are all paralyzed. Emerson is going to Georgia again on Friday, Mc-Kinney is going to Washington for a press photographers' dinner, Asger seems to have disappeared again, and Rita Ortiga spends most of her time shopping for her wedding. "Can't you understand that nobody cares any more?" Rita said. "Nobody cares what happens."

We were discussing the fiasco again, Mooney and I, and I was arguing that the failure of the *Post* illustrated all the failures of American business, that the bankruptcy of the magazine symbolized the bankruptcy of the system.

"You don't understand—bankruptcy is the great purgation," Mooney cried, suddenly a little manic, a fierce light in his eyes. "Bankruptcy is a cleansing. Bankruptcy is how the system washes away the filth and debris of its failures. Like the Curtis Publishing Company."

"But we can't keep destroying everything that doesn't make a profit," I said. "Lots of the best things we have don't make a profit, and once they're gone, they're gone forever."

"If that's the price we have to pay to keep the system alive, by punishing incompetence and failure, then it's worth it."

"Euthanasia," I said. "Kill the stragglers and the unfit."

"Yes!" Mooney retorted.

"The Metropolitan Museum should be burnt to the ground, by your rules, and all its paintings destroyed, because the institution can't support itself."

"All right, Otto, you can keep the museums."

"And the opera, and the universities, and the poor old *Herald Tribune*. And Central Park, too, I suppose, and all the great old buildings that your system turns into parking lots."

"But now you're turning everything into museums," Mooney said. "If you want life, there has to be death, because the system needs room for new things to grow."

"Heard on the Street" is the title of a regular feature in the *Wall Street Journal*, and, as we had always known that we would finally learn our fate through the newspapers, we learned it here on the morning of April 17, 1968:

The two men who run Curtis Publishing and Perfect Film & Chemical are scheduled to meet this morning in Philadelphia. . . . Both J. M. Clifford, president of Curtis Publishing, and Martin Ackerman, chairman and president of Perfect Film, would make no comment on the slated meeting. Financial sources say Mr. Ackerman will offer the deficit-ridden publishing concern $5 million in working capital from Perfect Film in exchange for his election as Curtis' new president.

The story went on to say that Perfect Film was an amalgamation of four companies, including the United Whelan drugstore chain, and that it engaged in film-processing and mail-order drug sales. The natural suspicion was that Ackerman wanted Curtis mainly for its subscription lists and would sell or liquidate everything else. Emerson called together his editorial staff, however, and assured them that there was no reason for anxiety. "There have been lots of meetings and lots of offers from lots of different people," he said, "and none of them involves the folding of the *Post* because the *Post* is the biggest consumer of the company's other goods and services. So I think it's reasonable to say that the *Post* is in pretty good shape."

Steve Kelly was even more explicit. Not only did he assure all his salesmen that the meeting with Ackerman was of minor significance, but he went on to say that the salesmen should be of good cheer because the prospects for this year were only slightly worse than last year (when the company lost almost $5 million).

". . . The reported meeting discussed in the Wall Street Journal article would be one of many that have been held over the past several years," Kelly said in a teletype message to his staff.

. . . Let your customers know that the strong second quarter enables us to have a first half only slightly off budget and about 9% off last year's first half. . . . This will improve and we should have a second half equal to or only slightly below last year's. . . . I fully realize that you are flying in the face of a lot of flak. The strengths of The Saturday Evening Post as an advertising medium and the strengths of your management in its belief in the product and its dedication to the continuation of that product are, we hope, self-evident. . . . Good luck and good selling.

Book III

THE LAST GAMBLE

With *Usura* . . .
no picture is made to endure nor to live with
but it is made to sell and sell quickly
with usura, sin against nature,
is thy bread ever more of stale rags
is thy bread dry as paper. . . .

—Ezra Pound, *Canto XLV*

BOOK III

THE LAST GAMBLE

18

"I am Marty Ackerman"

At seven o'clock on May 2, 1968, I found myself hopelessly lost somewhere in the thickly carpeted corridors of the New York Hilton Hotel, searching for Martin S. Ackerman.

It had been barely a week since his election as the president of the Curtis Publishing Company, but I had already begun receiving a stream of cheering messages from our new chief executive. The first was a letter to me as "dear Curtis staff member," declaring that Ackerman wanted to "take this opportunity to say how pleased I am to be associated with you. . . . Curtis is one of the finest companies in the country, and with new and continued cooperation of everyone, we will record major achievements for Curtis in the months and years ahead. . . . Please be assured that I am with Curtis to enhance our company, and to offer each of you a greater opportunity for personal participation in its future. . . ."

The next message was more specific. "Martin S. Ackerman . . . cordially invites you to join him for cocktails and buffet supper. . . ." The invitation, which had been sent to every Curtis employee in New York, some four hundred people in all, announced the meeting place as the Hilton's Trianon Ballroom. And now, having presented myself at the Trianon Ballroom, and having found it full of bankers with badges on their lapels, I was lost. The corridors were full of waiters, delegates, and wandering tourists, but nobody had ever heard of either Martin S. Ackerman or the Curtis Publishing Company. I asked an official-looking person for information and was directed to another ballroom, where I found myself at a reunion of

Niagara University. I asked another official-looking person and was directed to still another ballroom, and here, finally, I began to recognize some of the people standing around in nervous clusters, clutching at their drinks. It was a gigantic place, with a stage at one end, a balcony above, and a buffet table that measured not less than twenty feet across. The table was loaded with the customary bounty of hotel buffets—roast turkey, potato salad, cold cuts, chicken salad, cole slaw, and so on—all of this surmounted by a gigantic wreath of the sort that used to be called, when laid on gangsters' graves, a "floral tribute." The Ackerman style was, if nothing else, somewhat more dramatic than that of J. M. Clifford.

After an hour or so of eating and chattering, we became abruptly aware of irritable static from a microphone at the left side of the stage. There, at a lectern, stood a small, dark figure, fidgeting with the microphone, impatient to speak. "Good evening," he said as we put down our coffee cups and lapsed into silence. "I am Marty Ackerman, I am thirty-six years old and I am very rich. I hope to make the Curtis Publishing Company rich again." In that opening statement were the two main elements of the Ackerman creed. The first was a guileless, almost childlike belief in the mesmeric powers of his own self. "I am Marty Ackerman"—the words were intended not for his benefit but for ours, a trumpet call of leadership in these dark times. The second element was the equally guileless, equally childlike belief in the mesmeric powers of money, the root not of all evil but of all good. To be rich—that was what everyone wanted, wasn't it? And that was the goal toward which Marty Ackerman would now lead us.

He began by reassuring us that he approved of us. "One of the greatest assets of any corporation," he said, "is its people. You, the employees." The crowd stirred in pleasure. No previous president of Curtis had ever invited us all to dinner at a Hilton ballroom; no previous president had ever praised us as a corporate asset. We looked with furtive satisfaction at one another and then back at the speaker. But we were truly an asset to the company, he continued, only if we all thought in terms of the good of the company. He had once hired a psychological testing firm to check on what his employees were thinking about, and "it turned out that they were thinking about themselves." This was not right. "There cannot be one good Curtis magazine and one bad Curtis magazine, one successful division and one unsuccessful division. Every Curtis magazine must be good. Every division must be successful. We must all work together to make the whole company good and successful."

Obviously, this was only an introduction. As Ackerman began to discuss the problems confronting the company, it became apparent that we were not going to hear only praises and promises. "This company has been without leadership," he said. "The editors have talent, but they need leadership. The printing division is working hard, but it needs leadership. Now, good intentions are fine, but if I just listened to people's good intentions, I'd be very poor instead of very rich. In addition to good intentions, we must have *performance*. If the circulation people can't get the right circulation for us, then they aren't doing their jobs. And an editor who can't write so that people can understand him isn't a good editor. So the people who can do the job will get the job, and they will get rich. People who can't do the job will go. And decisions are going to be made. They will be hard, and you may not agree with all of them, but decisions will be made. And on balance, there will be more right decisions than wrong ones."

Life would be difficult, then, but it would not be without a purpose. "I'm 98 percent certain that we'll continue publishing the *Post*," Ackerman said—and for the first time, the threatened employees applauded their new leader. "It may not necessarily be in its present form or size," he warned, "but it will continue. I met this afternoon with the First National Bank of Boston, and they assured me that we'll get all the money we need. Now I have promised them that this money won't just go down the tube, and they know me well enough to know that when I say it won't go down the tube, then it *won't go down the tube*. But I can tell you that *money is not going to be a problem*."

Once again, there was applause, and once again Ackerman offered his sequences of lures and threats. The company would "move forward, make money," and the return of success would bring more success. "When we start to move," he said, in a startling series of metaphors, "we're going to move like a rolling stone, and then we're going to get the smell of a winner, and when we get the smell of a winner, everybody wants to get on the bandwagon." And we, the faithful employees, would share in all this. "I have a theory that every company should be at least partly owned by its employees. Then they feel differently about the assets of the company, and they treat those assets differently. So we'll never have profitable magazines unless the editors of those magazines—you people—own shares in them. . . . But one last thing. These next few months are going to be hard, and we're going to have to work as we've never worked before. And I want to say this. Anybody who can't stand heat had better get out of the kitchen. Anybody who's nervous, who wants security or the easy way—get out now, and run as fast as you can. Because we've got one big job ahead of us, to turn this great company around again and make it as rich and profitable as it was in the past."

The applause was moderate—not grudging, not hostile, just moderate. We had been promised that the *Post* would continue, and that more money would be available, but the promises had been so interspersed with threats and warnings that the prospect before us seemed rather ambiguous. And then, when we thought the ceremony was over, we heard a new voice at the microphone. We looked up, and there was G. B. McCombs, who had been serving at the right hand of Mac Clifford only a fortnight ago, now pleading the cause of his new master. "Yes, we may have some hard days ahead," G.B. declared, grinning, "and like Marty just said, anybody who can't stand the heat had better get out of the oven. But I want to tell you that even though I've only known Marty Ackerman for just a few days, I want to tell you that he's a great guy, and he's going to do a great job at Curtis. So let's give him another big hand!" There was another round of applause, but still moderate, and then we heard low voices commanding us: "Up! Up!" We looked around and saw a number of advertising salesmen, who are responsive to such things, lurching to their feet. Ultimately, with some more urging, about two-thirds of Marty Ackerman's new employees rose and gave him what he might have considered a standing ovation.

One of the striking things about Martin S. Ackerman was his total obscurity. Not only the employees but many of the top executives at Curtis knew nothing whatever about him. And wherever we called for more information, we could find almost nobody who had ever heard of him. Ackerman's passionate love of personal publicity soon changed all that. Not since the muzzling of Joe Culligan, four years ago, had we seen any Curtis official stage so many press conferences, grant so many interviews, speak so volubly to the bemused press. The campaign reached its climax on August 23, when Ackerman achieved one of the supreme heights for an American businessman, a lead article about himself on the front page of the *Wall Street Journal*. "*Marty in Action*," said the headline. "Aggressive but Likable Tycoon Applies Tough Techniques at Curtis." In that same story, he also enjoyed one of the supreme rewards to which an ambitious young man might aspire—the *Journal* had interviewed his mother.

Mrs. Louis Ackerman, of Rochester, New York, provided retrospective insights that we should not otherwise have gained. She considered him, as mothers generally do, a humanitarian. Once, she recalled, a high school boy had to stand shivering on a bridge all day for the sake of some fraternity hazing, and young Marty had run home to get his mother to make a thermos of cocoa for the victim. Mrs. Ackerman thought it understandable that her son should eventually become an executive in the field of film-processing, since he had once had a two-dollar Brownie and "took at lot of pictures and developed them in the cellar." He also saved his weekly allowance of twenty-five cents. Mrs. Ackerman reported further that her son had political aspirations and had once been president of his senior class in high school. The *Wall Street Journal* delicately inquired whether young Marty might someday become President of the United States, and it delightedly quoted her answer: "I don't know. He's Jewish, you know."

The Ackermans appear to have been a closely knit family, of moderate means. "I didn't come from poor folks," Ackerman said. He went to Rochester's Ben Franklin High School, a name not without future significance, and he took pride in the fact that he drove his own car at the age of sixteen. He took no less pride in the fact that he went through the University of Syracuse in only two and a half years, and then won a scholarship to Rutgers, from which he emerged in 1956 with a Bachelor of Law degree.

As a lawyer, Ackerman skipped and jumped rather quickly toward the field of corporate mergers. Just out of Rutgers, he spent a little more than a year as clerk to a judge of the Appellate Division of the State Superior Court in Elizabeth, New Jersey. Then he went to New York, for a year at Louis Nizer's firm of Phillips, Nizer, Benjamin, Krim & Ballon, then to the firm of Rubin & Rubin, which specialized in corporate acquisitions and securities regulations. In 1961, he established his own practice, engaging in corporate work for other firms. "I was a lawyer's lawyer," he said, "and I did very, very well." In 1962, he became a partner in Cooper, Ostrin, DeVarco & Ackerman, another specialist in corporate mergers and acquisitions, but that same year he decided to go into business for himself.

After investigating various possibilities, he selected a small and unhappy company named Perfect Photo, Inc., a collection of small photo-finishing stores that had never been properly integrated. In fiscal 1962, it earned only $401,000 on sales of $21.2 million. "When the market soured in '62," said one of Ackerman's aides, "the owners wanted out." Ackerman and some associates bought 300,000 shares, a 21 percent interest and sufficient for a takeover, at a price of $4, the market price being $6.38. Ackerman himself bought 50,000 shares and took charge, cutting costs, combining expenses, and, oddly enough, moving out of New York to the Long Island suburb of Great Neck. "We were beating our brains out traveling back and forth," said Perfect's vice president, Bert Samit. "We both lived out here so we decided to run it on the Island, get away from the traffic and put in more hours." (Ackerman later moved the company to Manhasset, even farther from New York and nearer to his own home in Roslyn.)

Ackerman's labors failed to solve the company's problems, however, and so he looked for a solution through merger. He thought he saw it in the United Whelan Corporation, the drugstore chain. Once he had maneuvered into control of United Whelan, he began to apply the Ackerman technique—basically the same technique by which men like James Ling and Charles Bluhdorn were building the great conglomerates—a dismantling of the acquired corporation, a reintegration of its profitable parts, and a sale or liquidation of the unprofitable ones. In the case of Whelan, Ackerman sold the Company's discount stores, used the money to buy Hudson National, Inc., and Equality Plastic, Inc., and then merged all four companies into a new firm named Perfect Film & Chemical. By the time Ackerman undertook his Curtis adventure, he had turned Perfect Film into an enterprise that grossed $58 million a year, netted a profit of $2.5 million, paid its president a prodigious salary of $200,000, and ran virtually by itself.

Even before he came to Curtis, Ackerman had enjoyed roving far from Long Island to pursue various business opportunities. The most bizarre of these was an enterprise called Cemeteries of America, owner of five cemeteries in Kansas, in which Ackerman was a major stockholder from 1960 to 1963. This enabled the *Gallagher Report* to greet Ackerman with one of its pungent nicknames, "Mortician Marty," and to predict that his only function at Curtis would be to bury the cadaver of the corporation. On a more cheerful note, Ackerman took a proprietary interest in two bank reorganizations. "I became so intimately involved in those two deals that I decided I wanted to own a bank myself," Ackerman said. He therefore bought two small banks on the West Coast and combined them into the Republic National Bank of California. "This is for my kids," he said. "It's an investment for the future. You see, my philosophy is that you shouldn't be the owner of a bank unless you don't need anything."

At some point early in 1968, Marty Ackerman discovered the Curtis Publishing Company. The reasons for his interest are not wholly clear. Ackerman himself usually explained the move in terms worthy of a Chamber of Commerce: "I felt I could make a contribution."

Unsympathetic observers have been more cynical, attributing Ackerman's maneuvers to a desire for greater prestige and publicity. At one point, Ackerman claimed that he had had a life-long interest in magazines. "I've always been a prolific magazine reader right from the time I was in high school," he said. "I read every magazine I can get my hands on. On Saturday mornings I go out and buy up fifteen dollars' worth of magazines at retail. I get everything from analyst journals to women's magazines. You just name it, I read it." But then, as though this might sound amateurish and ridiculous, and as though he would be unwilling to sound amateurish and ridiculous, Ackerman reverted to the conventional statement of commercial faith: "I went into it because I want to make money."

Whatever his motives, Ackerman began investigating Curtis's finances. "I got a yellow sheet on the company from Standard & Poor's and saw two names on the board. One was Mac Clifford and the other was Milton Gould." Ackerman knew Gould from previous deals at Perfect Film. "I called Milt and told him I was interested and that I thought I could be helpful." Ackerman quoted Gould as saying, "Curtis is too tough for anyone, but I can't stop you from going to Clifford if you want to." Gould later recalled his own reaction in more forceful terms. "Curtis was hopelessly bankrupt," he told an interviewer. "I was ready to force liquidation. It would have been a social, commercial, and moral disaster, but I was ready to do it. . . . Then, when Marty said he was willing to take a crack at it, I told him, 'You can't handle it. It's a man-killer. It will destroy you.' But he wanted to go ahead anyway." To another reporter, Gould was even more vehement: "No one but a nut would pay $5 million to become captain of a *Titanic!*" Once he was convinced of Ackerman's determination, personal finances, and bank support, however, Gould simply told him, "I'll get you in."

The first rule of the organization is that it resists efforts to make it change its ways.

On April 22, the day that a special board meeting was convened to elect Ackerman to the presidency of Curtis, Emerson and I were summoned to the thirty-second-floor conference room by one of Mac Clifford's vice presidents, Roy V. Whisnand. Roy Whistlenut, as Emerson called him, was a tanned and dapper man of perhaps fifty, fond of cigarillos, and Clifford had assigned him to the field of mergers, acquisitions, and the "development" of Curtis assets. The purpose of this meeting, therefore, was to discuss a proposal by Milton Bradley & Company to use *Post* and *Holiday* covers for jigsaw

puzzles. So for about an hour, we all sat around the gleaming conference table, with the view of all Manhattan, and discussed with the
head of Milton Bradley's Puzzle Division the aesthetics and economics of jigsaw puzzles.

To this portly, white-haired gentleman, the aesthetics were a
matter of passionate concern. Puzzle art was not like other art, he
explained to us, but he would know a specimen whenever he saw one,
and so he made periodic inspection trips through the antique shops
and even bars along Third Avenue, searching for painted sunsets and
snowscapes, "the kind of picture that makes a great puzzle," and then
buying the puzzle rights for $200. The *Post* archives of more than
three thousand covers represented an enormous cache, and the
Milton Bradley puzzle-makers proposed to select six, offering royalties
of 5 percent on sales of 100,000 puzzles at $1 each, meaning that we
could anticipate a total payment of $5,000. As an advance, one of the
puzzle-makers suggested the "out-of-the-blue-sky" figure of $2,500.
Nobody treated this relatively infinitesimal sum as either surprising
or unsurprising. We simply chatted on for a while, the seven of us
assembled in this skyline conference room, and then promised to
think it over and meet again.

When I got back to the editorial floor, I checked the bulletin board
to see if there was any news of Ackerman's takeover, but the only
announcement there was one from W. E. Linke, director of personnel, informing us that Daylight Saving Time would begin on April 28.

ACKERMAN SEEKS 'POSITIVE PLAN' FOR CURTIS,
BUT DENIES HE INTENDS TO FOLD THE POST
—Headline in *Wall Street Journal*,
April 24, 1968

Mike Mooney was indignant at our apathy toward the new regime.

"If he tells people that he's looking for a 'positive plan,' that means
he's talking to everybody in town, and the only people who aren't
talking to him are you and Emerson, and probably Kelly."

"We're busy putting out a magazine," I said.

"No, you're not," Mooney said. "You're busy hiding from the fact
that you haven't got a 'positive plan,' to publish the *Post* at a profit."

"Sure I have, I've got lots of plans—cut the circulation, increase
the subscription price, and all the rest."

"Then make Emerson tell it to Ackerman, and make Ackerman
listen to him, because he's sure as hell listening to G.B. and all those

old fogy-boppers telling him to fold the *Post,* and he's sure as hell listening to all the fast-buck guys all over town, and they're all telling him to fold the *Post* too."

"I can't see that I'm the one to make Emerson tell Ackerman anything," I said, "or to make him listen to anything. Hell, I've never even met the guy."

"Well, if you can't put through a plan to publish the *Post* at a profit, then you aren't doing your job," Mooney said, "because that's what they pay executive-type salaries for, and expense accounts and stock options and all that, for people to figure out how to make money."

"You don't understand, Mike," I said wearily. "We're a defeated army. We've got frostbitten toes. You're telling us to stage another cavalry charge, when all we want to do is to get warm. Making money is Ackerman's problem, not mine."

"Then they're going to fold the *Post* on you," Mooney said, "and you'll all deserve it."

Exactly two weeks elapsed between the first mention of Martin Ackerman in the *Wall Street Journal* and his speech to us at the Hilton Hotel. During those two weeks, he was fiercely busy. On Monday, April 22, he was named to the presidency and elected to the board, without salary. One of his colleagues, E. Eugene Mason, was also elected to the board and replaced Gloria Swett as secretary to the corporation (both Gloria and Clifford seemed to vanish without a trace—no farewells, no statements, nothing). That same day, the board approved the sale of the Philadelphia headquarters building for $7.3 million. The next day, April 23, Ackerman took over the whole thirty-second-floor executive suite that Joe Culligan had once ruled, but he didn't like the exalted extravagance of the penthouse offices. "He arrived at 8:45," said one survivor of that period, "and looked around and said, 'My God, I can't stand it. Lease the goddamn place.' And it was leased two days later."

That same day, Ackerman had lunch with the editors and publishers of all the Curtis magazines and made a considerable impression on them. "He said he was only here to make money, and he was going to make money, and we were all going to make money," Emerson reported later. "He says the trouble with Curtis is that it always thought it was a printing company, but he says that's all b——, that he's only interested in publishing the magazines, and that's how we're going to make money. He says his book editor over at Popular Library pays himself eighty grand a year, and he says, 'Maybe some of you guys don't make that much.' Well, I tell you, I never had any objection to working with a well-trained pit viper."

Within a week, Ackerman had arranged a two-month extension of all overdue bank loans and ended once and for all the rumors surrounding the rise and fall of Curtis common stocks on the New York Stock Exchange. Informed that the Exchange was "considering" a delisting of Curtis securities, Ackerman coolly announced that "Curtis does not at present meet the assets and earnings requirement for continued listing, and does not expect to meet this requirement in the immediate future." As a result, the company decided "not to oppose the New York Stock Exchange action." From then on, Ackerman publicly and repeatedly referred to the common stock as "worthless." The cynics among us interpreted this as an attempt by Ackerman to drive down the price of Curtis stock so that he could eventually buy it up at bargain rates. But since he never actually did buy any substantial number of shares, and since the market price did eventually drift down to almost nothing, Ackerman may quite simply have been announcing from the start a basic truth that the owners of Curtis had never wanted to face.

Within that same first week, Ackerman had a private conference with Steve Kelly and outlined his plan to steer the *Post* into the black. We would cut the circulation from 6.8 million to no more than 3 million, perhaps less. (Ackerman proposed to Kelly a reduction to one million, but Kelly's alarm and anxiety dissuaded him.) We would promote it as a magazine of "class, not mass." And we would make a profit of $2.8 million a year.

"Are these figures real?" I asked Kelly.

"Well," he said, shaking his head in the familiar gesture of bewilderment, "I just don't know."

On the day after the Hilton dinner, I arrived to find the office in a turmoil. Ackerman's chief assistant, a short, stocky man named Lavere Lund, had announced that Emerson's conference room would serve very well as Ackerman's new office, and so the moving men were carrying in his furniture forthwith. "And there's this Chinaman," my secretary said in an unbelieving voice, "who acts like he's in charge of things too."

Ackerman was now ready to begin concentrating on the *Post*, and so he summoned us—a half-dozen editors and another half-dozen advertising men—to a private dining room on the third floor of the Brussels, an expensive restaurant in an elegant old house near our offices on Fifty-fourth Street. At high noon, we arrived in a small band, joking our way up the circular staircase, and found Ackerman waiting all alone. "Hiya," he said nervously as Emerson introduced us, "hiya. Go on over to the bar there and have a drink." He was even smaller than he had appeared to be when he stood high on the distant rostrum of the Hilton, and for that reason, I suppose, somewhat less prepossessing. In principle, we no longer judge men by their size or physical strength, but some primal instinct nonetheless puts us relatively at ease in the presence of a man we could knock down, and conversely, I suppose, no badge of authority can ever completely eliminate the instinctive uneasiness of a small man surrounded by vassals who are bigger than he is. Face to face, then, Ackerman appeared to be just another ambitious little man, about five feet eight, plump, stoop-shouldered, rather pale, with straight brown hair, a sharp nose, and a nervous squint that contorted his face when he smiled. From the bar, we saw him shaking hands with Kelly's arriving troops—and then greeting his own men, Lavere Lund, and the Chinese, Bob Yung, both of whom were short and stout, like Ackerman himself, and finally, inevitably, smiling in all directions, G. B. McCombs. The bartender had not even finished serving the drinks when we heard Ackerman, already seated at the table, calling out, "Okay, okay, let's get going." At his place, he had his own drink, a glass of tomato juice, and as we gathered in our chairs around his table, he reached a fork into the glass, speared a hidden clam, and popped it into his mouth.

"Okay," Ackerman said, hunching over the glass and gnawing on the clam, "the proposition for discussion is an evolutionary *Post* of three million circulation. Now Kelly and I have just been over talking to Bill Bernbach, who's a friend of mine, and he likes this idea, and he may even agree to join Curtis as a consultant. But the point is, when we try this idea on Madison Avenue, they like it. And I like it. So are we all set to go?"

"Why don't you just spell it out a bit more for the men, Marty?" Kelly said.

"Okay, here's the deal. Is somebody taking notes? We get out of the numbers game with *Life* and *Look*—we're not getting anywhere that way, and it's losing us money—and we cut back the *Post* from six point eight million to three million, and we make it a high-class magazine for a class audience. Not a radical change, but *evolutionary*. Concentrate on the audience we want to reach—maybe 90 percent in Nielsen A and B counties. Now is that something you can sell or isn't it?"

"With that A and B, it sure is," one of the salesmen cried.

"You bet your life it is," said another one.

But then they began to wonder how they were going to explain this to their advertisers. It all sounded convincing here in the comfort of a New York restaurant, but out there in Cincinnati or Los Angeles, it might sound like just another nervous spasm at Curtis, yet another "new *Post*." And so they began appealing for Ackerman himself to come and talk to their customers. "You come across real strong," said Joe Welty, the advertising director. The mixture of flattery and necessity had never failed. The advertising men had once lured Blair into making speeches for them, and for a time they had kept Emerson feverishly occupied in selling ads, and now they had a new showpiece to offer. Ackerman, unable to resist, sat there writing down dates and appointments for himself in Chicago and Detroit on the following week.

But what we really wanted to know, and what Ackerman really wanted to tell us, was the future of the Curtis Publishing Company. Somebody had just delivered a letter to him, on a silver plate, and he had hastily glanced through it and stuffed it in his pocket; now he pulled it out again and drew three boxes on the back of the envelope, redrawing and darkening the boxes with his pencil as he spoke. "What Curtis really is, basically, is three different operations, all mixed up together in one company. One is circulation—the circulation company—one is publishing—the magazines—and one is manufacturing—the printing plant and the paper mill. Now what we're going to do, essentially, is we're going to divide this company up three ways." He paused and looked around at us to see whether we had understood him so far. We had understood in theory, but it still seemed unreal to imagine the ancient Curtis Publishing Company, which had always owned its own timber, its own paper, its own printing presses, suddenly torn apart. We nodded sagely, however, as Ackerman moved on to the next point.

"Now everything is screwed up by the preferred stock, which Cyrus Curtis handed out back in the Twenties, when he was feeling charitable. Nobody even knows who these preferred stockholders are or what they want. But as things stand now, you can't make a move, you can't even blow your nose, without the approval of the preferred stockholders. But we're not going to be quite as charitable as Cyrus Curtis. So we divide up the company. Now here, off to one side, I've got a nice little company that's making money, Perfect Film & Chemical, and we're going to merge the Curtis Circulation Company into that. And then, once we prove that the publishing company can make money on its own, we'll merge that in too. And that will leave the preferred stockholders owning the printing and paper plants, plus a piece of the other companies. But we're not going to go on just being charitable. We figure that was Cyrus Curtis's problem, and we're going to let him worry about it, and if the preferred stockholders have any complaints, they can take them up with Cyrus Curtis." Laughter. "Of course, some of these preferred stockholders may try suing us, but we've got plenty of lawyers, and they've got strong backs, so we'll deal with that problem when we come to it." More laughter.

"I think you all agree that no previous management has ever taken us into its confidence this way," old G. B. McCombs spoke up from the far end of the table, "though one of Marty's predecessors perhaps would have, if he'd known what his confidence was, which he didn't." It was a memorable demonstration of how a man survives in a corporation for thirty years by bowing before each new president. And once again there was laughter.

Ackerman was making jokes to ingratiate himself with us, but there was nothing indulgent about either the jokes or the laughter. Jacobins are always Puritans, for the emotions that compel men to overturn social conventions also compel them to deny social pleasures. In this elegant restaurant, therefore, we all had only one drink and only one course, because that was what Ackerman ordered, and as we ate, it became clear that Ackerman's Puritanism extended far beyond the dinner table. He talked of corporate economies, and the abolition of executive extravagances. The suite of offices on the thirty-second floor must go; the company plane must go. He wanted everyone at work by nine; he himself arrived at eight.

And then, as he talked on, it turned out that he disapproved even of secretaries. In fact, he particularly disapproved of secretaries. He had just been out to California, where a Curtis advertising office had four salesmen and four secretaries, "and they need four secretaries like I need a hole in the head." This judgment, furthermore, applied to all of us. "I mean, out in our place in Manhasset," he said, "we do a $50-million-a-year business on one and a half floors, and one floor is the computers, and the half is my office." What really seemed to bother him, though, was not the quantity of secretaries but the fact that the average man, if given a choice, tends to prefer pretty secretaries to plain ones. "I mean, these Vassar girls in short skirts look great," Ackerman pressed on, still trying to explain his disapproval to a puzzled audience, "but think about trading in four of them for a little old gray-haired lady who knows how to type. You know? I mean, if you want to get laid, great, but get laid on your own time. Okay? I mean, I think the money ought to go on what's really important, like the quality of the product."

Ever since I had first seen Ackerman, I had been bothered by a sense of partial recognition. He reminded me of somebody, and it irritated me that I could not identify my own memories. Only during this peculiar monologue on secretaries did I recall that I had heard a similar outburst of Puritanism one night four years earlier. And once I remembered, the other details struck me as astonishingly similar. The same small figure, the same nervous energy, the same awkwardness of manner, the same squint of the eyes. Even the same geographical origins in upstate New York, for both of them had gone to the University of Syracuse, within a few years of one another. It occurred to me, finally, that we had been possessed by the ghost of Marvin Kantor.

The clock of St. Peter's Lutheran church struck one, and we all looked at our watches for verification, and we saw that it was time for the next meeting. As we left the restaurant, I succumbed to the temptation to look at the bill that had been submitted to Steve Kelly. It was $131.74. *Service non compris.*

It was Ackerman's plan, apparently, to apply his concept of "leadership" to each department of the corporation. Each department in turn would receive an infusion of Ackerman's ideas, criticisms, proposals, and judgments. This therapy would be administered sequentially, starting with editorial problems and then moving on to advertising, circulation, production. There would be some overlapping, of course, for no department would ever be free from the leader's attention. But at the top of every list of Curtis's difficulties came the *Post,* and the most interesting aspect of the *Post* was the question of what it should publish. And so, Emerson and I suddenly realized, Ackerman had made us the first problem to be solved.

We adjourned from lunch at the Brussels to the thirty-second floor of the Curtis building, and the advertising men were all dispersed, all except Kelly. The conference room filled with other Curtis editors, and with a number of additional Ackerman adjutants we had never seen before. One of the adjutants closed the door and placed a full box of Antonio y Cleopatra cigars on the table in front of Ackerman. He scattered a few around the table, then took one for himself, unwrapped the cellophane, looked around him, and said, "Does anyone have a match?" There was a pause, and then Peter Wyden, sitting at his left, pulled out a pack of matches. ("It was weird," Wyden said later. "I remember thinking, 'Why doesn't he carry his own matches?' And then I thought, 'Well, I have a book of matches, so 'I might as well hand them over.' And then I saw that he was leaning forward, with the cigar in his mouth, waiting for me to light it for him. So what can you do?")

"Okay, we all here?" Ackerman said, taking a deep puff. "Now the reason I got you guys together is to talk about the *Post*. As I said last night, I don't want you just thinking about yourselves, and your own problems. I want all of you to be thinking about all the different areas of the whole company. We may have more meetings like this, to talk about the other magazines, but right now I want to get you thinking about the evolutionary *Post*. What can all of you contribute to the *Post*? Ideas. Maybe even some of your manuscripts, or pictures. Now I was talking with Bill Bernbach, who's a friend of mind, and he thought there were two big troubles—the graphics—the magazine just doesn't look very good—and the definition. A magazine needs a clear definition. A personality. Now how about it? Does that make sense? Who's going to start the discussion? You?"

"Well," said Wyden, savoring one of Ackerman's cigars. "I think the fundamental problem of the *Post*, of any magazine, is to define its *function*. Why is it here? What does it have to say that nobody else is saying?"

"Who's that?" whispered the Chinese, Bob Yung, a chubby and amiable-looking young man, who had slipped into a chair just behind mine.

"Peter Wyden," I whispered back.

"What does he do?"

"Executive editor of the *Journal*."

"Okay, who's next?" Ackerman was saying. "Caskie?"

Caskie Stinnett, now nervously established as the editor of *Holiday*, offered the opinion that the *Post* should be "more popular, more like the *Reader's Digest*," that it should publish "popular articles on medicine, that kind of thing."

"Okay, is somebody taking notes?" Ackerman asked. Again, as at lunch, a number of people fished pieces of paper out of their pockets and began taking notes. Ackerman himself had a tablet of lined yellow paper in front of him, and he had already written on it the words "EVOLUTIONARY" and "FUNCTION" and "POPULAR."

From behind me, Bob Yung now spoke up and said he thought each issue of the *Post* should be devoted to one subject, "like foreign affairs, or literary criticism, or the theater." Since this suggestion seemed ominously specific, and since I assumed that Yung spoke for Ackerman, I thought I'd better intervene, and so I said that there really were very few subjects that were worth an entire issue. As Yung looked at me in surprise, Hub Cobb, editor of *American Home,* spoke up to say that magazines should devote more attention to the specific interests of the thoughtful professional or businessman. "Like, when there's a crisis in Czechoslovakia," Cobb said, "does this open up new markets for American businessmen?"

That suggestion brought the conference to a total halt, and so Ackerman stepped in with a new question: "Should there be more fiction?" "A fiction issue?" Yung added. "No," Emerson and I said, almost in unison. "Every survey shows," Emerson added, "that fiction has the lowest readership of anything we publish." "How about a different kind of fiction?" Ackerman offered. "A lot of the most popular stuff nowadays," said Wyden, coming to our rescue, "isn't much more than pornography." Finally it came the turn of John Mack Carter, the bright-eyed little Kentuckian who had restored the commercial success of the *Ladies' Home Journal,* and who now offered what he called "an idea that nobody will like." He proposed that the *Post* give up on the audience that Madison Avenue was hungering to reach, the college-educated urban and suburban middle class, and turn back to its traditional audience, which everyone else was ignoring, the common folk, the older people, the inhabitants of farms and small towns.

It is possible that Ackerman sincerely thought that editors could simply drop their natural competitiveness and help other editors for the greater good of the corporation. It is possible that these editors offered these ideas in good faith as proposals for the improvement of the *Post;* it is also possible, however, that they wanted, not without malice, to steer the *Post* away from the course that their own magazines were following. But it gradually came to me, as this hour of "constructive criticism" droned on, that the truth and quality and sincerity of the various proposals were all equally irrelevant as criteria.

What was taking place here, I realized, was not a discussion of the *Post* but rather an event that might be called, in Maoist terms, a mock trial of the *Post*'s landlords. As in the China of the early Fifties, the other Curtis editors were playing the role of peasant militants, offering helpful suggestions on how Emerson and I, the landlords, might improve ourselves. We were not specifically accused of anything. On the contrary, we were repeatedly told that the purpose of the meeting was to help us, to help us find what we had done wrong and purify ourselves by promising reform. And within the next half-hour or so, Emerson and I passed through every phase of psychological self-protection, from innocent incomprehension to forthright rebuttals to excuses and alibis, and finally to the beginnings of a guilty and confessional sense that we had indeed failed our corporation, and that we wanted only a new chance to prove ourselves worthy of its confidence. And it was not the shrewdness or aptness of our colleagues' suggestions that brought us to this state—indeed, the folly of their views served our sense of guilt just as well—but rather the mechanism of a meeting that somehow acquired the power of a trial.

But it was only a mock trial, and the effectiveness of a mock trial depends on the ability of the judge to call it off at his whim—and on the consequent sense of relief and gratitude in the defendant. And so, after this meeting had lasted about an hour, someone came in to tell Ackerman that there was a telephone call from the legendary Bernard Gallagher, and he strode out to answer it, leaving the rest of us looking at one another in silence. When Ackerman returned, he told us that he had "explained the new *Post*" to the *Gallagher Report*, and then he dismissed the People's Court, keeping only Emerson and Kelly and me behind. This meeting had "served a valuable purpose," Ackerman said, and now it turned out that the purpose had been not to indict the *Post* but to expose its accusers. "There's been a lot of second-guessing of the *Post*," Ackerman said. "A lot of people have been knocking it without ever saying what they'd do to fix it, so my idea was: Let's get everybody together and get it all out in the open and see if anybody has any real ideas worth talking about."

"Yes, get it out in the open," said Bob Yung, who seemed to have become Ackerman's proconsul in charge of the *Post*.

"And as you can see—*nothing*," Ackerman said.

So the mock trial had ended in our acquittal, and that seemed somehow to put us in debt to the benevolent Marty Ackerman, obligating us to carry out his wishes, if only we could figure out what his wishes were. "I've got to be able to show evidence of change, and fast," he said. "So how soon can you guys produce this evolutionary *Post*?" Before we could decide on that, we needed a clearer idea of what the "evolutionary" *Post* was supposed to be—not a repetition of the famous "new" *Post* of 1961, for we realized that Ackerman had already been warned on that subject—and how the smoothly evolutionary *Post* was supposed to differ from the unregenerate, nonevolutionary *Post* we had been publishing until now. Specifically, I asked Ackerman to leaf through a copy of the May 18 issue, the latest one published, and to tell us what he liked and didn't like, what he wanted changed and what he wanted continued.

It so happened that the May 18 issue was a good one, marred only by a conventional cover story on teen-age shoplifting, the kind of story that editors doggedly keep publishing in an effort to sell more copies on the newsstands. Aside from that, Ackerman liked everything he encountered. He liked the "Speaking Out" by Abe Raskin of the *Times*, criticizing the conservatism of the American working class; he liked the regular columns by Stew Alsop and John Gregory Dunne; he liked Lewis Lapham's article on the Beatles visiting their Guru in India; he liked Nick Pileggi's article on the Harvard Business School; he liked Charles Portis's new novel, *True Grit*, which was beginning as a serial in that issue, and he liked Roger Kahn's *The Passionate People*.

"You know, they tried to stop us from publishing that, Mac Clifford and G.B.," Emerson said, on cue. Emerson had a theory, in fact, that G.B.'s strong opposition to the book had come from his advance knowledge of Ackerman's arrival, and if G.B. had miscalculated both Ackerman's judgment and ours, then let him pay the consequences. "G.B. said it would offend a lot of Jews, but we told him he didn't know what he was talking about," Emerson went on. "We told him we'd resign—Otto and me—if he tried to stop us from running it." Ackerman did not bother to feign surprise or even interest in these revelations, and one could only suspect that G.B. had already taken the trouble to tell his version of the tale, and had been absolved for his role in it.

But what, to return to the point, was the goal of evolution? The real goal, Ackerman said again, was to provide evidence of change. There must be nothing so noisy as the "new" *Post*, but there must be a sense of direction, of forward movement, an illustration of what the *Post* would like to become. "Well, if you like what we're publishing now," I said, "then what we'd like to become is fatter, with full-page Cadillac ads. What makes the magazine look sick is that it's so thin, and so loaded up with quarter-page ads for dog food and kitty litter."

It was agreed, consequently, that the issue then being worked on, the June 15 issue, known in the office as *Post* No. 12, would be immediately followed by an evolutionary variant issue, to be known as *Post* No. 12A. This variant issue would not be the usual eighty pages but at least a hundred, and it would be printed on heavier and glossier paper, in a run of twenty thousand copies for display to skeptical advertisers. It would contain slightly different treatments of the stories in the regular *Post* No. 12, plus ten or twelve pages of special and theoretically "classy" editorial material. It would contain many full-color ads (since none of the advertisers would have to pay for these ads, after all) and none of the trashy ads that appeared in our regular issues.

"Now, can you guys do this yourselves?" Ackerman asked. "Or do you need a special staff?"

"We can do it ourselves," I said quickly.

"It'll be a hell of a job," Emerson elaborated, "but we can do it."

"And Bob will help you," Ackerman said.

We were not exactly overstaffed after four years of Mac Clifford's cost-cutting, and the prospect of putting out two magazines instead of one was rather forbidding, but we did at least know the first rule for dealing with boarders trying to take over a ship: Keep control of the tiller. On the other hand, Bob Yung also knew the first rule for the other side: Get on board the ship. There followed, then, this rapid dialogue:

"How about graphics?" Yung asked. "Don't you think you have problems there?"

"Yes," Emerson said.

"Do you need a new art director?"

"Yes, probably."

"What are you doing about it?"

"Well, we're talking to people all over town."

"Have you talked to Herb Lubalin?"

"Not yet, but we're talking to Wolf and a lot of other people."

"Ah, Henry," Yung said with a vague smile. "Well, can we all meet first thing Monday morning?"

"Sure—no, I'm making a speech to the liquor industry in Washington on Monday morning."

"Okay, Monday afternoon?"

"Well . . ."

"How about three o'clock?"

"Okay."

Within half an hour of Emerson's agreement, he received a written memorandum from Yung confirming that an appointment at Lubalin's studio had been scheduled for 4 P.M. on Monday. It was a small thing, perhaps, but as a contrast to Mac Clifford's system of delaying for months on a secretary's raise, it was another clear sign that we were confronting a brisk, new way of doing business. "It's funny," Emerson said. "I'd sort of looked forward to quitting this week, and now I'm surprised at my own optimism."

To reach the studios of Herb Lubalin, one entered a small, brick building on East Thirty-first Street, climbed two flights of narrow wooden stairs, and then arrived at a sort of citadel of pop art. There were framed advertisements on the walls, and antique clocks, and the lights looked like London street lamps in the days of Sherlock Holmes.

Lubalin, whom I had never heard of until the previous Friday, was actually something of an institution. Once a five-dollar-a-week letterer at the New York World's Fair of 1939, he had gone on to jobs as varied as teaching architecture students at Cornell and designing the lettering on the men's rooms of the Ford Foundation Building. Almost inevitably, he had played a part in the creation of the "new" *Post* of 1961, although nobody could now say how large that part was. A search through the files, however, did reveal some bizarre layouts with Lubalin's signature on them. One, for example, presented a short story, "Where the Wind Blows Free," with the title in blurred and billowing wind-blown type; another, even more literal, was entitled "The Crooks Get All the Breaks," and all the letters in those words were broken. For this kind of thing, Lubalin had acquired a reputation that was often expressed in the same phrase, "very good with type." His greatest celebrity in the field of magazine design, however, came from his work on Ralph Ginzburg's periodicals, *Eros, Fact,* and *Avant Garde*. It was Lubalin, in fact, who did the layout for the celebrated *Eros* picture story on interracial sex, which played a considerable part in Ginzburg's being sentenced to prison. An art director who can get his own editor sentenced to prison may be said to have achieved the highest goal to which an art director can aspire. Despite these difficulties, however, Ginzburg remained appreciative of his colleague's talents. Lubalin, he said, is "the Michelangelo of the commercial art world."

After keeping us waiting for half an hour, the Michelangelo of the commercial art world came bouncing out of some back office—a short, thick-set man of about fifty, with horn-rimmed glasses and long gray sideburns. "I don't really know what this is all about," he said by way of introduction. Emerson slowly began to tell him, that we wanted to make some changes in the *Post,* to appeal to a smaller and more sophisticated audience, that we didn't like the layouts and general appearance of the magazine, and that we wanted him to help improve it. We were going to begin producing some variant issues, Emerson said, and we wanted to know if he would design them. Lubalin, if he didn't know what this was about, seemed remarkably unsurprised. His first question was eminently practical: How much time did he have to design this variant issue? The answer was: ten days.

Other people began to drift in. First Bob Yung, trailed by a long-legged blonde in a miniskirt, who established herself on a sofa in the corner and began taking notes on everything that was said. Then came Henry Wolf, a dark, frail, shaggy man of about forty-five, perhaps best known as the former art director of *Esquire*. It was not at all clear what his role was. He said he didn't think any American magazines looked good. "I only look at them for the ads," he said, and snickered. Wolf and Lubalin then began to talk to each other, and to laugh over the appearance of the newly revived magazine, *New York*. "If you can't be *exciting*, graphically," one of them said, "you shouldn't try to be graphic at all."

As for the *Post*, Lubalin finally announced that it was bland, and he offered the conventional prescription. "You've got to do things that make people love you or hate you," he said.

"But let's not equate the two," I protested.

"You've got to stir them up," Lubalin went on.

"But if the result is that they hate you, what have you accomplished?"

Lubalin lapsed into silence, brooding. Emerson and Yung made conversation. Then Lubalin suddenly declared that the *Post* was the wrong size, too big, too thin. He said he thought it should be the size of *Vogue*. "Yes, yes, much better," Wolf agreed. And bound with a square backing, like *Vogue*. "Yes," Wolf said again.

"And the name," Lubalin said. "It should be not just the *Post* but the *Saturday Evening Post*, like in the old days, and maybe a slightly old-fashioned look to it. Don't you think?"

And so it became clear that without any specific offer having been made or accepted, and without money having been even mentioned, Herb Lubalin was already at work in redesigning the *Post*.

By the time I returned to the office, I could see that Ackerman had moved in. The dark, cork-lined conference room, where Clay Blair had mobilized his troops for *"Der Tag,"* where Mac Clifford had confronted the angry editors, where farewell parties had traditionally been given for those who were leaving us, now had the standard Lexington Avenue executive look. Against the near wall stood a long orange leather sofa, ending in a circular glass table on a cast-iron base. On the opposite wall, where Emerson used to post the editorial schedules listing the contents of the issues he was closing, Bob Yung had tacked up facsimiles of *Post* covers from the old days, doughboys returning from World War I, Pa and Ma driving the family runabout, children joining in prayer. Against the window at the far end, there stood a large modern desk, heaped high with folders full of papers. Behind the desk, with his feet propped up on top of it, a cigar in his mouth and a telephone crooked under his ear, sat Marty Ackerman.

Two days later, I wandered into Emerson's office and found him conferring with Mike Mooney. There was a pause, and then Mooney said, "Otto might as well hear this too. I've decided that Friday is going to be my last day here."

"Well, that's certainly a decisive reaction to something or other," I said.

"The assumption has always been that Mac Clifford and G.B. and all those people would have to go someday," Mooney said. "Otherwise, this place was hopeless. Now we've had a chance to look at the whole corps of replacements, and *they're* hopeless. So I'm going."

"You have another job?"

"No. I'm just getting out."

The Last Day of the Saturday Evening Post

Waiting for official word of the *Post*'s death, Emerson joked to keep up spirits. At top, managing editor Otto Friedrich.

Every few minutes, phone calls brought new rumors, commiserations, job offers.

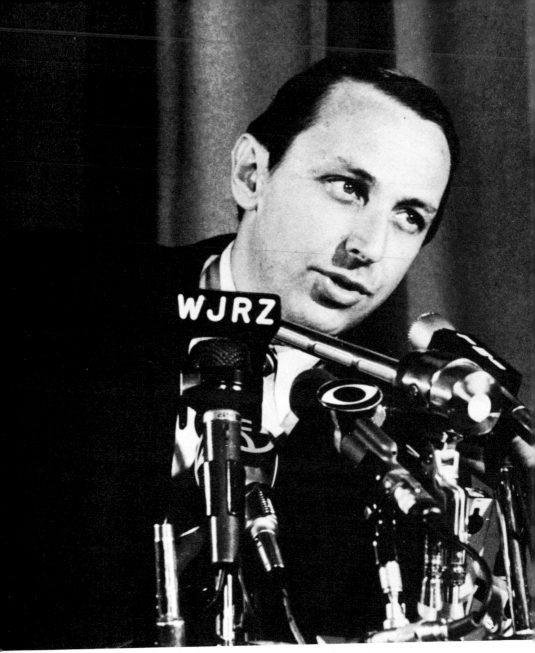

"There just is not a need for our product," Ackerman said, delivering his verdict to a press conference.

Bill Emerson listening as his
magazine was killed. At right, production manager Rita Waterman
weeping after the announcement.

Back at the office after the
execution, Steve Spencer, the
Post's oldest editor, began packing.

Don Allan, the foreign editor,
bought roses to cheer the women
of the staff.

Glumly the younger editors opened wine to toast their dead
magazine.

"Where was St. Anthony?" sobbed Louise, the cleaning woman,
as she kissed Emerson goodbye.

The television spotlights cast a glare upon Emerson's farewell to his staff. Seated in foreground, from left: editor Chris Welles, production manager Rita Waterman, editors Otto Friedrich, Don Allan, John Kobler. Behind them, from left: editors Robert Poteete, James Atwater, William Ewald, and Don McKinney. At center is Emerson's secretary, Barbara O'Dwyer.

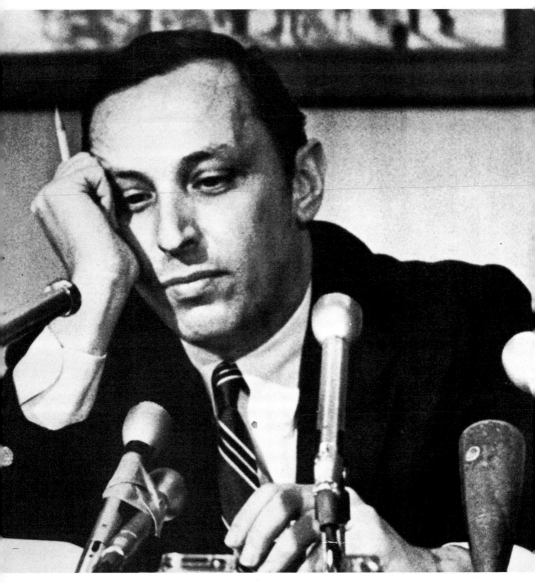

End of an empire: Litigation and controversy led to Ackerman's own departure from Curtis.

19

"I want the magazine to reflect me"

It is probably inappropriate for any writer ever to accuse anyone else of enjoying the sight of his own name and picture in print, but the shameful desire for personal publicity is nonetheless endemic among the rulers of publishing corporations. This passion may be sublimated in the form of publicity for the publisher's favorite charity, or for his daughter's social career, but none of these sublimations prevents the publisher from enjoying—in secret, if his conscience requires secrecy —the awesome view of himself as a public figure.

Marty Ackerman did not bother with sublimation. When the Perfect Film & Chemical Corporation returned a customer's processed film, for instance, the envelope showed a sample photograph, and that sample was a picture of Marty Ackerman sitting on his brick steps with his wife and children. And now that he had a whole publishing company at his disposal, he thought it quite natural to apply the same principles to its magazines. "You guys have been putting out a good magazine, but that's not enough," he said. "It must be successful, and to be successful, it must be *considered* successful. And it can't get there on its own right now, because of all the troubles in the past. So the only way it can achieve that aura of success is by being attached to my own personal success, see? When they write stories about me, those stories will help the *Post*."

"Joe Culligan used to have a similar theory," I said, thinking that a lawyer might be mildly interested in precedents, but this was not a subject for ironic comment. Ackerman shrugged slightly, as though I had struck him, but with only a glancing blow.

We were sitting in my office, Ackerman and Emerson and I, because Ackerman, in these early days of turmoil, had filled up his own office with negotiators and petitioners, then invaded and temporarily occupied Emerson's office with another corps of conferees—and then followed Emerson to the sanctuary of my office. "I've got to get away from those bankers for a while," he said, relighting his cigar. "They can make you dizzy."

"What are you doing in there anyway?" I asked.

"I'm forcing through my reorganization of the company, the one I told you guys about."

"What if the board doesn't like it?" I inquired.

"Then they'll have to get themselves a new president," Ackerman said fiercely.

Despite these portents of great events, Emerson decided to take this opportunity to settle some editorial problems, specifically the problem of the editorial page, which I wrote and which Ackerman wanted to dominate. Since Emerson knew that Ackerman hoped to write some sort of editorial statement in the first of our variant issues, Post No. 12A, he began on a conciliatory note by saying that he had discussed it with me, and we had no objections. Ackerman raised an eyebrow at this, as though he had just been told by some servant that the kitchen staff had no objection to his carving his own Thanksgiving turkey, but all editorial problems were such a fascinating novelty to him that he immediately turned to the new subject.

"Here's my point on that," he said. "We've got to have more editorial excitement, all through the Post, on every page. Now I happen to be particularly interested in the editorial page, and I think we probably all have something to contribute, so I think each editorial should be signed by whoever wrote it, you or me or Bill or whoever."

"Those wouldn't be editorials any more," I said. "They'd just be columns. Editorials are anonymous because they represent the whole magazine."

"I don't give a s—— what you call them," Ackerman said. "But let me just make one thing clear: I intend to participate in the editorial direction of the Post, okay?"

"Depends on what you mean by 'participation,'" I said.

"Okay, then I'll explain. Now I don't have any terribly strong political opinions, no ideology or anything like that, but I want to be able to commit the Post—and not just the Post, but all the magazines—to, say, a presidential candidate, or to anything else I believe in."

"Let's get this clear," I said carefully. "You mean, you want to have all the Curtis magazines say: 'I, Martin S. Ackerman, support Hubert Humphrey for President'?"

"Well, not quite that way," Ackerman said.

"Well, what way then?"

"Put it like this," he said. "I've put my five million dollars on the line. I've staked my reputation, my career, and my money on the proposition that I can get Curtis to make a profit. Now if I make that kind of a commitment, I'm going to *participate* in the editorial direction of these magazines, okay? Because if I can't participate, then I'm not interested in putting up my five million dollars, okay? So what I mean is, I don't want to edit the magazine, but I want the magazine to reflect me. I want it to reflect my personality."

"The only way a magazine can reflect your personality is if you edit it yourself," I said. "*The New Yorker* is Shawn's magazine because he controls every word in it, and *Playboy* is Hefner's not because he owns it but because the assigning and choosing and changing all add up to what a magazine is."

There was a pause, and then Ackerman said, "Well, we've got lots to talk about." He got up, went through the ritual of tucking in his shirt, then clapped Emerson on the shoulder and returned to business. "I want to tell you, this company is in terrible shape," he said. "Just terrible." Emerson laughed and cheered him on, but there was one point he wanted to make clear.

"Now about this damn statement of yours in 12A," Emerson said, "I want you to write it yourself, because none of us can say whatever it is that you want to say."

"I understand, I understand," Ackerman said, opening my door and preparing his return to the bankers. "But I may need somebody to make it—you know—literate."

The fact that Marty Ackerman reveled in personal publicity, the fact that he regarded the Curtis magazines as the newest and brightest toys in his young life, did not mean that the *Saturday Evening Post* did not genuinely need some editorial rejuvenation. All its main editors had been working together in the same harness for five years, and a certain weary staleness was predictably evident. And while Ackerman was no editor, there were a number of experienced editors who would have agreed with his statement to an interviewer from the *Wall Street Journal:* "The *Post* can't make it in its present format. It can't compete with television."

By now, therefore, we were already engaged in the production of *Post* No. 12A, the "evolutionary" *Post*. We had begun by scheduling only a few variations on the regular *Post* No. 12, but then Emerson came to me and said, "I finally figured out what this *Post* No. 12A really is. It's a test of whether *I* can put out a magazine that they'll accept. You know what Yung said to me? He said, 'We want this to be your magazine, not Otto's magazine or somebody else's magazine.'"

"Okay, it's all yours," I said.

"So what I thought," Emerson said, "is why not do something very jazzy and very special and very pictorial? Why not do a big picture story on this new musical, *Hair*?"

"It's all yours," I said again. "Yours and Yung's and Lubalin's."

And Ackerman's. It was about noon when Ackerman popped into my office and said he wanted a copy of all the articles scheduled for *Post* No. 12A. I promised I would send them to him.

"And how about the editorial?" he asked.

"I haven't written it yet," I said.

"Okay, I want that too, as soon as it's written."

A few minutes later, the telephone rang, and G.B. said, "Marty says he wants all the copy for 12A."

"I know," I said. "He already told me."

"Well, I guess we're going to have quite a bit of that from now on," G.B. said with a nervous laugh. "Where Marty asks me for something and then goes and gets it himself."

"There's a name for that, G.B.," I said. "It's called inefficiency."

"Well . . ." G.B. said, with another nervous laugh. "Just so you give him what he wants . . ."

The next day, Ackerman called Emerson from Chicago, where he was selling ads for his new, evolutionary *Post*. "And since this is what I'm selling, I've got to believe in what I'm selling, right?" he demanded.

"Right," Emerson agreed.

"Now this Marshall Frady story about Governor Wallace is great, and, let me see, *True Grit*, I like that too. But this little story about the lady racing driver—that just isn't up to the level of the new magazine that I'm telling people about."

"Okay, we can live without it," Emerson said.

"Understand—you can do whatever you want in the regular issues. It's just the 'A' issue I'm talking about. And this story about Lady Bird's tour of Texas—I mean, it's all right, but it's awfully folksy for what we're trying to do."

"Okay, no Lady Bird," Emerson said.

"And this story about the moon rocket—it's pretty heavy going—"

"Now wait a minute," Emerson protested. "If you're going to talk about being urban and sophisticated, then you'd better give them a few pieces that'll make them think, and that's a good solid article."

"Okay, I buy that," Ackerman said. "But you'll get something else instead of those other two, okay? And listen, everybody out here thinks our new program is just great. They're real excited about it."

Back in New York, Ackerman continued to read the copy, and he continued to demand improvements. He didn't like a short story by Shirley Ann Grau. He didn't like the new column by John Gregory Dunne, a memoir on the baseball players of his youth. "Well, that's the only column we've got," I snapped back at Emerson when he brought these tidings. "For Christ's sake, it's the easiest thing in the world to sit there and say you don't like things—as though this were some kind of a restaurant—so if he wants something better, let him produce it himself."

We did remove the Grau story, however, and replace it with a memoir by William Saroyan. It was difficult to argue with Ackerman, not just because he was the president of the corporation, or because he spoke very forcefully about what he liked and didn't like, but because he was often right. He liked, in every instance, our best stories; what he disliked was the merely acceptable, the average, the usable, material that editors necessarily publish for want of anything better. Perhaps because of his inexperience, Ackerman was pursuing the theory that if he kept demanding something better, something better would be found.

From the *Gallagher Report:*

May 14:

"MORTICIAN MARTY" ACKERMAN CATCHES EDITORIAL FEVER. Major blunder. Curtis Publishing's problems financial, management, sales—not editorial. Marty's proposal to get Saturday Evening Post "in tune with people it serves," write editorials insult to editor Bill Emerson. . . .

May 21:

. . . Staffs jumpy. SEP editorial floor chaotic. Marty's men all over place with "bright" ideas, no experience . . . Marty talks to press about breezier layouts, subtle cartoons, more sophisticated articles. . . .

From *Newsweek,* May 20:

Ackerman . . . has moved into an office alongside Emerson's at the Curtis headquarters in New York City. "The Post should be the class book," he says. "We want quality rather than quantity." What happens if the class instead of mass formula doesn't work? Ackerman says he will keep the magazine going. "As long as I am here," he promised skeptical advertising men in Chicago last week, "there will not be a last issue of The Saturday Evening Post."

"There has never been a company with problems like this one," said Bob Yung, laughing. Emerson and Yung and I were in a taxi, driving down Lexington Avenue to Lubalin's studio. "You wouldn't believe the problems we've been finding."

"We believe them," Emerson said.

"Everywhere you turn, more problems," Yung said. "The book division—millions of copies of books sitting in warehouses. You wouldn't believe it."

"We believe it," Emerson repeated.

"Then why is Marty spending so much of his time on *Post* editorial," I asked, "when we're one of the few Curtis departments that function?"

"He's getting more and more impressed with the idea of Ben Franklin's magazine," Yung said. "When we first went down to Philadelphia to take over the company, everybody told us to get rid of the *Post*. They all said that was the first move to make. And all we said was that we'd look it over, and then come to a decision. But now—"

"It hooks everybody," I said. "The spell of Ben Franklin."

"That *Newsweek* statement that there would never be a last issue of the *Post*," Yung said. "When I saw that, I said to him, 'Marty, that's quite a commitment.' And he just smiled. And I said, 'Whatever became of Marty Ackerman, King of the Conglomerates?' And he just smiled."

It came time, finally, for Ackerman to produce his editorial statement at the beginning of *Post* No. 12A. We had agreed that this would be the editorial page, and that, as a special case, it could carry Ackerman's portrait and by-line and signature. But now, as often happens, it turned out that Ackerman suffered from the Achilles' Heel of the Press Lord—he didn't really know quite what he wanted to say, or how to say it. In short, he couldn't write, and neither could his myrmidons.

Emerson told me this with a certain satisfaction, and we assigned one of our senior editors, Tom Congdon, to ghost-write a statement for Ackerman. Congdon had a flair for promotional writing, and he also wanted passionately to guide Ackerman into a genuine rejuvenation of the *Post*, so he set to work with great ardor. In midafternoon, I looked in on him, and he said, "I'm having fun." The first few paragraphs had already been composed, in the manner of something destined for marble:

On a fair June day exactly half my lifetime ago I graduated from high school—not just any high school but Benjamin Franklin High School. . . . Today I find myself the chief executive officer of the company that publishes Franklin's magazine. That heritage alone compels dedication, demands that I pledge to you, its millions of mid-20th-century readers, that the fundamental resolve of this management is to perpetuate *The Saturday Evening Post.* . . .

"You have a great future in public relations," I said.

"I know, but I've always tried to hide from it," Congdon said.

When I left at seven, Congdon had sent for a hamburger and was planning to work on into the night. He had shown the statement to Yung, and Yung had praised it and taken it to Ackerman, and Ackerman had praised it too, and now they had given Congdon a management statement to Curtis stockholders, to be "edited." I laughed. "Ambition is gnawing at the vitals of Thomas B. Congdon, Jr.," I said, "as he sees himself earning a place in the confidence of the president of the corporation."

"Stop," Congdon said.

"This is the point in that movie where Jack Lemmon sees a chance to get off the fourth floor and onto the thirty-second floor, with a key to the executive washroom."

"Go home and let me work," Congdon said.

From this point on, a strange power struggle began to develop. The very next day, at the regular Thursday morning meeting of the editorial staff, Bob Yung appeared with several of the layouts for *Post* No. 12A, notably for the picture story by Clive Barnes and Pete Turner on *Hair*. Emerson and I had seen these layouts before, and so we showed no particular approbation, but many of the other editors seemed to experience a sudden flowering of enthusiasm, not just because of the layouts on *Hair*, or because of Lubalin's lavish and dramatic use of pictures, but because they saw for the first time something more concrete than speeches and prophecies: a genuinely new look to their battered magazine. One of the young female editors burst out with the exclamation: "I love it!"

Bob Yung, who had hitherto played a rather enigmatic part in our lives, now assumed the role of triumphant impresario. He accepted the editors' praises for Lubalin's new look as his own just due. And

this was typical of the enigma of Bob Yung. He had come in with
Ackerman, he hovered at Ackerman's heels, he seemed to carry
Ackerman's seal of office, and this naturally gave him a proconsular
power. From the little cubicle he had appropriated, on the executive
end of the main corridor, he wandered in and out of the editors'
offices, asking questions and inviting gossip—but never making it
quite clear what he actually did or what his responsibilities really
were.

(Part of the mystery about him was that despite his fluent,
unaccented, and slightly high-pitched English, he was unmistakably
Oriental. Perhaps inevitably, and to nobody's credit, the editors began
to compete in proposing secret nicknames for him. "Blooper boy" was
Emerson's first choice, in honor of Yung's vaguely sybaritic figure, but
all the rest of the nicknames were purely racial—Fu Manchu, Charlie
Chan, Dr. No, Oddjob, and finally the one that lasted, The Yellow
Peril, or The Peril for short. It would have sounded pompous, I suppose, if anyone had protested against these racial nicknames—all of
which were supposed to be comic, in the sense that the Heathen
Chinee used to be a comic character like Sambo and Paddy—but it is
probably worth noting that the people who used these nicknames for
Yung, myself included, would have thought it vulgar to use similar
terms for any Negro or Mexican.)

On this Thursday in May, in any case, Bob Yung acted as though
he had become—or perhaps would soon become—our editorial director. And the staff responded as deferentially as any new editorial
director could wish. They asked respectful questions about Ackerman's plans for the magazine, about the shortcomings of the printing
plant, about the need for better promotion. Yung answered all their
questions with a mixture of authority and benevolence, and then,
when there seemed to be no more questions, he said he had an
appointment and departed. He left behind him an editorial staff that
now seemed in a state of euphoria about the prospects for salvation,
and I thought it best to remind them that very little had really
changed or was likely to change, that the "A" issues might look nice
but were not genuine magazines, if only for the reason that they were
economically impossible to publish. At that, there began a general
outcry against my pessimism, and a general insistence that the
evolution heralded by the "A" issues somehow must and would be
carried out. "We're going to have to be with it and *go*," Congdon said
heatedly. "And we're not going to be able to limit ourselves to heavy
things and worthy things. We're going to have to be light and

sophisticated—and if that means more pictures of naked ladies than they've ever seen in Kansas, then I for one am glad."

Within a few weeks, it now appeared, the evolution of the evolutionary *Post* had served to isolate both Emerson and me, and particularly me, not only from the management but from our own staff. Because Mac Clifford had shunned contact with the staff, a hierarchical structure had developed, with authority flowing in clearly marked channels from top to bottom. Because Ackerman, by contrast, had encouraged and even solicited contact with the staff, and because Ackerman and the staff shared a yearning for the *Post* to become fashionable, in the Manhattan manner, everyone could imagine his own individual ideas prevailing. As a consequence, the hierarchical form of authority had begun to crumble. And so, after all the years of trying to keep the badly wounded *Post* alive by a policy of prudence, moderation, and responsibility, of pressing to the limits and occasionally beyond the limits of what a frigidly conservative management would permit, Emerson and I suddenly saw ourselves cast as the heirs of Cardinal Ottaviani and the Curia, no longer defenders of the faith but symbols of reaction and repression.

Emerson, like Montini, proved adaptable enough to work with anyone, even people as alien to his nature as Yung or Lubalin, and to maintain a kind of equilibrium among his own authority, Ackerman's demands, and the hopes of the staff. I myself, however, largely abandoned the "A" issues, concentrating instead on the "regular" issues, which, after all, were still being published for seven million subscribers, and which I took to calling "the real *Post.*" This peculiar diffusion of power, a temporary reorganization in response to stress, obviously could not last very long. In due time, Ackerman would realize that his "A" issues were an extravagance, and the two concurrent magazines would have to be united. Then there would be an interesting conflict over the question of who would decide what the renovated magazine would publish.

On the day after the noisy staff meeting, I received an unhappy memo from Congdon, indicating that the forces of change and progress were less unified than I had thought. Bob Yung, it turned out, was not always affable after all. "I walked into the conference room a little while ago," the memo said,

and Bob Yung was telling Jeannette Wagner that he had attended a meeting of advertising writers, and that all those guys thought Emerson was no good, a washout. I said nothing. Jeannette said lightly: "Well, you can't be a good editor without offending people." Yung said: "Well, they were unanimous. They all felt the same way about him." Then he turned to me and said, "What is this editorial column of Emerson's supposed to be, the one on the contents page?" I said, "What do you mean?" He said, "What is it? What's it supposed to do?" I said I thought it was a grace note at the start of an issue, and also that it was meant to personalize the editor. . . . All these were very aggressively put questions, and Jeannette's and my responses were obviously not those that Yung was seeking.

The memo also reported on another problem. Ackerman had approved of Congdon's editorial declaration for *Post* No. 12A, and now he wanted Congdon to ghost-write another editorial with an Ackerman signature in the next issue. "For me, I think this is the end of the line," Congdon's memo said.

I will not ghost editorials for Ackerman, don't want to work for the kind of magazine that prints editorials ghosted for the company's president. . . . But the immediate problem is not what I am going to do about this, but what you and Bill are going to do about it. . . . What I was trying to say in the meeting yesterday is that you just can't let the magazine be eased out from under you. I wanted to make it clear that I—and Ewald and Atwater and most of the rest of the staff—had been in favor of the new kind of *Post* long before any of us ever heard of Ackerman.

My first response was to take the memo and hand it to Emerson, and his first response was to vow that he would not work one more day in the same offices with Yung, and that Ackerman would have to choose between them. "I'm *sick* of all these f—— midgets!" he shouted. "I'm sick of their cigar butts all over the place and the cheese sandwiches sent up for lunch, and I'm sick of finding them using my goddamn bathroom. And now this—it's just one load of s—— too many." I was sick of the situation too, not of the cigars and sandwiches but of the constant confusion about who was supposed to be in charge of what. If Ackerman wanted Yung to run the magazine, and ghosts to write the editorial page, then let him say so, and I would join in Emerson's resignation.

"When the enemy advances, we retreat," said Chairman Mao. "When the enemy retreats, we advance." On the largest scale, of course, Mao's theories were demonstrated in the conquest of China— and, later, Vietnam. On a microcosmic scale, and with Americans as subjects, they were applied in different ways in the prison camps of Korea. And at the Orofino State Mental Hospital in northern Idaho, a psychiatrist named Dr. Myrick Pullen has organized work camps where mental patients create their own social structure, elect their own leaders and collectively choose their own system of labors, rewards, and punishments. "The camp was suggested," one chronicler wrote, "by the actions of the Communist Chinese in Korea, who took away their prisoners' leaders, rewarded informers, split up the prisoners' groups, and produced something a lot like schizophrenia. Dr. Pullen felt that if we could reverse this process, it might reduce schizophrenia."

It is difficult to escape from a prison if there are no walls or bars, or to resign angrily on a matter of principle if no commanding officer can be found. Ackerman was away, unreachable, and it was not until midafternoon that Emerson could find Ackerman's chief deputy, Lavere Lund. After half an hour with Lund, he came into my office, shut the door, and said, "Things are never what they seem." According to Lund, Bob Yung had never had any authority of any kind over the *Post*. An hour later, Ackerman himself made a brief reappearance at the office, and Emerson got the same verdict from him. Yung had only been working for Ackerman for two months, he was an "idea man," and his only function was "to stimulate people."

At the time, this revelation came as a relief. Emerson had been unequivocally told, "You're in charge." Only somewhat later, when I knew Ackerman better, did I realize that this had been an example of what he called "abrasive management." In other words, he had apparently intended from the start that Yung irritate us, and he had counted on us to fight back. If we had failed to do so, we would have been unworthy of our jobs, but once we had reacted as our position required, then Yung could be sacrificed, or moved on to some other project. Only much later, when the corporation had again begun to founder, did I realize that "abrasive management" is a workable theory only when a corporation has a surplus of managerial talent. In such a case, the winners of the struggle provide the corporation with the best available management, because even the losers are capable men who get good jobs somewhere else. I realized this because I realized that Ackerman had brought to the echoing void on the upper levels of Curtis no new management except himself.

Bob Yung ended that phase of the power struggle with characteristic style. Late Friday, Emerson was acting as host at a small farewell party for two departing secretaries, and Yung inevitably made himself one of the guests. He wore a double-breasted white twill suit with a scarlet necktie and a matching scarlet handkerchief protruding from his breast pocket. Having probably been briefed and warned by Ackerman on the day's unpleasantnesses, he made a point of approaching me with hand outstretched. "Thanks for your cooperation during this difficult week," he said as we shook hands. "From now on, it will be better."

Even though Ackerman was devoting much of his energy to playing editor of the *Post*, his greatest immediate problem was the reduction of the magazine's circulation. It was easy to announce that the circulation would be cut in half, but a magazine subscription is a contract, and the reader who subscribes has a legal right to the magazines that have been promised him. Furthermore, the halving of *Post* circulation threatened every other part of the corporation. The paper plant would henceforth be asked for only half as much paper, and the giant printing presses would stand idle for hours every week.

Ideally, however, Ackerman figured that there must be some way of fitting the reduction of the *Post* together with the expansion of some other magazine. Most publishers, after all, spend lots of money to gain new subscribers, and therefore some magazine should be willing to pay for the *Post*'s subscribers. And once that magazine had acquired its new subscribers, it would need more printing presses, bindery machines, circulation workers. Ideally, in other words, Ackerman could find some publisher who would not only enable him to save money but pay him to save money.

There were two obvious choices, *Life* and *Look*, which had both outrun Ben Hibbs's *Post* in the suicidal circulation wars of the 1950's—coming to rest, exhausted, at a level of slightly more than seven million readers. *Look* had ended the race slightly ahead of *Life*, at terrible expense, and had remained ahead ever since, standing now at 7.8 million to *Life*'s 7.6 million. (It was an unfair competition, since *Life* appeared weekly and thus sold roughly twice as many copies as the biweekly *Look*, but advertising and circulation wars are not waged on a basis of fairness.) So what could be more natural than for Ackerman, seeking a customer for his unwanted subscribers, to offer *Life* a chance to achieve supremacy and to offer *Look* a chance to beat back that threat? *Look* declined the gambit, but *Life* could not resist the temptation of a blitzkrieg, and so Ackerman reached toward his first major victory. A dollar a name seemed a minimal price, and that could net him up to $3.8 million, with millions of additional dollars erased from the *Post*'s subscription liabilities. And by getting rid of the rural readers, those listed as living in Nielsen C and D counties, the *Post* would automatically become more attractive to advertisers.

"It sounds great," said John Mack Carter, when Ackerman began boasting of his victory as early as that first conference on the future of the *Post*, "but why is *Life* willing to buy your C and D circulation when most magazines don't want that kind of circulation at any price?"

"Well, they're doing it as a sort of favor to us," Ackerman said. "They want to help us get back on our feet because it would be very bad for the whole magazine business if the *Post* goes under."

It would have been undiplomatic for Carter to suggest that Ackerman's statement was highly implausible, and so he simply smiled and said, "I'm sure you know that any time the big wheels over at Time Inc. tell you they're doing you a favor, anything they propose ought to be looked at *very* closely."

Life, as it turned out, had no intention of buying any C and D circulation, or any name that was already on its own lists, or any subscription of less than a year. Nor, in fact, was it prepared to pay any cash for even our best circulation. What was finally announced, on May 17, was a deal that benefited both corporations, but within reasonable limits. *Life* acquired "a substantial number" of *Post* subscribers (apparently one million), of whom at least 500,000 were "expected" to switch permanently to *Life*. In exchange, Time Inc. agreed to advance $5 million to Curtis as a prepayment for $3 million worth of printing and $2 million worth of distribution service. By any estimate, *Life,* far from doing us a favor, drove a very hard bargain, but its talent for negotiation was equaled by its talent for public relations. Somehow, the deal was made to sound as though Time Inc. had acted out of charity. "Time Inc. . . . is coming to the aid of Curtis," said the lead in the *Wall Street Journal*. The *Times* reported that "in a further move to help Curtis reduce its burdensome publishing costs, Time has agreed to take over a substantial part of the circulation of *The Saturday Evening Post*." As for the future, Jerome Hardy, publisher of *Life,* declared: "We expect that *Life* will be clearly established as the No. 1 magazine in the United States in every respect."

And as for the future of Curtis, the announcements on this same day disclosed that all its circulation subsidiaries had been turned over to the Perfect Film & Chemical Corporation. Specifically, Perfect acquired the Curtis Circulation Company, National Magazine Service, Inc., Keystone Readers' Service, Inc., Moore-Cottrell Subscription Agencies, Inc., and Curtis Distributing Company of Canada. The announcement said that the sale price had not been worked out, but added that it would be paid by means of a new issue of Perfect Film preferred stock.

The day after the announcement of the deal with Time Inc., Ackerman publicly acknowledged that Curtis had suffered a "large loss" in the first quarter of 1968 and would lose a lot more during the rest of the year. Since the Curtis stock had been removed from the New York Stock Exchange, however, there was no need for a quarterly statement of profit or loss, and so Ackerman did not provide one. "We want a chance to go in and review the numbers," Ackerman said.

Once again there was a meeting. This time, Ackerman wanted to see the entire editorial staff, which sounded ominous, but he went to great lengths to sound reassuring. He seemed to want to explain everything to everybody. He explained the circulation reduction, and he explained the deal with *Life*. He explained the need for economies, and the need for everyone to come to work early, and the need for editors to think about profits and losses. At times, he seemed defensive—"Not all of us went to Harvard or Yale," he said—and at times incoherent—"We've got to mirror editorial and business decisions together," he said, "uh—we've got to *marriage* them." On the future of the *Post*, however, he was full of enthusiasm.

"Listen, I can absolutely guarantee you that the *Post* will make money in 1969," he said. "In fact, I can guarantee you that the *Post* will make money *even* if it doesn't make money. What I mean is, if I had been president of this company over the past couple of years, I never would have admitted that the *Post* lost money. Because—see?—when the *Post* loses money, it makes the whole company look bad. So we've got all these other operations, the book division and all that stuff, well, let them lose the money, and nobody would pay any attention. They'd think the company was in great shape."

There are people who take pleasure in boasting of their talents for deception, generally assuming that friends can all rejoice in the bewilderment of enemies, and they never realize that some of their listeners may take their boasts more literally than they expect. Clay Blair sometimes talked that way, and so did, to a lesser extent, Emerson. It is a trait of the political man, I think, of the salesman, and of diplomats and poker players. Conversely, it is a practice disapproved of by those who make a living by weighing the truth or falsity of other men's statements. Priests, teachers, and editors tend to believe that anyone who boasts of his skill in trickery may not be entirely trustworthy. It was with some misgivings, therefore, that I heard Ackerman tell the assembled staff, with an expression of the utmost sincerity, that he had made no efforts to find any new editors, and that he had no intention of making any such efforts. "I have complete confidence in Bill and Otto and the rest of you guys," he said, not once but several times.

I felt a dull sense of recognition, therefore, of prophecy confirmed, when Congdon joined Don McKinney and me en route to Grand

Central at the end of that day and said that he had spoken with Ackerman both before and after the staff meeting. "And Ackerman said, 'I think we may lose Otto, and maybe Emerson too.'"

"What is that supposed to mean?" McKinney asked. "That they just get misplaced, like old shoes?"

"Did he say this as something to be regretted or something to be wished for?" I added.

"I don't know, I don't *know*," Congdon said unhappily. "I told him that you were a great asset to the magazine, but he just said, 'Well, I don't think our minds really mesh.'"

"Is that the requirement, for Christ's sake?" I asked. "That you have a mind that *meshes* with his?"

"I don't know, I tell you," Congdon repeated. "And he said, 'I think Emerson just isn't the kind of editor who can bring off this new *Post*.'"

"Well, too goddamn bad for old Marty," I said. We had arrived at Grand Central, and I veered off to continue to Penn Station, keeping cool, and thinking: *I'm keeping cool.* And then, of course, great waves of paranoia began to sweep over me. If Ackerman felt this way, then Yung must have been acting as his agent after all, and Ackerman had simply denied his own agent when challenged. Or was Congdon playing *agent provocateur*? Playing off everyone against everyone else, in the hope that he would emerge at the top? Or was this all hallucination?

We are creatures of routine, as Mao teaches, and we cling to our routines as marks of order and sanity in the world. When these routines are broken—and this is true for individuals and organizations alike—we respond with a kind of temporary insanity (like the prisoners in Korea), which lasts until we can create and justify some new routine. "Disorientation" is a technical word for this madness, a sense that things are not where they are supposed to be, and therefore a sense that one has lost contact with one's environment. Suspend a man in lukewarm water, comfortable but separated from all sight and sound, and he begins to see visions.

And yet the preservation of social order is surely not the highest of values. When any new regime takes power, it must, for the sake of its own survival, crack open and master the old order. Hadn't Clay Blair confronted much the same problem more than five years ago? And hadn't he acted much the way Ackerman was acting? And hadn't I been equally hostile, equally concerned about the affronts to tradition and the violation of my own inconsequential prerogatives?

There were even more elaborate and ambiguous analogies in Europe. When the Nazis occupied a country (or the Americans, for that matter), their first action was not the massacre of all women and children but rather the establishment of a system to govern an alien and hostile land. In Occupied France, for example, there were many German officials who spoke French, admired French culture, and yearned for peaceful accommodation. The techniques were mixed, and so were the results. One technique was to assign a military governor to take charge of the conquered territory, work with the local people, decide which ones were reliable. But such a man was always an alien, isolated, mistrusted. Another technique was to recruit or coerce supporters among the native population, to convince them that the new order represented both progress and inevitability. These native recruits would know what the problems were, how things worked. But wouldn't they, too, soon become isolated and mistrusted? That depended on the alternatives open to the natives. The occupiers' first rule, therefore, was to break up and disperse the old social structure, for then the occupied population would have no choice but to support the new order. How neatly everything fitted, from Ackerman as the swaggering governor general to myself as the crusty old Baron de Friedrich, tending the rose garden—or was this all hallucination too?

Well, *damn* Ackerman, I finally decided, late that night. As long as Emerson and I were at the *Post*, it was our magazine and not his, and if we had to play the part of the old order, then so be it. We would be very correct.

On May 29, Ackerman confronted the stockholders, who had always unnerved his predecessors, and completely overawed them. He admitted that losses in the first quarter, before he arrived at Curtis, had been about $1.6 million. He also announced that he was replacing the accountants, Price, Waterhouse & Company, with a different firm, Touche, Ross, Bailey & Smart.

"We will be changing a great deal," he said once again. "We will be moving forward. And if you can't stand change and heat, get out of Curtis, because things will change."

The changes would place greater importance on the magazines, he said, and less on the printing operations. "In our present posture, it makes no sense for us to own a paper mill and a printing plant," he said. "We hope very soon to be a magazine company and not a manufacturing company. Our goal is to develop our magazines."

As for the staff, he said, "I'm not firing anybody. I think we have a good, qualified group of people."

During this period of spring maneuvers, Ackerman and I began playing a ridiculous game of who's-got-the-office? Every two or three days, I would come to work and find one of Ackerman's acolytes sitting at my desk, and every time it happened, I would throw the invader out.

It is possible that the game was simply a conflict of cultures, not a contest. Just as Ackerman believed that people should share secretaries, he seemed to believe that they should share offices, as though nobody could consider his place of work anything more than a temporary and impersonal piece of space. I believed just as strongly that my office, where I had to spend more waking hours than I spent at home, was my territory, a place where I lived. On Ackerman's side of the case, it was true that the corridor outside our offices was an inadequate waiting room for all the people coming to see him, but I couldn't believe that his visitors would keep invading my office unless they had been told that it was unused, and I couldn't help feeling that these encounters kept occurring because of the hours I kept.

This may seem picayune to anyone who has not been forced to engage in office warfare, but just as men and animals will kill in defense of their territorial rights, so they will fight bitterly over their choice of when to sleep. Stalin, for example, was a man of nighttime habits, and so he enjoyed the power of summoning his sleepy cabinet to midnight meetings. Ackerman, by contrast, was a devout disciple of Ben Franklin ("Early to bed, early to rise . . ."), and he could never understand why other people didn't like to wake up at dawn. Since I preferred to keep Stalin's hours rather than Ben Franklin's, I usually read manuscripts until one or two in the morning and arrived at the office at about 10:30.

At my desk, a stranger would look up in surprise, sometimes in the middle of a telephone call, and I would put my briefcase down in front of him, take off my coat, and scowl. The dialogue was generally much the same:

"Oh, is this your office?" the stranger would say.

"Yes, it is," I would say, as unpleasantly as possible.

"They told me it was empty," the stranger would say.

"Well, it isn't."

"Do you mind if I make a few phone calls?"

"Yes, I do mind."

"Oh. Well, where can I wait for Mr. Ackerman?"

"Out in the hall."

Very few people chose to go through this experience twice, but

Ackerman's supply of visitors was limitless, and I had to stage the same scene two or three times a week. This odd contest lasted all summer, until one day when the man I had to evict turned out to be Ackerman's younger brother, Lennie. It was a very unpleasant scene, and after he departed, the game ended, as mysteriously as it had begun.

"Well, Otto, what do you think of *that?*" Ackerman came barging into my office, with Yung tagging behind, and holding aloft the first preliminary copy of *Post* No. 12A. It was, finally, a magazine in which he had "participated." It carried his name and his picture (a rather evil-looking one; he seemed unable to distinguish between flattering and unflattering portraits of himself) and the philosophical statement that Tom Congdon had written for him ("The *Post* will speak with a clear, sure voice to its natural readership, the cultivated Americans who want a quality of information and entertainment the mass media seldom provide—the people who like to have their intelligence honored, their opinions challenged, their personal worlds expanded").

It was a good issue because the original *Post* No. 12 had been good, dominated by Marshall Frady's richly ornate portrait of Governor George Wallace and by the Gothic conclusion of Charles Portis's novel, *True Grit*. And then, to the regular issue, we had added a profile of J. K. Galbraith by Jack Skow, the picture story on *Hair*, a humor column by Alan Brien, and the Saroyan memoir, which McKinney had artfully entitled "Best Wishes to a Former Mistress and Carl Sandburg and a Dead Armenian and Other People I Lost Track Of." But all that, essentially, was just more of the same old *Post* that the nonreading critics called stodgy and conventional.

The important difference came in layout and design, for Lubalin had provided dramatic changes. The David Levine illustration of George Wallace, for instance, had changed from a black-and-white pen-and-ink drawing into a red-white-and-blue cartoon that took up virtually all of the opening page. The hippies of *Hair* gamboled through eight pages of color, and even so relatively staid a figure as Professor Galbraith was illustrated with a full-page photograph of his professorial fist. There was also an important change in the treatment of text: Lubalin had switched to Times Roman type and set everything in a larger size, with more space between the lines, which made a page of solid text look attractively readable rather than dense and forbidding. Along with these signs of progress, there were excesses and extravagances of the kind that appear whenever an art director is allowed too much "creative freedom." The subtitle of Sandy Brown's story on the moon rocket, for example, had been set in red type, all squashed together underneath a photograph of a rocket launching, so that the blur of red type could convey the impression of the rocket's exhaust. The "Speaking Out" title, similarly, had been given the form of a comic-strip balloon, so that the author could be shown to be truly speaking out, and since the author was a priest, the title emerging from his lips had been set in Gothic script.

To the Madison Avenue jaybirds who talk of "visual excitement," this sample issue was a radical improvement over anything the *Post* had published in years. And yet much of the visual improvement had little to do with pictures. One reason for it was that Ackerman had decided to print the entire issue on heavier, glossier, and more expensive paper, which would, of course, have added enormously to the printing costs of the regular issues. The second reason was that Ackerman had told the heads of the manufacturing division that he wanted *Post* No. 12A to be the most beautiful printing job Curtis had ever done, and that any of the usual ink smears and broken letters would bring terrible retribution. The third reason was that Ackerman had listened to my warnings about the aesthetic influence of advertisements, and therefore all the little offerings of mail-order shoes and suppositories and courses in hypnotism had been thrown out. In their place, *Post* No. 12A carried thirty-six full-page color ads (as compared to twenty-five in the regular No. 12). And with a total of fifty-three advertising pages, and fifty-eight editorial pages, the new issue looked undeniably handsome and opulent, a Potemkin village among magazines.

"Well, a lot of it is good," I said, in answer to Ackerman's question, "and some things I don't like at all."

"Listen, Otto," Ackerman said grimly. "It's great. It's just great. This is the kind of magazine we want to put out."

"Great," said Bob Yung.

For the next month or two, we all had a great deal of work to do, and we all tried to cooperate. *Post* No. 13A was not very different from *Post* No. 13—though we added an extra article on Ravi Shankar to soothe Ackerman's yearning for culture—but Lubalin once again redesigned everything to make it look more dramatic, and that meant new titles and captions, and another revision of all the copy. And by now, Ackerman was beginning to have lots of ideas about what he wanted in future issues. At one point, in fact, he handed me five pages covered with sixty scribbled ideas for articles:

. . . How about future inventory?
1. Charles Bluhdorn
2. Banking—how does the U.S. banking system work?
3. Profile Mike Nichols
4. What it's like to get old
5. What to do in the summer—guide to a new kind of summer
   vacation
   a. what the poor do
      what the middle class do
      what the rich do
6. What's left of the famous hotels
   Beverly Hills Hotel—a week there?
   Broadmoor—in Colorado Springs
   Grossinger's
7. Howard Baker of Tennessee—Tennessee politics
8. Senator Harris of Oklahoma
9. Story on The New Yorker Magazine . . .

Some of Ackerman's ideas—the working of the banking system—
were unrealistic. Some—Mike Nichols—we had already undertaken.
Some—the great hotels—seemed well worth assigning. It was among
the ironies of Ackerman's regime, as a matter of fact, that one of the
articles he had urgently requested, an expert evaluation on how the
United States could get out of Vietnam, ultimately turned out to be
the lead article by A. J. Langguth in the last issue of the *Post*.

Once he had an editorial foothold on the *Post* as a whole, Ackerman
was ready to abandon the experiment of the "A" issues—"G.B. tells
me they're costing us an extra hundred and fifty grand," he said with
a bitter laugh—but then we stumbled into "the family series." Back in
the dark days of the previous autumn, when Mac Clifford seemed
determined to kill one or two summer issues, we had worked out a
devious strategy to block his plan by commissioning a series of six
articles on "The New American Family," then scheduling them in six
successive summer issues and selling space in those issues to advertisers. Now Clifford was gone, and almost no advertisers had responded to our appeals—"a million-dollar idea," Steve Kelly had
called it in the first moments of enthusiasm—but the manuscripts
were still coming in from people like Phyllis McGinley and Arthur
Schlesinger and James Beard. Ackerman, seeing no need for a
summer series, wanted to put everything together in a year-end
special issue in December. We protested that a series designed for
summer would need to be completely revised for winter, and so the
"A" issues were extended to include one devoted to the American

family. "The attached issue," said Kelly, in a memo to the usual list of advertisers and agencies, "represents still another effort in the program of constant enrichment."

One benefit of all this extra work was that it helped to resolve much of the feuding and intriguing of the previous weeks. The Puritan ethic works. *Labor omnia vincit.* Because Ackerman wanted to accomplish so much, he needed all the editorial help he could get, and therefore he looked more charitably on all our eccentricities. Because Congdon was one of our best editors, we loaded him up with so much work (including all the supervision of the issue on the family) that he had no time or energy to think of anything else. And because Bob Yung was not a magazine editor at all, his whole editorial role gradually faded away.

While the editors could stand the extra work, however, the extra expense of the "A" issues was beginning to pain Ackerman, and so, after two months of what Kelly had called "constant enrichment," we were approaching the time to drop the charade and resume normal publication. It was a prospect that filled Kelly with foreboding. He had warned everyone against talk of a "new *Post*," but once the redesigned "A" issues began floating around Madison Avenue, nobody could prevent people from calling them "the new *Post*." And once Kelly heard that people actually liked "the new *Post*," he began worrying about what would happen when the "A" issues stopped.

"If the next issues don't live up to the 'A' issues," he said gloomily, "we'd better just get out of town."

"They can't possibly live up to the 'A' issues," I said, "because the 'A' issues have ten extra editorial pages and ten extra pages of unpaid-for ads, and we can't afford to go on that way for long."

"I'm quite aware of the cost," said Kelly, who always got huffy when I talked about money, "since that happens to be my area of responsibility."

"Okay, the first issue after the 'A' issues is going to be No. 16, the August 10 issue, so the only question is how many pages Ackerman wants to publish."

The next morning, Ackerman and Emerson appeared in my office, and we set to work on the problem. Ackerman began by suggesting that we abandon Mac Clifford's limit of forty-four editorial pages and return to the old limit of fifty-one pages.

"Fine," I said, "but we now have only 60 ad columns, so the book will be 264 columns, which makes 66 pages. Is a 66-page issue going to satisfy you after you've been showing everybody the 'A' issues of more than 100 pages? Here, look at it."

I took from my desk drawer a recent issue of sixty-eight pages, a pitifully thin issue, all the more pitiful because of its large page size, made for the two-hundred-page *Posts* of George Horace Lorimer. I held it up by one corner and waved it slowly in front of Ackerman as though it were a dead animal.

"Okay, how much more do you need?" Ackerman asked.

"You tell me," I said. "Whatever you think will look respectable and make Kelly happy. We can provide any amount you want, but it's going to cost you at least $6,000 per page."

"How about another four or five pages?" Ackerman pleaded.

"That makes seventy-two pages," I said, reaching into my desk drawer again. "Here's a seventy-two-page issue. Is that going to be enough?"

I held it up, and it looked as limp and starved as the sixty-eight-page specimen.

"Jesus, let me see some more of those," Ackerman said in desperation. I handed him several issues of different sizes, and we finally agreed on eighty-four pages.

"I'll just tell Kelly to get some more ads," Ackerman said hopefully, "and I'll get some myself, and we'll fill up some of that space."

"Okay, great," I said, "but our ads have a habit of fading away, and it's possible that we might end up with less ads than we have now, so are you ready to make eighty-four pages your permanent minimum, even if we have to replace dropped ads with more editorial copy?"

"Yeah, let's stick to that," Ackerman said.

"And how about the next issue, and the one after that? Hold the line at eighty-four pages?"

"Yeah," Ackerman said. "Let's hold the line there."

Perhaps I should not have challenged Ackerman in that way, knowing that he could not resist a dare. Perhaps I should have warned him that his bravado would cost him (and us) a small fortune. But Ackerman had repeatedly told us that he had plenty of money, and Kelly had repeatedly told me that publishing costs were none of my business, and so I thought, *Well, at least he'll be spending his money in a good cause.*

We had already begun building this issue around a major study of the Negro ghetto by Ben Bagdikian, and Ackerman had requested that we ask all the presidential candidates what they proposed to do about the problem—not a bad idea, incidentally—and so we had assigned Bill Davidson to interview them all. Now that we had more space, we added one of Emerson's pet projects, a three-year study by Dick Lemon on the state of psychiatry (that alone took up fourteen pages of solid text), and as more space kept opening up, we kept adding more articles until we ended with sixty-six editorial pages, twenty more than in the previous issue. All these details are significant primarily because of the cost that Ackerman had accepted on my dare—well over $100,000 in extra expense on this one issue, just to try to make an impression on Madison Avenue, and in the middle of August.

The one thing that Ackerman dearly hoped to have in that issue was not there. Ever since he had experienced the intoxication of seeing his own name and picture above the sonorous editorial that Congdon had written for him in No. 12A, he had tried to devise some way of repeating the pleasure. Congdon's refusal to ghost-write any more editorials, combined with my hostility to his being on the editorial page at all, had deflected him for a time. But Congdon, in trying to steer him away from the editorial page, had rashly suggested that Ackerman write a presidential column on matters of business and economic policy. Ackerman considered this a happy solution and promptly set to work, producing half a dozen such columns in the next two weeks. It was typical of Ackerman, and perhaps typical of all the impatient executive figures who wish they could write, that he undertook simply to dictate these columns to his secretary. They emerged, therefore, beautifully typed on expensive paper, but with words missing and the syntax in a state of anarchy. It is traditional, at this point, for the executive to turn such a "draft" over to some assistant with a lordly suggestion that perhaps a little editing might not be amiss. Congdon, inevitably cast in this role, had struggled to convince himself that the column was a good idea and that Ackerman really could produce it.

"Here's the pitch for the column," Congdon said in a memo to Emerson, covering Ackerman's first six entries.

A column addressed not to rank-and-file readers but to the key people in advertising and industry. These people already know Ackerman as an ingenious and successful businessman, and they will be more likely to honor his right to speak in these areas. In fact, the column, if done right, should even draw the attention of these people into the magazine. And lots of ordinary readers too, many of whom are businessmen, or investors, or otherwise money-minded . . . The first column, as yet unwritten, should introduce and explain the feature. Ackerman has worked out rough drafts of subsequent columns; most of them have the germ of a good idea but need lots of work, research, etc. . . . . There's a precedent: Ben Franklin talked about money and thrift and success in these pages.

Congdon's theory was reasonably sound, but the six drafts of Ackerman's columns provided very little for any editor to work with. The first was called "A Revolution—But What Kind?": "People want a new order. They're not sure what it's to be, but they're sure it should come. . . . Very few seem really concerned about getting out into the world and making a living or they will starve. Things are pretty good without having to make a living. The issue of revolt keeps deluding them and all of us. While it's presently the War in Vietnam, the draft in the United States, and better wages in France, these are only sparks that set off the mobs. . . ." Then came "The Little League": "Well, it's an interesting phenomenon when you see how well organized we can become when we, the nation, really want to accomplish something—like teaching the little boys how to play baseball. . . ." And "Business Is Business but Everyone Likes the Movie Business": "It's funny how hardened businessmen react when they get a chance to be glamorous. Apparently there is business that is business, strict, correct, not very exciting, and then there is the movie business which everyone is trying to get into. . . ." And "Television—It's Missed It's Opportunity": "The idea of a really stimulating program is a once-in-a-while occurrence and except for sports is probably the only time most of us are watching television today. . . ." And "It's Lots of Fun—If You're Not the Chairman": "Since so many people have recently become 'shareowners in America' or just old-fashioned stockholders, they are starting to wonder about what really happens at a Shareholders' Meeting. . . . It's lots of fun (if you happen not to be the chairman) and recommended as a real experience and almost a dividend to the new shareowners in America. . . ." And "The S.E.C.": "Well, we have come a long way since 1933, but the basic tenure of the Securities Act has always remained full disclosure. Theoretically, you can sell securities in a good or bad company as long as you disclose the facts. This is not also so under some of the state security laws where the Securities Commissioners decide if it is a good or bad buy and, if a bad buy for the general investor, they won't let it be sold. . . ." And finally, "Why Does the Price of a Stock Go Up?": ". . . I wish I knew. It's all quite confusing to me, and I have been around for some time."

For those who knew Ackerman and might want to know him better, these little columns undoubtedly provided a few insights into his personality. The ingenuousness of his views on the Little League, for example, was as characteristic as his fascination with the "glamour" of the movie business. For those who worked for him, however, and listened to his continuous demands for higher editorial quality in

the *Post,* the columns provided a different kind of insight. To mis-
appropriate T. S. Eliot's remark about Henry James, "He had a mind
so fine that no idea could violate it." But because Congdon had told
Ackerman that the columns had promise, the company president was
already badgering Emerson, like a nervous author, on when and how
he proposed to "get them into shape." We had a conference, Emerson
and McKinney and I, on which hack writer we should offer as the
executor of Ackerman's literary ambitions. McKinney proposed
A———, who was sensible and professional but a little slow-witted.
"Ackerman is too quick," I said. "He's not going to be satisfied with
somebody plodding along behind him." Emerson proposed B———,
who was quick and competent but deviously ambitious. "Look, anybody who ghost-writes a column for Ackerman is going to turn into a
kind of court scribe," I said, "and he can make a lot of trouble for us
if we pick somebody we can't really trust."

"Well, I haven't yet heard you propose anybody who's good and
quick and trustworthy," Emerson said.

"Why do we have to provide Ackerman with a ghost at all?" I
complained. "Why can't we just tell him the column is no good?"

"Do you want to take on the job of telling him that?"

"Sure, if you want."

"Look, it's not going to do any good," McKinney said. "This guy
really wants to see his name in print, and nobody's going to talk him
out of it."

We agreed, finally, on C———, who was quicker than A———
and more trustworthy than B———, but we also agreed that Emerson would offer him up as Ackerman's ghost only after making a
serious attempt to argue Ackerman into abandoning the column.

Two or three days later, I wandered by Ackerman's office and saw
that Emerson was already in the middle of his argument.

"You just haven't got the professional experience to write a column
for national publication, Marty," Emerson was saying. "And it would
take you several years to acquire it."

"Yeah, I see what you mean," Ackerman said, hurt and embarrassed but trying to be reasonable.

It must have been rather difficult, on a matter so personal, for
Emerson to tell the president of the corporation that his work was
hopelessly inadequate. When Emerson got himself mobilized, however, he was almost irresistible. And by being bold, he overwhelmed
all opposition.

"Now we could provide you with a ghost writer," Emerson went on,
sensing his victory, "and he could come in here and listen to your

ideas and take notes and patch together something for you to sign—"

"Yeah, I see—"

"And you could *lie* and tell people that you wrote it yourself, but honestly, Marty—"

"Okay, let's forget it," Ackerman said.

Once the four "A" issues were finished, and the "evolutionary" *Post* No. 16 was properly organized and under way, I felt an overwhelming desire to get away from Ackerman and the *Post* and the offices at 641 Lexington, and so I took my wife on a week-long drive to Montreal and Quebec. When I came back, I found that all the pressures and conflicts of the past two months had burst like some great blister. Emerson and McKinney had completed the work on *Post* No. 16, and Emerson had written an editorial about the Negro ghetto, which so impressed Ackerman that he had it reprinted as a full-page ad in the *New York Times.* In fact, Emerson reported that Ackerman now seemed to think the whole editorial department had finally proved itself, and that he was consequently turning to other things.

At the time, this seemed like a great blessing. We could finally return to our proper business of editing the *Post* as we saw fit, without having to worry about the sudden inspirations of Ackerman and his favorites. Over the course of two months, we had demonstrated to a very skeptical judge that we knew how to produce a good magazine. We had accepted and carried out his ideas when we thought they were good ones, but we had also resisted his ideas when we thought they were bad ones, and so we had retained our control of the magazine. And this was important to us as a matter both of professional pride and of principle.

In retrospect, however, it seems possible that we may have made a major miscalculation, and that our checkmating of Ackerman's literary ambitions may have been a Pyrrhic victory. For if Ackerman's counselors had all advised him to kill the *Post*, and if all the statistics of business logic supported that advice, then perhaps the only thing that deterred him was the incandescent vision of himself as the successor to Ben Franklin. Even Ackerman himself probably could not say how much this vision might have meant to him, nor could anyone say how badly it was damaged when Emerson persuaded him to abandon his column. Emerson's argument was perfectly reasonable, of course, and Ackerman quite reasonably accepted it. Just as reasonably, Ackerman knew that he had other problems to deal with, and that there were limits to the amount of time and energy he wanted to devote to the *Post*'s editorial affairs. But in that triumph of reason and logic, we unwittingly cast aside the armor of Ackerman's emotional involvement in the *Post*. If we were all going to be reasonable about editorial decisions, then there was no reason not to be reasonable about commercial decisions, no reason, in short, not to pay proper attention to those advisers who counseled liquidation. To put it another way, the final decision to kill the *Post* made (or seemed to make) sound business sense, but if each issue of the *Post* had been carrying a column of opinion signed by Ackerman, then Ackerman might not have been so coldly sensible.

None of these consequences could have been foreseen at the time. For the moment, Ackerman had simply decided that the *Post* editors were no longer a problem, and so he turned to his most immediate cause of financial loss, the payroll. The payroll cost him nearly a million dollars in cash every week, and consequently it was never far from his thoughts. In our first meeting at the Brussels restaurant, he had complained about the number of secretaries, and in his first gathering of the editorial staff, he had remarked that the company could hardly need all of its 5,500 employees. "It's costing us $41 million a year, and I figure, with a payroll that size, there've got to be 10 percent that don't work, so there's $4 million saved." By the time he brought me the first copy of No. 12A, his plans had become more definite. "The way I figure it now," he said, "we're going to lose $8 million this year no matter what we do, so I'm just going to take that much out of the payroll—$4 million from Philadelphia, $2 million from New York—not from you guys, from the bureaucracy—and $2 million from the offices in the field."

On the day I returned from Canada, I learned that the ax had struck its first blow. Four hundred of what Ackerman had publicly called "a good, qualified group of people" had just been fired in Philadelphia, and fifty more in New York. None of the victims came from *Post* editorial—after all, we had proved ourselves, hadn't we?—and so we reacted as people usually do in such circumstances, with indifference and even approval. It seemed splendid that we finally had a management that would deal with all that waste and inefficiency in Philadelphia. It seemed fine that the payroll could be cut without any of us losing a penny, that somebody else could be sacrificed for the good of the corporation.

20

"I'll sell it myself"

There was an unmistakable gleam in Ackerman's eye. He could hardly contain himself long enough to say hello and ask after my good health. Then he burst out with his news.

"Well, I just bought another magazine," he announced. "That ought to shut up those people who keep saying we're going to go out of business."

"Great," I said. "What magazine is it?"

"*Status*," he said.

The name was something of an anticlimax. *Status* had been founded in 1965 by Igor Cassini, after Peter Maas and I had helped to end his career as Cholly Knickerbocker, and it purported to describe what fashionable people were doing. In the course of three years, it had taken over a mildly competitive magazine called *Diplomat* and struggled upward to a circulation of 145,000, but despite its name and its ambitions, I couldn't recall ever having seen a copy or having heard anyone discussing its revelations. So I failed to show the enthusiasm that Ackerman had hoped for, and we stared at each other for a moment.

"Great," I said in a different tone. "Do we get Cassini too?"

"No, he's leaving."

"What did you pay for it? Not much, I hope."

"I just agreed to pay their debts—two hundred grand—and that's it."

"Do they make any money?"

"No, but they don't lose too much—maybe forty grand this year—and that's because they haven't got any sales staff. With our sales staff, they can't lose.

"I've got this plan, see?" Ackerman went on. "What we've been doing is, we've got all these different sales staffs selling the different magazines as though they didn't have any connection with each other. Now my plan is: the Curtis Network." (*Joe Culligan used to have that theory,* I thought again, but this time I kept it to myself.) "It's sort of like a triangle, see? At the bottom, the *Ladies' Home Journal* can be the big family magazine at six- or seven-million circulation. Then comes the *Post,* politics and Americana and all that, at about three million, and slightly higher demography. Then *Holiday* at one million—when I get it fixed up so that it's the magazine of leisure, top demography. And then comes *Status,* the real status magazine, the jewel in the crown, with maybe 200,000 circulation, absolutely top quality, nobody making less than twenty-five grand a year."

It was characteristic of Ackerman that he always had a theory to explain and justify every move he made, and that most of his theories were quite sound. Obviously, a salesman who could offer an advertiser a whole array of magazines and a whole spectrum of audiences and demographies could sell space with great efficiency. But after one had heard a certain number of Ackerman's theories, one began to judge each new offering with a certain skepticism. I had no doubt that the gleam I had seen in Ackerman's eye was the gleam of acquisitive passion, and yet I couldn't help comparing his delight over *Status* to his more moderate enthusiasm about another acquisition he had recently made.

McKinney and I had encountered him in an elevator a few weeks earlier, and he had smiled with that grimace we had already come to recognize as a sign that he had just figured out some profitable deal that he was not really proud of. "What you guys don't know about the publishing business!" he had said, shaking his head sadly. "I've just been talking to this guy who publishes more than twenty magazines, comic books, things you never heard of, and he makes a couple of million dollars' profit every year. We're going to buy his whole company."

The man's name was Martin Goodman, and his company was called Magazine Management, Inc., and the magazines included *For Men Only, Stag, Men, True Action, Man's World, Screen Stars, My Confession, Movie World, Laugh Parade,* and *Complete Crosswords,* plus the comic books, *Marvel Tales, Fantastic Four, Strange Tales, The Avengers, The Amazing Spider Man.* Ackerman did take over this company, but very quietly. He made no move to merge it into the Curtis publishing empire, and he never mentioned it as part of his "Curtis Network." *Status,* by contrast, appeared to be not just a financial proposition but a source of personal prestige. Perhaps Ackerman, alone of all the magazine's 145,000 readers, took Cassini's title at face value.

"You have an editor in mind?" I asked.

"Yeah. Frank Zachary." Once again, as when he had first spoken the name of his new magazine, we stared at one another, I with an obvious lack of enthusiasm, he with a defensive belligerence. I had nothing in particular against Zachary—a stout, ducklike man of about fifty, who looked rather like a David Levine caricature of himself— but he was now in his second term as the art director of *Holiday,* and I was convinced that no magazine run by an art director could ever amount to much. Ackerman quickly admitted that he had doubts of his own. "Zachary doesn't want to be an art director for the rest of his life. He wants to edit his own magazine. So can he do it? Hell, I don't know. Maybe I'm making a mistake, but I figure it's worth a try."

Regardless of what Zachary might accomplish, the prospects of the magazine, and of the Curtis network, depended on Ackerman's plans for selling ads, and his plans were to rely on the same ragged system that was failing to sell even the *Post.* It was failing for the most fundamental of all reasons for organizational decay—a steady decline in the quantity and quality of the staff. Back in the days of Joe Culligan, there may have been too many advertising executives getting in one another's way, but since Culligan's departure, there had been four years of attrition. The only newcomer of any note had been Steve Kelly, and his arrival had led to the departure of key executives, first at *Holiday* and then at the *Post.* In that last *Putsch* against Jess Ballew, the victim's two chief deputies had both been promoted, Jack Connors to replace Kelly as publisher of *Holiday* and Joe Welty to replace Connors as advertising director of the *Post.* And then, just three weeks after Ackerman's arrival, Welty resigned his new position for the less prestigious but presumably more secure job of advertising director of *House Beautiful.* This left the *Post* without any advertising director at all, and when I asked Kelly who his choice would be, he affected great annoyance at my impertinence. "I mean that's just not a problem at all," he said. And while the advertising revenue kept going down and down, Kelly never again filled the job.

Ackerman did not consider this a problem either, for he had already selected a new advertising director, himself. As early as that first meeting at the Brussels restaurant, Ackerman had succumbed to the ad salesmen's argument that he alone could explain the new regime and the new *Post* to America's captains of industry. "No door," Joe Culligan had said, "is ever closed to the president of the Curtis

Publishing Company." And so Ackerman had started out with appointments in Chicago and Detroit and any other city where the ad salesmen called to his ambitions.

It is still a mystery how anyone sells ads, because it is still a mystery how advertising itself sells goods to potential customers. "I know half the money I spend on advertising is wasted," John Wanamaker once said, "but I can never find out which half." Because of this uncertainty, different salesmen have developed different approaches. They may be summarized under five broad categories.

The first approach is pure numbers. One magazine has more readers than another, and the ad salesman promises that, for a price, a certain number of people will see the ad. This provides the most basic advertising measurement, cost per thousand, known in the business as CPM. The fact that CPM provides a measurement means that it rules against some people—television, for example, provides larger audiences at a lower CPM than any magazine—and the losers naturally want to change the rules. Among magazines, *Life* demonstrated that picture magazines get passed around in barbershops, and *Life*'s "passalong readership" thus gave it a "reach" or "total audience" about five times as large as its circulation. The *Post,* by contrast, argued that the advertiser got little benefit from one flickering glance by a skimming viewer; new tests showed that an average reader spent more time with a text magazine (and its ads) than with a picture magazine. Despite all this, CPM is still basic.

The second approach is demography. The salesman demonstrates to the advertiser that he is wasting money by sponsoring TV commercials addressed to millions of people who don't want his product. The salesman promises that his magazine can provide a better "demographic audience," which is usually described in terms of the magic words, "young," "urban," "sophisticated," and "affluent." Specifically, these terms are defined as follows: "Young" means that a known number of the magazine's readers are between eighteen and thirty-four; "urban" means that a certain number live in the A. C. Nielsen Company's nationwide list of A and B counties; "sophisticated" means that a certain number went to college; "affluent" means that a certain number earn more than $10,000 a year. For any mass magazine, the actual figures in these categories are depressing. In a 1964 Politz study of eleven large magazines, for instance, *Life* had the best demography, and yet only 35 percent of its readers had finished college (12.5 percent hadn't gone beyond grade school), and only 28.9 percent earned more than $10,000 (21.6 percent earned less than $5,000). The chief beneficiaries of the demographic arguments are smaller or more specialized magazines—*Time* and *Newsweek*, *Esquire* and *Scientific American*—which have prospered during a period of general magazine decline.

The third approach, much favored by those who don't like to talk about numbers or don't have persuasive numbers to talk about, is "editorial vitality." In principle, the advertising salesman is only selling space in the magazine that his editors produce, and therefore advertising will theoretically be attracted to well-edited magazines. In fact, however, no advertiser has any way of knowing what will be in the issue that contains his ad, and advertisers are not great readers anyway. "Editorial vitality," therefore, consists mostly of buying expensive books for serialization and then taking big ads to boast about them.

The fourth approach is to be fashionable. Madison Avenue people like to think of themselves as fashionable, or at least aware of what is considered fashionable. This approach is related to the third, since "editorial vitality" is considered fashionable, but a magazine can also acquire a reputation as a "hot book" simply because people regard it as a success. The best example in recent years, probably, is *Playboy*.

The fifth approach, when all else fails, is to sell ads by making friends with the advertisers. It is hard to estimate how much advertising is sold by sheer charm, but apparently enough to support a whole way of life—expensive lunches, evenings at the theater, repeated trips to the golf course. "Media buying remains as personal a matter as anything else in advertising," Martin Mayer observed in his book, *Madison Avenue, U.S.A.*, "a business of hunches and intuitions, of favors done and favors received."

When it came to selling advertising in the *Post*, none of these approaches worked very well, and they hadn't for years. The circulation wars of the 1950's had ended with the *Post* far behind *Life* and *Look*, and demographic surveys indicated that its readers were older, poorer, more rural, less educated. Some critics liked to blame this on the magazine itself, but magazines are bought and sold like any other commodity, and circulation is gained or lost according to the amount of money and energy invested in it. High-demography circulation is expensive to acquire, so Curtis had saved money by not acquiring it. As for "editorial vitality," or being fashionable, many people still thought of the *Post* in terms of Norman Rockwell, others in terms of Clay Blair's "sophisticated muckraking," and Curtis again saved money by not taking ads to promote itself. Not only was the *Post* not fashionable, it was so damaged by the company's recent history of instability that some advertisers actually feared to place orders. In explanation, they sometimes cited David Ogilvy's malicious comment,

"Nobody likes to have his ad appear in the last issue of a magazine."

Without facts or fashion to support their arguments, left with little except their desire to be friendly, the *Post* salesmen had become a dispirited lot, far more despondent than the most mournful editors. A number of the good ones had already gone to happier companies, and the rest simply waited for help to come from somewhere. Ackerman, knowing that they had been deprived of their golfing trip to Ponte Vedra, Florida, summoned them all to New York for a series of conferences at the Drake Hotel. We met for lunch in the hotel's discothèque, Shepheard's, decorated with palm fronds, and sphinxes staring from the pillars. And in that bizarre setting, Ackerman addressed us as though he were Lord Nelson.

"This magazine *will* be successful," he cried into the microphone. "Not this year, of course, but the work we're doing right now will *assure* us of a profitable year in 1969. And I'm not just guessing or predicting. I'm telling you!"

The weary, middle-aged faces began almost perceptibly to regain a little life. An awed silence spread through the room as the salesmen listened eagerly to every word of hope.

"There will be some cost-cutting," Ackerman said, "but this will be a streamlining operation. It will make us more efficient. It will help us to make money in 1969. We *will* be successful!"

The salesmen got no time off, no rest or recreation. That afternoon, they had to hear more speeches, by G.B. and Kelly and Emerson, and then a dinner address by the head of a large advertising agency, B.B.D. & O. Deprived of their golf, the salesmen had nothing to occupy them that night but cards and whiskey, and some of them were a little red-eyed the next morning, but the sales meetings resumed promptly at nine. Emerson and McKinney and I were organized into a sort of task force that moved from group to group, answering any questions the salesmen might have about the "evolutionary" *Post* we had just begun publishing. And then, back in Shepheard's for lunch, we heard G.B. make a speech in honor of Ackerman, in terms that used to be characteristic of *Pravda* on Stalin's birthdays. Never in G.B.'s long memory had Curtis had such leadership, such opportunities, such a glowing future. And all of us would have to work harder to be worthy of our new president. With that, the salesmen were all sent back to the battlefields to resume the struggle.

There is one other way to sell advertising. It is a rather unreliable method, like poison gas, and many publishers avoid it as much as they can. But, again like poison gas, it does work. And so I learned from Emerson that Ackerman had promised some executives in charge of Ford advertising that the *Post* would put Henry Ford's picture on the cover of its October 5 issue.

I realized that it was too late to talk about ethics, and so I tried to argue in terms of commerce.

"General Motors isn't going to like that," I said.

"That's the first thing I said to Ackerman," Emerson said. "So we decided to put the heads of all four auto companies on the cover. After all, Marty didn't tell the Ford people what else might be on the cover."

"But we do have readers, too, and they're not going to want to buy a magazine with four fat businessmen on the cover."

"I'm sorry, but I can't help that now," Emerson said. "By now, they're already selling Ford the whole inside of a gatefold cover."

"Well, think about this as an alternative," I said. "Why couldn't we put the new cars on the cover instead? That's what the companies want to sell, and that's what the readers are interested in. Then maybe we could put the businessmen on the inside of the gatefold."

This was obviously the right solution, so Emerson suggested that we present it to Ackerman. We did, and Ackerman vetoed it.

"Look, this is what happened," he said. "I was out there myself, selling ads for the auto issue—that's sometime in October, when the new models come out—and the top ad guy for Ford said they'd decided to take all their ads out of that issue. He said the future of the *Post* was just too uncertain. Well, I told him everything I could think of, but it just didn't have any effect. He kept saying the *Post* was too uncertain. And this wasn't just a couple of pages, this was $400,000 worth of advertising. So I said, 'You know, I really can't understand why you'd take all your advertising out of this issue when we're going to have Mr. Ford's picture on the cover. I mean, Mr. Ford might not like that.' So he did a sort of double take—boy, you should have seen that double take—and he said, 'Well, maybe you're right. Maybe we'd better leave the ads in that issue.' So you see? I've got to have Ford himself on that cover."

If we must, we must. But I couldn't help thinking that this issue would be an embarrassing failure on the newsstands, and an even more embarrassing success on Madison Avenue. To anyone connected with advertising, I thought, a picture of four auto magnates on the cover of an issue filled with auto ads would mean that the cover of the *Post* was for sale. In this case, the price had been $400,000. In future cases, it would be subject to negotiation. As these thoughts occurred to me, I also remembered two previous episodes.

"This magazine has got to swing, like other magazines swing," Ackerman had once said, and he had not meant simply that it should be fashionable but that it should be aware of the way society moved. He was speaking of a concept of business in which everything was negotiable, not just value for value but favor for favor. "You know why that story in *Time* was written that way?" he asked, referring to a favorable story about his move into Curtis. "Because they're doing business with me, that's why." On another occasion, he expressed a similar judgment on *Life*. "I know lots of stories that got written, but once they got up to the business office, they never got published," he said. I did not believe him, but it seemed useless to argue at the time. He was new to the publishing business, and we were new to each other, and my denials of his accusations against other publishers would have had little effect. The point was that he did not think his statements were accusations at all; he did not see anything wrong with editors "bending to the profit," as he put it. That was simply the way business was done, in publishing as in anything else, and anybody who thought differently was naïve.

From time to time, Ackerman would disappear for a day or two, and nobody seemed to know his whereabouts more specifically than "somewhere on the Coast" or "out of the country." Then we would read in the *Wall Street Journal* that he had bought or sold something, as, on July 15, we read that he had bought a film-processing company for $11 million in cash. And on the next day, he would dart into my office, firing questions: "What's up? What's going on? Anything happening?"

"Nothing much," I said on this occasion. "What's with you? I hear you just bought another company."

"Yeah," he said, grinning. "I have to buy companies like that to support the *Post*. Listen, it's a fantastic situation. This guy just puts a couple of ads in the papers, and he grosses $16 million a year, without really doing much of anything, and $3 million of that is profit. And here we are busting our asses trying to put out this magazine, and we can't make any money on it. I tell you, it's a commentary on our whole society!"

"Swinging," as a way of life, implies a certain kind of misbehavior, but nobody will admit there is anything improper.

We were talking again about what had already come to be known as "the auto issue," and Ackerman suggested that we include a long and rather critical article that Richard Whalen had written about the highway program.

"The Ford people aren't going to like that," I said.

"Listen, Otto, I do not want an ass-kissing auto issue," Ackerman said. "I want a group of articles about automobiles, but I want them to be honest articles."

"That sounds great," I said, "but what's the point of putting Henry Ford on the cover to make them happy and then putting something on the inside that will make them mad? I mean, we might as well not have started on this project in the first place."

"Well, how about something with some real ideas, by somebody like Galbraith," Ackerman said.

"They're not going to like that either," I said. "Galbraith is liable to say something unkind about automobiles."

"Well, I don't give a damn what you do," Ackerman said. "But it better be good. I don't want it to be like—[here he named another magazine]. They're just pimps to the auto industry."

"But this year we're challenging their supremacy in that field," I said.

"Okay, be a wise guy," Ackerman said. "But I've told you, this magazine has got to swing."

The auto issue was still several weeks in the future. We were working on the September 7 issue, and Ackerman wasn't satisfied with the lead. I showed him a different one, but that didn't satisfy him either. I offered him yet another, and he agreed to it, but only reluctantly.

"My theory is," he said, "that every issue has got to be better than the previous one."

"But listen, Marty," I said, "that theory has got to come to a breaking point."

"I know," he said.

"There comes a time when a new issue simply can't be better than the last one. It's got to be worse."

"Okay, okay," he said. "But we've got to make this one better because I'm fighting for my life."

These were new words, and spoken in a new tone, quite different from the rash enthusiasm that we had heard in his various speeches. "He told me," Emerson said later that day, "that he wakes up in the middle of the night in a cold sweat about this company."

With the passing of every week, every million-dollar payroll, every money-losing issue of the Curtis magazines, Marty Ackerman was seeing with increasing clarity that he had acquired not just a company with some troubles but an insatiable monster. Only four years ago, after all, a buried mountain of copper and zinc had been discovered in Ontario and sold for $24 million, and the monster had already swallowed all of that. Now it stood ready to devour Marty Ackerman and his chauffeured Cadillac and his house in Roslyn and his little film company and the bank he had bought for his children.

In the spring, he had thought that his arrival, his investment of new capital, his talk of editorial "evolution," would all help to bring back the advertisers, and that he could ride forth and sell the advertising himself. By July, however, he began to realize that the audience on Madison Avenue enjoyed and applauded his antics but had no intention of supporting the *Post*. Two months had been spent on the "A" issues, and now another two months had passed, and there still weren't many ads, and the accountants informed him that the extra costs of the "A" issues and the eighty-four-page minimum since then had amounted to about $1 million. "And then he had lunch with some old friend in the ad business," Emerson said. "I don't know who it was—maybe Bill Bernbach—but somebody he trusted. And this guy told Marty that nobody on Madison Avenue really gave much of a goddamn about him or his new *Post* or his press conferences or any of the rest of it. And that really shook him, because he'd gotten so happy with his book of press clippings that he couldn't believe everybody didn't love him. So what he says now is: 'We're going to wait just a couple more weeks to see whether Steverino can hack it. And if that doesn't work, we'll have to consider the disaster plan.' "

Ackerman's disaster plan for the coming year, as Emerson defined it on this first occasion, consisted of cutting the *Post* to a skeleton staff, "just McKinney and Ewald and a handful of others putting out a semblance of a magazine." The following week, Emerson heard a few more details. Ackerman's computer had proposed specific figures. "Could you cut the payroll by 50 percent and the materials by 33 percent?" Ackerman asked. Emerson said he could not, and I agreed. But what we said was not strictly true. We could indeed make cuts of this size, but only by making radical changes in the nature of the *Post*. Lorimer himself, after all, had not always been a distributor of largess. There had been times, back at the start of the century, when the *Post* paid very little and was content to publish what it could afford. The same was true of newer magazines. Henry Luce and Britton Hadden had founded *Time* in a basement apartment, and Hugh Hefner had dummied the first issues of *Playboy* on a kitchen table. At the other extreme, there were magazines like *Coronet* and

Pageant, which, having died, lived on as zombies, recreated in cheaper forms by other publishers. And so, although it would have been possible to cut the *Post*'s editorial budget almost in half, it would have been very difficult to keep together enough of a staff to produce the kind of magazine that Ackerman said he wanted. "Even Potemkin villages need a certain amount of paint," I said to Emerson. "Otherwise, the empress will suddenly say, 'Potemkin, those are the worst-looking villages I've ever seen. In fact, they're practically slums.'"

Ackerman had an appointment with Senator Harris of Oklahoma, and he invited me to come along. I declined because I was going to the opera. Rossini's *Otello*. It was a cue that Ackerman could not resist.

"We have season tickets at the Met," he said.

"I've about given up even trying to get to the Met," I said. "They always seem to be sold out two weeks before they even announce what the opera is."

"Yeah, I know, but somebody told me that the way to get in is to become a patron, so I became a patron."

"What does that cost you, about a million dollars?"

"No, just a thousand."

"And then what happens?"

"Then you get tickets."

At the beginning of August, nothing short of war could stop Emerson from taking his family back to Georgia for the month. And so, when Ackerman next wanted to talk about the disaster plan, the only audience he could find was me.

The disaster plan, I soon learned, was much more elaborate than anything I had heard from Emerson. It began with—was rooted in—a passionate sense of loss. "By now I've put seven *million* dollars of my own money into this f—— company," Ackerman said, "and it's all gone, down the drain. Which is exactly what I said was not going to happen." It was this sense of personal loss that filled him with such an unreasoning anger against the secretaries whom he passed in the corridor every morning, gossiping, like secretaries everywhere, on the telephone. And in Philadelphia, the bureaucracy had taken the previous month's blow of the ax and then, hydra-like, begun to heal itself. "They've been hiring people back, secretly," Ackerman said. "We've *got* to make this company more flexible, and that means cutting the fixed costs. But in all the work I've done so far, I've only managed to get rid of a hundred people out of the whole five thousand." This, too, filled him with anger, and a desire to cut harder.

"I think I've got to get rid of the whole corporate superstructure," he said, "There's just no room for G.B. and all those people. And all those regional sales bureaus." *No room for G.B.? I thought. After all those thirty-eight years of smiling and trying to be agreeable—no room?*

"I think I've got to fold the *Journal* too, or else sell it," Ackerman said.

"I thought the *Journal* was one of the few things around here that made money," I said.

"Yeah, but not much. See, I'm probably going to have to shut down the printing plant, because once we cut back on the *Post*, then the plant loses money. And our plant is the only one that can print the *Journal*, so the *Journal* is what's keeping us at the plant."

"Why can't you print the *Journal* somewhere else, at Donnelley or McCall's?"

"Because they won't take it unless we pay for the new presses they'd need to handle it."

At the time, the conversation was going too quickly for me to follow all the implications of Ackerman's reasoning, but even then the sequence of closings seemed bizarre. According to his argument, the reduction of *Post* circulation would put the printing plant at Sharon Hill so irremediably into the red that it would have to be liquidated. And because Sharon Hill printed the *Journal*, the *Journal* had to be disposed of. If this was true, how could such an obvious set of developments have been miscalculated at the time Ackerman decided to reduce the *Post* circulation? In fact, however, Ackerman's information was at least partly wrong. ("I can never get the right figures around here," he complained periodically.) It turned out later that the McCall plant was quite capable of printing the *Journal*, and at a lower rate than the Curtis plant charged. And it was only then that the idled printing plant was shut down by Ackerman's successors.

As for the *Post*, it would simply have to find a new break-even level. Ackerman was already tired of soliciting ads. "I'm not going to go on sucking around for advertisers," he said. "Screw that." Instead, he had decided to start making the readers pay for the magazine— finally—by subscriptions at eight dollars instead of the present four dollars (often discounted to two dollars). But it would take time to win new subscribers and work off the old ones, and until this new course became profitable, the costs would have to be cut. "I believe in the philosophy of pay as you go," Ackerman said. "The *Post* will have to find a level where it can pay its own way."

"Now we've fed all these figures into the computer," Ackerman went on, "and, as I told Emerson, the figures show that we should cut the *Post* payroll by 50 percent and materials used by 33 percent. Now can you do that and still maintain the quality at the same level as what we've been publishing?"

"No," I said. "You can cut as much as you want, but you're going to be cutting the quality too."

"Well, how much can you cut?"

"I don't know. I wouldn't know until I tried it."

"Okay, good, then that's settled," Ackerman said, and I realized that I was agreeing to what Emerson had already rejected.

"Wait a minute," I said. "All I've said is that we can try. And I'm saying that on the assumption that either I say it or you find somebody else, or the magazine gets shut down. Is that it?"

"That's it," Ackerman said. There was a pause, and then he added dreamily: "You know, sometimes I plan this all the way to the ultimate cut. You know what the ultimate cut is? That's when I go down to Philadelphia myself, and I stand in front of the plant, and whenever anybody comes out, I hand them a paycheck, and I say, 'That's it. Good-bye. Don't come back.' To everybody. Every single one of them. And then I lock up the building, and I sell it as real estate."

Ackerman wandered into the office of Frank Kilker, who had replaced Asger Jerrild as art director, and saw on the cork wall the cover of the September 21 issue. It was a greenish painting of Fran Tarkenton throwing a pass, to illustrate our condensation of Eliot Asinof's book on the New York Giants, *Seven Days to Sunday*.

"That really is great, but why have you only got half of it?" Ackerman asked. He took the picture down from the wall and unfolded it so that the opened-up gatefold showed Homer Jones charging downfield to catch Tarkenton's pass.

"Because they couldn't sell the inside of the gatefold," Kilker said.

"Well, they've got to sell the gatefold," Ackerman said. "Where's Kelly?"

Kelly happened to be sitting morosely in a nearby office, telling his sorrows to Don McKinney, and so he was brought in to defend himself.

"Now look, Marty," Kelly protested, "the boys did everything they could. They tried everybody."

"Listen, I want that gatefold sold, if I have to buy it myself," Ackerman said. "Better, I'll sell it myself. I'll show you."

"But today is the deadline," said the former Rita Ortiga, now Rita Waterman.

"Okay, I'll sell it before the end of the afternoon," Ackerman said. And within an hour, he had sold it.

From the *Gallagher Report*, August 13:

"MORTICIAN MARTY" ACKERMAN PEDDLES CURTIS MAGA-ZINES. Needs money. Curtis president offers Ladies' Home Journal, American Home as package. Marty gave Time Inc. president Jim Linen first refusal. . . . Jim turned down deal. Marty approached McCall Corp., Cowles Communications, Times Mirror Co., National Periodical Publications (Kinney subsidiary). Marty mentions no price. Plays buyers off against each other. LHJ income provides $1.6 million surplus after operating expenses, breaks even with inclusion of corporate expenses. American Home breaks even on operations, loses money after corporate expenses. . . .

I came out of the office one evening and encountered the small and fugitive figure of John Mack Carter, editor and publisher of the *Journal,* standing on the corner of Lexington and Fifty-fourth Street and waving vainly for a cab.

"Hello, John Mack, how're things?" I said. Carter paused a moment and looked me up and down to make sure I was friendly, and then he smiled and said, "If I told you, I'd be lying."

Two days later, the *Wall Street Journal* broke the news that the Curtis board was to meet to consider "several offers" for the *Journal* and *American Home.* The only offer that was publicly identified came from Downe Communications, Inc., proposing a swap of 100,000 shares of its own stock, a market value of about $5.4 million. The story pointedly recalled that Ackerman had "stated as recently as May 15 that 'we're not selling any of our magazines,' " and then added that Ackerman "said his decision to sell the magazines was based on a conviction that Curtis should concentrate on publishing magazines for 'class' rather than 'mass' audiences."

That same morning, Peter Wyden, executive editor of the *Journal,* came to work early. "It wasn't even eight o'clock yet, maybe 7:55," he said later, "and as I rounded the corner of Lexington Avenue and Fifty-fourth Street, who should I see come out of the Curtis building, in his blue shirtsleeves, but Martin S. Ackerman? He came out to the curb, and he looked up at the sky, and then he went back inside again, and I couldn't help thinking, 'He looks just like the owner of a supermarket going outside his store to look at the weather to see if the ladies are going to come and get today's special in tomatoes.' "

In that day's special, Curtis gave up its two most profitable magazines and acquired in exchange 9 percent of the outstanding stock of
Downe Communications, Inc., a company which was best known as
the publisher of *Family Weekly*, the newspaper supplement, but
which also held a large share of Bartell Media Corporation and its
collection of movie and detective magazines. These interests, Ackerman said loftily, put Downe "in a better position to develop the
magazines than Curtis." In addition, Downe owned such miscellany
as Jacquet, Inc., a cosmetics company; Greenland Studios and Madison House, two mail-order merchandisers; Zenith Industries, a pet
supply company, and a magazine called *Cat Fancy*.

The thirty-nine-year-old builder of this empire, Edward R. Downe,
Jr., once a staff member at *True* and *Argosy*, seemed to be living a
life even more frenetic than that of Marty Ackerman.

Mr. Downe is usually at his desk by 7 A.M. and often has two breakfast
meetings because he gets to work so early [the *Times* reported]. He works
late too, seldom leaving until long past the normal dinner hour. "I'm 39
mentally but 80 physically because I work so long and so hard," he
said. Why does he work so long and intensely? Mr. Downe explained it
this way: "If you want to get ahead these days you've got to do it in your
own business and do it when you are young enough. And the reason you
have to be young is because you must be willing to work three times as
hard as the next guy."

"The real question with people like this," said Peter Wyden, "with
Martin S. Ackerman, thirty-six, or Edward R. Downe, thirty-seven, or
whatever he is, is: *What does he want to be when he grows up?* Press
lord? Great liquidator? Conglomerate king? What? The trouble with
these people is that they don't know themselves, half the time. But as
far as I can see, so far, Ackerman is just holding an auction, one
thing at a time. And I think that if he could find anybody who would
take the *Post* off his hands, even for *nothing,* he'd be happy to wrap it
up in some old newspapers and deliver it."

It was traditional, during the Clifford years, for bills to go unpaid
during the middle of the month, particularly in late summer. Writers
and agents would call and complain, and we would offer vague
excuses about the bureaucracy in Philadelphia, about the accounting
department being short-staffed because of vacations, about checks
being somewhere in transit between Philadelphia and New York. On
about the first of every month, some advertising revenue would come
in, and the accountants would rush to clear up the backlog of unpaid

bills. Now, however, we learned from our chief bookkeeper, Elena Dardano, that no bills had been paid since July 23, almost a month earlier, and that the August 1 revenues had all been turned over to other departments.

I asked Ackerman what he wanted us to do about this.

"Stall 'em as long as you can," he said, picking at his teeth. He found some cigar debris and spat it out on the floor.

"Well, look," I said, "here's Milton Viorst, who wrote the story on Mayor Daley in the August 24 issue, which is already out on the newsstands. What am I supposed to tell him?"

"If it's a special case, give me a memo on it, and I'll see that it's taken care of."

Ackerman had always been high-strung, but now he seemed more nervous than ever. He spoke in short bursts, and his head twitched from side to side. He seemed irresistibly attracted to my Scotch tape dispenser, which he kept unrolling, two or three inches at a time. He would tear off a short segment of tape and roll it between his fingers, while he spoke, until it was reduced to a shiny little ball. Then he would drop the ball into my ashtray and tear off a new strip of tape.

"Listen, that's all secondary," he said. "The main thing is that I'm going to have to get moving with the budget cuts I told you about."

"I thought that was for next year," I said.

"Next year nothing. The deadline is going to be September 30."

"You mean you want to put that 1969 austerity budget into effect for the last quarter of 1968, is that it?"

"That's it, exactly."

The next afternoon, he was in my office again, tearing at the Scotch tape dispenser again, and talking about money.

"I tell you, Otto, there's no f—— money," he said. "There's just no f—— money."

The tone in his voice was unmistakable. Ackerman was exasperated, but underneath that exasperation lay fear.

"I've put five million of my own f—— money into this f—— company, and it's all gone," he said. "I've got maybe two million more, and that's it."

I couldn't help remembering that Ackerman had told me quite recently that he had already put seven million, rather than five, into Curtis. On the other hand, a week after telling me that he had only two million more to invest, he told me that he had invested another five million. I began to realize that Ackerman's sense of numbers was not that of an accountant, for whom two and two always make four, but more nearly that of an advanced mathematician, for whom numbers form a language, capable of expressing an emotion or a view of the world. Our children nowadays are taught a "new math" in which arithmetic equations are said to represent "sentences." To convey an opinion, then, "I've put five million into this f—— company" is probably just as accurate a mathematical sentence as "I've put seven million into this f—— company."

Embittered and frightened, Ackerman turned once again to the hated payroll, and to the plan that would eviscerate the monster. Throughout the company, he said, he would ultimately cut the number of employees from more than five thousand to about eight hundred.

"Have you given any thought to the problem?" he asked.

"Sure, I've given it a lot of thought," I said.

"Okay, can you start cutting people next week?"

"I guess so, but I've got to talk to Emerson first."

"Talk to Emerson, then, but let's get going."

Now that the deadline had been set, I worried, while I tried to reach Emerson in Georgia, whether I had made a mistake in dutifully promising to carry out Ackerman's demands, whether Emerson's habitual tactics of delay and circumspection might not be a wiser course. And if we cut the staff, were we doing it to save the *Post* or simply to provide Ackerman with a cheaper product to sell to somebody else?

When I finally reached Emerson and told him of Ackerman's demands, his first reaction was one of despair.

"Maybe this is the time we should both get out, while it's still a respectable magazine," he said.

"Well, okay, but I'm going on the assumption that if we both walk out, the magazine will die, so do you want to make this the moment to kill it?"

Emerson agreed to fly north over the weekend and fire whoever had to be fired.

And still the struggle to sell advertising continued. Emerson had told Ackerman at some point that we were going to publish a long article by John Gregory Dunne about the recovery of Twentieth Century Fox, and Ackerman had promptly turned that prospect into "our movie issue." In the past, he had often requested that a major article be ornamented by secondary stories (like the presidential candidates' responses to the problem of the ghetto), and now he wanted coverage on the other big studios and their top executives. This time, however, his reasons were not purely editorial. "You know what I'm going to do with those guys?" he asked me in an unguarded moment. "I'm going to sell an ad to every single one of them." Having boasted that he would sell these ads himself, he then gave Steve Kelly a list of Hollywood executives who would figure prominently in "our movie issue" and told Kelly to go and sell ads to them. Kelly called me to ask what I specifically planned to do about this list of executives, and I said I hadn't seen any such list and hadn't yet made any plans at all.

"I guess I'd better wait a while, then," Kelly said sarcastically, "before anybody tells them we're putting them on the cover or something."

"Right," I said.

On Emerson's return from Georgia, he agreed to Ackerman's demands for a staff cut, but I had been worrying more and more about the course we were taking, and I had decided to tell Ackerman that we didn't want to fire a lot of people if the magazine we were trying to salvage would prove unworthy of respect.

"I don't know what you mean by that," Ackerman said.

"I mean there's no point in saving the *Post* if it's going to publish schlock issues on Hollywood with pages full of pictures of all the advertisers."

"Well, let's get this straight now," Ackerman said, the hackles rising, and we both knew that I had finally opened the argument that had hovered unspoken between us since the first time we met. "Is it your idea that there's something wrong about our going to the people who are the most interested in our Hollywood issue and trying to sell them some pages?"

"Yes, I do," I said.

"What?"

"Yes, I do think it's wrong."

"Well, you're just crazy!" Ackerman cried in disbelief. "There's nothing wrong with it at all. How can you say it's wrong?"

"It just isn't done," I said doggedly.

"Oh, that's what you think!" Ackerman retorted. "How about the *New York Times*? That's good enough for you, isn't it? And you don't think they do things like that?"

"No."

"Hey, where have you been all these years? How do you think they sell all those travel ads every Sunday? And those real-estate ads? And those special supplements on spring fashions? You think those things

just happen by themselves? You think those advertisers would put
their ads in just any old section?"

"Well, I don't think those Sunday sections count as the real *Times*,"
I said, without much conviction.

"Seems to me they're as real as anything else," Ackerman said. By
now he was quite agitated, and he repeatedly took pieces of copy
paper from Emerson's desk and began tearing them up into small
pieces, folding the pieces, then tearing some more.

"The only thing that worries me," he said. "You know the only
thing that worries me? That the advertisers may look at the magazine
someday and say it's not good enough. That's the only thing that
worries me, that it's not good enough."

"Well, okay," I said, "but the basic fact is that you're telling us
what to do with editorial pages, and then you're selling ads against
those pages, and that's just bad policy—"

"I am not doing that—" Ackerman broke in.

"—because it means you're giving away editorial pages to the
advertisers."

"I am not doing that," Ackerman repeated. "I am not selling ads
against editorial pages."

"You are too," I said. "You told Kelly to sell ads to all those guys
who were going to have their pictures in the magazine."

"Well—" Ackerman said, thinking quickly, tearing at the folded
bits of paper. "I didn't tell you what to say about them. You can't give
me one example where I ever told you to say something on the editorial pages for business reasons."

"Why, sure I can. The whole auto issue—"

"I didn't tell you what to say in the auto issue. You could have said
anything you wanted to. All I said was, I wanted some articles on
automobiles, and what's wrong with that? People like to read about
the new cars. I like to read about the new cars. Is that supposed to be
some kind of—uh—prostelation? Tell me what's so terrible?"

"You said we couldn't put the new cars on the cover. We had to put
Henry Ford on the cover because you'd promised it to the Ford advertising people. And I wasn't the only one who was appalled. The whole
staff was appalled."

"Now look, we can talk about all this in terms of your integrity or
my integrity or we can talk about it in terms of keeping the magazine
alive. So I don't see how anybody can accuse me of prostelizing,
because I have just as much integrity as you do, Otto, just as much,
every bit as much, and maybe more than a lot of your editors—"

"Let's not get into a personal argument," I said. "The Ford thing happened once, and I realize it was a time of crisis, and it's all over now. But what I'm trying to warn you against is doing that kind of thing as a matter of regular policy."

"Well, if you guys want to edit a magazine just for yourselves, then you should put up the millions of dollars that it costs to publish a magazine, and then there wouldn't be any complaints. I wouldn't complain."

"Why would I want to edit a magazine for myself?"

"But if you want to work in the magazine business, then you've got to learn about business, because every editor in the magazine business has got to work one-third for the readers, one-third for the company itself and one-third for the advertisers—that's the way I see it—and anybody who calls that proselyting just doesn't know what the hell he's talking about!"

"Let's not get sore, Marty," I said.

"I'm not sore. But I'm just telling you that certain things are going to be done around here, whether you like it or not, and it's very simple—you can decide any time whether you want to go along or whether you want to leave."

"I know that perfectly well," I retorted.

"Well, okay, then," Ackerman said and looked at Emerson and laughed harshly. Now that he had reminded me once again of his wealth, now that he had asserted his prerogatives by threatening me, now that he had proclaimed his integrity and his innocence of prostitution, a word that his lips seemed unwilling to pronounce, he soon lapsed into an amiable exhaustion. The table in front of him was littered with bits of torn and folded paper. "I mean, I've got no hard feelings," he said. "You understand. We've got tough times ahead of us, and we've all got lots of work to do. Right?"

A "consent decree" in antitrust litigation has been defined as a document in which the defendant corporation denies that it has done anything wrong but promises to stop doing it. Ackerman, having stated his case and rendered a judgment in his own favor, never again mentioned the idea of using the editorial pages for the benefit of the advertisers. If he had ideas along those lines—and I suspect he did—he kept them to himself.

"Well, Jack Connors just got dumped," Emerson said.

"How did that happen?" I asked.

"Ackerman wants to merge the sales staffs of the *Post* and *Holiday*, and Kelly and Connors were both told to say what they'd do as Number One, and I guess Kelly came out on top." And so, with the departure of the publisher of *Holiday,* the twelfth of Clay Blair's fifteen rebels to go, we began the second great Ackerman purge.

Cutting a staff is not really as painful as one might think. One starts by drawing up a list of those who must go, and one can judge fairly easily where the surplus is—a department that is obviously overstaffed, another that isn't really needed at all, and a few people who were never much good anyway, who had stayed on largely because it was easier to keep them than to find replacements. Contemplating the list of expendables, and adding up their salaries, one soon convinces oneself, with the logic of the homicidal maniac, that the dismissals should have taken place long ago, that the victims have been wasting the company's money for too long, that it is an act of moral justice to dispose of them. At the same time, one convinces oneself, and not without good reason, that the victims will all do better elsewhere. After all, these are times of full employment, and many companies pay higher wages, and change is always invigorating.

We started with an added advantage because of the attrition that had worn down the staff during the past year. Asger Jerrild, for example, had never really been replaced on the payroll, since we had simply given the title of art director to Frank Kilker. Joe Sapinsky, the photography editor, had been replaced by a younger man who got barely half of Sapinsky's pay. Tom Congdon had been offered a good job at Harper & Row, and he had decided to move onward. Jeannette Sarkisian Wagner had gone to *Cosmopolitan* as articles editor. Mike Mooney had gone to Crowell-Collier-Macmillan. By simply making these vacancies permanent, we cut the staff substantially before we fired anybody at all.

As for those on the list, ten in all, Emerson worked his way through the whole ordeal in less than two hours, telling each victim that this was not a dismissal but a layoff, that we were not making any judgment on the victim's merits, that we had no choice. And nobody really seemed to mind. Indeed, the victims began to revel in euphoric daydreams of bright new jobs ahead. It was the survivors who gathered morosely in one another's offices and moped about the dark prospects confronting them.

All these observations, however, apply only to the young, to those under thirty, or at most forty. It is unwise, in the long run, to cut a staff by cutting the young, for the young are essential to the future of the organization (and they are also the lowest paid). But to fire an older man, a gray-haired veteran whose twenty-odd years of service leave him just short of a pension, is like shooting a defenseless farm animal. He may not be the most efficient of workers any more, but he has nowhere else to go. The young, on the other hand, leave quietly and cheerfully, without fear. And so, after an abortive attempt to retire a couple of older men, we took the easy course.

At the end of that morning, we told Ackerman that we had cut our payroll by about $200,000, slightly more than a third of the total, and he said, "Yeah? We just cut the sales staff by $700,000." The merging of advertising staffs had forced Kelly to choose, in every sales office, between *Post* and *Holiday* salesmen. Perhaps by necessity, perhaps by choice, Kelly had not limited himself to the young expendables but had slashed away a number of highly paid executives who had been with the company for many years. But when he had finished, the publicity releases could announce not dismissals but "major promotions in the newly combined advertising sales staffs," and that rated two paragraphs in the *Times*. By the end of the week, Kelly looked sad and shaken as he came to my office and shut the door behind him. "This is the last time," he said. "If there's another round, like dropping to one million circulation on the first of January—have you heard that one?—well, we can't sell that proposition. So if you hear that coming, you'd better dust off your résumé."

Perhaps partly to cheer himself up, Kelly took out a full-page advertisement in the *Times* on the day after Labor Day. To executives returning from vacation, it said, "Welcome back!" It then proceeded to address them in the Madison Avenue vernacular that Kelly loved so well:

Some summer, wasn't it. For Julius Boros and the Czechs and the stock market . . .

The headlines about The Saturday Evening Post had the second-guessers working on thirds and fourths. A lot happened. For the good. There's more and better ahead.

To bring you up-to-date. The POST's circulation was distilled down to a manageable 3 million from a high of 6.8 million. . . . Acceptance by advertisers and their agencies tell us the moves are right. Advertisers who did a mark-time have taken a second look and are back. . . . And cheers and thanks to those running advertisers who hung in and gave us courage with their confidence. . . .

The POST is now in tune with the times and perhaps a bit beyond. . . .

21

"Now I'm the circulation director"

Aside from the final destruction of the *Post,* the one action that inundated Marty Ackerman in criticism and controversy was his decision to cut the magazine's circulation in half. In theory, it was a perfectly simple measure—the subscription lists would be fed into a computer, and the computer would execute the required number of cancellations. It was also a perfectly understandable measure—the advertisers were increasingly unwilling to have their ads make up the deficits created by millions of cut-rate subscriptions, so it was extravagantly uneconomical to continue such subscriptions.

Despite the logic of the move, however, there were no precedents for it. There had been cases of magazines reducing their commitments by letting expiring subscriptions lapse, and of magazines abolishing all their subscriptions for the greater profits of newsstand sales, and of magazines selling their subscription lists as part of the process of liquidation. But no magazine had ever before announced that a certain number of subscribers, who had already paid their money in advance, were no longer acceptable and would no longer receive the magazines they had paid for. Perhaps because no such announcement had ever been made before, Ackerman's decision was greeted with a considerable amount of indignation. It was not just that the subscribers had a legal and moral right to their magazines but that they seemed to believe they had a personal relationship with the *Post.* They thought that when they subscribed, the editor rejoiced, and when they canceled, he grieved. Now they were learning that they were nothing but names on a computer tape.

Many of the problems could have been solved if Curtis had been willing simply to send a refund to the unwanted subscribers, but that would have cost millions of dollars that we didn't have. While we suspected that our readers had a legal right to their magazines or their money, we believed Ackerman was fully justified in doing his best to give them a substitute. Not only could we not afford to continue our ruinous circulation policies, but we convinced ourselves that we had every right to change those policies for the salvation of the corporation. The only question was how to carry out the change. One solution was simply to let the unwanted subscriptions expire, since about forty thousand expirations occurred every week, but although that sounded like a great number, it added up to only two million in an entire year, not much more than half of the 3.8 million we wanted to eliminate immediately. Another solution was to fulfill the unwanted subscriptions with other Curtis magazines, but while this would benefit the *Post*, it would be correspondingly damaging to the other magazines, and the corporation as a whole would gain nothing.

The only real solution was to find some other publisher who would take over Curtis's obligations, and Ackerman thought he had won the battle when he found that *Life* wanted *Post* subscribers. The trouble was that *Life* wanted only about a million of them, and only a million of the best. To understand the dimensions of this problem, we must pause to consider some statistics and the implications of those statistics. As of the June 29 issue, cited as a standard in the annual statement of ownership, the *Post* had a total of 6,551,963 subscribers (plus a newsstand sale of 347,050). A little more than 70 percent of those 6.5 million subscribers—about 4.5 million—lived in the magic A and B counties. Thus, even if we had planned to limit our new circulation of 3 million entirely to subscribers within A and B counties (and we actually had promised only that 80 percent of the new circulation would be A and B), we would still have to dispose of not only 2 million subscribers in the C and D counties but at least 1.5 million of the cherished A and B subscribers. These statistics of A and B circulation do not have any intrinsic significance, of course. I have used them simply because this was the standard by which Madison Avenue judged circulation and therefore the standard by which magazine managements judged their own readers. The assumption was that the A and B readers not only lived in the best market areas but were consequently above average in education and income. They were the readers everybody wanted; C and D readers, whatever their virtues might be, were wanted by no one.

"So on about the first of August," Ackerman explained at his first meeting with the editorial staff, "we're going to send a form letter to one million A and B readers, saying, 'We can't send you the *Post* any more, and unless you notify us within ten days, you're going to get *Life* from now on.' "

"What if they don't want *Life?*" somebody asked.

Ackerman shrugged.

"We're counting on the fact that a lot of people don't answer their mail," he said.

As for the C and D readers, who were unworthy of the *Post* and unwanted by *Life*, Ackerman laughed and said, "We haven't worked that letter out yet. We'll give them some kind of magazines, but we don't know which ones. If anybody has any ideas on what the letter should say, please speak up."

In a society that demands advance and growth, even the most necessary retreat must seem like a defeat, and no organization is ever willing to admit defeat. In Korea, for instance, when the advancing Chinese Communists compelled the United Nations Command to evacuate more than 100,000 of its troops from the besieged city of Hungnam, U.S. authorities claimed that the move was not an evacuation but a redeployment. "Evacuation is when you pull out and go home," an army spokesman insisted, "but redeployment is when you move your troops to a better position to fight back." In redeploying our circulation, then, we declared not that we were cutting our losses but that we were improving our position, canceling subscriptions not because we couldn't afford to fill them but because we didn't choose to.

"You've been hearing some good things about The Saturday Evening Post," Steve Kelly's people proclaimed in full-page ads in the *Times* in mid-July. "Here's the long and short of it. Post reduces circulation from 6.8 to 3 million. Eliminates subscribers not living in A and B markets. . . . The Post has gotten out of the box-car number business and into station wagon statistics." Even if we had in fact limited ourselves to "eliminating subscribers not living in A and B markets," the boastful tone of Kelly's ads would have been somewhat misleading. It could be argued, on the other hand, that it is well within the bounds of advertising ethics to be misleading so long as one is not actually dishonest. In actual fact, however, we were not simply eliminating C and D readers but selling to *Life* no less than one million of our very best subscribers from A and B counties. And we were not only selling them to *Life* but taking ads to denounce them as worthless country bumpkins.

The first complaint I heard was from my sister-in-law, an attractive widow in her mid-thirties, a graduate of Wellesley, and a resident of the expensive Long Island suburb of Manhasset. She was indignant both at being cut off and at the tone of the form letter that had announced her fate. When I mentioned this to Emerson, he answered that his mother in Atlanta had also been rejected. So had my mother in Cambridge, and Ben Hibbs, and *Newsweek*, and the William Morris Agency. So had Mrs. William Kerby, wife of the president of Dow Jones, publisher of the *Wall Street Journal*, and the *Journal*, after some inquiries, published a story under the headline: "Sorry, Mr. Rockefeller, You Don't Quite Pass the Income Standard." The *Journal* had discovered that our victims included Winthrop Rockefeller, Governor of Arkansas. The computer also cut off a subscriber named Martin S. Ackerman.

The letter that went to all these subscribers, and aroused such anger in my sister-in-law, carried the printed signature of Noble Acuff, vice president and director of circulation for the Curtis Publishing Company. It also carried no return address other than a post office box number in Chicago, which, together with Acuff's unusual name (Emerson invariably called him Noble Acorn), led a number of angry subscribers to argue that the letter was a hoax.

"Dear Post subscriber," it said,

I am sorry to tell you that we will be unable to continue sending the Saturday Evening Post after the July 27th issue. Unfortunately the economics of publishing often dictate major changes in policy, and occasionally this means a program of austerity. We are very fortunate, however, in having arranged to replace the remainder of your POST subscription with LIFE magazine for an equivalent number of issues. . . . With LIFE each week you'll be an eyewitness to the dramatic events that shape our lives . . . the raw tension of our fighting men in Vietnam. . . . You'll have a grandstand seat as the race to the White House turns into the homestretch. . . .

We know you'll love LIFE. However, if your attachment to the POST is absolutely unbreakable, we could continue your subscription but only if you notify us within the next ten days. . . .

You can count on the wonderful world of LIFE every week. All you have to do is relax and enjoy it.

Whether Ackerman was right or wrong in thinking that most people didn't answer the mail, he had apparently decided that there was no reason for Curtis to do any better. The regiment of women in the subscription fulfillment department, which was not the most efficient department at the best of times, had been cut back for the sake of corporate economy. The departmental computers, which were no better than the clerks who tried to manage them, became paralyzed by the flood of messages from subscribers. As a result, many subscribers who sent back postcards to say they didn't want *Life* didn't get either *Life* or the *Post*. Others selected other magazines. Still others who wrote to complain or ask questions got neither answers nor magazines. The mail simply piled up in Philadelphia. (The C and D readers, incidentally, were offered their choice of *Ladies' Home Journal, American Home, True, Rudder,* or *Electronics Illustrated,* and most of them, through apathy or stoicism, offered no protest over their fate.)

The press seemed unable to understand what was happening. Columnists and reporters all accepted Kelly's ads at face value and made clumsy attempts to be humorous about the idea of the *Post*'s discarding lower-class subscribers. James Wechsler, editorial page editor of the New York *Post,* wrote a little scenario dramatizing the moment when Mrs. Myrtle Jones learns that her *Post* subscription has been canceled. Art Buchwald wrote a similar scenario involving a man named Feneker, of Hopscotch, Nebraska. "No one came right out and said they knew the Saturday Evening Post had canceled his subscription, but the atmosphere in the town changed. The bank refused him a loan for a new wing on his house. He had trouble cashing checks in the grocery store." *The New Yorker*'s "Talk of the Town," from which one might have expected more subtle humor, resorted instead to scornful sarcasm: "The *Post*, we feel, has dealt with . . . the freeloading reader, the inconsiderate and economically unviable person who buys magazines and newspapers for the information and entertainment he can get out of them, without ever considering that he has an obligation to buy the many lovely products advertised in their pages."

But if the press was obtuse about what Curtis was doing, Curtis was equally obtuse about the criticism. Both Ackerman and Kelly, far from being dismayed at being denounced as welshers, professed to be delighted with the publicity. "If we'd paid Buchwald, he couldn't have done better for us," Ackerman said. "Stories like that are practically ads. They tell everybody that the *Post* is a class magazine, and that not everybody can get it. That's great."

In this dismissal of criticism, Ackerman was continuing the traditional Curtis attitude toward the subscribers. "Do you know why we publish the *Ladies' Home Journal?*" Cyrus H. K. Curtis had said. "The editor thinks it is for the benefit of the American woman. That is an illusion, but a proper one for him to have. But I will tell you the publisher's reason. . . . To give you people who manufacture things that American women want and buy a chance to tell them about your products." In contrast to Curtis's certitude, however, Ackerman was already beginning to realize that there were several different ways of regarding circulation, and that Curtis's traditional way might have been one of the fundamental errors that had caused the company's ruin.

To an editor, if he thinks of circulation at all, the millions of subscribers are simply "the readers," the anonymous mass toward whom the magazine is theoretically directed. On general magazines, a confident editor provides his readers with a judicious mixture of what he thinks they would like and what he thinks they ought to have; on more specialized magazines, editorial confidence defers to a more rigid view of the subscribers as young or old, male or female, scientists or salesmen, and the editor feels obliged to publish only what suits the readers' special interests. In either case, though, the editor thinks of the readers as his clients or consumers, the reason for the magazine's existence. Since editors rarely have any control over a magazine's circulation policies, however, this view is idealistic to the point of irrelevance—"an illusion," as Curtis called it.

To an advertising manager—and advertising managers came to dominate Curtis publishing policies during the 1960's—the subscribers represent an "audience" that can be sold to advertisers for large sums of money. To satisfy these buyers, magazines have spent and misspent fortunes on circulation, first to acquire more and more readers at almost any price, and then to "refine" their subscription lists by soliciting only those categories that meet with Madison Avenue's approval. This policy inevitably gains justification from the fact that advertisers, and not readers, pay most of the costs of the magazine. They thereby win the right to say whether the magazine's audience suits their needs. When it does not, the magazine's publishers can hear the toll of doom.

In addition to these two views suggested by the statement of Cyrus Curtis, there are two other views, more purely financial, of a magazine's subscribers. To a circulation manager, the subscribers are customers, which is not necessarily the same thing as an audience. The customer pays a fair price for a product; an audience is simply a collection of people who have gathered to listen. Like an advertising manager, a circulation manager wants the circulation to grow and flourish; unlike an advertising manager, he wants the subscribers to pay for what they get, and when they pay, he considers all his customers equal. Unfortunately, because of Curtis's traditions, the *Post* didn't have a circulation manager. Its circulation was managed and manipulated by the autonomous Curtis Circulation Company, according to whatever cost-cutting directives were handed down by the corporate management.

The fourth view of the subscribers—and by no means the least important one—is the accountant's view. To an accountant, a subscriber is neither a reader nor a customer, nor is he part of an audience. He is a liability, and he is carried on the books as such. In exchange for the money he has paid, the magazine owes him future issues, and the accountant lists the cost of those issues as part of the long-term debt. Shrewd publishers put aside at least part of their subscription earnings to pay those future debts. Curtis, inevitably, had played the role of the grasshopper in the Aesop fable, and its subscription liabilities in the spring of 1968 totaled, according to Ackerman, the almost incredible sum of $60 million. To fulfill those obligations, the company had only the hope that advertisers would someday return to the fold.

"This whole mass-magazine business is exactly the same as the Ponzi game," Ackerman said. "You remember the Ponzi racket? Where Ponzi said, 'Send me a dollar and I'll send you back two dollars in a month.' Remember? Well, that's what mass-magazine publishers do. They tell the subscriber, 'Send me two dollars now, and I'll send you five dollars' worth of magazines in the next year.' And it just can't be done. They're heading for trouble, every one of them. Just like Ponzi."

On August 21, Ackerman issued a report on Curtis income during the first six months of 1968. It showed a loss of $7,136,000 on operating revenues of $58,424,000, compared to a loss of $370,000 on revenues of $63 million during the first six months of the previous year. For the year as a whole, Ackerman said that operating losses could total between $10 million and $15 million. With special write-offs, he said, the loss could amount to $25 million.

He also disclosed that Perfect Film had taken over Curtis's bank loans of $13.2 million from the First National Bank of Boston and its group of associated banks. The interest was 1 percent above the prime rate (then 6.5 percent), he said, and maturity "is on demand." And so farewell to the spirit of Serge Semenenko.

"The problem with Curtis," Ackerman said to the New York Times, "is that it has too many fixed expenses. The company is so thoroughly integrated it has become a bureaucracy and functions like the Post Office. . . . The hope and future of Curtis Publishing is to shrink it to size and then build it up again."

And of the Post, he said, "I think we have made it."

One morning, I encountered Ackerman on his way to the elevator. He stopped, asked whether I had a minute to spare him, and then led me into the nearby editorial library.

"I'm sure you've got lots of good writers on your staff," he began. "Right?"

"That's true," I said.

"I hear you're a good writer yourself—"

"That's true too."

"—so why can't you people develop some ideas on how we can sell subscriptions at eight bucks a year?"

"Well, because we're not advertising copywriters," I said. "Why don't you go and get the best ad writers in New York—"

"They're no good," Ackerman said.

"—and tell them this is their greatest challenge?"

"Hopeless," Ackerman said, almost to himself. "Hopeless."

"But look," I said. "Advertising is a special business, and it takes a certain amount of time to learn it. There must be somebody on Madison Avenue who knows how to sell subscriptions."

"No, nobody," Ackerman said. He seemed surprisingly firm in his conviction that no outsider could help him, and I saw that my arguments only made him feel gloomy, deserted. He had decided, as he had said in a previous meeting, that the salvation of the *Post* lay in first cutting the circulation and then rebuilding it by selling subscriptions at a profit, at eight dollars a year. Since Curtis had no staff and no machinery that could accomplish this purpose, Ackerman had convinced himself that he must solve the problem alone, aided only by whatever kindred souls he could recruit.

"This is the most important single problem we face right now," he said, taking out a piece of paper and starting to draw another one of his outlines.

"I know," I said. "That's why you ought to hire a good circulation manager."

"No, we've got to figure it out ourselves," he said. He wrote at the top of the paper, in large block letters: "HOW TO IT." He looked at the paper, and then at me, and he knew there was something wrong, but he couldn't figure out what it was. In his mind, the words "to" and "do" had somehow elided, the way similar sounds sometimes do. As he read the three words, they undoubtedly appeared as four. After a moment, he scratched out the whole phrase, put the paper back in his pocket and said, "Well, think about it. See what you can do."

Late that night, I decided that it wouldn't do any harm to try organizing some of the arguments in favor of eight-dollar subscriptions. I drafted half a dozen ads in all, and then I put them in a drawer until I had a better idea of what would happen next. What happened next was that I found myself enmeshed once again in the nets of the smiling Bob Yung. Emerson had succeeded in banishing him from the *Post* but not from Ackerman's entourage, for Yung, like a true courtier, was quite skillful at making the king's problems his own. If selling subscriptions was now Ackerman's concern, then Yung stood ready to dedicate himself to selling subscriptions. He had already written a full-page ad to run in the next issue of the *Post*, proclaiming that the magazine had improved so dramatically since Ackerman's arrival that any reader could see it was worth eight dollars a year.

"Is there anyone in editorial who could check this ad?" Yung wondered. I asked what he meant by "checking," and he just smiled. "Marty said he wanted it checked by somebody in editorial," he repeated. I read through the ad, and everything became clear. Ackerman had wanted an ad, but there had been nobody to write one, and so Yung had undertaken the job. Then, once Ackerman had seen it, he knew he needed somebody to fix it, but he didn't know who should fix it or how. It said things like "This was must reading at the recent G.O.P. convention."

"And that's true," Yung said eagerly, "because we delivered a copy to every delegate."

"Yeah, but it just doesn't sound very interesting," I said. "Why don't you write an ad based on what's in the next issue?"

"But I don't know what's in the next issue," Yung said sadly. "Could you help me? Could you dictate to your secretary just a few words on each article?"

I reluctantly agreed to provide Yung's material, but when I asked him the next day how the revision of the ad had turned out, he only said, "Marty decided to postpone it."

So there's nobody in this one-man band who can write an ad, I said to myself. And if Ackerman didn't have anybody who could produce an ad that would sell subscriptions, then he wasn't going to sell very many subscriptions.

"Problems, problems," said Marty Ackerman. He had wandered into my office again, apparently just to find somebody to talk to. "Everybody is crazy around here, just crazy, all of them. I tell you, they could *never* pay me enough to make up for what I'm going through for this company.

"And the craziest thing is, I still can't get any accurate figures out of anybody. That f—— printing plant. First they told me it would be cheaper to shut it down. I could sell it for real estate for $7 million. Now they tell me it would be cheaper to keep operating it. They told me I'd need $2 million until the end of the year, and then it turned out I had to put in another $2 million just last week. And the figures are still no good. People lie to you.

"The lesson of Curtis, Otto, is that they never made it follow the entrepreneurial system. Competition. They just went on tolerating waste and inefficiency, year after year. You must have the entrepreneurial system, each department paying for itself on a competitive basis. That's the only way. That's the lesson of Curtis."

Throughout all Ackerman's difficulties with advertisers and accountants and printers, he still kept worrying about the question of how to sell subscriptions for eight dollars. One day, he came bursting into my office with what he thought was the solution.

"Listen, I got a great idea," he cried, flinging himself into a chair.

"How many companies have you bought since we last saw you?" I asked. The question had become sort of a ritual joke that I offered whenever he seemed suspiciously full of enthusiasm, but he always answered very earnestly.

"Well, I could have bought the Longines-Wittnauer Company," he said, "but it was too much money, basically, so I said, 'To hell with it.' But listen to my idea. It came to me in a flash."

The idea that Ackerman proceeded to explain did indeed sound like a stroke of promotional genius. The basic problem in selling subscriptions by mail, he said, was that the sales message—the "mailing piece" that was sent out to prospective subscribers—generally wasn't much good because it was written by hacks, who had little understanding of either magazines or salesmanship. At the same time, these mailings were so expensive—often ten dollars or more per name, depending on the quality of the list of names—that nobody could afford to make the thorough tests that were required for successful mail-order selling. Ackerman's solution ended both problems. As soon as we had put together a regular issue, we would put together a free sampler consisting of any twelve editorial pages from that issue and another twelve pages of ads, which would appear only in the sampler. The opening spread of this sampler would explain our purpose and urge the reader to buy a subscription. The twelve editorial pages would then provide the prospective subscriber with a much better idea of the *Post* than he would ever get from the standard mailing piece. And the advertisements would pay for the whole thing. In theory, then, we could inundate the country with millions of our solicitations, and we could even solicit the same families over and over again. The cost of acquiring subscriptions, for which publishers generally paid millions of dollars, could be reduced to nothing, and every subscription that we sold would bring us a profit.

"Doesn't that sound like a great idea?" Ackerman said.

"It really does," I said.

By midafternoon, the art department had produced a dummy of what Ackerman had started calling the "preview mailer." He had requested this dummy so that he could show it to prospective advertisers, and it looked splendid. In fact, it looked too splendid—it contained eighteen editorial pages and only six pages of ads. Ackerman ignored such details, however. He was in a state of high euphoria.

"This is it!" he said, tilting back and putting his feet on my desk.

"Hey, don't do that!" I said. "You'll break George Horace Lorimer's chair."

Ackerman docilely tilted forward again and then reached toward the Scotch tape dispenser, tearing off a strip and starting to finger it.

"If this deal will work," Ackerman went on, "I've really solved the whole problem. The whole problem. I told you I could do it. I tell you, Otto, the human mind . . ."

Ackerman stopped and shook his head in awe at his own feat. I was on the verge of laughing at his self-admiration, but some inner voice told me not to disturb his moment of triumph. I decided instead to go and get the art department to draw up a new dummy that would show what the preview mailer would actually look like. ("I'm just trying to convert 'A' issues into reality," I said to Emerson. "How typical of you," Emerson said, "when most people would say that the road to success lies in converting reality into 'A' issues.") At the end of the day, I brought the new and rather less impressive dummy to Ackerman, but it could not diminish his enthusiasm.

"I've been on the phone to the Book-of-the-Month Club and Capitol Records and all kinds of people like that," he said, "people who could use a good mailing piece for their own coupons, and they think this idea is just sensational. And you know, we can send out three million copies, but just to people in A and B counties, with incomes over ten grand, or whatever we want. Because controlled circulation is the name of the game nowadays."

"So are they going to take ads?"

"Sure. They say the cheapest they can get on a mail-order piece is fifteen bucks a thousand, and here we're offering them a CPM of five."

"That doesn't sound right," I said.

"Let's see, how does it work out?" Ackerman said. "Let's say it costs them twenty-five bucks per thousand, and we . . ."

He was making pencil marks on one of his yellow pads, but they didn't seem to produce an answer, and he looked expectantly up at me.

"As far as I can see, it's costing something like fifty bucks per thousand," I said.

"Well, some of them say it costs them seventy-five or eighty per thousand."

As each new statistic came spilling out, each quoted as a figure that had been cited by prospective advertisers, I felt more and more like Prince Hal listening to Falstaff's tale of battling two, four, seven, nine rogues in buckram suits. Whatever the correct figures might be, though, I still shared Ackerman's view that this project might save us, and so I volunteered to write the sales spiel that would introduce the twenty-four-page issue and sell the eight-dollar subscriptions. "Fine," Ackerman said. "You and Yung work it out."

I went to Yung and asked whether I should write a draft for him to consider or whether he would write a draft for me. The moment I asked the question, I realized that it was absurd, and Yung, having been offered an unprotected pawn, took it. "I don't want to avoid the problems," he said, smiling, "but I think it would be good if you wrote it." But having lost my pawn, I challenged one of his. I proposed that each of us write a draft and show it to the other on the following Monday. I had worked that way on several projects with Emerson, but Yung was not Emerson. We both agreed to do our best.

I double-crossed Yung first by writing the advertising copy and then taking it directly to Emerson and Ackerman, both of whom approved it. Yung, on the other hand, told the art department that Ackerman didn't really like my copy and wanted his version used. I double-crossed Yung again by taking both versions to Ackerman and demanding that he tell me which one he wanted. "What do they say? What do they say?" said Ackerman, shuffling the two pieces of paper and pretending to read them.

"Can't you combine them somehow?" he asked plaintively.

"No," I said. "They're quite different. You have to pick one."

"Okay, this is the one I want," he said, approving my copy for the second time.

"Now, I'm going to tell that to Yung, so we don't keep going around in circles, okay?"

The next confusion involved what is called—I was getting a whole education in the mail-order business—"the premium." The most familiar way to sell goods through the mails is to discount them—a $10 value for only $7.98. But our goal was to abolish the discounting of *Post* subscriptions, which were still being offered at $1.98 a year, less than eight cents a copy, and the technique in such cases is to offer something extra—free, absolutely nothing to pay, when you place your order—and this is called the premium. The trick, obviously, is to offer something that is cheap but seems expensive, and so, since we boasted of our millions of dedicated readers, Ackerman naturally thought of books.

"What's a hot book we can offer as a premium?"

I suggested Charles Portis's *True Grit* and Stewart Alsop's *The Center*, both of which had clear associations with the *Post*. "And you can get the paperback version of the Alsop for the asking," I said, "because the rights were just bought by your own paperback company."

"Oh, they were? Hey, that's great!"

"But let's try to use the hard-cover edition," I said. "That's more like something worth getting."

"Okay, who should call the publishers, you or me?"

Not without malice, I suggested that Ackerman do the telephoning himself, and he agreed. Instead of calling the publishers, however, he called the head of his own paperback house, Frank Lualdi of Popular Library. The next day, Ackerman returned with what he thought was a splendid proposal by Lualdi. As a premium for new subscribers, we could offer free paperback editions of not only the Alsop book but Thornton Wilder's last novel, *The Eighth Day*, a collection of adventure tales from the *Post*, and a "treasury" of writings by Nobel Prize winners.

"What's Lualdi trying to do, clean out his warehouse?" I asked. "Does he think people want their mailboxes suddenly stuffed full of paperback anthologies?"

"Yeah, I guess you're right," Ackerman said. "But I can't get any hard-cover premium."

"Who have you asked?"

"Well, I've been on the phone to Lualdi. He knows a lot of people."

Once again, I recognized the thinness of Ackerman's management. It was gossamer. He railed against the quantity of secretaries, and then he assigned clerical work to his handful of executives. And he seemed quite indifferent to the gaps created by his demands, indifferent to the fact that a book publisher and a magazine editor must leave a certain amount of their own work undone if they are suddenly assigned to the chores of an assistant circulation director.

Despite our intermittent efforts, however, the "preview mailer" seemed to drift along in a world without time. Partly because nobody was directly in charge of it, everybody ducked whatever responsibility he could. The printers said they couldn't print it until the advertising plates had been delivered, and the salesmen said they couldn't sell the space until the dummies were finished, but the dummies depended on what ads could be sold, and in such a state of confusion, nobody could figure out what anything cost.

"The circulation people say we can produce three million of these things for eight cents apiece," Ackerman said happily.

"Sounds good," I said. "But how about the ads?"

"They've all been sold," Ackerman said. "Ten pages. For a CPM of five."

"Can we break even at that?" I asked.

"Well, almost," Ackerman said.

In Ackerman's language, that meant we could not break even. The only question was how much we would lose. After he had gone, I began to do some figuring. If we produced three million copies at eight cents apiece (assuming that figure was correct), that would cost us $240,000. If we were selling ads at a rate of $5 per thousand, that meant $15,000 per page, or a total revenue of $150,000—and that meant a loss of $90,000 on the very first attempt in a project that Ackerman had conceived as perpetually self-sustaining. If Ackerman kept cutting the budget and demanding that we fire people, then how could we justify spending $90,000 on this untested experiment? And even if we had $90,000 to invest in a mailing—for that was very cheap compared to ordinary prices for subscription mailings—we had nonetheless lost sight of the original idea, that the self-sufficiency of the mailing would enable us to send it to millions of people, week after week.

I took my figures to Emerson and convinced him that we should either reorganize the whole project or else scrap it. Then we went together to present the case to Ackerman. His first response, characteristically, was to change the figures. The CPM was six dollars, not five dollars, he said. That would only cut our loss from $90,000 to $60,000, I said, and what would we get for it?

"Listen, all we need is a 1 percent return, and we'll be delighted," Ackerman said. "One and a half percent and I'd be jumping up and down on the table."

"Well, 1 percent of three million copies is only thirty thousand subscriptions, so you're losing two dollars for every subscription."

"It would be worth it," Ackerman said.

"And that's just a beginning. If you want to sell three million subscriptions at that rate, it's going to cost you six million dollars."

"It's worth it," Ackerman said. "You have to realize that it only costs us about five dollars to produce the magazines for a year, so an eight-dollar subscription gives us three dollars toward the cost of obtaining it, see? So if we can get it for only two bucks, that's great."

When I finally saw the finished dummy of the preview mailer, based on the October 19 issue, I saw that Ackerman hadn't sold the ads at all. He had donated them, from all the provinces of his empire, himself. Next to the contents page was a full-age ad for Ackerman's flashbulb Perma-Cubes; next to the lead page of Bill Emerson's interview with Hubert Humphrey came an ad for Ackerman's dress patterns; in the center fold came a full spread for Ackerman's United Film Club, then a full page for Ackerman's sets of pens, five for $1.25, another spread for a series of Curtis books on Napoleon, Michelangelo, and other great men, all translated from the Italian, and finally the back cover offered all of Ackerman's Hudson vitamins at half-price. And once again, Ackerman had an explanation.

"The best kind of ads for a thing like this are mail-order ads, but I've got to prove the ads will pull, and then I can go to the advertisers and say, 'Look, it works, we proved it.' But until then, we've got to go on faith, and Perfect Film has faith in this project. Hell, this may be a better advertising medium than the *Post* itself. It's cheaper, and it has a more selective audience."

When everything was finally arranged, the printers announced that they didn't have enough time to print three million copies of the preview mailer and get it out into circulation on the same day as the regular issue. "Tell them," Ackerman said to Emerson, "that they're going to print this thing and print it on time, or I'm going to shut down the whole f—— plant." Faced with this prospect, the printers suddenly discovered that they could print the mailer on time after all. And so it was done, and everybody was pleased. "That's class, that's real class," Ackerman said as he held up one of the first copies.

The only trouble was that it didn't sell any subscriptions. Millions of copies went out and nothing came back. The return was about one-eighth of 1 percent, which was the equivalent of a total loss. If anybody wanted to analyze the disaster, there were several answers. It could be argued that the idea itself was no good; it could be argued that the sales spiel I had written was no good; it could be argued that the book premium was no good; it could be argued, finally, that eight dollars was simply too much to charge for a mass magazine. But I had my own theory, which I pursued into the innards of the circulation company. Who, I wanted to know, had actually received these solicitations, and how had we selected them? Had we searched out people who might be interested in the magazine we were publishing, and who could easily afford the eight dollars we were asking, or had we once again sent the mailing to the wrong people, because that was the cheapest way of picking names? The mailing had been sent, I finally learned, to a list of people who had once subscribed to the *Ladies' Home Journal* and *American Home,* and who, through apathy or dislike, had let their subscriptions lapse.

"And how in hell did we figure that those were the people who would want to subscribe to the *Post?*" I asked.

"Well," said the man in the circulation company, "we figured that we'd have to give up the names before too long, because we'd sold the magazines to Downe, so we might as well use the lists while we had them for free. But you just can't sell subscriptions for thirty cents a copy when *Life* and *Look* are still selling for ten cents. No matter what Marty says, it won't work."

We had cut the *Post* editorial staff down to forty-one employees, but Ackerman and his accountants were still searching for further economies. In mid-September, Ackerman decreed that we would have to schedule our next issue, *Post* No. 23, at only 176 editorial columns. So it had taken us only four months, since the euphoria of the opulent "A" issues, to return to the bleakest austerity of the Clifford regime. A magazine of only forty-four editorial pages was scarcely a magazine at all; it was a revelation of impending death.

Steve Kelly came by that afternoon, still spreading his new message of cheer. "I'm hearing nothing but compliments about the magazine," he said. "Really amazing. Really looks good."

"I'm glad you like it," I said, "because there's only going to be 176 columns of it from now on. Or haven't you heard that we're cutting back again?"

"No, I hadn't heard that," Kelly said. "That would ruin my whole day if that were true, so I'm sure glad I haven't heard that."

In Philadelphia, where most of the payroll was spent, the ax began to cut more deeply. There was, for example, a huge department called subscription fulfillment. The reason why it took weeks to start a subscription, why checks got lost and orders misaddressed, why numbers of readers found their subscriptions mysteriously cut off and others got two copies of every issue—all this was the handiwork of the four hundred people in the subscription department. For their labors, they were paid, assuming an average of at least $75 a week, a collective wage of more than $1.5 million a year. On September 13, a Friday as it happened, Ackerman announced that all this work and the four hundred workers were being turned over to the A. C. Nielsen Company, which had a division called Neodata that handled such problems for thirty-five other magazines.

Still, he kept scratching at the editors too. We had been trying for two weeks to cut our budget from $3 million to $2 million (there were rumors that further retrenchment would be required at the end of the year), but we couldn't figure out how to make such cuts without serious damage. And then Ackerman told Emerson that $2 million wasn't good enough; we would have to come down to $1.8 million.

"Well, we just can't do it," I said.

"That's what I told him," Emerson said, "and he said, 'Cut it to one point eight or we'll have to close it down.'"

"Oh, to hell with him," I said.

"So I said, 'Then close it down,'" Emerson said.

"And what did he say to that?"

"He backed off. He just said, 'Well, do the best you can.'"

It came time, finally, near the end of the presidential campaign, to make a Hobson's choice. Ackerman, who had once talked of committing all Curtis magazines to whichever candidate he favored, now seemed to have nothing to say. Emerson wanted to come out for Humphrey, but I argued that it was impossible to endorse anyone who supported the war in Vietnam. I took a poll of the editors and found them equally undecided, and so I wrote an editorial that equivocated. I called both candidates "inadequate" and applied to both of them Eliot's phrase about "decent godless people, their only monument the asphalt road and a thousand lost golf balls." I myself was sick of the familiar argument of "realism," that everybody had to make a choice between the candidates no matter how inferior they might be. If one had to choose, I wrote, then Humphrey was a better man than Nixon. But because of his commitments to Lyndon Johnson and the war, we did not endorse him.

"You're a hard man, Otto," Ackerman said, striding into my office with a copy of the editorial. Now if there were going to be any objections from him at this point, I thought, we would have a really memorable argument. We both managed, however, to evade the problem. I refrained from asking whether he approved of the editorial, and he refrained from saying that he did (or didn't). Instead, he began to recite back to me many of the arguments in the editorial, as though I might find his views informative. Personally, he said, he had given a check to Humphrey, "because I figured he needed the money," and in turning over the check, he had taken the opportunity to tell Humphrey's fund-raiser what he, Ackerman, thought about the state of the nation. Humphrey must adopt an independent stand on Vietnam or it would cost him the election. He had said that to Humphrey's man, and now he was saying it to me. And there it was on the *Post* editorial page, I answered, already set in type.

"You're a hard man, Otto," Ackerman repeated. "I'd hate to think what you'd say if I was running for President."

"Oh, I'd endorse you, Marty," I said. "You can count on that."

Most magazines send about 90 percent of their copies to subscribers and sell about 10 percent on newsstands, but, by the nature of magazine publishing, the newsstand sales get most of the attention. One reason is that newsstand sales provide an index, however inaccurate, for editorial success. One issue sells better than another; consistently high sales convince everyone, including the editor, that the editor knows his job. Another reason is that Madison Avenue believes in newsstand sales. Each newsstand purchase is an act of individual free choice, paid for in cash, and thus convinces the advertiser that people respond to the magazine (it should also be noted parenthetically that virtually all newsstands are in A and B counties, the promised land). And the final reason is that newsstand circulation is profitable circulation. If a magazine costs between ten and twenty cents to produce, publishers have discovered that they can make a profit by selling it at the newsstand for twenty-five or thirty-five or even fifty cents. One might think that this would inspire them to raise the price of subscriptions, which account for 90 percent of their circulation, but instead they simply yearn for more newsstand sales.

In the old days, at five or ten cents, the *Post* had sold hugely at the newsstands, more than a million copies a week. As late as 1962, when I came to Philadelphia, Sherrod proudly told me that the *Post* regularly outsold *Life* and *Look* combined. The price then was only twenty cents, however, and I suspect that the profits were marginal. Since then, all mass magazines had been raising their newsstand prices and selling fewer copies at bigger profits. In mid-1968, when our sales had dropped to less than 400,000 copies at thirty-five cents,

Ackerman abruptly decreed that the newsstand price would be increased to fifty cents on the next issue. Sales promptly dropped another 75,000 copies. This struck me as a perfect example of classic economic theory, but Ackerman rejected such arguments as defeatist. Having lost patience with his unsuccessful "preview mailer"—which he had tried twice more, on a small scale, with equally apathetic mailing lists, and then abandoned—he now decided that there must be some merchandising stunt that would increase newsstand sales.

Ackerman's first proposal was that we stick a paperback book into every newsstand copy. That would be a premium, free. I answered by putting a paperback book into one thin copy of the *Post* and showing him what a lump it made; a stack of such magazines couldn't even stand up straight on a newsstand.

"Well, why couldn't we do something like this?" he wondered, opening up the paperback so that it made less of a lump. "Or how about this?" He took the magazine and tore loose its twenty middle pages and folded them in half. "Maybe on special paper?"

"Okay, but that isn't going to turn into anything that anybody would want to put on his bookshelf," I said.

Ackerman threw down the torn magazine and glared at me.

"How can we afford these things anyway?" I went on. "The new budget allows less than $50,000 for all the editorial material in an issue, and the rights to any new book cost at least $5,000, and usually more. Just for some extra newsstand sales."

It was curious to watch Ackerman's reaction to this net of logic that I kept throwing at him, for his irritation was probably characteristic of men who have become accustomed to command. He couldn't overcome my objections, but he wouldn't accept them either. He didn't argue. He simply looked fretful and unhappy, obviously wishing that the problems didn't exist, and making it clear that their existence was my fault. It was easy to see why he liked having courtiers who would follow at his heels and keep saying, "That sounds great, Marty."

The following week, Ackerman had a new idea. He wanted to take the cover of the next issue, a photograph of Bob Dylan, and turn it into a poster, four times the size of the cover, to be bound into newsstand copies. This time, we got as far as proposing the idea to the printers, who said, as usual, that it couldn't be done. Once again, they had to be bullied into agreeing to do their job. But the printing and binding costs would amount to $15,000, and we would need to pay an additional fee to the photographer, if we could get the rights to manufacture such a poster at all.

"It'll come to almost $20,000," I said, "and you only make ten cents a copy in profit on newsstand sales, so you'd have to sell an extra 200,000 copies just to break even. So why are we doing it?"

"Because," said Ackerman, "I want to startle the s—— out of people."

("You keep talking about art," said G. B. Shaw to the movie producer, "when I am talking about commerce.")

We were saved from this new extravagance by the fact that we couldn't reach the photographer to buy poster rights. But I had begun to believe, as I usually did, and as Ackerman intended me to believe, that I might as well join in thinking up projects that would end in profits rather than simply criticizing projects that would end in losses. Within a few days, I had hatched a plan that struck me as worthy of Ackerman himself.

"I've got an idea that will help newsstand sales, and also provide something new, and also sell subscriptions at eight dollars," I said, "but there's one catch, and that is that I'm not going to do the donkey-work of carrying it out."

"Well, I can take care of that," Ackerman said.

"Okay, now every issue we publish has some article in it that has some kind of a connection with a new book. The issue we're doing now has Schanche's article about Eldridge Cleaver, so there's a natural connection with Cleaver's book, *Soul on Ice*, which is already selling pretty well. So on the newsstand copies, we glue a tab on the cover that says: 'Free book offer. Black militant's best-selling auto-biography. See page so and so.' So they buy the magazine and they turn to page so and so, and there's Schanche's article about Cleaver, and in the middle of it, bound right into the magazine, there's a postcard that they send to us, and we'll give them Cleaver's book free if they subscribe to the *Post* for eight dollars. All you have to do then is to get the book for two dollars wholesale from the publisher, and I've already got them to agree to that. So how can you lose?"

"It's good," Ackerman said. There was an odd look on his face, of interest, curiosity—almost of gratitude. At last, he was not the only one trying to figure out ways of making money.

"And you can provide a different book in every issue," I went on, "and after a while, you can even turn the surplus into a sort of book club. The *Saturday Evening Post* bonus books."

"It's good," Ackerman said. "Let's do it."

"Okay, but not me, remember. Isn't there anybody in your circulation company who can handle these chores?"

"No, I'll do it myself," Ackerman said. "I'm better than they are."

After a few preliminary phone calls, however, Ackerman became involved in other problems, and the mess was all turned over to Don McKinney, who cleaned it up and took care of the book deals from then on. By now, Ackerman had a new idea.

"Why couldn't we put a record into every newsstand copy?" he asked. "I hear you can buy them from the manufacturers for as little as eight cents apiece."

The record we agreed on—two Rowan and Martin comedy routines, to be inserted in a TV issue—eventually cost twenty-one cents instead of eight, and the printers were by now in a state somewhere between mutiny and hysteria. Ordered once again to do as they were told, they had to hire extra workmen to come in at overtime rates and spend a whole weekend stuffing 100,000 records into stacks of magazines.

And so we continued through the fall. Each new issue contained a different book offer for subscriptions. One issue contained a poster by Sister Corita for one set of newsstands and a record produced by the Beatles for another. Cartoon editor Charles Barsotti produced a cartoon calendar that could be bound into all the magazines destined for expiring subscribers, reminding them that it was time to renew for eight dollars. I tried periodically to persuade Ackerman to hire some competent circulation director to handle all these problems, but he consistently refused to delegate the responsibility. At one manic moment, he cried: "Now I'm the circulation director! I'm the circulation director!" But when I argued that the job needed full-time attention, he pleaded helplessness. "Who can we get? You want to put everything in the hands of somebody like ————?" (He named one of our old-line bureaucrats.) "I tell you, you find me somebody .who knows this field, and I'll certainly be happy to interview him for the job."

Late in November, just six weeks before the *Post* died, Ackerman was still struggling with this intractable problem. He summoned me late in the afternoon to his new office in what he liked to call "the town house." I let myself in out of the cold darkness of Park Avenue and found the brightly lit building apparently empty. Then, from the second floor, I heard Ackerman howling my name in welcome: *"Otto!"* I met him halfway up the stairway and followed him to his office.

"We've got to talk about these goddamn subscriptions," he said. "I've got some new ideas."

Now that he owned and operated the Curtis Circulation Company, Ackerman had mixed feelings about the traditional methods of selling magazines, for his own magazines were losing money to his own circulation subsidiaries. "The first thing you have to understand about all these subscription systems," he said, "is that the publisher doesn't get anything at all. Take the school plan. Kids out selling subscriptions. The kid doesn't get anything. The school gets 50 percent of the revenue. And 15 percent goes to the salesman who acts as liaison between the school and the circulation company. So what's left for the publisher?"

The circulation company salesmen were now having a convention—"On any given day in the year," Ackerman said, "somebody in this goddamn company is going to a convention"—so he was planning to fly south with a new plan: The schools could continue to get the same amount in dollars but not the same percentage of the increased subscription price, and the salesmen would get only 5 percent.

"Circulation salesmen are not people who take cuts in their percentages," I said.

"Well, they all work for Perfect Film now," Ackerman said, "so we'll see what we can do."

No matter how much he might coerce his salesmen, however, he still had not solved the basic problem—the same problem he had placed before me at that odd meeting in the editorial library three months earlier—the problem of the message, the advertisement, the sales spiel, something that would persuade millions of people to pay a fair price for their magazines. By this time, he had at least attempted to enroll some advertising agencies in the search, but he could find nothing that satisfied him. One of the agencies wanted $10,000 a month to deal with the problem, and another had produced samples that he didn't like. He dug through a stack of papers and then held up one of the dummies.

"We've thrown out the MUSH of the dear old *Post*," the advertisement said, "and turned it into a CEMENT FIST that HITS YOU BETWEEN THE EYES."

Ackerman looked at me, and I looked back at him.

"I mean, what s——," he said.

"Pretty bad," I said.

"What I think," he said, "is that I ought to write a personal letter to every single subscriber who expires this year. There's a million of them, and hell, they've got to be our best prospects. And a million subs at eight bucks—that would be pretty nice. They've got computers that write letters now, you know, very personalized, just like a real letter. Here, let me read it."

Ackerman fished out another paper from the clutter on his desk and began reading. The subscriber might have heard, the letter said, that the *Post* was cutting its circulation so that only the best people would get this new and improved magazine. Because of some expirations, however, there were still a few openings available, and the *Post* wanted to fill them with successful and sophisticated people like you. . . . The letter was rather conventional, not dissimilar to the letters that go out periodically from *Newsweek* or *Forbes* or *Sports Illustrated,* but it was not at all bad either. It had that rare and under-appreciated quality of technical competence, saying what needed to be said, making the points that needed to be made. What struck me, though, was the awed and reverential tone in which Ackerman was reading aloud to me every word in this standard sales message, and reading with real feeling, sincere.

"That's pretty good," I said when he finished. "Who wrote it?"

"I did," Ackerman said offhandedly. "Now here, look at these."

Under more papers, he had more advertising dummies, which he proudly held up. As before, he began reading aloud.

"Accept a sporting offer from the publishers of The Saturday Evening Post," said one. It offered to give anyone who sent in the coupon three free issues of the *Post,* and then, unless the reader stopped it, a year's subscription.

"Test yourself," said another. It listed ten future articles in the *Post.* The reader was supposed to check which ones he would like to read. If he achieved a "passing" score of six, then he should send in the coupon and subscribe to the *Post.*

Like the letter, the ads impressed me as conventional but not at all bad—better, in fact, than most of the ads produced by our supposedly professional advertising people.

"You wrote those too?" I said. "Every word? No helpers?"

"Every word," he said grimly.

"Who did the layouts?"

"There's a little ad agency out in Manhasset, near where I live, and they'll do whatever I tell them. I mean, they don't do anything very creative, but they can carry out instructions. But what I was wondering was, now that I've roughed in some ideas, couldn't you guys carry out the rest of it?"

"No, dammit," I said, but mildly, knowing that he couldn't understand why I (and the other editors) didn't want to do the same work he was doing. "I'm just not an advertising man, and every time I get involved in one of these projects, I get screwed up in my own work."

"I understand, I understand," Ackerman said, with that hurt look of irritation that I had come to recognize as his response to rejection, meaning that he didn't understand at all. "But there's got to be some way we can work this out. There's got to be some way I can get the message across. You know, the people who have been reading the *Post*, at least in the six months I've been here, what with all the problems in the world, and what we've been telling them, they're *better people* than they were six months ago."

22

"The whole thing will be almost
as big as Time Inc."

In mid-October, Ackerman moved his headquarters out of the Curtis building and into his "town house," a five-story stone building on Park Avenue at Thirty-eighth Street. If it is true that one of the fundamental goals in life is the control of one's own environment, then the town house doubtless represented to some degree the ideal that Ackerman envisioned for himself. I asked him, the first time I saw it, how he had happened to select it, and he answered with another Gatsbyan revelation. "I used to come driving in from Manhasset every day, and I used to go past this place, and it was always sitting here empty. It had been empty for ten or fifteen years, I don't know why. So about two years ago, long before I had anything to do with Curtis, I bought it, and I gave my wife the job of doing all the decorating, and so she's spent the last year and a half getting it all fixed up."

Emerson liked to refer to the town house as "the pickle factory," conjuring up images of Ackerman and his diminutive assistants laboring over vats of boiling brine, but it was actually an elegant building, reflecting, as it was intended to reflect, the $700,000 that Ackerman had invested in it. The front was narrow, a little more than twenty feet wide, with a stone balcony across the front of the second story. Inside, just beyond a reception foyer, there was a hall with marble floors and red carpeting, leading past the billiards room back to the dining room. The first time I went there, I heard sounds of banging from this dining room, for the redecorating was still going on. An electrician on a stepladder was working on an exposed wire, and two spattered painters were wandering around. In the middle of the hall, a curving stairway, also carpeted in red, led upward past a gigantic portrait of Ackerman, very formal, in a striped necktie, holding a copy of the *Wall Street Journal*, and staring out into space. It looked like a posthumously commissioned portrait of someone who had died young.

"I see you've had your portrait painted," I said, not without a certain sarcasm.

"Yeah, my employees gave it to me," Ackerman said. I tried to imagine the scene. What extraordinary pressures must have been applied to the serfs of the Perfect Film & Chemical Corporation to extort from them this tribute to their leader.

"That's what they call the cult of the personality," I said. Ackerman, bounding up the stairs ahead of me, muttered something I couldn't hear.

(In times to come, Ackerman seemed to vacillate between pride in his own portrait and embarrassment about this display of vanity. In February of 1969, Kent MacDougall of the *Wall Street Journal* paid a visit to the town house and noted that the portrait had disappeared. "The facts surrounding the disappearance of the painting suggest that Mr. Ackerman can at times be confused, if not untruthful," MacDougall wrote. "Visitors to the town house insist the painting hung on the wall until last week, shortly before a Wall Street Journal reporter was invited to the town house. Asked about the missing portrait, Mr. Ackerman first denied it had ever left Perfect Film's Long Island headquarters, where employees had presented it to him for Christmas in 1967. Confronted with testimony of visitors who had seen it at the town house, he conceded it had been there briefly but was now in storage. Later he said the frame was too heavy, and the picture was taken down to be reframed.")

At the head of the stairs, a corridor led forward to the library, where callers were asked to wait. The library was a handsome room, with a large fireplace, a sofa, and windows looking out over Park Avenue. The walls were lined with bookshelves, but Ackerman apparently had no appropriate books to put in them. Instead, he had filled one wall with a large set of rather ugly brown lawbooks and the other with maroon volumes of the *Post*. For the floor, the decorator had indulged herself in a white rug. After a few minutes here, a secretary came to announce that Ackerman was waiting in his own office at the other end of the corridor.

It was a dark, funereal sort of place, suitable, one would think, for a retired French diplomat. The walls were entirely paneled in dark

DECLINE AND FALL

oak, and even the fireplace was of brown marble. The three windows overlooking the courtyard held heavy red draperies that cut off most of the light. Ackerman's desk was of dark wood and leather, ornamented with golden figureheads and leaves and curlicues, in the manner of the Napoleonic era, and on the wall facing the desk hung another oil portrait, this one of Mrs. Ackerman. It was an impressive room in which to receive visitors, who sat in frail Empire chairs around the giant desk, but Ackerman himself seemed somewhat ill at ease in his new splendor. He had littered the place with piles of papers, and whenever the phone rang, he leaped to answer it, as though anxious for contact with the outside world.

An environment not only expresses a man's ambitions; it also changes his perspectives. The Ackerman who sat enthroned in the town house was not the same man who bustled in and out of offices on our editorial floor. Now, he received us only by appointment, negotiated through one of his two secretaries, and we appeared not as the managers of our own domain but as emissaries to his castle. And in the act of physical withdrawal from the Curtis building, he inevitably withdrew, to some extent, from his intense physical involvement in the day-to-day problems of the *Post*. This was quite understandable, too, for in six months of hard labor, his involvement had really accomplished relatively little. And so, as all executives like to fall back on the specialties that originally brought them their success, Ackerman in his town house began to revert to what he had been before he ever came to Curtis, a financier, a maneuverer of stocks and corporations, an expert at mergers and acquisitions, a banker and millionaire.

We had seen but failed to understand the portents that summer, when Ackerman sold the *Ladies' Home Journal* and *American Home*. A man who has serious plans to manage a magazine empire does not lightly dispose of a magazine as large, as good, as venerable, and as profitable as the *Journal*. The reason he had offered me, that publication of the *Journal* committed him to the printing plant, made little sense at the time, and made even less in retrospect. Most moves of such dimensions have a good many reasons, however, and the complications of the printing plant may well have been one factor. But there were other reasons for the sale of the *Journal*. One of them, if one considers Ackerman purely as a liquidator and auctioneer from the beginning, might have been the simple fact that the two profitable magazines were probably the easiest to sell. And even if Ackerman was only partially a liquidator, he might have been tempted to sell the magazines that interested him least.

There may also have been personal conflicts. John Mack Carter, as editor and publisher, controlled all departments of the *Journal,* and he was quite independent in his ideas about its future. And there was still another reason, which Ackerman repeatedly stated, and which most people discounted: Ackerman simply didn't believe in mass-magazine publishing. The *Post* could theoretically be reduced in size and turned into something unique, whereas the *Journal,* trailed by smaller magazines like *Good Housekeeping* and *Redbook,* was committed to the pursuit of a mass audience. There were obvious economic reasons for Ackerman's distrust of mass publishing—the Ponzi game—but it also had roots in something deeper, in his patronage of the opera, in his portrait and his town house.

At the time he sold the *Journal* and *American Home,* however, the explanation that sounded the most logical to me was simply that Ackerman needed money. This had been, after all, a summer of unpaid bills and disaster plans. And the price—100,000 shares in Downe Communications, Inc., then valued at an estimated market price of $5.4 million—seemed low enough to evoke the image of a fire sale. And even that value was theoretical, for the shares were "letter stock"—an issue that could not immediately be sold on the open market. To the *Times,* Ackerman said on the day of the sale, "Basically, we'll keep the [Downe] stock," and the paper added that he "stressed that the Downe stock could be used by Curtis for an additional $5 million of loans if that becomes necessary."

Ackerman soon found, however, that it was difficult to use the Downe stock as collateral for loans, and so, a month later, he had Curtis turn over the stock to Perfect Film for $4.5 million, which was applied against the Curtis loans that Perfect had taken over from Serge Semenenko. Then, once Ackerman had the Downe stock in the possession of Perfect Film, he sold it privately through the Wall Street firm of Oppenheimer & Company to two banks and two investment funds. The sale at $50 a share was not so difficult as might have been anticipated, for Downe shares by this time were selling on the open market at 74. In fact, Downe shares, originally offered on the market at 10, later rose as high as 180—a theoretical increase of $13 million over the price at which Ackerman disposed of them.

But if Ackerman had sold the *Journal* to raise money, his series of deals showed no sign of it. The same day that his sale of the Downe shares was disclosed, it was announced that Perfect Film was spending $9 million to buy from Gulf & Western two Desilu film studios in Culver City, California, the fourteen-acre Culver Studio and the twenty-nine-acre Culver Backlot, both of which were being used by Paramount and various television producers.

Soon after this series of transactions, Ackerman told me he wanted to buy a book-publishing company.

"What's for sale?" he asked.

"I don't know," I said. "I suppose most of them are for sale if the price is right."

"Well, name one," he said.

I named three small publishers, without any idea of whether they were really for sale, and Ackerman declared that he would investigate all three of them.

All of this interested me greatly, because I saw in it a bizarre fulfillment of a daydream I had had since I was about twenty. I even had a name for it: Otto Enterprises—the culture cartel. In my daydream, I was the ruler of a vast empire, including Otto Books, Otto Magazines, Otto Newspapers, Otto Records, Otto Movies, Otto Concerts, and so on. In theory, each one of these divisions would be a monopoly within its own field—in other words, Otto Books would absorb all other book publishers and publish all books in the country —a daydream rather like Pirate Jenny singing, "Kill him now, or later?" I realized, of course, that the Justice Department disapproved of such practices and would probably coerce me into permitting a revival of competition, but Otto Enterprises would gain its real powers through the interrelationship of all its different divisions. An idea conceived by an Otto author would become, in sequence, a serial in Otto magazines, a best seller from Otto Books, a play staged by Otto Productions, a movie from Otto Films, and so on.

These daydreams may sound absurd, but as I grew into middle age, still dependent on a weekly paycheck, I watched a good number of more prosperous entrepreneurs create their own modest versions of my cartel. The Washington *Post*, which already owned several television stations, bought *Newsweek;* RCA bought Random House, which, in turn, controlled Knopf; Crowell-Collier merged with Macmillan and then expanded into remote areas, a secretarial school, a dance studio; Time Inc., perhaps the most classic form of my culture cartel, started a book division, sold records, invested in television stations and newspapers, bought Little, Brown, and acquired an interest in M-G-M. And though all this had passed me by, I now found myself involved with an equally megalomaniac entrepreneur with a rather similar vision.

The Ackerman empire at this point was a curious collection of companies, still largely unintegrated and, to use a clumsy word, unrationalized. At the center, of course, stood the Perfect Film & Chemical Corporation, that mysterious amalgamation of four companies, which still paid Ackerman $200,000 a year as president and still seemed to run all by itself out in Long Island. Its basic business was processing film, but with the help of its various subsidiaries, it also sold vitamins, pens, camera flashbulbs, and dress patterns. Then, with its apparently limitless supply of Perfect Film stocks and bonds (the stocks that Ackerman had bought at $4 rose, after a four-to-one reverse split, to a peak of $88.50 that June), it had acquired a magazine circulation company, two film studios, and a number of publishing enterprises. As a publisher, the empire controlled Curtis, with its four remaining magazines; Popular Library, a paperback publishing firm; and Magazine Management, Inc., a collection of two-dozen pulp magazines and comics. The first and biggest of these three had not really been acquired yet, however. Perfect Film had invested virtually nothing in the Curtis shares that Ackerman repeatedly called "worthless"—preferring instead to take over Curtis's bank loans, at a profit to itself, and Curtis's management. Obviously, the rationalization and reorganization of this conglomerate depended on what could be done with Curtis. But Ackerman did not want to limit himself to magazines, any more than he wanted to limit himself to film-processing. He wanted to move forward into books and movies, and for that, he needed a well-organized company from which to operate. And so we came to a new version of The Plan.

"Some guys just worked this out for me," Ackerman said, his voice alive with anticipation, "and I really think it's going to work. Now here's what we do." He had his yellow pad with him, and he began drawing another one of his organizational charts. First a box at the top, marked "Curtis Pub," then another box marked "N & P," then a third marked "SEP Comp." "Basically, we're going to turn Curtis into a holding company, and we're going to divide its holdings into two separate companies. The first is the New York & Pennsylvania Company, which we've already got anyway as a subsidiary in the paper-making business, so they're going to get the paper mill and the printing plant, see? Now the second company is going to be a completely new company, which we're going to call the Saturday Evening Post Company, and that ought to show people that we're in business to stay. And this will be the company that publishes the magazines.

"Now the next step is that I found ten million dollars," Ackerman continued, with a little smile. "And if you want to know where I found it, I won't tell you, because it's none of your business." (As it later turned out, the repeated reductions in the payroll had left a substantial surplus in the Curtis pension fund.) "So we give three million to the printing plant, and we put seven million into the bank for the magazines. Now once we have this new company set up, free of all Curtis obligations, and with seven million in cash in the bank, I can go right down to Wall Street and sell it to Harvard and Yale and the other institutions. I can issue five million in convertible securities in the Saturday Evening Post Company, backed up by Perfect Film securities, and these institutional investors will buy them up in no time. So we add their five million to the seven million we've already got, and we have twelve million dollars in a brand-new company, still owned by Curtis, and all set to go. I think it'll work. I really think it'll work."

Dick Ficks, the nervous little man who was head of Curtis public relations, had drifted into the Ackerman entourage, working at the town house and generally trying to make himself useful. Now he wandered by and asked what we planned to do about new stationery. I said I hadn't really given the matter any thought and planned to go on using whatever stationery I had until it was gone.

"As far as I can make out," Ficks said, "they're planning to take every scrap of Curtis stationery and set it on fire—fifty thousand sheets of it, if necessary."

"What on earth is the good of that?" I asked.

"Well, as soon as this new company gets going, the Curtis Publishing Company really won't exist any more. There won't be anything left of it but G. B. McCombs and his secretary."

Ackerman's description of The Plan had been mistaken, or else he had changed his mind again. In a subsequent meeting with the advertising staff, he said that Curtis wouldn't be a holding company after all. It would retain the printing plant and paper mill in its own name. And the figures for the Saturday Evening Post Company were all different. Now, as he explained it anew, Curtis would hand over the magazines, which would be valued at $5 million, and it would also provide $5 million in cash. The institutional investors, whom Ackerman repeatedly referred to as "Harvard, Yale, and the Guaranty Trust," would provide another $10 million, not just for the operation of the magazines but for the acquisition of other publishing properties by the Saturday Evening Post Company. There would be 400,000 shares of common stock, half for Curtis and half for the investors. Once all this was accomplished, there could be no doubts about the *Post*'s future, "because we'll have something that nobody else has, we'll have fifteen million bucks in the bank."

One of the advertising salesmen dared to suggest that he was still encountering questions about whether Ackerman might not, despite the name of the new company, sell the *Post*. "I'd sooner sell my wife," Ackerman promptly replied. There was cheerful laughter at that, but the subject recurred later, and Ackerman responded more seriously and more ominously. "I gave this company the name of the Saturday Evening Post Company because I'm so dedicated to the idea of the continued publication of this great magazine," Ackerman said. "I've put everything I have into this—money, reputation, time, energy, because I believe it will work. Now, if it doesn't work—if, despite all our efforts, nobody wants to read the magazine, and nobody wants to buy advertising in it—well, Emerson will just have to get another job." The laughter was slightly more subdued than before, and one of the salesmen broke in to ask whether he could quote Ackerman in public about selling his wife before selling the *Post*. "Sure," Ackerman answered with a shrug.

The public announcements soon followed. Ackerman chose, for some reason, to proclaim his plans in Boston, at a lunch given by the Boston Advertising Club. The reorganization would "assure" the future of the *Post*, he said, adding that it "will become a very profitable magazine." The *Times*, for one, was not impressed; it carried only a few paragraphs from a wire service. To the staff, Ackerman sent a memo on November 1, declaring: "The Saturday Evening Post Company has now been established. It is an entirely new company incorporating an old name—a name which in itself reflects determination to continue this great magazine as a mainstay of our publishing operations."

Soviet intelligence agencies apparently spend huge amounts of time in establishing false identities for their spies, and when we study their activities in detail, it seems surprising that such large and powerful organizations should devote so much energy to seeking out obscure Social Security numbers and duplicating the trivia of immigration reports. It is surprising, however, only because we forget the quantity of trivia that is necessary to establish an identity in the contemporary world. Every bride who takes a new name, after all, discovers the nuisance of obtaining a new driver's license and new credit cards. And although Ackerman had decreed the Saturday Evening Post Company to be "established," it never did gain more than a phantom existence.

Ackerman was president, of course, because he had to be president of everything he touched, but beneath him the Saturday Evening Post Company had no corporate structure except for one accountant, who had been turned out during the first purge at Curtis and then rehired after three months of unemployment to supervise the finances of the SEP Company. There were several meetings devoted to the creation of some kind of hierarchy, and it soon became apparent that Steve Kelly wanted to be the head of the new company. A publishing company in which all the editors acted independently would be "hydra-headed," Kelly argued, and he asked who would "provide the over-all direction." Ackerman's answer was that he would provide that direction himself. The new company's only other organ, finally, was a seven-man board of directors, drawn entirely from the Curtis board, but this group's very existence was generally unknown until Ackerman called its members together in January to settle the fate of the *Post*.

Whatever reality the new company acquired, then, had to evolve from its accumulation of identity papers. All our contracts with writers and agents had to be redrawn. Purchase forms had to be revised and reprinted. Our paychecks began arriving on different paper, headed with the new title: the Saturday Evening Post Company. Nobody seemed able to take any of this very seriously, however. Just as the bride feels that her new name isn't really her own, we all felt that we were playing a complicated game, which we didn't understand. The host had asked us all to put on masks and become masqueraders, and as long as the orchestra kept playing, we saw no reason not to oblige him.

In business, the difference between games and reality is often even less clear than in ordinary life. The creation of a "holding company," the "merger" of two disparate organizations, the act of "going public"—many of the basic events in corporate life are forms of make-believe. Let's pretend, for example, that the Curtis Publishing Company, having a theoretical will of its own, wants to divide itself in half and create a new company. Let's pretend that it wants to give all its magazines to the new SEP Company in exchange for some pieces of paper, and let's pretend that those pieces of paper are worth $5 million. Since the rules for these games can be made or changed by the executives in charge of their companies, the games can veer off at any time into pure fantasy. In an attempt to standardize the rules, and to permit any player to take part in other people's games, we have created the stock markets, which establish a consensus on prices, values, and the basic rules. Curtis Publishing, of course, had been delisted by the New York Stock Exchange. For the Saturday Evening Post Company to achieve a real existence, therefore, it needed some kind of stock-market listing that would certify its otherwise imaginary figures.

"Yeah, I've already got that figured out," Ackerman said. "Here's what we do. There's a little company called Plume & Atwood that we're going to buy, see? Now Plume & Atwood has three things. It makes copper and brass, and it's got a little chain of theaters up around Boston, and it's got a listing on the American Stock Exchange. So we sell off the copper business for maybe ten million, which is probably more than we'll need to buy control of the whole company, and we keep the movie theaters, because they might come in handy later on. And as soon as the Post Company is on its feet, we can merge it with Plume & Atwood, and that'll get us the market listing."

It is traditional for magazine editors to take writers and agents out to lunch and to charge the company for their meals. There is undoubtedly a large amount of waste in this practice, but the total sum of money involved is not ruinous. The custom bothered Ackerman, however. Instead of forbidding or circumscribing these lunches, he decided that we should eat only in certain restaurants, where, in exchange for the restaurants' advertisements in our various magazines, food would be available at great discounts.

"They're perfectly good restaurants—Longchamps, places like that," Ackerman said to Emerson and me. We just looked back at him blankly, and he took our silence as a criticism.

"Look, go to the Pavillon, if you want to," he went on, his voice rising excitedly. "I've got three thousand dollars' worth of credit at the Pavillon, and somebody's got to eat it up. But I save seventy-five cents on the dollar on deals like this. What's the matter, is it a crime for me to want to save seventy-five cents on the dollar?"

I don't know what Ackerman ever did with the names of the three book-publishing houses that he was going to investigate, but I soon heard from Emerson, in the darkest secrecy, that Ackerman planned to buy the firm of Simon & Schuster.

"I don't believe it," I said.

"That's what he says, though," Emerson said.

"They're at least as big as we are, and much more prosperous," I said.

"That's still what he says. And Curtis was a lot bigger than Perfect Film when he took it on. In this business, the little fish sometimes eat the big fish."

"You know what I think he may be doing?" I said. "It's like when I was living in Paris, and I didn't have a nickel, and I would go into an art gallery and say, 'How much is that Modigliani over there?' And they'd say something like, 'Twenty million francs, Monsieur.' And I'd nod and thank them. It used to brighten up my whole day to go and get the price on some antique harpsichord."

Whatever was in Ackerman's restless mind, he went on sniffing at possible acquisitions throughout the fall, and rarely did he keep the prospects to himself.

In October, he said he wanted to start a joint venture with some book publisher to develop *Post* articles into a series of Saturday Evening Post Books. I myself spent a considerable amount of time in developing this plan.

In November, he talked of buying Ed Downe's newspaper supplement, *Family Weekly,* or, if he couldn't get that, some other Sunday supplement. He also wanted to buy a group of movie theaters in New Orleans.

That same month, he said he wanted to buy a Southern newspaper chain, which he said would cost "a couple of million" but was making a profit. "Maybe we ought to go into newspapers," he said. "Who've we got who knows about newspapers?"

In December, he said he was ready to buy the Cosmo Book Distributing Company, which handled shipments to department stores, and the Arco Publishing Company, which specialized in hobby books. "But what I'd really like to buy is Harcourt, Brace," he said. "I think they're the Tiffany's of book publishing."

I suspected that there was no coherent plan behind these periodic confidences—nothing more than Ackerman's sheer enthusiasm at the sight of all the enterprises that were waiting to be bought. I asked him, nonetheless, what all his acquisitions would add up to, and so he treated me to yet another version of The Plan. This time, the first thing he set down on his yellow legal pad was not "Curtis" but "PFO," which stood for Perfect Film. From there, a pencil line descended vertically and then swooped off to the right, ending in the letters "P/A," which stood for Plume & Atwood. This he subdivided into $10 million worth of brass and copper works and $3 million worth of theaters, and then he added the figure of $10 million for the customary sale of securities to "Harvard and Yale." "They love me," he said happily, "the banks and those people, they think I'm just great." Below this, he wrote "SEP," representing the Saturday Evening Post Company, with its magazines and its $10 million from Harvard and Yale. His pencil then began drawing swirls around "SEP," ending in an arrow pointed at "P/A," representing a merger in March of 1969. Then more swirls around the two companies and an arrow that led back to "PFO."

"The whole thing will be a $200 million company, almost as big as Time Inc.," Ackerman said, matter-of-factly. "Maybe 100 million in publishing, 50 million in films, and 50 million in entertainment services, theaters and so on.

"The whole pitch," he went on, "is what this country will be doing ten years from now. Leisure is the growth field. Entertainment, movies, books, magazines, that's what's going to be important. That's the way I see it."

Every month, the advertisers seemed to demand more and more concessions in exchange for their smaller and smaller number of ads. They did not try to interfere with what we said on our editorial pages—either they had given up on that or they had ceased to care—but they tried without interruption to achieve an equally basic goal: to make an ad dominate the page that contained it. Under pressure from our advertising department, we had given up trying to restrict the number of *"Reader's Digest* units"—small ads placed at the center of an editorial page rather than at the side. We had reluctantly opened the front of the magazine to "junior pages"—ads that occupied everything but an L-shaped remnant of editorial text along the edges of a page. We had even permitted the "Letters to the Editors" to be sliced up by "zebras"—single-column ads separating each column of letters. And now it was time for the final assault.

"These people will guarantee us two spreads like this in every issue," Steve Kelly said, depositing a layout on my table. "Look, here's the way it's going to be in *Holiday.*"

The layouts showed two columns of small mail-order ads on the outside of every page, and the inner two columns contained an array of pictures designed to look like the *Post*'s own recommendations on things to buy: shoes, kitchen utensils, ornaments for the lawn. And we were looking at these layouts with Ackerman because Emerson had announced that we didn't want to publish them.

"We can call it 'The Trading Post,' " Kelly pressed on, "or whatever title you guys want."

"Okay, any objections?" Ackerman said.

"Yes, we object," I said.

"Why? What's the matter?" Ackerman asked in surprise.

"It's fake editorial copy, that's what's the matter," I said. "They want us to pretend that the *Post* is endorsing all this stuff, and that's cheating the readers."

"Ah, come on," Kelly said angrily. "Every other magazine does it."

"Well, they shouldn't do it," I said. "I always thought those things were produced by the magazines themselves."

"Say, I don't know where you've been all these years," Kelly said.

"*Life* doesn't do that kind of thing," Emerson said. "*Look* doesn't do it, I don't think."

"Well, all the women's magazines do it, and all the home magazines," Kelly said. "I tell you, it's absolutely standard. And it's business that we need, badly."

"So you guys are really against it?" Ackerman asked.

"Historically, Marty, we've never done anything like this before," Emerson said. "We've always insisted that ads that try to look like editorial copy have to carry the word 'Advertisement' at the top of the page."

"Well, how about that?" Ackerman asked Kelly. "Can't we do that?"

"That would kill the deal," Kelly said desperately. "They just won't allow that."

"Then we're against it," I said. "It's a trick at the expense of the readers."

Ackerman looked at Kelly and shrugged.

"They're against it," he said. Kelly shook his head, swept up his layouts, and marched out.

On December 16, I got home late and found that the day's mail included an invitation from the American Jewish Committee to attend a dinner at the Hotel Pierre for the presentation of the AJC's annual Human Relations Award to Martin S. Ackerman. The invitation contained a photograph and description of Ackerman. It said that in his half-year at Curtis he had "made dramatic changes in the business and editorial approach of the firm that have won widespread recognition . . . from the business world." I looked on the back of the invitation and saw that the dinner was being run by an executive committee loaded with Ackerman's associates and employees—G. B. McCombs, Dick Ficks, a representative of Ackerman's accounting firm, another from his bank. "Black tie," the invitation said. "No solicitation of funds." The price was $150 per person or $1,500 for a table of ten. R.S.V.P.

"I just can't figure this company out," Ackerman complained. "Never before have I seen a business where I had such a hard time figuring things out."

He had taken to wearing a sheepskin coat these days, and he hung it up behind my door and then opened a whole sheaf of budget figures. Ackerman liked to wave sheets of statistics in front of me, but he rarely surrendered them long enough for me to study them in any detail.

According to these new figures, which lumped together all three magazines of the SEP Company, monthly advertising revenues totaled $1.5 million and manufacturing costs totaled $1.4 million, leaving only $100,000 for all editorial costs, corporate salaries, and everything else. And since all those non-printing costs amounted to $500,000, the figures guaranteed a loss every month of more than $400,000, adding up to about $5 million a year. "And that's just more than I'm going to pay," Ackerman said. "It's insane. Every business I look into, every different kind of business, I find everybody doing one-tenth of the work that people do in publishing and making ten times the profits. So what are we all doing here?"

"Damned if I know," I said. "How's the brass and copper business?"

"The more I look at the brass and copper business, the better it looks," he said. He was sitting in Lorimer's chair again, poking at his ear with a tightly rolled bit of paper.

"The only solution I can see," he went on, "is the printing plant. There's got to be a reason why the printers chew up every penny we earn. Look at these figures from McCall's on the *Journal.* I got Ed Downe bound in with a contract until next June, but here's McCall's coming in with a printing bid that's 18 percent less than what our plant charges—that's $180,000 less per month—more than $2 million a year. Now how the hell can McCall's print the *Journal* for $2 million a year less than we're charging? And if that's all waste and inefficiency at the plant, how much could we be saving on the cost of printing the *Post?*"

"A lot," I said.

"That's what you ought to be thinking about," Ackerman said. "That's the most critical problem we face right now—that and circulation. Somehow, we've got to figure it out."

"Okay, I'll see what I can do," I said.

"Where I miscalculated," Ackerman said moodily, "was in keeping the *Post* in the mass-magazine business at all. I should have cut it to one or two million, but everybody got so panicky that we compromised at three million. So we're still carrying a couple of million nonpaying subscribers on our backs."

"Well, we'll get rid of them eventually," I said.

"Yeah, but we can't keep going this way. If there's any real hope of selling eight-dollar subscriptions, then we've got a chance. But I think it's going to take too much time, more time than we've got. I can put in more money if I can see a solution, but if it's just more money down the drain, then I have to start thinking about my obligations to my backers."

I looked at him, still poking at his ear, and I suddenly realized what he was saying. For the first time, he had dropped the imperial first person, had stopped citing himself as the sole authority for what we were going to do. For the first time, he had introduced those anonymous others who are always invoked to justify the unjustifiable.

At the lower levels of the organizational hierarchy, the orders always come from "them." "Always remember," a veteran at *Newsweek* had once said to me, "that it's their magazine." "They" are the ones who impose policies on us and demand our obedience. To a certain extent, this is undeniably true, but it is also true that the very existence of "them" permits the underling to do wrong without any protest from his conscience. "They" order bombings and the killing of captives, and there is nothing one can do. Unless one chooses to deny "them." Even in Auschwitz, according to the testimony of a surviving prisoner, Frau Ella Lingens, M.D. and LL. D., there was one block run by an SS officer named Flacke, where the prisoners were fed and treated relatively well.

"Do you mean to say," asked the astonished judge at the Frankfurt trial, "that everybody at Auschwitz was able to decide for himself whether to be good or bad?"

"Exactly," said Dr. Lingens.

As we rise higher in the organization, we gradually free ourselves of those anonymous superiors whom we call "them." Instead of simply accepting the rules, we first break them whenever it suits us, and then we start making rules for others. Finally, however, we realize that we can never escape from "them," for "they" simply change form, embodying whatever coerces us. A President of the United States speaks helplessly of his inability to get a piece of legislation through Congress, while Congressmen speak fearfully of the administration's terrible powers of retribution. Arrayed against us, then, we see "all that most maddens and torments; all that stirs up the lees of things."

The most curious aspect of these power relationships is that the pressure can come not only from above, or from the side, but from underneath. George Orwell provided one of the best descriptions of this subterranean pressure in his memoir, *Shooting an Elephant*. Orwell, the lone policeman, armed, was pursuing a runaway elephant but was himself being followed by a bloodthirsty crowd of Burmese onlookers.

I did not want to shoot the elephant. I watched him beating his bunch of grass against his knees, with that preoccupied grandmotherly air that elephants have. It seemed to me that it would be murder to shoot him. . . . It was perfectly clear to me what I ought to do. I ought to walk up to within, say, twenty-five yards of the elephant and test his behavior. . . . But I also knew I was going to do no such thing. . . . If anything went wrong those two thousand Burmans would see me pursued, caught, trampled on, and . . . some of them would laugh. That would never do. I shoved the cartridges into the magazine and lay down on the road to get a better aim.

In whatever direction one sees "them," therefore, one can see a justification for one's sins. And since there are few endeavors that cause so many sins as does the pursuit of corporate profit, the whole structure of business is designed to permit a continual shifting of responsibility. Acts that hurt the corporation can readily be blamed on one or two individuals, who can be punished by dismissal, but acts by which the corporation itself does harm are seldom blamed on anyone in particular. The workers labor for the foreman, the foreman for the departmental boss, and so on up to the president, who serves the interests of the board of directors, just as the board serves those of the anonymous mass of stockholders. And as we get higher in the hierarchy, we find not an increasing tendency to sin for its own sake but an increasing willingness to sin for the benefit of the corporation. While a workman may steal some supplies for himself, a vice president will shut down a whole division and throw hundreds of men out of work purely for commercial reasons of state. He cites his obligations to others, to corporate management, to the stockholders. To make a profit is "good business"; to lose money is "bad business." If the elephant is more trouble than it's worth, shoot it. There are no other rules.

"Did you realize it would be all this complicated when you started out last April," I asked Ackerman, still sitting across from me, on the other side of Lorimer's desk.

"Well, I knew it wasn't going to be easy," he said.

"So what are you going to do next?"

"I'm going to take my wife and children on a ten-day vacation to the Bahamas."

"No, I mean in the long run."

"Oh, I never plan more than a year ahead."

In this last month of our existence, we noted a number of minor absurdities, which, in view of later events, had a certain irony. One was that Ackerman wanted all the editorial offices redecorated, and so Lavere Lund began wandering around with various decorators and painting contractors.

The basic plan, apparently, was to have each office painted white on three walls and apple green on the fourth. Protests against the apple green arose immediately, and each editor was given the alternate choices of all white or all green. There was yet another option— a wall of imitation cork tiles—and several of the more aesthetic editors selected that. The painting of offices was only the beginning, however. Once that was finished, the decorators covered the corridors—previously painted white to make up for the lack of natural light—with a kind of wallpaper that looked amazingly like wood paneling. It gave our central corridor the effect of a hunting lodge, but it also made the whole space seem smaller and darker, as though the hunting lodge were somehow buried deep underground, like a Swedish bomb shelter. The final touches of elegance came in the lavatories. In the four-by-four-foot area that separated the men's room from the corridor, the decorators had decreed a thickly textured yellow paper that was supposed to look like silk; in the similar area outside the ladies' room, the color scheme was olive green and mauve.

I couldn't help remembering how Parkinson's Law on new buildings had predicted the fall of Culligan and Blair, and I made a halfhearted attempt to find out who had instigated this extravagant redecoration. Nobody seemed to know. One theory was that Ackerman was papering the offices with leftovers from the town house; another was that the change had been ordered by "the next tenants." In any case, whoever did the decorating apparently had Ackerman's full support, for the idea of covering walls with artificial wood somehow coincided with his views on the proper way to run a business. "As you know, we are having the offices at 641 Lexington Avenue painted," he said in a memorandum to Emerson.

I think the first of the year would also be a good time to get the place generally straightened up, the files put in place, the desks cleared off and the offices looking presentable. There is a tendency on the part of editorial people to let things pile up. We should have a massive cleanup program so that we will at least look like we are in business. . . . The pressure is really going to be put on right after the first of the year for performance. As you know, every dollar we spend that is unnecessary is coming right out of our pockets. Please see that everyone gets the message.

Now that his new headquarters was open, Ackerman passed the word through his publicity man, Dick Ficks, that he wanted to have a state dinner each time a new issue of the *Post* appeared, bringing to the town house a select gathering of writers, celebrities and advertisers. It was a perfectly good idea—many magazines stage lunches for various dignitaries, as Mike Mooney used to remind us when he was experimenting with the same plan at the Stanhope Hotel, and Hugh Hefner even turned the idea of *Playboy* parties into a weekly TV show—but there was a doomed quality to the way Dick Ficks scurried around in search of guests. Our first issue of the new year was a rather good one, but I was not at all certain that its contributors were available for lunch. Arthur Miller, for instance, might have other things to do, and so might Milovan Djilas, who had returned home to Yugoslavia. In fact, very few of the contributors were in New York—Tom Wicker in Washington, Garry Wills in Baltimore, Martin Mayer on a trip to the Middle West, Joan Didion in California, John Skow in Austria.

"Is he going to pay people's expenses to come here?" I asked Emerson.

"No, you don't pay people's expenses when you invite them to lunch," Emerson said.

"Well, you don't ordinarily ask people to come to lunch by airplane either."

"We'll just let Ficks worry about that."

There were problems about the advertisers too. Steve Kelly had delegated the selection of guests to some subordinate, and the subordinate had invited people whom Ackerman didn't want. Dick Ficks sounded very irritated when he called Emerson's secretary to say that the whole lunch was canceled. But we would try again, he said, when the next issue appeared. That next issue, as it turned out, was to be our last.

A week before Christmas, we were still struggling to sell eight-dollar subscriptions. After months of talk, the only system that had achieved any success at all was my scheme to give away a book with every subscription. "That Eldridge Cleaver book has really been moving," Ackerman said on the phone from the town house. "It looks like this is something that really works. Almost three thousand so far."

"Oh, have you got new figures?" I asked. "The last I heard was twenty-five hundred."

"Yeah—well—twenty-five hundred, almost three thousand. Listen, you multiply that by eight bucks and that's twenty-five grand. But what you need is to increase the pull, see? Instead of just a postcard, you ought to take a full-page ad for these premiums. Because if you could double the pull, why that'd be fifty grand. That would pay all the editorial costs for the whole issue."

I was struck once again by the way Ackerman used figures to suit his emotional needs. Somehow, in his desire to find solutions, he was able to convince himself that 2,500 was almost 3,000; that 3,000 times 8 made 25,000; that a full-page ad could double this, and that $50,000 in subscription revenue would not be needed to provide magazines to the subscribers but could be used for editorial costs instead. It was as though Ponzi had started sending money to himself.

"Okay, I'll do an ad," I said. "But listen, while I've got you, I need some figures on the printing problem that you wanted me to work on. Like what's the printing plant's expected profit for 1969?"

"A small profit," Ackerman said.

"Okay, but how much?"

"Well, I'm going to get some new figures on all the printing operations next week," Ackerman said, "so we can talk about it then."

"Next week? I thought you were going to the Bahamas. When are you leaving?"

"Monday," Ackerman said.

Then how in hell can we talk about printing costs? I asked myself.

"Well, *bon voyage*," I said.

23

"There is just not the need for our product"

The last act of a Verdi opera customarily begins with sounds of agitation from the violins and a rhythmic chorus of trumpets and trombones. The dark music heralds the dark end that we know is coming, and we feel a satisfaction in watching the inexorable *forza del destino*. But does poor Leonora know that her brother is going to stab her? Does Manrico really expect to be beheaded, or Aida buried alive?

Throughout the entire decade of the 1960's, people had been predicting the death of the *Post*, and so we must have known, somehow, that it was doomed. These prophets were not only critics and enemies, of whom there were many, but also friends and colleagues, people who had taken part in the fight to save the magazine and had seen how every effort ended in failure. Clay Blair had predicted the disaster at the time of his own downfall, and he blamed it on his enemies. Don Schanche had predicted it and blamed it on the Curtis philosophy of business, Mike Mooney had predicted it and blamed it on our lack of commercial sense, Peter Wyden had predicted it and blamed it on the general decline of the magazine industry. "One day," Wyden had said, back during the euphoric days of the Blair regime, "you guys will put out the best issue any magazine ever published— and *it'll be the last one.*"

And yet we continued to survive, living and partly living, through all rumors and past all prophecies. We had survived our friends and our enemies, employers and competitors, Clay Blair and Joe Culligan, Mac Clifford and Gloria Swett, we had survived Serge Semenenko and

Raymond DePue McGranahan and A. Edward Miller, we had survived the *New York Times* and the *Gallagher Report,* and we had even survived, finally, our own mistakes and miscalculations. By now, we had watched over more than two hundred issues—Emerson, and McKinney, and Ewald and the rest of us who had come to Philadelphia in the fall of 1962—and month after month, year after year, we had seen each new issue start to take shape, grow to completion, come to life, and then give way to its successor. And so, although we must have known that the magazine would die, we had lived through so many death sentences, and so many reprieves, that we must have thought, like miniature Fausts, that our doom could somehow be postponed forever. *Lente currite noctis equi.*

On the morning of January 6, 1969, Emerson stopped at my office on his way to the town house and asked whether I had any problems I wanted him to discuss with Ackerman. This would be the first meeting since Ackerman's return from the Bahamas, and I just offered a few of the standard problems—overdue raises, a change in the company's medical program, a new plan of mine to place institutional advertising for the *Post* at almost no cost. I then settled down to discuss some future assignments with a writer, Anne Chamberlin, who had just turned in her story on the Florida Gold Coast for the February 22 issue.

"Have you heard today's rumor?" McKinney asked from the doorway.

"No, what?"

"They're supposed to be folding the *Post*—today."

"Oh, they're always folding the *Post* today," I said irritably.

"And Ackerman has summoned you and Emerson to the town house to get the news."

"Well, Emerson's down there, but I'm not. And Emerson didn't think it was anything but routine when he left here. Where did you hear this one?"

I had always suspected that if the death sentence came, we would learn of it from the outside, from some stockbroker or gossip columnist. As it turned out, the news came from Jeff Brown, a former *Post* fiction editor who had gone to work at *Life* but still liked to keep in touch with old colleagues. It was probably inevitable that we would hear the news not just from an outsider but from a victorious competitor—the news that Lee is coming to offer his sword is not a very well-kept secret among Grant's adjutants. But because *Life* and *Look* had been the sources of many malicious rumors in the past, and because Jeff Brown was on a relatively low echelon, I shrugged off the rumor as a matter of little consequence.

Emerson did not return until midafternoon, and then I followed him directly into his office, asking, still without any particular anxiety, "Do we have a problem?"

"Well, yes, as a matter of fact, we do."

Ackerman had summoned "the editors and publishers"—a group that seemed a parody of Clay Blair's once-vociferous Curtis Editorial Board, now reduced to only four people: Emerson, Kelly, Stinnett, and Zachary. There were new figures from the accounting firm of Touche, Ross, according to Ackerman, and they predicted that the Saturday Evening Post Company would lose at least $3.7 million in 1969.

"Those aren't new figures," I said. "Ackerman knew them before he went to the Bahamas, three weeks ago."

"Well, he says they're new, and he's acting as though they were new," Emerson said.

Ackerman had announced to the group that he could not stand such a loss. One million, perhaps, but not four million. Having stated the problem, Ackerman began to suggest solutions. One was to sell *Holiday*. Another was to fold the *Post*.

"He actually said that?" I asked, unbelieving.

"He sure did," Emerson said.

"Just a few weeks ago, he said he'd sooner sell his wife."

"Well, maybe he's thinking about selling his wife too."

Steve Kelly had proposed other alternatives. One was to ignore the Touche, Ross figures, since they were based on the assumption that Kelly could not sell the one thousand advertising pages needed for the *Post* to break even in 1969. The Touche, Ross prediction was 820 pages. Kelly growled that he had every expectation of selling the thousand pages he had promised to sell. But if Ackerman didn't believe that, then Kelly had another proposal: Abolish the entire advertising staff, and Kelly would regroup it as an independent organization, selling ads on commission and charging the *Post* only for the ads he actually delivered.

Ackerman promised to think about all this, but he had to go to lunch with Ed Downe, who was threatening to take all his printing business to the McCall plant. Then he had to go to a meeting of the Curtis board's executive committee, and he said he didn't know "what my recommendation will be."

"It's most unlike him not to know what his recommendation will be," I said.

"That's what I told him," Emerson said.

"If he's going to do something bad, he's going to try to spread the blame," I said.

The final decision would be reached, Ackerman had told them, at a special board meeting on Friday. It seemed strange, after a year of Ackerman's autocratic leadership, to hear him invoke the board of directors. That corporate supreme court, that final arbiter, had barely been mentioned since Ackerman's accession. Its monthly meetings no longer attracted any attention in the newspapers, and even its membership had become less than certain. At the time of the last annual report, the board had consisted of the familiar factions: Clifford and a small management group, Cary Bok and the Philadelphia old guard, and Milton S. Gould. That spring, Gould had won board seats for two new allies representing the preferred stockholders, Lawrence Kessel and Thomas Hyland, and Ackerman had acquired seats for himself and Eugene Mason, the corporation secretary. G. B. McCombs, who once was a Clifford member, was now an Ackerman member. Cary Bok had finally retired, due to ill health, but the Philadephia wing had been reinforced by two newcomers named Hedburg and Patterson, representing the Bok family. Clifford and McGranahan had also retired, and who else remained? The two remaining old-timers— Moreau Brown and Walter Franklin? And Ellsworth Bunker, our distinguished Ambassador to South Vietnam.

All that evening, according to Steve Kelly, the *Times* kept asking him for some statement on the newest rumor. "I kept fencing until about eleven o'clock," Kelly said later, "and then they called back and said, 'You want to hear what your boss has to say?' And I said, 'Yeah.' And they read it to me."

"And what did you say to that?" I asked.

"I don't know what I said to that," Kelly said.

The headline on Tuesday morning appeared on, of all places, the society page:

END OF SATURDAY EVENING POST
TO BE WEIGHED BY ITS EXECUTIVES

"Amid reports in publishing circles that the Saturday Evening Post may be discontinued," the story began, under the familiar by-line of Robert E. Bedingfield. "It's all up in the air," Bedingfield quoted the voluble Marty Ackerman as saying. "We don't know what it looks like for the Saturday Evening Post. We don't know whether we can make it." Under four successive presidencies, no major Curtis official had ever announced anything but gains, improvements, and successes, and still the company had lost more than $60 million. If the president of the corporation now chose to say that the future was uncertain, he was announcing, by analogy, the death of the *Post*.

Kelly was not the only one to react with despair. The entire staff read the story and interpreted it in exactly the same way. The only hope was to reach Ackerman and get him to issue a new statement like those he had been making all year—the future of the magazine assured, a "very profitable" year ahead, or a restatement of that promise of the previous spring: "As long as I am here, there will not be a last issue of the *Saturday Evening Post.*" But Ackerman could be reached only at the town house these days, and the secretaries there said that he was out of town. It seemed an incredible time for him to disappear. The only explanation was that he was hiding either from the press or from us, or both. That afternoon, Kent MacDougall of the *Wall Street Journal* was also trying in vain to find Ackerman, and when I asked him what he had heard, he said, "I'm sorry to say that I hear it's all over." He blamed the story in the *Times* on Milton Gould, but when I asked the source of his own information, he only said, "Somebody who should know."

Kelly finally discovered where Ackerman was—in Montreal—but not what he was doing there. Kelly himself was by now in a sad state. His silver hair and gray suit were as immaculate as ever, but he suddenly looked older and fatter than he had looked the day before.

"They've been telephoning all day to cancel ads," he said unhappily, shaking his head. "And the damnedest thing is that we were just getting moving again with the new look—we're well ahead of last year's figures—acceptance in the market is just great—and now this. I tell you—"

I remembered the summer afternoon, a year and a half earlier, when Jess Ballew had been fired, making way for Kelly to take over as publisher. I had wondered then how an advertising manager could keep prophesying success even on the day of his dismissal for failure, but now I saw that this quality was inherent in the breed. It was a series of advertising directors who had guided Sir Walter Raleigh in search of El Dorado and Ponce de León toward the fountain of youth.

Kelly had convoked a meeting with Emerson, Stinnett, and Zachary, but nobody seemed to have any idea of what to do next. Emerson wondered whether it was time to start shopping around for someone who might buy the *Post.* Kelly said it was too late. "The contract with *Life*, in case you don't know it, says that if the *Post* folds, *Life* gets everything—the subscription lists, you name it." I asked Kelly whether he thought the *Post* was salable. "No, I don't think so," he said. Stinnett was only slightly more sanguine. "If you think you've got any kind of prospects," he said to Emerson, "then start shopping."

Emerson was very secretive about prospective buyers, but he

thought he knew at least four—wealthy corporations, interested in communications, with a top management to which he had access— the Washington Post Company, the Encyclopaedia Britannica, Whitney Communications, and, oddly enough, Coca-Cola. He was still uncertain about Ackerman's plans, however, and he worried that a premature effort to sell the *Post* might lead to his own ruin. Ackerman had declared from time to time that the *Post* could not be sold, but Emerson had said to him at their meeting the previous day: "It would do less harm to your own pride and prestige if the *Post* were sold instead of folded." Ackerman had answered: "I know." Still, Emerson had neither asked nor received permission to try to sell the magazine, and without that permission he could not know whether Ackerman would even agree to such a sale. By this Tuesday afternoon, however, it seemed academic to worry about risks.

"Get hold of Ackerman in Montreal, if you really think you need to," I said, "but let's not wait until Friday's board meeting before we go into action."

Emerson did not call Montreal. He called Frederick S. Beebe, chairman of the board of the Washington Post Company. This was probably his best prospect, for the Washington Post Company, through its acquisition of *Newsweek*, had successfully entered the field of magazines and yet owned nothing comparable to the *Saturday Evening Post*. It was also a very prosperous company—"Down in the basement," Peter Wyden joked, "they have a printing press that prints flawless United States banknotes"—and finally, there was a network of many editors and writers who had worked for both magazines: Emerson, Stew Alsop, Wyden, Bill Ewald, Roger Kahn, me. At the end of an hour, Emerson reported that Beebe was "very, very slightly interested." He interpreted this as a sign of hope. To me, it sounded like the closing of another escape route.

On the next morning, Wednesday, a two-paragraph story in the *Wall Street Journal* gave us a good indication of where Ackerman had been the previous day. Plume & Atwood, the story said, "has purchased all the issued and outstanding stock of Gold Star Sales Ltd., a privately held Montreal sales-incentive company [a variation of supermarket green stamps], for $10 million in cash." The main story that concerned us, however, was the *Journal's* evaluation of the *Post's* fate, and it was forbidding. "The ailing Saturday Evening Post appears to be near death," the story began. "Persons familiar with [Ackerman's] thinking said he seems disposed to fold the Post. . . . Milton Gould, the only member of the seven-man Post board who has also been a Curtis director for more than two years, is reported to be among those strongly inclined to fold the magazine."

"Our presentation was so popular that they're asking us to restage it," Steve Kelly said as he entered my office that morning. His words made no sense to me, but Kelly was by now highly distraught. I could only listen politely and hope that I would gradually begin to understand. It soon became clear that Kelly had asked his depleted and demoralized advertising staff to create a "presentation," showing that the *Post* was ahead of its comparative position the year before and would undoubtedly sell the one thousand advertising pages required for 1969. A "presentation" is a popular advertising technique (I have always suspected that it is a very bad way to sell advertising), which can involve movies, slides, or various other forms of graphic paraphernalia, but in its simplest form it involves a large, loose-leafed book, which the salesman holds open before his victim, turning over page after page and reading aloud the statistics shown on a series of graphs and charts.

"I stayed up half the night rehearsing it," Kelly said bitterly, throwing the presentation book on my table. I gathered that Kelly had been preparing himself for a meeting scheduled with Ackerman at ten o'clock that morning, but Ackerman had abruptly canceled it, leaving Kelly with nobody to whom to make his presentation. "I realize it's all academic by now," Kelly said to me, "but just look at this." Since I was the only audience he could find, I would have to listen to the presentation. "Look at this," Kelly repeated, opening the book. The charts had been hastily drawn with Magic Marker, but Kelly pressed relentlessly forward. Advertisements on order on the previous day were 32.9 percent greater than those on the same day in 1968. A series of charts showed that advertising is a seasonal business, and the final chart in the series showed that current figures would project a total of 535 pages of advertising for the first six months of 1969. We flipped on through the plastic pages of the loose-leaf notebook, in a folder of artificial leather with gold lettering, and at the end Kelly noted that there was something wrong. He looked it over for a moment, puzzled. "Now I see," he said finally. "The cover has been put on backward."

Kelly was very disturbed about our situation. His normally red face was flushed. He often broke off in the middle of a sentence and stared into space for a few moments. From time to time, he whipped out a large white handkerchief and noisily blew his nose. One of the things that bothered him most was that he wasn't to be allowed even to state his case to Ackerman. He left the presentation book with me, to give to Emerson, and asked that we present the arguments on his behalf. But even as he made this proposal, which undoubtedly embarrassed him, he saw no hope for salvation. "We should have seen what he was like from the beginning," he said. "He was after the buck, that was all. But we were blind. We didn't want to see."

Shortly after Kelly left, I got another call from Kent MacDougall of the *Wall Street Journal*, who reported a bizarre announcement by Barney Rosset, president of Grove Press, calling a press conference for the following day to "reveal a Grove Press offer for the purchase of the *Saturday Evening Post*." By coincidence, the cover story in the current *Post* was about Rosset, and it was billed as "How to sell 'dirty books' for fun and profit." MacDougall wanted to know whether there was any connection, and I told him that there wasn't. Then, finally, at about two o'clock, I got a call from Ackerman.

"Hey, how're things going?" he asked.

"Jesus, you're the one who ought to tell how things are going," I said.

"Well, I don't really know," Ackerman said.

"What do you mean, you don't know?" I said.

"Well, the board is divided into factions, see? One faction wants to close the *Post*, and another faction wants to keep going for a while, maybe put in another two-three million."

"And which faction are you in?" I asked.

"I just don't know," Ackerman said. "I haven't made up my mind. The trouble is, I don't think the next few months are going to cost just two million but maybe more like five million."

"Quite likely," I said, thinking, *You said you had plenty of money.*

"*Yeah,*" Ackerman said.

"Meanwhile, the publicity is killing us," I said.

"Yeah, nobody you talk to can ever keep his mouth shut," Ackerman said. I laughed at the disingenuousness of that complaint. Ackerman wanted to know where Emerson was. I said he was out having lunch with John Le Carré, but I could find him if necessary. Ackerman said there was no hurry and invited us both to the town house at four.

When Emerson and I arrived there at dusk, we found the whole front door of the building missing. A kind of plastic sheet flapped over the hole, and behind it the front hall was empty. A sign next to the missing door said: "Use basement door." Behind the railing, we found an iron gate, and then we crept down an iron stairway, past some heavy gratings that looked like the entrance to a dungeon. "That's where we're going to keep Bob Yung," Emerson remarked. At the side of the basement entrance, a doorbell was hanging loose at the end of a wire. The door itself opened easily, and a steel door behind it was also open, and so we wandered through the empty basement until we found a narrow circular stairway that snaked upward to an obscure door next to Ackerman's office. He looked up from his desk and greeted our abrupt appearance without surprise.

"Well, how are you?" Emerson asked.

"Oh-h-h," he groaned, quite cheerfully, "I don't know whether my stomach can stand this business. Here, let me take your coats. Reporters on the phone last night, frightening the children. I finally had to disconnect the phone so I could get some sleep."

"It hasn't been easy for anybody," Emerson said. "I might as well say right off that we're all waiting for some kind of word from you."

"I really don't know what the word is," Ackerman said. "I got these new figures from the accountants, and they make it look pretty bad."

"Now, Kelly, as you know, has been putting together his own figures to show that—"

"Look," Ackerman interrupted, "the basic fact is that Kelly can't produce the ads."

"Well, he's got this book that says he can," Emerson said, "and he's upset that you won't listen to him, so I promised to bring his collection of figures over here and get you to look at it."

"Oh, I'll talk to him, I'm willing to be polite to the guy," Ackerman said, taking Kelly's loose-leaf presentation book and thumbing through it without interest. "But I don't think it's going to make much difference. See, Kelly's figures are all based on these letters of intent. He got his salesmen to go out and get these letters of intent from the advertisers, but they ain't worth s———."

"Well, the point Kelly wanted to get across," Emerson said, "is that ad sales are seasonal, and these accountants may not appreciate all the complexities."

"I understand, I understand," Ackerman said. "But look, the fact is that Touche, Ross just don't accept Kelly's predictions. So if I put Kelly's estimates before the board, the board is going to ask me whether the accountants agree with them, and then I've got to say 'No.' And then the question is: Do I *know* that Kelly's estimates are accurate? Do we stake millions of dollars on Kelly's estimates?" He shrugged. We all shrugged.

"Here, look at this," Ackerman went on, fishing around among the papers on his desk. The telephone rang just then, and Ackerman snatched it up with one hand while shoving a letter at us with the other. "Yes, Milt," he said into the phone.

"Dear Mr. Ackerman," said the letter from the accounting firm of Touche, Ross, Bailey & Smart, dated that Monday, January 6,

As you requested, we have adjusted the 1969 Pro Forma Profit and Loss Statement for The Saturday Evening Post Company. . . . The adjusted Pro Forma Statement (Exhibit I) shows a net loss of between $3.7 and $7.0 million compared with a net profit of $1.1 million in the October 11 Pro Forma Statement. . . .

"I understand," Ackerman said into the phone, after a long silence. "Yeah, well maybe they can find some new capital."

"The adjustments," the accountants' letter continued,

are based on the assumption that the present rate of advertising sales will continue throughout 1969. This assumption appears to be reasonable in the absence of any additional advertising stimuli. This advertising sales rate would yield 558 advertising pages for *Holiday* and 578–819 pages for *Post*, compared to 800 *Holiday* and 1,000 *Post* pages projected by Curtis personnel and used in our October 11, 1968 Pro Forma Statement. . . .

"Okay, Milt," Ackerman said into the phone. "Yeah . . . Well, we'll see. . . . Okay . . ."

"That was Gould," Ackerman said. "He's the head of the faction in favor of killing the *Post*. He says the Bok family seems to be kicking up some trouble. They're mobilizing their forces to keep the *Post* going. Well, okay, nobody has any objections if they can find the money to pay for it."

"Why is Gould so keen on killing the *Post*?" I asked.

"He says it's the absolute *duty* of the board not to go through another year of losing more money on the *Post*. He says, 'I've heard wrong figures over and over again.' And now he says these new figures from Touche, Ross confirm his judgment. And Gould, as you may know, is *very* persuasive. So what's the answer?"

"Who knows?" I said.

"It's not that the magazine isn't good," Ackerman said. "We've delivered everything we said we would, and I think the *Post* is without question one of the finest magazines on the newsstands. But that doesn't solve the problem. And you know what I think? I think the next four years are going to be very rough in this business. The guys from *Life* were telling me they're expecting a drop in '69 too. Because, see, the businessman is going to think that these next four years under Nixon are the big chance for expansion, for conglomerates, for everything that business can get away with. And what they always cut down on in a situation like that is the advertising dollar. That's what I predict."

It struck me as unusual theory, but I had no reason to dispute it.

"What about your investors?" I asked. "Do you have any kind of a commitment to them to fold the *Post?*" I asked.

"No—well—I promised that I wouldn't use their capital just to operate the *Post* if it kept on losing money. If that's a commitment—yeah—"

"How about the drop in the price of Perfect stock? How much of a problem is that?"

"Not too much. Of course, if the stock is selling at 80 when you offer to swap it at 70, then a lot of people think you're a great guy, and if it drops to 60, then you're a bum. But Perfect Film is in good shape, so we don't worry too much about that."

"Well, now, what's going to happen at this board meeting?" Emerson asked.

"You never know," Ackerman said. "I have some votes, and Gould has some votes, and then there's ———, if he's functioning. That's why we have board meetings at ten in the morning, so we can have them while ——— is still functioning. Because when he's functioning, he's fairly intelligent, and you can talk to him, persuade him. He's a real swing vote. So we'll just have to see."

"But the main vote is yours," I said. "You say you haven't made up your mind, but what are you going to say at that meeting?"

"What I think now is, if nothing changes between now and Friday, I'm just going to be absolutely neutral."

"I don't see how you can be neutral when you're running the whole company," I said.

"Well, I'll tell you what I can do. I can present the problem and say I don't know the solution. Let's listen to somebody else try to come up with a solution for a change. I'm ready to listen."

"You once said you'd say the *Post* was making money even if it wasn't making money," I said, still trying to draw him into the conflict.

"Yeah, but you can't do that now," Ackerman said. "The loss is just too big. I've always said I could lose a million, or even two, but five million—that's too much, and you can't hide it.

"And even if I put in the five million," Ackerman went on, as though he were arguing with himself, "the worst part is that it would all be gone in a year, and we'd still be right where we are now. I mean, nobody has figured out how to make a profit in 1970, or 1971 either. It's just more of the same, year after year. And I've been running long enough to know that you can get a heart attack that way."

"And nobody wants a heart attack," Emerson remarked.

"Well, I don't want one, I know that. So the basic decision to be made is: Can the *Post* stand another year of struggle? And the next question is: Is it worth it? I mean, is it *worth* it?"

"I think the answer to both questions is yes," I said.

Ackerman shrugged. My views were about as valuable to him as Steve Kelly's charts and figures.

"This isn't just a business proposition," I said. "The *Post* is a national institution. You know that yourself. Ben Franklin High School."

"Yeah, well—" Ackerman sighed. "You know, I had a talk with Jock Whitney when he was losing millions of dollars on the *Herald Tribune*. And he said—national institutions—they're not that different. . . ."

We all sat there in the near-darkness of Ackerman's funereal office, and we knew that rhetoric would accomplish nothing. There had been times in the past when Emerson and I had made impassioned speeches on behalf of the *Post*, and perhaps they had helped to keep it alive a little longer. Perhaps even now we might have shouted and shamed Ackerman out of his post-Bahamian lethargy and into a new round of battle. Perhaps, indeed, that was why he had summoned us, to see whether we still had any inspiration to offer and whether it would be strong enough to revive his spirit. If so, we must have disappointed him. Maybe we were simply too war-weary, Emerson and I—or too familiar with all the arguments why the *Post* must die. Every course that we could propose had already been explored. Finally, it was simply a question of who would spend several million dollars to keep the magazine alive for another year, and neither Emerson nor I had those millions. No matter how exalted our titles or our theoretical responsibilities, we were only salaried employees, after all, and, as Ackerman said, national institutions are not that different.

"Well, let's come back to the idea of selling the damn thing," I said. "Who have you tried?"

"Everybody," Ackerman said. "Of course, you could sell it to some right-winger, somebody like H. L. Hunt, or that guy out in Chicago— he might like it for a year or two."

"But among respectable people?"

"Well, all the main magazines. And Annenberg. And Casey of the Los Angeles *Times*. He was a good man, and pretty interested, but after he looked at the figures—see, you'd need fifteen million bucks in the bank just to run the operation for a year, and you'd have to count on losing five million of that. And the worst thing is that you'd have to accept the subscription obligation of eighteen million. That has to go right on your books as a debit on the day you take over the magazine. And who wants that?"

"Eighteen million!" Emerson sighed.

"Hell, you know what it was when I started?" Ackerman asked. "Sixty million. Sixty million bucks' worth of subscriptions owed to all those folks out in the country. But what I did, I matched it off against the tax loss."

"You mean that famous tax-loss carry-forward has all disappeared?" I asked. "I thought that was the great bait for a merger."

"There's a few million left, but that's about it," Ackerman said.

"Let me ask you—do you have any objection to our trying to sell the magazine?" Emerson inquired.

"Not at all, not if it's a respectable deal," Ackerman said.

"How about the Washington Post Company? Have you tried that?"

"No, that'd be great. But I don't think they'll take it. With those figures, it just won't work. Look, some things you just have to accept, even when they're unpleasant. Maybe we can try something different, a book business. I could put half a million into it, and if we lose it, well . . . But it doesn't do any good to try to duck the decisions that have to be made. Let's face it—there are winners and there are losers, and that's just the way it is."

A bell rang downstairs, and Ackerman started to his feet. He had asked Marvin Whatmore, the president of Cowles Communications, Inc., to come with his advisers to the town house, and for some mysterious reason he did not want the rulers of *Look* to meet the two chief editors of the *Post*. And so we departed down the same back stairway up which we had come, like a pair of Verdian conspirators, while behind us we heard *il principe* loudly welcoming the enemy delegation from across the waters.

Thursday, the next day, was the day on which we gradually gave up our loosening grip on hope. The morning newspapers brought a few more details on Barney Rosset's offer on behalf of Grove Press, and Rosset's press conference confirmed the suspicion that his proposal could not be taken seriously. "We would return the editorial direction of the *Saturday Evening Post* to the spirit of Ben Franklin, adapted to the demands of the modern world in ferment," Rosset declared. All he asked of Ackerman was that the *Post* be given to him "with the understanding that the Saturday Evening Post Company would assume all current obligations and specifically the responsibility for the fulfillment of its unexpired subscriptions." Ackerman dismissed Rosset's gesture as a "gross publicity stunt." And this was not the only such stunt. Bill Ewald got a call from a prosperous rock 'n' roll production group that wanted to pay $250,000 for the chance to turn the *Post* into a pop music magazine.

Much of the day was spent in efforts to find more serious buyers. Fritz Beebe at the Washington Post Company was sufficiently interested to have Ackerman arrange a conference that afternoon with the accountants from Touche, Ross. Who else, then, might want to buy a famous magazine? Who also had enough financial power to commit several million dollars without the delays involved in consulting some committee? I got Emerson to try calling Edgar Bronfman, head of Seagram's and a major stockholder in both Time Inc. and M-G-M. I got somebody else to try John Diebold, head of the management firm called the Diebold Group. Ewald began drawing up lists of possibilities: IBM, Lord Thompson, Hugh Hefner, the Kennedys. . . .

Steve Kelly was still determined to fight on in the same trenches. Having failed to get past Ackerman's door, he sent him a long letter restating his figures—the 32 percent gain over 1968 orders, the projection of 2,135 columns for the first six months, and all the other estimates that nobody believed any longer. He then restated his idea of turning the whole advertising staff into an independent company, which he claimed would save $1.6 million. He also suggested that the *Post* could be reduced to the size of a news magazine, another theoretical saving of $2.2 million. Kelly concluded that his "optimistic view for the future . . . has to be realistically dimmed by the events of the last two days," but he nonetheless "did want you to have this in your records and would hope that you would see fit to discuss the contents of this letter with the members of your board. If I in any way agreed with the assessments that the Touche Ross people have made, I would be the first to tell you so since I hope that in our dealings you are aware of my honest candor."

By this time, even the production machinery had begun to break down. It was difficult to keep lashing the editors to work on the February 22 issue, but we did continue shipping manuscripts and layouts to Philadelphia, only to learn that some of them were simply piling up at the printing plant, ignored. The cover, specifically, was being left unfinished in the engraving department while everyone waited for the results of the next day's board meeting. As soon as Emerson heard of the delays, he angrily ordered all work resumed. The *Post* was not dead yet, he declared, and as long as it still breathed, everybody had a duty to keep working on the next issue.

But the death watch had begun. Reporters from the newspapers and news magazines were calling various editors for comments on the impending collapse. A TV crew from ABC invaded the editorial library and began stripping down the shelves to prepare for some shots of old *Post* covers. And Don Schanche, the *Post* recruiter who had originally invited me to come to work for Curtis more than six years earlier, the militant reformer who had written Blair's manifesto against Culligan, now wandered in to ask whether he could "hang around for a couple of days" to write an obituary memoir for *Esquire*.

As the day drew to an end, the rejections began coming in. Fritz Beebe of the Washington Post Company said the figures indicated that the obstacles were too great. John Diebold didn't even need to look at the figures to come to the same conclusion. Bronfman said he had enough problems trying to cope with M-G-M. On the other hand, Gil Kaplan, publisher of the *Institutional Investor,* said he had offered Ackerman $15 million and been told he would need $35 million. Kaplan was puzzled at the rejection and remarked that Ackerman must have already made up his mind to close the *Post*. I myself suspected that Ackerman wanted a more substantial buyer and would sell only if there were no possibility of later complications.

Throughout all this, Ackerman's painters kept doggedly repainting the editorial offices, and by now they had covered Emerson's walls with a sticky new layer of white. There were various placards on top of chairs and cabinets saying: "WET PAINT." Emerson himself was sitting at his desk with a slice of ham, a pickle, and a glass of red wine. It was seven o'clock, and I was going home.

"I've just been on the phone with Hugh Hefner's money man, and he sounded pretty interested," Emerson said. "And I've got another call in to that guy in Texas, Judge Hofheinz. He's interested too."

"Why are you eating supper so early?" I asked.

"Supper! That's my goddamn lunch," Emerson said.

Television was first. On the CBS eleven o'clock news on January 9, the announcer smiled as he made his statement: "The *Saturday Evening Post* is dead." There was no source, no equivocation, and no fear of denial or retribution.

The Friday morning *Times* was equally definite. "The end will come today for The Saturday Evening Post," the front-page story by Bedingfield began. "Directors of the once-dominant publication . . . will declare it officially dead this morning and arrange for its burial in the subscription lists of Life and other magazines. Thus will end the 147-year publishing history of a magazine that has outlived the more rural, insular America it once served." The story went on to say that Ackerman had called a press conference for that afternoon, at which he might have "something to announce" about merging the Post Company with the LIN Broadcasting Corporation of Nashville. LIN owned two TV stations, six radio stations, and interests in several record companies, art galleries, answering services and mail-order firms. Its most notable possession was the Miss Teen-Age America Pageant. In the previous year, it had earned $1.7 million on revenues of about $25 million, according to President Frederic Gregg, who was expected to sell his 80,000 shares (a 4 percent interest) to Ackerman.

We knew, then, that there was no more work to be done. We were there only to wait until the official announcement came. Emerson arrived late, almost noon, and said that he had been on the telephone most of the night with various prospective buyers, and that he had called several board members to plead for more time. But none of these efforts seemed to matter any more. The war was over, and we had lost. Defeat is worse than war, Lieutenant Henry had said, but one of the Italian soldiers had answered: "I do not believe it. What is defeat? You go home."

Don Allan, the foreign editor, who had been managing editor of the *Reporter* when it was killed just a few months earlier, brought a bunch of orange roses and handed one to each of the girls on the staff. It was a theatrical gesture, but by now we had all become characters in a melodrama called "The Last Day of the *Saturday Evening Post*." No sooner had I arrived at my office than I looked up to see a small, dark figure hovering in the doorway and taking pictures of me. I scowled at him, but he simply went on taking pictures. "I'm Steve Schapiro of *Life*," he said at last, as though that explained and excused everything. By this time, the last-day writers had become a regiment, many of them familiar figures from the past. In addition to Schanche, we now had Tom Congdon on assignment for the *New York Times Magazine*, Tom Hyman and Chris Welles of our own staff both writing for *New York*, Mike Mooney for *Playboy*, Al Aronowitz for *True*, Pete Hamill for the *Village Voice*. A number of reporters from the newspapers and news magazines were there too, and a young lady in a miniskirt, named Jill Krementz, climbed and crawled around, taking photographs from various positions on the furniture, radiators, and floors. All these people spent the day sitting around in our offices, watching us pretend to lead normal office lives, and waiting for something poignant to happen. Precisely because they were all flocking around, of course, nothing could possibly happen, and so they eventually went away and wrote that the end had come quietly.

The board meeting lasted longer than we expected. It had started at ten, in Ackerman's town house, and it continued until almost two, the hour at which Ackerman had scheduled a press conference at the Overseas Press Club. Six of us had hamburgers and beer around the corner from the office, then piled into a taxi and drove over to West Fortieth Street, just behind the Public Library. We arrived at the second-floor auditorium in time to see Ackerman standing in the glare of the TV lights and blinking as he read his announcement.

"This is one of the saddest days of my life," he was saying, reading the words calmly in his slightly nasal voice, "a sad one for me, for our employees, officers and directors; indeed, it is sad for the American public. However, no other decision was possible in view of the sizable predicted losses which continued publication would have generated. Quite simply, this is an example of a new management which could not reduce expenses nor generate sales and income fast enough to halt mounting losses. . . . Having refinanced the Saturday Evening Post Company with $15 million in new capital, I assured directors and stockholders of the company that regardless of my own personal feelings, if we could not return a profit we would have to shut down the *Post*. Apparently there is just not the need for our product in today's scheme of living."

That, in any case, is the official record of what he said. I found myself unable to listen. The news had been in that morning's *Times*, after all, and this was just the ritual confirmation. The news had been recorded before it had happened, in other words, and the actual announcement of the actual event was just a scene staged for the TV cameras. On a chair in front of me, I saw a foot-high stack of press releases, and when I took one of them, I saw that it carried the printed text of what Ackerman was saying. To listen to the formal reading seemed unnecessary. Instead, I looked deafly at the man himself, standing so confidently before the row of microphones, and nicely browned by the sun of the Bahamas. I wondered if he had not perhaps applied some tan makeup in preparation for the TV appearance. I wondered, for that matter, whether he could see beyond the television cameras to his full audience. I was standing directly in front of him, not more than fifty feet away, and he looked directly at me as he spoke his funereal words. But between us stood the TV lights, shining only on him, and as Brecht observed at the end of *The Threepenny Opera*: "*Man siehet die im Lichte/Die im Dunkeln sieht man nicht.*"

I remembered the first time I had heard Ackerman make a speech, that festive occasion after dinner in the Hilton, when he had warned us that we must become successful and make profits for the corporation. "And decisions are going to be made," he had said. "They will be hard, and you may not agree with all of them, but decisions will be made." Yes, he had lived up to that promise. He had promised that there would be a great effort to make the Curtis magazines successful, and that those of us who could help him in that effort would all get rich, but that any failures would be punished with dismissals and liquidations. "People who can't do the job will go," he had said. Yes, many were gone by now, and many more would have to follow. That was the law of the profit system.

There were desultory questions. Ackerman confirmed his purchase of the shares of LIN Broadcasting, but not the reports of a merger. He guessed that the *Post* had lost about $5 million during 1968 but that Curtis as a whole had broken even. He admitted that he couldn't be sure of this because there had been so many changes in the company's structure. He would do his best to find new jobs for all *Post* employees, and the loyal subscribers who had done so much to kill the *Post* would "receive full value in the form of magazines they wish to receive as substitutes for the *Post*."

After the questions, we all milled around a large table where dozens of cups of black coffee were standing ready, and I kept thinking, simultaneously, two contradictory things: *This is not real, it is not happening*, and, on the other hand, *So this is the way it all ends*. I saw Don McKinney take up a cup of coffee and begin sipping it, smiling feebly in all directions, and then I saw Emerson dazedly answering reporters' questions, and then I saw our slender production chief, Rita Waterman (nee Ortiga), reacting the way a good Italian girl reacts. Tears streamed down her cheeks as she ran out of the auditorium and into the elevator. "Come on, let's get out of here," I said to Schanche, and we walked down the circular stairway and out into the street. It was cold and clear, and I couldn't help observing that most of the world was thinking about other things. At Fifth Avenue, we passed the debris of the parade that had gone by that morning, honoring the first three Astronauts to fly around the moon.

"Are you really sad?" I asked Schanche.

"Yes, I really am," he said. "More than I'd ever thought I would be."

Back at the office, the television crews were established in full force. The glaring lights had been set up in the main corridor, and a crowd was milling around just outside the copy department. Emerson

was making some kind of a statement, but the TV people were interviewing anybody they could find, more or less at random. I took
Emerson by the arm and led him away from the pursuing interviewers and told him that he ought to gather his staff for a farewell
meeting.

"What should I tell them?" he asked.

"I don't know. Tell them whatever comes to mind. Tell them they
did a good job."

And so Emerson did gather them all together in his office, barring
the press at the door. These were the last survivors, and a woebegone
group they were. A dozen editors or so, a few people from the art
department, and a handful of secretaries. The previous spring, I had
told Mike Mooney that we were a defeated army; now we were a
defeated platoon. And Emerson, for the first time since I had known
him, had very little to say, no jokes, no stories about his uncles in the
South. He thanked everyone for the work done, and he apologized for
any shortcomings of his own. He said it had been a great voyage, and
a great attempt to save a magazine that had deserved better of its
owners. And that was all. He asked whether I had anything to add,
and I said I didn't. He asked Don McKinney, and he had nothing to
say either, but Don Allan, believing that Emerson had called on him,
said he did have something to add. "God bless you all," he said.

Having been excluded for fifteen minutes, the press began banging
on the doors, demanding group pictures, and then a television crew
marched in. If it had been strange to be interrogated and photo-
graphed in the morning, it was even stranger to be pursued by television in the afternoon, for if reporters and photographers distorted
the reality they were trying to cover, the equipment-laden TV crews
completely shattered it. There were four members of this crew: a
lighting man who drowned us all in the white glare of his floodlights;
a cameraman who bent gnomelike under the burden of his camera
and aimed it in any direction where there were signs of movement; a
gray-haired sound man, who docilely carried a large box, resembling
a hurdy-gurdy with dials, on a strap around his neck, and finally a
snappy young "reporter," who maneuvered his team around like a
sheep dog, asking an occasional question and then holding forth a
microphone while cameraman and sound man captured the answer.
Having little to say, Emerson held aloft Charley Barsotti's Valentine's
Day cover, drawn for the February 22 issue that would never be
published, and one of the girls read out the caption Barsotti had
written underneath his lonely heroine: "If I can't have a knight in
shining armor, bright star, how about a little action?"

At about five, the television crews took their cameras and went away, and people began bringing out bottles of whiskey, and it took very little time for the liquor to spread a kind of artificial and slightly bitter conviviality. "Laughter is supposed to keep a man young," Ring Lardner had written, "but if it's forced laughter it works the opp." It seemed incredible that only four days had passed since Emerson had asked whether I had any problems to take up with Ackerman on his return from the Bahamas, but now our only real topic of conversation was what the severance pay would be, and how one enrolled for unemployment insurance, and where the next job would be found.

Some advertising people drifted up from the third floor and brought us the news that Steve Kelly had officially resigned that morning, just before the announcement of the *Post*'s closing.

"A grand gesture," I said. " 'You can't throw me out, I quit.' "

In due time, Louise the cleaning woman appeared, snuffling, and Emerson hugged her fiercely and told her that it was against the rules for anybody to cry. "It's-a true? It's-a true you going away?" asked Louise, the last one to have faith that somebody might yet prevent the debacle. Emerson told her it was true, and Louise cried out: "Oh, where was Saint Anthony?"

There had once been two of them, Louise and Lena, sisters, both immigrants from Italy, and they had become our cleaning women on our first day in New York, more than six years ago. Lena had gone on to scrub floors in Wall Street, but Louise had remained with us, bringing cookies and cheeses, cleaning out coffeepots, and greeting everyone with a shy grin.

"When my husband died," Louise said, "he look at me and say, 'Louise, they never make another like you.' That's you guys." Then she burst into tears.

"Hush, now, Louise," Emerson said gently. "You'll make us all cry. Have you ever seen fifty people cry in unison?"

Someone had given Emerson several samples of a new drink, a Martini that came ready-mixed in a plastic bag, and now he put his arm around Louise and offered her a sip of the concoction. "Tonight, Louise," he said solemnly, "you and I are going to get together and drink hard liquor. You better be ready, too, or I'm gonna raise hell and kick the baseboard. Now here—this is something that you shouldn't drink until you're lying down. You'll take three steps and fall heavily."

"You gonna take me with you?" Louise asked confusedly.

"We're all going to meet in seven years and start all over again," Emerson said.

"You told me everything was gonna be all right," Louise sobbed. "I told myself, 'You fulla s——.' "

"Death is inconvenient, Louise," Emerson said. "Here, have another drink of this, and don't cry. We're going to be around here for a while yet. I'm planning to hide in the men's room for months."

As it drew near to seven o'clock, people began congregating in Rita Waterman's darkened production room, waiting for the television news. (On the door of that production room, I noticed that Ackerman's imitation-wood wallpaper had already started to tear loose and hang down in tatters.) Television had played a large part in killing the *Post*, of course, not malevolently but simply by coming into existence, the new medium, more dramatic, more immediate, and cheaper. The heirs of Cyrus Curtis and George Horace Lorimer had been strong when television was weak, and there had been a time when they could have bought control of a whole network, but they had chosen instead to ignore the new competition. And so it took away Curtis's audience and Curtis's money, and then it came with lights and cameras to record the death of Curtis's old magazine, and nobody really seemed to mind the intrusion. Everyone wanted to take part in the show.

As I was about to leave for home, with my last armful of office possessions, I heard Charley Barsotti shouting: "Otto!"

"What's the matter?"

"I just think there's something we ought to say to each other," Barsotti said, "but I don't know what it is."

"If you think of it, let me know," I said.

When I passed Rita's production room, on the way out, they were all sitting in the darkness, watching themselves on television.

That night, I succumbed to the same temptation and watched the closing as one of a dozen items on the eleven o'clock news. Ackerman's elaborate press conference had been cut to two or three sentences, and Emerson looked hot and flustered under the lights in the corridor, but the TV people knew how to package a story within a minute or two. They closed with a shot of Rita, who looked very pretty as she said, "This was a family, and everybody here was part of it."

The next week, I found out how unpleasant it is to be deprived of all function and all authority. We came to work on that Monday without any real job to do, and without any clear announcement on how long we would remain on the payroll. All such questions would be decided by Ackerman himself, or by Lavere Lund, or by two of their young lieutenants, a round, partly bald man named Dick Brigdon and a thickly mustachioed accountant named Ernest Linneman. In sudden contrast to times past, the editors' writ no longer applied. Payments that we had approved simply ended on Linneman's desk, awaiting his decision. And we no longer had any political power with which to settle arguments. We could no longer use our control of the magazine, for we had no magazine. We could not threaten to leave, since we were supposed to leave anyway.

We had only two functions left. One was to dispose of the inventory of articles, stories, and pictures that we had acquired before the collapse. The other was to see that the staff was reasonably paid off and helped toward new jobs. We began these tasks in a leisurely way, but the sense of leisure lasted only through that first Monday morning. On Monday afternoon, a memo from Ackerman's office announced that severance pay would be only one-half week for each year's service, with a minimum of two weeks' pay and a maximum of twelve. There are very few unions in the country that would accept such terms, and Mac Farrell, the bearded fiction editor who had lived through the failures of *Collier's, Coronet, Everywoman's,* and *Show,* promptly announced that an employee committee would contest the issue, by a lawsuit if necessary. Emerson and I refused to join the committee but said we would try to negotiate a settlement. Ackerman, however, now claimed he was too busy to see us.

On Tuesday, Emerson reached Ackerman by telephone just long enough to hear him say that the severance terms were final. And Linneman asked Emerson how many people could be removed from the offices by the end of the week. "Why, all of us," I said. Emerson frowned at that and said some people needed more time to look for jobs. But the more I thought about it, the angrier I got. "Let's tell Linneman that we'll all go out of here together," I said again. "On any day they choose."

"The rest of the staff may not be so eager to be sacrificed so soon," Emerson said sourly. "They'd probably planned to stay around until they could get new jobs."

"Then let's call them in and tell them what we're doing, and let's tell them that if they don't want us all to go out together, they can form their own committee to decide which people get thrown out first. But let's not us do it."

Emerson announced this decision to Linneman the next morning and reported that Linneman was surprised, incredulous. But Emerson himself was suddenly more cheerful. He had been in a foul temper at the beginning of the week, still afflicted by a terrible sense of guilt over the death of the *Post*, still feeling that he, as the editor, should have found some way to avert the collapse. And now that his fundamental managerial position had been destroyed, he could feel a great sense of relief in abandoning the management entirely and shifting to the side of the employees. If any of them had to go, we would all go. It was very simple. Lavere Lund soon came by and said that our plan was "impractical" and "unreasonable," but I answered that Ackerman's harsh closing terms were just making him a lot of enemies. I urged Lund to persuade Ackerman to be more generous, and he promised that they would discuss it.

Thursday was spent in maneuvering. Ackerman had made an appointment to see Emerson and me, but his secretary called up to postpone it until Friday. Ackerman's lieutenants brought word that we could carry out our request to send all accepted but unpublished manuscripts back to the authors for resale (a liquidation of about $300,000), but they were adamant on severance pay. It was a matter of company policy, they said, and all other departments had accepted it. The American Society of Magazine Editors happened to be meeting that day, and, at the behest of Harold Hayes of *Esquire,* the assembled editors drew up a collective statement saying that Ackerman's terms were far below the standards of the industry. As soon as Emerson learned of this, he had the statement delivered by hand to Ackerman's town house. But Ackerman was busy with other things. That day's mail brought me a last notice from the American Jewish Committee. "Make your reservation today," it said. That very evening, at the Hotel Pierre, before an audience paying $150 each, Ackerman would receive the Committee's annual "human relations award."

On Friday, January 17, which happened to be Ben Franklin's birthday, we were all summoned to the production room to hear Ackerman's people announce our future. The chief speaker was to be Dick Brigdon, with Lund sitting beside him for moral support, and Linneman at the back of the room. It began very politely. Brigdon, obviously nervous, told us quite directly that we should get out of the offices at the end of the day.

"I am representing the management," he said, "and I am here to inform you that your employment with the Saturday Evening Post Company is terminated as of today, and you will be expected to leave by the end of the day. For you to linger would be a disadvantage to you. We have no intention of continuing your services. There is really very little work left to do, and your services are no longer required."

The employees' committee had decided to respond only with a series of polite questions. What about vacation pay? There would be no vacation pay, Brigdon answered. What about contracts with writers? They would all be turned over to the legal department. What about the two weeks' notice required by state law? There was no such law, and the management had decided that two weeks' severance pay would be final.

As I listened to these formal exchanges, I once again became angry at the way an anonymous force called "management" could expect docile compliance with whatever it decreed to be "company policy."

"I'm glad everybody is being so polite," I finally said, "and I hope it continues that way, but I'd like to make a statement which I think will have the support of everybody here. The man whom you euphemistically call 'management' once promised that he would never close down this magazine, and that he would lead it to great prosperity, and many of us believed his promises. Now that what you call 'management' has decided to close down the magazine he promised not to close, I think the offer of a half-week's pay for every year worked is grossly inadequate and grossly immoral. And that we should be thrown out onto the street on one day's notice is an absolute outrage!"

Before I had even finished, everybody in the room burst into violent applause—except, of course, for Ackerman's lieutenants, who looked at me in silent accusation, as if to ask how I, a member of management, could indulge in such demagoguery. As soon as the applause died down, Emerson joined in and denounced the severance terms as "mean" and "heartbreaking," reflecting "a management that does not deserve its employees." The questions then became increasingly strident. How could Ackerman keep boasting of his millions and then treat his employees so shabbily? Why had he come to Curtis in the first place?

Lund, a cocky little man, intensely loyal to Ackerman, could not remain silent any longer.

"When we came here last spring, you all wanted raises," he shouted, "and you all got them, didn't you?"

"No! No!" The answer was a chorus.

"You didn't get raises?" Lund asked, uncertain now.

"We got nothing but promises!" cried Elena Dardano, the bookkeeper.

The questions became still sharper. Why had the advertising salesmen received a Christmas bonus? These were management policies, Brigdon said, over which he had no control. Then who was in charge of things? Management had issued its instructions, Brigdon said, and that was that. "As you can gather," Mac Farrell shouted over the turmoil, "your proposals are unacceptable to the staff. We do not accept the severance pay, we do not accept the loss of vacations, we do not accept the whole package."

Brigdon, rather white-faced by now, turned to Lund and said, "Well, there's no point in staying here any more." The two of them pushed through the boisterous crowd and out the door.

"I don't really care whether they like me or not," said Lavere Lund, sitting in my office a few minutes later, drinking a cup of coffee. "After all, I'm not paid to be liked. Let them all work off their frustrations. The worst thing that can happen to me is what I really want anyway, and that is that I go back to teaching school."

"What did you teach in school?" I asked aimlessly.

"Business and administration," Lund said. "At the University of Washington. In Seattle. But I got the feeling that it was immoral to teach something when you didn't have any firsthand experience of it. Those textbooks on how business works, that just isn't the way it is."

At the town house, where I was to meet Ackerman and Emerson that afternoon, the front door had been restored, but nobody answered it. Now that I knew the dungeon route, I decided to try that, and once again the door opened easily. The hall was barred, however, by a second door of black iron grillwork. I heard voices in the background, so I called out. Two maids in black uniforms skittered past the end of the hall, and then a butler appeared in evening dress. When I explained who I was, the butler let me through the iron door and led me to an elevator, where we both stood for a while.

"Nothing seems to work around here," I said.

"No, we haven't got all the bugs out yet," the butler said.

"There are stairs around here, aren't there?" I said. And so we started up the same circular stairway that Emerson and I had discovered on our last visit. We emerged at the ground floor, and I heard a deafening surge of movie music coming from the dining room. "What's all that?" I asked the butler. He didn't answer, but another maid came darting out of the pantry and hurried to close the doors to the dining room. The butler led me to the reception desk in the front hall, which was now occupied by an ancient Negro.

"He says the front doorbell doesn't work," the butler said.

"The doorbell doesn't work?" the Negro repeated.

"Well, nobody answered it," I said. The Negro and the butler looked at one another as though unable to decide what to do next. A secretary whom I had never seen before suddenly appeared.

"Look, I have an appointment with Mr. Ackerman," I said to her. "Isn't Bill Emerson already with him by now?"

"No," she said. "Come, will you wait on the third floor?"

I walked ahead of her up the curving stairway, and by the time I reached the third floor, I heard her calling me back again. Now she silently held open the doors of Ackerman's office and waved me in.

Ackerman was talking on the telephone, obviously to some reporter, and Emerson sat in a nearby chair, looking rather unhappy. "Well, if I hadn't come in and taken over last spring, there wouldn't have *been* any *Saturday Evening Post,*" Ackerman said into the telephone, "and there wouldn't have been any severance pay at all, because there wouldn't have been any payroll, they were that broke. . . ." I slipped off my coat and took another seat, next to Ackerman's desk. I noticed that on a table just to the right of his desk he had put on display the "human relations" plaque presented to him at the dinner the night before. "Well, this is company policy," Ackerman said into the telephone, "and it was accepted by all the other departments, but the editors apparently think they're better than anybody else. . . ." After a few more statements of the same kind, Ackerman hung up and turned to Emerson in a state of great indignation.

"Your guys seem to want to play Russian roulette," he snapped, "and if they do, they've come to the right guy, because I love to play Russian roulette."

"In case you don't yet have a copy of this," Emerson said quietly, "here's a copy of the employees' statement to the press."

Ackerman snatched it and glared at it, his hands trembling.

"Considering the devotion, hard work and loyalty of the staff to the magazine through many difficult years . . . the attitude of the management strikes me as not only callous but immoral," MacLennan Farrell, the *Post*'s fiction editor, said. The staff has formed an employees committee . . . and is seeking two weeks' pay in lieu of notice . . . payment of accrued vacation time, and two weeks' severance pay for each year of employment. . . . The committee has retained legal counsel, Taylor, Ferencz, and Simon, and, said one committee spokesman, "We intend to pursue vigorously all available remedies."

"You know what I think of that?" Ackerman said, throwing the statement to one side. "It makes me want to throw up. It makes me want to *puke!*"

"You understand that Otto and I are not taking part in this suit," Emerson said.

"They're your people," Ackerman said. "It's up to you to control them."

"No, it isn't," Emerson said. "They're quite capable of acting on their own, and they're doing it because they feel they're being treated unfairly."

"And then going to the press before I even hear about it," Ackerman snarled. "It's blackmail, that's all it is—*blackmail!*" He shouted the last word and banged his fist loudly on the top of his gilded desk.

I had thought that Ackerman would feel guilty about his destruction of the *Post,* and that a sense of failure and loss would make him behave a bit less like a conquistador. I had thought, in other words, that he would be inclined toward generosity and apologia. I found exactly the opposite. Aided by all those traditional arguments of commerce—the well-being of the corporation, the need to cut losses and make profits, the interests of the stockholders—and probably aided even more by the flattery of his entourage, Ackerman seemed to have convinced himself that his action had been not just necessary but quite acceptable, even admirable, forceful, brave, and quite beyond criticism.

"You talk as though you were some kind of a victim, Marty," I finally said, "as though you were being persecuted by your employees."

Ackerman nodded in agreement, apparently happy to see that someone had finally understood his position.

"But you're the villain of this story," I said.

"Huh?" Ackerman gasped. He looked as though I had struck him. His eyes widened, and he seemed unable to speak.

"Yeah, you're that character known as The Boss," I said. "The one who wears a big top hat and stands in the window looking out at the workers shouting back at him. You're the man who killed the *Saturday Evening Post.*"

"Now listen, I tried like hell to save the *Post,*" Ackerman protested. "I worked like hell on it. You know that."

"Sure, I believe you," I said. "But I'm one of the few people who do."

Ackerman could have argued that he had acted out of necessity, or that the president of the corporation had a right to do as he chose, but Ackerman was too argumentative and too moralistic to settle for such a resolution. It seemed clear to me that he wanted to believe that he had done the right thing, and to believe that, he had to persuade us. His cause was a weak one, but he would not give it up. He returned again to the argument that he was being threatened.

"We tried to talk to you Marty," I said, "but all we got from you was that telephone call to Emerson, when you said you wouldn't budge on the severance."

"And now I get a statement to the press," Ackerman said bitterly. "That's blackmail."

"But you wouldn't talk to us," I said again. "As a matter of fact, I told all this to Lund two days ago. Now did he tell you about our conversation?"

"Of course."

"Well, then you knew exactly what was coming before anybody said anything to the press."

"Yeah, but you should have told them to keep their mouths shut, and we could have worked this out."

"Look, I know your mind is made up, and we're not really getting anywhere with this argument," I said. "But I'd just like to tell you that what we're urging on you is for your own good. Because if you have any future plans in the field of publishing and communications, and if you care about your public image in this field, then you're making things unnecessarily hard for yourself in the future. If you insist on pinching pennies now, you're going to be sorry you did this five years from now."

There was an element of hypocrisy in my little sermon, of course, and Ackerman answered it in kind.

"Well, if it were just a matter of my own self-interest, perhaps I could make some kind of a deal," he said, "but this involves money that isn't mine, and it's a matter of principle. What I'll do for your people, I'll help them get jobs. And anybody with any hardships, we'll take care of them."

"That's grand old-fashioned paternalism," Emerson said. "You sound like a Southern textile mill owner."

"What did I say that was so terrible?" Ackerman protested. "You talk as though severance pay was some kind of penalty that I had to pay."

"That's exactly what it is," I said. "And they want it as their right, not as your charity."

"Well, I just can't see that," Ackerman said. "There are thousands of employees in this company, and they've all got to be treated evenly. I can't break the rules for the editors."

"Sure you can," I said. "You pay them higher salaries than you pay the printers. And I can't imagine that this company has any rules that you couldn't break if you wanted to."

"Well, how about this?" Ackerman finally said. "Suppose I appoint you guys as a committee of two, and I give you $50,000 to settle the hardship cases, and you can spread it around any way you want. I don't care what you do with it. I don't even want to know. I'll tell the board that it's for hardships. It's not severance. But you handle it any way you want."

It is a little surprising, after one has given up all hope, to receive $50,000, but the essence of good bargaining is to accept victory gracefully.

"We'll be happy to take that back to the employees' committee and see what they say," Emerson said. "And we'll get right back to you as soon as they decide."

Suddenly, there was no more argument. It seemed a good offer— averaging out to an extra week's pay for each year of employment— and we rightly assumed that the staff would accept it as a settlement. But having put up the money, Ackerman wanted the last word.

"You know, looking back on it, maybe Kelly wasn't so bad after all," he said. "I think better of him than of your people."

"How's that?" Emerson asked.

"Well, he said he wanted to resign, and he said, 'I don't want any severance pay at all.' Whereas you guys all want the payoff."

"I can't see that at all," I said. "Kelly's resignation was meaningless."

Ackerman just smiled and shrugged. He helped Emerson into his coat, and we stood for a moment in embarrassment.

"Marty," I said, holding out my hand, "I'm sorry it all ended this way."

"Well, you know," he said, shaking hands, "it always does."

Then, once again, he undid his trousers and began tucking in his shirt. It was a gesture of preparation, somehow, for all the battles that were to come.

Book IV

EPILOGUE

"If I wasn't real," Alice said . . . "I shouldn't be able to cry."
"I hope you don't suppose those are *real* tears?" Tweedledum
interrupted in a tone of great contempt.

—*Through the Looking Glass*

24

The Aftermath

"Sure Marty fell on his ass with the *Saturday Evening Post*," Milton Gould said to a reporter from *New York*. "But Curtis is not bankrupt. It's got equity. It's $10 million richer. The creditors are happy. I'm happy. We're all happy. Marty's a great kid. He did a good job. He's one of the ablest, most dynamic human beings I know."

By the rules of the profit system, then, Marty Ackerman had done well. And yet it was not without significance that Ackerman's predecessors had all felt a mysterious sort of fear at the idea of killing the *Post*. They must have sensed, somehow, that whoever did the deed would be marked forever after. And so it happened. I myself left with the rest of the *Post* staff in mid-January of 1969, and so I had to depend on the *Times* and the *Wall Street Journal* to report on new developments. They did not tell a great deal, but they told enough to show that the fates had suddenly shifted against Marty Ackerman.

On February 3, the lawsuits began. Philip P. Kalodner, a thirty-eight-year-old Philadelphia lawyer who popped up every spring to make complaints at the Curtis stockholders' meeting, filed a suit in Common Pleas Court in Philadelphia. A Philadelphia accountant named Frank M. Tait served a similar complaint on Curtis in New York. Kalodner's suit specifically accused Ackerman of "illegal, oppressive and fraudulent" actions that had "misapplied and wasted" more than $45 million of Curtis assets. It said Ackerman had sold the *Journal* and *American Home* and the Curtis Circulation Company at prices "substantially below fair market value." Ackerman immediately denied these charges and denounced them as "sheer nonsense."

"Nobody has wasted the assets," he said. "On the contrary, we have preserved the assets."

Later that same week, the trustees of the estate of Cyrus H. K. Curtis began a far more powerful assault. They, too, accused Ackerman of dissipating the Curtis assets, and they publicly demanded that he resign from the presidency by noon on the coming Saturday, February 8. They also demanded the resignations of his closest allies on the board of directors—Milton Gould, Eugene Mason, and G. B. McCombs. The trustees were vague in their accusations, citing only "conflict of interest," but Cary Bok told a reporter who telephoned his home in Camden, Maine: "That company is in such a damn mess that it's time we got into it—don't you think?" The question sounded reasonable enough, so much so that it might well have been asked a few years earlier. But even though the Bok family's apathy had permitted the corporation to drift into its present condition, the Boks' sudden offensive was hard to resist, for the family controlled 32 percent of Curtis common stock and 22 percent of the preferred. In effect, the family was asserting that it still owned the company that it had failed for so long to manage. Now it rose from its torpor to declare itself, in the words of a spokesman, "dissatisfied with, and disturbed by, the Ackerman management."

Ackerman's initial defense was that the family's two representatives on the board, Robert Patterson and Robert Hedburg, had approved all his major moves. To this defense, the trustees' anonymous spokesman offered an unusual rebuttal: "The directors were bamboozled. They went along, but they still didn't know what they approved and what they didn't approve." In searching for more details of the family's unhappiness, the *Wall Street Journal* printed a story saying that Ackerman had recently transferred $6 million out of the $34.4 million Curtis pension fund and used the money for corporate expenses. Another irritant was the management's failure to produce any minutes of monthly board meetings. "He'd say he was going to do one thing," the trustees' spokesman said of Ackerman, "and then he'd do another." Under this pressure from the major stockholders, the board itself began to disintegrate. Alfred E. Driscoll, former Governor of New Jersey and former head of the Warner-Lambert Pharmaceutical Company, and Harry C. Mills, former vice president of J. C. Penney, both turned in their resignations.

The very next day, February 7, the Curtis Council of Unions, which had been recognized as bargaining agent only during the last summer of the Clifford regime, stepped forward to file a lawsuit of its own. The council, a group of six union locals representing seventeen hundred production and maintenance workers in Philadelphia, charged that Ackerman, McCombs, and Mason had "improperly" removed the $6 million from the pension fund. "We are seeking the appointment of a court-appointed trustee to oversee the pension fund," a union lawyer said, "as well as the removal of the three trustees and a complete accounting to determine how much has been misappropriated."

During these developments, Ackerman was on another vacation in the Caribbean. When the *Times* finally reached him in San Juan, Puerto Rico, he responded with an outburst of indignation. The charges against him were "false" and "ridiculous," he said, and they had "wrecked" two deals he had undertaken for the liquidation of Curtis's remaining physical assets. He said he had been negotiating to sell the paper mill to the Oxford Paper Company and the printing plant to a syndicate of Philadelphia businessmen. The syndicate would have paid $7.5 million in cash and $3 million worth of shares representing a 30 percent interest in a new printing venture. "This would have secured jobs for the employees in Philadelphia," Ackerman said, "but I think these are now wrecked by what has happened." And as for the labor unions' criticisms, Ackerman answered that staff cuts permitted a corresponding reduction in the pension fund. "There has been available for some time $10 million of surplus funds in the Curtis pension plan," he said, "which legally belonged to the Curtis Publishing Company, not to the Curtis Council of Unions."

"It comes down to a question of their honesty or ours," Ackerman said of his accusers. "The Curtis trustees claim that there is a conflict of interest, and the charge is untrue. Each and every action has been approved by the independent boards of both Curtis and Perfect Film. . . . I personally have not gotten anything out of all this. I only own a few hundred shares, and I only went to Curtis's help as a public service because I wanted to save it from bankruptcy. Perhaps it should all have been expected. I come from New York, I'm anti-establishment. They're establishment. But they have had twenty years to save this company and instead they've wrecked it. If the trustees continue their wrecking operation, the shareholders will lose all that they have, and I will say to myself, 'If they don't appreciate all you've done to save this company, who needs it?' . . . I'm honest—if there's anything I am, it is honest. I borrowed millions of dollars on the basis of my honesty."

The following Monday, the trustees filed their suit, in the name of Cary Bok, charging Ackerman with conspiracy to defraud Curtis by the unlawful disposal of assets. And from this point on, Ackerman's fortunes began to decline rapidly. The next week, he suffered his first specific personal defeat. The board of the LIN Broadcasting Corporation, which Ackerman had so ostentatiously announced as his new acquisition on the day he killed the *Post*, removed him from its presidency after a tenure of just over one month. Three brokerage houses also had seats on the LIN board, and they were described as being "uneasy" about the lawsuits and accusations against Ackerman. One reason for their uneasiness may have been the precipitous decline in the price of LIN shares. Ackerman had bought his shares at almost 44, when the market price was 28, and on the day of his dismissal the price was 18¼. Ackerman doggedly voted against his own dismissal but then decided to retire peacefully "because I don't want to do anything to hurt" LIN Broadcasting. "All the adverse publicity convinced them that I was more of a detriment to LIN than a help," he said.

At about this time, the *Wall Street Journal* devoted its second front-page lead story to Ackerman. The first such story, entitled "Marty in Action," had appeared the previous summer, and it had been extravagantly laudatory. The new story, "The Trials of Marty," paid somewhat more attention to the critics who argued that Ackerman's press notices "went to his head," that his juggling of corporate divisions "looked lousy," and that he sometimes seemed to be "doing deals for the sake of doing deals." Even worse, in some ways, was the recapitulation of Ackerman's stock ventures—Downe shares having been sold at 45 and then soaring to 180; LIN shares bought at 44 and then dropping to 18; even Perfect Film, cornerstone of the empire, dropping from 88½ the previous June to 69 at the end of the year to 43 at the end of February (it fell to 20 by July). "A smart lawyer stays out of court," one observer said. "Even if Marty wins, he has lost." Ackerman himself was characteristically tart: "Wall Street hates complications, but complications is how I've built a company from crap."

The ultimate power in the American corporation, however, remains with those who own the largest block of stocks, no matter who they are, no matter how inadequately they carry out their responsibilities. In the final contest between Ackerman and the Bok family, Ackerman had no weapon except a sharp tongue. The two sides managed nonetheless to work out a compromise plan, in which Ackerman and the trustees would each get half the seats on the board. Ackerman would remain as president until the annual stockholders' meeting in April, but the trustees would be represented inside the management by Thomas W. Moses, the recently retired chairman of the First

National Bank of Minneapolis, who would become executive vice president of Curtis.

The trustees refused to drop their suit until they had regained complete control of the corporation, however, so the compromise plan soon collapsed, and each side accused the other of "impugning the integrity" of its opponents. Ackerman was particularly angry at the Boks' chief lawyer, W. James MacIntosh, of the Philadelphia firm of Morgan, Lewis & Bockius. "MacIntosh is the culprit," he declared to the *Times*. "He wants to run Curtis, which is all right. But he shouldn't shoot first and ask questions later. If he's so smart, let him run the company. . . . It's unbelievable." Ackerman then summoned a special board meeting for the following Monday, March 3, to elect a new president. He said that he himself would nominate MacIntosh for the position. MacIntosh called this a "facetious suggestion" and "not worthy of serious comment." The only avowed candidate, then, was the original plaintiff against Ackerman, Philip Kalodner, who modestly announced: "I'm available if the directors wish to turn to me." Ackerman himself predicted: "Only God knows what will happen at that meeting."

What happened was that the board, with "reluctance and great regret," accepted Ackerman's resignation as president. And into the presidency, after thirty-nine years of survival, went the old gray fox of Waxahachie County, G. B. McCombs. In 1930, when G.B. had joined the company, Cyrus H. K. Curtis was still the president, and George Horace Lorimer was the editor of the *Post,* and Martin S. Ackerman had not yet been born. G.B. had dug in and G.B. had survived.

At that same meeting, the Curtis board attempted an aimless reorganization of itself. Philip Kalodner, who held only one hundred shares of stock, was given a series of positions, as a vice president, director, and member of the executive committee, in return for agreeing not to press his lawsuit against the company. Ackerman's ally, Eugene Mason, secretary of the corporation, resigned, but Ackerman himself vowed to remain on the board "because I want to see what they call me to my face." None of these maneuvers placated the furies, however. "From the viewpoint of the shareholders," MacIntosh said, "this is no reorganization at all. . . . The only healthy move at this stage is to clear out the present management group."

Ackerman did finally resign from the board at the end of March, but by then he had already made a more fundamental decision. On March 20, 1969, he observed his thirty-seventh birthday by announcing that he was abandoning the entire world of business enterprise.

"Who needs the aggravation?" he said. Ackerman's corporate castle, which had been halted in mid-construction, its beams and girders suspended and exposed in mid-air, would simply be patched together and sold to another conglomerate, Commonwealth United Corporation, which already had investments in entertainment, real estate, and oil. To that end, Ackerman turned over his own 52,000 shares of Perfect to Commonwealth United for the astonishing price of $100 per share, almost three times its market price, and he added 24,000 shares held by friends and associates for a total sale of $7 million. The merger never took place, however, because of what one insider called "the tight money market" and "other problems." In June, finally, Perfect Film hired a new president, Sheldon Feinberg, formerly the financial vice president and treasurer of Revlon, Inc., and Ackerman agreed to remain only temporarily as chairman of the board.

Ackerman now said he would return to the practice of law. He was still a partner in Cooper, Ostrin, DeVarco & Ackerman, and he said he would henceforth be "an active, very active partner." As for Curtis, he planned to recount all his experiences in a book. "I intend to make it my lifework to see that MacIntosh and Bok pay for the attack," he said, according to the *Times*. "I'm going to take my time, but they will fight for every tooth and nail they have for making the most fantastic, wild charges." Aside from that, Ackerman sought tranquillity. "I intend to get out of the public limelight," he said.

At Curtis, meanwhile, the presidency of G. B. McCombs lasted, like the reign of certain late Roman emperors, for only five weeks. During a stormy board meeting on April 10, G.B. announced that he was resigning as president and would return to New York as chairman of the Curtis Circulation Company (which was still in the hands of Perfect Film). G.B. issued a two-page statement grieving over his decision to resign and explaining that a "series of baseless lawsuits have had devastating effects on Curtis operations" and made it "virtually impossible for us to conduct our normal day-to-day operations."

At this point, Philip Kalodner once again put himself forward as a candidate for the presidency, but the board once again rejected him. According to Kalodner's subsequent statements, however, it was he alone who kept the board from throwing the company into bankruptcy. The board itself, depleted by the latest resignations of Ackerman, Gould, and McCombs, now consisted of only six members (one of whom was serving as U.S. Ambassador to Saigon). Three of these had been allies of the departed Milton Gould, and they all favored a petition of bankruptcy. "But I spoke up against them," Kalodner said. "In fact, I filibustered against them." The board meeting went on for five hours, and then ended inconclusively. And the day after the crisis, Kalodner simply decreed himself to be, if not the president of Curtis, then "chief executive officer." Once again, Curtis was without a president.

The deadlock lasted through most of April, and then, on April 24, it was broken long enough for Kalodner, like yet another Roman emperor, to become president. In that capacity, he offered repeated invitations to the unhappy trustees to "join" him in salvaging the wreckage of the company, but the trustees had no intention of collaborating in Kalodner's presidency. Kalodner alone, therefore, had the responsibility of announcing that the Curtis operating loss during the Ackerman year of 1968 had been $18.3 million. He also had to admit that the Curtis contract to print the *Ladies' Home Journal* and *American Home* for Downe Communications would run out at the end of June. "The contract," said the *Wall Street Journal* "is practically the only on-going venture Curtis has left."

Despite the company's pitiful condition, and the inexorable return of the Bok family, Kalodner determined to cling to his newly won authority. And so both sides devoted the early weeks of May to the printing and mailing of six different proxy statements to every stockholder in anticipation of the May 21 stockholders' meeting. Kalodner fired the first round on May 1 by nominating his own slate of seven prospective directors, which the incumbent board refused to approve. In addition to Kalodner himself, the slate included two surviving Curtis executives and four outsiders, leaving four places vacant for the trustees. Kalodner said the trustees' 30 percent ownership entitled them to these four seats, but no more. The trustees, however, called a special stockholders' meeting for May 12 and nominated their own full slate, headed by Thomas W. Moses, the former chairman of the First National Bank of Minneapolis, and Arthur R. Murphy, former president of the McCall Corporation, who were offered as the prospective chairman and president of Curtis.

Once the battle was joined, the tone of the proxy statements began to get sharper. Kalodner's second entry criticized the trustees for having spent "the past decade in sitting idly by while the Company's fortunes and the stockholders' investments went plummeting downward." Now, he charged, their special meeting represented "a shockingly arrogant attempt . . . to seize control of the company." The trustees responded by criticizing the "attempt by Mr. Kalodner to preserve himself in power although he has no significant investment in the company." They also accused Kalodner of rising to power through "an agreement with the Ackerman management." Of themselves, they said, "We offer you a fresh start." Kalodner, in turn, denied any connection with Ackerman and boasted of having been the first to sue him. He accused the trustees of having "during the past decade . . . supported three successive managements—including Martin S. Ackerman—in annual elections." On the basis of the trustees' own record, Kalodner said, "I submit the trustees cannot themselves be entrusted with the control of the company."

It was up to the stockholders, finally, to decide the fate of this ruined corporation. And so we all gathered, in the dusty heat of May, in the Crystal Ballroom of the Ben Franklin Hotel. It was a somewhat faded institution, four blocks from the Curtis building, but it was doing its best to keep up appearances. A string band played beneath the potted palms in the lobby, and the Crystal Ballroom sported three large chandeliers, golden draperies, and a row of white pillars along the walls. About two hundred stockholders had gathered for this final battle, but the crowd contained none of the familiar figures of the recent past—Ackerman, McCombs, Gould, none of these had come to witness the confrontation.

Kalodner began the meeting by calling on Robert T. Smith, a beefy young man, now the Curtis attorney and secretary, to read the minutes of the 1968 session. Smith droned through a page or so of minutes, and then he was interrupted by shrill outcries from a woman named Mrs. Evelyn Y. Davis. A short, slightly hunched woman of about forty, wearing a yellow dress ornamented with a large pin that said "SOCK IT TO ME," Mrs. Davis was a professional participant in stockholder meetings. When people tried to shush her, she began shrieking imprecations, in an accent that sounded Hungarian. "Both of your slates are having hands in the till," she shouted into her microphone. "I will not be intimidated by stooges."

When Mrs. Davis had finally been silenced, and Smith had finally finished the minutes, Kalodner announced that he wanted to avoid any suspicion of partisanship, and so he turned the gavel over to the neutral hand of William R. Spofford, a red-faced Philadelphia lawyer of about sixty. Spofford placed Kalodner on the right side of the dais and called up to the left side the trustees' chief candidate, Thomas W. Moses. Each side then nominated its candidates for the board, and the head of each slate spoke in favor of his group, and so we finally had a chance to appraise and judge the rivals.

In the newspapers and proxy statements, Philip P. Kalodner had seemed an implausible candidate, a usurper with very little support for his pretensions. On the dais, however, he was somewhat less implausible. Tall, slim, dark-haired, he had a long nose and a rather sour, downcast look, but he spoke confidently of the work he had done and expected to continue doing at Curtis. He told us how he had checked the attempt to throw the company into bankruptcy and how he had made a series of deals to get some new revenue. He had made "a handshake deal" for the sale of the paper mill, he said, and "a handshake deal" that would settle the controversy over the $6 million that Ackerman had taken from the pension fund. Liquidation of the company would bring "no money for the common stockholders," he said, and therefore it was "unacceptable." On the contrary, he planned to rescue all the company's magazines, and "to invest in our magazines, to invest in publishing. That is the only course that is sensible and reasonable."

Thomas Moses, by contrast, seemed to have very little to propose. "Our philosophy," he said, "is to take a hard look at all the assets of the corporation and then either to continue operating them or to dispose of them according to the best interests of the stockholders." He did take a very definite view, however, of one aspect of the prospective regime. "The era of the medicine men at Curtis is over," he said, "and the era of the businessmen is here." Medicine men? Businessmen? To a layman or an outsider, the distinction is not so easily grasped. Fuller, MacNeal, Culligan, Clifford, Ackerman— which of these was not a businessman?

Moses had a cherubically pink but square-jawed face, silvery hair cut athletically short, and a distinguished gray suit with a bright red boutonniere. As I looked at him, I was struck by his resemblance to the man who had nominated him, a partner in the Boks' law firm of Morgan, Lewis & Bockius. The lawyer, too, had distinguished gray hair, also cut short and emerging in a V over his forehead, and a dark gray suit that fitted him better than any suit would ever fit Marty Ackerman, or Clay Blair, or me.

In fact, as I looked at the whole Bok group, all clustered together in the far left corner of the Crystal Ballroom, they all looked more or less alike. They represented the famous Establishment, not in the sense that they really ran things—for the men who run things are generally more unorthodox—but rather that they had been reared and trained to serve the people who own things. "Ivy League," an outsider would have said, implying a ruling class, but there was something almost too methodical about their gray suits and their haircuts and their Caribbean tans—and those trim waists that implied more weekend tennis than anyone obsessed with making a fortune would ever find time to play. These were not climbing, scrambling people, and by the time they reached college, whatever college it might be, they already knew (or believed or sensed) that they would quite peacefully become executives of whatever corporation they joined, partners in whatever law firm, managers of whatever bank. They expected these honors because they expected to dedicate themselves to the service of their class, and in that dedication they took a rather solemn pride.

The stockholders were not like that at all. They were crass and noisy—Mrs. Davis broke in repeatedly to proclaim her views, often with raucous laughter—and a number of them spoke with the accents of the streets. Not a single one asked a single question about the killing of the *Saturday Evening Post,* or about any other aspect of the company's publishing problems. Instead, they rose up to demand explanations for the loss of the company's assets. What had happened to the tax-loss carry-forward? That was a very complex area of tax law, Kalodner said. And what about Curtis debts? Down to about $1.6 million, Kalodner said. And why was Moses less committed to the continuation of the company than Kalodner? Moses denied it. Most of all, though, the stockholders seemed bitter. "Where were all you people," shouted one middle-aged lady with dyed blond hair, "when all this Ackerman jazz was going on?" The response from Moses was typical: "I can't answer that question, for obvious reasons."

But Moses didn't need to answer. In spite of all the recent theories about the managerial revolution and the power of the technostructure, Moses was here (Bok didn't even need to come) to assert the most basic claim in the capitalist system: ownership. The trustees did not need to announce any plans for the salvation of the Curtis Publishing Company. They simply said, like children on a playing field: It's ours—give it back to us. And so the stockholders cast their votes, and when the votes were counted, the trustees had won nine of the eleven seats on the board of directors. Moses thus became chairman and Arthur Murphy president (the fourth in three months). The two remaining seats went to Kalodner, who took one for himself and gave the other to his brother, a professor at the New York University Law School.

In due time, Murphy took full control, as chairman as well as president, and all the litigation was settled. Curtis got back its remaining magazines (*Holiday, Jack and Jill,* and *Status*), and Perfect Film kept the circulation company. Various financial demands were submitted to arbitration, subject to court approval, and although the

Federal Trade Commission still pressed its claim for a refund to all the *Post*'s subscribers, all charges against Ackerman were dropped. (Also in due time, early in 1970, the Bok family's iron control of the company was loosened by the death of Mary Louise Curtis Bok Zimbalist, aged ninety-three. From then on, the future of the family trusts was open to negotiation.)

There remains one other fact to be recorded. The new management's first major announcement was that the printing plant in Sharon Hill would have to go out of business. On July 14, 1969, it said, all seventeen hundred employees would be sent home, and Walter Deane Fuller's great monument would be shut down forever. And that sad event provided the final demonstration of how the rulers of Curtis had misunderstood their own corporation for so many years. For here was clear proof of the argument that the Curtis magazines had been supporting and subsidizing the Curtis machinery right up until the end. Left to itself, the gigantic printing plant could not survive six months after the death of the *Saturday Evening Post*.

"I have always preached . . ." Mark Twain said in his *Autobiography*. "If the humor came of its own accord and uninvited, I have allowed it a place in my sermon, but I was not writing the sermon for the sake of the humor."

What lessons, then, can be learned from our years of ruined effort?

The first instinct is always to search for someone to blame. Marty Ackerman blamed the death of the *Post* on Madison Avenue, on society in general, on "today's scheme of living." In return, many people blamed Ackerman himself as a marauder and destroyer. It is undeniably true that Ackerman carried out the public execution, but it is also true that other people played an important part in his decision. Milton Gould, for example, who had once been the sponsor of Joe Culligan, had brought Ackerman to the presidency and had finally insisted that Ackerman kill the *Post*. And Cary Bok, whose power was sufficient to dictate an entirely new board of directors, obviously had the power to stay the execution, but he failed, as he had failed for so many years, to exercise that power. So if I were to draw up a list of all the people who were responsible for the death of the *Post*, those two would be on it. But the list would be a long one. It would also include Walter Fuller, who made the mistakes of the 1940's, and Robert MacNeal, who made those of the 1950's, and Mac Clifford, who did so little when so much needed to be done, and Serge Semenenko, who arrived with such fanfare but accomplished so few of the predicted triumphs.

But let us return to the day of the execution and observe how the press regarded the disaster. The press has a natural tendency to exaggerate the importance of writers and editors, unfortunately, and now it seemed disposed to place a good share of the blame for the killing on the *Post*'s own editors. There was much mourning for the grand old days of Lorimer and Hibbs, and then the vague charge that the great editors' heirs had failed to keep up with changing times, and that the advertisers had therefore drifted to newer media. The *Times* even turned to some advertising agencies for enlightenment on the evolution of publishing, and these arbiters of elegance hastened to defend their own innocence. "The more educated reader today needs a magazine that is much more contemporary than the *Post*," said one of these experts, Joel Davis, media director of the Marschalk Company. "There is plenty of money available to support magazine publishing, but the advertisers want to be sure the publications are attractive to the reader," said another expert, Clifford Botway, a partner in Jack Tinker & Partners. "The *Post* folded," said a third, Sam Vitt of the Ted Bates agency, "because it could no longer survive the years of mismanagement and editorial floundering."

The press itself was ready to throw the second stone. *New York* magazine, constantly struggling to appear fashionable, derided "the *Post*'s stodgy editorial formula—really its lack of any clear formula or sense of what it was trying to say." A littérateur in the *Village Voice* attempted an image of bathos: "I was sorry to see it [the *Post*] go out the way it did, like a showgirl of the '30's dressed in powder and rouge and a miniskirt getting run over in the slush on a wintry side street."

The *Times* asked vaguely on its editorial page "whether the demise of the *Post* could have been averted," and then answered its question by saying: "It is, unfortunately, almost impossible to cast any light on that question." *Newsweek* did make an effort to cast some light, and it decided that "it would be unfair to place all the blame on the ad agencies and their clients. In truth, editorially the Post has been an uncertain trumpet in recent years. . . . A former SEP editor adds: 'When the crunch was on, real genius was required. The Post's top men were talented, energetic—but none of them were geniuses.'"

Bill Emerson responded to all these posthumous judgments with admirable vigor. "I hope that all the one-eyed critics will lose their other eye," he said at a post-mortem convened by the Society of Publications Designers. "I'd like to cast a malediction. I hope it will wither them through the spring, and by early summer they will be all flaky and ready to go. My spirit is one of pure malice. I look from the other side of the grave, which is my peculiar advantage."

Still, before we cast maledictions, it may be appropriate to confess our sins. For in any final judgment of the *Post,* it can very well be argued that we all failed it, and thus we were all inadequate, all of us, to our mission. Not by the specious standards of Madison Avenue but by our own standards of what a magazine should be, and what an editor should be, we failed repeatedly to demand enough of each other, and of ourselves. Like the aged editors whom we had routed out in 1962, we gradually became prisoners of our own routines, of our own group of favored contributors, and of everyone's natural desire for peace and quiet. It is so much easier to accept mediocrity, and make a friend, than to demand improvement, and make an enemy. And so, all too often, we took the easy way, failing to search beyond the conventional, to discover what was hidden, to foresee what the future promised.

After that *mea culpa,* however, it seems reasonable to inquire further for the names of those editorial geniuses whose achievements we failed to equal. As one surveys the men who now produce the major magazines, *Life* or *Time* or *Look* or *McCall's,* one is not immediately impressed by the name of anyone celebrated as an editorial wizard. The only editor who resembles that popular image is Hugh Hefner of *Playboy,* and his wizardry is based so directly on neurotic public obsessions that it hardly serves as a model for others to emulate. People who talk of editorial genius are not generally referring to anyone currently engaged in magazine publishing, however, but to the distinguished founders of magazines that became successful a generation ago—Harold Ross of *The New Yorker,* or Henry Luce of *Time* and *Life,* or DeWitt and Lila Wallace of *Reader's Digest.* Except for Ross, though, the genius is not remembered primarily for his editorial perceptions but for his dedication to a commercial idea that led to immense profits.

My purpose here is not to denigrate the success of America's great publishing institutions but to argue against the popular theory that magazines rise and fall because of editorial genius. It does happen sometimes, of course, but not often enough to support the theory. As far as the *Post* is concerned, I think that, despite its lapses and failures, it was a very good magazine throughout its last five or six years of commercial decline, as good in substance as any magazine in the country. I also think, and have tried to show, that the magazine's long descent toward ruin had very little to do with its editorial quality. Better articles (or pictures) would not have kept it alive longer; neither would worse ones. Nor could salvation have been found, as occasionally suggested, in some kind of "formula." An "editorial formula" provides a good basis for promotion campaigns, and a good talking point for advertising salesmen, but any magazine that is really edited according to a formula is a magazine in a rut.

The decisive fact is that the *Post* was part of our competitive economic system—a system it had glorified as long as it suffered little competition itself—and magazines, like everything else within this system, survive not because they are good or bad but because they make a profit. And they make a profit not because of their inherent quality but because somebody is hard at work on the relationship of costs to revenues. That involves the price of ink and the weight of paper and the financing of subscription offers and many other details that do not interest people who like to talk about the publishing business as a matter of changing life styles. To be a successful magazine editor today (and perhaps in any day) means to leave the actual process of editing to someone else and to join in the process of managing a business, and to manage a business, in turn, means to control costs, to negotiate contracts, to make speeches, to sell the product, and to lead a public life far beyond the level of the people who actually create what the company sells. What I am saying, to put it another way, is that a skillful management could have made a profit from Emerson's *Post*, or Blair's *Post*, or even Sherrod's *Post*, but that no amount of editorial genius could have made up for the failings of the various rulers of the Curtis Publishing Company.

Looking beyond this question of immediate responsibility, it is interesting to speculate on what the death of the *Saturday Evening Post* implies about the shortcomings of the competitive corporate system as a whole. Some people might immediately answer that it implies very little. Publishing is an unorthodox and very volatile business, after all. Many companies rise and fall, and it could be argued that the failure of one particular magazine is neither very typical nor very important. It seems to me, however, that the sad events at Curtis were quite typical, for I suspect that there are many other corporations that also suffer grievously from insufficient leadership, misguided policies, encrustations of past mistakes, and a basic conflict between the professional goals of the technicians and the commercial goals of the shareholders. And if the difficulties at Curtis were typical of other corporations, then they may help us to understand some of the flaws in the profit system itself.

The Curtis story has been called a classic case of corporate mismanagement, and it is classic because the fault lay with no one man but with a whole series of men, and, I think, with the system that brought them to power. Mismanagement is not a peculiar characteristic of the American capitalist system, of course. On the

contrary, armies, churches, universities, and nationalized railways all
have their share of managers who prove inadequate to their jobs.
Indeed, it can be argued that American capitalism, by rewarding
efficiency, has developed a relatively high proportion of competent
managers. Still, when hereditary princes turned out to be incom-
petent governors, when caste systems produced arteriosclerotic oli-
garchies, we found it reasonable to indict the societies that based
their decisions on heredity or caste. If a major corporation stumbles
to the verge of bankruptcy, then, it seems equally reasonable to
question the premises on which decisions are made by privately
owned corporations. The two basic premises of the capitalist system,
if I may oversimplify a little, are that the man who provides the
capital can rule the corporation, and that the protection of his capital
outweighs any consideration of the public interest. Specifically, the
owners of Curtis ignored the internal rotting of their corporation so
long as it made a profit, and then, when the money mysteriously
stopped, they turned to anyone who could promise to restore their
profits. And finally, Marty Ackerman became president of Curtis not
because of his ability or experience but because he invested $5
million in new capital, and he killed the *Post* not because of any
faults he saw in it, not because it failed to entertain and edify its
millions of readers, but because he couldn't figure out how to prevent
the magazine's losses from endangering his investment.

Joe Culligan accused me, not long ago, of being hopelessly prejudiced against all businessmen and against the whole system of
private enterprise. "The most dismaying remark you made was to the
effect that 'businessmen' killed the *Post*," Culligan said. "You couldn't
be more in error—*editors* killed the *Post*. . . . Businessmen (including me) kept the *Post* alive from 1961 through 1968." I hastened to
deny Culligan's accusation, but perhaps he was at least partly right
about my prejudices. I do believe that there is something essentially
wrong with an economic and social system that is based so solidly on
the instincts of greed and aggression. Over the years, we have continued to rely on this profit system partly because of its spectacular
success in building our country and partly because we keep hoping
that it will give us a chance to satisfy our own personal ambitions.
What we still try to ignore is the extent to which the system destroys
and wastes and corrupts for the sake of its building. It is, in other
words, an exceptional system for the production and distribution of
goods, for manufacturing cars and shoes and moon missiles, and
even for growing chickens at phenomenally low prices. But it is also,
as a number of critics have pointed out, a system that poisons rivers,

ravages land, adulterates food—and fails in many of the less-profitable services that any properly organized society should provide: mass transport, urban housing, medical care.

Perhaps it is precisely because we have been provided with so many material goods that we increasingly sense a deficiency in the intangible qualities of the life we have provided for ourselves. In some fields, particularly those that we consider cultural, we have already decided that a basically Darwinian economic system, one that remorselessly kills off any venture that fails to return a profit, does not serve our best interests. And so we have found other methods for judging value. We support hundreds of colleges, for example, without ever demanding that they return a profit. Every city of any size boasts its own symphony orchestra, and not a single one of them makes a profit. We do not demand money from the Red Cross, for that matter, or from our libraries, or from Yellowstone National Park. The press, however, remains an anomaly within our economy, partly protected by the Constitution, partly subsidized by cheap postal service, and yet subjected to all the destructive risks and uncertainties of the profit system.

Institutions like the *New York Times* are virtually a fourth branch of the government, but anyone who is ready to pay the price can buy control of a newspaper or magazine for whatever purpose he chooses. At the start, the new owner usually announces that he has acquired a public trust; eventually, he feels quite free to kill any periodical that does not return him a profit on his investment. If all things in our system were as interchangeable as tenpenny nails, this system might work better than it does, but the laws of profit make no allowances for time and tradition. When Jock Whitney and Hearst and Scripps-Howard all joined in mourning the death of the unprofitable New York *Herald Tribune,* there was no way in which any of them could create a newspaper that could replace the paper they had destroyed. We still have the *Times,* of course, and it is good to know that it produces a profit of about 2 percent on gross revenues. But it is natural to wonder how long the Sulzberger family would support the *Times* if it began to lose several million dollars a year. How long would it be before somebody asked Marty Ackerman's question: "Is it worth it? I mean, is it *worth* it?"

If the press were purely a business enterprise, produced only to satisfy a "market," then perhaps we could watch with complacence while newspapers merged for greater efficiency, and old magazines died to make way for new ones. But the vitality of the press lies in its variety, in the competitiveness of ideas rather than of advertising rates. This is a matter not just of differing editorial views but of differing tones and styles. The *Post*, admittedly, was not part of the press in the sense that it covered the week's news, but in its major articles on subjects like the black revolution, in its editorials about Vietnam, in its regular columns of dissenting opinion, and even in its support of serious fiction, it certainly fulfilled the function for which the First Amendment to the Constitution was designed. The *Post* published good writing on every aspect of contemporary history, and, perhaps even more important, it circulated its message far out into the country, reaching millions of middle-class, mid-American families with information they could get from no other source.

And it spoke to its readers with an authority that was inseparably connected to its great age. It is easy, I suppose, to romanticize our national institutions, and to venerate them for their contributions to the past rather than to the present. But it is also easy, and much more dangerous, to underestimate the importance of preserving the things that enrich our lives precisely because their weather-worn traditions make them different from anything we could create today. When we tear down a musty and pillared opera house in order to erect a more "efficient" music center of steel and glass, for example, we are destroying something that can never be restored to us. And so it is with everything that has survived a century or more. If all of Harvard University were somehow obliterated, to suggest another example, and the entire faculty moved to a brand-new campus called the University of Eastern Massachusetts, the program of education might remain exactly the same, but its nature and quality would be quite different. I do not mean, of course, that all our traditional institutions must be preserved forever as fossils (and the *Post* of 1960 was undoubtedly becoming a fossil). On the contrary, it is the constant process of internal renewal that keeps these old institutions alive and valuable. The *Post* was, I think, such an institution, genuinely renewed, and it deserved to live. When it was killed, therefore, we lost not only an independent voice in American society but an irreplaceable part of our own national past. And I think that a system that favors such losses is a system that is fundamentally indifferent to the requirements of civilized life.

People who carp and criticize are supposed to provide solutions, and I really have no solutions. Or rather, whatever solutions I have are largely theoretical, and probably Utopian. I do think that the *Post* should have been saved, but it would have taken more money, more time, more managerial skill—and the recognition that the press provides our society with something more than profits.

"It's time," the announcement said. "In fact, it's way past time, for a reunion of the world's greatest editorial staff." We could recognize the affectionate but authoritarian tone of our former production chief, Rita Waterman, and so we each paid four dollars for the right to unlimited drinks in the dark and ill-ventilated back room of a place called T.T.'s Cellar, on East Fifty-fifth Street. If it was time for our first reunion, in the summer of 1969, then it was time to find out what had become of us.

Rita herself looked as sleek and svelte as ever, dressed in a blue-gray pants suit, presiding over the doorway and embracing all her favorite editors. And she, of course, had fared well. She was now the production chief for a new book-publishing firm called Winchester, at a salary one-third higher than what she had earned at the *Post*. And this was fairly typical of the technicians among us. Most of them had easily found new jobs with greater responsibilities and higher salaries. Don McKinney, to take the best example, moved first to the New York *Daily News* and then became the managing editor of *McCall's*. Bill Ewald turned down offers from *Life* and the *News* to become an executive at the Literary Guild. Jim Atwater went to Washington to become a special assistant to President Nixon.

But these were only the last survivors of all the talented and ambitious people who had played a part in the final years of the *Post*. There were others who didn't come to our reunion at T.T.'s Cellar, and plenty of others who weren't invited. Where was Joe Culligan nowadays, and what had become of Ben Hibbs? Where were Mac Clifford and Gloria Swett?

Those who left first did the best for themselves. Ben Hibbs, for one, still lived very comfortably in Philadelphia, contributing articles from time to time to *Reader's Digest*. Bob Fuoss also tried the *Digest* for a while—indeed, the *Digest* provided a haven for numerous veterans of the "old *Post*," notably its art director, its science editor, and its lone European correspondent—but Fuoss experienced some difficulties in Pleasantville, and now he was living in Cincinnati as a vice president of Federated Department Stores, the chain that owns such enterprises as Bloomingdale's in New York and Filene's in Boston. Men like these, however, had had time to move onward with the sedate caution of the old *Post* itself. What of those who had been thrust to the top in the times of crisis—and then thrust out? Among many of them, there is a curious pattern.

Joe Culligan, to begin there, spent only a brief time at the Burns Detective Agency, and then, in the fall of 1966, he stepped into the presidency of the Mutual Broadcasting System. At the start, he sounded full of the old vigor, and *Variety* quoted him planning to expand the radio network's news coverage, including commentaries from *Post* correspondents like Bob Sherrod and Stew Alsop. Only two years later, however, there was another one of those announcements: Culligan was resigning from Mutual "to launch a number of communication projects of my own." Once again, at the age of fifty, Culligan started with a cannonade of hopeful promises. The Culligan Communications Corporation, capitalized at $1 million, was designed to become what Culligan called "a major force in public media working toward conversion of public knowledge into understanding."

The letterhead of the Culligan Communications Corporation was printed in a distinguished shade of blue, and it proclaimed a fashionable address in the East Sixties, but when I went there to seek out Culligan, without any appointment, I found that the address marked one of those bleak new apartment buildings that dot the East Side. A uniformed doorman directed me to an upper floor, and as I walked along the silent corridor, I smelled the faint smell that suffuses all such buildings, the smell of new wall-to-wall carpeting combined with that of last night's cooking. There was a pause after I knocked at Culligan's suite, and then the door was opened by his secretary, a delicious blonde with a bright blue dress and an English accent. She professed to believe that I was a messenger boy and asked whether I wanted to leave the manuscript that I was carrying. Culligan himself was talking on the telephone in an inner office, but when he heard that I was waiting on his doorstep, he welcomed me with surprising cordiality—surprising to me, at least, for Culligan had no reason to regard me with anything but distrust and dislike. But Culligan's vocation for salesmanship was so deep, and yet so irrepressible, that he had to regard even me as a potential customer, a challenge, someone to be conquered.

Yes, the Culligan Communications Corporation was flourishing. Incorporated only in January of 1969, it had four radio stations in Providence, Dallas, and Houston. He referred to "our paper," meaning the *Town Crier*, published in Westport, Connecticut. He spoke of Pilgrim Productions, a movie outfit that was going to film two novels by Robin Moore, the author of *The Green Berets*. "And here, look at this." He thrust on me a book, of which the back cover contained a photograph of himself presiding over the venerable Curtis board of directors. It was the dust jacket for his own forthcoming book, *The Curtis-Culligan Story*, but it hadn't yet been printed, so he had wrapped the new dust jacket around some other book. "It's good for presentations and speeches and that kind of thing." By now, he said, he was already at work on a sequel, to be called *The Rape of Curtis,* "about what happened after I left." He might publish that himself, he went on, for the Culligan Communications Corporation also had a publishing house, Phaedra Publishers, Inc. "We publish Nabokov and Saroyan and lots of the greatest writers." And if I had any trouble in getting my own work published, he added, perhaps I would like to consider Phaedra. No? Well, was there anything else he could do for me? I thanked him. Culligan looked at his watch.

"Listen, I've got to catch a plane for Dallas," he said, "but can I give you a ride anywhere between here and the airport?"

It was only as we walked out the gray, stale corridor together, Culligan carrying his bulging suitcases with almost too much ease, that he began to speak more openly, and more bitterly. "What do you hear of Blair these days?" he asked, and then, hardly waiting for my answer, he told me some dark reports that he himself had heard. That was only an opening. With scarcely a pause, and without any change in tone, he began reopening the wounds of the great battle, recalling that his own children had once come home from school and told him some wild rumors that were being spread about him. "Even my eye, for Christ's sake, they were saying that was some kind of a fake. I tell you—the character assassination attempted on me—I've never heard anything like it."

I could only nod and shrug, and the strange thing was that Culligan and I kept doggedly smiling at each other as we rode down together in the little elevator. "It's easy enough for Blair to go and write a book, and you can write a book," Culligan said, "but in the world of business, it's not so simple. Everything depends on your reputation, and when they try to ruin your reputation—I can tell you—starting all over again is pretty tough. Flying all over the country—fifteen-hour days, week after week—I mean, we're going to make it with this new company, but the work we'll have to put into it—I've done it before, and I can do it again, but I shouldn't have to be going through all this at my age. I'm just too old for this kind of thing."

As soon as the elevator doors opened, however, Culligan seemed to leave his weariness behind. He picked up his suitcases and marched across the foyer, smiling his acceptance of the doorman's salute. Outside the glass doors, he looked around for a taxi, as though he expected one to be waiting for him. Behind him, the doorman waved vaguely at the traffic.

"You sure I can't give you a lift anywhere?" Culligan said to me.

"No, thanks."

"Say, would you like to go back upstairs and use my phones—whatever you need?"

"No, thanks, really."

Then a taxi arrived. Culligan flung in his suitcases, shook my hand, wished me well, and set off for the airport.

"What do you hear of Joe Culligan?" asked Clay Blair. "I mean, what's he doing? How's he living?"

I shrugged. We were sitting in Blair's suite at the Algonquin Hotel, where Blair had set up temporary headquarters while he gave interviews to promote his new books. Blair was still dark and heavy—he was wearing a green turtle-neck, slacks, and loafers—but he seemed to have lost all the old passion. He spoke peacefully and benignly of the past battles, as though they had happened to someone else. And yet the appearance was deceptive. Blair was as curious about Culligan as Culligan was about him, for in the imagination of these two antagonists, the struggle for Curtis had ended in 1964, and they would forever remain, like the figures on the Grecian urn, fixed in combat. To them, nothing that had happened in the last five years at 641 Lexington Avenue had any reality whatever.

Blair had spent those five years trying to fulfill his old ambition of becoming a writer. As he looked back on it now, he had never wanted anything else, and he had made a great mistake in accepting Ben Hibbs's invitation to the editorial offices in Philadelphia. Blair had begun by writing about his experiences at Curtis, but after a thousand pages, written at a breakneck pace of about five thousand words a day, he had abandoned that. "I felt I had to find out more about myself, about who I really was," Blair said. "I thought I could find out by writing, and I did." For several years, then, Blair had faded out of sight, and there were only sporadic rumors, among people who had once known him, that he had written a novel about the publishing business, or a novel about his childhood, or two novels, or three, that he was leaving New York and moving back to Washington, that he was getting divorced from his wife.

Finally, in the spring of 1969, he published a novel called *The Board Room*, which, according to the dust jacket, told of an editor, "Leland Warwick Crawford Jr., brilliant, moody, dedicated magazine journalist hired to revitalize the Marshall Company's weekly *Tribune*," and of his ally, "Jerry Roth, Wall Street wizard with a soft spot for journalism," and of the corporation president, "Michael Cade . . . glib-talking promoter." The novel was heavily advertised, but the reviews were lukewarm, and many people along Madison Avenue read it with smiles. That same spring, Blair also published a paper-back book about James Earl Ray, the murderer of Martin Luther King, and the reviews of this were rather chilly. By now, Blair had moved to Miami, and he was working on a new novel entitled *The Archbishop.* "I always thought," he wrote me not long ago, "that if we succeeded at the *Post,* I would make a lot of money and retire so I could live well and write novels. I did the starving-in-the-garret bit at Columbia and wanted no more of that. . . . In a curious way, I have achieved what I sought then. Except I don't have any money, and don't want any. I won't go into this now, but my whole outlook on life has changed since the Curtis days."

This, then, is the pattern—getting out of the system and working for oneself, often with no more than a faint hope of future riches. Marvin Kantor, to recall another name from the past, invested in a small company that exported scientific and technical books to Europe. And Hank Walker, the onetime Marine photographer, moved to Florida and bought a radio station. In due time, he and Kantor joined forces in what Bill Emerson called "the world's smallest and strangest conglomerate." Under the name of C.V.R. Industries, it engaged in building and book-selling in New York, trucking in Ohio, boat construction and retail liquor sales in Florida, and according to Blair, both Kantor and Walker were "well on their way to becoming millionaires." "Matters at Curtis are long since buried in the subconscious," Kantor wrote me, "and I have no interest nor desire to reconstruct the affairs of six years ago. I do wish you the very best."

Mike Mooney, too, after a time at Crowell-Collier-Macmillan, decided that the secret of publishing was the distribution system, and that the best way to make money was to sell books to schools. With characteristic gusto, he founded a company, which he called Connex Systems, and he hired a number of salesmen to start working the school circuit with a series of books reproducing and explaining the great works of art. In his first year, he claimed a sale of several million dollars and a profit of several hundred thousand.

Peter Wyden, more orthodox but no less energetic, also abandoned the magazine business and founded Peter H. Wyden, Inc., a book-publishing company that produced twenty books within its first year of operations.

And one morning, walking past the Curtis building at 641 Lexington Avenue, I encountered Bob Yung, smooth and smiling as always, and I asked him what he was up to these days.

"I have my own company now," he said, "right in the same building here."

"Really?" I said. "What does your company do?"

"Well, we work with Comsat," Yung said. "With television relay stations."

"What does that mean?" I persisted. "What do you do with television relay stations?"

"Well, we help to build them," Yung said.

"That sounds very promising," I said, and so we shook hands, and smiled and parted.

On lower Fifth Avenue, a few days later, I went looking for Bill Emerson. After seeing him every day for several years, I thought it strange to be wondering where he was, and what his office looked like, and what he was really doing.

In the days immediately after the fall of the *Post,* I had suspected that he might return to the South. There was some kind of an opening at the upper levels of the Atlanta *Constitution,* and another at the University of Georgia, and throughout the nationwide network of Southern editors, writers, talkers, and public figures, there was a constant shifting and maneuvering. But the killing of the *Post* had been a greater shock to Emerson than most people realized, and the prospect of high-class job-hunting was more than he wanted to face. And besides, among all those expatriate Southerners who control such extraordinary powers in the alien North, the desire to return home is a desire to return with laurels, not in shamefaced defeat.

And so Emerson told me that he was already involved in a small new company called EduVision. In theory, it was a splendid venture, for anyone who considered the future knew that television could not be dominated forever by the networks' offerings of situation comedies, games, and old Westerns. The networks' own scientists had already developed a technique for inserting cartridges into TV sets, enabling the viewer to watch prize fights, ballet, Jack Benny reruns, a concert by Horowitz, or whatever movie he chose. At present, the cartridges were expensive, but once the system caught on, the demand would be limitless. And to produce such shows, Emerson had become "editor-in-chief" of EduVision.

Lower Fifth Avenue, however, is a forgotten quarter of New York. Across from Emerson's office, derelicts lounged on the scratched and peeling benches in Madison Square Park. I took the elevator to the top floor and wandered through bare corridors until I found a half-open door marked with the name: EduVision. It was just one large loft, containing a dozen or more desks, partly separated from one another by masonite partitions. I saw one lonely woman typing near the doorway, and so I asked her if she knew where Emerson might be.

"He's not here," she said, "but his assistant is over there."

I looked across the length of the loft and saw one other figure, Emerson's secretary, Barbara O'Dwyer, talking on the telephone. I walked across the bare, echoing floor, past a mysterious pile of children's blocks—the company apparently had something to do with the sale of educational toys—and took a seat next to Barbara's battered desk. She looked up in surprise and then put down the telephone.

"Well, for heaven's sake," she said.

"Where's the great man?" I asked.

"He's out on a speaking tour," she said. "He won't be back until tomorrow."

"Quite a place you've got here," I said, getting up and wandering over to the window.

"Yes, isn't it?" she said.

"You know what this view looks like, in a funny way? That sleepy park—it looks like Independence Square, across from the old Curtis building in Philadelphia."

"Really? Well, you know, none of us stay here at the office any more than we need to."

I saw Emerson from time to time after that, but never at his office. He was living primarily on savings and Barbara on unemployment insurance. Occasionally, he gave lectures. "There wouldn't be any sense in putting money into one side of the company and taking out a salary at the other," he said. "By now, just about everything I've got is tied up in this. It's all a gamble—I know that—but I've got a lot of shares, and we're going public soon. So in a couple of years, I may make a couple of million dollars, or I may make nothing."

Not everyone at Curtis went into business for himself, of course. Many of us simply went on working at what we considered our vocations. All the *Post*'s writers continued at their trade, for other magazines, and a number of editors who had once been writers returned to their original profession. Bob Sherrod was laboring over a book on the American mission to the moon; Don Schanche went to Laos to write about an Ugly American; Roger Kahn set to work on a recreation of the Brooklyn Dodgers of his youth, and I myself began research on a book about Berlin in the 1920's.

And the salesmen went on selling. Jess Ballew tried to help launch a new magazine called *Homemaker's Digest,* and when that fell on hard times, he moved on to become publisher of the New York *Law Journal*, and when there were difficulties there, he moved on yet again, to *U.S. News & World Report*. Hungry John Veronis, now president of the company that produces *Psychology Today*, hired Jack Connors as the magazine's publisher. Steve Kelly took over the presidency of the Magazine Publishers Association, and he could be heard periodically in the advertising section of the *New York Times*, announcing that the magazine business was better than ever.

Then there were those who retired to a quieter life. Mac Clifford, for one, returned to his home in Santa Barbara, where he eventually joined a law firm that was thereupon renamed Brazelton, Bletcher, and Clifford. Gloria Swett, who received a handsome settlement on her employment contract, moved to her family's home in Teaneck, New Jersey. Asger Jerrild, the Danish art director, went back to Denmark and began building himself a house by the sea. And somewhere, in the uncertain peace of old age, lives Maurice Poppei.

And there were those who survived. The *Post* editorial offices at 641 Lexington Avenue were invaded by the bureaucrats of the Curtis Circulation Company, and a large corner office, once occupied by the *Post*'s fiction editor, and then by its art editor, was ultimately turned over to G. B. McCombs. And Ackerman? Late in 1969, he turned up at the Four Seasons restaurant, serving as co-chairman of a "kitchen party" to raise money for charity. "I'm unemployed," Ackerman said, to explain the amount of time he was devoting to good works. "But Mr. Ackerman wasn't asking for charity," the report in the *Times* continued. " 'I'm 37 years old and very rich,' he announced."

A cynic might say that many of us abandoned the corporate life because we could not find new positions there. Were we not branded, after all, by the mark of failure? And despite the restlessness of American society today, the great organizations still expect a certain kind of loyalty, a willingness to work upward through twenty years of corporate promotions. Would any such corporation pass over its dedicated subordinates to take on mavericks like Culligan or Emerson or Blair or Mooney or me?

Perhaps not. But I believe there are other reasons for the pattern. One of these reasons, I think, is the effect of age. When a man reaches forty—and most of us were near that point when we had to make our decisions—he becomes acutely aware of problems that he never even considered a decade earlier. He becomes aware, to say it as simply as possible, that he is within sight of his own death. Sometimes he reacts with an almost hysterical rejection of what he sees before him. He undertakes an affair with his secretary, or, at the very least, he starts frantically experimenting with new diets and new exercises. Even the calmest of men, however, must begin wondering whether the life he is leading is really the life he wants to lead, whether it will ever bring him any of the satisfactions he once thought it would bring. Quite often, with a rebelliousness far more profound than his own adolescent children have ever contemplated, he realizes that he is on the wrong course, and that a change in that course is a matter of his own survival.

We come back again to the corporate system. When we were young, we assumed, on trust, that the corporations were the indestructible engines of our national life. They were run by wise men, and they would harvest profits forever and ever. But as we watched the rich, powerful, age-old Curtis Publishing Company lurch to its doom, we felt, in a small way, the same shattering of confidence that the nation as a whole had felt during the Depression. The system was not invulnerable after all. The rulers were not infallible. The corporation was not immortal. It, too, could die, just as we ourselves could die. And so, if our days were numbered, we might as well set out to live our own lives as best we could.

The party in the smoke and noise of T.T.'s Cellar was not a great success. We all enjoyed seeing each other again; we enjoyed flirting with the secretaries and exchanging gossip about what had become of us. But when Rita Waterman had said on the day the *Post* died that we had all been a family, nobody had added a postscript on what eventually happens to families. We grow older, and we grow apart, and our own children return to us only on Christmas visits, as strangers.

A Note on Sources

This book is essentially autobiographical, rather than historical or reportorial, and most of its observations come from my own experience. I have made use of other views from time to time, however, and I want to acknowledge them here.

The traditional books about the Curtis Publishing Company are the following: *George Horace Lorimer and the Saturday Evening Post*, by John Tebbel (1948); *A Man from Maine*, by Edward Bok (1923), and *The Americanization of Edward Bok*, by Edward Bok (1923). More recently (1968), Bruce and Beatrice Gould published a memoir of their years at the *Journal*, entitled *American Story*. The only journalistic book about the company's internal warfare is *The Curtis Caper*, by Joseph C. Goulden, expanded from a series that Goulden wrote for the Philadelphia *Inquirer* in 1965. *The Curtis Caper* suffered somewhat from a Philadelphian point of view, an assumption that everything was better in the good old days, but Goulden worked hard and discovered a lot.

During the past year, 1969, two of the major combatants finally published books of their own, both extremely personal. *The Curtis-Culligan Story*, by Matthew J. Culligan, provides the former president's account of his two-year rule at Curtis. He is alternately heroic and rueful in tone. Clay Blair, Jr. published a novel, *The Board Room*, about a young executive's efforts to revitalize an ancient publishing company. Its tone is almost entirely heroic. Blair also wrote two manuscripts that were never published. One, a thousand-page draft of a book entitled "The Crack in the Liberty Bell," tells Blair's side of the Curtis story in considerable detail but breaks off at the end of 1963, before the climactic crisis began; the other, a hundred-page article entitled "Adventures of a Not-So-Sophisticated Muckraker," retells the story to its end, but in a very condensed form. In addition to these, Blair wrote or edited much of the 350-page dossier of reports compiled by his 1962 "Study Group." Both Culligan and Blair generously made their manuscripts available to me, and I have quoted freely from all of them. (Martin Ackerman's book, *The Curtis Affair*, appeared in the spring of 1970, after these pages had already gone to press.)

After reading the documents, I found that I still had a lot of questions to ask. A number of people took time and trouble to answer these questions, even though they had no idea how their answers would be used. For contributions large and small, I should like to thank (in alphabetical order): Andrée Abecassis, Stewart Alsop, Jesse Ballew, Robert E. Bedingfield, Clay Blair, Jr., Moreau D. Brown, Hubbard Cobb, John Connors, Matthew J. Culligan, E. Clifton Daniel, William A. Emerson, Jr., William Ewald, C. Richard Ficks, Deborah Harkins, Roger Kahn, James Kobak, A. Kent MacDougall, Don McKinney, A. Edward Miller, Michael Mooney, Kathryn Powers, Sally Reukauf, Norman Ritter, Verginia Robinson, Don A. Schanche, Ann Sciullo, Robert L. Sherrod, Caskie Stinnett, Philip Strubing, C. Davis Thomas, Rita Waterman, Chris Welles, Margaret Wilkinson, Peter Wyden, Daniel Yergin, and Sam Young. Several others expressed a desire to contribute their observations but were prevented from doing so because of their involvement in litigation over the events at Curtis.

I also want to thank two other Curtis veterans who helped in getting this book published. One, Don Gold, negotiated the financial terms as a representative for the William Morris Agency. The other, Tom Congdon, who appears several times in these pages as a militant critic of the status quo, welcomed and assisted my work in his new position as an editor at Harper & Row.

My original statement remains fundamental, however. This is my story, and the responsibility for it is entirely my own.

Index

THE POWER STRUGGLE AT CURTIS

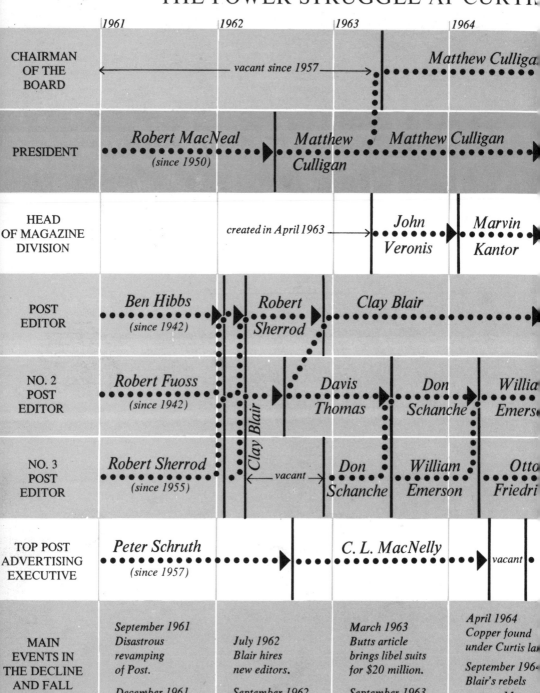

	1961	1962	1963	1964
CHAIRMAN OF THE BOARD	← *vacant since 1957* →			*Matthew Culligan*
PRESIDENT	*Robert MacNeal (since 1950)*	*Matthew Culligan*	*Matthew Culligan*	
HEAD OF MAGAZINE DIVISION		*created in April 1963* →	*John Veronis*	*Marvin Kantor*
POST EDITOR	*Ben Hibbs (since 1942)*	*Robert Sherrod*	*Clay Blair*	
NO. 2 POST EDITOR	*Robert Fuoss (since 1942)*	*Clay Blair*	*Davis Thomas* / *Don Schanche*	*William Emerson*
NO. 3 POST EDITOR	*Robert Sherrod (since 1955)*	← *vacant* →	*Don Schanche* / *William Emerson*	*Otto Friedrich*
TOP POST ADVERTISING EXECUTIVE	*Peter Schruth (since 1957)*	*C. L. MacNelly*		*vacant*
MAIN EVENTS IN THE DECLINE AND FALL OF CURTIS	September 1961 Disastrous revamping of Post. December 1961 Curtis loses money for the first time.	July 1962 Blair hires new editors. September 1962 Post moves to New York.	March 1963 Butts article brings libel suits for $20 million. September 1963 Semenenko loans Curtis $35 million.	April 1964 Copper found under Curtis land. September 1964 Blair's rebels meet at Manero. October 1964 Blair-Kantor dismissal.